D0354361

Discarded by
Santa Maria Library

943.604
Bridge, F. R.
The Habsburg monarchy among
the great powers, 1815-1918
New York : Berg :
Distributed exclusively in
the US by St. Martin's

HL MAY 04

GAYLORD MG

The Habsburg Monarchy among the Great Powers, 1815–1918

F.R. BRIDGE

The Habsburg Monarchy among the Great Powers, 1815–1918

BERG

New York / Oxford / Munich
Distributed exclusively in the US and Canada by
St. Martin's Press, New York

First published in 1990 by
Berg Publishers Limited
165 Taber Avenue, Providence R.I. 02906, USA
150 Cowley Road, Oxford OX4 1JJ, UK
Westermühlstraße 26, 8000 München 5, FRG

© F.R. Bridge 1990
All rights reserved.
No part of this publication may be reproduced
in any form without the written permission of Berg Publishers Limited.

Library of Congress Cataloging-in-Publication Data

Bridge, F.R.
  The Habsburg monarchy among the great powers. 1815–1918 / F.R.
Bridge.
    p. cm.
  Includes bibliographical references.
  ISBN 0-85496-307-3
    1. Austria–Foreign relations—1867–1918. I. Bridge, F.R. From
Sadowa to Sarajevo.
  DB86.B74   1990   89–28947
  943.6′04—dc20   CIP

British Library Cataloguing in Publication Data

Bridge, F.R. (Francis Roy) 1939–
  The Habsburg Monarchy among the great powers, 1815–1918.
  1. Austrian Empire & Austro-Hungarian Empire
  I. Title
  943.6′04

ISBN 0–85496–307–3

Printed in Great Britain by
Billing & Sons Ltd, Worcester

For Maximilian

Contents

Illustrations

Plates

1. Clemens Prince Metternich
2. Felix Prince Schwarzenberg
3. Karl Ferdinand Count Buol
4. Johann Bernhard Count Rechberg
5. Alexander Count Mensdorff
6. Friedrich Ferdinand Baron (1868 Count) Beust
7. Julius Count Andrássy
8. Heinrich Baron Haymerle
9. Franz Joseph I
10. Gustav Count Kálnoky
11. Agenor Count Goluchowski
12. Alois Baron (1909 Count) Aehrenthal
13. Leopold Count Berchtold
14. Stefan (1900 Baron, 1918 Count) Burián
15. Karl I
16. Ottokar Count Czernin.

The plates are reproduced by kind permission of the Picture Archives of the Austrian National Library, Vienna.

Acknowledgements

I wish to acknowledge the kind permission of the officials of the Haus-, Hof-, und Staatsarchiv, Vienna; of the Public Record Office, London; of the Archives Nationales, Ministère des Affaires Étrangères, Paris; and of the Bayerisches Staatsarchiv, Munich, to make use of the archives within their care.

I am indebted to the late Count Johann Aehrenthal for permission to use the Aehrenthal papers; to Mrs Elizabeth Cartwright-Hignett for permission to use the Cartwright papers; to Dr H. Rumpler of the Kommission für Neuere Geschichte Oesterreichs for permission to use the transcripts and microfilms of the Berchtold papers; and to Dr E.R. von Rutkowski of the same Kommission for permission to use the Mérey papers.

My thanks are also due to my friends and colleagues, Dr E.J. Adams, Dr M.J. Allison, Professor K. Bourne, the late Dr R.J. Bullen, Dr H.P. Cecil, Dr M.J. Cornwall, Professor D. Dakin, Professor D.N. Dilks, Professor R.J.W. Evans, Professor R.M. Hatton, Mr C.H.D. Howard, Mr M. Hurst, Professor J. Joll, the late Professor C.J. Lowe, the late Professor W.N. Medlicott, Professor A. Polonsky, Professor J.C.G. Röhl, Dr A. Sked, Dr D. Stevenson, Professor N. Stone, Mrs S.M.D. Wheeler and Dr K.M. Wilson, for their invaluable comments on some or all of this volume, or on my earlier book, *From Sadowa to Sarajevo* (London 1972), a shortened, revised and updated version of which is incorporated in the present work; to Professor A. Wandruszka, Dr P. Urbanitsch, Professor F. Fellner, Dr L. Höbelt, Dr K. Koch, and the late Professor R.A. Kann for their encouragement during the writing of my contribution to *Die Habsburgermonarchie 1848–1918, VI: Die Habsburgermonarchie im System der internationalen Beziehungen* (Vienna 1989), some of which is again used here; and to the members of my special subject class 'The Great Powers and the Balkans' at Leeds University, whose opinions proved both enlightening and reassuring.

Finally, my thanks are due to Alan Haigh and Des O'Hara, of the Graphics Unit, Leeds University, for the elegant maps; and to Ann Dale and Margaret Walkington, for their invaluable assistance in the production of the manuscript.

F.R.B.
Leeds, 1989

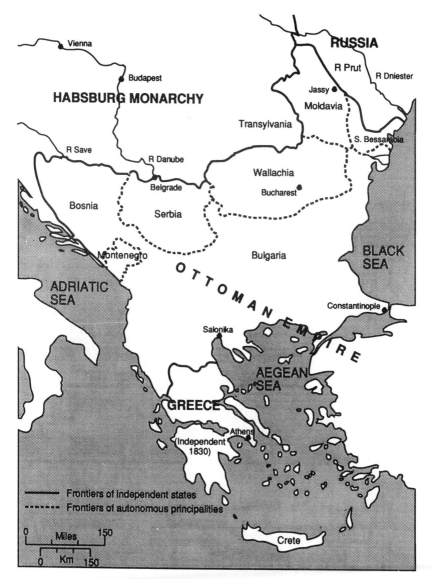

1 The Balkans, 1815-1878

2 The Balkans, 1878–1908

Vienna

RUSSIA

R Dniester

Graz

Budapest

R Save

R Prut

Agram (Zagreb)

ROMANIA

R Danube

Bosnia

Belgrade

Bucharest

SERBIA

Sarajevo

Uvac

Nish

Vama

Herze-
govina

Novi Bazar

Bulgaria

MONTE
NEGRO

Mitrovitza

Sofia

Eastern
Roumelia

BLACK
SEA

Antivari

Üsküb

Philippopolis

ADRIATIC
SEA

Macedonia

Adrianople

Constantinople

Monastir

Salonika

AEGEAN
SEA

Albania

Larissa

GREECE

Athens

Frontiers of independent states
Frontier between the
Dual Monarchy and
the occupied territories
Boundaries inside the
Ottoman Empire
Railways

0   Miles   150

0   Km   150

Crete

3 The Balkans in 1914

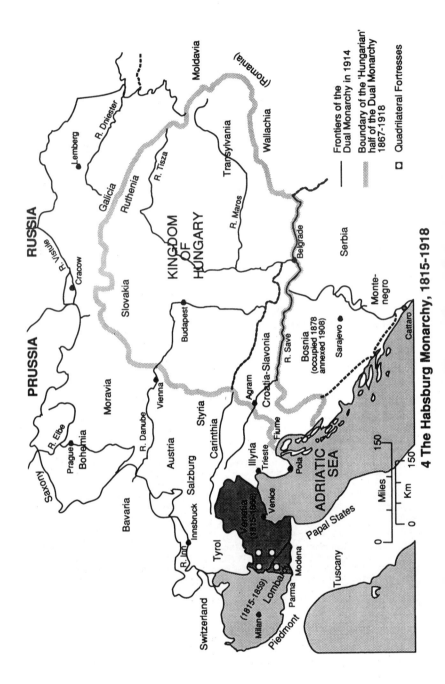

4 The Habsburg Monarchy, 1815-1918

- Frontiers of the Dual Monarchy in 1914
- Boundary of the 'Hungarian' half of the Dual Monarchy 1867-1918
- □ Quadrilateral Fortresses

PRUSSIA

RUSSIA

Saxony
R. Elbe
Prague
Bohemia
Bavaria
R. Danube
Moravia
Vienna
Austria
Salzburg
Styria
Carinthia
Innsbruck
R. Inn
Tyrol
Switzerland

Cracow
R. Vistule
Lemberg
R. Dniester
Galicia
Ruthenia
Slovakia
Budapest
R. Tisza

KINGDOM OF HUNGARY

Moldavia
(Romania)
Transylvania
R. Maros
Wallachia
Belgrade
Serbia

Agram
Croatia-Slavonia
Fiume
R. Save
Bosnia (occupied 1878 annexed 1908)
Sarajevo
Monte-negro
Cattaro

Illyria
Trieste
Pola
Venetia (1815-1866)
Venice
ADRIATIC SEA

Lombardy (1815-1859)
Milan
Piedmont
Parma
Modena
Papal States
Tuscany

Miles
Km
0   150
0   150

1

The Making of Foreign Policy in the Habsburg Monarchy[1]

'Je n'ai jamais vu de plus joli petit congrès':[2] thus Metternich on the Congress of Aix-la-Chapelle, which in November 1818 finally set the seal on the arrangements made in the post-Napoleonic peace settlement, a settlement which had established the Habsburg Monarchy as the lynchpin of the European order. It was a verdict that was echoed in other capitals: the British, for example, observed with satisfaction that 'the territorial system of Europe, unhinged by the events of war and revolution, has again been restored to order'; and they readily joined with all the other Great Powers in a declaration acclaiming 'the accomplishment of the work of peace and the completion of the political system designed to secure its solidity'.[3] Just one hundred years later, in November 1918, the Habsburg Monarchy was staggering to defeat and dissolution, and Great Britain and her coalition partners were determined on a peace settlement in which 'Austria-Hungary must be wiped off the map of Europe as an empire'.[4] Yet the very fact that this dramatic

1. The following works are of particular relevance to this chapter: Adam Wandruszka and Peter Urbanitsch (eds), *Die Habsburgermonarchie 1814–1918, VI: Die Habsburgermonarchie im System der internationalen Beziehungen* (Vienna, 1989), hereafter cited as *Habsburgermonarchie VI*; Alan Sked, *The Decline and Fall of the Habsburg Empire, 1815–1918* (London 1989); C.A. Macartney, *The Habsburg Monarchy, 1790–1918* (London 1968); A.J.P. Taylor, *The Habsburg Monarchy, 1809–1918* (London 1949); Idem, *The Struggle for Mastery in Europe, 1848–1918* (Oxford 1954); Istvan Diószegi, *Hungarians in the Ballhausplatz: Studies in the Austro-Hungarian Common Foreign Policy* (Budapest 1983); H. Ritter von Srbik, *Aus Oesterreichs Vergangenheit* (Salzburg 1949); A. von Musulin, *Das Haus am Ballplatz* (Munich 1924); F. Engel-Janosi, *Geschichte auf dem Ballhausplatz* (Vienna 1963); F. Klein (ed.) *Oesterreich-Ungarn in der Weltpolitik, 1900–1918* (Berlin 1965), H. Benedikt, *Die wirtschaftliche Entwicklung in der Franz-Joseph-Zeit* (Vienna 1958); W. Wagner, 'Kaiser Franz Joseph und das deutsche Reich 1871–1914', Doctoral dissertation, Vienna, 1951; F.R. Bridge, *Great Britain and Austria-Hungary 1906–1914: A Diplomatic History* (London 1972).
2. Richard Metternich, (ed.), *Mémoires, Documents et Écrits Laissés par le Prince de Metternich*, 8 vols., (Paris 1880–4), III, p. 267.
3. Castlereagh memorandum, October 1818, in H.W.V. Temperley and Lillian M. Penson, *Foundations of British Foreign Policy* (Cambridge 1938), p. 40; W. Allison Phillips, *The Confederation of Europe* (London 1914), p. 187.
4. See below, p. 368.

reversal of fortune took a century to accomplish would seem to suggest that it was by no means inevitable. The century had witnessed serious, sometimes violent, threats to the internal structure of the empire; but none of them had been fatal. In fact, on the eve of war in 1914 the domestic situation in the Monarchy was a good deal less troubled than it had been ten years before. In peacetime, the government had enough resources at its disposal to cope with internal opposition: the Army had intervened successfully in Hungary in 1849, and was preparing to do so again, if the need should arise, in 1905. Internal weaknesses there certainly were; but it was only when in 1918 they combined with defeat in war that the Monarchy collapsed – an interrelationship best encapsulated in Otto Brunner's observation that 'if one has a weak heart one should not go mountaineering'.[5] This raises the questions, of course, of what provoked the decision-makers of 1914 to throw half a century of caution to the winds; and why was the impact of the actions of the other Powers in the succeeding four years so fatal for the Monarchy? In fact, the Monarchy's fortunes throughout the 'long nineteenth century' from 1815 to 1918 were very much determined by its position among the Great Powers.

The imposing position the Monarchy had attained in 1815, controlling Italy and Germany and backed up by the Quadruple Alliance of the victorious coalition, concealed the fact that its responsibilities far exceeded its resources; and that it was not so much maintaining as being maintained by the power constellation of 1815. So long as the real Great Powers, Great Britain and Russia, worked to maintain the system and to uphold the sanctity of the treaties of 1815, all was well; but when the Monarchy lost their support and at the same time found itself confronted, as in the decade after 1856, by other Powers determined to replace treaty rights with sheer force as the basis of international relations, the power of the Habsburg Monarchy was reduced to accord with international realities. The loss of its position in Italy and Germany it survived; but the challenge in 1914 in its sole remaining sphere of influence, the Near East, seemed, in the minds of the decision-makers in Vienna, to pose the alternatives of war or voluntary withdrawal from the ranks of the Great Powers into the role of a kind of super-Switzerland. This latter prospect had for some time appealed to pacifists and others outside the political élite, and it

---

5. Otto Brunner, 'Das Haus Oesterreich und die Donaumonarchie', in *Südost-Forschungen*, 14, (1955), pp. 122–44, cited in A. Wandruszka, 'Vorwort', *Habsburgermonarchie VI*, p. xv.

would at least have allowed the Monarchy to continue to exist as an independent state.[6] But it was always regarded by Franz Joseph and his advisers as quite incompatible with the honour of the dynasty of the state. As it turned out, their alternative course of action did not save the situation either; and by 1918 the Monarchy had, under the stress of war, become so inextricably entangled with its German ally that it faced either defeat and destruction at the hands of the Entente or victory in harness with an all-powerful Germany – which would equally have spelt the end of its existence as an independent Great Power.

For most of the nineteenth century, however, the Monarchy was able to maintain both its Great Power status and its independence. Threats to its position were never far to seek – even Metternich had found himself dangerously isolated at the end of the 1820s. But thanks to a combination of ingenuity and flexibility in Vienna, on the one hand, and a largely favourable international situation, in which most Powers were disposed to uphold the status quo, on the other, the threats were overcome. In the decade after 1856 the opposite situation prevailed: a highly unfavourable international situation, with three Powers challenging the isolated Monarchy in Italy and Germany, was compounded by an utter inflexibility and stiff adherence to high principles on the part of the emperor and his advisers, which led them simply to confront all challenges head-on, without even seriously attempting to secure allies or divide their opponents. The psychological effects of the consequent disasters may well have been one factor in the return to flexibility after 1871, when for nearly half a century the decision-makers in Vienna manoeuvred unceasingly to defend the Monarchy's interests without recourse to war. Fortunately for them, the international situation, while less favourable than that of the Metternich era, was, at least until 1914, both fluid and manageable enough to allow these manoeuvres to succeed.

At the apex of the decision-making structure of the Habsburg Monarchy stood the emperor, who to the very end selected the men who determined the behaviour of the Monarchy among the Powers. In practice, until 1848 foreign policy decisions lay in the hands of Metternich. The emperor Franz I (1792–1835) had learned to value Metternich's skills in successfully concluding the twenty-year war with France that had dogged him since the beginning of his reign; and he was even more appreciative of his activity in fighting the Revolution in Germany and Italy. (It was not the defeat

6. Stephan Verosta, *Theorie und Realität von Bündnissen* (Vienna 1971), pp. 271ff.

of Napoleon, but the defeat of the revolution in Naples in 1821, which earned Metternich the title of Chancellor.) Under the feeble-minded emperor Ferdinand (1835–48) Metternich's rivals for control of the government, however ill-disposed towards him, were impressed enough by his proven talents to allow him a pretty free hand in foreign affairs. (It might be noted, however, that even Ferdinand was dimly conscious of a certain responsibility in that field, witness his observation on hearing, in his retirement, of the loss of Lombardy in the disastrous war of 1859: 'I too could have managed that!') At the end, the brief reign of Karl I (1916–18) saw the twenty-nine-year-old emperor launching his own peace initiatives in 1917, and, a year later, summarily dismissing a foreign minister who was one of the most forceful personalities of the Monarchy. It was in the seven decades of Franz Joseph's reign, however, that the most momentous decisions were taken; and the monarch himself was ultimately responsible for all of them, either directly or through his choice of advisers, almost without exception men after his own heart. Of his own responsibility Franz Joseph was never in any doubt whatever. In the prime of life he rebuked an Austrian politician in – for him – unusually sharp tones: 'You are always talking of Andrássy's policy; do not forget that it is my policy';[7] and towards the end of his life he used almost exactly the same language in rebuffing the attempts of the chief-of-staff to interfere in foreign policy matters: 'Policy – it is I who make it; that is My policy, . . . in this sense My minister of foreign affairs is conducting My policy.'[8]

It is not always easy to pinpoint the emperor's influence in specific decisions of foreign policy,[9] many of which were taken after verbal consultation between the monarch and the minister, with no written record being kept as to how a particular decision was reached. But the emperor's marginal comments on foreign ministry papers (which he read daily with prodigious industry to the end of his life) are remarkably consistent, and give a fair idea of the general drift of his policy.

It is true that for the first three years of his reign Franz Joseph[10]

7. Helmut Rumpler, 'Die rechtlich organisatorischen und sozialen Rahmenbedingungen für die Außenpolitik der Monarchie', in *Habsburgermonarchie VI*, p. 45.
8. Franz Conrad von Hoetzendorf, *Aus meiner Dienstzeit* (Vienna 1921) II, p. 282.
9. Wagner, 'Kaiser Franz Joseph', *passim*.
10. Josef Redlich, *Kaiser Franz Joseph von Oesterreich* (Berlin 1928); Hugo Hantsch, 'Kaiser Franz Joseph und die Außenpolitik', in Engel-Janosi, *Ballhausplatz*; F. Engel-Janosi, 'Der Monarch und seine Ratgeber', in F. Engel-Janosi and H. Rumpler (eds), *Probleme der franzisko-josephinischen Zeit* (Vienna 1967).

allowed himself to be guided by Schwarzenberg (although even here, in the confrontation with Prussia in 1850, it seems that the young emperor's reluctance to start his reign with a German civil war was an important factor restraining the Chancellor from pushing things too far – to the latter's subsequent regret.) Certain characteristics the emperor displayed throughout his reign of sixty-eight years: he was always extremely conscientious and hard-working, and anxious to become an effective ruler of his peoples. (It must also be admitted that his toughness and perseverance were combined with a certain inelasticity of mind and lack of imagination, which at least partly explain why his ideas on his role never really changed during the whole sixty-eight-year period.) It was hardly surprising, given the traumatic circumstances of his accession, when liberalism and nationalism stood revealed as threats to the very existence of his empire, that he never developed any real sympathy for the two most powerful forces for change in the nineteenth century. Although he was forced in 1861 to accept a limited accommodation with liberalism at home, he never faltered in his unshaken conviction that with nationalism there could be no accommodation, at home or abroad. Not that his was a barren conservative policy devoid of ideals; nor did he regard the state, as some extreme conservatives did, as merely a chattel of the dynasty. His insistence that outside the Habsburg dynastic state there could be no security for a collection of small peoples faced with infinitely more powerful historic races in Germany and Russia, was in a sense justified after his death; and for much of his reign, until old age and the desire for a quiet life led him to abandon the Slavs to the hegemony of the German Austrians and the Magyars, he made a genuine effort to realise his vision of himself as the sovereign of all his peoples. But essentially, his determination to uphold the empire as established by treaties, in terms of both territory and influence – like his obstinate refusal to cede territory unless it had been lost on the battlefield – stemmed from a passionate sense of dynastic honour reminiscent of a bygone age.

In practice, the emperor's legitimist convictions account for the essential consistency of Austrian policy from the Metternich era to the end of Franz Joseph's reign. Naturally, given the Monarchy's ultimate dependence on a changing European power constellation to maintain its position, this consistency was more successful in some periods than in others. For over a decade after the Crimean War, when most European governments were indifferent, or even actively hostile, to the 1815 settlement, Austrian insistence on legitimacy and treaty rights – for which the emperor himself bore a large share of the responsibility – led the Monarchy into diplomatic isolation and military defeat. After 1871, when most European governments were satisfied with the status quo and doctrines of monarchical solidarity were again in vogue, Austria was more in tune with the times; and once Franz Joseph had abandoned positions in Italy and Germany that the Monarchy, ever since 1815, had lacked the strength to hold unaided, Austria's objectives were altogether more in line with her resources. In the Monarchy's remaining area of influence, the Near East, the threat to its territorial integrity was less direct than it had been in central Europe, and could usually be countered by finding support elsewhere or by compromise agreements with the threatening Power itself, Russia This suited the emperor, whose confidence in himself as a military commander had been shattered by two unsuccessful wars; and while he remained consistent in his ends, he adopted a flexible attitude as to means, supporting over the next forty years a whole succession of diplomatic devices and manoeuvres to defend the Monarchy's interests short of war. When, however, the threat again appeared to be directed at the territorial integrity of the Monarchy – in 1914 – Franz Joseph again resorted to the arbitrament of war. As the alignment of European forces was by then unfavourable to the Monarchy, the decision proved as disastrous as those of 1859 and 1866. Indeed, like those decisions, it was to a large extent motivated by the conviction that the international situation had become unfavourable to the defence of the Monarchy's position by diplomatic means; and the mentality behind the decision was essentially that revealed by Franz Joseph in 1859 and 1866: to defend one's position as long as possible, to do one's duty, and if that fails, to go down with honour.

Of the other members of the imperial family, only two played any significant role in foreign affairs: Archduke Albrecht and Archduke Franz Ferdinand, as Inspectors General of the Army from 1869 to 1895, and from 1913 to 1914 respectively. Archduke Albrecht, Franz Joseph's uncle and the victor of Custoza, was one of the emperor's most trusted advisers. His own view of the Monarchy was strictly dynastic – the state was no more than a family possession – and he generally exerted his influence in favour of monarchical solidarity, especially with the court of St Petersburg. Although his attitude towards Germany was never entirely free from the rancour dating back to 1866 that he usually reserved for Italy, he also supported the idea of a Three Emperors' Alliance. In all this he stood squarely in the tradition of those high-ranking military men who, mindful of Russia's services to the dynasty in

Hungary in 1849, led the opposition to Buol's pro-western policy at the time of the Crimean War – a tradition that was carried on by Beck, the emperor's and the archduke's most trusted adviser on military affairs, and chief of the general staff from 1881 to 1906.

The emperor's nephew, Archduke Franz Ferdinand, displayed elements of the same tradition. Although he was less drawn to St Petersburg than to Berlin – he developed a close personal friendship with Wilhelm II – he was always profoundly opposed to the idea of war with Russia, and never entirely lost hope of some day seeing the *Dreikaiserbund* restored. But his pro-Russian, pro-Romanian, and on occasion pro-Slav inclinations were also a reflection of his hatred of the Magyars, whose separatist ambitions he regarded as a mortal threat to the Monarchy. This hatred was one of the two great ruling passions of his life. The other was a fanatical clerical-ism, which added fuel to the flames of the deep personal loathing he felt for the usurping Kingdom of Italy: not for nothing had Franz Ferdinand of Habsburg-Este, a grandson of the last king of the Two Sicilies, inherited the title and the fortune of the last duke of Modena. Yet, fiercely held though his convictions were, he was, to his intense frustration, for most of his life in no position to influ-ence his uncle's policies – especially when he faced in Aehrenthal an Italophile foreign minister who enjoyed Franz Joseph's full con-fidence. It was in vain that he stormed and raged – so much so that the emperor was said to be considering excluding him from the succession on grounds of insanity.[11] It was only when the more pliable Berchtold was at the Ballhausplatz that the archduke, who kept up a fairly regular correspondence with the minister, gained a measure of influence over policy, and eventually exercised, together with his imperial uncle, what was perhaps a decisive restraining influence on Berchtold in the summer of 1913.

The responsibility for the routine management of foreign policy in the Habsburg Monarchy rested with the foreign minister. It was, however, only along general lines laid down by the emperor that he performed his function of translating the imperial will into the day-to-day decisions of policy that made up the substance of Austria's relations with the other Powers. If he was unsuccessful (like Buol in 1859) or if, worse, he presumed to attempt to bend the emperor to his will (as Beust did in 1871) it was the emperor who dismissed him. Moreover, the foreign minister was by no means the em-peror's only adviser; and he was obliged in practice, and after 1867

---

11. [Public Record Office, London,] F[oreign] O[ffice series] 371/ [File] 1047, Cartwright to Nicolson, private letter, 25 May 1911.

in law, to take into account the views of others, such as the emperor's military and financial advisers. Even Metternich had had to bow to their opinions on the hopelessness of taking a stand against Russia in the 1820s, or on the inadvisability of seeking admission to the Zollverein in the next two decades. Moreover, Franz Joseph himself, especially in his earlier years, once he emerged from the domination of Schwarzenberg, was distrustful of advisers who might become too powerful, and deliberately resorted to tactics of divide and rule as a device to retain control of policy in his own hands. After Schwarzenberg's death he lost no time in dismantling the accumulation of powers the Chancellor had built up; and in the early sixties he played off a whole series of advisers, official and unofficial, against the foreign minister.[12]

After the *Ausgleich* settlement of 1867, which finally established the constitutional basis on which the Monarchy rested until its collapse in 1918, the foreign minister was under an actual constitutional obligation (the Hungarian Law XII of December 1867) to take into account the views of the Hungarian prime minister. Indeed Andrássy declared in 1882 that the Hungarian prime minister was directly responsible for everything that happened in foreign policy.[13] And as the Hungarian government was itself responsible to the parliament at Budapest, the opinions of the magnates and gentry dominating that body carried a weight never gained by their counterparts in Austria. (There, neither ministers nor parliament had any constitutional right whatever to be consulted about foreign affairs.) Both the law and political realities, therefore, obliged the foreign ministers to consult the Hungarian prime minister before taking any major decision. In 1914 there was no question of going to war until Tisza's consent had been extracted. This is not to say that the Hungarians could dictate the foreign policy of the Monarchy: the warlike demands of Budapest in the later 1880s were ignored by the Ballhausplatz. Altogether, the degree of mutual dependence established by the *Ausgleich* was probably just one more factor making for a generally passive foreign policy. A policy of action that commended itself to Budapest was always liable to come up against opposition from the Ballhausplatz, and vice versa. So, more often than not, a negative, waiting attitude would be adopted.

The non-Hungarian parts of the Dual Monarchy, loosely known

---

12. Rumpler, 'Rahmenbedingungen . . .', in *Habsburgermonarchie VI*, pp. 15ff.
13. J. Galantai, 'Die Außenpolitik Oesterreich-Ungarns und die herrschenden Klassen Ungarns', in Klein (ed.), *Weltpolitik*, p. 266.

as 'Austria', presented the foreign minister with an easier task. For the domestic situation there was much more fluid. The German elements, whatever their social position, never exercised a political dominance comparable to that of the Magyars in Hungary. They were always challenged, often successfully, by Czechs, Poles, Italians and South Slavs; and from this plethora of nationalities a foreign minister could always find a substantial body of opinion to support any policy he chose to pursue. And although the Austrian government had no constitutional right to be consulted about foreign affairs, the foreign minister generally kept in touch with the ministers in Vienna – not least because they could sometimes be called on to override the opposition of Budapest.

A third constraint on the foreign minister was the fact that about certain matters, not themselves directly within the purview of the foreign minister, but nevertheless of vital importance to the management of foreign policy, the governments in Vienna and Budapest simply had to be consulted – for example, the building of strategic railways and the adjustment of tariffs by commercial treaties. Indeed, every foreign minister spent long and wearisome hours in conference with the prime ministers and finance ministers of the two governments about these matters. And many were driven almost to despair by the attempt to reconcile the economic interests of Austria and Hungary. These rarely coincided: the Austrians sought to protect their industries against German competition and favoured the importation of cheap Balkan food (in the hope of reducing pressure for higher wages); whereas the Magyars sought to protect their agricultural prices from undercutting by Balkan producers, and their infant industries from Austrian competition. As a British observer noted in 1910, it was 'as impossible to please Budapest and Vienna as it is to serve God and Mammon'.[14] This disharmony accounts for a good deal of the tension that afflicted the Monarchy's relations with both Germany and the Balkan states by the end of the century; and it also lay at the root of the great crises that shook the Monarchy every ten years when the common commercial institutions established by the *Ausgleich* settlement came up for revision. The decennial prospect of deadlock and the subsequent break-up of the Monarchy into two separate states in economic – perhaps even in political – terms, earned for Austria-Hungary the sobriquet of a 'Dual Monarchy on short notice [*auf Kündigung*].

Now this was a serious matter. For the common institutions of

14. F.O. 371/827, Howard to Grey, No. 34, 22 April 1910.

the Dual Monarchy – the Common Ministry of Foreign Affairs; the Common Ministry of War, which controlled the Imperial and Royal Army (as opposed to the home-guard forces administered by the war ministers of Austria and Hungary); and the Common Ministry of Finance, which supervised the revenues of the other two Common Ministries (and after 1878 administered Bosnia and the Herzegovina) – functioning above and largely separate from the Austrian and Hungarian governments, were absolutely essential to the preservation of its position as a Great Power. It was for this reason that in the settlement of 1867 the emperor-king, while he conceded that the common economic arrangements might be the subjects of negotiation between the governments of Vienna and Budapest, had taken care to ensure that control over the common political and military institutions was clearly vested in the prerogative of the Crown. In defence of his prerogative rights over these common institutions the emperor was always absolutely unbending. Never would he yield to the demands of Magyar extremists who saw in them an infringement of Hungary's liberties and sought to control them or whittle them away. The crisis of 1903–6 between Franz Joseph and the Magyars over the Common Army was the most serious in the whole history of the Dual Monarchy, and, in so far as it threatened to paralyse it altogether for external action as a Great Power, far more serious than anything it was facing in 1914.

Friction over the Common Ministry for Foreign Affairs was less of a problem – although in the crisis of 1903–6 the Magyars included in their grievances the complaint that the principle of equality established in 1867 had never been extended to foreign affairs, that the diplomats and the foreign minister resided at Vienna, not at Budapest, and that Hungary had not had her fair share of personnel in the diplomatic corps and at the Ballhausplatz. It is true that apart from Andrássy and perhaps Berchtold (who possessed both Austrian and Hungarian citizenship) none of the foreign ministers of the Dual Monarchy down to 1914 was drawn from the kingdom of Hungary. (Kálnoky was a Bohemian German, despite his deceptively Hungarian name.) On the other hand, Magyars were well represented in the diplomatic corps: of the occupants of the ten highest-ranking embassies in 1914, six were Hungarians. And the emperor was several times influenced in practice by Magyar views on the incumbents of the Ballhausplatz – for example, in accepting the resignations of Kálnoky and Goluchowski and in appointing Aehrenthal. But he still insisted as a matter of principle – and despite occasional grumblings from

Budapest this was never seriously challenged – that the appointment of the minister for foreign affairs lay solely within the prerogative of the Crown.

The only institutional constraint on the foreign minister under the constitution of 1867 was his responsibility to the Delegations – a common assembly, consisting of sixty members drawn from the Austrian, and sixty from the Hungarian parliament, which voted the budget for the Ministry of Foreign Affairs. But this body was never able to exercise any effective control: on the contrary, its establishment had been a manoeuvre on the emperor's part to put an end once and for all to any notions of parliamentary control of foreign policy. Over the years, the manoeuvre proved effective. Debates in the Delegations were usually retrospective, and could in no way be said to determine policy. Occasionally, a foreign minister might present to the Delegations a survey of the political horizon; and this would be avidly studied abroad for indications of his intentions. Hence the Delegations might be used for specially emphatic speeches when the minister wanted to make an impression abroad. Sometimes they provided a useful sounding-board for public opinion – but usually only if it suited the foreign minister to lend an ear. In 1908, for example, Aehrenthal thought it useful to remind Berlin that speeches by members of the Delegations – in this instance, by Poles who were outraged at the expropriation of Polish landowners in Prussian Poland – had a certain 'symptomatic value', which Germany would be unwise to ignore.[15] (Vienna was naturally anxious lest such an important section of opinion as the Poles, staunchly anti-Russian and an invaluable support in the *Reichsrat*, be forced into opposition to the Dual Alliance and the government at home.) On other occasions, the Delegations could be important indicators of the intensity of Magyar feeling: the rough handling they gave to Goluchowski in 1906 certainly contributed to his fall. In practice, however, the Delegations were never able to dictate a line of policy to a minister. They met irregularly – usually only once or twice a year for a couple of weeks (but sometimes not at all – for example, between the end of 1908 and late 1910). They certainly did not provide a channel by which public opinion could influence foreign policy. According to a British observer they were 'a body which is, from its constitution, out of touch with the general public; and any interest which has been excited almost immediately subsides;[16] . . . in neither of

15. [Haus, Hof- und Staatsarchiv, Vienna,] P[olitisches] A[rchiv, series] I/ [Karton] 484, Aehrenthal to Bülow, private, 11 March 1908.
16. F.O. 120/825, Stronge to Plunkett, No. 16, 7 March 1905.

the two halves of the Dual Monarchy has the institution of the Delegations been able to secure any real measure of popular sympathy. Its forty years' existence has not helped to enhance its prestige or increase public confidence.'[17]

Infinitely more important than such formal constitutional mechanisms was the distinctly informal conference of ministers,[18] which met on an *ad hoc* basis when important business arose. In essence, this body had changed little since it originated in the Metternich era, and it remained to the end the supreme organ of decision-making in the Habsburg Monarchy – if organ it can be called, for its composition tended to vary according to the business in hand. After 1867 it always included: the foreign minister, who took the chair when the emperor did not preside in person; the Common Minister of War; the Common Minister of Finance; often the chief of staff; the prime ministers of Austria and Hungary, their ministers of finance, and occasionally, their ministers of war, commerce, or agriculture. Here, various influences could indeed be brought to bear on the foreign minister. But they were usually effective only in a negative and general sense – for example, a refusal to grant money for an armaments programme. It was extremely rare in the Dualist era for a foreign minister to find himself overruled and obliged to endorse a particular course of action he disapproved of. Even when, as in the Scutari crisis of 1913, Berchtold was outvoted in a conference that recommended the sending of an ultimatum to Montenegro, he was able in the end – thanks to the support of the emperor – simply to ignore the decision of the conference.

His predecessors had not always been so fortunate. When, in the early sixties, the emperor was resorting to tactics of 'divide and rule' to maintain his own control of policy, foreign ministers sometimes found that the emperor sided with other ministers against them: both Rechberg and Mensdorff found themselves pushed into taking a more demonstrative line against Prussia than they would themselves have wished. Conversely, Andrássy found himself hopelessly isolated when he tried to persuade councils of ministers to consider the possibility of war with Russia in 1878. In the later years of the dualist era, however, the most striking feature of the debates in the conference of ministers is the way in which the foreign minister, confident of imperial support, generally got his

---

17. F.O. 371/599, Cartwright to Grey, Annual Report, 1 February 1909.
18. M. Komjathy, 'Amtsgebarung der oesterreichisch-ungarischen Monarchie zur Zeit des ersten Weltkrieges', in Klein (ed.), *Weltpolitik*, pp. 285ff.

own way: Kálnoky's policy of peace prevailed (admittedly with the support of the Austrian ministers as well) against Magyar belligerence in 1888; and even the easy-going Goluchowski could, when he bestirred himself, overrule both Austrian and Hungarian governments on extremely important Balkan issues in 1906. Indeed, by the twentieth century the role of the conference of ministers in the actual formulation of policy was declining before an increasingly autocratic handling of affairs by the foreign minister. Whereas Andrássy had allowed the occupation of Bosnia to be fully debated in conferences of ministers in 1878–9, Aehrenthal was much more perfunctory in regard to the annexation in 1908; and Berchtold, in 1914, short-circuited the conference of ministers altogether in order to circumvent and override the stubborn opposition of the Hungarian prime minister.[19] By then, indeed, it seemed that the foreign minister of the Dual Monarchy had assumed the powers of the Chancellor of the old Austrian Empire. Clad in the mantle of Metternich, even the weak Berchtold could compel one of the most forceful statesmen the Monarchy ever produced to bow to his will.

The circumstances of July 1914 were, however, exceptional. For the most part, the foreign ministers of the Habsburg Monarchy after Metternich did not exercise anything like the powers of a Chancellor. This was particularly clear in relation to domestic affairs and their impact on foreign policy. It is true that for a few years after the great upheavals of 1848–9 the young Franz Joseph had been prepared to allow Schwarzenberg as Chancellor a fairly free rein in both foreign and domestic affairs. But his successors as foreign minister were largely confined to their own *ressort*; and although Beust, called in after the Monarchy's second escape from destruction in 1866, was granted exceptional powers as Chancellor to implement the *Ausgleich* settlement, and did, indeed, attempt to institutionalise them by setting up his own *Reichskanzlei* alongside the foreign office, this was allowed to wither away after his departure.[20] After this, no foreign minister enjoyed either the title of Chancellor or the power that it carried in domestic affairs. Both Kálnoky and Aehrenthal bewailed the absence in Austria-Hungary of a post of real authority comparable to that of the Chancellor in Germany; but they made no impression on an emperor who remained determined to retain overall control of the state in his own hands.

The upshot, in terms of foreign policy, was that if the foreign

---

19. Ibid., pp. 289–90.
20. Rumpler, 'Rahmenbedingungen . . .' in *Habsburgermonarchie VI*, pp. 30ff.

minister was remarkably free to take decisions on high policy with little regard for the wishes of the Austrian, and even Hungarian, governments, these bodies were equally free to determine such matters as came within their purview without regard for the views of the foreign ministry, even when these matters had serious implications for foreign policy. The foreign minister was not represented in either parliament; and if the parliaments could never dictate to him, he could rarely influence them. This could be particularly embarrassing in regard to commercial questions and tariffs, which could have far-reaching effects on the Monarchy's relations with its neighbours; and successive foreign ministers lamented the deficiencies in matters of defence arising from the parsimony of the Austrian and Hungarian governments, or from the periodic lapses into chaos in the last two decades of peace – all of which deficiencies the foreign minister was precluded from alleviating by virtue of the constitution of 1867.

Both the formulation and the implementation of policy depended to some degree on the diplomats in the field and the officials of the Ballhausplatz.[21] The influence of the latter varied according to the personality of the minister. For Metternich, the officials of the central office were never much more than clerks; indeed, Schwarzenberg was so appalled at their mediocrity that he embarked on a veritable purge. Partly as a consequence of this, the Ballhausplatz of the fifties and early sixties was characterised by capable and strong-minded officials who took it upon themselves to interfere in the formulation of policy and even to defy the minister, under the diffident Mensdorff virtually assuming personal responsibility for communications between Vienna and Berlin. The more insubordinate of these officials were eliminated by Beust and Andrássy; but both these ministers tried to introduce men of ability into the Ballhausplatz, and to create there a forum they could draw on in the formulation of policy. Kálnoky, by contrast, the 'prototype desk-minister [*Schreibtischminister*]' concentrated the formulation of policy very much in his own hands, and confined the officials largely to routine business.[22] Goluchowski was more prone to trust the advice of experts, such as Zwiedenek, the long-standing head of the Eastern Department; and, impressed from his time at the Paris embassy by the French system, made a point of restoring Andrássy's ministerial secretariat (*Kabinett des Ministers*) as the central organ of the office. This his successors

21. Ibid., pp. 51ff.
22. Ibid., p. 79.

continued to use until 1918; but the scope allowed to officials still depended on the personality of the minister. Aehrenthal kept all his officials, including the younger, more spirited men, under tight control; whereas Berchtold was more inclined to give them their head. Indeed, the leading modern authority on the subject even talks of Berchtold's consciously fostering the growth of a 'war party' in the office.[23] Yet the fact remains that the 'war party' was kept well under control throughout the hazardous months of the Balkan wars; and the final decision in July 1914 was taken on higher authority than that of the Ballhausplatz officials.

As for the diplomats in the field,[24] their activities *en poste* might well be the making of a future foreign minister – apart from Andrássy, all Franz Joseph's foreign ministers had served as heads of diplomatic missions, usually in St Petersburg; but they did not have much impact on the making of foreign policy. The chief function of such diplomats in the Habsburg foreign service was simply that of reporter; and in this capacity it must be said that the general level of competence was high. It is true that even after Schwarzenberg's introduction in 1851 of examinations – chiefly in languages, law, and history – for admission to the foreign service the academic attainments, as opposed to the social qualifications, of all too many of the foreign ministry officials (who by 1914 accounted for an élite of 832 out of a total of 6,293 ministerial officials in Austria) was mediocre; but the handful who achieved ambassadorial rank were both intelligent and industrious, and bore comparison with any of their colleagues in the other diplomatic services of the day. Aehrenthal, for example, even as an honorary attaché at St Petersburg in his early twenties, made quite a name for himself as an authority on all aspects of Russian society (and was one of the few members of the service to have command of Russian). Certainly his chief, Kálnoky, found him 'indispensable'.[25] And Kálnoky set high standards: his own fourteen-year incumbency of the Ballhausplatz was something of a landmark, in that it saw the foreign service develop into an institution for the collection of information that certainly equalled the other great foreign offices of the day; and the indefatigable minister – like Bismarck and Salisbury – instituted a system of regular correspondence with his leading ambassadors in which he debated issues of policy with

23. Ibid., pp. 84–5.
24. Ibid., pp. 88ff.
25. Haus, Hof- und Staatsarchiv, Vienna, Nachlass Klemens Erb von Rudtorffer, manuscript, 'Geschichte des Außenministeriums 1848–1918', henceforth cited as 'Erb MS'.

them at length. Certainly, Kálnoky was one of the best informed foreign ministers of his day. His successors, even Goluchowski and Berchtold, kept up this network of communications; and whatever charges may be levelled at Austro-Hungarian foreign policy in 1914, it cannot be said that decisions were taken on a basis of ignorance. If the decisions then taken were fatal, that was not due to any deficiencies in the technical functioning of the machine.

On the contrary, the system of internal correspondence developed by Kálnoky promoted reasoned debate between well-informed experts, and ensured that controversial issues were aired. This did not always make for harmony. In the last resort the minister always retained the final decision in his own hands, and diplomats in the field might still feel that their advice had been too little taken into account by blinkered officials at the centre. The latter, of course, replied that only those at the centre could take an overall view and see things in perspective. This sort of conflict became increasingly acute between the St Petersburg embassy and the Ballhausplatz in the decades after 1870, when the possibility of agreement with Russia formed the central issue and main debating point of policy. The embassy invariably pleaded for a conciliatory and trusting attitude towards Russia, whereas the Ballhausplatz stressed the need for scepticism and caution. During the embassy of Aehrenthal at St Petersburg (1899–1906) the debate almost reached the point of a public row; and although the ambassador's arguments may have contributed to a softening of his government's line, most notably in the Neutrality Agreement of October 1904, on the main issue Goluchowski prevailed absolutely.

If even an ambassador of Aehrenthal's quite exceptional energy and determination could have so little influence on the formulation of policy, it was not surprising that the impact made by his more diffident colleagues was even less (although the garrulous Khevenhüller on two notorious occasions exposed his government to embarrassment through his incompetence). The usual reaction of a diplomat who found his advice consistently ignored was simply either psychic – or in the case of Goluchowski at Bucharest and Liechtenstein at St Petersburg – literal – resignation. That *feu sacré* that inspired men of the stamp of Schwarzenberg, Andrássy and Aehrenthal with a desire to do great things was a rare phenomenon in the Habsburg foreign service. Most of Franz Joseph's foreign ministers served simply – and often reluctantly – out of a sense of duty to the dynasty and the state; and the same attitude pervaded the rest of the diplomatic corps. It was one which reflected the education and upbringing of these people. At the Oriental (from 1898 Consular) Academy through which most of them passed the 'problem-oriented study, discussion and critical debate [characteristic of] Anglo-American higher education were somewhat eclipsed by the acquisition of knowledge. This was quite in conformity with the aims of the institution to educate, not reformers and revolutionaries, but reliable functionaries to administer and maintain the Monarchy and to represent it abroad.'[26] Revolutionaries they were certainly not; indeed, it has been suggested that the high proportion of men from aristocratic families 'still themselves rooted in the countryside [*Boden*] and inclined from their personal experience to be sceptical about the influence that human beings can exert over elemental things'[27] imbued the whole service with that conservative resignation that accorded so well with the emperor's own temperament.

A simple 'black and yellow' loyalty to the existing order of things in Franz Joseph's dominions was the most marked characteristic of those who served the emperor in the foreign service (and in the Army and bureaucracy too). It was a loyalty that paid no regard to social origins – and coherence of the service was in no way diminished by the steady increase in non-noble personnel (almost 50 per cent by 1914).[28] Above all, nationality meant absolutely nothing. In the days of the Monarchy's leadership of Germany the Habsburgs had never had any hesitation in drawing on the states of the Confederation for their servants – Metternich, Biegeleben, Rechberg, Schmerling and Beust being only the most notable examples. Of the senior personnel in the Ballhausplatz in 1914 only one – Hoyos – was a German Austrian.[29] This supranational loyalty to the dynasty inspired the political élite of the Monarchy to the end – or almost to the end: the anti-dynastic furore unleashed in German-Austrian circles by the Sixtus affair, which led to open conflict between foreign minister and emperor, and the outright rejection by the government in Budapest of Habsburg attempts to save the Monarchy by federal reform, showed that the dynasty could no longer count on the absolute loyalty of even the élite; and that the Monarchy had perhaps indeed outlived its days.

Foreign policy in the Habsburg Monarchy, then, was the concern of a small, supranational élite – the emperor, his close advisers,

---

26. Heinrich Pfusterschmidt-Hardtenstein, 'Von der orientalischen Akademie zur k. u. k. Konsularakademie', in *Habsburgermonarchie VI*, p. 170.
27. Rumpler, 'Rahmenbedingungen . . .' in *Habsburgermonarchie VI*, p. 91.
28. Ibid., pp. 106ff.
29. Ibid., p. 114.

and their officials. The influence of public opinion on its formulation was negligible. It is true that the state of public opinion – for example, the sullen indifference of the German bourgeoisie and the outright hostility of the Magyars to the absolutist regime in 1859 – could contribute to the disastrous outcome of a particular policy decision. But the decision was taken by the élite on the basis of external rather than – in 1859, indeed, despite – internal considerations. Similarly, the government's response to the defeat of 1859 was not to change its foreign policy, but to attempt to buy off the domestic opposition by constitutional concessions, in order to defend the Monarchy's position among the Powers all the more effectively. For Franz Joseph and his advisers primacy lay with foreign, not domestic, policy. It is also true that in the constitutional era the state of public opinion was sometimes an element in the background against which decisions of the greatest moment were taken: it would have been a hazardous undertaking for Beust to launch a war of revenge against Prussia in 1870 in defiance of the well-known inclinations of German-Austrians, who regarded France as the traditional enemy. Equally, in the late eighties Kálnoky could point to the doubtful loyalty of the non-Polish Slavs to counter Hungarian arguments in favour of preventive war against Russia. On the other hand if the external arguments were compelling enough – as in 1914 – doubts about the state of public opinion would not sway the issue. And the only war that would have met with almost universal endorsement from public opinion – war against Italy – was, when it came in 1915, not of the Austro-Hungarian government's volition.

In a very general and negative sense, admittedly, public opinion could indeed affect foreign policy, by restricting the options open to decision-makers. For example, the parliamentary bodies controlled the military expenditure of the Monarchy; and the eternal parsimony of the Austrian and Hungarian governments and their parliaments was one root cause of the relative weakness of the Monarchy's military forces, an underlying factor that any foreign minister had to take into account. From the 1890s until 1912 the Monarchy fell steadily behind the other Great Powers in military potential; and in naval construction Italy gained a lead over the Monarchy in the later nineties that she was never to lose. By 1903 Franz Joseph's subjects were spending more than three times as much money on beer, wine and tobacco as on the entire armed forces of the Dual Monarchy.[30] And in the next six years, whereas

30. A. von Wittich, 'Die Rüstungen Oesterreich-Ungarns von 1866 bis 1914', in *Berliner Monatshefte*, 1932, p. 868.

Russia and Italy spent nearly a quarter of their revenues on armaments, and Great Britain nearly two-fifths, the Monarchy could hardly manage more than an eighth.[31] In this situation, it was hardly suprising that Austro-Hungarian foreign ministers generally felt they had to do everything possible to avoid an appeal to the arbitrament of war.

Equally, in very general terms, the agitated state of public opinion over nationality questions was sometimes a factor influencing the Monarchy's standing among the Powers and restricting the options open to the decision-makers. In the 1890s the Czech–German language dispute, or rather Berlin's attempts to meddle in it, contributed to the poor state of Austro-German relations at that time. Far more serious, the great crisis that raged between Franz Joseph and his Hungarian subjects for nearly ten years at the turn of the century paralysed the Monarchy for action abroad, and cast doubt on its chances of survival even if peace were maintained. However, the situation improved after the settlement of the Hungarian crisis in 1906, and especially after the Monarchy's display of vitality in the Bosnian crisis. By 1910 the British press was almost universally agreed that the Monarchy had never appeared stronger, and that the recent troubles which so many had taken for death-throes had in fact been 'a lusty re-birth'.[32] The enthusiasm for Serbia displayed in some South Slav circles during the Balkan wars certainly irritated the government, and perhaps contributed to its determination to take drastic action in 1914. On the other hand, there is not much evidence that the state of public opinion was a factor in the deliberations of the decision-makers during the July crisis.

There was nothing unusual in that. Indeed, it is difficult to point to an instance where public opinion had anything approaching a determining effect on the making of Habsburg foreign policy. Foreign ministers might make opportunistic references to it in defending their actions from criticism at home or abroad; but public opinion was never able to take the lead or force the hand of a foreign minister, prescribing a particular direction for day-to-day decisions of policy. In the first place, there was among the political institutions of Austria no constitutional forum for the expression of views on foreign policy. (The Liberals fell from power in 1879 for attempting to transform the parliament into just such a forum.) In the second place, public opinion in such common institutions as existed for the discussion of foreign policy – the Delegations – was

31. F.O. 371/1296, Russell to Grey, No. 223, draft, 29 December 1911.
32. *Daily Graphic*, 18 August 1910.

never united; and the foreign minister could generally collect enough support for whatever policy he chose to pursue. Most important of all, it was simply impossible to devise a policy that would have a hope of being acceptable to 'public opinion', so various were the strands of which it was composed[33] – from Kramář and the Czechs, who advocated alignment with Russia, to the Magyars and Poles, who abhorred such an idea, and the Germans, who demanded an alignment with Berlin, or even longed for the day when German troops would march in to put an end to the Monarchy and annex its German territories. In the age of nation states, the Habsburg Empire was indeed, as Franz Joseph himself observed, 'an anomaly';[34] and opinions being so diverse, and a consensus so obviously impossible of achievement, it was perhaps as well that the Ballhausplatz took its decisions in accordance with what it considered to be the great interests of state, and did not attempt to devise a policy to suit 'public opinion'. Even on the exceedingly rare occasions when public opinion was more or less united – in hostility to Great Britain during the Boer War, for example – it was ostentatiously ignored by the government.[35]

In Hungary after the *Ausgleich* public opinion – or, rather, the opinions of the Magyar ruling élite – carried a certain weight by virtue of the 1867 constitution. And as neither Világos nor Sadowa had been forgotten, Magyar opinion was both violently anti-Russian and firmly opposed to any attempt to reverse the verdict of 1866 at home or abroad. But this did not prevent Beust from pursuing his schemes against Prussia in the 1860s, nor Andrássy and Kálnoky from co-operating with Russia in the seventies and eighties. With the waning of the Russian threat and the constitutional conflict at home at the turn of the century Hungarian opinion turned inwards, so much so that by 1905 a British consul-general could write[36] that there were 'few countries in the world where foreign affairs are less discussed and understood than Hungary'. The typical politically aware Hungarian (and the opinions of the masses remained, if they existed, an inscrutable mystery) seemed to be 'indifferent to the international standing of the Monarchy. He has always been the subject of a Great Power and perhaps

33. Thomas Kletecka, 'Außenpolitische Vorstellungen von Parteien und Gruppen in Cisleithanien', in *Habsburgermonarchie VI*, pp. 457–8.
34. A. Wandruszka, 'Vorwort', *Habsburgermonarchie VI*, p. xi.
35. Bridge, *Great Britain and Austria-Hungary*, pp. 3, 10. Idem, 'British official opinion and the domestic situation in the Habsburg Monarchy, 1900–1914', in B.J.C. McKercher and D.J. Moss (eds), *Shadow and Substance in British Foreign Policy* (University of Alberta Press 1984), pp. 77, 82–3.
36. F.O. 120/825, Stronge to Plunkett, No. 16, 7 March 1905.

for that reason he fails to appreciate the advantages of his position' – hence his complaints about the cost of the Common Army, and his opposition to any activity in foreign affairs that seemed to be to the advantage of Austria and the dynasty. In short, the account concluded, there was little likelihood of political and commercial circles in Hungary being stirred by issues of foreign policy unless events threatened to close the markets of Turkey and the Balkans to Hungarian trade. On this, the Magyars did in fact feel strongly – as they did about Vienna's inclination to offer commercial concessions to their rivals in the Balkan states. It was Hungarian opposition that frustrated Aehrenthal's attempts to end the tariff war with Serbia in the hope of winning that state over to a position of commercial dependence on the Monarchy. The Magyars felt equally strongly about anything that might affect the balance of races within the Monarchy – even in 1914 they vetoed any policy that involved the incorporation of more Slavs; and ministers of foreign affairs generally accepted, or bowed reluctantly to, such shibboleths. The fundamental conviction of almost all Magyar politicians was, however – and here the British consul-general had misjudged them – that it was only as part of a Dual Monarchy that Hungary, surrounded as she was by a sea of Slavs, could hope to survive as a Great Power, or indeed survive at all. So long as this held true – as it did until 1918 – the foreign minister could generally count on their support; and the Ballhausplatz did not need to pay any more attention to calls from minority groups in Hungary – such as Michael Károlyi's pleas for a western orientation of policy – than it did to the demands of Kramář and some Czechs for a Russian orientation.

Nor was public opinion as reflected in the press[37] a factor of much importance in the formulation of foreign policy. On the contrary, in so far as there was any dependent relationship between policy-makers and the press, it was the former who sought to influence the latter.[38] In the *Vormärz* period, government activity was confined almost entirely to negative censorship. Only in the absolutist era were more positive efforts made to exploit the press, especially abroad, by establishing journals to put the government's case; but by the middle sixties this tactic was considered to have been ineffective, if not even counter-productive. Beust was more publicity-minded and more sophisticated, and concentrated on

---

37. K. Paupié, *Handbuch der österreichischen Pressegeschichte*, II (Vienna 1966), pp. 105ff.
38. Leopold Kammerhofer, 'Diplomatie und Pressepolitik 1848–1918', in *Habsburgermonarchie VI*, pp. 459ff.

developing contacts with, and placing articles in, existing organs that had a reputation for independence; and he set up a regular press bureau, the Literarisches Bureau, in the Ballhausplatz to organise journalistic support for his diplomatic campaigns against Prussia and Russia. This was certainly a bold innovation – indeed, in the eyes of the British *chargé d'affaires*, a decidedly shocking one:[39]

> He has done more in five years than any other statesman could have effected in fifty years to lower the tone of political morality at Vienna. . . . He has habitually employed . . . the secret service money of the state in purchasing panegyrics of himself from the home and foreign press. [During his occupancy, the Imperial Chancellery] has been the notorious resort of stock-jobbers, journalists known for their venality and other persons whose intimacy would be a discredit to any private, and a disgrace to any public man.

Certainly, none of Beust's successors was inclined to cultivate the press to quite the same degree; but the Literarisches Bureau in the Ballhausplatz continued to function until 1918. Not that its activities were wholly nefarious, even in British eyes: indeed it was to the foreign ministry's control of the press that one British observer attributed the lack of influence of the military over public opinion and foreign policy.[40] And certainly, in 1911 Aehrenthal quashed an attempt by the Army to set up a rival office of its own for feeding information to the press.[41] To others in the British foreign office, however, it seemed by 1910 that 'of all press bureaus, those at Vienna and Berlin are the vilest. Those who deliberately work them are responsible for their direct and indirect effects, which . . . constitute not only the most shameful, but also the most dangerous feature of modern politics.'[42] Certainly, on two notorious occasions – the Friedjung and Prochaska affairs, each of which ended with the resignation of the head of the Bureau[43] – the attempts of the Literarisches Bureau to prepare the public mind for tough action against Serbia did a good deal to poison the international atmosphere and to damage the Monarchy's reputation abroad.

Even so, perhaps British strictures on the all-pervasive intrigues of Germany and her alleged satellites throw more light on British

39. F.O. 7/791, Lytton to Granville, No. 62, 18 November 1871.
40. F.O. 120/853, Goschen to Grey, No. 171, 3 November 1908.
41. *O[esterreich-] U[ngarns] A[ußenpolitik]*, (eds L. Bittner and H. Uebersberger), 8 vols (Vienna 1930), III, Nos. 3057 and 3149.
42. F.O. 120/883, Crowe to Akers-Douglas, private, 6 April 1911.
43. Kammerhofer, 'Pressepolitik . . .', in *Habsburgermonarchie VI*, p. 491.

preoccupations than on the actual state of affairs. In fact, the Austro-Hungarian government had nothing like complete control of the press. The strongly – often hysterically – pro-German tone of much of the Austrian press in the last years of peace was less the result of government inspiration than of the simple fact that the Austrian and Hungarian press was largely in the hands of German-Austrian Jews with German nationalist sympathies of a liberal kind. These people were men of considerable means and independent views, and were naturally sympathetic to Germany and hostile to the anti-semitic Tsarist government (and also to Great Britain, as Anglo-German relations deteriorated in the twentieth century). And all this quite regardless of the wishes of the Ballhausplatz. Indeed, in the 1880s and the early 1890s the warlike language of the Hungarian press was a constant embarrassment to Kálnoky; just as the raucous hostility of the Austrian press towards Great Britain during the Boer War, and its gloating about Russia's defeats at the hands of Japan, aroused the Ballhausplatz to impotent fury in the next decade. The Hungarian press joined heartily in the campaigns that helped to drive Kálnoky and Goluchowski from office; and in Austria both the clerical *Reichspost* (which had close links with Archduke Franz Ferdinand) and the Germanophile press on occasions launched sustained attacks on the incumbents of the Ballhausplatz – most notably (and with the encouragement of the German embassy) against Aehrenthal in his last years of office. If press attacks on Berchtold's pacific policy during the Balkan wars were indeed a factor in determining him to resort to force in 1914 it would have been the first time the press had exercised a significant influence on the making of policy. For if the foreign minister's influence over the press was more tentative and sporadic than was often assumed, there is no evidence that the influence of the newspapers over the Ballhausplatz had grown since the days of Andrássy, who assured the emperor in 1876 that, whatever the press might say, 'it can in no way at all restrict our freedom of decision'.[44]

Nor could other pressure groups outside the narrow circle of decision-makers do much to determine policy, at least in a positive sense. True, a foreign minister might make use of them, just as he might point to the attitudes of this or that national group, in the course of debates within the decision-making élite: thus Aehrenthal used the complaints of commercial interests suffering from a Turkish boycott during the Bosnian crisis to bring the Austrian and

44. Ibid., p. 476.

Hungarian governments to accept the need to pay financial compensation to Turkey. But for the most part Austrian and Hungarian commercial interests were sluggish and unadventurous: it was Berchtold, not the capitalists, who in 1913–14 took the initiative with plans for an excursion into the colonial field in Asia Minor; and even then commercial interests were exasperatingly slow to respond. It is true that economic pressure groups did on occasion exercise a significant influence in a negative, blocking sense: in the Metternich era, the opposition of Austrian industrialists fearing German competition (and enjoying the sympathy of Metternich's rivals and of the emperor) frustrated the Chancellor's plans to take Austria into the Zollverein – although the experiences of his successors who pressed on regardless showed that Prussian opposition might have defeated his plans in any case. In the constitutional era the demands of Hungarian agriculturalists for protection against Balkan competition seriously hindered the efforts of Kálnoky to hold on to Romania and of Aehrenthal to conciliate Serbia. But, as in other fields, these were factors that could restrict the freedom of manoeuvre of a foreign minister, limit the effectiveness of his policy, and, indeed, even damage the Monarchy's standing among the Powers; but they could not prescribe a positive policy for the Ballhausplatz.

As in the case of public opinion, economic factors were perhaps most significant in their broadest and most general sense – as constituting one aspect of the background against which the élite made its decisions. Here the fundamental fact was, of course, that Austria-Hungary was a relatively poor, agrarian country. Nor, as the nineteenth century progressed, did her relative position in the ranks of the Great Powers improve. On the contrary, the gap widened; and when the loss of her Italian possessions was followed by a world slump in the 1870s and the race to establish tariff barriers (which had a depressing effect on trade without yet doing enough to protect Austrian industry from German competition) she was hard put to it to maintain even her mediocre prosperity. Nor did the jealousy with which Austria and Hungary each sought to hamper the industrial development of the other help matters: as a Hungarian newspaper complained in 1900, 'the curses of Austria are launched against every fresh chimney-stack erected on Transleithan ground'.[45] This general economic weakness, at a time when more advanced industrial rivals, particularly Germany, were rapidly developing their economic activities in the Near East, did a

45. F.O. 7/1303, Thornton to Plunkett, No. 55, 25 October 1900.

good deal to undermine the Monarchy's position in its one remaining sphere of interest; and also lessened its chances of holding its own by diplomacy. At the same time, its economic weakness made itself felt even more painfully in the field of armaments. If diplomacy should prove an inadequate shield for its vital interests, the Monarchy could hardly look forward with relish to the prospect of war, even if, as in 1859, 1866 and 1914, the defence of its honour should demand it. Throughout the 'long nineteenth century' from 1815 to 1914, to seek salvation in the military capacity of the Monarchy was very much a counsel of despair.

2
Austria and the European States System of 1815[1]

The Metternich Era, 1815–1848

The Vienna settlement of 1815[2] left the Habsburg emperor, Franz I, in possession of an empire more extensive, but at the same time more compact, than any of his predecessors since Charles V. In addition to the central and eastern territories retained throughout the Napoleonic wars – Austria, Bohemia, Hungary and Galicia – Lombardy and Tyrol, lost during the wars, had been recovered; and Salzburg, Venetia and the Adriatic lands, annexed and lost again, had been finally regained. The Austrian Empire was thus firmly established in northern Italy, and by virtue of dynastic links with the central Italian duchies and a treaty with the king of the Two Sicilies, in a good position to fulfil the role assigned to it by the peacemakers of 1814–15 as a barrier against the resurgence of French power anywhere in the peninsula. In Germany, too, Austria was the acknowledged head of the new Confederation, which, like the Italian settlement, was, for all its deficiencies from a liberal or nationalist point of view, an eminently sensible arrangement in terms of the stability of the European states system. The German Confederation of 1815 combined a realistic recognition of the existence of the Austrian and Prussian monarchies with the creation of an organisation in central Europe strong enough to resist pressure from the 'restless' flanking Powers, France and Russia, and yet – in favourable contrast to anything that succeeded it – not cohesive enough to form in itself a disturbing source of pressure on its neighbours.

1. The following works are of particular relevance to this chapter: F.R. Bridge and Roger Bullen, *The Great Powers and the European States System, 1815–1914* (London 1980); A. Sked (ed.), *Europe's Balance of Power, 1815–48* (London 1979); Barbara Jelavich, *The Habsburg Empire in European Affairs 1814–1918* (Chicago 1969); and the works by C.A. Macartney, A.J.P. Taylor, A. Sked, and Adam Wandruszka and Peter Urbanitsch (eds) cited in Chapter 1, note 1.
2. D. Dakin, 'The Congress of Vienna 1814–15 and its Antecedents', in Sked, *Balance of Power*, pp. 14–33.

Not that the Austrian position was without weaknesses. Indeed, some of these arose from that very accretion of disparate territories under Habsburg rule that was one of its most imposing features. For instance, the Habsburgs might have done better to abandon Galicia, an exposed plateau lying beyond the Carpathians, the natural defensive frontier of the Monarchy in the north-east. This province, constantly at the mercy of the tsar's armies lately established in the puppet kingdom of Poland, was virtually indefensible unless Austria chose to burden herself with the odium of a preventive northward strike. To that extent Galicia remained something of a pledge of good behaviour to Russia throughout the nineteenth century. The annexation of the turbulent Republic of Cracow in 1846 could do nothing to alleviate this basic problem. Similarly, in the south-west, the long Dalmatian coastal strip relied for its defence on tenuous maritime communications, being cut off from the rest of the Monarchy by the Ottoman provinces of Bosnia and the Herzegovina. These provinces were themselves, so long as they remained under Ottoman rule, a constant source of disorder, strife and costly border raids. Yet Vienna was reluctant to seek a remedy by taking control of Bosnia at the risk of weakening the Ottoman Empire and creating perhaps even greater instability in the south-east.

Even so, these strategic deficiencies were of minor importance, compared to the fact that the apparent strength of the Habsburg state itself was to a great extent a mirage. By 1815 the Monarchy had achieved, by dint of a skilful diplomacy that exploited both the combined efforts and the divergent interests of its allies in the war against Napoleon, an imposing position that it would be difficult to maintain in the long run. The Monarchy simply lacked the resources to hold unaided what it had acquired only thanks to the assistance of the real Great Powers, Russia and Great Britain, acting temporarily in co-operation. In economic terms the Monarchy was a weak, agrarian Power, unable to compete with Great Britain and France in terms of industrial development, and lacking the manpower with which Russia made up for her deficiencies in that respect. The first years of peace, which saw a major financial crisis in Austria and the revival of British industrial and Russian agrarian exports, soon revealed the hollowness of the domestic basis of Austria's Great Power position. Even a little expedition against a handful of rebels in Naples in 1821 threw the finances into virtual bankruptcy, and undid much of the work of recovery since the Napoleonic wars.[3] For the Austrian Empire, with a population of

3. Adolf Beer, *Die Finanzen Oesterreichs im XIX Jahrhundert* (Vienna 1973).

30 millions and an army of a mere 230,000, the argument of force, the *ultima ratio* that alone could give reality to a claim to Great Power status, was lacking.[4] The mirage that had been conjured up by diplomatic skill and finesse would have to be maintained by the same means. The first time a Great Power seriously challenged it by force, it would vanish into air.

The Monarchy was confronted by threats to change the status quo to its disadvantage in three areas: in Italy and Germany, until the Austrians finally abandoned their position there between 1866 and 1871; and in the Near East, throughout the last century of the Monarchy's existence. Although the threat that arose in Italy and Germany from indigenous liberal and national movements chafing under the yoke of Habsburg dynastic conservatism could usually be contained by police measures and the occasional military demonstration, if ever a great military Power should lend its support to these movements, the problem for the Monarchy would be of an entirely different order.

In all three areas, such a Great Power challenge to the Monarchy's position was certainly a possibility. In Italy, every French government after 1815 was concerned to exploit anti-Austrian feeling and to re-establish French influence – possibly even as a first step towards the destruction of the whole 1815 settlement; and on occasion the French enjoyed the effective support of liberal circles in St Petersburg – witness, in the years after 1815, their successful encouragement of the resistance of the Italian states to Metternich's attempts to make good one of the deficiencies of the 1815 settlement and strengthen Austrian control of Italy by establishing a league of Italian states along the lines of the German Confederation.[5] In Germany, the final renunciation by Austria of the Holy Roman Empire and the defence of the Rhine had inevitably strengthened the position of a Prussia that had not forgotten the traditions of Frederick II, and which was steadily developing its economic ties with non-Austrian Germany through the Zollverein. Here again, the emperors of Russia, mindful of their dynastic links with the South German states (and in Nicholas I's case, with Prussia), were to prove allies of doubtful loyalty in upholding that Austrian supremacy which Russia had helped to establish in 1815. Finally, in the Near East, it had been clear since the Serbian Revolt

4. A. Wandruszka and P. Urbanitsch (eds), *Die Habsburgermonarchie 1848–1918, V: Die bewaffnete Macht* (Vienna 1987).
5. Roger Bullen, 'France and Europe, 1815–48', in Sked, *Balance of Power*, pp. 122–44; Alan J. Reinerman, 'Metternich, Alexander I, and the Russian Challenge in Italy, 1815–20', in *Journal of Modern History*, 46, (1974), pp. 262–76.

of 1804 that the Ottoman Empire might some day be replaced by a congeries of revolutionary nationalist states, some of which might have irredentist claims against the Monarchy itself, and all of which might look to St Petersburg for protection. For the Austrians it had been axiomatic, ever since Leopold II had abandoned his brother's policy of co-operation with Russia against the Turks in 1791, that the Ottoman Empire, for all its faults, was the best possible neighbour for the Monarchy, which should do nothing to weaken it. But the problem remained of how a weak Power like the Monarchy should respond if ever its mighty northern neighbour should seek to establish its control over the Ottoman Empire, or to replace it with a string of Russian satellites. Certainly, the Monarchy's freedom of action as an independent Great Power – already undermined by the establishment of the Russian satellite kingdom of Poland on its northern border in 1815 – would be gravely jeopardised if the Eastern Question so developed as to produce a complementary Russian encirclement of the Monarchy in the east and south.

It was the recognition of this simple fact, that the Monarchy was too weak alone to maintain the position that had been created for it by a coalition, which explains Metternich's unwearying efforts to enlist the support of at least one of the leading Powers of that coalition in defence of the established order in Italy, Germany and the Near East.[6] Essentially, this was an attempt to perpetuate in peacetime that spirit of solidarity which had fleetingly appeared in the final stage of the struggle against French hegemony.[7] Not that this was an entirely unrealistic aspiration. In the first place, the decision-makers in St Petersburg, London and Berlin all saw in the 1815 settlement their salvation after twenty years of social upheaval and international disorder. They broadly accepted Metternich's view that social and international upheaval were merely two sides of the same coin, and the view of his secretary, Gentz, that the peace settlement was designed to contain 'the restlessness of the masses and the disorders of our time'. In fact, so long as memories of the revolutionary and the Napoleonic eras remained fresh, these decision-makers were more than ready to endorse Austrian hegemony in central Europe and Italy, and even the need to maintain

6. Robert A. Kann, 'Metternich: a Reappraisal of his Impact on International Relations', in *Journal of Modern History*, 32, (1960), pp. 333–9; and for a discussion of the literature, see Paul W. Schroeder, 'Metternich Studies since 1945', in *Journal of Modern History*, 33, (1961), pp. 237–60.
7. F.R. Bridge, 'Alliance Diplomacy in Peacetime: the Failure of the Congress System, 1815–22', in Sked, *Balance of Power*, pp. 34–53; Irby C. Nichols, *The European Pentarchy and the Congress of Verona* (The Hague 1971).

the status quo in the Near East, as essential safeguards against a return to disorder. In the second place, Metternich was often able to make use of the very threats to the existing order themselves in his efforts to maintain it. The futile activities of alienated students in Germany could be painted in lurid colours to frighten the tsar and the king of Prussia – by 1818 the latter was even taking Metternich's advice in selecting his ministers; and France, where the restored monarchy not only seemed unable to contain revolutionary ferment at home, but was itself notoriously seeking to break out of the international restraints imposed on her by the 1815 settlement, was often Metternich's best ally in his efforts to persuade the other Powers of the need to perpetuate the coalition against her.[8]

There was, of course, nothing particularly noble about that stubborn insistence on the sanctity of treaties and legitimacy in international relations that made Austria, in Talleyrand's words, 'the House of Lords of Europe'. This was only common sense for a Power whose position, unlike those of the real Great Powers, could never rest ultimately on sheer force. Nor was there anything particularly enlightened or forward-looking in Metternich's devotion to the experiment in international organisation that historians have termed the 'Congress System': this was, after all, only an attempt to prolong into peacetime that coalition diplomacy of 1814–15 to which the Monarchy owed its salvation and its exalted position. It was no mere coincidence that, when France was formally admitted into the Concert at Aix-la-Chapelle in 1818, the Quadruple Alliance against her was renewed at the same time. For Metternich, as for Castlereagh, concert diplomacy and talk of international solidarity were a cover for a practical political alignment to preserve the status quo.

In the first years of peace the Austrians seemed to find a natural ally in Great Britain.[9] Nowhere did the interests of the two Powers clash: the concern of the British for their position in the Mediterranean and the Ionian Islands led them to welcome Austria's presence in Italy as a guarantee against a recrudescence of French influence there; their concern to preserve the balance of power against both France and Russia convinced them of the need for a strong central Europe based on Austrian control of Germany; and their fears for the land route to India through Turkey and Persia made them as averse as the Austrians were to the prospect of Russian domination

8. Guillaume de Berthier de Sauvigny, *Metternich et la France après le congrès de Vienne*, 3 vols (Paris 1968–71).
9. C.K. Webster, *The Foreign Policy of Castlereagh, 1812–22*, 2 vols (London 1925).

of the Ottoman Empire. Thus Castlereagh endorsed Austrian intervention against threats to the established order in Italy and Germany: the Carlsbad decrees might be met with murmurs of disapproval from France and Russia, but they were enforced without demur by the Hanoverian ministers of George IV; and when, during that monarch's visit to his German dominions in October 1821, Metternich paid a ten-day visit to Castlereagh, the two co-ordinated their tactics very successfully to dissuade the tsar from moving in support of his Greek co-religionists in their rebellion against the sultan. Similarly, Metternich had been unfeignedly relieved when French and Russian schemes to increase their influence in Spain by organising international intervention against the revolution of 1820 were thwarted by Castlereagh's state paper of 5 May. Indeed, throughout these years, Castlereagh and Metternich managed to frustrate the tsar's attempts to activate his Holy Alliance, through which he hoped to bring the Bourbon monarchies into play against the overweening maritime power of Great Britain, and to insist instead that international relations remain based on the Quadruple Alliance – a neat device whereby they both isolated France and contained Russia in a minority of three to one.

Unfortunately for Metternich, as for Maria Theresa before and Franz Joseph after him, a British alignment could never offer absolute security. It was not merely that Castlereagh, although personally as anxious as Metternich to continue in peacetime the habits of co-operation that had served the allies so well in 1813–15, was confronted at home with an isolationist and liberal public opinion that regarded as futile Metternich's attempts to unite the alliance in blank opposition to all changes in Germany, Italy and the Near East. There was the deeper problem that if ever Austria did secure British support, this always tended to drive France and Russia closer together, conjuring up the ghosts of 1803 and Tilsit. Moreover, even if Castlereagh could carry his policies against the groundswell of British opinion, the fact remained that Great Britain, since the demobilisation of her army in 1815 almost exclusively a naval Power, could do precious little to assist Austria in practical terms if she drifted into a confrontation with France and Russia. In the last analysis, if Great Britain could do little to help Austria, Russia could harm her infinitely more.

Metternich himself admitted this in the late summer of 1820 when he yielded to French and Russian pressure for a congress at Troppau to deal with the revolution that had broken out at Naples. His first instinct had been to intervene single-handed on the basis of an Austro-Neapolitan treaty of 1815; and Castlereagh, recognising the threat the revolution posed to Austria's position throughout the peninsula, had given him moral backing by strengthening the British Mediterranean squadron. The French, however, were absolutely determined that Austria must not be allowed to 'conquer Italy on the pretext of punishing the revolutionaries', and they hit on the idea – which found favour with some of the tsar's leading advisers – of internationalising the question and establishing a liberal regime at Naples which would put an end to Austrian influence there. This presented Metternich with a serious problem. He had no relish for a confrontation with France and Russia: British diplomatic, or even military and financial, support could not save Austria in the last resort. His acquiescence in the demand for a congress was logical enough; but the fact that he had to accept a mandate from the Alliance to intervene in an area that was after all supposed to be Austria's sphere of influence was nevertheless a remarkable confession of weakness. It also, on the point of principle, temporarily estranged his British friends, who insisted that intervention was a matter for individual Powers whose interests were threatened, not for the Alliance.

In the event, the affair turned into the greatest triumph of Metternich's career.[10] By a supreme feat of diplomatic skill he managed at Troppau to frighten the tsar out of his liberal proclivities, and to convince him that the Revolution was a universal menace with which compromise was impossible; and, when the congress adjourned to Laibach in January 1821, that the intervention in Naples should in practice be purely Austrian and reactionary in character. Never before or since did Metternich seem to be so much in control of events as at Troppau and Laibach, whence a French diplomat reported in disgust, 'j'ai vu le prince de Metternich dans tout l'orgueil de son triomphe'.[11] The altercation with Castlereagh over the theoretical purpose of the Alliance proved to be of no lasting significance, and the French were soon noting bitterly that Great Britain and Austria were 'like college friends, who can say anything to each other without breaking up [*se brouiller*]'.[12] Indeed, by the autumn of 1821 Metternich seemed to have squared the circle, and to have gained the support of both leading Powers of the old coalition: the measure of control over Russian policy that he had established at Troppau was complemented by the restoration of close relations with Castlereagh at

---

10. Paul W. Schroeder, *Metternich's Diplomacy at its Zenith, 1820–3* (Austin, Texas 1962).

11. H. Contamine, *Diplomatie et diplomates sous la restauration* (Paris 1970), p. 60.

12. De Sauvigny, *Metternich et la France*, II, p. 486.

Hanover. The Monarchy seemed to enjoy an altogether unprecedented security.

It was a fragile security all the same, dependent entirely on Metternich's ability to convince the decision-makers in the capitals of the real Great Powers that their interests were the same as Austria's. Hence, the catastrophic decline in Austria's position among the Powers in the 1820s. The role of personal factors should not be underestimated. By the time the Congress of Verona met to discuss the Greek and Spanish revolutions, Castlereagh was dead and his successor, Canning, intensely jealous of Metternich's pretensions to be the 'coachman of Europe', was simply not interested in co-operation with Austria. That in these circumstances Metternich was powerless to prevent French intervention in Spain was hardly surprising; but this intervention, the first independent French action since the Hundred Days, was clear evidence of the decay in the west of that concert of Europe by which Metternich was striving to contain France and to reinforce the 1815 system generally. Even worse was to come in the east, once Metternich could no longer count on British co-operation to restrain the tsar in the Greek question. True, Alexander I was in any case beginning to lose patience with Metternich's strictly negative advice; and it must be said that reports of Metternich's foolish boasting of his control over Russian policy made their own contribution to undermining his influence in St Petersburg. From 1825, however, the new tsar, Nicholas I, was in any case determined to free himself from Metternich's leading strings. When he proceeded to lend diplomatic and even military assistance to the rebels, and when both western Powers supported him, there was simply nothing Metternich could do. In 1827 financial stringency again dictated a reduction in the military budget, to such an extent that, according to the finance minister Kolowrat, Austria was 'armed for perpetual peace'.[13] By 1828, when Russia was involved in outright war against the Ottoman Empire, Metternich's isolation was complete; and he could only watch helplessly as the Russo-Turkish Treaty of Adrianople (1829) established a Russian protectorate over the Danubian principalities, marking an ominous advance of Russian influence along the south-eastern frontiers of the Monarchy.

The harsh fact was that in the power constellation of the late 1820s – a power constellation that had been created by factors largely outside Austrian control – Austria's interests, in both east and west, were more seriously imperilled than at any time since

13. Sked, *Decline*, p. 13.

1815.[14] If in 1821 Austria had enjoyed the support of both leading members of the wartime coalition, by 1828 she could count on neither. Metternich's fleeting hopes of restoring an effective working relationship with the British, who were, indeed, becoming increasingly uneasy about Russia's ambitions, came to nothing in the face of the confused party-political situation in London and the lack of clear direction in British policy after the death of Canning. With St Petersburg, his relations were decidedly bad – not surprisingly in view of the direct conflict between Austrian and Russian approaches to the eastern crisis. But again it must be said that the estrangement owed something to Metternich's own blunders, notably his gloating language about the difficulties the Russians encountered in the 1828 campaign. This contrasted starkly with Prussian expressions of sympathy; and relations between the tsar and his Prussian brother-in-law were exceedingly close. It was the obvious disarray in the old coalition that gave the French the opportunity to launch an ambitious diplomatic campaign to gain the support of Russia – 'notre allié naturel' – and Prussia, against Great Britain and Austria – 'nos ennemis vrais, implacables, éternels' – with a view to combining extensive territorial changes in the Near East with a revision of the 1815 settlement on France's borders.[15] Charles X speculated excitedly that 'perhaps a war against the Court of Vienna would be useful to me, in terminating the internal debates and occupying the nation *en grand* as it desires'.[16] True, at the last minute Metternich managed to head off the danger by his old tactic – prevailing on both his imperial master and the king of Prussia to harangue the tsar during his visit to Berlin, and to depict France as a dangerous hotbed of revolutionaries. But a price had to be paid all the same – namely Austrian acquiescence not only in a Russian advance in the east, but in a Prussian advance in Germany, with the extension of the Zollverein to embrace reluctant states in central and south Germany in these years.[17] Altogether the 1820s had demonstrated the interdependence of Austrian interests in the Near East and in central Europe, and pointed out the lesson – which was to be underlined even more painfully in the 1850s and 1860s – that the Monarchy depended for its security on the voluntary support of at least one of the leading Powers. Even Metternich could only lead if others were prepared to follow.

14. K. Hammer, *Die französische Diplomatie der Restauration und Deutschland* (Stuttgart 1963) pp. 128ff.
15. Ibid., p. 152.
16. Ibid., pp. 147–8.
17. Ibid., pp. 166, 194.

The 1830s showed, nevertheless, that Metternich's alarm had perhaps been exaggerated. Of the Great Powers, only the France of Charles X had been implacably hostile to Austria, whose isolation in the 1820s had been more an accidental by-product than the conscious aim of the other Great Powers. At any rate, events on the wider European scene in 1830 proved to be as beneficial to Austria's position among the Powers as those of the 1820s had been detrimental. The July Revolution in Paris not only eliminated the adventurous regime of Charles X, but replaced it with one that, from its origins to its end, was execrated by Nicholas I as the very embodiment of the Revolution.[18] The establishment of the July Monarchy banished for a whole generation the spectre of a Franco-Russian combination that had haunted the Austrians ever since Tilsit. Certainly, none of the Powers of the wartime coalition had as yet any desire seriously to weaken the position of Austria as established in 1815; and the Austrians were consequently able to maintain that position with relative ease against such indigenous forces as sought to undermine it in Germany and Italy.[19] Apart from an irritating French counter-demonstration at Ancona, there were no objections from the other Powers to Austria's suppression of the revolutionary disturbances of 1830–1 in Italy and the German states. Indeed, in the latter, Prussia was decidedly co-operative, readily according priority to the struggle against the revolutionary menace, and accepting Austria's leadership in further amending the constitution of the Confederation to deal with it.

It is true that the Austrian position in Italy rested solely on bayonets. For want of any federal organisation comparable to that at Austria's disposal in Germany, Metternich found himself in the distinctly unenviable position of having to prop up incompetent and exasperatingly wayward satellite regimes – which defiantly rejected his proposals for limited reforms – simply in order to stave off at all costs the triumph of even more overtly anti-Austrian forces on the Left. It is also true that Metternich was able to make little progress with his more constructive plans to develop commercial links with the Italian states, in the hope of giving not only their rulers, but also their commercial classes a vested interest in the maintenance of Austria's political predominance.[20] Here he was confronted with a variety of obstacles, some of which were to

18. Bullen, 'France and Europe', in Sked, *Balance of Power*, p. 136.
19. Alan J. Reinerman, 'Metternich, the Papal States and the 1831 Italian Crisis', in *Central European History*, 1977, pp. 206–19.
20. Ugo Cova, 'Oesterreich(-Ungarn) und Italien', in *Habsburgermonarchie VI*, p. 630.

bedevil Austrian attempts to develop the Monarchy's commercial interests in Germany and in the Balkans later in the century: protectionist interests at home, and competition from more advanced industrial states – in this case, France and Great Britain, who dominated the trade of Naples, and, through the establishment of Leghorn as a free port in 1815, the maritime trade of Tuscany. The great variety of economic conditions prevailing in Italy only added to the problem. At one extreme the Papal states were so backward in comparison with Austria that the papal government shrank from a customs union with Austria for much the same reasons that Austrian industrialists shrank from association with the Zollverein. In the case of Naples, Metternich was unable to prevail on his colleagues in Vienna to grant tariff reductions to relieve Austrian trade of discriminatory duties that worked in favour of the Western Powers; and the 1830s saw an actual tariff war between Austria and the Kingdom. Of the more advanced states, Piedmont's adoption of free trade in the 1830s was followed by such rapid economic development that she became herself a focus for rival plans for an Italian customs union; and while Tuscany remained too fearful of the frowns of Great Britain to co-operate in such plans, she would not listen to Metternich's proposals either. For the present, however, the Austrians had bayonets enough – at least more than their opponents had; and they remained defiantly determined to hold on: in 1838, for the first and last time, an Austrian Emperor was ceremonially crowned as King of Lombardy-Venetia in Milan.

Perhaps the greatest stroke of luck for the Austrians in these years was the radical change in Russia's policy. If in 1829 the Russians had already shrunk from throwing in their lot with French adventurism, and had opted for a policy of conserving and influencing, rather than demolishing, the Ottoman Empire, the events of 1830 in Paris, Belgium and Poland converted Tsar Nicholas to the doctrine of absolute respect for the established order everywhere. The upshot was the Austro-Russian Münchengrätz agreement of September 1833, pledging the two Powers to do nothing to upset the status quo in the Ottoman Empire. It is true that this agreement, like almost all later Austro-Russian agreements on the subject, was essentially negative: Metternich never responded to Russian hints that it might be developed to take account of possible changes in the status quo.[21] Indeed, Austro-Russian

---

21. G. Bolsover, 'Nicholas I and the Partition of Turkey', in *Slavonic and East European Review* (1948), pp. 115–45.

co-operation in the Near East always rested on the presumption that Russia must not seek to alter the status quo to her advantage. Even so, Metternich was able, as in the 1820s, to take advantage of St Petersburg's renewed apprehensions about an international revolutionary conspiracy; and when Münchengrätz was followed by a demonstration of Austro-Russo-Prussian solidarity against the Revolution, in the Berlin Convention of October, it seemed that Austria had recovered that security based on co-operation with the two eastern monarchies which she had first attained at the Congress of Troppau.

The rift with Great Britain took longer to heal, primarily for reasons of state: Palmerston had come to regard Austria's Russian friends as even greater threats to the status quo than France. Discerning – quite mistakenly – in the Münchengrätz agreement a deep-laid plot to partition the Ottoman Empire, he was striving to construct a quadruple alliance with France and the Iberian monarchies against the revived Neo-Holy Alliance.[22] Ideological differences, sharpened by the dramatic events of 1830, also played their part. On the one hand, if the Old Whig faction in the British government, stuck in the traditions of the 1790s, were sentimentally inclined towards an alliance with France, the mother of liberty, Metternich regarded Great Britain, after the Reform Act of 1832, as herself something of a revolutionary Power. On the other, the two Powers were kept apart by Metternich's own rigidly legitimist attitudes, expressed in his stubborn but quite futile efforts to support reactionary pretenders in Spain and Portugal against the liberal monarchs patronised by France and Great Britain, and by his equally futile encouragement of the resistance of the King of the Netherlands to the implementation of the Concert's decision on the frontiers of the new Belgian state. Finally, personal factors made their contribution; notably the rivalry between Palmerston and Metternich for the leadership of the Concert to which they both professed their allegiance.

When, however, the Eastern Question again became acute in 1839, with France seeking to promote the designs of her protégé Mehemet Ali against the integrity of the Ottoman Empire, and Russia making clear both her concern to preserve it and her willingness to co-operate with Great Britain to that end, Palmerston was cured of his ill-founded suspicions of St Petersburg, and, like Russia herself nearly a decade before, returned to the conservative

---

22. Roger Bullen, 'The Great Powers and the Iberian Peninsula, 1815–48' in Sked, *Balance of Power*, pp. 54–78.

fold. Metternich was quick to bring Austria into line with this dominant – and most congenial – combination; and he was rewarded when the conference that announced that the settlement of the Mehemet Ali affair was a matter for the Great Powers was held in Vienna. In the end, however, it was in London that the Concert of Europe was centred; and although the Austrians made a useful military contribution to the British naval action against Mehemet Ali, it was Anglo-Russian rather than Anglo-Austrian co-operation that restored the Near East to order. Once the two leading Powers of Europe saw eye to eye, they had no need for the mediation of a second-class Great Power such as Austria.

In some respects, however, the Eastern crisis of 1839–41 marked an undoubted improvement in Austria's position among the Powers. In so far as the security of a weak Power is better safeguarded by the consensus of a united concert than by membership of an embattled bloc, Metternich could count it a success that he was able to restore the Concert, and secure the admission of France to the five-Power treaty that finally ended the crisis (though here he owed much to the support of Russia and of pro-French elements in the British court and cabinet in moderating Palmerston's implacable hostility to France.) At the same time, in case the unity of the Concert should fail, the Monarchy's position among the Powers had improved, in that France's warlike posturing during the crisis had revived memories of alliance solidarity against her, and had called forth a heartening demonstration of support of Austria on the part of the German Confederation. As Metternich himself observed, France had done more for German unity in six weeks than Austria herself had been able to do in thirty years. All in all, the Austrian Monarchy, now supported by a combination of the two strongest Powers of Europe, who were again intent on containing, and if necessary resisting, French attempts to disturb the status quo, whether in Italy, Germany, or the Near East, seemed to enjoy a greater security than at any time since 1821.

There were differences, however. Whereas in 1821 Austria had herself held the key position, having established close relations with a Great Britain and a Russia who remained distant from each other and desirous of Austrian support, in 1841 she could never exercise that same measure of influence over a Great Britain and a Russia who had now found a basis of co-operation of their own. It was not simply that in the 1840s the Eastern Question, the principal basis of co-operation between Austria and the Anglo-Russian *entente*, remained dormant. The hard fact was that for Russia, so long as she had hopes of working with Great Britain – a real Great Power, and one, moreover, who seemed to the tsar not unwilling to discuss the future disposition of the sultan's territories – Austria was a Power of secondary importance. Nicholas I was in fact becoming increasingly bored, indeed irritated, by Metternich's despairing immobility. Even when the Austrians took firm action – in suppressing the Galician Revolt of 1846 – Nicholas had in effect to push them into extinguishing the independent Republic of Cracow, which had for many years been giving shelter to Polish dissidents. (Although arguably the republic had been in breach of its obligations under the Treaty of Vienna, its suppression was the first violation of the terms of the Treaty by a Great Power, and, in the light of the events of the following two decades, Austrian misgivings about setting such a precedent were perhaps understandable.) Finally, the sudden collapse of the Metternichian order in the face of what were after all relatively minor disturbances barely a year later seemed to the tsar yet further proof of the fatuity of Austria's claim to be taken seriously as a Great Power.

If the Monarchy's links with Russia in eastern Europe had become somewhat tenuous, it could no longer count on the support of Great Britain in Italy,[23] where from the 1830s a nation-wide revolutionary movement had arisen under Mazzini's leadership; and where from 1846 Metternich was faced in Pius IX with the disconcerting spectacle of a 'liberal' pope. True, the Austrians made some progress on the economic front:[24] in 1846 Metternich was able to overcome the objections of protectionist ministers at home, and a trade and shipping agreement with the Kingdom of the Two Sicilies at last secured a mutual reduction of tariffs, and put Austrian trade on a basis of equality with that of France, Great Britain and Spain. In 1847 he was able to put pressure on Naples and Modena to frustrate a Papal proposal for an 'Italian customs union' that would have excluded the Austrian lands; and he not only occupied Ferrara, as a warning to Pius IX, but secured alliances with the rulers of Parma and Modena, granting Austria rights of occupation in the event of an external threat to the Lombardo-Venetian kingdom. As far as international support for their stance was concerned, however, the British had long ceased to accord to the Austrians in Italy that positive support that Castlereagh had accorded them in the years after 1815. For Palmerston, the most effective barrier against a recrudescence of French influence there

23. A.J.P. Taylor, *The Italian Problem in European Diplomacy, 1846–49* (Manchester 1934).
24. Cova, 'Oesterreich(-Ungarn) und Italien' in *Habsburgermonarchie VI*, pp. 634–5.

was not Habsburg dynasticism, but its enemy, Italian national feeling. There could be no co-operation between a Palmerston encouraging the governments of the Italian states to adopt liberal constitutional reforms as the best prophylactic against revolution, and a Metternich exhorting them to adhere rigidly to absolutism. Indeed, according to Palmerston, Austria would do well to abandon the Lombardo-Venetian kingdom to Piedmont and concentrate on guarding the Near East against Russia – not an attractive proposition when it is remembered that Lombardy and Venetia were the two richest provinces of the impecunious empire, and that if Austria attempted to defend her Near Eastern interests by direct confrontation with Russia she might only find herself used as a battering ram by a Great Britain too distant to lend any effective support.

Needless to say, the Austrians could not find much support for their position in central Europe from their potential opponents. Metternich's efforts to establish a working *entente* with the increasingly conservative July Monarchy after 1847 produced very little. In the Swiss civil war of 1847–8 Austro-French diplomatic efforts to rally the concert in defence of the conservative and Catholic cantons of the Sonderbund were defeated by Palmerston's dilatory tactics, and by the French government's fear of provoking the liberal opposition in Paris too far; and at the Italian courts, for all his professed desire for an Austrian *entente*, Louis-Philippe could not resist the temptation to exploit Austria's growing unpopularity in the hope of enhancing France's position. In Germany, Prussia was increasing her economic and political influence over all the member-states of the Zollverein, to which Austria, to Metternich's chagrin, in 1841 again failed to gain admittance on terms that would satisfy Austrian industrialists fearful of German competition. At the same time, the replacement in 1840 of the strictly conservative Friedrich Wilhelm III by a king whose romantic notions inclined him to make concessions to popular and nationalist feeling made Prussia a less reliable ally against the Revolution than she had been in the 1830s.

As Metternich himself despairingly observed in March 1847, 'le monde est bien malade, et chaque jour le gangrène s'étend'. Although externally no Great Power as yet posed a direct threat, as the 1840s wore on the Austrians were finding themselves increasingly isolated in defence of their position in Germany and Italy; and the growth of nationalist tensions inside the Monarchy, especially between Magyars and Croats, and between Magyars and the central government, portended a serious weakening of the state itself.

The raising of all three problems at once and in an acute form, in 1848, nearly brought about the disruption of the empire even without the intervention of a hostile Great Power.

The Revolutionary Challenge Confronted and Defeated, 1848–1853

For three years after 1848 the revolutionary movements unleashed in that year posed a serious challenge to the position of the Habsburg Monarchy as established by the peace settlement in 1815. But the empire survived. The military power of the dynasty was still adequate to deal with threats that were not backed up by Great Power intervention.[25] The Austrian army defeated the attempt of Piedmont and the Italian states to drive the Habsburgs out of Italy, crushed the revolution at home, and, at Olmütz, forced Prussia to abandon her hopes of dominating a new Germany. The truth of Grillparzer's apostrophisation of Radetzky seemed self-evident: 'in deinem Lager ist Oesterreich'.

Even so, that the Army was able to ensure that the Monarchy in the end maintained its position among the Powers was largely due to the international situation, which still remained in its essential features that which had given the Monarchy its exalted position in the first place. It was the international situation that enabled the Army to deal with the dynasty's opponents unhindered. Although the Austrians had failed to establish particularly close relations with any Power in the 1840s, with the overthrow of the July Monarchy France once again became an object of suspicion to all the other governments; while of the two Great Powers that, themselves unaffected by revolution, now dominated the European states system more than ever – Great Britain and Russia – neither had any interest in seeing Austria disappear altogether from the ranks of the Great Powers. The Czech patriot Palacky's famous dictum of 1848 – 'if Austria did not exist, it would be necessary to invent her' – found a ready echo in both St Petersburg and London. And unsatisfactory though it might be for a Great Power to base its existence on the fact that other Powers could think of nothing better to put in its place, Austria was to continue, even after the fall of Metternich and after the disastrous wars of 1859 and 1866, to draw an illusory strength from this simple fact.

---

25. Alan Sked, *The Survival of the Habsburg Empire: Radetzky, the Imperial Army and the Class War, 1848* (London 1979).

Nicholas I, for example, although he might be scornful of Austria's demonstrable feebleness, and reluctant to involve himself too closely in her affairs, rendered the Habsburgs two valuable services: he helped to limit the impact of revolutionary disturbances on the south-eastern frontiers of the Monarchy, eventually even lending the sultan armed assistance to suppress the revolution in the Danubian principalities; and in the south-west, his clear warning to Paris that Russia would regard as a *casus belli* any move by the French against the system established in Italy by 'les actes dont elle est le garant' certainly had a sobering effect on the one Great Power that even contemplated striking a serious blow against Austria.[26] As a result, the authorities in Vienna were allowed a relatively free hand to deal with the problems that confronted them.

These were serious enough. If the political movements in Vienna and Prague left the government little enough time for foreign affairs, the movement in Hungary, which had an army behind it, and those in northern Italy, where indigenous movements against the status quo of 1815 now received military assistance from Piedmont (and, for a time, from the constitutional regimes established in Naples and Rome) fully absorbed the military capacity of the Monarchy until well into 1849. But perhaps the most serious consequence of the events in Hungary and Italy was that they paralysed the Monarchy's capacity to make good its interests in Germany, where the national movement was carrying all before it. Representatives from the German provinces of Austria were soon attending the new parliament at Frankfurt and participating in the debates about the future configuration of Germany; and in June 1848 even the Habsburgs felt obliged to bow to Frankfurt and allow Archduke Johann to assume the supreme office of *Reichsver-weser* in the service of the Assembly.[27] By the end of the year the latter body was even including in its speculations the absorption of the emperor's Austrian territories – to be linked henceforth only by a personal union with the rest of the empire – into the future German state.

At first, it was the threat to the Monarchy's position in Italy that appeared the more urgent and spectacular, with Piedmont sending its army against the Austrians, France waiting for an opening to come forward as the patron of the Italians and replace Austria as the dominant Power in the peninsula, and Great Britain pressing

26. P. Renouvin, *Histoire des relations internationales* (Paris 1954), V, p. 198.
27. Brigitte Hamann, 'Die Habsburger und die deutsche Frage im XIX Jahrhundert', in Heinrich Lutz and Helmut Rumpler (eds), *Oesterreich und die deutsche Frage im 19 und 20 Jahrhundert* (Vienna 1983).

Vienna to abandon northern Italy to Piedmont in the hope of thereby creating a more effective barrier to French influence than Austria herself had been. For a time it seemed that the hard-pressed incumbents of the Ballhausplatz in the Liberal era – Ficquelmont, Lebzeltern and Wessenberg, all septuagenarian diplomats of the Metternich school – might be prepared to cede at least Lombardy in the hope of securing British support. But in the event the issue was decided on the battlefield by Radetzky, whose forces proved more than a match for the local Italian forces at Custoza. The French were restrained, not only by Russia, but by Great Britain, from going beyond diplomatic gestures: and the British were in the last resort reluctant to press the Austrians too hard at the risk of opening the door to French influence. By the autumn, therefore, military success and the diplomatic stand-off between the Western Powers had allowed the Austrians to carry out an effective holding operation in northern Italy. True, the affair had distracted them from any effective intervention in Germany; and they had to leave it to Great Britain and Russia to force Prussia to suspend the military operations she had undertaken against Denmark in Schleswig-Holstein on behalf of the Frankfurt parliament. By the end of the year, however, there were signs that in Germany, too, Austria might be about to embark on a more determined policy, with the appointment of Prince Felix Schwarzenberg as Chancellor in November, and the replacement of the ineffective emperor Ferdinand by Franz Joseph on 2 December.

From the start, Schwarzenberg[28] enjoyed the young emperor's full support: as late as 1907 Franz Joseph still remembered him as 'my greatest minister'.[29] The new Chancellor, an experienced diplomat and a tough and clever *Realpolitiker*, had more faith in the Monarchy's future and a higher opinion of its capabilities than Metternich and his successors, and a lower opinion of the capabilities of the revolutionaries, already riven by internal dissent. He immediately made it clear that there were to be no concessions to the Revolution on any front – in Austria, Hungary, Germany or Italy. On 12 December a council of ministers resolved, with the emperor's full approval, that all the territories of the Monarchy must remain united in one great empire, and that there could be no question of any secession of the Austrian provinces into a new German state: on the contrary, if there were to be changes, then the

28. Rudolf Kiszling, *Fürst Felix zu Schwarzenberg. Der politische Lehrmeister Kaiser Franz Josephs* (Graz–Cologne 1952); Kenneth W. Rock, 'Felix Schwarzenberg, Military Diplomat', in *Austrian History Yearbook*, 11, 1975, pp. 85–100.
29. Erb MS.

empire ought 'in its entirety' to join the new 'league of states [*Staatenbund*]' to create an 'Empire of Seventy Millions' that would confirm Austria's lead over Prussia in Germany once and for all. As the German question was still a matter for theoretical debate at Frankfurt, this pronouncement did not have any immediate consequences. But it showed that a new wind was blowing in the Ballhausplatz; and by the spring of 1849 Schwarzenberg's uncompromising attitude provoked an intensified challenge in Italy and Hungary, with the renewal of the war by Piedmont, and formal declarations in Budapest of the deposition of the Habsburgs and the independence of Hungary. By the late summer, however, the dynasty's opponents in Italy and Hungary had been crushed and the Monarchy's position, on the surface at least, restored.

Again this was due in large measure to the favourable international situation, and to the fact that no Great Power was willing to lend material aid to the insurgents. In Italy, the diplomacy of Great Britain and France was still paralysed by their mutual suspicions, with the result that Radetzky was again able to defeat the Italian forces and impose peace on Piedmont on the basis of the status quo of 1815. Even so, British diplomatic pressure had been effective in restraining the Austrians from exploiting their victory to establish their political and military domination over Piedmont – by forcing her to abolish the *Statuto* granted in 1848 and to cede the important frontier fortress of Alessandria. In fact, in general terms the Austrian position was if anything somewhat weaker than it had been before 1848. Piedmont, who had after all launched an aggressive war against the 1815 settlement, had survived unscathed, had retained her liberal constitution despite Austrian objections, and was now a clearly recognisable focus for Italian hopes of future liberation. She continued, moreover, to make capital throughout the 1850s of the ready welcome she extended to political exiles from Lombardy and Venetia, whose well publicised, if hardly unmerited, tribulations served further to blacken Austria's reputation as a bastion of inhumanity and reaction among their numerous sympathisers in high places in London and Paris.

In Hungary, too, there was never any question of distant Great Britain and France lending effective help to the rebels. Indeed, Palmerston, for all his sympathy for Hungarian liberalism, and for all his talk of the Austrians as 'the greatest brutes that ever called themselves by the undeserved name of civilized men',[30] still saw in a strong and united Austrian Empire an essential barrier against the

---

30. R.W. Seton-Watson, *Britain in Europe 1789–1914* (Cambridge 1937) p. 266.

extension of Russian power in central Europe and the Near East. Hungarian liberalism would have to be sacrificed on the altar of the balance of power. Nicholas I, for his part, saw in a strong, conservative Austria an essential barrier against the spread of western liberalism to the borders of his empire; and it was the ominous presence of 10,000 Poles in Kossuth's army that led him to lend the Habsburgs actual armed assistance against the Hungarian rebels. Here again, however, a refugee question arose to plague Anglo-Austrian relations in the early 1850s; and even as regards Russia, the Austrian position was not quite what it had been before 1848, let alone in the days of Troppau and Münchengrätz. Russian assistance in Hungary was not entirely welcome to the Austrians: General Paskievich's telegram to the tsar after the capitulation of Világos – 'Hungary lies at the feet of Your Majesty' – was resented in Vienna, as was Russian criticism of the harsh treatment meted out to the defeated; and the suspicion that the tsar regarded Franz Joseph as somehow beholden to him for the recovery of Hungary brought an element of unease into Austro-Russian relations, whether or not Schwarzenberg ever made his famous boast: 'Austria will astonish the world with her ingratitude.'[31] The Habsburgs could, after all, have recovered Hungary even without Russian assistance. But it would have been a slow business, and in the summer of 1849 a speedy end to the war in Hungary was essential because of developments in Germany.

There, the Habsburg position had seemed to collapse entirely in 1848; and perhaps the most serious aspect of the situation was that in Germany the Monarchy was to find itself challenged by another Great Power: Prussia.[32] Vienna watched helplessly as liberal deputies in Frankfurt and royal ministers in Berlin discussed possible substitutes for the Confederation of 1815, culminating in March 1849 with the Frankfurt parliament's offer of the crown of a united Germany – excluding Austria – to the king of Prussia. As in Italy and Hungary, however, the Austrians were rescued from serious local difficulties by a favourable international situation. Neither Great Britain nor Russia was keen to see any significant alteration of the 1815 settlement in Germany (although the mildly sympathetic attitude of Queen Victoria and Prince Albert towards

31. Kenneth W. Rock, 'Schwarzenberg versus Nicholas I, Round One: The Negotiation of the Habsburg–Romanov Alliance against Hungary in 1849', in *Austrian History Yearbook*, 6/7, 1970/71, pp. 109–42.
32. Helmut Rumpler, *Die deutsche Politik des Freiherrn von Beust, 1848 bis 1850* (Vienna 1972); Roy A. Austensen, 'Austria and the "Struggle for Supremacy in Germany," 1848–64', in *Journal of Modern History*, 52, 1980, pp. 195–225.

kleindeutsch proposals was fiercely resented at Vienna, and lingered on as yet another legacy of the revolutionary years to the coldness that marked Anglo-Austrian relations in the early 1850s). On the main issue, however, if Russia since the eighteenth century had seen her security and her opportunity in the continued existence of both Austria and Prussia as Great Powers balancing each other, the British had no desire to see a monolithic and probably protectionist state controlling central Europe from the Alps to the North Sea. Both Powers had been quick to indicate their disapproval when Prussia began to pose a threat to the approaches to the Baltic and the North Sea by taking up the German cause in Schleswig-Holstein against Denmark. Nicholas I astutely played the legitimist card, hinting ominously that, as head of the house of Romanov-Holstein-Gottorp, he might be obliged to assert his own rights in the duchies, under the terms of a treaty of Catherine II, if the Danish royal house should lose possession. As with the French in Italy, the tsar's arguments made an impression. Similarly, a Russian warning to Berlin in March 1849 was sufficient to deter Friedrich Wilhelm from accepting the crown offered by the Frankfurt Assembly. With that, the radical-popular threat to the 1815 settlement in Germany disappeared.

The next threat came from the middle states, when the rulers of Saxony and Hanover reached agreement with Prussia in the Three Kings' Alliance of May 1849.[33] This envisaged a narrower confederation, tightening the links between Prussia and the non-Austrian states, within the framework of the original Confederation of 1815. Here, it was not external pressure, but Prussia's own greed and stupidity, that played into Austria's hands. Her transparent opposition to the admission of Bavaria as a fourth member, and her clumsy attempts to use the Alliance to secure complete domination over North Germany, drove the middle states to abandon it and turn to Austria with their plans for reform. Not that Schwarzenberg was any more interested than the Prussians in a genuine sharing of power with the liberal middle states.[34] He dallied with them simply to set the seal on the disruption of the Three Kings' Alliance, while himself settling for the *Interim* of 1849 – an agreement with Prussia providing for the joint control of the Confederation by the two leading Powers until a final settlement could be devised.

This in itself settled nothing: the real Austro-Prussian struggle

33. Rumpler, *Beust*, pp. 170–94.
34. Ibid., pp. 287ff.

was only just starting. Prussia continued to manoeuvre for a North-German Confederation under her own leadership, until, in November 1850, Schwarzenberg made a determined move to restore the authority of the old Confederation, summoning the Diet to act in support of the Elector of Hesse, who was at odds with his subjects. At first, the Prussians were defiant – 'we shall not tolerate the entry of foreign troops into Hesse, and if it comes to war, so be it' – and a few clashes with Bavarian troops occurred.[35] Schwarzenberg was undaunted, however. He had already assured himself of Russian support in two meetings with the tsar, and at the Olmütz conference – where the Russian ambassador played a decisive mediatory role – managed, on 29 November, to force Prussia to accept a return to the Confederation of 1815.

Of course, the Prussians had been bluffing. The Austrians, even without Russian support, still had the balance of military power in Germany on their side. Indeed, Schwarzenberg himself wondered whether he might not have done better to let it come to war, in order to crush Prussia once and for all.[36] With the benefit of hindsight, it can certainly be argued that his decision to settle for a compromise, in the hope of arriving at a tolerable *modus vivendi* with Prussia, was one of the great missed opportunities of Austrian history, comparable to Aehrenthal's letting Serbia escape with a promise of good behaviour at the end of the Bosnian crisis seventy years later. On the other hand, the condition of the Monarchy in 1850 was hardly such that any war could be undertaken lightly: even Schwarzenberg had recently exclaimed that without financial help from Russia, 'God knows what will become of us!'; and financial help was just what Russia had been unable to supply.[37] Moreover, no one was to know at the time of Olmütz that Austria was to be deprived so soon – by Schwarzenberg's sudden death fifteen months later – of the guidance of Franz Joseph's 'greatest minister'; nor was there, as yet, much evidence in Berlin of the energy and drive that Bismarck was later to inject into Prussian policy. It seemed at the time that the Austrians had managed to restore, with the acquiescence of a chastened Prussia, the position of 1815.

Not that Schwarzenberg managed to advance beyond that position in Germany any more than in Italy. Nor, perhaps, did he even wish to do so.[38] True, at the Dresden conference in 1851 he put

35. Erb MS.
36. Ibid.
37. Ibid.
38. Roy A. Austensen, 'Felix Schwarzenberg: "Realpolitiker" or Metternichian?

forward a plan for the admission of the whole Monarchy into the Confederation, on the face of it another bid to create and control an empire of seventy millions. But that was, perhaps, as he himself said, 'a scarecrow [*eine Popanz*]' to strengthen his hand in the practical negotiations with Berlin. (Austrian proposals for a customs union embracing the whole of central Europe owed more to the finance minister Bruck than to Schwarzenberg.) At any rate, Schwarzenberg did not press these plans once Russia spoke up for Prussia and the arrangements of 1815. For all his determination and energy, his own ideal for Germany was, perhaps, at bottom little different from that of Metternich: 'a close relationship with Prussia in a league of states under Austrian leadership'. But, as in Italy, the Monarchy's position in Germany was, if anything, rather weaker than it had been in 1848. The revolutionary years had shown how far Prussia was determined to go in her bid for leadership. And if Franz Joseph and Schwarzenberg had been misled, by her apparent submissiveness at Olmütz, into hoping for a period of genuine co-operation between the two great conservative German Powers against the Revolution as embodied in Cavour and Napoleon III, the experience of 1848 would not be forgotten by those who saw Germany's future with Prussia.

Finally, although the events of 1848–9 had seemed to vindicate the conservative Austro-Russian alliance in defence of the European order established in 1815, that order was in fact less securely based than before 1848, even in international terms. True, Great Britain and Russia had both defended the 1815 order, *faute de mieux*, in 1848–9; but they had not really co-operated in its defence. On the contrary, the tsar's diplomatic and military triumphs in central and south-east Europe had created in London a resentment and suspicion of Russia that was to lead, within a few years, to an Anglo-Russian conflict which was to shatter the international foundations of the 1815 system. Moreover, the reactionary policies adopted by the Vienna government after 1849 earned it the declared disapproval of Liberal ministers in London, and for the next few years kept the option of a British alignment closed to the Austrians – not that the latter, in turn resentful of British expressions of sympathy for their defeated opponents, were inclined to seek one anyway. In international terms, therefore, the Monarchy emerged from the revolutions of 1848–9 weakened both in Italy and Germany, and dangerously dependent on Russia for support.

The Evidence of the Dresden Conference', in *Mitteilungen des österreichischen Staatsarchivs*, 30, 1977, pp. 97–118. (Series hereafter cited as *MöSta*.)

The Eastern Crisis and the End of the Holy Alliance, 1853–1856

Despite the underlying weaknesses of its external position, the Habsburg Monarchy in the 1850s presented a confident, not to say defiant, face to the world. At home, at least, the emperor's authority had been restored; and for the next ten years Austria was governed in accordance with the lessons of 1848, as a military autocracy. No regard was paid to Magyar nationalism, which had at last thrown off the mask, and stood revealed as the mortal enemy of the dynasty. Indeed, no regard was paid to nationalism of any kind, which, with the failure of the various liberal and federalist attempts to devise satisfactory constitutions in 1848–9 had proved, in the eyes of Franz Joseph and his advisers at least, to be no viable basis for governing the empire. In the 1850s the Habsburg throne was said to rest on four supports: the army, standing; the priest, kneeling; the bureaucrat, sitting; and the spy, rampant.

Yet events were to show this rather theatrical authoritarian regime to be dependent in the last resort on military success; and from the start it concealed serious internal weaknesses that were in the end to have a disastrous effect on Austria's standing among the Powers. The Hungarians had been silenced, but not cowed – let alone reconciled to the regime, which was to be seriously embarrassed by their unreliability in the external crises of the 1850s. Even more serious was the parlous condition of the state's finances throughout the decade.[39] It is true that Austrian commerce and industry profited from the prolonged Europe-wide boom that followed the discovery of gold in California in 1849; but Great Britain, France and Prussia made even more striking advances, and the decade was one of relative decline in terms of the Monarchy's ranking in the European states system. In any case, the state was unable effectively to tap even such wealth as was created – for example, by attracting loans from a liberal bourgeoisie that found itself denied any role in the political life of the state, and that, since the bloody suppression of constitutionalism by the army, regarded that particular mainstay of Habsburg power as a hostile, almost alien, element in society. The divorce between the state and bourgeois society was certainly one of the reasons why the chronic lack of revenues that had undermined Metternich's attempts to assert Austria's authority abroad continued in the 1850s to limit the

---

39. Harm-Hinrich Brandt, *Der österreichische Neoabsolutismus: Staatsfinanzen und Politik 1848–1860*, 2 vols (Göttingen 1978).

effectiveness of Austrian diplomacy in the Eastern crisis. Indeed, it led in 1859 to diplomatic and military catastrophes of such magnitude as to convince even the emperor of the bankruptcy – both figurative and literal – of centralised absolutism.

Initially, however, the salient feature of the domestic scene in the 1850s was the triumph of the forces of order, and the underlying internal weaknesses of the regime had no more visible impact on its policies and attitudes than had the fundamental precariousness of its position among the Powers. Abroad, Russian support gave the Austrians a new confidence, and Schwarzenberg was able to make a show of implementing such 'strong' policies as he wished. No concessions were made to the Monarchy's opponents anywhere. After disturbances in Milan in 1853 the government pressed ahead, quite undeterred by the indignant protests of the Western Powers, with the sequestration of the estates in Lombardy of known enemies of the regime who had taken refuge in Piedmont. In Germany, Franz Joseph's hopes of an Austro-Prussian alignment, in which Prussia voluntarily accepted second place, seemed to move a stage nearer realisation when, in 1853, Prussia conceded a commercial treaty that left the door open to Austria's admission to the Zollverein.

In the Near East too, again with Russian support, the Austrians made determined efforts to assert their interests by displays of power. It is true that a counter-demonstration by Anglo-French naval forces at Constantinople was sufficient to frustrate their efforts in 1849 to compel the sultan to extradite a number of Hungarian rebels – including Julius Andrássy – who had taken refuge in Turkey. Three years later, however, they registered a notable success. At the end of 1852 the brutal suppression by the Ottoman governor of a rising in Bosnia was causing such indignation in neighbouring Montenegro that there seemed reason to fear the outbreak of actual hostilities. In February 1853 the Austrians, with Russian support, sent Count Christian Leiningen to Constantinople with a peremptory demand for the dismissal of the offending governor. The Turks complied immediately, and the Austrians seemed to have achieved a striking success. It should be noted, however, that the Russians drew two dangerous conclusions from the affair: that the sultan would always give way to such pressure; and that, if Russia ever wished to apply it, Austria was now under an obligation to lend her support.

In so far as the Leiningen mission documented Austria's direct interest in the affairs of Bosnia, it pointed to the possibility of a radical departure from her traditional conservative policy in the

Near East. Since 1815 the Monarchy's strategic position in the south had suffered from the fact that the kingdom of Dalmatia relied for its defence on tenuous maritime communications, the long coastal strip being cut off from the rest of the empire by the Ottoman provinces of Bosnia and the Herzegovina. Moreover, so long as these provinces remained under Ottoman rule, they were not only a constant source of disorder on the frontier of the Monarchy; they might at any moment produce an open conflict between the neighbouring semi-independent states of Montenegro and Serbia and Constantinople, which might in turn set the Balkans ablaze. It was not surprising, therefore, that demands were heard in Vienna – demands which met with some sympathy from the youthful emperor – that the Monarchy should itself take control of Bosnia.

These demands were not acted upon. In the Ballhausplatz, Metternichian views prevailed: that nothing should be done that might weaken the Ottoman Empire; and that an absolute respect for the status quo was an essential precondition of continued co-operation with Russia. When, in March 1852, the forceful Schwarzenberg was succeeded at the Ballhausplatz by Karl Ferdinand von Buol Schauenstein,[40] a cautious career diplomat of strictly conservative principles, these doctrines were even more firmly entrenched than ever; and the tsar decided that the *entente* between Austria and Russia, somewhat uneasy under the independent Schwarzenberg, would now be more than ever complete. He had no hesitation whatever about supporting the Leiningen mission. For Buol, too, the mission was not so much a new departure, let alone a forward move to advance Austria's special interests, as a precautionary measure to defuse a potentially explosive situation between Turkey and Montenegro before it caused a serious conflict on the very borders of the Monarchy. Similarly, the diplomatic support that Buol had accorded to Napoleon III in his promotion of the claims of Catholic monks against their Orthodox rivals in the Holy Places question at the end of 1852 had only reflected his solicitude for Austria's prestige as the leading Catholic power, with rights of protectorate of its own in the Ottoman Empire (in Albania) since 1606. It was in no sense meant as part of the challenge to Russia that Napoleon intended. Under Buol, as under Metternich, Austrian policy in the Near East was still essentially conservative.

The 1850s nevertheless saw a complete transformation of the

---

40. Roy A. Austensen, 'Count Buol and the Metternichian Tradition', in *Austrian History Yearbook*, 9–10 (1973–4) pp. 173–93.

international situation; and this was not the result of any change in Austrian policy, but of a change in the relationship between the two leading upholders of the 1815 settlement, Great Britain and Russia. In the summer of 1853 Russia made a bold attempt to change the balance of power in the Near East decisively to her advantage. Prince Menshikov was sent on a mission to Constantinople, to demand, not only satisfaction in the Holy Places question, but the recognition of the tsar as protector of all the Orthodox subjects of the sultan, some two-fifths of the population of the empire. This was nothing less than an attempt by Russia to demonstrate to Europe her primacy at Constantinople; and it evoked in Great Britain an equally uncompromising determination to destroy Russia's position at Constantinople and her influence in the Ottoman Empire, and to put an end to the dominant position she had seemed to occupy in Europe since 1849.

Faced with this conflict of Titans, Buol, with the resources of what was after all only an impecunious second-class Great Power at his disposal, not surprisingly proved no more able to control events than Metternich had been when faced with Anglo-Russian co-operation against the Ottoman Empire in the 1820s. Moreover, it was axiomatic for Buol, as it had been for Metternich, that there could be no question of Austria's continuing to co-operate with Russia if that Power was seeking to alter the status quo in the Near East to its own advantage. The Menshikov mission demonstrated that Russia had broken with that policy of respecting the status quo which had been the basis of the Austro-Russian *entente* since Münchengrätz. Indeed, Russia's subsequent attempts to browbeat the sultan, by occupying the Danubian principalities (July 1853), and by stirring up unrest in the western Balkans, posed a direct strategic threat to the Monarchy.

In terms of Austria's general position among the Powers, however, there were weighty reasons behind Buol's desperate attempts to resolve the crisis by diplomacy before it produced an actual war between Russia and the Western Powers. Such a war would confront Austria with the dilemma of having to make a choice between the belligerent Powers – a choice which, given her vulnerability both in the Near East and in Italy, she was ill-equipped to make. Unfortunately for Buol, however, his determined and patient efforts, by means of a series of compromise proposals within the framework of the Concert and of the Holy Alliance, to enable Russia to retreat from her threatening posture without losing face, came to nothing. On the one hand, the British were persistently obstructive, not trusting the tsar to keep his word, and being above all determined to document the humiliation of Russia before Europe;[41] on the other hand, the tsar, ever mindful of the services he had rendered to the Habsburgs in 1849, and more recently over the Leiningen mission, would be content with nothing less than full support, and regarded even Buol's compromise proposals as treason to the Holy Alliance. In this situation, Austria was helpless. By the spring of 1854 Great Britain and France were at war with Russia, and both the Concert and the Holy Alliance, which had given Austria her security since 1815, lay in ruins.

Although the Austrians were immeasurably exasperated at the uncompromising attitudes of both parties, it was Russia who seemed to pose the more direct and more immediate threat. Even in the years when she had held loyally to the conservative *entente* of Münchengrätz, her activities had on occasion injured Austrian interests. For example, in her determination to protect the grain exports of southern Russia from Romanian competition, she had made use of her territorial advance in 1812 to the Danube delta, and the protectorate she had acquired over the Danubian principalities themselves in 1829, to obstruct the operations for improving the navigation of the Danube – to the detriment not only of Romanian, but also of important Austrian trading interests. Her latest pretensions seemed to Buol absolutely unacceptable. In the long debate that ensued in Vienna, in the spring of 1854,[42] he set his face firmly against suggestions from the pro-Russian military party at court in favour of making a common cause with Russia against Turkey, and establishing Austrian control of the western Balkans – even though the emperor himself was quite attracted by the idea. Like every Austrian statesman after him, Buol considered the price of such co-operation prohibitive, both in terms of weakening Turkey, and of establishing a dangerous Russian strategic threat to the Monarchy in the eastern Balkans. In Buol's view, recent events showed that even the status quo of 1853 hardly gave the Monarchy adequate security: not only could there be no question of allowing Russia to make further advances in the Balkan peninsula; she must actually be pushed back from the position she had held in 1853. Austria must find her security in a permanent weakening of Russia in the Near East that would deprive the latter of any springboard

41. Paul W. Schroeder, *Austria, Great Britain and the Crimean War: The Destruction of the European Concert* (Ithaca 1972).
42. Paul W. Schroeder, 'Austria and the Danubian principalities, 1853–6', in *Central European History*, 2 (1969) pp. 213–36; Idem, 'A Turning Point in Austrian History in the Crimean War: the Conferences of March 1854', in *Austrian History Yearbook*, IV–V, (1968–9), pp. 159–202.

from which she might launch further advances against Turkey, either militarily, or diplomatically, in the manner of the Menshikov mission.

To strengthen his hand for the impending confrontation with Russia, Buol managed to extract a limited degree of support from Prussia and, eventually, the other German states, in the form of a defensive alliance to maintain the status quo (April 1854).[43] The long-term consequences of this for the Monarchy's position among the Powers were to be very serious. In the first place, it drove Nicholas I to new paroxysms of rage, finally setting the seal on the destruction of the Austro-Russian alliance: 'the time has come, not to fight the Turks and their allies, but to concentrate all our efforts against perfidious Austria and to punish her severely for her shameful ingratitude'. In the second place, it weakened Austria's position *vis-à-vis* Prussia within the German Confederation. Bismarck, now the Prussian representative in the Diet at Frankfurt, astutely exploited the reluctance of the German states to be drawn into a conflict – in which their interests were, after all, hardly directly involved – to convince them of their common interests with Prussia in restraining the 'warmongers of Vienna'. The resounding defeat in the Diet, in February 1855, of an Austrian proposal to mobilise the forces of the Confederation, was a telling illustration of Prussia's enhanced position within that body. At the same time, Prussia's insistence on the strictly defensive character of the alliance of April 1854, and her interpretation of her own neutrality in a markedly pro-Russian sense – for example, her allowing Russia to use Prussian ports to evade the Anglo-French blockade – stood in stark contrast to Austria's threatening troop movements, which tied down so many of Russia's forces as to condemn her to a position of relative inferiority, and to humiliating defeat, in the Crimean theatre.[44] In St Petersburg, these things were long remembered; and in so far as the Austro-Prussian struggle over the future of the 1815 settlement in Germany was as much an international as a purely German affair, the consequences for Austria's position among the Powers were to be embarrassing in the extreme.

In the Near Eastern arena, and in the short term, Buol's policy was more successful. By July, an Austrian ultimatum to St Petersburg, threatening intervention on the side of the Western Powers, had forced Russia to withdraw her forces from the Danubian

43. Ernst Rudolf Huber, *Deutsche Verfassungsgeschichte seit 1789*, 7 vols (Stuttgart, 1960–), III, pp. 239ff.
44. Winfried Baumgart, *The Peace of Paris, 1856* (Oxford, 1981), p. 2.

principalities. This gave the Monarchy immediate strategic security – especially as the theatre of the war then moved to the distant Crimea. At Turkey's request, the Austrians then proceeded to occupy the principalities themselves, in a move to strengthen both the military threat they posed to Russia and their own negotiating position in St Petersburg. More than this, Buol went on to draw up, in consultation with the French, the Four Points of 8 August, expressly designed to prevent any Russian advance in the Near East in future: not only was Russia to be deprived of her capacity to threaten Turkey in the Black Sea, she was to give up her claims to protect any Christian minorities whatsoever in the Ottoman Empire. Of course, some of these claims, notably those in Serbia and in the Danubian principalities, had been established at considerable sacrifice of Russian blood and money, expressly sanctioned in international treaties, and implicitly recognised by Austria at Münchengrätz. The Four Points, by which Buol committed himself to altering the status quo in the Near East – in this case, naturally, to Russia's disadvantage – showed that Austria too had finally broken with the policy of the Holy Alliance.

Buol had embarked on an ambitious policy; but he was in no position to pursue it by military means. Indeed, although he was always prepared to consider diplomatic pressure, and even threatening military gestures, he was absolutely determined to avoid any commitment to support the Western Powers in actual war. After all, the Monarchy was still convalescent from the upheavals of 1848–9: several provinces were still under martial law as late as May 1854, and at the end of 1855 the demands of financial stringency even forced the government to reduce its expenditure on the army. Above all, it was clear to everybody in Vienna that if Austria joined the war, it would be transformed from a Crimean war into a great European war – one that would be fought chiefly on Austrian territory, and in which the Western Powers could be of little direct assistance.[45]

Whether Buol would be able to achieve his aims through skilful diplomacy remained to be seen. It was, of course, advantageous to him that the Western Powers had their own good reasons for compelling Russia to submit to the Four Points. Buol, for his part, gave them all the support he could, short of actual military assistance; and even in the theatre of war itself, the effect of the pro-Western neutrality of Austria (and Sweden), which obliged the tsar to employ the vast majority of his forces in defending Russia's

45. Ibid., pp. 40ff.

western frontiers, was of enormous importance. After all, in Buol's view, Austrian interests too were at stake in the Crimea. His pro-Western orientation did not spring from any fear that France might otherwise stir up Piedmont (an ally since January 1855) against Austria: when, in December 1854, he signed an alliance with the Western Powers pledging Austria to work with them for the implementation of the Four Points, he had taken care to extract from France a guarantee of Piedmont's good behaviour for the duration of the war. It was simply that Buol had come to the conclusion that the Monarchy could expect no lasting security in the Near East unless Russia could be forced to admit defeat, draw back from the position from which she had launched her advance in 1853, and mend her ways.

Not that Austria's relations with her partners in the alliance of December 1854 were really cordial. Buol was often exasperated by the intransigence of the Western Powers – in the spring of 1855 for example, when the governments of London and Paris disavowed their own negotiators, and brought to nothing a compromise proposal based on the idea of an agreed balance of naval power in the Black Sea, which had already been agreed in principle by Buol and the ambassadors of the belligerent Powers in conference at Vienna. The Western Powers, for their part, had only scorn and indignation for Buol's stubborn refusal to commit Austria to war, and he in turn was coldly indifferent to their pleas – the December alliance had not committed Austria to military intervention, and if the Western Powers had signed it under the misapprehension that this would be the eventual outcome, that was their affair. On the necessity of somehow bringing Russia to heel, however, Buol and his alliance partners were still fundamentally agreed.

Hence Buol's endorsement, despite his original misgivings, of his allies' demands for the actual neutralisation of the Black Sea – an unprecedented infringement on the sovereignty of a Great Power; hence his own insertion into the preliminary peace proposals of the allies of the demand that Russia cede to Moldavia the Bessarabian bank of the Danube, which Russia had held since 1812; hence his threat, in an ultimatum of January 1856, to break off diplomatic relations with Russia – as a result of which Russia at last agreed to open peace negotiations on the basis of the allied proposals. The demand for the cession by Russia of Southern Bessarabia, intelligible enough in terms of Austria's narrower commercial and strategic interests, was perhaps a fateful error. Since the 1820s Austria's Great Power status had depended, not on control of the Danube delta, but on a good relationship with Russia. The cession of Southern Bessarabia – the first loss of territory by Russia since the time of Peter the Great, and, to make matters worse, at the dictation of a Power that had not even fired a shot – was regarded in Russia as a greater slur on Russia's honour than any of the demands of her opponents on the battlefield.[46] Hatred of Austria rose to new heights of intensity – and not only in St Petersburg, but at the Russian embassy in Vienna, whence the ambassador, Gorchakov, was about to be recalled to assume the direction of Russian foreign policy.

In the short term, and in relation to the Monarchy's local problems in the Near East, the Treaty of Paris of 30 March 1856 was a success for Buol's policy. The possibility that Russia might once again attempt to establish control of the Ottoman Empire, as she had done in 1853, was certainly reduced – by the neutralisation of the Black Sea; by Russia's renunciation of her established rights of protectorate over Serbia and the Danubian principalities in favour of the Concert; by the admission of the Ottoman Empire itself into the Concert; and, most strikingly, by the tripartite treaty of 15 April 1856, by which Great Britain, France and Austria gave Turkey a unilateral guarantee against any future Russian attack. As for Austria's particular interests, although she had not managed herself to retain control of Moldavia and Wallachia, the clauses in the Treaty of Paris prohibiting a union of the two principalities and confirming their status as provinces of the Ottoman Empire under the sultan's suzerainty seemed to offer some guarantee against the creation, on the south-eastern frontier of the Monarchy, of a unitary nationalist state, possibly with ambitions in Transylvania; and the removal of Russia from the mouth of the Danube gave the Monarchy more security in that quarter than it had enjoyed since 1812.

In the long term, however, and in relation to Austria's position in the European states system as a whole, the Treaty of Paris left the Monarchy far from secure. The trouble was that the European alignments on which the treaty rested were exceedingly unstable.[47] Even at the Congress of Paris itself, there had been sharp altercations between Austria and her former allies and co-signatories of the tripartite treaty: on 8 April, the British raised the issues of the misgovernment of the Papal states and Piedmont's complaints against Austria; and if the debate came to nothing, the Austrians were nevertheless immensely exasperated by it. They were almost

---

46. Ibid., p. 49.
47. Werner E. Mosse, *The Rise and Fall of the Crimean System, 1855–71* (London 1963).

equally indignant at French suggestions that they hand over the Lombardo-Venetian kingdom to Piedmont in exchange for the primitive Danubian principalities. The Congress of Paris was the first occasion since Troppau at which Austria's position in Italy had been openly questioned at an international gathering; and the Austrians drew the obvious conclusion that they could not hope for much support from France or Great Britain if that position should be called in question at any future congress.

Even more serious, perhaps, Russia, hitherto the chief supporter of the established order in Europe, was now the revisionist power *par excellence*; and she was more than willing to countenance revision of the 1815 settlement in the west – primarily to the disadvantage of Great Britain and Austria – in the hope of setting a precedent for, and gaining the *quid pro quo* of, revision of the 1856 settlement in the Near East. Her closest supporter on the continent was Prussia, whose studied benevolent neutrality in the late war contrasted markedly with Buol's activities, and who was not in the least concerned to enforce the 1856 settlement. In France, Napoleon III, intent on replacing Austrian influence by French in Italy, was about to pursue revision in the west as an end in itself; and if Russia could not yet bring him to countenance openly the revision of the 1856 settlement, he could certainly not be counted on to support Great Britain and Austria in enforcing it. As for Great Britain, if she had a common interest with Austria in the Near East, she had a healthy fear of a Franco-Russian *rapprochement*, and was anxious to hold on to her *entente* with France for general European purposes.

It was such considerations that brought Great Britain, in 1857, to yield to French pressure and to cease supporting Austria's efforts to enforce the restrictions imposed by the Treaty of Paris on the unification movement in the Danubian principalities.[48] The constitutional changes that were implemented there in 1858, under French patronage and in defiance of the Treaty, were an ominous first step towards the creation of a Romanian national state. That even autocratic Russia, despite her resentment at Moldavia's possession of Southern Bessarabia, supported these changes was proof enough that the tsar, like Napoleon III, saw in them primarily a means of distracting Austria and undermining her capacity to defend her interests elsewhere. This early defeat in the Romanian question was taken very seriously in Vienna: indeed, according to Buol's successor, it was the chief reason for that minister's fall in

---

48. F. Engel-Janosi, 'Drei Jahre der Orientfrage, 1856–59', in Idem, *Geschichte auf dem Ballhausplatz*; Lawrence R. Beaber, 'Austria and the Emergence of Roumania, 1855–61', in *East European Quarterly*, XI (1971) pp. 65–78.

the spring of 1859.[49] At any rate, it was eloquent of the total isolation into which Austria had fallen by the end of the 1850s.

Of course, these disastrous developments cannot simply be ascribed to the alleged mistakes of Austrian statesmanship during the Crimean War. Austria's failure to secure the support of any of the former belligerents in the troubles she faced after 1859 is sometimes attributed to Buol's ill-advised policy of neutrality in 1854, which alienated Russia completely, while it only irritated the Western Powers. This theory is attractive for its simplicity; but for the rest, there is little to be said for it. As far as the Western Powers were concerned, they had hardly been well disposed towards Austria's position in Italy, even before the Crimean War; and their unhelpful – indeed hostile – attitude at the end of the fifties, was less an expression of some irrational desire to 'punish' Austria for her actions some five years before, than of their assessment of their own interests in the question at issue in 1859. Then, the parlous position in which Austria found herself among the Powers was the consequence of these harsh realities, and of her own activities in the years after, rather than during, the Crimean War. As far as Russia was concerned, Alexander II's high regard for the obligations of honour and Gorchakov's injured vanity may have injected a more personal element into policy-making; and Buol can indeed be accused of a certain lack of foresight when he created in the Bessarabian question such a formidable – indeed, in Russian eyes, symbolic – barrier to any *modus vivendi* with St Petersburg after the war. Yet, here again, it must be said that it was not Buol, but the tsar, who had first abandoned the status quo policy of Münchengrätz; and unless Austria had been prepared actively to connive at a Russian advance in the Near East – something that even Metternich had always refused to contemplate – the Holy Alliance could not have been saved anyway. Nor could the Austrians, if they might perhaps have done less inadvertently to promote it, have done much to prevent the developing *rapprochement* between Russia and Prussia. Russia's attitude towards Austria's predicament in 1859, like those of the Western Powers, reflected her assessment of her own interests at that time, in relation to Austria's activities since, rather than during, the Crimean War.

Even so, the Eastern crisis of 1853–6, and the realignment of the first-class Great Powers that resulted from it, marked the end of an era in terms of Austria's position in the European states system.

49. [Archives Nationales, Ministère des Affaires Etrangères, Paris, Correspondance politique] Autriche 479, Moustier to Thouvenel, No. 42, 28 April 1861.

3
The Fruits of Isolation, 1856–1871[1]

The End of the 1815 Settlement in Italy

The collapse of the Holy Alliance in the Crimean War was followed within a decade by the violent overthrow of the 1815 settlement in Italy and Germany. These events were not unconnected: without the support of either Great Britain or Russia, Austria was simply too weak to sustain that position in central Europe which the flanking Powers had secured for her and helped her to uphold for a generation. Yet the very comprehensiveness of her fall from power, which left her by 1871 with her position in Italy and Germany shattered and her interests in the Near East still under threat, has brought down on the decision-makers of Vienna the severe criticism of historians.[2] It is, of course, impossible to say whether a willingness to make concessions in one of the three threatened areas would actually have saved the Austrian position in another; but the fact remains that Austria's refusal to conciliate Russia in the Near East, combined with her confrontation with the Western Powers over Italy, won her no supporters in her most decisive and most disastrous conflict, that with Prussia over Germany. On the other hand, there was perhaps something to be said for the Austrian argument that even the most modest display of willingness to abandon unimpeachable treaty rights in one area would only have undermined the Monarchy's position in others, and would have amounted in effect to a renunciation of the very *raison d'être* of the Habsburg dynastic state. And in any case, the simple fact was that the very idea of adopting the opportunist tactics of Cavour, Bismarck and Napoleon III, for whom expediency was everything and honour nothing, was something quite foreign, indeed repugnant, to the young Franz Joseph, to whom

1. Of particular relevance to this chapter are the works by A. Wandruszka and P. Urbanitsch (eds), C.A. Macartney, A.J.P. Taylor, A. Sked and F. Engel-Janosi cited in chapter 1, note 1; and by Barbara Jelavich and F.R. Bridge and Roger Bullen cited in Chapter 2, note 1.
2. Cf. the discussion in Sked, *Decline*, pp. 167ff.

honour was everything, expediency nothing. Certainly, the ultimate responsibility for the policy of attempting to defend Austria's position in three areas at once must rest with the emperor himself, who after Schwarzenberg's death in 1852 began to take a much more active interest in foreign affairs, and appointed three foreign ministers in succession to pursue that very policy.

Of the areas under threat, it was always Germany that touched Franz Joseph's honour most nearly. As he himself succinctly defined his position: 'I am a German prince [*Ich bin ein deutscher Fürst*]'; and he attached perhaps even more importance to the 'princely' than to the 'German' attributes of his role.[3] Indeed, he always regarded the German Confederation primarily in dynastic terms, as a league of German rulers. He had himself more German than Habsburg blood in his veins; his mother was a Bavarian princess, whose sisters were married to the kings of Prussia and Saxony; and his own marriage in 1855 to Elizabeth of Bavaria both symbolised and reinforced in these years his consciousness of the ties that bound the House of Habsburg into the German dynastic system. For German nationalism, by contrast, which had inflicted such humiliations on him at the start of his reign, he never felt the slightest affection; indeed, he never ceased to regard it as a potential threat to himself and his fellow German rulers, and to cherish the hope until well into the sixties that all these rulers, including the king of Prussia, would in the last resort make common cause against it. This hope was, of course, an illusion: by the 1850s Prussia was determined to challenge Austria's primacy in the Confederation, and was prepared to make use of German nationalism to undermine it. Franz Joseph, however, seemed unable or unwilling to grasp this, and continued to cling to both elements of Metternich's prescription for the management of German affairs: that the Confederation should be controlled by a conservative alliance of the two leading monarchies; and that Prussia should continue to accept the role of Austria's loyal lieutenant. The emperor, and later Rechberg and Mensdorff, were inclined to put the emphasis on the first; Schwarzenberg, by contrast, very definitely on the second: and it was because he expected Karl Ferdinand Count von Buol-Schauenstein to take a firm stand against any Prussian challenge to Austria's leadership that the dying Chancellor recommended him to Franz Joseph as his successor.

---

3. Brigitte Hamann, 'Die Habsburger und die deutsche Frage im XIX Jahrhundert', in Heinrich Lutz and Helmut Rumpler, eds, *Oesterreich und die deutsche Frage im 19 und 20 Jahrhundert* (Vienna 1983).

In fact, Buol's German credentials were not all that impressive.[4] True, he was the son of a mediatised imperial count who had served as Austria's first presidial representative in the Diet at Frankfurt after 1815; and he himself had served for nineteen years in German posts before Schwarzenberg sent him as ambassador to St Petersburg (1848–51) and London (1851–2). Even so, he still displayed in 1852 what his rival Bismarck remarked on as a 'really incredible' unfamiliarity with the German question, and, indeed, openly confessed his inability to understand it. Certainly, his handling of the Germans was no great success; and his overbearing manner, vanity and notorious irascibility gave much needless offence to Austria's potential friends in the Confederation. (He also – perhaps significantly for his diplomacy in the eastern crisis of 1853–6 – failed to establish any rapport with the Russians during his years at St Petersburg, and left London, according to Prince Albert, without having made a single friend.) Not that any of this detracted from his own confidence in his ability: 'I wish', Bismarck exclaimed, 'that I could be but for one hour of my life that which he takes himself for all the time'. Metternich had no opinion of him either, describing him as 'a knife with a sharp point but no cutting edge', and making the extraordinary suggestion that the emperor appoint him foreign minister on a temporary basis only, 'to try him out'. In the view of some historians Buol, admittedly one of the least successful of Franz Joseph's foreign ministers, has been treated too harshly by critics who underestimate the obstacles with which he had to contend. Yet it is difficult to avoid the conclusion that his own deficiencies as a statesman, particularly his narrow bureaucratic outlook, and his inability to establish a clear order of priorities between different aspects of Austrian policy and co-ordinate them into a coherent whole, made their own contribution to the failures of that policy in these years.

Not that Buol emerged particularly badly from the first test of his abilities, which came, not over Germany, but over the Eastern Question. At any rate, he managed to steer safely between the most obvious hazards, refusing to become the cat's-paw of either Russia, to further the advance of that Power along the south-eastern frontier of the Monarchy, or of the Western Powers, at the cost of transforming Franz Joseph's dominions into the battleground of a Europe-wide conflict. But even in these early years Buol was short-sighted in pressing the Bessarabian question to the extent that Russia emerged from the crisis as the Monarchy's mortal foe; and

4. Erb MS.

the lack of tact and judgement he displayed in handling the neutrality issue in the German Confederation played into the hands of Bismarck, and left the Monarchy with a difficult inheritance in Germany, which now, along with Italy, moved into the foreground of Austria's external preoccupations.

Indeed, it is for his performance in these areas, rather than in the Near East – where the choices facing the Monarchy were perhaps impossibly difficult – that Buol is most open to criticism. Not that the position in Germany was easy. In the later fifties the Austrians were unable to make any progress whatever towards integrating the Monarchy into the economic affairs of the Confederation, which Prussia, in her determination to retain exclusive control of the Zollverein, was tending more and more to exclude from the debates of Frankfurt. Perhaps not much could be done about this: the economic development of the German states was making giant strides during these years, while the Austrian economy, still languishing under the economic effects of the Near Eastern crisis, fell ever further behind; and whereas the states of the Zollverein weathered the world recession of 1857 by increasing production, industrialists in the Monarchy again took refuge behind an impenetrable 'Chinese wall of Austrian custom duties'.[5] On the political front, however, errors of judgement were made that had serious repercussions on Austria's standing, not only in the Confederation, but in Italy.

The Neuchâtel affair,[6] for example, while not particularly important in itself, was almost a textbook example of the interconnection between Austria's position in Germany and in Italy. In the principality of Neuchâtel, since 1707 a personal possession of the Hohenzollerns, and also, under the Vienna Settlement of 1815, a canton of the Swiss Confederation, a republican regime had seized power in 1848; and ever since 1852 the Swiss had been defying a declaration of the five Great Powers restoring the king of Prussia's rights. Matters came to a head in September 1856 when the Swiss imprisoned and threatened to try for treason the leaders of an abortive royalist coup in the principality. The Prussians brought the affair to Frankfurt, arguing that a threat to the non-German territories of a member state of the Confederation constituted an injury to the whole Confederation; and invoked Article 47 of the Federal Act, which obliged members to support each other in

---

5. Klaus Koch, 'Die außenwirtschaftlichen Beziehungen der Monarchie', in *Habsburgermonarchie VI*, p. 548.
6. Ernst Rudolf Huber, *Deutsche Verfassungsgeschichte seit 1789*, 7 vols, (Stuttgart, 1960–), III, pp. 249ff.

defensive wars. In December, Friedrich Wilhelm IV personally implored his imperial nephew to endorse a Prussian military strike against Switzerland. This was certainly an opportunity the Austrians might have seized to tie the Confederation to an interpretation of Article 47 that they might themselves some day find useful in the event of a challenge to their position in Italy. Buol, however, insisted that the matter was one for the signatories of the 1852 declaration to deal with, and vainly urged the rulers of the South German states to deny Prussia the right of transit through their territories. In the end Napoleon III managed to persuade the Swiss to release the imprisoned royalists and the king resigned himself to the renunciation of his rights in Neuchâtel, duly recorded by the five Great Powers meeting in conference in Paris. Prussia had been put in her place. But the whole affair had done nothing for Franz Joseph's reputation as the leading *deutscher Fürst*; and it was a defeat – endorsed, disturbingly enough, by the Concert – for dynasticism and the legitimist principle. Most ominous of all, perhaps, was the fact that the only ruler to speak up for Prussia was Napoleon III. The longer-term consequences of the Neuchâtel affair for the Austrians were only seen when they themselves sought to invoke Article 47 against Napoleon's challenge to their position in Italy two years later.

Indeed, even before this there were signs that the Austrians might some day find themselves confronted in Italy with a baleful combination of Piedmont, France and Prussia. Until 1857, the efforts of Bruck to build on Metternich's foundations and reinforce Austria's political position in Italy by developing her economic links with the states of the peninsula had been by no means unsuccessful. The renewal of Metternich's commercial treaty with the Kingdom of the Two Sicilies in 1856 saw a further lowering of tariffs on both sides; and by the end of that year a whole network of agreements had been completed between Austria, the Papal States and the Central Duchies on postal and telegraphic communications, and for the building of a Central Italian railway. When in 1857, however, Bruck and Buol began to press seriously for an Italian customs union, to be linked ultimately to the Zollverein to form a big Central European customs union, with Austria at the hub of the whole system – a plan, in effect, 'to isolate Prussia in Germany and Piedmont in Italy' – the scheme came to grief. Even the first link in the chain – a customs union between Austria and Parma concluded in October 1857 – had to be abandoned in the face of objections from Piedmont and – orchestrated by Prussia – from the Zollverein. It was no nearer achievement when war broke out in 1859.[7]

Not that the 1859 crisis in Italy was the result of any Austrian initiative. The Austrian position in northern Italy was essentially the same as it had been for the past four decades; and if neither Palmerston nor Napoleon III would shed any tears to see Austria ousted by Piedmont, neither had dared to make any serious moves to bring this about at the last major European congress in 1856. Indeed, for most of the 1850s there seemed little to choose, from a Piedmontese point of view, between Franz Joseph established in the north and Napoleon III scheming to reinforce French influence in the Papal states (where a French garrison still upheld the authority of Pius IX in the capital) and – possibly through a Muratist restoration – in the Kingdom of the Two Sicilies. Without Great Power support, Piedmont's sulky refusals to respond to Austrian proposals for solving the refugee problem could not seriously threaten the peace of Europe.

The situation changed suddenly in the summer of 1858, when Napoleon, as a preliminary move in his schemes to revise the whole 1815 settlement, pledged himself at Plombières to assist Piedmont in a war to conquer Lombardy and Venetia and to reorganise the peninsula as a confederation of four states – provided only that Austria could be brought to assume the role of aggressor. (The proviso was important, because Austria could call on the assistance of the German Confederation in a defensive war.) Napoleon III's icy observation to the Austrian ambassador at the New Year's reception in the Tuileries – 'je regrette que nos rapports ne soient pas aussi bons que je désirerais qu'ils le fussent' – was widely interpreted as an indication that war was soon to be expected;[8] and by the spring of 1859 both Austria and Piedmont were openly preparing for war. At this juncture a short-lived Tory government in London, sympathetic to the traditions of 1815, and above all apprehensive of French designs, proposed a congress to defuse the crisis. This move, designed to help the Austrians, failed when the latter suddenly presented Turin with an ultimatum demanding that Piedmont immediately cease her military preparations, and on 29 April precipitately invaded the kingdom.

These Austrian actions were not incomprehensible. The effort involved in preparatory military measures was more debilitating and costly for the cumbersome Monarchy, whose finances after four years had still not recovered from the expenditure incurred in the Near Eastern crisis, than it was for Piedmont. Indeed, the latter

7. Ugo Cova, 'Oesterreich (-Ungarn) und Italien', in *Habsburgermonarchie VI*, p. 652.
8. Alexander von Hübner, *Neuf ans de souvenirs* (Paris 1904), p. 238.

could only enhance its position *vis-à-vis* the Monarchy the longer the tension continued. It was also psychologically impossible for a ruler of Franz Joseph's temperament, with his rigid sense of honour and his deep feelings of righteous indignation at the blatant challenge to Austria's unimpeachable treaty rights, to respond to the threats of France and Piedmont by humbly agreeing to enter into negotiations, the purpose of which was to deprive the Monarchy of territory, without having recourse to the arbitrament of war. (His instinctive reactions were to be much the same in 1866 and in 1914.) Buol was less set on war; and it seems that he endorsed the ultimatum in the hope that it might somehow end the crisis with a diplomatic victory for Austria: even if France had squared Russia, Buol was apparently counting on British and Prussian support at a congress. At any rate, if Piedmont could be forced at the outset to humble herself before Austria by accepting the ultimatum, Austria could face with composure a congress that could then hardly do other than endorse the status quo. If Piedmont continued defiant, however, then even Buol admitted that war was inevitable.

In the event the Austrian move was disastrous, and immediately plunged the Monarchy into total isolation. Buol and Franz Joseph had paralysed the diplomacy of Austria's friends in London, and at the same time deprived her of the right to invoke the support of the German Confederation in a defensive war. Buol paid the price of his diplomatic miscalculations with the loss of office (4 May); Franz Joseph, with the loss of most of Lombardy: for diplomatic errors were compounded by weaknesses at home which deprived the Monarchy of any advantage of surprise that might have accrued from the precipitate declaration of war. Not only did the war bring the Monarchy itself to the very brink of financial collapse, and expose the total inadequacy of the brittle military–bureaucratic regime that ruled Austria in the 1850s; the unappeased unrest in Hungary, and the unreliability of the Hungarian forces in Italy, had disastrous consequences on the North Italian campaign itself; and this was made worse by the timidity of the mediocre Austrian commanders in the field, who failed to strike down Piedmont before French assistance could arrive. The result was defeat at Magenta and – in the presence of Franz Joseph himself – Solferino.

Meanwhile, the international situation had taken an ominous turn. In London, the replacement of the Tories by a Liberal government headed by the Italophile triumvirate of Palmerston, Russell and Gladstone, finally killed any hope that the British might in the end speak up for the Italian settlement they had helped to establish in 1815. Events at Frankfurt were even more depressing. Although opinion in the middle states, and amongst German nationalists, was on Austria's side, it was Prussia who held the key to the situation; and the wretched state to which Buol and Bismarck had reduced Austro-Prussian relations now bore bitter fruit. Any forlorn hopes which Franz Joseph may have cherished that 'perhaps Germany and this despicable scum, Prussia [*dieser schmählicher Auswurf von Preussen*]⁹ will yet stand by us in the end' were dashed, as Prussia single-mindedly exploited Austria's embarrassments to improve her own position in the Confederation. She eventually mobilised six army divisions on the Rhine to show the Austrians that she had something to offer; but she adamantly refused to commit them to action unless the Austrians would concede to her the command over the northern forces of the Confederation. After their defeats, the Austrians were prepared to concede even this, which virtually implied a position of equality for Prussia, not only in the action in question, but in the affairs of the Confederation generally. But the Prussians, never seriously interested in fighting, began to raise legalistic points; and when they shifted their ground to demand that command be exercised in the name of the King of Prussia, rather than in that of the Confederation, the negotiations finally broke down.¹⁰ The Austrians were disappointed and bitter; and they were even more dismayed to discover that Prussia was putting out feelers to London and St Petersburg with a view to imposing a mediated peace settlement.

They were not totally without resource, however. It is true that their hopes for a return to the Holy Alliance were disappointed. Indeed, Russia positively welcomed the weakening of Austria as a weakening of the 1856 system. No help could be expected from the new government in London; and Prussian support in Italy could only be bought at a price Franz Joseph was unwilling to pay. There remained, however, France herself. At the eleventh hour Austria, isolated, and facing the prospect of expulsion from Italy by the diplomatic intervention of the Concert, was saved by the embarrassments of Napoleon III.¹¹ Magenta and Solferino had done nothing to weaken the Austrian defensive position in the fortresses of the Quadrilateral – a fortification system that had never yet been taken by an enemy. Napoleon, already disillusioned by Piedmont's annexationist ambitions in central Italy, which went well beyond

9. Hamann, 'Die Habsburger und die deutsche Frage . . .' in Lutz and Rumpler, eds, *Oesterreich und die deutsche Frage*, p. 218.
10. Huber, *Deutsche Verfassungsgeschichte*, III, pp. 260–3.
11. Richard Blaas, 'Die italienische Frage und das österreichische Parlament, 1859–66', in *MöSta*, 22 (1969) pp. 151–245.

the Plombières agreement, and facing the prospect of a long and bloody war with no certainty of the continued neutrality of Prussia and the German states, decided that he might do well to settle with the Austrians direct. The Austrians, too, decided that they stood to lose less by direct negotiations with the foe, which in any case accorded better with Franz Joseph's sense of honour: 'je n'eusse jamais cédé à un Aréopage européen'.[12] The upshot was the armistice of Villafranca of 11 July, formally confirmed in the Treaty of Zurich of 10 November. To avoid all semblance of any concession to the revolutionary principle of nationalism, Franz Joseph ceded most of Lombardy, not to Piedmont, but to Napoleon III (who in turn bestowed it on Victor Emmanuel). At the same time, Austria retained Venetia and her defensive position in the Quadrilateral; the Central Duchies were assigned, not to Piedmont, but to their exiled lawful rulers; and Austria herself was to be a member of the confederation into which the Italian states were to be organised.

On the face of it, the Habsburgs had done extraordinarily well. Despite their defeats on the battlefield, they had retained a good military position on the Mincio, both for defensive purposes, and perhaps even as a springboard for an attempt to recover the territories signed away in Lombardy: 'those, we shall get back in a couple of years [*die werden wir uns in ein zwei Jahren wieder holen*]', Franz Joseph declared.[13] But the apparent success was an illusion. On the one hand, it remained an open question whether the terms of the Treaty of Zurich could ever be enforced. On the other hand, in failing to relieve Austria once and for all of Italian commitments that were only realistic in terms of the states system of 1815, which had vanished beyond recall, Villafranca and Zurich proved for the Habsburgs a veritable *damnosa hereditas*, perpetuating the isolated and exposed position in which they had found themselves since 1856.

Meanwhile, in Bernhard Count von Rechberg-Rotenlöwen,[14] Buol's successor as foreign minister (and from 1859 to 1861 also president of the council of ministers), Franz Joseph had found an adviser after his own heart. Born in 1806, son of the Bavarian representative at the Congress of Vienna, Rechberg had entered the Austrian foreign service in 1828, serving mainly in German posts,

---

12. Ibid., p. 159.
13. Ibid.
14. Friedrich Engel-Janosi, *Graf Rechberg. Vier Kapitel zu seiner und Oesterreichs Geschichte* (Munich 1927); Richard B. Elrod, 'Bernhard von Rechberg and the Metternichian Tradition', in *Journal of Modern History*, 56 (1984), pp. 430–55; Sked, *Decline*, pp. 175ff.

and gaining a reputation, under Metternich's tutelage, as something of an expert in the German question. In 1848 he had voluntarily accompanied Metternich into exile, and had remained in close touch with him throughout the 1850s. His recipe for handling the German question, with which he was chiefly concerned as Austrian representative at Frankfurt between January 1855 and April 1859, was thoroughly Metternichian: control of the Confederation in close partnership with Prussia, while insisting on upholding Austria's presidential rights, her 'birthright'. Of course, not much progress was made in this particular direction. The time for Metternichian solutions was clearly past; and even if Buol had not seemed so intent on gratuitously humiliating Prussia – as in the Neuchâtel affair – Berlin was set on achieving absolute equality. But Rechberg, conciliatory in negotiations, and, in contrast to his chief in Vienna, well informed, made enough progress towards restoring Austria's links with those middle states whom Buol's high-handed methods had been driving towards Prussia to catch the eye of the emperor, who had marked him out as Buol's successor even before the war of 1859.[15]

Once in office, Rechberg set about re-establishing Austrian policy on a thoroughly conservative, Metternichian basis. Not that, in terms of style and personal appearance, there was very much that was Metternichian about this 'dry, sober, highly-strung and fidgety [*nervös und zappelig*] bureaucrat', who according to Bismarck looked 'more like a lawcourt official [*Kammergerichtsrat*] than a diplomat and Count Rechberg'. Nor was there much of Metternich's urbane nonchalance in his handling of subordinates at the Ballhausplatz: *Referent* Meysenbug, who had complained about his salary, was sharply reminded that he was free 'to resign and sue me in the courts . . . Agitation and opposition I do not intend to tolerate'.[16] But the principles of his policy would have had Metternich's full endorsement: 'We have always stood out against policies of annexation [*le système d'annexions*] because to substitute for treaties by which territorial limits have been fixed by the Powers in concert [*d'un commun accord*], geographical necessities, or plebiscites [*votations populaires*] or strategic guarantees would be, in our view, to deprive international relations of every element of security.'[17]

The difficulty was, that these principles were not endorsed by the foreign governments with whom Rechberg had to deal. The

15. Erb MS.
16. Ibid.
17. Archives Nationales, Paris, Correspondance politique, Autriche/476, Rechberg to Metternich (copy), 29 March 1860.

French, for example, who were by no means blind to the advantages of striking a bargain with Austria over Italy, found it difficult to establish any close rapport with a man who explained 'everything that has happened in Italy in terms of the intrigues [*menées*] of Piedmont' and the 'exaggerated expansion of higher education, which has created a kind of literary proletariat furnishing perpetual recruits for the revolutionaries' – while any suggestion that 'Italian patriotic feeling' might be a factor provoked an outburst of rage.[18] Co-operation with Great Britain was perhaps out of the question anyway, in view of the policies of the Italophile Liberal government in London; but Rechberg objected equally strongly to their methods – the publication of Blue Books was 'a veritable plague [*peste*], which rendered impossible any confidential relations with the government of Great Britain'.[19] As for Russia, she made it brutally clear that none of Rechberg's preaching about monarchical solidarity would induce her to support Austria in Italy; while the Eastern question, which Rechberg, self-confessedly no expert, left in the hands of the Oriental department and Prokesch – who he admitted was '*très Turc*'[20] – offered no hope for co-operation either. It seemed that despite the change of minister, and despite Franz Joseph's hopes of France and Prussia, Austrian isolation was set to continue.

This being the case, Rechberg's policy – like Buol's essentially one of upholding the Monarchy's treaty rights in three threatened areas at once – was over-ambitious. The emperor's dreams of securing German help in order actually to reverse the decision of 1859 in Italy was, of course, entirely divorced from reality. But even Rechberg's more modest objective, of simply enforcing the Treaty of Zurich – an objective which Franz Joseph was to endorse and pursue doggedly until 1866 – was only one aspect of a policy that was *in toto* quite beyond the resources of the Monarchy. In Germany, Rechberg's and the emperor's hopes of maintaining the status quo with the assistance of a submissive Prussia were to prove equally unrealistic. In the Near East, Austria's determination to uphold the system of 1856 continued to form an insurmountable obstacle to a *rapprochement* with Russia. It is true that Rechberg himself, as a sincere Catholic, felt some sympathy for French and Russian moves to protect the Christians of Syria, Montenegro and the Danubian principalities from what seemed to him to be a cruel

18. Ibid., Moustier to Walewski, No. 3, 30 December 1859; to Thouvenel, No. 13, 11 February 1860.
19. Ibid., Moustier to Thouvenel, No. 36, 30 March 1860.
20. Ibid., Autriche/479, Moustier to Thouvenel, No. 13, 28 January 1861.

Muslim regime at Constantinople.[21] But the arguments of the entrenched body of conservative Near Eastern experts in the Ballhausplatz, and his own suspicions that the unrest in Montenegro and the principalities might be inspired by the unholy trio of Kossuth, Klapka and Garibaldi, soon persuaded him of the wisdom of a strict adherence to the status quo.[22] Fortunately, the Near East remained relatively calm in the early sixties. But as it was, Rechberg's strict insistence on maintaining the Monarchy's treaty rights in even two of the threatened areas at once – Italy and Germany – led to new disasters.

In practical terms, the hopes that the Austrians rather naïvely placed in Napoleon III – if only because they had nowhere else to turn – brought very meagre rewards.[23] At the end of 1859 Prince Richard Metternich was sent as ambassador to Paris to work for this '*entente désirable*'; but it was soon clear, from Napoleon's connivance (at great cost to his own reputation amongst his clerical supporters) at the publication of the pamphlet *Le Pape et le congrès*, advocating the incorporation of the Papal states into Piedmont, that Napoleon was engaged in a deadly competition with Great Britain for influence in Italy, and would do nothing to enforce the Treaty of Zurich. For fear of precipitating matters, the Austrians now ceased to press for a congress to discuss the future Italian confederation. But matters were precipitated all the same: in 1860 Piedmont proceeded to the formal annexation of the Central Duchies, the Kingdom of the Two Sicilies, and most of the Papal States, the Kingdom of Italy being formally proclaimed in March 1861. The Austrians were dismayed, and along with the other continental Powers broke off relations with Turin; but they were in no position to intervene militarily to arrest the course of events. They were still exhausted after the war of 1859, and in the throes of a constitutional reform which, if it appeased German liberal centralists, left the Magyars as hostile and unreliable as ever. Franz Joseph learned from his meeting with the Prussian regent and the tsar at Warsaw in October 1860 that there was no hope of assistance from Austria's former Holy Alliance partners. Devious Napoleon was still Austria's only resource; and it was, as much as anything, the desperate concern to do nothing which might spoil the chances of achieving the '*entente désirable*' that restrained the Austrians from action

21. Ibid.
22. Ibid., Autriche/477, Moustier to Thouvenel, No. 72, 30 July 1860.
23. Richard Blaas, 'Il problema veneto e la diplomazia austriaca', in *Conferenze e note accademiche nel centenario dell'unione del Veneto all'Italia* (Padua 1967), pp. 14–15.

against Piedmont in 1860. At the same time, however, they were almost fanatically determined never to recognise the new state of affairs. For the next six years they adamantly refused to discuss any Italian questions whatever, except 'on the basis of the Treaty of Zurich, the non-execution of which is at the root of the situation which preoccupies Europe'.[24]

This attitude was not incomprehensible. True, the emperor's judgement was clouded by emotion: as late as 1866 he was declaring that to make a diplomatic approach of any kind to the Kingdom of Italy – even for a mutually beneficial commercial treaty – would be 'a scandal' incompatible with his honour. But there were weighty reasons of state, too, why Franz Joseph, as ruler of a multi-national empire founded on the dynastic principle, should insist on conducting foreign policy on the basis of established treaty rights; and why he could not recognise the national principle, on which the Kingdom of Italy was founded. To do so would be to open the door to the loss of Venetia – already being demanded by Italian irredentists – and of the South Slav and Romanian-inhabited territories of the Monarchy.

It was with such considerations in mind that Rechberg, and Mensdorff after him, always refused to listen to pragmatic British suggestions for finally winding up Austria's Italian responsibilities by handing over Venetia to Italy, in exchange for a much-needed pecuniary compensation. In domestic terms, Venetia was in any case still regarded as of considerable strategic and economic value. In international terms, other proposals for solving the Venetian question, such as those of Napoleon III, appeared to the Austrians as contrary to elementary principles of statesmanship and common sense. During the Polish revolt of 1863, for example, Napoleon certainly gave the Austrians an opportunity to escape from their isolation through a French alliance. But Austria was to pay for this, not only by ceding Venetia to Italy, but by joining France in a war against Russia and ceding Galicia to a liberated kingdom of Poland. Franz Joseph would not for a moment consider ceding two provinces merely to improve Austria's diplomatic position. Napoleon's proposal of April 1866 for the cession of Venetia in exchange for the Danubian principalities, again at the risk of war with Russia, fell on equally deaf ears in Vienna. The Venetian question was, nevertheless, fatal to Austria's hopes of escaping from isolation by a *rapprochement* with France. Indeed, as the Kingdom of Italy had been recognised by all the other Great Powers by 1862, and in 1865

24. Ibid., p. 23, n. 27.

even by Catholic Spain, the Austrians' stubborn adherence to the Treaty of Zurich, their delusion that what they pleased to term the '*fantôme de l'unité italienne*'[25] would prove a fleeting phenomenon on the international scene, led the Monarchy into a world of unreality, and isolated it totally from all the other Powers. It was certainly no viable basis for an effective policy in the developing struggle over Germany.

The Struggle for Mastery in Germany, 1862–1866

The situation in Germany after the war of 1859 was problematical.[26] Although in theory Austria was still, as in 1815, undisputed head of the Confederation, in practice she had relied, ever since 1815, on a partnership with Prussia to control the other German states. Now relations with Prussia had been seriously embittered by the war of 1859; by Prussia's coldly calculating attempts to exploit the embarrassment of the Austrians; and by Franz Joseph's publication of the 'Army Order of Verona' of 12 July, putting the blame for the catastrophe in Italy on Prussian disloyalty.[27]

In the sixties the conflict sharpened. In Vienna, the February Patent of 1861 established a constitutional regime that found favour with the German-Austrian bourgeoisie (to whom the government was desperately looking for loans); and their patron, Anton Count Schmerling, whose voice as *Staatsminister* counted for even more than Rechberg's on this issue, was determined to exploit Austria's new image as a liberal, centralised, German state, not merely to uphold, but to strengthen and develop her position within the Confederation. Prussia, for her part, was equally determined to exploit to the full her leading position in German economic life, as she showed when in 1862 she concluded, and eventually forced the other members of the Zollverein to accept, a commercial treaty with France that lowered tariffs to a degree that virtually ruled out the admission of Austria to the union.[28] Franz Joseph and Schmerling were undeterred. Overcoming his distaste for the German national movement, the emperor arranged to celebrate his birthday

25. Blaas, 'Die italienische Frage', p. 166.
26. H. Rumpler, 'Oesterreich und die Gründung des deutschen Reiches' in *Europa und die Reichsgründung*, (Historische Zeitschrift, Beiheft 6) (Munich 1980).
27. Blaas, 'Die italienische Frage', pp. 166–8.
28. Koch, 'Die außenwirtschaftlichen Beziehungen', in *Habsburgermonarchie VI*, pp. 549ff.

on 18 August 1863 under the red–black–gold flag in an imposing assembly of all the rulers of the Confederation: the *Frankfurter Fürstentag.*[29] There, he and Rechberg revealed their plans for a reform of the Confederation, to exalt the position of Austria and reinforce her links with the middle states in a strengthened executive. The blank refusal of the Prussians even to attend the gathering brought these proposals to nothing, however, exposing Austria's impotence to modify the Confederation to her advantage by peaceful means, and demonstrating that the two leading German Powers had at last manoeuvred themselves into a position of stalemate.

Even so, despite the success of Prussia's blocking manoeuvre, the attendance of every German ruler but one at Frankfurt bore witness to their instinctive regard for Franz Joseph's position as the leading *deutscher Fürst*, and to the fact that Austria was undoubtedly more popular than Prussia in Germany as a whole. Indeed, in so far as the 'German question' could be regarded as the internal affair of the German states, Austria indisputably had the edge on Prussia. In most states of the Confederation liberal views prevailed, and Prussia, after the outbreak of the constitutional conflict in Berlin in 1862, was coming to be regarded askance as a reactionary, militarist state. Of the two associations set up in the late fifties to promote a greater degree of unity within the Confederation, the *großdeutsch* *'Reformverein'*, which looked to Vienna and saw in the leadership of Germany by a multinational empire a guarantee of the multifaceted character (*Vielfältigkeit*) of German political life, was making great strides, while the Prussian-oriented *Nationalverein* lapsed into embarrassed silence. Similarly, the liberal noises of disapproval that Austria made on the occasion of Russia's suppression of the Polish revolt of 1863, while completely ineffective – even disastrous, in terms of relations with St Petersburg – accorded better with the prevailing state of opinion within Germany than did Prussia's slavish collaboration with Russia.

On the Right, however, conservatives of the stamp of Franz Joseph and Rechberg failed to make the most of these opportunities. Perhaps their conclusion, after the experience of the *Frankfurter Fürstentag*, that nothing much could be achieved with the middle states alone, was wise and realistic; but their sanguine assumption that Bismarck was bluffing, that in the interests of monarchical solidarity Berlin would in the end accept second place in a conservative alliance against the Revolution, was totally unrealistic.

---

29. Hamann, 'Die Habsburger und die deutsche Frage', p. 221.

It was, indeed, a delusion comparable only to Franz Joseph's naïve faith in Napoleon's loyalty after Villafranca. The Prussian regent, who became King Wilhelm I in 1861, had, unlike his predecessor, neither a romantic-sentimental respect for, nor any family ties with, the House of Habsburg; and Bismarck cynically mocked the Austrians: 'Austria will believe I am bluffing right up to the eve of the battle.'[30] Franz Joseph was himself to confess that in these years 'we were very honourable but very stupid [*sehr ehrlich aber sehr dumm*]'. Nevertheless, it was on this delusion that Franz Joseph's and Rechberg's German policy was based in the early 1860s.

The Austrian decision in January 1864 to ally with Prussia to fight Denmark over the Schleswig-Holstein question marked the apogee of this policy. It is true that even conservatives like Rechberg had for years been adjuring Denmark to respect the interests of the German-speaking elements in the duchies. After all, here was a question over which German opinion of all shades was unanimous;[31] and if Austria's claim to the leadership of Germany was to mean anything, there could be no question of allowing Prussia to act alone in defence of the German cause, as in 1848. Nor was Franz Joseph willing to resign himself to the humble role of executor of the middle German states, promoting the claims of the Duke of Augustenburg to the duchies. True, the Austrians had no fundamental objection to the creation in north Germany of a new middle state, potentially a useful ally against Prussia in the debates at Frankfurt. But the claims of Augustenburg were of doubtful legality – indeed, the popular demonstrations in his favour in the duchies gave them a distastefully revolutionary air; and there could certainly be no alliance with Prussia on this basis. On the grounds of both inclination and policy, therefore, Franz Joseph opted for an alliance with Prussia, ostensibly with the eminently legitimist aim of enforcing the five-Power Treaty of London of 1852 that regulated the position of the duchies; but in fact in the hope of broadening it into an alliance of more general application for use in Italy. In so far as the January alliance said nothing about the future of the duchies should the treaty of 1852 prove unenforceable, it left Prussia dangerously free to seize control of the duchies herself; but by the same token the Austrians had left their hands free for a possible alliance with the middle states to resist Prussia should that Power play false.

---

30. Blaas, 'Il problema veneto', p. 92.
31. Autriche 479, Moustier to Thouvenel, No. 10, 22 January 1861.

In the short term, Austrian policy was successful: the war against Denmark was short and victorious; and Austrian naval action against the Danish fleet – which might otherwise have held command of the sea – did much to compensate for the fumbling performance of Prussian commanders on land. The claim of the two German Powers to be acting in the name of the treaty of 1852 confused the other signatory Powers, and made it difficult for them to co-ordinate any effective opposition; whereas Denmark's outright rejection at the London conference of May 1864 of any settlement on the 1852 basis freed the German Powers from even that constraint. By the Treaty of Vienna of 30 October Denmark ceded the duchies to Austria and Prussia jointly. Austrian diplomacy registered its first success since the Crimean War.

Yet in so far as Austrian diplomacy was based on the assumption that co-operation with Prussia would continue, and would even be extended to wider issues, it was a monumental failure. Bismarck was by now determined to deprive Austria, not only of her 1864 position in the duchies, but of her 1815 position in Germany; and the struggle for control of the Confederation was resumed. True, Bismarck was still prepared to work for his ends by negotiation: if Austria would abdicate her position in Germany, Prussia would help her to recover her old position in Italy – that was the gist of the offer he made to Rechberg in the Schönbrunn draft of August 1864, which Rechberg, as always anxious to avoid a conflict with Prussia, was certainly prepared to consider. The king of Prussia, however, had no desire to be dragged into Austria's fatal Italian entanglements, and refused to endorse Bismarck's proposal; and he further allowed his ministers, despite Bismarck's advice, to administer a final humiliating rebuff to Rechberg by rejecting his proposals for a commercial treaty that would have left the way open for Austria's admission to the Zollverein at some distant date. These failures only strengthened the position of a powerful body of opinion in the Ballhausplatz, led by Ludwig von Biegeleben, head of the Western department, who argued that Rechberg's policy of conciliating Prussia was futile and undignified.[32] Franz Joseph himself had already rejected the Schönbrunn draft, being no more willing than he had been in 1859 to sacrifice one iota of his rights in Germany, even in exchange for support in Italy. On 27 October, Rechberg resigned.

The emperor's choice – significantly, on Rechberg's advice – of

32. Rüdiger Freiherr von Biegeleben, *Ludwig Freiherr von Biegeleben. Ein Vorkämpfer des Großdeutschen Gedankens* (Vienna 1930).

Alexander Count Mensdorff-Pouilly to succeed him certainly did not suggest that the Austrians were now set on an armed confrontation with Prussia. It is true that Mensdorff was acutely conscious of Austria's position in the wider German world: his mother was a Princess of Saxe-Coburg-Gotha and a cousin of Queen Victoria; his wife, Princess Alexandrine von Dietrichstein, the richest heiress in the Empire. It is also true that Mensdorff was 'a soldier in every fibre of his being'[33]: apart from a brief spell as ambassador at St Petersburg in the early fifties and more recently as *Statthalter* of Galicia, his career had been entirely military; and he had fought with distinction in twenty-two battles between 1848 and 1859. But even stronger than his passion for the military life was his sense of duty to the emperor; and it was simply this that led him to accept the offer of the foreign office, where he always felt rather out of his depth. At first, however, the auspices were favourable. It is worth noting that the Prussian ambassador described Mensdorff approvingly as the only suitable candidate; and there is no reason to doubt the sincerity of Franz Joseph's assurances to Wilhelm I that the appointment did not herald a breach. Indeed, in so far as it heralded an attempt to restore co-operation with Prussia (for example, by eliminating the influence in Vienna of the liberal Schmerling, always a *bête noire* of Berlin); and in so far as Mensdorff, like Rechberg, was a declared devotee of co-operation between the two leading German states on a conservative basis, it seemed that Austro-Prussian relations were set to improve.

That was not be, for Mensdorff's hopes were based on false assumptions. Like Rechberg, he had failed to appreciate just how far Bismarck was prepared to go, and that his aim was now nothing less than the expulsion of Austria from Germany. This, no Austrian government could accept without a fight. It must also be said, however, that Mensdorff's efforts to cultivate Prussia were to some extent undermined by his own personal qualities. These were not unattractive: Ballhausplatz officials high and low were delighted to discover in Mensdorff an urbanity that had been quite foreign to his predecessor. 'He did not give orders to his staff, but only requests. The most lowly clerk who handed him a document or brought him a file he would accompany right to the door and open it himself'.[34] This was all very well; but it all reflected a lack of self-confidence of which the masterful senior officials of the Ballhausplatz took full advantage, acting with a degree of independence that was to remain

33. Erb MS.
34. Ludwig Ritter von Przibram, *Erinnerungen eines alten Oesterreichers*, 2 vols (Leipzig 1910–12), I. pp. 132ff.

without parallel until – perhaps significantly – the days of Berchtold. Moric Esterházy – *der stille Moritz* – appointed as minister without portfolio to assist Mensdorff with the routine work of the office, would always appear and sit with him while he saw foreign representatives; Biegeleben, who drafted almost all the papers relating to Prussia, would lecture him, and present him with ready written, excellently worded, memoranda, which Mensdorff would never presume to alter even when he was of an entirely different opinion. Under such a regime, it was not surprising that, despite all Mensdorff's goodwill, relations with Prussia soon took a sharp turn for the worse.

It was indicative of the government's firmer stand against Prussia that the decision was now taken to open negotiations with the Hungarians, with a view to modifying the constitution to remove that Magyar discontent which had had such a debilitating effect on the war machine in 1859. But until these wearisome negotiations could be concluded, and so long as the finances continued in desperate straits, Vienna was reluctant to force a confrontation with Prussia. Indeed, in the Gastein Convention of August 1865, which assigned the administration of Schleswig to Prussia and that of Holstein to Austria, the Austrians even bought time at the price of conceding to Prussia extensive military rights in Holstein that made their position there virtually untenable by force of arms. But by February 1866 it was clear that the Austrians were no longer basing their position on bilateral arrangements with Prussia, or on local conditions in the duchies – even though opinion there was largely on their side – but on their stronger position in the Confederation as a whole. They had at last abandoned hope of co-operation with Prussia in favour of an alignment with the middle states, and they began openly to espouse the cause of Augustenburg in Holstein. The Prussian government, for its part, now determined on war, not only to seize the duchies, but to expel Austria from the Confederation once and for all. This decision was in itself an admission of Prussia's failure to win the diplomatic battle in Germany, and an eloquent testimony to the success of Austrian policy in terms of the Confederation. It was striking that when the final confrontation came, with Austria's appeal to Frankfurt over the Schleswig-Holstein issue in June, not a single German state of any significance took the Prussian side[35] or questioned the continuing validity of the 1815 arrangements in Germany, which Prussia now declared void.

35. Huber, *Deutsche Verfassungsgeschichte*, III, pp. 540ff.

Yet, although in local terms Austria's position in Germany in 1866 was stronger than, say, her embattled position in northern Italy in 1859, the problem was that the German question could not be handled simply in local terms. It had to be seen in European terms, as in 1815, 1803, 1779 or 1648. The position Austria had achieved in Germany in 1815 had been the result of a favourable constellation in Europe, and her retention of that position depended on at least the passive approval of the Powers who had helped to establish it. In this respect, Austria's position in Germany had been seriously weakened by 1866: in European terms, Austria had just as decisively lost the diplomatic battle as, in local terms, she had won it.

Of the two leading Powers of the 1815 settlement, Russia had ceased to underwrite Austria anywhere since the Crimean War; since then, she had also found Prussia a congenial ally to be fostered – all the more so in view of Austria's cultivation of the Poles, and her stubborn refusal to purchase security in Germany or Italy at cost to her Near Eastern interests by supporting Russian demands for the revision of the Treaty of Paris. And the Austrians could expect little help from the British, who had no desire to risk another direct intervention in the maelstrom of continental affairs – partly as a result of the particular humiliations they had suffered at the hands of the German Powers in the Schleswig-Holstein affair, and partly from more general considerations. Although they deplored a conflict that threatened to jeopardise the strong central Europe they had laboured to create in 1815, they were on the whole prepared to see in a strengthened Prussia an adequate substitute barrier against France.

With regard to Italy, there were more opportunities for Austrian diplomacy: an offer to recognise the Kingdom and cede Venetia to it would certainly have secured Italy's neutrality – and this was important, given that even Moltke thought Prussia too weak to risk war unless Austria could be distracted by a second front in the south. But the Austrians were just not interested in neutralising Italy, partly because they cherished the illusion that they could defeat Prussia and Italy combined; but even more because they felt that vital principles of a more general nature were at stake. As late as June 1866, in a statement whose Metternichian tones rang oddly in a Europe that had experienced the diplomacy of Bismarck, Napoleon III and Cavour, Mensdorff explained to the British ambassador that there could be no question of purchasing Italy's neutrality:[36]

36. F.O. 7/707, Bloomfield to Stanley, No. 313, 2 June 1866.

What was the Austrian monarchy? It was an empire of nationalities. If she gave up Venetia today to please King Victor Emmanuel . . . where would his ambition lead him? . . . Would he rest satisfied before he had wrested all the Austrian possessions in the Adriatic from their rightful owner? . . . The Prince of Hohenzollern might some day find out that there was a considerable Romanian population in Transylvania, and therefore it would be right that it should be added to Moldo-Wallachia. The Prince of Serbia might also claim the Serbs in Austria, . . . in fact, . . . we are determined to take our position in defence of our principles and our rights, which are based on treaties, and if war should be the consequence we shall do our best to protect the various possessions and interests of which the Empire is composed.

In the long term, perhaps Mensdorff was right: dynasticism and nationalism were ultimately incompatible. In the short term, Mensdorff's principled stance was fatal; not so much because it condemned Austria to a war on two fronts, but because it undermined Austria's bargaining position among the Powers generally. It must be emphasised that Austrian diplomacy in the summer of 1866 proceeded from the – as it turned out, completely mistaken – assumption that Austria was in a position to defeat both Prussia and Italy. At the same time, even the boldest spirits in Vienna recognised that she could not hope to prevail against a combination of three Powers. The attitude of France was, therefore, decisive. Mensdorff's absolute refusal to contemplate direct negotiations with Italy had the inevitable consequence of putting the Monarchy at the mercy of Napoleon III.

Now in the spring of 1866 Napoleon III was anything but well-disposed towards Austria. Whatever gains he might have been expecting in the Rhineland from a long-drawn-out Austro-Prussian war that left both combatants exhausted, his chief preoccupation was to restore his credit with the Italians. So long as Austria frustrated his attempts to secure Venetia for Italy by diplomacy, his policy was bound to remain fundamentally anti-Austrian. Indeed, his notorious speech at Auxerre (6 May) – 'je déteste ces traités de 1815' – was essentially a *ballon d'essai* to test French reactions to the idea of actively intervening in a German war on the side of Austria's opponents. Similarly, his pressing Italy to enter into negotiations with Berlin – which finally led to the alliance of 8 April – was at bottom merely a manoeuvre to frighten Austria into ceding Venetia in return for the Danubian principalities. For Napoleon, Austria was, at least until Sadowa, a Power to be intimidated, not one to be protected.

In these circumstances it was, to say the least, sanguine of the Austrians to imagine that they could persuade Napoleon to sacrifice French blood and money for their cause. Yet, at the eleventh hour, Franz Joseph offered, in return for active French assistance in recovering Silesia from Prussia, to cede Venetia to Napoleon (who could then hand it over to the Kingdom of Italy). Even at this stage the Austrians were above all concerned to avoid any appearance of making concessions to the national principle, such as a direct transaction with Italy would have implied. In fact, the proposal was typical of Franz Joseph's diplomacy in the sixties, in which questions of form were considered no less important – indeed, even more important – than questions of substance. If the Austrians could have steeled themselves to buy Italy off in the opportunistic manner favoured by their opponents, they could have negotiated for French support from a position of equality. As it was, by their principled refusal even to recognise the Kingdom of Italy, let alone negotiate with it, they had put themselves in a hopeless position. Napoleon saw no need to pay for what he could get for nothing, and he exploited his advantage to the full. On the very eve of the conflict he simply rejected Franz Joseph's conditions, demanded the cession of Venetia to France whatever the outcome of the war, and offered only French neutrality in return – otherwise, France might join the war on the Prussian side. Richard Metternich in the Paris embassy could not bring himself to put his name to such shameful terms, and the negotiations were transferred to Vienna. In the Ballhausplatz, Moric Esterházy still thought that Napoleon might be bluffing, that the French 'pistol' pointed at Austria's chest might not be loaded. A conference of ministers chaired by the emperor decided, however, that the Monarchy simply could not risk a confrontation with three Powers at once, and that the 'cursed robber' in the Tuileries would have to be bought off.

The upshot, the notorious (and often misunderstood)[37] Treaty of 12 June was in fact, as a diplomatic instrument, by no means such an unmitigated disaster for Austria as the emperor and some of his advisers thought. It provided for the cession of Venetia to Napoleon only in the event of Austria's emerging victorious from the war in the north and strengthening her position in Germany; and it included a guarantee of Austria's remaining possessions in Italy. At

---

37. H. Ritter von Srbik, 'Der Geheimvertrag Oesterreichs und Frankreichs vom 12 Juni 1866' in *Historisches Jahrbuch*, 57 (1937), pp. 454–507; Michael Dendarsky, 'Das Klischee von "Ces Messieurs de Vienne". Der österreichisch–französische Geheimvertrag vom 12 Juni 1866', in *Historische Zeitschrift*, 235 (1982), pp. 289–353; Cf. Sked, *Decline*, pp. 179ff.

least some of the Monarchy's interests had been safeguarded for the future. For the present, the treaty reflected Vienna's decision to entrust the fate of the Monarchy not to negotiations with a Europe that showed so little sympathy for Austria's cause, but to the arbitrament of war.

As the Seven Weeks' War showed, the Austrians had miscalculated. Although French intervention, which would have had unthinkable consequences, had been staved off, even Italian intervention proved damaging enough when taken together with Austria's other difficulties. In the north Benedek, whose spirited performance as a corps commander at Solferino, coupled with his popularity in the army (especially among the Hungarians) had dictated his assignment to the principal theatre, proved a sad disappointment as a campaign commander; and the allies in the German Confederation did not fight well (their spirited performance against the French in 1870 was to give rise to some bitter comment in Habsburg circles).[38] Altogether, however, the performance of the Austrians exposed a variety of weaknesses that called in question the Monarchy's capacity to face the test of modern warfare. On the one hand, the efficiency of the war effort was hardly enhanced by continuing uncertainty as to the structure of the state itself: unsettled conditions in Hungary, which Bismarck, through his contacts with Hungarian extremists, was doing his best to exploit, had a debilitating effect. as in 1859. On the other, problems arising from the Monarchy's rudimentary railway communications were compounded by Prussia's technical-military superiority: Prussian infantry armed with breech-loading rifles that could be fired from a lying position wrought havoc among the Austrians armed with muzzle-loaders. At any rate, by the end of June the Austrians, despite their victories in Italy, were facing a steadily growing Prussian threat in Bohemia.[39]

On 2 July, therefore, they appealed to Paris for diplomatic assistance in bringing about a cease-fire with Italy, and offered to hand Venetia over to Napoleon whatever the outcome of the war in the north. Franz Joseph and his advisers had finally taken the decision to sacrifice the Monarchy's position in Italy in the hope of maintaining, and possibly developing, its position in Germany. In the event, however, they lost their position in Germany too. After the battle of Sadowa (3 July) the decision-makers in Vienna had

38. Hamann, 'Die Habsburger und die deutsche Frage', p. 227.
39. K. Koch, *Franz Graf Crenneville, Generaladjutant Kaiser Franz Josefs*, Militär-geschichtliche Dissertationen österreichischer Universitäten, 3 (Vienna 1974).

little stomach for continuing a war that was obviously unpopular at home: the Viennese had greeted the news of Austria's defeat with pacifist celebrations in the streets; and, for the first time in his life, the emperor had felt the need for a cavalry escort to accompany him from his summer palace at Schönbrunn to the capital.[40] True, the Italians had been defeated on land and sea, at Custoza and Lissa; but the Austrians had already abandoned their position in Italy on 2 July.

Yet the decision to abandon the Monarchy's position in one of the spheres of influence it had held since 1815 must be seen against the background of a continuing determination to hold on in the two others: in Germany and the Near East. And in neither was everything yet lost. In fact, Austria's position in Germany now rather resembled her position in Italy after the war of 1859. True, the battle of Sadowa, which exposed the capital itself to an enemy thrust, was a more severe defeat than Magenta and Solferino. On the other hand, the Austrians were now in a position to move forces from the Italian to the northern theatre; and non-belligerent Powers such as France and Russia were beginning – out of fear or hope of gain – to offer their mediation. Bismarck was, therefore, just as anxious to conclude a speedy peace by direct negotiations with the enemy as Napoleon had been in 1859. After the Nikolsburg Armistice (26 July) and the Peace of Prague (23 August) the Austrians emerged – as they had done after Villafranca and Zurich – in a rather better position than might have been expected.

True, Bismarck forced them to renounce their political ties with the states of the former German Confederation. (Franz Joseph was for the moment thoroughly disillusioned with those states anyway, and told his wife that 'we shall get out of Germany altogether, whether it is demanded of us or not, and after the experiences we have had with our dear German allies I hold this to be a blessing for Austria'.) But that did not mean that the Austrians were prepared to concede to Prussia complete domination over Germany. The military and commercial arrangements Bismarck had forced on the four South German states showed that he certainly hoped to draw Germany south of the Main into Prussia's orbit in the long run. On the other hand, in Article IV of the Treaty of Prague, he had had to accord to the South German states an 'independent international existence': they were in fact free to gravitate in any direction they chose; and as the Austrians were not only themselves determined –

---

40. P. Hohenbalken (ed.), *Heinrich Graf Lützow. Im diplomatischen Dienste der k.u.k. Monarchie* (Vienna 1971), p. 5.

even to the point of war – to see this article upheld, but could count on the support of a France apprehensive of any further increase in Prussian power, the Treaty of Prague still left the way open for Austria to make her voice heard in German affairs. In fact, the Austrians had no more given up hope of exerting influence in Germany in 1866, than they had renounced their role as an Italian Power in 1859; and whereas the Treaty of Zurich had been a dead letter from the start, the restrictions imposed by the Treaty of Prague on an extension of Prussian control south of the Main were to remain in force for half a decade. During that time the Austrians continued to strive to maintain, with a view to ultimately restoring, their position. Not until 1871 did they finally abandon the last shreds of the role assigned to them in Germany by the peacemakers of 1815.

Coming to Terms with Realities, 1866–1871

Of course, in the immediate aftermath of defeat, the Austrians had to move with extreme caution. The war had left Austria in a state of military, economic and financial collapse. Politically, the very nature of the state was completely uncertain, the 1861 constitution having been suspended in 1865 pending negotiations with the Hungarians. Economically, the prospect was also bleak: with a national debt that had risen from £82 million to £291 million since 1815, a war indemnity to pay, an annual deficit in the budget, and harvest failures and floods in Hungary, the government was faced within a year with the prospect of Austrian bonds being excluded altogether from the exchanges of western Europe. Clearly, the immediate need was for a period of peace.

Above all, a system of government had to be devised for the Habsburg Monarchy. For this purpose, Friedrich Ferdinand Baron Beust,[41] until 1866 foreign minister of the king of Saxony, proved ideally suited. Untainted with any past record in Austrian politics, and with a good streak of opportunism inherent in his character, he could cut through the tangled undergrowth of the Austrian political scene. Within a bare two months of taking office under Franz Joseph he had reached agreement with the Hungarians on the broad outlines of the *Ausgleich* settlement, and 1867 saw stable liberal governments established in Vienna and in Budapest – where Franz Joseph was at last crowned King of Hungary in June. Beust was

41. Heinrich Potthoff, *Die deutsche Politik Beusts* (Bonn 1968).

rewarded with the title of Chancellor, previously held only by Kaunitz, Metternich and Schwarzenberg. No minister after him enjoyed either this title or the power it carried in the domestic affairs of the Monarchy. If the liberal reforms of the next few years helped to bring the social and economic structures of the Monarchy into line with those of western Europe, a succession of good harvests after 1867 and the euphoria that prevailed in the financial world after the end of the German crisis inaugurated a period of general prosperity, indeed, 'a perfect orgy of speculation', that was to last until the great crash of 1873. The new prosperity permitted a rapid development of the railway network. And the importance of this was not only strategic – in Galicia, for example – but commercial and political. The Vienna–Constantinople projects of the later 1860s promised much for Austro-Hungarian trade and influence in the Balkans. Similarly, the spate of commercial treaties[42] – with Prussia (1865–8), France (1865), Italy (1867) and Great Britain (1868) – which represented the high-water mark of free trade in Austria, were not without political significance. In the case of the British treaty, Beust explicitly stated that the advantages of a possible *rapprochement* must outweigh the Austrian industrialists' fears of competition. Altogether, Beust hoped that these internal political and economic developments would be of service to the Monarchy externally, both in ending its political isolation and in reinforcing its influence as a modern, German, liberal state in Germany south of the Main.

In the event, these hopes were disappointed. The British, for example, remained isolationist despite the commercial treaty; and after the financial crash of 1873 the whole free-trade policy was called in question. Above all, although the total collapse that had threatened in 1866 had been averted, the Austro-Hungarian authorities still lacked the resources to raise the Monarchy to the ranks of the first-class Great Powers, or to equip it to act effectively in a crisis demanding an intimidating show of force or involving a risk of war. Financial and constitutional objections from the parliaments in Vienna and Budapest delayed the projected military reforms until 1868, with the result that the Monarchy faced the great crisis of the Franco–German war of 1870–1 with its armed forces still in the throes of reorganisation and totally unfit for action. In the years after 1866, the constraints of internal weakness forced Beust and Franz Joseph to confine themselves to diplomatic manoeuvres for

---

42. Karl F. Helleiner, *Free Trade and Frustration. Anglo-Austrian Negotiations 1860–1870* (Toronto 1963).

very limited objectives. Unless a favourable international situation brought it some external support, the Monarchy could take few initiatives.

The fears of the foreign press that Beust might disturb the peace with an active revanchist policy soon proved unjustified. It is true that it was the catastrophe of 1866 that had brought Beust and Franz Joseph together. Indeed, considerations of honour may have been one element in the favour shown by the emperor to the minister: Beust had sided with Austria before the war, and as a result of it faced political ruin, the victorious Bismarck having forced the king of Saxony to dismiss him as a condition of peace. A policy of *revanche* was ruled out, however, not only by the lack of material resources, but by the state of public opinion. In the first place, Magyar opinion, a powerful force to be reckoned with since the *Ausgleich*, was united in opposition to any attempt to reverse the decision of 1866 in Germany: not only would that be an irresponsible distraction from the Monarchy's main task – guarding against the threat from Russia; but the restoration of the Habsburgs' pre-1866 position in Germany might well mean the end of those concessions which Hungary had managed to extract from Franz Joseph in the hour of his defeat.[43] Nor was there any enthusiasm among Franz Joseph's ten million German subjects for a renewal of the *Brüderkrieg*. It is true that in foreign affairs Beust was responsible to the emperor, not to public opinion; that for the emperor, as for Beust, a policy of actual reconciliation with Prussia was unthinkable; and that neither the emperor nor his minister was prepared to accept the verdict of 1866 as final. But for the present even Franz Joseph could see that a renewal of the conflict with Prussia must bring certain defeat, giving Prussia a chance to get hold of not only the South German states, but perhaps even the German provinces of the Monarchy. As he defined his aims to Beust on 1 September 1866, these were: to raise Austria to the position of a Great Power again by means of domestic peace; to strengthen her ties with the South German states and keep them out of Prussia's grasp; and to give up the idea of war 'for a long time [*auf lange Zeit*]'.[44]

The international situation too was hardly such as to encourage an active policy. Of the real Great Powers to whom Austria-Hungary might have looked for assistance, Russia was closely

43. Istvan Diószegi, 'Das politische und wirtschaftliche Interesse Ungarns an der gemeinsamen Außenpolitik', in *Habsburgermonarchie VI*, pp. 375ff; Idem, *Hungarians in the Ballhausplatz* (Vienna 1983), pp. 125ff.
44. Potthoff, *Deutsche Politik Beusts*, p. 46.

aligned with Prussia, and Great Britain was firmly isolationist. True, France, still smarting over Sadowa, was a possible ally; and at the diplomatic level, indeed, was co-operating fairly effectively with the Austrians in impressing on the South German states their obligation to stay clear of Prussian enticements and to uphold their independent international status, in accordance with Article IV of the Treaty of Prague. But for an Austria as yet in no condition to fight, an actual alliance with France might well prove positively dangerous. In the Luxemburg affair of 1867, Beust himself was appalled at the wave of national feeling that French adventurism stirred up, even in the South German states. He could only strive to restrain it, coldly rebuffing Bavaria's attempt by the Tauffkirchen mission to bring together the two great German monarchies and Russia in a revived Holy Alliance; and he consoled himself in the end by smugly pointing to the Prussian evacuation of the fortress of Luxemburg in the final settlement as a lesson to the German states 'of what Germany is or can achieve without Austria'.[45] But the whole affair had served to remind him of the dangers that might arise for the Austrian position in south Germany if France should ever start a war on an issue even moderately favourable to Prussia.

Already, on 23 April, he had shied off when the French ambassador, Gramont, had proposed an offensive and defensive alliance to secure the Rhine frontier for France and gains in south Germany for Austria. This he felt was the worst conceivable basis for a Franco-Austrian alliance. Franz Joseph could not possibly take his ten million German subjects into a war, the express object of which was to put German soil under foreign rule. A war against Russia over the Near East would be a very different matter: both German-Austrians and Magyars, would be only too willing to fight; and if Prussia intervened in such a war, then France could make her gains in Germany under the cloak of a general settling of accounts.[46] As Napoleon III's visit to Franz Joseph at Salzburg in August showed, however, France and Austria were at cross purposes. Beust still insisted that Austrian policy in Germany was for the present simply one of maintaining the Treaty of Prague by peaceful means. If the French stirred up German national feeling, they would paralyse any Austrian government; and in any case, Austria was as yet in no condition to fight a war at all.[47] Napoleon, for his part, had too much sympathy for the national aspirations of

45. Ibid., p. 115.
46. Haus, Hof- und Staatsarchiv, Vienna, Kabinett series, File 17, Beust to Metternich, confidential, 27 April 1867.
47. Ibid., Beust, reports to Franz Joseph, dated '1867' and 19 August 1867.

the Balkan Christians, and set too much store by his own links with St Petersburg, to take up Beust's alternative proposal for a conservative alliance to uphold the Ottoman Empire against the alleged designs of Russia.

This was a setback for the Austrians. For, if they had renounced Italy and could not do much about Germany for the present, they were faced with immediately pressing problems in the Near East. The Treaty of Paris of 1856 had not saved the Ottoman Empire; indeed, in so far as it sanctioned intervention by the Powers in conflicts between the sultan and his subjects, it had, if anything, weakened it further. By 1866 Crete was in rebellion, and Serbia and Romania were appealing to the Powers to relieve them of the last remaining vestiges of Ottoman suzerainty. All this worried the Austrians. They had no desire to see a general upheaval in the Ottoman Empire, which, if left unchecked, could eventually threaten the Habsburg Empire. (Beust was convinced that the Cretan rising was only part of an international revolutionary movement, with links with Kossuth, Mazzini and the Romanian nationalist leader, Ion Bratianu.) On the other hand, if Austria-Hungary simply supported the Turks, she risked driving the whole of the Christian Balkans into the arms of Russia, which would then encircle the Monarchy in the south. Beust's aims were essentially conservative; but he felt, as a liberal, that the old negative, conservative-legitimist methods would no longer suffice, and that mere repression would only produce an enormous explosion in the long run. According to the British *chargé d'affaires*, he waxed eloquent on these themes:[48]

> It has been the lot of Austria to attend '*les pompes funèbres*' of all those legitimate rights which she had most sincerely and staunchly supported. It had been so in Italy, and now she had seen the rights of the old German Confederation carried to the grave. He feared that the same destiny might still follow her were she to advise Turkey to continue to uphold certain, though incontestable, rights midst the difficulties that surround her.

Beust's solution was that of a 'middle way': to support the Turks in essential questions of the territorial status quo, while persuading them to settle legitimate grievances and make concessions to the Christians in non-essential matters. In 1867 he helped to persuade the Turks to withdraw their last remaining garrisons from Serbia;

48. F.O. 7/712, Bonar to Stanley, No. 87, 18 December 1866.

but he would have no truck with Serbian designs on Ottoman territory, say, in Bosnia. There was a further consideration involved here: Bosnia and the Herzegovina formed the hinterland to the Monarchy's Dalmatian coastline, and in Beust's view they 'must be either Turkish or Austrian, no third possibility is admissible.'[49]

Of course, the Austrians were in no position to enforce their policy of the middle way, unless it happened to be in the interests of a first-class Great Power to assist them. Throughout 1867 Beust failed in his efforts to rally the Concert round a programme of moderate concessions to satisfy the Cretan rebels: the British simply refused to put any pressure whatever on Constantinople; whereas the French and Russians talked of forcing Turkey to cede to Greece not only Crete, but territory on the mainland. It was only when, in 1868, the Turks managed to frighten the Powers by coupling an offer of virtual autonomy to Crete with an ultimatum to Greece, that the Powers met in conference in Paris and settled the Cretan question for the next thirty years along compromise lines such as Beust had been advocating.

Sometimes, the tactical errors of his opponents provided Beust with the chance to get his own way. Moldavia and Wallachia, for example, which since the summer of 1866 had enjoyed a *de facto* unity as 'Romania' under the suzerainty of Prince Carol of Hohenzollern-Sigmaringen, presented a constant source of friction and disorder on the Hungarian frontier. Indeed, Beust had long despaired of ever achieving tolerable relations with Carol's liberal prime minister, Ion Bratianu, 'the Romanian Cavour',[50] in whose eyes the very existence of a Dual Monarchy ruling over some three million Romanians in Transylvania constituted an offence, and whose whole policy was avowedly based on the assumption that the Monarchy's days were numbered. By the summer of 1868 a serious crisis was developing. The Romanian government was harbouring Bulgarian nationalists who were sending raiding parties into Turkey. In this, the Austrians discerned, as usual, a general conspiracy, with branches in Serbia, Greece and Montenegro, seeking to promote the dissolution of the Ottoman Empire. Worse still, the Romanian government was arming to the teeth. Prussia, with the connivance of Russia, was supplying weapons and military instructors; and Austrian officials were struck by the military bearing and strict discipline of large numbers of Prussian 'railway

49. K.P. Schoenhals, *The Russian Policy of Friedrich Ferdinand von Beust, 1866–71* (Ann Arbor, 1964), p. 39.
50. Kab. 17, Beust Memorandum, 25 September 1868.

workers' travelling to Romania via Galicia.[51] All this led Beust to conclude that the intended victim of the conspiracy (which included Prince Carol and his master, Bismarck) was not so much Turkey as Austria-Hungary.

Whether or not Bismarck was actively seeking – as he was to do in Spain the following year – to exploit a Hohenzollern connection in order to paralyse a potential opponent, his tactics on this occasion only played into the hands of Beust, who was quick to seize the opportunity to issue a public denunciation of the 'living arsenal' that was being created on the south-eastern frontier of the Monarchy.[52] Indeed, Bismarck had to beat a hasty and undignified retreat. To have persisted would have risked not only the estrangement of Prussia's friends in Budapest – still, after all, a surer guarantee against Habsburg revisionism than Romania, however well armed, could ever be; worse, Prussia might have found herself involved in an unpopular war on an issue remote from German interests, which might – as Beust indeed speculated – give France and Austria their chance to make their gains in Germany. When therefore in November Bismarck persuaded Carol to dismiss Bratianu, Beust had scored a notable success. Moreover, Austro-Romanian relations now improved steadily. The conservative 'boyar' government that replaced Bratianu continued to arm feverishly; but it eschewed all revolutionary propaganda; and by the spring of 1870 Beust decided that, as Russia was already treating the principalities as a united and virtually independent state, Austria-Hungary might do well to make some generous gestures too. The union, he decided, should be upheld – Wallachia was a useful restraint on Russophile Moldavia; so should Prince Carol, who had thrown off Prussian leading strings, and who at least kept Bratianu at bay. Indeed, in an effort to strengthen the prince's position, Beust even began to consider recognising him as 'Prince of Romania'.

Concern to prevent the encirclement of the Monarchy by Russian satellites in the south led Beust to adopt a similarly conciliatory attitude towards the other semi-independent Balkan states, even towards the most 'Russian' of them, Montenegro, which began to agitate in the spring of 1869 for a port on the Adriatic. On this, Beust refused to lift a finger: he had no desire to see a potential Russian naval base in the Adriatic. But he was accommodating enough with respect to telegraphic concessions and financial

51. Ibid., Beust, 'Résumé of information on political agitation among the states subject to Turkey', February 1870.
52. F.O. 7/739, Bonar to Granville, No. 164, 3 November 1868.

assistance. Towards Serbia, Montenegro's sister-state and rival, and at this time of all the Balkan states the least hostile to Turkey, he could be even more forthcoming. The assassination of Prince Michael Obrenović in June 1868 at last put an end to that ruler's disconcerting schemes for a league of Balkan states; and to Vienna the rule of his youthful and malleable son, Milan, even with a pro-Russian regency, was an infinitely lesser evil than a Serbo-Montenegrin union under Prince Nikita of Montenegro. By 1869, in fact, the Austrians were well pleased to discern very little Russian influence at Belgrade, and they successfully used their influence to secure Turkey's assent as suzerain to a new constitution for the principality.

Not that Beust would go as far as Andrássy and his protégé in Belgrade, Benjamin Kállay, who in their keenness to use Serbia as a stalking-horse for Austro-Hungarian influence in the Balkans, hinted to Belgrade that the Monarchy would not object if Serbia one day absorbed some Slav districts of Turkey. Beust still insisted that territorial acquisitions by Serbia would ultimately whet her appetite for Austro-Hungarian territory. Besides, Serbia might one day become a stalking-horse for Russia, to further the latter's 'great object . . . of extending her power towards the Adriatic'.[53] Hence, although he admitted to the British ambassador that, as Andrássy was an essential element in the government of Hungary, 'he had to bear much from him', he would have nothing to do with his 'attempts to meddle in foreign affairs'.[54] For his part, he continued to count on Turkey – at least a certain friend – and on railway construction to spread Austro-Hungarian influence in the Near East. In the spring of 1870 he at last persuaded the Austrian government to back a project for a railway from Vienna to Salonika, which a Franco-Belgian group had agreed to finance. In so far as the Eastern Question was, for Beust, one of securing Austria-Hungary's Near Eastern interests by maintaining reasonable relations with both Turks and Christians, it seemed by 1870 that his policy of the middle way was succeeding.

The fact remained, however, that for the Austrians, the Eastern Question was primarily one of security against Russia. Not that Beust was anxious to oppose her at absolutely every turn: indeed, he on occasion sought – quite abandoning the stiff legitimist stance adopted by his predecessors – to humour her by suggesting a revision of the Black Sea clauses of the Treaty of Paris; and the

53. F.O. 7/768, Bloomfield to Granville, No. 119, 27 November 1870.
54. Ibid., Bloomfield to Granville, No. 149, 13 October 1870.

threat of a Russian advance along the south-eastern frontiers of the Monarchy, either directly or by the establishment of satellite states, had for the time being been dispelled. But the military threat persisted; and Austro-Russian relations were, on the whole, thoroughly bad. If the Russians resented Beust's diplomatic successes in the Balkan capitals, and the advance of Austro-Hungarian influence in the Ottoman Empire, they were particularly offended by the privileged position accorded to the Poles of the Monarchy since the *Ausgleich*. With Potocki, in April 1870, Austria even had a Polish minister-president. Whereas the embassy in St Petersburg took a fairly nonchalant view of Russian complaints – 'the Muscovite colossus is afraid of the ghost of Poland as a murderer is haunted by the shadow of his victim'[55] – the tsar never tired of lecturing the Austrians:[56] 'You have to admit that Prussia's Germanification of the Poles . . . as well as our forceful Russification have been crowned with success. Your system, which is based on the opposite point of view, will produce regrettable discord between our two governments.' Beust, however, always refused to discuss what he insisted was a purely internal affair, and countered with complaints about Panslav intrigues among the Ruthenian peasantry under Polish rule in Galicia. On these issues, debate proved futile; and by the summer of 1870 the two courts had withdrawn their ambassadors and were communicating with each other through mere *chargés d'affaires*.

The Austrians, for their part, resented not only Russia's official support for Prussia in the international field – on the German question, according to Austrian reports from St Petersburg, 'the Russian tsar purely and simply used the language of the Prussian diplomatists'[57] – but unofficial influences, such as that of Moscow-inspired Panslavism on the Slavs of the Monarchy, particularly on the Czechs, whom the *Ausgleich* had left discontented. The underground activities of Russian diplomats, the language of the Russian press, the attendance of a sizeable Czech delegation at a so-called ethnographic Panslav Congress in Moscow in the summer of 1867, and the consequent flood of Panslav literature into the Monarchy alarmed the Austrian government. Indeed, the formally correct attitude of the Russian government, and its denial of responsibility for the activities of its agents and the language of its press, only made it all the more difficult to get to grips with the problem and clear it up in the interests of better relations between Vienna and St

55. Schoenhals, *Russian Policy*, p. 19.
56. Ibid., p. 129.
57. Ibid.

Petersburg. Even when full diplomatic relations were resumed at the beginning of 1870, the new Russian ambassador, E.P. Novikov, proved to be an ardent Slavophile; and the Panslav Benevolent Societies in Russia, offended by Austria-Hungary's Balkan railway projects, began to step up their activities among the South Slavs. The Austrians were particularly upset by the publication at this time of General R.A. Fadayev's book, *Opinion on the Eastern Question*, which advocated the forceful liberation of the Austrian Slavs, and declared that 'the road to Constantinople lies through Vienna'. More immediately, they lived in constant fear of some Russian military coup, such as the occupation of Romania. The military encirclement that would result from this would paralyse the Monarchy for action anywhere else in Europe; and it was this nightmare that was to preoccupy successive councils of ministers in Vienna throughout the crisis years of 1870–1.

The German problem, by contrast, was distinctly less worrying. If the governments of the southern states seemed responsive to French and Austrian admonitions about their obligations to preserve their independent international existence in accordance with the Treaty of Prague, particularist successes in the South German elections for the new German Customs Parliament in 1867 showed that aristocratic, clericalist and peasant opinion in the South German states was decidedly averse to establishing closer ties with the Protestant, liberal and militarist elements that set the tone in the North German Confederation. Indeed, distrust of Prussia and of Prussian methods – *Steuerzahlen, Soldatwerden, Maulhalten*[58] – was growing apace. The publication, at the time of the Luxemburg crisis, of the military treaties through which Bismarck had sought to bind the south German states to Prussia in wartime had been greeted with a storm of indignation in those states; and the treaties continued to be the object of increasingly critical comment south of the Main. Indeed, despite the apparent strengthening of Slav tendencies in Austria with the appointment of the Potocki government in March 1870, elections in Bavaria a few months later established the Austrophile Count Bray in power as prime minister in place of the pro-Prussian liberal Prince Hohenlohe. In short, Bismarck was facing defeat. He had been all too aware, ever since 1866, that any attempt to subject south Germany to Prussia by force would involve him in a hopeless war against France, Austria and the southern states combined. Yet at the same time, the ties of Zoll-

---

58. 'Pay your taxes, become a soldier, keep your mouth shut', quoted in Pothoff, *Deutsche Politik Beusts*, p. 385.

parlament and military treaties, through which he had hoped to secure the South German states as satellites without the risks or, indeed, the encumbrances contingent on their actual membership of the Confederation, were clearly inadequate. As a leading German liberal despairingly concluded on 20 July 1870:[59] 'It is not true that the South German states are being drawn gradually closer to us. They are of necessity becoming more distant from us the more legislation [*die Gesetzesorganisation*] progresses in the North. And what then? Division for eternity [*Zweiteiligkeit in Sempiternum*].' To that extent, certainly, Beust's policy was succeeding.

The Austrians had no desire to jeopardise this success by making rash commitments to Napoleon III. In November 1868 they began to investigate the possibility of a tripartite agreement with France and Italy. Austro-Italian relations were improving; and Beust now had his own quarrel with the Pope, who had condemned the Austrian government's liberal education laws. (Indeed, in another breach with the legitimism of the 1850s, he was even prepared to consider ceding south Tyrol to Italy if Austria could get compensation in Germany.) Moreover, he felt that a tripartite agreement with Italy would be safer than one with Napoleon III alone: it would be well 'to put the . . . wild and warlike French elephant between two tame ones'.[60] By the summer of 1869 he had in fact secured a draft agreement that was very favourable to Austria-Hungary, in that it committed her only to neutrality in the event of a Franco-Prussian war in which Russia did not intervene. Admittedly, this was partly intended for the consumption of the public, which was still not disposed to fight for the German mission of the House of Habsburg. That mission was well catered for in the final settlement envisaged in the draft alliance, however: an Austria restored to her pre-1866 position, a Prussia reduced even beyond her pre-1866 limits, and gains for the middle German states. Revenge for Sadowa was still the ultimate objective of Beust's German policy. But in the end, the project came to little. The Italians demanded territory on the Isonzo and the immediate evacuation of the French garrison from Rome, whereupon Napoleon at once broke off negotiations. An exchange of letters between the two emperors promising each other assistance if attacked was all that had resulted by September 1869.

Subsequent Franco-Austrian contacts – at the highest military

59. Gustav Freitag to the Duke of Gotha, 1 July 1870, quoted in Josef Becker, 'Zum Problem der Bismarck'scher Politik in der spanischen Thronfrage, 1870', in *Historische Zeitschrift*, 212 (1971), pp. 529–607, p. 542.
60. Potthoff, *Deutsche Politik Beusts,* p. 269.

level – were similarly inconclusive. They may, however, have made their contribution to the deterioration of the international situation in the summer of 1870. When, for example, Archduke Albrecht went to Paris in February 1870, his personal advice to the French to make an unassisted thrust at Nuremberg and then to await Austrian and Italian help, did not commit the Austro-Hungarian government; but it could hardly fail to encourage in Paris a cavalier belief in the warlike intentions of the Austrian military party. Equally reckless was the archduke's advice to the visiting General Lebrun in June: although there could be no question of any simultaneous offensive – both Austria-Hungary and Italy would need six weeks to mobilise – the French should still think in terms of an offensive through south Germany, with Italy and Austria-Hungary joining in the final grand battle in Saxony. All this betrayed a grave miscalculation as to both feeling in the South German states and Prussian striking power; but in this context it is perhaps not surprising that the French tended to discount Franz Joseph's own very explicit warning: if Napoleon appeared in south Germany as an invader, instead of as the defender of South German liberties against Prussia, Austria could not march at all in his support. Lebrun, at any rate, seems to have taken this lightly, and to have left Vienna well pleased.

It was in fact the foolhardiness of the French, and not the malevolence of Prussia and Russia, that was to strike the blow which was to destroy Beust's delicately constructed edifice of Austrian influence in south Germany; indeed, to put an end once and for all to the German mission of the House of Habsburg. In the early stages of the Hohenzollern candidature dispute Beust had been pleased to see a welcome embarrassment for Prussia: here was a dynastic, non-German issue, which might .well widen the gulf between Prussia and the South German states. But the speed with which the dispute flared up into a German national issue after Gramont's warlike speech of 6 July took Beust completely by surprise. He simply had no time to prepare the South German states psychologically. A hasty summons to neutrality now would have been widely interpreted as *undeutsch*, and would have damaged Austria's reputation in Germany beyond repair. He had hoped to assist the French to a peaceful diplomatic victory; but in this the French were not interested. Despite his warnings that he could only co-operate if he were properly consulted in good time, the French rushed recklessly ahead. For Gramont had formed his own optimistic assumptions about Austrian policy during his nine years' embassy at Vienna. On 15 July he coolly informed the Austro-

Hungarian ambassador that 'la guerre est décidée: si l'Autriche comprend ses intérêts elle marchera avec nous', and flew into a rage when the ambassador mentioned the word 'congress'.[61] On 19 July the French declared war on Prussia, and duly appeared in the Bavarian Palatinate as invaders; the South German states all fell into line behind Prussia in defence of the national cause, and the very situation arose that Beust had striven most to avoid.

In Vienna a conference of ministers had decided on 18 July that the Monarchy could not join in the fray.[62] As Beust made clear from the start, Austria-Hungary was under no obligation to France. On the contrary, it was against insistent advice from Vienna that France had gone ahead and transformed the Spanish question into a German national issue. True, the Common War Minister, the fiery Baron Kuhn, swore that 'the Prussians on the Inn mean *Finis Austriae*'. He was for immediate intervention and a general settling of accounts in a world-wide conflagration. But all the others held that intervention was unthinkable in view of the state of German, and much Hungarian, opinion, the total unpreparedness of the army – a memorandum by Beck, head of the emperor's military chancellery, envisaged a retreat into Central Hungary in the event of a Prussian attack – and the threatening attitude of Russia (a point much emphasised by Andrássy). The conference opted for neutrality and a series of defensive preparations on the Russian, rather than on the Prussian, frontier. Even if Beust was still toying with the idea of intervention later at the side of a victorious France, and had actually started to sound the Italians to this end, he dropped this plan with somewhat undignified haste at the news of the first French defeats in early August. Three weeks later another conference of ministers,[63] meeting under the shadow of a further series of what Franz Joseph termed 'frightful catastrophes'[64] in France, finally abandoned all thought of armed intervention.

The Austrians now fell back on the idea of mediation, and tried to get Great Britain and Russia to help in restraining Prussia; but the decisive Prussian victory at Sedan, and Prussia's insistence on seizing Alsace-Lorraine, soon ruled out that possibility of

61. Ibid., p. 344.
62. Istvan Diószegi, *Oesterreich-Ungarn und der französisch–preußische Krieg, 1870–71* (Budapest 1974); Friedrich Engel-Janosi, 'Oesterreich-Ungarn im Sommer 1870', in idem, *Geschichte auf dem Ballhausplatz*, pp. 207–231; E. Kolb (ed.), *Europa vor dem Krieg von 1870* (Munich 1987).
63. P.A. XL/285, Ministerratsprotokoll, 22 August 1870.
64. W. Wagner, 'Kaiser Franz Joseph und das deutsche Reich' (Vienna dissertation, 1951), p. 53.

compromise. Beust consoled himself with the thought that it might well be in Austria-Hungary's interests if Prussia acquired two indigestible provinces which would ensure her a permanent enemy on her western frontier. Finally, in a last desperate attempt to persuade the South German states unaided to stay out of Prussia's clutches and uphold the Treaty of Prague, Beust himself went to Munich. But Prussia's military triumphs, and the wave of national feeling they had provoked, rendered even this hope futile. On 5 December, while perhaps secretly hoping even now that the guerrilla war starting in France might eventually save the situation,[65] Beust resignedly informed Berlin that he would no longer uphold 'the formal right of the Treaty of Prague' against 'the logic of mighty events through which the leadership of Germany has fallen to the Prussian crown'.[66] Those mighty events had also finally destroyed any lingering hopes the Austrians might have had of eventually playing a role again in the affairs of Germany.

At the same time, the Austrians suffered a diplomatic defeat in the Near East; and unlike the defeat in Germany, this was to a great extent their own fault. For as far as Austro-Russian relations were concerned, the Franco-Prussian war presented what was perhaps one of the great missed opportunities of history.[67] Initially, the Russians were seriously alarmed at the prospect of a French victory that might encourage Napoleon III to pursue his Polish obsessions; and on 23 July Alexander II himself spoke in very conciliatory terms to the Austro-Hungarian ambassador, Count Chotek: if Austria-Hungary would help to localise the war, Russia would give her a territorial guarantee, secure for her a protectorate over southern Germany, and keep the Near East quiet. If, on the other hand, Austria-Hungary resorted to threatening military measures, particularly in Galicia, Russia would be forced to take countermeasures, and there was no knowing where such a process might end. Chotek, impressed by Alexander's evident sincerity, urged Beust to respond, and to help the tsar and the peace party to retain control of Russian policy. Beust, however, preferred to keep a free hand – as for a protectorate over south Germany, the Treaty of Prague suited Austria well enough; and Andrássy was extremely suspicious, declaring that it was only Russia's own military unpreparedness that had prevented her from attacking Austria-Hungary already. A conference of ministers on 24 August decided, therefore, to go ahead with the Galician fortifications.

65. Diószegi, *Französisch–preussischer Krieg*, pp. 222–6.
66. P.A. III/102, Beust to Wimpffen, 5 December 1870.
67. Schoenhals, *Russian Policy*, p. 171.

The tsar persisted with his offers for a time: after the first French defeats, new fears alarmed him, namely, an overweening Prussia, the fall of the dynasty in France, and the Revolution rampant. Again he urged the Austrians to cease their military preparations and to join Great Britain and Russia in their efforts to mediate. Again, however, Andrássy stiffened the conference of ministers against concessions: 'Austria's mission remains, as before, to be a bulwark against Russia, and only so long as she fulfils this mission is her existence a necessity for Europe.'[68] The Austro-Hungarian reply to Russia, accompanied by a catalogue of hoary complaints about Panslav activities, was not unnaturally considered profoundly unsatisfactory in St Petersburg. As a modern authority observes, Beust had just buried the tsar's offer in 'an avalanche of worn-out accusations'.[69] After a further rebuff on the same issue in September, the Russians simply gave up and went their own way. Perhaps the ministers in Vienna had been right in considering Russia's conciliatory offers to be merely the insubstantial result of her temporary embarrassment. The cost of rejecting them, however, was to be high.

For when the next crisis broke in the Near East Austria-Hungary was both on bad terms with Russia, and diplomatically isolated. By the end of October the Balkans were buzzing with rumours of some impending Russian coup. Vienna feared that this might take the form of an occupation of Romania; and it was in fact with some relief that Beust learned on 10 November that Russia had merely denounced the Black Sea clauses of the Treaty of Paris – the revision of which he had always been prepared to countenance. Public opinion was not unduly concerned either: the Magyars made warlike noises, but the Germans were conciliatory, and the Czechs even pro-Russian. Beust emphasised in a council of ministers on 14 November[70] that there could be no question of going to war; nor was there even any enthusiasm for an international conference, at which, as Franz Joseph rightly feared, both Prussia and France would only be out to humour the Russians. When nevertheless the other Great Powers decided on a conference, Beust made the mistake – admittedly under pressure from Andrássy, who was even talking recklessly of war – of setting Austria-Hungary's demands extremely high: Turkey, for instance, was to put a Black Sea port at the disposal of a permanent western naval force to counterbalance any fleet that Russia might build. As the Turks objected strongly to

68. P.A. XL/285, Ministerratsprotokoll, 22 August 1870.
69. Schoenhals, *Russian Policy*, p. 200.
70. P.A. XL/285, Ministerratsprotokoll, 14 November 1870.

this, and as the other Powers were not in the least interested in assuming such obligations, but simply regularised the new position with a series of anodyne declarations, the London conference of January–March 1871 marked another defeat for Austria-Hungary; and it again underlined the lesson that the Monarchy unsupported by a first-class Great Power was simply too weak to secure its objectives.

It was against this background that Beust undertook a thorough reappraisal of Austro-Hungarian foreign policy in a memorandum he wrote for the emperor on 18 May 1871.[71] After 1866, he argued, agreement between Austria and Prussia had been impossible because Prussia would neither allow Austria back into Germany, nor help her against Russia in the Near East. Now things had changed in so far as Austria-Hungary had abandoned all hope of re-entering Germany. The new German Empire, moreover, was a national state, which, by its connections with the Germans in Austria, could gravely embarrass the Habsburg government if provoked. The best policy for Austria-Hungary, therefore, would be to come to terms with realities and seek a *modus vivendi*, or even co-operation, with Berlin. Not that Beust, unlike Andrássy later, had illusions about the possibility of steering the Germans on to a positively anti-Russian course. On the contrary, he saw in a reconciliation with Berlin the chance of improving relations between Vienna and St Petersburg too – especially if some sort of co-operation against 'the Revolution' could be devised; and this might in turn enhance the Monarchy's security in the Near East. Altogether, therefore, Beust advised the emperor to abandon the illusions of past epochs and settle for a general understanding with Prussia. This would make the Central Powers predominant on the continent: no longer organically united, but side by side.

The new policy went into operation at once. It was not forced on Beust by Andrássy, as Wertheimer maintains,[72] let alone deferred until Andrássy replaced him at the Ballhausplatz. In July, the British ambassador remarked on the 'vast and rapid improvement' in Austro-German relations,[73] which was completed by Beust's meetings with the German emperor and Bismarck in August.[74] True, his first encounter with Wilhelm I at Ischl was marred by the emperor's lack of tact in suggesting that the Austrian government

71. P.A. XL/54, Beust, Memorandum for Franz Joseph, 18 May 1871.
72. E.v. Wertheimer, *Graf Julius Andrássy: sein Leben und seine Zeit*, 3 vols (Stuttgart 1910), I, 130–1.
73. F.O. 7/789, Bloomfield to Granville, No. 237, 11 July 1871.
74. Wagner, 'Kaiser Franz Joseph . . .', pp. 83–6.

ought to side with the German element against the Slavs in the political debate then raging in Vienna; and at Salzburg on 28 August Beust and Bismarck both recognised that there was no basis for an actual alliance: Austria-Hungary did not wish to bind herself to fight France, nor Germany, Russia. Nor were the Austrians, in particular the emperor, entirely free from their old suspicions: Franz Joseph, fearful for Austria's independence, refused outright a German offer of a post and telegraph agreement and an extended commercial treaty;[75] and even Beust, although he welcomed Bismarck's disavowal of all desire to annex the Germans of Austria – 'a nest [*Herd*] of Catholics' – still felt there was a need 'to keep a sharp eye open'.[76] But the two Chancellors promised to work for better relations based on the recognition that German and Austro-Hungarian interests no longer clashed, and they were both agreed that the International, which seemed to them to be pursuing its activities more openly and unashamedly – the Commune in Paris was barely three months dead – should be opposed by more definite co-operation between governments. Although only at the price of recognising Prussia's equality, Franz Joseph's old dream of the two German Powers standing together in a common conservative front against 'the Revolution' had in a sense been realised.

Despite Franz Joseph's reservations, the Austro-German meetings of the summer of 1871 marked the end of a decade and a half in which the Monarchy had found itself isolated – or, indeed, had isolated itself – among the Great Powers. Since the collapse of the Holy Alliance in the Crimean War the Monarchy had been striving to defend its position in Italy, the Near East, and Germany without a western ally and in opposition to both its northern neighbours. It had been only very gradually that Franz Joseph and his advisers had come to terms with reality, to the extent of admitting that they could not hold three positions at once, all of which depended on at least the tacit approval of the other Powers. It had taken two disastrous wars before they recognised the impossibility of holding the position even in Italy and Germany simultaneously. As for Germany and the Near East, even Beust after 1866 had not been entirely free from illusions. In the Near East he greatly overestimated the chances of securing support from a Great Britain that had, in fact, largely withdrawn from continental affairs. In Germany, it is true, he had enough sense to steer clear of Napoleon III's proposals for common military action against Prussia, which

75. Ibid.
76. Kab. 17, Beust, report to Franz Joseph, 28 August 1871.

would have been totally unacceptable to Franz Joseph's German subjects; and he managed to achieve his minimum goal of preventing any Prussian advance south of the Main (until Napoleon III upset the boat and presented Bismarck with a united Germany); but his encouragement of the emperor's hopes of re-entering Germany, and the vigorous efforts he made in the press to stir up feeling against Prussia and Russia, rendered any reconciliation with Berlin out of the question. By 1871, however, Beust had managed to raise Austria from impotence and isolation in 1866, to a fairly strong position by the spring of 1870; and when France collapsed, leaving the Monarchy isolated in the storms of 1870–1, he salvaged what he could and then had the resilience to change course and establish a link with Germany that might eventually also serve to take the edge off the conflict with Russia in the Near East – henceforth the focus of Austria-Hungary's external interests and the touchstone of her relations with the other Great Powers.

The realisation of the latter objective was, however, to be deferred for some years when Beust suddenly fell from power, to be replaced by the distinctly anti-Russian Andrássy. Although Beust had had little difficulty bringing the emperor to accept the need for reconciliation with Prussia in terms of the Monarchy's external interests, when he tried to compel Franz Joseph to bring the domestic affairs of the Monarchy into line he went too far. The emperor, ever since he had appointed a Slavophile ministry under Hohenwart and Schäffle in the spring, had been considering a constitutional reform to conciliate the Poles and Czechs. (Since the Germany of 1866 had gone, it was now less important for Austria to keep up appearances as a German state.) The complaints of Liberals, both in Vienna and Budapest, were loud; but it was not merely the demonstrative way in which Beust chose to display his sympathy for them that gave offence at court – as when, at a ceremony at the University of Vienna that degenerated into a riot in which two Slavophile ministers were violently ejected, he saw fit to remain on the platform, acknowledging the cheers of the German students. Perhaps even more galling to Franz Joseph was the memorandum[77] which Beust sent him on 13 October, tactlessly reminding him of the German emperor's admonitions, and stressing the need to humour Berlin at all costs. 'The group Germany–Austria–Italy guarantees us peace and security: if this combination is upset, we drive Russia and Prussia closer together and have then to expect the group Russia–Germany–Italy, and

77. Kab. 17, Beust, report to Franz Joseph, 13 October 1871.

where will the Monarchy find its support then?' Faced with such arguments, and the unpalatable fact that ten million hostile Germans and five million hostile Magyars could make more trouble than three million hostile Czechs, the emperor was obliged to retreat. On 25 October he dismissed the Hohenwart–Schäffle ministry and restored the Liberals to power.

Beust's triumph was shortlived. The emperor had recognised the weight of his arguments: he could not forgive the humiliation. On 1 November he suddenly asked Beust for his resignation. The Chancellor spent the rest of his active career as an embittered ambassador in London (1871–8) and Paris (1878–82), far removed from the centre of policy-making in Vienna. His legacy was nevertheless in some respects a lasting one. He had at last brought the emperor to abandon the illusions that had so bedevilled Austrian policy in the fifties and sixties. All of his successors accepted the desirability of maintaining good relations with the new powerful empire in the north; and none of them ever attempted to re-establish the Monarchy's 1815 position in Germany and Italy, the defence of which had led it into so many disasters. As regards the Monarchy's remaining sphere of interest, however – the Near East – the replacement of Beust by Andrássy showed that in some quarters illusions still persisted. Andrássy, in the words of his son 'an out-and-out Hungarian',[78] was by no means inclined to follow Beust in investigating the possibility of agreement with Russia. On the contrary, he came to office determined to build up a bloc, with Great Britain and the newly reconciled Germany and Italy, to confront and overawe Russia. This represented a fundamental misappreciation of the Monarchy's position among the Powers. Neither Great Britain nor Germany proved in the least inclined to play the role Andrássy had conceived for them; and it was to take another decade of experiments and bitter experiences before the Monarchy could devise a satisfactory basis for the defence of its interests in the last sphere of interest that remained open to it.

78. Julius Andrássy the younger, *Bismarck, Andrássy, and their Successors* (London 1927).

4
Seeking a Near Eastern Partnership, 1871–1881[1]

The internal political situation when Andrássy took office as minister for foreign affairs on 13 November 1871 was, from the new minister's point of view, more promising than at any time since 1866; and there seemed to be every prospect that he would be able to pursue his plans to reinforce the Monarchy's position among the Powers unhindered by any domestic complications. Although the recent ministerial crisis had been something of a humiliation for the emperor, it inaugurated what proved to be a decade of remarkable political stability. In Vienna, the German liberals were in a chastened mood after their narrow escape from political death; and, having defeated the Czechs, they were content to obey the emperor and Andrássy and grant some concessions to make sure of the Poles. Although, still centralists at heart, they had reservations about Andrássy, the incarnation of Dualism, they recognised in him a fellow Liberal; and although they sometimes jibbed at expenditure on the armed forces, they managed to avoid a serious clash with the Supreme War Lord, until the occupation of Bosnia provoked them too far. Hungary, after an upheaval in Deák's '1867' Party, settled down to a new era of stability in 1875 under the masterful Koloman Tisza, newly converted to Dualism by Andrássy. By and large, Andrássy could count on the backing of both the Austrian and Hungarian governments until after the

---

1. The following works are of particular relevance to this chapter: E. von Wertheimer, *Graf Julius Andrássy: sein Leben und seine Zeit*, 3 vols (Stuttgart 1910); T. von Sosnosky, *Die Balkanpolitik Oesterreich-Ungarns seit 1866*, 2 vols, (Stuttgart 1913–14); E. von Glaise-Horstenau, *Franz Josephs Weggefährte. Das Leben des Generalstabschefs Grafen Beck* (Vienna 1930); W.N. Medlicott, *The Congress of Berlin and After*, 2nd edn (London 1963); Idem, *Bismarck, Gladstone, and the Concert of Europe* (London 1956); Agatha Ramm, 'European Alliances and Ententes 1879–1885, a Study of Contemporary British Information' (MA thesis, London); A.F. Pribram, *The Secret Treaties of Austria-Hungary*, 2 vols (Cambridge, Mass. 1931); and the works by A. Wandruszka and P. Urbanitsch (eds), C.A. Macartney, A.J.P. Taylor, A. Sked and I. Diószegi cited in Chapter 1, note 1; and by Barbara Jelavich and F.R. Bridge and Roger Bullen cited in Chapter 2, note 1.

Congress of Berlin. In this respect, he enjoyed a degree of domestic support for a 'strong' foreign policy that was to be vouchsafed to none of his successors.

On the economic front, the indications were that a 'strong' foreign policy might indeed prove desirable. True, in Andrássy's first year at the Ballhausplatz prosperity continued and industry flourished: in the spring of 1872 Austrian stocks almost reached par, for the first time since 1848. Liberalism remained the doctrine of the day, and Austria-Hungary's network of commercial treaties was extended in 1870–3 to include Sweden, Spain, Portugal and some of the South American countries. The financial bases of this prosperity remained unsound, however. Speculation, especially in a host of dubious mushroom enterprises, reached new heights, until in 1873, the year which saw the great festival of economic liberalism in Austria with the Vienna International Exhibition, the inevitable crash occurred. This coincided with the start of a general European depression, and the later seventies in Austria-Hungary saw growing demands from industrialists for protection, only partly assuaged by a general 15 per cent increase in tariffs in 1878–82. For the government, too, 1873 saw the first of a decade of budget deficits; 1879, with the occupation of Bosnia to pay for, was the government's most impecunious year. Although a direct connection is not easy to prove, it would seem that these economic difficulties added a new note of urgency to the government's efforts to develop opportunities for Austro-Hungarian trade by means of commercial treaties with the Balkan states and by improving transport facilities by rail and water to European Turkey.

On the Near Eastern question, Andrássy's views at first diverged markedly from those of Beust. Whereas the latter seems in 1871 to have envisaged a possible adventure into Bosnia – at least, he approved of some speculative remarks made in this sense by Bismarck at Salzburg – Andrássy declared for a strictly conservative policy, rejecting all notion of territorial expansion. (This could only swell the Slav element in the Empire, a prospect that was anathema to the Germans, and even more to the Magyars.) 'The Hungarian ship is so overloaded,' he told the Russians in 1872 (*à propos* the Poles, in fact), 'that any addition, whether a hundredweight of gold or a hundredweight of dross [*Schmutz*], would sink it'.[2] Moreover, to the south, Austria-Hungary had some difficult neighbours – 'wild Indians who could only be treated like unbroken horses, to whom corn should be offered with one hand while

2. Wertheimer, *Andrássy*, II, p. 32.

they are threatened with a whip in the other'.[3] If these neighbours would abandon their territorial ambitions and their intrigues among the Slavs and Romanians of the Monarchy, they might be given corn; but for the present, the whip was needed. Serbia, particularly, was becoming a source of alarm to Budapest. Andrássy's exaggerated cultivation of Belgrade at the end of the sixties had borne bitter fruit: the first state visit of the young Price Milan in October 1871 had been paid to the tsar, and had conjured up the prospect of a territorially enlarged Serbia under Russian, not Austro-Hungarian influence. Since then, Panserbian propaganda had been flooding into the Monarchy, causing a great outcry in the Hungarian press; and the impecunious Serbian government had introduced fiscal tariffs to the detriment of Austro-Hungarian trade. As a result, Andrássy now professed himself 'entirely converted'.[4] He agreed with the Turks that Serbia's ambitions were indeed insatiable, and urged them to join him to watch her closely 'and crush her the moment she moves'.[5] Reforms would never satisfy the Slavs of Turkey, he told the British ambassador, and Great Britain should help Turkey to hold them down by brute force. By May 1872 he had decided that Turkey was Austria-Hungary's 'strongest and most reliable ally' in the Near East,[6] and that in the event of a Christian revolt Austria-Hungary should try to assert the doctrine of non-intervention, 'holding the ring' to allow Turkey to suppress it.[7] Beust's policy of cultivating Austro-Hungarian influence in the Balkan states, even at the risk of offending Turkey, had been swung violently into reverse.

At the same time, Andrássy was both more ambitious and less realistic than Beust in hoping to steer the Austro-German combination in an anti-Russian direction. He even hoped to enlist Great Britain and Italy in a four-Power combination designed, he explained to the British on 21 December 1871, to reinforce Austria-Hungary as a bastion of the status quo (particularly in the Near East) and to keep the restless Powers, France and Russia, 'on their good behaviour'.[8] Yet by the late summer of 1872 these hopes had all proved unrealistic. The British had fobbed him off with a completely non-committal answer. The Germans had assured him that the tsar had no designs against Austria-Hungary, and had

3. F.O. 7/812, Buchanan to Granville, No. 247, 7 September 1873.
4. F.O. 7/791, Lytton to Granville, No. 76, 23 November 1871.
5. Ibid.
6. P.A. XL/287, Ministerratsprotokoll, 17 May 1872.
7. F.O. 7/798, Buchanan to Granville, No. 223, 29 August 1872.
8. F.O. 7/791, Lytton to Granville, No. 108, 27 December 1871.

reminded him that Germany was very much indebted to Russia. Franz Joseph's return visit to Wilhelm I at Berlin (6 to 12 September) merely confirmed Andrássy's failure to enlist German support against Russia. For the tsar, worried about a possible Austro-German alliance, had secured for himself an invitation to Berlin at the same time, thereby substituting a demonstration of monarchical solidarity for the demonstration of Austro-German solidarity, with anti-Russian overtones, that Andrássy had intended.

Ironically enough, so far as relations between the three courts were concerned, it was only Austro-Russian relations that showed any noticeable improvement as a result of the three emperors' meeting at Berlin. The Russians, fearful of an Austro-German agreement, had every reason to be conciliatory; but there were also voices raised at Vienna in favour of a *rapprochement*, notably in the anti-Prussian military party, still smarting from the wounds of 1866: a memorandum from Archduke Albrecht warning the emperor to have nothing to do with the devious Bismarck had almost provoked Andrássy's resignation in the summer of 1872. Andrássy himself, once he got to Berlin, found both the tsar and his Chancellor surprisingly friendly. Gorchakov was even willing to endorse his doctrine of non-intervention in the event of upheavals in Turkey. But little of positive value emerged from the meeting. A formal declaration of war – the only war that could now be waged in Europe, according to Wilhelm I – was launched against the International. But there was little sign of any fighting, apart from some desultory discussions between the police authorities in Vienna and Berlin.

As for Austro-German relations, these had not progressed one jot beyond the stage where Beust had left them. An undercurrent of suspicion of Berlin still persisted at the Austrian court. Archduke Johann Salvator, who in the spring of 1875 fell into disgrace for publicly advocating war with Germany, was admittedly an extreme case. But even during the three emperors' meeting Franz Joseph had been disconcerted to hear of a Prussian scheme to buy a controlling share in the Austrian Southern Railway, a line of vital strategic importance; and as late as 1874 he vetoed an exchange of information on torpedo development with Berlin. In October of the same year Vienna shrugged off a German request for the nullification of Article V of the Treaty of Prague, which had burdened Prussia with the embarrassing obligation to hold a plebiscite in North Schleswig. The questions that most exercised Bismarck – the French threat, the *Kulturkampf,* and a combination of the two in a Catholic conspiracy against the new Germany – offered hardly any scope for co-operation between Vienna and Berlin. True, Austria-Hungary's relations with the Vatican left much to be desired. Franz Joseph had forbidden the promulgation of the dogma of Infallibility in his dominions; in 1872 he again refused asylum to the Pope; and in 1874 he pressed ahead, despite a papal threat of excommunication, with new laws to fill the gap left by the denunciation of the Concordat. Andrássy, certainly, was impressed by Bismarck's intense, almost obsessional, hatred of Pius IX: he had observed, during a visit in October 1873, how the blood always flushed to the rims of Bismarck's eyes at the very mention of the Pope.[9] He was, therefore, at some pains to assure the Germans – citing in evidence the King of Italy's visit to Vienna in September 1873 – that Austria-Hungary would never join any Franco-Papal alliance. Such a combination, he fully realised, could only drive Berlin closer to St Petersburg. At the same time, however, it was not for nothing that Franz Joseph bore the title 'Apostolic Majesty'. The emperor assured the Vatican, in April 1874, that there would be no *Kulturkampf* in Austria-Hungary, nor could Andrássy consider obliging Berlin by expelling the Jesuits, who were far too well entrenched at court; and they both discountenanced Bismarck's plans for a concerted diplomatic offensive against the Papacy, despite his insistence that the Curia was a far greater enemy of all governments than the Communists were.

There was equally little sign of co-operation against Bismarck's other great enemy, France. To Vienna, a monarchist regime in Paris seemed infinitely less dangerous than the possibility of a red republic under Gambetta. Moreover, although a French republic might suit Bismarck, because it could be more easily isolated in a monarchical Europe, this very reasoning made the prospect unattractive to Vienna. For the sake of the balance of power, Franz Joseph emphasised to the French ambassador in St Petersburg in March 1874, Europe had need of a strong France; and Andrássy told the British that if Bismarck was really trying to annihilate France as a Great Power, his brain must be disordered. He had no sympathy with Bismarck's campaign to depict France and the Vatican as warmongers in the spring of 1875: 'within the last six months his good sense seems entirely to have deserted him'. When things reached the level of an actual war scare in May, however, he was careful to stand aside and leave Great Britain, Russia and Italy to bell the German cat; and although Franz Joseph does in fact seem to have added his warning voice to theirs, he did so more

9. Wertheimer, *Andrássy*, II, p. 107.

discreetly.[10] The result could not have been more satisfying for Andrássy: Bismarck had been taught a lesson; France and the peace had been saved; best of all, any danger of an embarrassingly close Russo-German alignment had disappeared with Gorchakov's clumsy *démarche* in Berlin. 'Bismarck will never forgive him!', Andrássy exclaimed, and performed three exultant handstands on his office table.[11]

At the same time, Andrássy took good care, in the years following the three emperors' meeting, to cultivate his own relations with the Russians. True, Russia remained the only serious military threat to Austria-Hungary, whose whole military preparations remained directed against that Power; and a conference of ministers decided, on 8 January 1873, to push ahead with the fortification of Przemysl and Cracow in Galicia as bases for launching an offensive into Poland should it ever come to war.[12] Failing that eventuality, however, and granted that Andrássy had been unable to win German support for an anti-Russian policy, there was much to be said for attempting to live on good neighbourly terms with Russia. The latter's Balkan ambitions seemed to have abated, and as Vienna kept its constitutional concessions to Galicia within reasonable bounds, the Polish question too proved to be no insurmountable obstacle after all.

A definite step forward was made during Alexander II's visit to the Vienna Exhibition in 1873. The Schönbrunn Convention of 6 June, (see Appendix I)[13] concluded, to emphasise its permanence, between the monarchs rather than their ministers, was an important achievement. Admittedly, it was only an 'agreement to agree' in time of trouble; and its general endorsement of the status quo – significantly, even against Germany – did not go beyond what Andrássy and Gorchakov had agreed at Berlin the previous autumn. As regards the Near East, it simply implied that the two Powers could best preserve the peace by hopefully abstaining from meddling. All the same, an Austro-Russian agreement now existed. And when the German emperor acceded to it during his visit to Vienna in October 1873, an imposing Three Emperors' League was created, with the theoretical emphasis strongly on monarchical solidarity against 'the Revolution'. In reality, however, the

10. W. Wagner, 'Kaiser Franz Joseph und das deutsche Reich', Vienna dissertation 1951, p. 102.
11. Wertheimer, *Andrássy*, II, p. 243.
12. P.A. XI /287, Ministerratsprotokoll, 8 January 1873.
13. Text in *Die Große Politik der europäischen Kabinette, 1871–1914* (eds J. Lepsius, A. Mendelssohn-Bartholdy and F. Thimme), 40 vols (Berlin 1922–7), I, pp. 206–7.

League remained essentially an Austro-Russian arrangement. This was evident during Franz Joseph's return visit to St Petersburg in February 1874, which set the seal on the reconciliation of tsar and emperor, when Franz Joseph did pious homage at the deathbed and the tomb of Nicholas I. Andrássy told Gorchakov straight out that Austria-Hungary wanted good relations with Russia in case Germany should become expansionist again. This latent suspicion of the third partner was to be characteristic of relations within the Three Emperors' League.

It was, of course, an essential condition of improved Austro-Russian relations that Austria-Hungary should not feel menaced by Russian and Panslav activities on her southern frontier. In fact, the years 1872–5 saw a considerable relaxation of tension in the Balkans, partly, no doubt, because no major disturbance occurred to force Russia to defend her reputation as protector of the Slavs; but also because the Russian government, fearful of the new German empire, and above all of an Austro-German alliance, was at pains to cultivate its new *entente* with Vienna. The Austrians made good use of the situation. Andrássy spent a good deal of secret service money in combating Russian, and promoting Austro-Hungarian, influence in Bosnia by building Catholic churches and schools and encouraging the propaganda activities of the energetic Croatian bishop, Strossmayer. Indeed, his policy towards the Balkan states now became altogether more flexible and less nervously negative. Like Beust, he was now prepared, while remaining opposed to the territorial ambitions of the Balkan states, to consider minor concessions to ease relations with them. The 'wild Indians' were to be plied with corn.

In Bucharest, for example, he managed to take some credit, along with Russia, for securing international recognition of Prince Carol as Prince of 'Romania' – although he forced the prince to drop his claim to the title 'Prince of the Romanians', which would have implied a connection with the three million Romanian subjects of Franz Joseph in Hungary. Already Andrássy had his eye on Romania as a potentially useful barrier against the slavicisation of the Balkans; and he further increased his influence at Bucharest in 1875 when Austria-Hungary became the first state to conclude a commercial treaty with Romania, a state which, as a vassal state of Turkey, had no legal right to conclude treaties at all. It was not only politically astute to flatter the Romanians, but it also made good sense commercially (especially in view of Austria-Hungary's growing economic difficulties after 1873) to replace the haphazard *ad hoc* tariffs hitherto prevailing by a mutually agreed system.

Between 1874 and 1876 the Austrian State Railways duly built the Budapest–Bucharest line. In Serbia, too, Austro-Hungarian influence recovered after 1872, when Belgrade, finding St Petersburg unwilling to back its territorial ambitions, turned to Vienna. Although Andrássy, too, firmly advised the Serbs to forget about territorial expansion, the establishment at Vienna of a Serbian diplomatic agency furthered trade between Serbia and the Monarchy; and in the spring of 1874 Andrássy opened negotiations with the Serbs for the construction of the railway to Constantinople via Belgrade. Serbia, he was so bold as to inform St Petersburg, would always be commercially dependent on her great northern neighbour. As early as November 1873 Andrássy told the British ambassador that he had broken with the 'old' policy of simply supporting Turkey, because this only united the Balkan states in solidarity against Turkey and Austria-Hungary.[14] He was in fact returning to the policy of Beust.

Andrássy's decision to conciliate the Balkan states both reflected and exacerbated a strain on his relations with Constantinople. He had in fact soon become disillusioned about the identity of Turkish and Austro-Hungarian interests. In the autumn of 1872 he found the Turks unwilling to co-operate over the projected navigation works to clear the Danube (still Austria-Hungary's most important economic lifeline in the south-east); and in 1875 they unhelpfully raised legalistic objections to the Austro-Romanian commercial treaty. As regards the railways in which Austria-Hungary was interested – in the western Balkans – the Turks were dilatory in the extreme. Indeed, until the 1880s, such bits of railway line as the Turks constructed (a few lines into Macedonia from the Aegean) only worsened the commercial position of Austria-Hungary by furthering the penetration of cheap seaborne French and British wares into Macedonia. The Turks, for their part, were not without grievances against Austria-Hungary. The governor of Bosnia had been complaining since 1873 about her increasing 'cultural' activities there, and her designs on that province seemed to receive new confirmation in the spring of 1875, when Franz Joseph made a spectacular tour of the neighbouring Austrian province of Dalmatia. The effect was electric on the Christian populations of Bosnia and the Herzegovina, who sent delegations to greet the emperor and ask for his protection. Andrássy himself sensed that the visit might provoke serious trouble, and seems to have advised the emperor against it. A direct connection between it and the Bosnian

14. F.O. 7/814, Buchanan to Granville, No. 321, 17 November 1873.

revolt of July 1875 is difficult to prove: Prince Milan's triumphal progress through Serbia in June was equally inflammatory, and more closely coincident in time. Nevertheless, by June there were 4,000 rebels under arms in the Herzegovina, and the Christians of Bosnia rose in July. Andrássy's expectation that the Turks would soon suppress the rebellion proved unfounded. The Turks took no effective military measures until the Bulgarians rose in the following year. In the meantime, the question of the future of Bosnia had been posed in an acute form.

For the previous fifty years Bosnia had been a source of constant disorder on the southern frontier of the Monarchy.[15] The Austrian government had shown considerable restraint, however, abjuring any actions that might weaken the Ottoman regime – even in the face of incessant frontier raids by Muslim bands (which cost the Austrian government some nine million guilders, for example, in the years 1815–30 alone). This was no solution. Inside Bosnia conditions grew progressively worse, with bloody rebellions of the Islamised landowning beys against attempted reforms from Constantinople, or, when Turkish control was relaxed, rebellions of the Christian peasantry against the oppressive regime of the beys. So it is not surprising that as early as the 1850s voices had been raised in Austria suggesting intervention and military occupation as the only effective means of bringing peace to the frontier.

By the 1860s these arguments were gaining ground in military and naval circles. Already in 1856 Radetzky had maintained that the possession of part of the Bosnian hinterland was strategically necessary for the defence of the Dalmatian coastal strip, which contained no suitable land route for troop transports, and depended for its security on the ability of the small Austrian fleet to control the eastern Adriatic. With the loss of Venice in 1866 it became even more important, as Vice-Admiral Tegetthof pointed out, to make absolutely sure of Dalmatia, now the only possible base for the navy. Besides, Dalmatia could never flourish economically without its hinterland – an argument which lost nothing in force as Austria's Adriatic trade developed and as economic conditions became more difficult in the 1870s. To Franz Joseph himself, who had so far managed only to lose territories, the idea of acquiring a province naturally had its attractions; and as the devout heir to a three-hundred-year-old protectorate over the Catholics of the western Balkans, he could not feel completely indifferent to the appeals of his suffering co-religionists across the frontier. Above all, as Beck

15. Sosnosky, *Balkanpolitik*, II, pp. 108ff.

reminded him, Austria-Hungary must make sure that not only Bosnia, but the Herzegovina as well, did not fall into the hands of the Slav states, Serbia and Montenegro – otherwise, both Dalmatia and Croatia would soon be lost. The Sanjak of Novibazar, the strip of the vilayet of Bosnia separating Serbia from Montenegro, would be, as the gateway to Salonika, a doubly useful acquisition. It was in line with such thinking that Franz Joseph, during his tour of Dalmatia in 1875, told the governor, General Mollinary, that he would be put in charge of an occupying expedition if ever it seemed that the provinces were about to slip from Turkey's grasp.

Andrássy, by contrast, was as loath to see an Austro-Hungarian occupation of Bosnia as the emperor was keen. Personally, perhaps, he still felt some gratitude to the empire which had sheltered him, an exile under sentence of death for treason, in 1849. As a statesman he realised, like Metternich, that a feeble Turkey, tiresome though she might sometimes be, was still the best possible neighbour for Austria-Hungary, who would be foolish to do anything that might precipitate her collapse. On the other hand, it was obvious that there could be no question of fighting to uphold Turkey: that would merely play into the hands of a Russia seeking to pose as a patron of the Slavs. Indeed, although, as a Magyar, Andrássy had no desire to see more Slavs inside the Monarchy, he felt that even this would be a lesser evil than the expansion of potentially hostile South Slav states outside the Monarchy. Thus he reluctantly came to consider the possibility of an occupation, not, like Beck, as a forward, expansionist move, but simply as a preventive action to stop the Slav states sealing the Monarchy off from areas of trade and influence in the south. He defined his policy thus: 'not to push the Turks out of the two provinces, rather to support them as long as possible there, by giving advice and recommending reforms; nevertheless, should the occasion arise, to take their place should they lack the strength to defend their position'.[16]

The immediate situation in the summer of 1875 was menacing in two respects: the little Slav states, Serbia and Montenegro, might intervene in the Bosnian affair; or Russia herself might do so. As regards the first possibility, Andrássy hoped that the Turks would suppress the rebellion before the following spring, that is, before Serbia and Montenegro were militarily prepared. He was sceptical about the complaints of the Bosnian Christians and decided – especially in view of the stubborn refusal of the rebels to negotiate

---

16. Wertheimer, *Andrássy*, II, pp. 260–1.

with the Turks, and the excited language of the Slav press from Belgrade to Prague – that the whole rising had been organised by revolutionary committees. At the same time, however, he was reluctant to come forward alone in defence of the Turks: that would only draw on to Austria-Hungary the wrath of the whole Slav world. For the time being, therefore, he took refuge in the idea that the question was one for Europe, and particularly for Russia and Austria-Hungary together, to settle.[17] This raised, of course, the question of St Petersburg's intentions: the 1873 'agreement to agree' was about to be put to the test.

At first, the prospects did not look promising. In August, the danger that Russia might take advantage of the rising to increase her prestige among the Balkan Christians appeared very real, when the St Petersburg government, under great pressure to make some gesture to Panslav opinion, proposed that Bosnia and the Herzegovina might be granted an autonomous regime. Momentarily, Andrássy was thrown completely off balance, and in an excited letter to the emperor[18] revealed his deep-rooted suspicion of the Russians: they had not changed their spots after all. For any Russian government, even for that of Alexander II and Gorchakov, Russia's historic mission would always count in the last resort for everything, and consideration for Austro-Hungarian interests for nothing. Gorchakov's proposal he described as the 'purest nonsense': autonomy might be practicable for an entirely Christian region, such as Bulgaria, but such a weak system of government would never be able to maintain order in Bosnia, with its warring Muslim, Catholic and Orthodox populations. The chaos on the Monarchy's southern frontier would only intensify. Moreover, the Russian proposal would provoke similar claims from Bulgaria, and declarations of independence by the Turkish vassal states: 'everything that should be kept stable will then really begin to move'. Eventually, Andrássy calmed down. After all, the hard fact was that a weak Power such as Austria-Hungary, without an ally, was in no position to take a strong line; and unless Russia could be seen to be co-operating with the Monarchy in the search for a compromise solution, the rebels would never be brought to negotiate with Turkey. There was much to be said for seeking agreement with St Petersburg. Luckily, Gorchakov did not press his autonomy proposal for the present; and towards the end of the year Andrássy managed to persuade him to agree to a moderate programme of

17. Kab. 18, Andrássy to Franz Joseph, 27 August 1875.
18. Kab. 18, Andrássy to Franz Joseph, 30 August 1875; Diószegi, *Hungarians in the Ballhausplatz*, pp. 173ff.

reforms, which was put before the Powers in the so-called Andrássy Note of 30 December 1875. He hoped by this means to preserve Turkey by encouraging her to remove the causes of the upheavals that were weakening her; to take the initiative himself and wrest from Russia the role of protector of the Slavs; and possibly also to stake out a claim to Austria-Hungary's prime interest in the Bosnian question, to facilitate any occupation that might become necessary.

Be that as it may, the Note came to nothing. It was clear by the spring of 1876 that Andrássy had been wildly optimistic in thinking that his proposals – essentially a repetition of the still unfulfilled Turkish promises of 1856 – would remotely satisfy the rebels. The latter gave the Note very short shrift; and the crisis assumed a more serious aspect, from the Austrian point of view, when Gorchakov seized the initiative again, asking Andrássy to meet him during Alexander II's forthcoming visit to Berlin in May. Indeed, on his arrival in Berlin, Andrássy was greatly taken aback when Gorchakov presented him with a full-dress programme for intervention by the Concert, in the form of a memorandum that condoned the rebellion and envisaged armed intervention and a congress to discuss further means of coercing Turkey. He told Gorchakov that his proposals were quite unacceptable, and complained bitterly to the Germans about 'this unnatural thing that calls itself the Three Emperors' League'.[19] Luckily for him, however, the tsar was in no mood to risk a clash with Austria-Hungary; and in the face of Andrássy's decided stand, Gorchakov became 'soft as butter' and modified his original proposals beyond all recognition.[20] The 'unnatural thing', or, rather, the anxiety of the Russians to preserve it, had its uses after all. The upshot was that the so-called Berlin Memorandum of 12 May was drafted largely by Andrássy. This document merely urged the Turks to grant an armistice to the rebels and to institute reforms on the lines of the Andrássy Note. A vague hint of stronger measures – probably a naval demonstration – if the Turks refused, was all that Gorchakov could salvage from his original proposals for intervention. Not content with this success, Andrássy took advantage, a week later, of a British refusal to consider any kind of pressure on the Porte to scrap the Berlin Memorandum altogether. He seemed to have foiled the Russians completely.

The Three Emperors' League had survived; but events beyond

---

19. R. Hegedüs, 'The Foreign Policy of Count Julius Andrássy', in *Hungarian Quarterly*, III No. 4 (1937) pp. 632–3.
20. Kab. 18, Andrássy to Franz Joseph, telegram, 12 May 1876.

its control gave the crisis a new and dangerous turn. A palace revolution in Constantinople in June removed all hope that the Turks would soon master the rebellion; and at the beginning of July Serbia and Montenegro declared war on Turkey. (The Bulgarians had already risen, and had been subjected to fearful massacres as a result.) Fortunately for the peace of Europe, however, both Russia and Austria-Hungary were, above all, anxious to avoid being dragged into war with each other by these untoward events. While Gorchakov, increasingly apprehensive about Panslav pressure for action if Serbia were defeated, was naturally keen to keep in touch with his partners in the Three Emperors' League, Andrássy, for his part, had little alternative. Working within the League was the only policy that could offer Austria-Hungary the slightest hope of support from Berlin; and there was precious little hope of aid from any other quarter. Although the British, Austria's allies of old in the Near East, might still fight for the Straits and Constantinople, they were now chary of lending support in the Balkan peninsula to the government responsible for the Bulgarian massacres. At most, Great Britain might be a factor to be held in reserve in Andrássy's calculations. For the present, he simply had to rely on the Three Emperors' League. He welcomed, therefore, the Russian sugges- tion for a meeting between himself, Gorchakov, and their two imperial masters at the Bohemian castle of Reichstadt in July.

At Reichstadt (8 July 1876) Gorchakov and Andrássy achieved their aim of effectively eliminating the war between Turkey, Serbia and Montenegro as a possible source of conflict between Russia and Austria-Hungary. They agreed that, if Turkey were victorious, she was to be prevented from exploiting her victory to change the status quo; if she were defeated, however, she was to be virtually expelled from Europe. In the latter case, Russia would recover Southern Bessarabia, and Austria-Hungary would take Bosnia. (According to Andrássy's view – there was no agreed statement in writing – Austria-Hungary was also to occupy the Herzegovina.) Serbia and Montenegro were to expand to a common frontier in the Sanjak of Novibazar. Greece was to gain Crete and Thessaly, and the remaining provinces of European Turkey – Bulgaria, Rumelia and Albania – were to receive autonomous regimes. On the whole, Andrássy could be well content. Turkey might after all survive; but even if she collapsed, Austro-Hungarian interests had been fairly well secured. Serbia and Montenegro would not gain possession of Bosnia and the Herzegovina. True, by absorbing the Sanjak, they would effectively seal off Austria-Hungary from the rest of the Balkans in a strictly territorial sense; but at this stage

Andrássy seems to have thought the Reichstadt agreement a sufficient guarantee that Austro-Hungarian influence would prevail in the western Balkans generally. His growing faith in the Three Emperors' League seemed to have been rewarded; and at Salzburg in August he gave the German emperor the gist of the agreement. It was significant, however, that he left the other Powers pretty much in the dark. Indeed, whereas the Andrássy Note and the Berlin Memorandum had been drawn up for presentation to the other Powers, the Reichstadt agreement marked a major step towards the withdrawal of Austria-Hungary and Russia from the Concert of Europe.

Certainly, it was in the framework of the League, rather than that of the Concert, that, as the crisis became more menacing, the two Powers addressed the question of Russian armed intervention. By the autumn, the crushing defeat of the Serbs had made Constantinople less willing than ever to consider concessions to the Christians; and it took a Russian ultimatum – ominous sign – to bring the Turks to grant an armistice to Serbia at the end of October. As Panslav excitement mounted, Gorchakov had to face the prospect of war with Turkey, and to try to secure, if not the actual co-operation, at least the acquiescence of Austria-Hungary. That Austria-Hungary might actively co-operate in weakening Turkey was, in fact, always out of the question, as the ensuing negotiations showed. Indeed, the negotiations were not so much a plot between two accomplices, as yet another attempt by Andrássy – like those at Berlin and Reichstadt – to restrain Russia and secure Austria-Hungary's vital interests. In September, Alexander II had made a tentative approach with a letter to Franz Joseph suggesting that temporary occupations of Bosnia and Bulgaria by Austria-Hungary and Russia respectively might bring Turkey to heel. Andrássy had given very short shrift to this 'absurd proposal'. Yet by 23 October the Austrians were engaged in discussing with St Petersburg the conditions on which they would be prepared to acquiesce in a Russian attack on the Ottoman Empire.

The unpleasant fact was, of course, that Russia could not be effectively opposed unless Austria-Hungary were willing to go to war in defence of Turkey, sacrificing her position *vis-à-vis* the whole Slav world, both outside and inside her frontiers, and putting her own existence as a Great Power at risk. Her diplomatic position had not improved since the summer: she still had no ally in Europe, and was in the last resort as isolated as in 1866 and 1871. As far as Germany was concerned, so long as the old emperor lived there did not seem to be the slightest chance of winning her support for any action against Russia: Bismarck warned the Austrians on 29 November that he was not prepared to come forward against Russia, and that they should square her at Turkey's expense. As for Great Britain, her commitments were likely to be of an extremely limited nature, hardly going beyond the defence of Constantinople. Indeed, in December Salisbury told Andrássy to his face that British public opinion would not permit the government to fight for the Ottoman Empire.

The military situation was equally depressing. Moreover, the persons most qualified to speak on it, Archduke Albrecht and Beck, were both old-style conservatives, deeply distrustful of Berlin and inclined by temperament towards the court of St Petersburg. The advice the emperor received from military circles was, therefore, to co-operate with Russia at all costs, and to work out some agreement with her. Beck even had visions of the Monarchy's expanding as far as Salonika by these means. War with Russia, by contrast, was not to be contemplated: the army was not ready; it would take a long time to defeat Russia, as Napoleon I had discovered; and there was even a serious risk that Germany and Italy might seize the opportunity to attack Austria-Hungary. Moreover, according to military thinking at Vienna, as represented in a memorandum presented to Franz Joseph by Archduke Albrecht and Beck in November,[21] 'long wars cannot be borne by a modern [*Kultur-*] industrial state employing universal conscription'. They were too exhausting, as had been proved in 1866 and 1870–1.

> Therein Russia has the advantage over all the other Powers. Least of all, therefore, should Russia's nearest, half-encircled neighbour, Austria-Hungary, who cannot like the Western Powers withdraw from the war when she thinks fit, be among the first to take the field. She must rather preserve her full strength to the end, and then the decision will lie in her hands.

Not even Andrássy, although he felt that the Monarchy ought to arm as fast as possible, so as to be in a position to take the offensive if its interests required, could contemplate war with Russia without apprehension: it would last for generations, and end only with the destruction of one or both combatants. It would be wise, therefore, while avoiding helping or encouraging Russia in her designs on Turkey, to see whether Austria-Hungary's more immediately im-

21. Glaise-Horstenau, *Beck*, p. 191.

portant interests could not be secured by some bilateral agreement.

The ensuing negotiations, culminating in the Austro-Russian Budapest Convention (15 January 1877) defined the military conditions on which Austria-Hungary would acquiesce in a Russo-Turkish war. War was not yet certain: since December the Concert had been trying, by means of an international conference at Constantinople, to persuade the Turks to concede a large measure of autonomy, under European supervision, to Bosnia and Bulgaria. (Andrássy had thought these proposals rather drastic, but had fallen in with them rather than risk offending their chief authors, Great Britain and Russia, and driving those two Powers together.) But when in the new year the Turks rejected the proposals, the Russians became extremely anxious to proceed with their military preparations in case war should become necessary in the spring. They consequently showed themselves as accommodating towards Vienna as in the previous summer. The Austrians, for their part, by pledging themselves to benevolent neutrality and to preventing mediation by the Powers or the application of the Austro-Franco-British guarantee to Turkey of 15 April 1856, again demonstrated their faith in the Three Emperors' League as opposed to the Concert of Europe. They seemed to be well rewarded. For example, they had been very worried lest Russia march into Serbia and transform the war into a revolutionary Slav-Orthodox crusade, which would have grave repercussions among the Slavs of the Monarchy. This point was adequately safeguarded in the Budapest Convention: Russia promised to confine her military operations to the Eastern Balkans. As for the results of the war, they were apparently to be minimal: Bosnia and the Herzegovina were to receive a measure of autonomy on the lines of the Andrássy Note, and Bulgaria a rather more far-reaching autonomy. At the same time, Andrássy reserved the right to occupy both Bosnia and the Herzegovina – forcing Gorchakov to recognise the Austro-Hungarian version of the Reichstadt agreement, and documenting anew the Monarchy's prime interest in these provinces. Possible more far-reaching changes were reserved for a later, additional convention.

This additional convention, dated 15 January to correspond with the original convention, was concluded at Budapest on 18 March, and dealt with the possibility that, under the strain of war with Russia, the Ottoman Empire might collapse altogether. It was essentially a re-statement of the Reichstadt agreement, and awarded Southern Bessarabia to Russia, Bosnia and the Herzegovina to Austria-Hungary, and territorial gains to the Balkan states. The only significant difference was that, whereas Andrássy still agreed to the partition of the Sanjak of Novibazar between Serbia and Montenegro, there was now to be a 'later agreement' guaranteeing to Austria-Hungary the use of commercial routes through the strip. By this means Andrássy hoped to safeguard Austro-Hungarian trade and influence in the western Balkans, without the burden of annexing yet more territory. On the whole, the Budapest Convention and the Annex of 18 March bore the stamp of their place of origin. Andrássy made the somewhat sanguine calculation that, if Russia observed them, her territorial gains would be minimal, and she would have by no means established her influence in the peninsula – especially as her military presence in the eastern Balkans was to cease with the end of the war. And if she broke her word, she would be in the worst conceivable military position – weakened by war, with over-extended lines of communication, and facing the hostility of Austria-Hungary and, possibly, Great Britain.

It should be emphasised that neither the Russians nor the Austrians were actually seeking war. Indeed, Andrássy still hoped that the day would never come when it would be necessary to implement the Budapest Convention. The Russians, for their part, joined readily with the other Powers in a last effort to keep the peace – the anodyne London Protocol of 31 March, which reduced the Powers' January proposals to a mere recommendation to the sultan to adopt reforms. It was only when the Turks rejected even this that the tsar declared war (24 April); and his behaviour for the next eight months gave Andrássy no reason to doubt his loyalty and moderation. In any case, this 'war between the one-eyed and the blind', as Bismarck termed it, seemed unlikely to precipitate the much-feared collapse of the Ottoman Empire. In the summer, the Russians, held up completely before the fortress of Plevna, were using remarkably restrained language at Vienna. On 26 July Alexander II assured Franz Joseph[22] that he had no intention of permanently occupying Bulgaria, or of introducing any 'democratic' elements there; that the Powers would be able to assert their interests in the final peace settlement; and that Russia intended to hold scrupulously to the Reichstadt agreement. This being the case, Franz Joseph and Andrássy were careful to keep the more turbulent spirits in the Monarchy under control: anti-Russian feeling was particularly strong in Hungary, where a Szekler volunteer force had to be restrained from marching into Romania when the Rus-

---

22. P.A. I/469, Memorandum by Aehrenthal, May–June 1895, on Austro-Russian relations 1872–94, hereafter cited as 'Aehrenthal Memorandum 1895'.

sians crossed the Danube. The Turks made an astute move at this time in restoring the treasures of the medieval kings of Hungary to Budapest, where massive demonstrations were held in support of Turkey. But Andrássy felt that, thanks to Tisza's continued support, he could ignore this 'foolish excitement'.[23] Clearly, he felt that his confidence in the Three Emperors' League had been justified at last.

Of course, Andrássy was always aware of the possibility that the League might yet prove a broken reed – if, for example, the Russian military on the spot should carry all before them and spread the war to the whole Balkans in defiance of the Budapest Convention. It was for this reason that he did not wish to lose touch entirely with the British. But both Andrássy and the emperor felt the need for great circumspection in handling London. They were always apprehensive lest the British might only be trying to use Austria-Hungary as a means of frightening Russia into making an agreement – perhaps to secure their interests in the Straits by giving Russia a free hand in the Balkans. Nor was Andrássy himself willing to tell the British exactly how closely he was tied to Russia. Anglo-Austrian soundings in the summer of 1877, therefore, never proceeded beyond the most tentative stage. On 20 May Andrássy rejected a British suggestion for an agreement over the Straits (an area of more importance to Great Britain than to Austria-Hungary). And he was not, even in the Balkans, quite in line with London, attaching more importance to making sure that Russia did not establish a permanent military presence in Bulgaria than to defining the future territorial limits of that province. Although on 26 July he agreed to keep in touch with the British, he would still undertake no commitments to fight; and so long as the tsar kept his word, Franz Joseph would not commit himself to Great Britain.

Even when it appeared that the Russians, having broken Ottoman resistance at Plevna and advancing on Constantinople, might not keep their word after all, and when in a letter of 9 December to Franz Joseph the tsar talked ominously of ceding parts of Bosnia to Serbia and Montenegro and of occupying Bulgaria for two years, the Austrians still refused to join with the British to oppose them. They attempted, rather, to settle their differences directly with the Russians: after all, in 1873 the two emperors had pledged themselves in the League to 'concert together' in this very 'event of their countries appearing to diverge over particular questions'. On 9 January 1878, therefore, Franz Joseph reminded the tsar that the

Ottoman Empire had not collapsed: hence there could be no question as yet of implementing the Reichstadt agreement. At the same time, he pointed out that Austria-Hungary's right to occupy Bosnia was contingent on Russia's recovery of Southern Bessarabia; not on her establishing a military presence in Bulgaria, to which, moreover, Austria-Hungary would object. And in any case, a definitive peace could only be made by all the Powers together, whose protection Turkey had enjoyed since 1856. These objections made little impression on Alexander II, who, in a threatening reply of 16 January, dismissed them as based on 'irrelevant assumptions and prejudices'.[24] Although he conceded that Austria-Hungary could take Bosnia in her own good time, he insisted on occupying Bulgaria and on recovering Southern Bessarabia, not by virtue of the Reichstadt agreement (which St Petersburg too admitted did not apply to the existing circumstances), but because Russia had only lost the latter as a result of Austria's treachery in the Crimean War. Franz Joseph was prepared to accept this last argument, but maintained his objections to the projected Russian military presence in Bulgaria.

Whatever hopes the Austrians may have set on 'concerting together' with St Petersburg were soon to be dashed. In the intoxication of victory even Gorchakov, while conceding that Austria-Hungary was still free to occupy Bosnia, nevertheless insisted on occupying Bulgaria; and coolly explained that Austria-Hungary's objections to the creation of a compact Slav state had been overridden by *force majeure*. The final formulation of the Russian terms in the Treaty of San Stefano (3 March) was, not surprisingly, completely unacceptable to Vienna. In a strictly legal sense, the Austrian position was not all that strong: Russia was not herself obliged to secure Bosnia for Austria-Hungary; and both Russia and Austria-Hungary were agreed that the conditions had not arisen that would bring the Budapest Convention into force, namely, the actual collapse of the Ottoman Empire. Nevertheless, Vienna could not unreasonably argue that the Treaty of San Stefano was a flagrant violation of the spirit of the convention, and a serious threat to those very interests which Andrássy had been concerned to safeguard at Reichstadt and at Budapest. Russia had chosen to settle single-handed questions which for the past thirty years had been the concern of all the Powers, and particularly of Austria-Hungary. By creating an autonomous Bosnia and a Big Bulgaria, which would be occupied by Russian troops for two years, and,

24. P.A. I/469, Aehrenthal Memorandum 1895.

what was worse, by doing this in the face of advance warnings and protests from Vienna, the Treaty of San Stefano portended the annihilation of Austria-Hungary's prestige and influence in the Balkan peninsula.

The Austrians had in fact been racking their brains as to how to stave off such a disaster ever since it became clear at the beginning of the year that Russian policy had definitely changed. The prospects of attempting to reverse the situation by military means remained as bleak as ever. Andrássy shrank from the prospect of a war with Russia, which, even if temporarily successful, would leave such a legacy of hatred between the two nations that Austria-Hungary would be burdened for generations with the enormous expense of standing permanently on guard and armed to the teeth against her mighty eastern neighbour. In view of this, and of the all too well-known opinions of the military, he did not even suggest war as a feasible policy to a conference of ministers on 15 January.[25] Nor did the conference show any enthusiasm for his suggestion that Russia might be brought to reason by a military demonstration, such as Austria had undertaken in the Crimean War. The military authorities present could not in any case agree as to where this might best be attempted.

There was, moreover, throughout these months, a strong anti-war current at court. Although Russia's behaviour aroused universal indignation, the idea of a war with the tsar was not attractive to the more conservative aristocrats, like Archduke Albrecht; and some, like the Court Chamberlain Prince Hohenlohe (who had large estates in Russia), even had a material interest in avoiding it. In military circles too there were many – notably the military attaché at St Petersburg – who still regarded Bismarck as the chief enemy of Austria-Hungary, and who used all their influence with Beck to make the most of the political and military-technical objections to war. Indeed, Beck is described by his biographer as the chief counterpoise to Andrássy in the crisis.[26] As a German centralist and defender of the Common Army, although his influence on foreign policy was unofficial, it was none the less weighty: as head of the emperor's military chancellery, he saw Franz Joseph every day. On 14 February he told the emperor straight out that the military position was worse than it had been in 1859 or 1866. Any war would have to be fought on four fronts – against Russia, the South Slavs, Germany and Italy. But to what purpose? Public

25. Wertheimer, *Andrássy*, III, p. 63.
26. Glaise-Horstenau, *Beck*, p. 186.

opinion might understand a war to conquer half the Balkans; but a war costing 600 million Gulden just to drive Russia back? – the parliaments would never vote the money. 'The whole thing is a Hungarian policy, a war of revenge for Világos.'[27] Three days later Franz Joseph assured him that the conference of ministers had decided that there could be no question of war. With the offer of only a loan, not a subsidy, from Great Britain, Austria-Hungary was virtually bankrupt (*auf dem Trockenen*).[28] She simply could not afford to go to war. In view of these harsh realities, when Andrássy and Tisza seemed to lose their nerve in a conference of ministers of 24 February, making what amounted to an appeal for war, the isolation of the two Hungarians was virtually a foregone conclusion.[29] It now remained to be seen whether Russia could be brought to reason by diplomatic means.

Andrássy proposed an international conference to discuss the settlement. This choice of diplomatic weapon was significant. He still preferred to give Russia the chance of saving face under cover of the Concert, rather than to risk a deadlock and war by openly challenging her, say, in conjunction with Great Britain. Indeed, although Great Britain was equally strongly opposed to Russia's proceedings, Vienna's doubts as to her usefulness remained as strong as ever. Any Anglo-Russian war would be an inconclusive fight between the shark and the wolf, Andrássy declared, and it would fall to Austria-Hungary to bear the brunt of the fighting.[30] Indeed, the British might only be seeking in Austria-Hungary a battering ram for use against Russia, to be discarded when convenient. And if Great Britain might be unable to lend effective assistance, Germany was decidedly unwilling. At the end of February Bismarck again warned Andrássy that, although Germany would not obstruct Austria-Hungary's diplomacy, she would lend it no assistance against Russia. Bismarck wanted above all, for the sake of his own relations with St Petersburg, to stay clear of the dispute; and he was in fact somewhat embarrassed when Andrássy and Gorchakov eventually agreed on Berlin (rather than Vienna, as Andrássy had originally proposed) as the venue of the conference. It is true that Austro-German relations improved a little at this time. Andrássy skilfully offered Bismarck the bribe of the nullification of Article V of the Treaty of Prague, and a secret agreement to this effect was concluded on 13 April. But Crown Prince Rudolph

27. Ibid., p. 200.
28. Ibid., p. 201.
29. Diószegi, 'Das Interesse Ungarns', in *Habsburgermonarchie VI*, p. 379.
30. Wertheimer, *Andrássy*, III, p. 70.

received in Berlin only the somewhat cold comfort of an assurance that Germany would never let Austria-Hungary actually perish in a war; and although on 25 March Franz Joseph could declare that Austro-German relations were 'of the best' [*das beste*],[31] the underlying assumption of even this tepid support from Berlin was that Andrássy should seek to square Russia. Hence his decision to try, even at this late date, to save the Three Emperors' League, and to seek a solution in agreement with Russia, if the latter were still amenable to reason.

At first, the Russians seemed willing to co-operate. They had, of course, a real interest in handling their chief opponents, Great Britain and Austria-Hungary, separately, and to this end they sent Ignatiev, Russian ambassador at Constantinople and chief architect of the Treaty of San Stefano, on an exploratory mission to Vienna in March. Andrássy spoke frankly to Ignatiev. Basing himself on the spirit (not, of course, on the inapplicable text) of the Reichstadt and Budapest agreements, he again insisted on Austria-Hungary's right to a voice in the settlement. The new Bulgaria, he said, was just such a big Slav state as had been forbidden in the agreements; and Russia could occupy it for at most six months, not two years. In addition, he now demanded possession not only of Bosnia and the Herzegovina, but of the Sanjak of Novibazar: Russia having proved herself so untrustworthy, Austria-Hungary could only be satisfied with a clear territorial access to the western Balkans. Only if Russia respected these interests, Andrássy emphasised to Ignatiev, would Austria-Hungary stay inside the Three Emperors' League and refrain from seeking agreement with the British. No definite agreement was reached, however; and in the ensuing months Russia showed that she was not particularly interested in one. For she managed herself to come to terms with the British in May, agreeing in principle to reduce the size of Big Bulgaria, and to submit the whole of the San Stefano treaty to the Congress. Her attitude towards Austria-Hungary stiffened in consequence. By 8 May she was talking of giving the whole of the Sanjak to Serbia – a suggestion which even Bismarck termed 'frivolous'.[32] The Three Emperors' League had proved a broken reed after all.

On the eve of the Congress of Berlin, therefore, the diplomatic position of Austria-Hungary was by no means brilliant. The Three Emperors' League had broken down, and Germany was offering no more than platonic expressions of goodwill. Nor was there any

31. Wagner, 'Kaiser Franz Joseph', p. 109.
32. Wertheimer, *Andrássy*, III, p. 100.

support inside the Monarchy for a strong stand: the most Andrássy could extract from the governments in Vienna and Budapest was a special grant of a mere 60 million Gulden to lend some credibility to his diplomacy – and that only at the price of a pledge that he did not intend to use it for war. Yet the outlook was not entirely bleak: the Treaty of San Stefano had so alarmed all the non-Bulgarian races of the Balkan peninsula as to make all of them – possibly even the Turks – potential clients of Austria-Hungary; the British had already brought Russia to agree to a reduction in the size of the new Bulgaria; and on 6 June they promised Andrássy their support in the Bosnian question.

In the event, the Congress of Berlin marked the apogee of Andrássy's diplomatic career. With his Magyar panache and colourful uniform, he was certainly one of the most striking figures at this, the biggest international gathering since the Congress of Vienna. In the case of the Congress of Berlin, the programme was much less ambitious; and the negotiations, conducted in a brisk and businesslike manner, with special commissions of the most interested Great Powers to sort out the details before the plenary sessions met, were concluded within a month. The decision to tackle the thorny Bulgarian question before dealing with less contentious matters, also made for the expeditious dispatch of business. Andrássy early forced his way into the Anglo-Russian special commission on Bulgaria, where he joined with the British in forcing Russia to reduce the size of Bulgaria by two-thirds, and the duration of the Russian occupation from the two years of San Stefano to nine months. The Bulgarian settlement of the Treaty of Berlin was, therefore, fairly satisfactory for the Austrians; and, far from producing the Anglo-Russian rift that Bismarck desired as a preliminary to reviving the Three Emperors' League, by giving some substance to Anglo-Austrian co-operation it only stiffened Andrássy in his resistance to Bismarck's plans.

Similarly, it was on the British, and not on the Three Emperors' League or Germany, that Andrássy relied in handling the Bosnian question: Salisbury agreed to put the case for Austro-Hungarian occupation to the Congress. The Germans offered no help at all: indeed, according to one of Andrássy's aides, as late as 28 June Bismarck himself sent his son Herbert to visit Andrássy, in a vain attempt to persuade him to drop the Bosnian question for the sake of relations with Russia.[33] From home, Andrássy was given no

33. A. Novotny, *Quellen und Studien zur Geschichte des Berliner Kongresses, 1878* (Graz 1957), 2 vols, I, p. 52.

clear lead. He was well aware, on the one hand, that the emperor wanted to annex Bosnia and the Herzegovina outright in full sovereignty; on the other, that public opinion was dead set against annexation, which would, moreover, raise the unanswerable question of the final destination of the provinces within the nicely balanced constitutional structure of the Dual Monarchy. It would also more than likely require the use of force – possibly, Andrássy feared, even a war with Turkey. Public opinion would not stomach such a policy, which would look like complicity with Russia in despoiling the Ottoman Empire. In this situation, Andrássy held doggedly to his limited aim of occupation. For him, the conclusive argument was that unless Austria-Hungary established herself in the provinces, they would sooner or later be bound to fall from the hands of Turkey – now weakened and partially dismembered – to Serbia and Montenegro. He decided for occupation rather than annexation, in the hope that this could be achieved peacefully with the consent of the Turks. He sought, moreover, an occupation on the basis of a mandate from the Congress, which would represent the public endorsement by Europe of Austria-Hungary's role as a guardian of order in the Near East.

As far as the European mandate was concerned, Andrássy was completely successful. On 28 June, he presented to the Congress the case against a continuance of Ottoman rule in Bosnia, which could offer at best the risk of anarchy or, in the event of the establishment of a weak autonomous regime, the near certainty of civil war between the Christian and Muslim populations. Salisbury then proposed the occupation, endorsing Andrássy's arguments, and adding that if Serbia and Montenegro were ever to acquire the provinces, this would create a chain of Slav states threatening the other races of the Balkan peninsula. Serious resistance, however, came from the Ottoman representatives, who, under fierce pressure from the Sheikh-ul-Islam and conservative circles in Constantinople, at the last minute refused their consent. The Turks were completely unmoved by Andrássy's talk of the advantages to them of giving Austria-Hungary a territorial base from which she could help them to preserve what remained to them in Europe; and they could only be brought to drop their opposition when Andrássy made them a formal (albeit secret) declaration on 13 July, stating that the occupation would only be temporary, and expressly reserving legal sovereignty over the provinces to the sultan. The settlement of the final details was reserved for a separate Austro-Turkish agreement. This contretemps was to cause Andrássy a good deal of trouble later, and to spell ruin to Anglo-Austrian hopes of an *entente* with Turkey. But for the moment Andrássy seemed unconcerned; and although he assured the Turks that, as far as the Sanjak of Novibazar was concerned, he was interested only in military and commercial routes, not in occupation, he took care to extract from Russia a promise not to oppose an eventual occupation of the strip.

With most of the remaining decisions of the Congress, Andrássy had good reason to be pleased, in that they documented an increase in Austria-Hungary's political and economic influence in the Balkan peninsula. Ironically enough, it was perhaps Russia herself who had done most to bring this about. The Big Bulgaria she had created at San Stefano, and her seizure of Southern Bessarabia from Romania, had driven all the other Balkan states to seek the protection of Austria-Hungary and the Western Powers. (Only Montenegro, the state least threatened by San Stefano, remained on reasonably good terms with Russia.) Andrássy made the most of the opportunity, willingly sanctioning the independence of Serbia, Montenegro and Romania, and earning the gratitude of the Serbs by helping them acquire Nish – thereby directing their gaze southwards, away from Bosnia and the South Slav provinces of the Monarchy – and of the Romanians by securing for them slightly more compensation than had originally been intended (albeit only in the barren Dobrudja). More than this, the Monarchy's economic interests had been well safeguarded. The projected railway from Vienna to Constantinople moved a step nearer realisation when Turkey, Bulgaria and Serbia assumed, under the Treaty of Berlin, the obligation to complete their railways in the direction of the Austro-Hungarian frontier. True, railway construction in the Balkans was a slow business: the final negotiations with Serbia and Bulgaria were not completed until the early eighties, and it was not until 12 August 1888 that the first train left Vienna for Constantinople. As regards the Danube, which for the present remained the Monarchy's most important commercial route to the Near East, Andrássy managed to check the increased influence of Russia (now re-established on the delta) by strengthening and giving more permanence to the international commission. He even managed to free Austria-Hungary from the millstone of Turkish 'co-operation' in clearing the river of obstacles to traffic, and to secure for her the right to undertake the work single-handed. Altogether, Andrássy could fairly claim to have consolidated at least the foundations for the spread of Austro-Hungarian commercial influence in the Balkan states and European Turkey.

The prospects for Austro-Hungarian political influence were

more problematical – at least as far as the Ottoman Empire was concerned. In the first place, the actual process of occupying Bosnia proved to be a very messy business, in stark contrast to Andrássy's recent triumphs on the international stage. For some weeks he delayed action, in the hope that the Turks would eventually recognise the ultimately pro-Turkish intention of his policy and conclude the agreement embodying their final consent to the occupation. (Tisza had warned him on 30 June that he could not defend a violent conquest before public opinion in Hungary.) The Turks, however, had no intention of smoothing the way, being less impressed by the deeper conservative motives of Andrássy's policy than by the fact that they were about to lose two provinces. This being the case, Andrássy's apparent hesitations merely encouraged them to hold out; while his advice to the emperor to keep the size of the occupying force to an absolute minimum (to avoid any appearance of a war against Turkey, or further recourse to the parliamentary bodies for funds) proved to be little short of disastrous. The upshot was that at the end of July an inadequate occupying force of 160,000 men advanced into extraordinarily difficult terrain against hostile natives ensconced in numerous fortresses abandoned by the Turks. Not until 20 October was the last of these mopped up. Certainly, as a demonstration of the Monarchy's capacities as a great military Power, the occupation campaign was hardly likely to impress Constantinople.

The final settlement with the Turks was in fact not at all easy to achieve, for the sultan was not only genuinely fearful of popular uprisings if he signed away Muslim territory, but hopeful that growing criticism of the occupation campaign inside the Monarchy, particularly in Hungary, might come to his rescue. It was not until April 1879 that he could be persuaded to accept a draft convention that omitted all reference to the provisional character of Austria-Hungary's occupation rights in Bosnia and the Herzegovina. Andrássy, for his part, tried to be conciliatory: he was content with garrison, not occupation, rights in the Sanjak of Novibazar, and those only in the western half of the Sanjak. But it won him little credit at Constantinople, and Austro-Turkish relations showed no sign of improvement for several years to come.[34]

This was all the more disappointing for Andrássy in that the British were trying hard in these very months to persuade the sultan to improve his relations with Vienna and to keep a watchful eye on his chief enemy Russia and her attempts to break the fetters

34. Medlicott, *Congress of Berlin*, pp. 262ff.

imposed on her by the Treaty of Berlin. Certainly, the supposed Russian menace was a fruitful source of Anglo-Austrian co-operation. Until the summer of 1879 the two Powers worked together against Russia on the boundary commissions that defined the frontiers of the new Bulgaria and Eastern Rumelia. And in May Andrássy took advantage of rumours that Russia was about to refuse to evacuate Bulgaria to make a gentlemen's agreement with the British: henceforth, London and Vienna were to take no steps in the Near East without consulting each other. In this respect, Andrássy seemed to be making progress towards establishing that great defensive bloc against Russia that he had sketched out in 1871. All the more so as 'the chancellors' war' between Bismarck and Gorchakov was fast blighting any hopes there might have been in Berlin for a restoration of the Three Emperors' League. But how-ever encouraging the long-term prospects might be, the Anglo-Austrian *rapprochement* was proving of little immediate effect in improving Austro-Turkish relations, or in fulfilling British hopes that an Austro-Hungarian guarantee of Turkey-in-Europe might some day complement the British pledge to safeguard the Ottoman possessions in Asia.

Meanwhile, the occupation of Bosnia had had embarrassing consequences on the domestic front. In the first place, Andrássy had to fend off a renewed demand for outright annexation from the military circles round the emperor, who now argued that Bosnia was Austria-Hungary's by right of conquest – an argument that was to be revived in 1908. Against these demands he stood firm, although he admitted resignedly to the Empress Elizabeth that 'the emperor does not understand the Eastern Question and will never understand it'.[35] The Monarchy, he insisted in successive confer-ences of ministers, must stick strictly to the Treaty of Berlin, and not give Russia any pretext to evade its stipulations respecting Bulgaria.[36] Not that he had any intention of ever evacuating Bosnia: Europe had put Austria-Hungary there as a check on Serbia and Montenegro, to prevent a forcible slavicisation of the Balkans. His views on the Sanjak of Novibazar were equally sober and equally firm: 'the possible occupation of the Sanjak . . . is by no means intended as a stage in the march on Salonika as public opinion wrongly conceives it. Its only object is to protect our position in Bosnia and it can only be carried out in complete agreement with Turkey and in the sense of the Treaty of Berlin.'[37]

35. Hegedüs, 'Foreign Policy', p. 369.
36. PA XL/290, Ministerratsprotokoll, 24 August 1878.
37. PA XL/291, Ministerratsprotokoll, 16 February 1879.

Some Austro-Hungarian presence there he held to be essential. For the Sanjak was to Bosnia what the Straits were to the Black Sea: a gateway to the east which must be kept open. If Serbia and Montenegro held it, Bosnia would become a cul-de-sac, not a base for Austro-Hungarian influence in the Near East; and a Turkey completely cut off from Austro-Hungarian support could not long survive. Worse still, if Serbia and Montenegro took the Sanjak, they might then unite to form one big Slav state, which would then turn for further expansion towards Bosnia and Dalmatia.

Yet the grumblings of the annexationist party at court were as nothing compared to the storm the occupation unleashed among the public. Such qualified approval as Andrássy's policy earned came from the Slavs and from military-aristocratic circles, who mistook an essentially negative preventive move for a first step on the road to expansion and a great role in the Slav world. Otherwise, there was no trace of patriotic feeling among the inhabitants of the Monarchy: Andrássy's return from the Congress stood in the most glaring contrast to the reception accorded to Beaconsfield in London. Both Germans and Magyars saw only the potential threat to their predominance within the Dualist structure. Moreover, to the Magyars, who since 1849 looked askance at anything connected with the Imperial Army, and to German Liberals, who regarded the army as the very incarnation of reaction, the military character the occupation assumed gave only further cause for offence. The Magyars felt that, if there were any fighting to be done, it should be to resist Russia, not to despoil Turkey, Hungary's friend. The German Liberal's grievance was – in form at least – constitutional: that Andrássy had carried out the occupation without consulting the parliaments. Constitutionally, they were on extremely thin ice, for the Treaty of Berlin was not one of those lesser commercial treaties over which the parliaments had the final word. As far as Austria-Hungary was concerned, Andrássy was undoubtedly constitutionally correct in stating unequivocally that 'foreign policy in the monarchical-constitutional state is the sphere in which the Crown has the right to act without the previous assent of the legislature'.[38] The emperor, too, was jealously on guard against any attempt to usurp his prerogatives, and even suspected that the Liberals were trying to make him look foolish in the eyes of Europe by rejecting a treaty which he had already ratified.

In fact, there was no question of this: by March 1879 the treaty had been approved by both parliaments. But apart from encouraging the

---

38. Wertheimer, *Andrássy*, III, pp. 195–6.

Turks to delay their recognition of the occupation in the hope that it might be abandoned, the storm had far-reaching repercussions in domestic politics. Neither Andrássy nor his German Liberal critics long survived it. For the latter, of whom the emperor had now had more than enough, ruin was sure and swift. For in contrast to Hungary, where perhaps nothing could be done, in Austria an alternative government stood ready to hand in the feudal, clerical and Slav fractions. The emperor had perhaps, in his innermost heart, never finally written them off, even in 1871; they had remained well represented at court throughout the 1870s, particularly in military circles; and in view of their patriotic response to the occupation, they now stood higher in favour than ever. In August Franz Joseph dismissed the German Liberal government and appointed as minister-president his boyhood friend, Count Eduard Taaffe, a conservative Tyrolean nobleman of Irish extraction (and still a viscount in his own right in the peerage of Ireland). Taaffe, as 'the Emperor's Minister' duly set to work to form a government of clerical, conservative landowners, with a view to winning Slav support in general and to conciliating the Czechs in particular.

This, of course, was hardly to the liking of Andrássy, who had opposed just such a policy, as a threat to Dualism, in 1871. The wrangles over the occupation had certainly weakened his position, costing him the support of the German Liberals, in parliament and press, on the one hand, and of the military-annexationist party at court on the other. Nor could he rely, even if he had wished to, on the continued support of Slavs and federalist nobles. In this situation, the support of the emperor would in the long run not be enough. Andrássy decided that perhaps the time had come for him to go. He had in fact, for some time, even during the Congress of Berlin, been attracted to the idea of leaving office at the zenith of his career. Besides, although he was only fifty-six, thirteen years of high office had undoubtedly taken their toll, and a marked deterioration in his health was no doubt another factor moving him to offer his resignation (in May and on 6 August 1879) – and in moving the emperor in the end to accept it.

Despite his passionately held feelings, Andrássy had, during eight years at the Ballhausplatz, managed to display, to a perhaps remarkable degree, that flexibility and adaptability which were absolutely essential in a minister wishing to safeguard the interests of an inherently weak Power such as Austria-Hungary. Although his original grand design of a quadruple *entente* against Russia – towards which he, as a Magyar, leaned instinctively – had been impossible to realise, thanks to the indifference of his intended partners, he had set to work to make the best of the situation, and managed between 1872 and 1875 to establish tolerable relations with Russia. When the eastern crisis burst upon him in 1875 he strove patiently to maintain the Three Emperors' League, partly out of a desire to humour Berlin, but chiefly because he realised the necessity, given the military weakness of the Monarchy, of trying at all costs to defend Austro-Hungarian interests without recourse to war. With the Panslav triumph of the spring of 1878, the Three Emperors' League was unable to cope; but Andrássy made a good recovery at the Congress of Berlin; and the final settlement, despite the awkward repercussions of the occupation of Bosnia on Anglo-Austrian influence at Constantinople, saw a strengthening of Andrássy's hopes of establishing an effective working relationship with Great Britain. True, Germany held aloof from this – an unpalatable fact that Vienna could do nothing to alter. Yet, ironically enough, after the emperor had accepted Andrássy's resignation, a change of mood in Berlin presented him with a chance to realise, at least in part, his original project of a defensive bloc, which for the past eight years had eluded him.

It was an undoubted stroke of luck for the Austrians that Bismarck was beginning, by the summer of 1879, to feel seriously unsure of Russia, even threatened by her. Her constant complaints about relatively trivial incidents arising from the enforcement of the Berlin settlement, her endless armaments, and the hostile language of the Russian press, had combined to produce (for a few gloomy months in the summer of 1879 at least) a radical change in Bismarck's attitude towards Russia. The news of Andrássy's resignation, coming at this juncture, caused the greatest consternation in Berlin. Bismarck's neurotic fear of anti-German coalitions reached a new intensity, as the prospect presented itself to him that the Taaffe government in Austria, once freed from Andrássy's influence, might complement its pro-Slav domestic policy by an alliance with Russia. Worse still, the clericals might bring in Catholic France as well, to create that combination most deadly to Prussia, a 'Kaunitz' coalition. In this situation, Andrássy's idea of an Austro-German alliance, which Bismarck had for years rejected as likely to cause hostility between Russia and Germany, now appeared to him as a possible remedy for a hostility that seemed already to have developed. When, on 15 August, the tsar sent a further list of grievances to his imperial uncle in Berlin, Bismarck took the opportunity to declare that Russia could no longer be relied on; and to familiarise the emperor with the idea of an alliance with

Austria-Hungary, both as a source of assistance in the event of war with Russia, and a means of ensuring that the Dual Monarchy would not join the ranks of Germany's enemies.

He had, in fact, already asked Andrássy to meet him at Gastein; and although he there discovered, on 28 August, that his apprehensions about a pro-Slav orientation of Austro-Hungarian policy after Andrássy's departure were groundless, he still wanted some firm guarantee for the future. So he came straight to the point and proposed an Austro-German alliance. What Andrássy had for so long sought in vain was now being offered for the taking; and he was quick to make the most of the psychological advantage he enjoyed over the anxious Bismarck. On the one hand, he welcomed the idea of an alliance; on the other, he was determined that any alliance must be on his own terms: it must be directed solely against Russia, and should not in the slightest jeopardise or restrict Austria-Hungary's relations with the Western Powers. Indeed, he hoped, as in 1871, that Great Britain would eventually join the combination. He made it clear to Bismarck, therefore, that the alliance must not be a general one: any suspicion that Austria-Hungary was abetting Germany against France would offend France's friends in London. Bismarck was slightly disappointed at this; but the two statesmen agreed to pursue the idea further after consulting their respective sovereigns; and Franz Joseph gave Andrássy his full support. The German emperor, however, fresh from a meeting with his Russian nephew, still refused to consider anything so offensive to the latter as an alliance directed solely against Russia, and authorised Bismarck to conclude an alliance only in general terms.

This was the central issue in the Vienna discussions between Bismarck and Andrássy (23–24 September). Andrássy would still not hear of a general alliance; nor would he have anything to do with a monarchichal league *à trois* with Russia. Austria-Hungary, he insisted, must be free to assure her friends in London that she had no commitments whatever against France, provided the latter did not join a coalition against the Central Powers. Any alliance must be clearly directed against Russia. Apart from this point, the two parties were already in broad agreement. The Austrians particularly liked the idea of a strictly defensive alliance, considering that the Monarchy had absolutely nothing to gain from an aggressive war against Russia, and might only risk being used as a battering ram by the Western Powers. They raised no objections either, when Bismarck suggested a communication to the Powers (and to Russia in particular) to emphasise the conciliatory spirit of the alliance and make its defensive purpose perfectly clear. In the end, Bismarck gave way. 'Accept my draft,' he said to Andrássy, rising from his seat and drawing himself to his full height, '. . . or I shall have to accept yours.'[39] On 24 September the draft was duly agreed, and, after a further tussle, Bismarck managed to extract the consent of the German emperor.

The alliance[40] was signed at Vienna on 7 October (see Appendix II), and Andrássy resigned on the following day. He could be well content with his work. The alliance pledged the two Powers to mutual support if either were attacked by Russia; if either were attacked by another Power, the other was only obliged to observe benevolent neutrality; but if the attacker were supported by Russia, the *casus foederis* again arose. These terms suited the Austrians exactly. Yet this was – for both parties – no ad hoc war alliance, like the opportunistic alliances of the 1850s and 1860s. However strictly limited its terms, it was always intended to have broader implications for the general policy of the contracting parties. Such implications had always been in Andrássy's mind during his quest for a German alliance in the 1870s; and were perhaps in Bismarck's during the summer of 1879. Franz Joseph, too, was aware of them; and was pleased at last to have realised his ideal of a conservative alliance of the two German Powers, which he had vainly sought from a hostile Bismarck in the early sixties and from an indifferent Bismarck in the early seventies. There was from the start, however, on the question of the broader aims and the ultimate purpose of the alliance, a wide divergence of view between Vienna and Berlin.

The tug-of-war that followed showed that Andrássy had been unusually fortunate in having to deal, in the summer of 1879, with a Bismarck who had temporarily lost his nerve. Indeed, the whole subsequent history of the Dual Alliance was to show that a Germany that had once recovered its nerve would be by no means so amenable to control by Austria-Hungary – after all, the weaker partner – as she had appeared to be in October 1879. Bismarck, for example, once he was confident of having dispelled the threat of a 'Kaunitz' coalition – if the threat had ever existed outside his own mind – and even before the alliance was actually signed, had begun to think that a conflict with Russia was perhaps not all that likely after all. He had been encouraged in this by the Russians themselves, who, on getting wind of the impending alliance, had

39. Ibid., p. 284.
40. Text in Pribram, *Secret Treaties*, I, pp. 25–31.

hastened to repair the wire to Berlin, hinting that they would welcome a restoration of the Three Emperors' League. This, of course, had always been Bismarck's ideal. It was also the implication of his boast to the Russian ambassador that in concluding the alliance he had succeeded in digging a ditch between Austria-Hungary and the Western Powers. In fact, nothing could have been further than the truth. The Austrians had, after all, taken scrupulous care in the negotiations to avoid anything that might cast a cloud over their relations with London and Paris; and Salisbury, in particular, had welcomed press reports of the alliance as 'glad tidings of great joy'.[41] For Andrássy, the Dual Alliance was a step towards the realisation of his old ideal of a grand alliance against Russia. For him, in contrast to Bismarck, suspicion of Russia was no passing mood. A 'warmed-up Three Emperors' League', he declared, would meet with great opposition from public opinion; Russia was 'full of perfidy';[42] and, after his recent experiences, he would hesitate 'not only as a minister but as a gentleman' to recommend an agreement with her on the Eastern Question.[43] Whereas the Dual Alliance was for Bismarck a stepping-stone towards a new Three Emperors' League, it was for Andrássy the tombstone of the Three Emperors' League. It remained an open question whether, faced with the newly confident Germany, Andrássy's successors would be able to realise his great objective, or whether they would be forced to fall into line with Bismarck's.

There could be no doubt about the personal inclinations of Andrássy's successor, Heinrich, Baron Haymerle. This cautious, unadventurous career diplomat, who had served at Constantinople, Athens and Rome, and as Andrássy's aide at the Congress of Berlin, was well versed in the details of the Eastern Question. The British were hopeful that 'his intimate knowledge of Turkish affairs'[44] would prove a serious obstacle to Russia's supposed designs. 'This', Beaconsfield confidently declared, 'is an anti-Russian appointment'.[45] By the same token, St Petersburg, where most of Russia's recent humiliations were ascribed to 'expressions insidiously inserted into the Treaty of Berlin by Baron Haymerle', was 'very little pleased'.[46] And it was not so much Haymerle's woebegone appearance or nervous manner, as his unwillingness to

---

41. *The Times*, 18 October 1879, p. 10.
42. Wertheimer, *Andrássy*, III, p. 297.
43. PA. I/469, Aehrenthal Memorandum 1895.
44. Ramm, 'European Alliances', p. 61.
45. Ibid., p. 86.
46. Ibid., p. 85.

venture into any agreement with Russia, that lay behind Bismarck's scornful comments on him: 'he is timid, he is not accustomed to high politics, he fears responsibilities'; and behind the notorious jibe attributed to Bismarck, that Haymerle always 'uttered an emphatic "No" three times on waking up in the morning, for fear of having undertaken some commitment in his sleep'.[47] From the start, he was determined to continue Andrássy's anti-Russian policy: to stand firm by the Treaty of Berlin, and if possible to enlist British support in forcing Russia to observe it.

Even unaided, the Monarchy was in a good position to pursue a strong Balkan policy. Of course, this policy would not be one of territorial expansion – the annexation of more Slav areas could fatally upset the balance of races within the Monarchy – but one of exercising a preponderant influence over the Balkan states. The prospects were inviting. By the 'unequal' trade treaties of 1861–2 with Turkey (to which Bulgaria too was explicitly subjected by the Treaty of Berlin) the Great Powers held the Ottoman Empire down as a ready market and source of raw materials. Customs duties, for example, were fixed at 10 per cent, and, according to the Capitulations, could not be increased without the consent of the Powers. Even without these measures, of course, the sheer weight of economic imperialism would in any case have served to hold the Balkan economy in fee to the Great Powers; and of all the Great Powers, Austria-Hungary was the chief beneficiary of this system. Over the Western Powers she enjoyed enormous geographical advantages: proximity and the Danube (which provided cheap transport) meant that Austro-Hungarian exports, chiefly light industrial goods, could easily command Balkan markets by virtue of their cheapness. Against Russia, who in Bulgaria temporarily enjoyed a measure of political control by virtue of the Treaty of Berlin, the Austrian position was even stronger.

Indeed, in Bulgaria Russia's political predominance was in fact counter-productive, and served mainly to offend the nationalist aspirations and foster the Austrophile inclinations of the Bulgarian bourgeoisie. Both Vienna and St Petersburg recognised the great importance of commercial channels as the conductors of political influence; and in Bulgarian railway construction, for example, Austro-Hungarian capital was completely dominant. In 1879 the Orient Railway Company, which controlled the Bulgarian section of the line to Constantinople, had passed from French to Austro-Hungarian control, and had transferred its headquarters to Vienna.

47. L. Ritter von Przibram, *Erinnerungen eines alten Oesterreichers*, II, p. 114.

In this situation, Russia found herself completely outmanoeuvred. Such capital as her own very primitive economy could spare generally went to easier markets in Asia; and Russian political pressure on Sofia to compel the Bulgarians to accept loans only aroused opposition and further undermined Russia's position in the principality. As for Austria-Hungary, although it is true that Bulgaria only accounted for about 6 per cent of her total trade, this 6 per cent was a huge amount for a state the size of Bulgaria. In fact, the Monarchy was able to impose successive renewals of the 'unequal' trade treaty and to maintain its position as Bulgaria's chief trading partner right down to 1914.

Although in the other Balkan states the Monarchy did not have a Russian-controlled government to contend with, it sometimes came up against the hostility of that very nationalism that worked in its favour in Bulgaria. The coldly calculating rulers of Serbia and Romania, however, were still very much haunted by the shadow of the Big Bulgaria created by Russia at San Stefano, and had no doubts as to where their chief enemy lay. True, in Serbia, the efforts of the fanatically Austrophile Prince Milan to develop the principality's commercial and railway links with the Monarchy were obstructed by the Liberal Ristić government, pro-Russian by instinct, sensitive to public resentment of the occupation of Bosnia, and fully aware that the taxes required to pay for the projected railway links would be deeply resented by their peasant supporters. Their resistance was encouraged by Russian agents, and, to some extent, by Great Britain, who still provided Serbia with one-third of her imports, and who strengthened her position with a commercial treaty in January 1880. By the summer, however, Milan had agreed to construct the railway line to Hungary before that to Salonika (which would only have furthered British trade); and when Ristić resigned in October, Serbia seemed to be moving steadily into Austria-Hungary's orbit.

Romania presented a similar picture, with fairly strong Austro-Hungarian political influence and nationalist and irredentist counter-currents. On the one hand, Austria-Hungary had been the first Great Power to recognise the independence of the principality in 1878; both Vienna and Bucharest recognised a common interest in ensuring that Romania, situated 'entre les deux Russies', as Bratianu remarked,[48] should not become a mere highway from

---

48. E.R. von Rutkowski, 'Oesterreich und Rumänien 1881–3, die Proklamierung des Königreiches und die rumänischen Irredenta', in *Südost-Forschungen*, 25 (1966), pp. 150–284; E. Palotas, 'Die außenwirtschaftlichen Beziehungen zum Balkan und zu Rußland', in *Habsburgermonarchie VI*, pp. 607ff.

Russia to Bulgaria; and Haymerle agreed with Andrássy and Prince Carol that the two states, which together formed a barrier to the slavicisation of south-east Europe, might some day even make a formal alliance. On the other hand, Haymerle, like Andrássy, was opposed to Romania's hopes of elevation to the rank of a kingdom, which he feared could only encourage irredentist designs on Transylvania and the Bukovina. The Romanians, for their part, like the Serbs, resented what they regarded as Austro-Hungarian attempts at commercial domination. The Congress of Berlin had subjected shipping on the lower Danube to a commission to be established by the Great Powers. For Austria-Hungary, the Danube was still the main commercial route to the Balkans; the Austrian Danube Steamship Company held a virtual monopoly of shipping on the river; and Haymerle was determined not to permit the subjection of these important interests to control by any Balkan state. When, however, in January 1880, he began to press, with German and Italian support, for a controlling interest for Austria-Hungary on the new commission, Romanian resistance, backed by Russia, led to serious tension between Vienna and Bucharest.

Austria-Hungary's position in the Balkans in 1879–80 was, therefore, strong but not unchallenged. And behind the threats to it, Vienna discerned everywhere the hand of Russia. Indeed, while Austro-Hungarian policy might be seen objectively, and especially by Russia, as aiming at predominance, it was conceived of in Vienna as defensive, as an attempt to prevent Russia from establishing her own predominance. Against the underhand designs of Russia, busily furthered by Russian agents and the Russian press, Haymerle saw it as his task to sound the alarm.

With Bismarck, he made no headway at all. Indeed, Haymerle's suggestions in the autumn of 1879 that the Central Powers enlist the support of Great Britain – as Andrássy had hoped to do when he concluded the Dual Alliance – only drew the crushing retort that the alliance was strictly for defensive purposes, and was not designed to support any particular policy in the Balkans whatever. In January 1880, following an irredentist demonstration in Italy, Haymerle tried another approach:[49] perhaps Great Britain could be persuaded to restrain Italy, he suggested, and even to join the Central Powers in a bloc so formidable that Russia would never dare to challenge it. A Romanian alliance would also be useful. Bismarck would have none of this. True, he wished to maintain the alliance with Austria-Hungary; but he was at the same time

---

49. Kab. 18, Haymerle, report to Franz Joseph, 7 February 1880.

immensely concerned to hold on to Russia. The latter, he told Vienna, was now suffering from nightmares about hostile coalitions, and should be comforted and reassured. Ramshackle Italy could be kept in order by threatening language; and as for Great Britain, who was gratuitously provoking Russia, her isolation was the price to be paid for Russian friendship.

The divergence of views over the ultimate purpose of the Dual Alliance had now come into the open. Certainly, if Bismarck imagined that the alliance had given him control over the direction of Austro-Hungarian policy, he was mistaken. 'So long as our interests in the Near East are so closely parallel with those of the English', Haymerle insisted, 'we should be unwise to abandon England.'[50] As for Russia, there was simply no basis for any *rapprochement*: this would be tantamount to a revival of the Three Emperors' League, which, Haymerle maintained, nobody in the Monarchy desired, and which Hungarian opinion would never permit. The emperor agreed. When the military attaché at St Petersburg reported on 21 April that the Russian press was full of talk of Russia's Slav mission; that official assurances were worthless in the face of such mighty currents of opinion; and that 'the sooner people admit this and stop deceiving themselves' about Russia the better, Franz Joseph minuted 'very sound assessment [*Sehr richtige Auffassung*]'.[51] In this frame of mind, the Austrians clung to the British even when Gladstone returned to power in April, after an election campaign in which he had denounced Beaconsfield's 'Austrian' foreign policy in very spectacular fashion. Tactful handling of the affair by diplomats in Vienna and London smoothed matters over, and even created what Haymerle was pleased to call 'an entirely satisfactory starting point for our new relations'.[52] He turned a deaf ear to Bismarck, who, secretly afraid that Gladstone's anti-Turkish views might tempt Russia and weaken her desire to restore the Three Emperors' League, tried naïvely to convince Vienna that Gladstone was a dangerous revolutionary. Indeed, in April he rejected yet another German proposal for an agreement with Russia precisely because – by enforcing the closure of the Straits to protect Russia from the British fleet, for example – it would alienate Great Britain. In short, pressure from Berlin failed completely to bring the Austrians to abandon their hopes of continued co-operation with the British in the Near East.

These hopes were nevertheless soon to be shattered. And it was

50. Medlicott, *Bismarck, Gladstone*, p. 52.
51. Wagner, 'Kaiser Franz Joseph', p. 123.
52. Medlicott, *Bismarck, Gladstone*, p. 62.

not the hectorings of Bismarck, but the loss of faith in the possibility of effective co-operation with Great Britain that caused the radical change of course in Vienna that was to lead to the Three Emperors' Alliance of 1881. As the Powers struggled in the summer of 1880 to settle the outstanding business remaining from the Congress of Berlin – the delimitation of the new frontiers of Greece and Montenegro – they were faced with stubborn Turkish opposition, and, in the case of Montenegro, with local Albanian armed resistance. On all these issues Gladstone began to take a decidedly anti-Turkish line; and one which Russian support made even more suspect in Austrian eyes. Haymerle had serious misgivings about the willingness of the other Powers to subject still more Albanians to Montenegrin rule. Already in 1878 the Austrians had seen in the spirited Albanian protests to the congress evidence of a potentially useful barrier against the compete slavicisation of the Balkans. More generally – and more seriously – he disliked the whole policy of coercion towards which the Powers, having exhausted their repertoire of paper condemnations of Turkey, were being steered by Great Britain and Russia in the summer of 1880. Not only might naval and military action bring British, and even Russian, forces to the shores of the Adriatic (which Vienna regarded as an Austro-Hungarian preserve); it might well provoke serious upheavals in Turkey – even her total collapse, with all the attendant risks of war. As a result, Haymerle began to come to the conclusion that his pro-British policy had been founded on a misapprehension; and that 'particularly since England is so actively trying to undermine Turkey and can no longer be counted on',[53] the Monarchy might do well to investigate the possibility of a cautious approach to Russia.

It was very much a question of facing up to unpleasant realities. There were certain developments – such as a union of Bulgaria and Eastern Rumelia – which the Monarchy would in any case be powerless to prevent. Gustav, Count Kálnoky, ambassador at St Petersburg, encouraged Haymerle in this train of thought: the Russians had probably already squared Gladstone on the Bulgarian question, he wrote; and Austria-Hungary herself might therefore do well to come to some agreement with St Petersburg to secure her own interests, especially her supremacy in Serbia, so necessary for the security of Bosnia and the Herzegovina. These latter, Kálnoky thought, might well be annexed. Bismarck, whom Haymerle sought out at Friedrichsruh (4–5 September) was all fire and

53. Ibid., p. 180.

flame for immediate tripartite negotiations; and although Haymerle thought these premature, he now agreed in principle to look into the possibilities of an agreement with Russia.[54] The Austro-Hungarian interests it would have to safeguard he was careful to spell out to Bismarck in the next few weeks: any union of the two Bulgarias must come about in the natural course of events, and not at Russia's instigation or behest; nor must it lead to further Bulgarian expansion into Macedonia, where the Monarchy had interests of its own; nor must it be seen as a condition of Austria-Hungary's annexing Bosnia and the Herzegovina – Russia had already agreed to that in 1877. The Dual Alliance must be in no sense weakened: on the contrary, it should be extended to cover a Russian attack on Romania. Finally, Russia must cease to oppose Austro-Hungarian influence in Serbia. What Haymerle was in fact demanding was the predominance of Austro-Hungarian influence in Romania and the western Balkans, and a fair measure of control over events in Bulgaria.[55] It was indeed sanguine of him to suppose that Bismarck would seriously press St Petersburg to accept all this.

Of course Bismarck, for whom the negotiations were primarily a means of making sure of Russia, did no such thing – as the Austrians were dismayed to discover when they received the Russo–German draft treaty on 23 January 1881. True, Franz Joseph recognised the desirability of cultivating conservative elements in St Petersburg, and liked the idea of an alliance that would demonstrate to subversive elements in Europe that monarchical solidarity could survive political differences. For the rest, however, the Austrians were not satisfied with Russia's promise merely to accept the status quo in Bosnia as defined by the Austro-Turkish convention of 1879 – that is, considerably less than the eventual annexation she had agreed to in 1877. And they rejected out of hand a clause that provided for the mediation of the third contracting party in the event of a dispute between the other two. This might some day be used by Bismarck to escape from his obligations under the Dual Alliance – for example, if Vienna felt obliged to reject the decision of mediators in Berlin. Similarly, on the point of Romania, they rejected Bismarck's counter-proposal for a blanket clause making the military occupation of any Balkan state dependent on the consent of the alliance partners: Austria-Hungary could never

---

54. Kab. 18, Haymerle, report to Franz Joseph, 19 September 1880. (The full text of Haymerle's reports to the emperor on the Friedrichsruh meeting is in W.N. Medlicott, 'Bismarck und Haymerle: Ein Gespräch über Rußland', in *Berliner Monatshefte*, November 1940, pp. 719–29.)
55. Medlicott, *Bismarck–Gladstone*, pp. 254–7.

accept such a restriction on her freedom of action against her South Slav neighbours. Throughout February the deadlock continued.

In the spring, the Austrians began to give way. In the first place, the uncomfortable diplomatic isolation in which they found themselves showed no sign of alleviation: the deadlock between Greece and Turkey, with its attendant risks that Great Britain might drag Russia along the path of violent coercion, was not resolved until the Turks suddenly surrendered in March. Secondly, Bismarck kept the Austrians under merciless pressure, informing them on 1 March that, if the negotiations failed, it would be his painful duty to tell St Petersburg who was to blame. Thirdly, Kálnoky's able dispatches from St Petersburg seem to have exerted an influence on both Haymerle[56] and the emperor (who greatly admired them). On 18 February, for example, Kálnoky put the case for co-existence with Russia very strongly: the Monarchy was simply too weak to adopt the only feasible alternative policy, of hurling Russia back into Asia for ever; and perhaps the present moment was the least unfavourable, and should not be allowed to slip away. For Russia was temporarily reasonable (having been weakened by a disastrous harvest in 1880); and whereas negotiations *à deux* would be dangerous for Austria-Hungary as the weaker party, she might do well to negotiate at a time when she could count on the backing of Germany by virtue of the Dual Alliance.

If the Austrians really set any store by this latter consideration, they were greatly in error. The subsequent negotiations saw one Austrian retreat after another, and all accomplished under brutal pressure from Bismarck himself. The Russians played their cards well. The assassination of Alexander II on 13 March presented them with an admirable opportunity to delay the negotiations; and they kept the Central Powers on tenterhooks for three silent weeks, rightly calculating that Bismarck would lose his nerve and put pressure on Vienna. In fact, the situation in St Petersburg was genuinely uncertain: the appointment of Ignatiev as minister of the interior was an ominous sign; and Kálnoky began to wonder how long the conservative Giers would retain any influence at the foreign office. In this situation, Bismarck bullied the Austrians mercilessly, threatening in April to conclude a treaty with Russia without them. During May Haymerle gradually gave way on all points except the right to annex Bosnia, the Herzegovina and the Sanjak. This should not only be recognised, but recognised in the body of the treaty as a quid pro quo for a clause reaffirming the

56. P.A. I/469, Aehrenthal Memorandum 1895.

principle of the closure of the Straits. Bismarck, surprised at the extent of Haymerle's concessions, promised his support; but when the Russians still held out, he again abandoned his Austrian allies. After another appeal from Kálnoky and another formal summons to surrender from Bismarck, the exasperated Haymerle again gave way. The eventual annexation of Bosnia and the Herzegovina ended up in an annexe, and as for the Sanjak, Russia merely reaffirmed her promise of 13 July 1878 to countenance an Austro-Hungarian occupation.

Nevertheless, considering the effective isolation of Austria-Hungary since the summer of 1880, and the extent to which her expectations of support from her German ally had even turned against her, the Three Emperors' Alliance,[57] signed in Vienna on 18 June 1881 (see Appendix III), was by no means an unmitigated defeat. The Dual Alliance had been formally declared to have survived unimpaired (18 May); and the obnoxious mediation clause had disappeared without trace. The main clauses of the treaty actually brought some positive advantages. True, Article III, endorsing the principle of the closure of the Straits, was a pure gain for Russia; but the sense of Article I at least gave Austria-Hungary cover against Italy, in exchange for her promise of benevolent neutrality in the event of Franco-German or Anglo-Russian wars. Article II, concerning the principles of action in the Balkans (spelt out in more concrete terms in an annexed protocol) really only dealt with developments that were in any case regarded as inevitable. And if the Austrians had to rest content with a mere reaffirmation of existing Russian pledges regarding Bosnia, the Herzegovina and the Sanjak, they had at least brought Russia to recognise Austro-Hungarian interests in Bulgaria: its union with Eastern Rumelia was not to be precipitated, nor was it to be extended into Macedonia. Haymerle had been careful to exclude the slightest hint of a division of the Balkans into Austro-Hungarian and Russian spheres of interest, such as would have abandoned Bulgaria to Russia (not that the latter would have been prepared to hand over Serbia and Montenegro to exclusive Austro-Hungarian control either). Thus, if the Austrians had perhaps achieved little in the way of positive gains, they had also given virtually nothing away.

Indeed, the very fact that the treaty said in effect so little, and placed no restriction whatever on the development of Austro-Hungarian influence, particularly economic influence, was a major

---

57. Text in Pribram, *Secret Treaties*, I, pp. 37–47.

advantage in Austro-Hungarian eyes; and one which the Monarchy intended to exploit. More than this, though Russia might not have pledged herself not to invade Romania, Austria-Hungary retained an equally free hand to coerce Serbia or Montenegro. Further, whereas the renunciation by the three contracting parties of their freedom of military action against Turkey (and Bulgaria was still technically part of Turkey) was an important sacrifice for Russia to make, it cost Austria-Hungary nothing, as she had no designs on Turkey anyway. Indeed, by the joint instructions to Russian and Austro-Hungarian representatives in the Balkan drawn up supplementary to the treaty in the course of the summer, and ordering them to co-operate and refrain from intriguing against each other, impecunious Russia had renounced what was perhaps her only effective weapon to counter the extension of Austro-Hungarian influence by means of trade. How far Russian diplomats on the spot would in fact obey the joint instructions was of course a point which no treaty could settle; but altogether the Monarchy's Balkan position was no weaker after the conclusion of the Three Emperors' Alliance than before.

So confident were the Austrians, in fact, that they even connived at a slight increase in Russia's political influence in Bulgaria at this time: in July 1881 Austria-Hungary became the spokesman of the Three Emperors' Alliance in bringing a reluctant Gladstone to accept a Russian-inspired authoritarian constitution to replace the unworkable liberal one granted to Bulgaria in 1879. True, the Austrians here formally abandoned the policy pursued since 1878 of co-operation with Great Britain to check Russian influence in Bulgaria. Yet they were perhaps only renouncing a policy inherited from Beaconsfield and Andrássy which Gladstone was highly unlikely to enforce. (Much the same may be said of Haymerle's conversion to the principle of the closure of the Straits.) Indeed, one thing on which all members of the Three Emperors' Alliance were agreed was the exclusion of Gladstone's influence from the Near East. This applied not only to the sultan's Christian dominions in Europe, where all three sought only to preserve peace, if not quiet; and to Egypt, where, in the face of British and French meddling in 1881 and 1882, all three paraded their scrupulous regard for the sultan's rights in an effort to ingratiate themselves at Constantinople: but also to Bulgaria and Serbia, where Austria-Hungary in particular was irritated by British commercial competition. In the latter principality Haymerle had just brought off something of a coup.

The accession of the Progressives – the party of Prince Milan – to power in Belgrade in October 1880 had not resolved the issues pending between Serbia and the Monarchy – the construction of the railway links agreed with Andrássy at the Congress of Berlin, and the negotiation of a commercial treaty. The first was delayed partly by the Austrian government, which until the autumn of 1880 refused to pay anything towards the cost of a line which would be built entirely in Hungary; and partly by the Serbs, who in the spring of 1881 were still toying with the idea of entrusting their section of the line to Constantinople to a British firm. As for the commercial treaty, when negotiations began in November 1880, even the Progressive government jibbed at what the British minister – admittedly an interested observer – described as Austria-Hungary's 'monstrous pretensions'.[58] By the early summer, however, these issues had been settled: the Serbian government placed the railway contract with the Union Générale, a French Catholic-monarchist bank with Austro-Hungarian affiliations; and further agreed to standardise Serbian railway rates with those of the Monarchy (to prevent underselling by British and French wares coming through Turkey from Salonika). Finally, on 6 June 1881 a commercial treaty was signed admitting Serbian livestock and agricultural produce into the Monarchy on favourable terms and securing the Serbian market for Austrian light industry.

The commercial treaty was followed by a secret political treaty[59] negotiated by Prince Milan in person during a visit to Vienna in June. As Milan saw the situation, Serbia, deserted by Russia at San Stefano and at loggerheads with her fellow Balkan states over the vexed question of the eventual partition of Macedonia, needed the diplomatic support of Austria-Hungary. This, the treaty of 28 June secured, in the event of Milan's wishing to bolster his position by raising himself to the rank of king, or of Serbia's seeking territory in the south in the event of the collapse of Ottoman rule in Macedonia. Serbia, for her part, was to abandon hope of acquiring the Sanjak or the occupied provinces. Indeed, she was obliged not to tolerate on Serbian soil any intrigues against the Monarchy. More than this, by Article IV – which Haymerle described as 'our greatest achievement'[60] – Milan bound himself to conclude no further treaties whatever without prior agreement with Vienna. This last article, too much even for the Progressive government,

---

58. Ramm, 'European Alliances', p. 371.
59. Text in Pribram, *Secret Treaties*, I, pp. 53–61.
60. A.F. Pribram, 'Milan IV von Serbien und die Geheimverträge Oesterreich-Ungarns mit Serbien, 1881–9', in *Historische Blätter*, 1921, pp. 464–94.

was eventually watered down; but Milan gave Vienna a personal assurance which in fact maintained it in its original vigour. The difficulty was that the treaty, and indeed the whole position of Austria-Hungary in Serbia, stood and fell with Prince Milan. The treaty had no roots in the wishes of the Serbian population; and Austro-Hungarian propaganda could never hope seriously to compete with that of Russia, which could harp on the enslavement of the occupied provinces. The best hope for the Austrians was to emphasise mutually beneficial commercial links (if agrarian Hungary could be persuaded to take a benevolent view of Serbian competition in the internal markets of the Monarchy), and to keep the population of Bosnia and the Herzegovina happy. Even this – admittedly a forlorn hope against such an inherently irrational phenomenon as nationalism – was in the long run to prove beyond the capacity of Vienna and Budapest. For the present, however, given that Milan was still master in Belgrade, the Austro-Hungarian position in Serbia was reasonably secure.

Only in Romania had the Austrians made no progress. When, in the spring of 1881, the Romanians had sounded the Central Powers with a view to declaring the principality a kingdom, Haymerle, seeing that no other Power would join him in forbidding this, rather clumsily tried to make his concurrence dependent on Romania's giving way in the Danube question and binding herself in general terms to the Monarchy. The Romanians thereupon – especially in view of rumours of an impending Three Emperors' Alliance which might freeze the Balkan situation – decided in March to go ahead with their proclamation regardless. Haymerle had been made to look rather silly, and in the end he had to join the Russians and Germans in recognising the new kingdom unconditionally. Worse still – as he and Andrássy had always feared – the proclamation did indeed give a boost to Romanian nationalism. A wave of demonstrations and spectacular excursions to and from Transylvania resulted, by August, in a veritable press war between Hungary and Romania.

Yet despite such setbacks, Haymerle had managed to build fairly successfully on the foundations laid by Andrássy at the Congress of Berlin. And he had surpassed Andrássy by establishing tolerable relations with Russia at the same time. Moreover, although the Three Emperors' Alliance, in contrast to the Three Emperors' League, was signed by diplomats rather than by sovereigns, and eschewed declarations of high principle in favour of a businesslike handling of specific Balkan problems, its significance as a demonstration of monarchical solidarity should not be underrated. Personal relations between the three emperors improved markedly: Franz Joseph saw Wilhelm I every summer after 1881; in that same year, he expressed his hearty approval of the Russo-German Danzig meeting, where the socialist menace was discussed; and in an affectionate exchange of telegrams with Alexander III he spoke of his solidarity with the tsar in the struggle 'contre des dangers qui menacent l'ordre social et qui sapent la civilisation chrétienne'.[61] If the easing of tension over the Near East gave the Russian government a breathing space to consolidate itself after the assassination of Alexander II, it also gave the Austrians time to establish the new order of things in Bosnia; and it may well have been a contributory factor to the firm stand taken by the Austro-Hungarian government against anti-monarchist elements generally in the early 1880s. For example, a spate of assassinations of officials between 1882 and 1884 was met with great severity: anarchists in the Monarchy saw their newspapers suppressed and their societies dissolved; and they lost their right to trial by jury.

Yet even after the conclusion of the Three Emperors' Alliance it was by no means clear that the Monarchy had managed to establish a realistic basis for the defence of its Near Eastern interests. Certainly, the Alliance was a far cry from the grand coalition to resist Russia that had been in Andrássy's mind in 1871. That, Andrássy had early been forced to abandon, in view of the recalcitrance of Great Britain and Germany; but he had managed, in the Three Emperors' League of 1873, to reach a *modus vivendi* with Russia that had, at least for three years, contained a potentially dangerous conflict on the Monarchy's south-eastern frontier. Of course, the League had collapsed when it proved unable to contain the waves of Panslav enthusiasm emanating from St Petersburg; but it must also be said that it had always been for Andrássy, with his ingrained distrust of Russia, something of a *pis aller*, and never a thing of the heart. Indeed, after his experiences in 1878 he set his face firmly against all German suggestions for its renewal. The alternative, however, an anti-Russian defensive bloc, which now again became his objective, continued to elude both him and his successor. Whereas Andrássy failed in the Dual Alliance of 1879 to secure any German support whatever for his policy in the Near East, Haymerle found himself confronted, once Gladstone returned to power in 1880, with a Great Britain that seemed positively hostile to the Monarchy's aims there. Hence Haymerle, like Andrássy in 1873, fell back on an agreement with Russia *faute de*

---

61. P.A. I/469, Aehrenthal Memorandum, 1895.

mieux. Indeed, in terms of the Monarchy's position among the Powers, the new agreement *à trois* was even less satisfactory than the old: it was explicitly anti-British; and the Germans, with their disconcertingly Russophile views, were now making their voice heard in Near Eastern questions. In short, the Monarchy was in some danger of finding itself cut off from the Western Powers and in a minority of one to two within the alliance of the three northern courts.

Even so, this latter danger at least might be countered if the Monarchy could itself establish a really cordial relationship with St Petersburg. Neither Andrássy nor Haymerle had ever believed this possible; but there were others who were ready enough to believe it both possible and desirable; and there were signs by the summer of 1881 that these groups were gaining an ascendancy in the political life of the Monarchy. Taaffe's regime was by then well established; and on 11 June Franz Joseph appointed Beck, for fourteen years the trusted head of his military chancellery, to the position of chief of the Austro-Hungarian general staff. (At the same time, the chief of staff was freed from all vestige of parliamentary control, being made responsible no longer to the war minister and the Delegations, but to the emperor.) Beck was certainly a staunch conservative – he got on well with the Inspector General, Archduke Albrecht; and in foreign affairs, too, he was an appropriate herald of the signature of the Three Emperors' Alliance of 18 June. Although naturally anxious that the Monarchy should be as well prepared for war as possible, he was just as anxious to prevent such a catastrophe for the conservative order by finding a *modus vivendi* with Russia. Five months later the trend towards strict conservatism was accentuated by a change at the Ballhausplatz, when, on 2 October, Haymerle died of a heart attack in his office. Andrássy was considered for the succession, but he could not bring himself to work with conservatives like Taaffe and Beck, whom Franz Joseph was absolutely determined to keep. When the emperor's choice finally fell on Gustav Count Kálnoky, another conservative devotee – indeed, one of the architects – of the Three Emperors' Alliance, it seemed that, for the first time since Metternich's day, the partisans of co-operation with Russia were fully in control. After ten years of frustration there at last seemed to be a chance, while always keeping the alliance with Germany in reserve as a deterrent, of securing Austria-Hungary's Near Eastern interests on a basis of a genuine attempt at *détente.*

5
Détente and Deterrence, 1881–1897[1]

Détente: the Three Emperors' Alliance 1881–1887

Gustav, Count Kálnoky, was born in 1832 of a German Moravian family which had emigrated from Transylvania in the eighteenth century – hence the deceptively Hungarian name. Having spent his early years as a cavalry officer, he always retained a stiff, military manner, and, like Bismarck, preferred to wear uniform for portraits and photographs: according to Lützow, most people, especially younger diplomats, dreaded having this dry, reserved man as a neighbour at table.[2] Entering the foreign office, he served from 1860 to 1870 in London, where, confronted with Palmerston's flounderings and Stanley's equivocations, he acquired a deep and lasting distrust of parliamentary foreign policy. In 1870, he was appointed to the Vatican; but, as a devout clerical, he soon quarrelled with Andrássy, who showed insufficient regard for the predicament of the Pope, and he left the service for a time in 1872. In 1879 he was appointed temporary ambassador to St Petersburg; but although he was a success – particularly, as a military man, with Alexander II – Andrássy would not hear of making him permanent ambassador. Kálnoky, for his part, was not ambitious – and certainly not for the foreign office, a post which he felt demanded someone with parliamentary connections. In his view, it was impossible for a mere diplomat to cope with the politics of

1. The following works are of particular relevance to this chapter: E.R. von Rutkowski, 'Gustav Graf Kálnoky von Köröspatak, Oesterreich-Ungarns Außenpolitik von 1881–1885', Doctoral dissertation, Vienna, 1952; Idem, 'General Skobelev, die Krise des Jahres 1882 und die Anfänge der militärischen Vereinbarungen zwischen Oesterreich-Ungarn und Deutschland', in *Ostdeutsche Wissenschaft*, 10 (1963), pp. 81–151; L. Salvatorelli, *La triplice alleanza, storia diplomatica* (Milan 1939); Margaret M. Jefferson, 'The Place of Constantinople and the Straits in British Foreign Policy, 1890–1902', MA thesis, London, 1959; and the works by A. Wandruszka and P. Urbanitsch (eds), C.A. Macartney, A.J.P. Taylor, A. Sked and I. Diószegi cited in Chapter 1, note 1; by Barbara Jelavich and F.R. Bridge and Roger Bullen cited in Chapter 2, note 1; by T. von Sosnosky, E. von Glaise-Horstenau, Agatha Ramm and A.F. Pribram, cited in Chapter 4, note 1.
2. P. Hohenbalken, *Heinrich Graf Lützow* (Vienna 1971), p. 75.

Austria, let alone those of Hungary, which so often impinged on foreign policy: the Monarchy needed a Chancellor on the German model.[3] In the end, however, he accepted the post out of a sense of duty.

The new appointment did not portend any change in the recent course of Austro-Hungarian foreign policy. On the contrary, it confirmed it: if Haymerle had been a somewhat reluctant convert to the concept of a Three Emperors' Alliance as a means of securing Austro-Hungarian interests by agreement with St Petersburg, Kálnoky's experience in Russia had given him a fervent conviction that war with that Power could never bring sufficient gains to compensate for the destruction and misery it would cause. Whereas Andrássy and Haymerle had both had an instinctively 'western' orientation – although diplomatic facts had worked against them in the end – with Kálnoky there was to be a distinct emphasis on the need for the three eastern empires to stand together against the Revolution and, of course, against the midwife of revolution, war. Kálnoky was sometimes prepared to pursue this policy at a cost to Austria-Hungary's freedom of action, and even state interests, that horrified Andrássy. But with the full support of Taaffe and his aristocratic, clerical and Slav satellites, Kálnoky was not usually perturbed by Magyar opposition. The British ambassador's assessment of him was fair enough: 'he clings to the alliance with Bismarck and to the Dreikaiserbund'.[4]

The Three Emperors' Alliance proved well worth clinging to in the first crisis with which Kálnoky was confronted, the Bosnian revolt of October 1881, which arose from the government's decision to impose conscription in the occupied provinces, and which took the Austro-Hungarian army some four months of hard fighting to suppress. The revolt raised a host of problems. On the domestic front, the argument was heard again that so long as Turkey was sovereign over the provinces, they would never settle down; and Kálnoky was more sympathetic to it than Andrássy had been, actually drawing up a draft annexation law in October 1882.[5] But this solution was not adopted: no progress could be made on the thorny problem of the ultimate destination of the provinces within the Dual Monarchy, the Magyars being violently opposed to anything smacking of Trialism. From abroad, Prince Milan told Kálnoky straight out that although he personally would be well

---

3. P.A. I/467, Kálnoky to Kállay, private, 14 October 1881.
4. Ramm, 'European Alliances', p. 250.
5. Rutkowski, 'Kálnoky', pp. 203ff.

disposed, the annexation of the provinces would rouse Serbian national feeling to a frenzy, and would certainly cost him his throne; and although the Russian government might be bound hand and foot by the Three Emperors' Alliance, Russian public opinion was a very different matter, and might force the government to precipitate a union of the two Bulgarias to recoup Russian prestige. Perhaps, in shelving the issue, Kálnoky had missed an opportunity. Russia's binding commitment was valuable, and should, perhaps, have been exploited while it still held. On the other hand, it was hardly unreasonable in 1882 to hope that the future might produce a rather more favourable situation.

More immediately, and more seriously, the Bosnian revolt had raised the problems of preventing foreign intervention and maintaining good relations with Russia. The attitude of the Russian government was, in fact, scrupulously correct; and, in that respect at least, the Bosnian revolt demonstrated the value of the Three Emperors' Alliance. On the other hand, the revolt caused a great stir in the Balkan states. In Bulgaria, the Russian minister, Hitrovo, was known to be supplying money and passports to volunteers who sought to help the rebels; and Montenegro had to be bought off by Vienna at the cost of some 100,000 Gulden. Most worrying of all, however, was the virulent reaction of 'unofficial' Russia. For four long months the Russian press raged against the Dual Monarchy; and the Minister of the Interior, the Panslav Ignatiev, whether personally approving or merely welcoming a diversion from the government's repressive domestic policies, seemed to do nothing to restrain it. Feeling ran particularly high in the army; and in January 1882 the popular General Skobelev made a much-publicised speech in a St Petersburg restaurant, drawing attention to the fight for faith and fatherland that was going on in Bosnia. He then went off to Paris, where he made a speech about the inevitable conflict between Teuton and Slav. True, with the end of the revolt, the Russian press calmed down; the appointment of the conservative Giers as minister for foreign affairs on 25 March was a reassuring sign; and Kálnoky was further gratified to hear in July of the sudden death, in a Moscow brothel, of Skobelev himself, 'the one man in Russia who might have prevailed against sensible people'.[6] But, for some months at least, Kálnoky's faith in the Three Emperors' Alliance had been shaken – and not so much by Skobelev's speeches, as by the government's, and especially the tsar's, timid reaction to them, as shown by their reluctance to respond to the

6. Rutkowski, 'Skobelev', p. 151.

appeals of their allies to summon Skobelev home. As the Austro-Hungarian ambassador at St Petersburg reported in March, there was undoubtedly a great conflict of political forces going on inside Russia, 'and no one can say whether the dam of the state's authority might not one day be swept away'.[7] In short, the very crisis that had demonstrated the tactical usefulness of the Three Emperors' Alliance had shown that it could provide no absolute guarantee of security.

The Skobelev crisis was in fact the starting point for a general reinforcement of Austria-Hungary's diplomatic and military defences against the possibility that the Three Emperors' Alliance might yet fail her. Beck, certainly, was seriously alarmed: 'from now on', he declared in February 1882, 'war against this Power [Russia] must be constantly kept in mind';[8] and in the next two years he laboured to strengthen the Dual Alliance with a military understanding. On the diplomatic front, an alliance was concluded with Romania, and an attempt was made to get a firmer grip on the Balkan states. More immediately, the Skobelev crisis precipitated the formation of the Triple Alliance.

Austro-Italian relations had not been particularly cordial in the later 1870s. In Italy, the government had been in the hands of the Left, traditionally associated with irredentist claims at the expense of the Dual Monarchy. Andrássy, for his part, had warned Rome that 'at the first sign of an Italian annexationist policy, Austria-Hungary would attack';[9] indeed, that Italy would not be permitted to gain territory anywhere on the Adriatic. As for public opinion in the Monarchy, according to the British ambassador, aggression by Italy would be met with 'a unanimous alacrity that would be wanting in the case of any other war'.[10] True, at the very highest level, irredentism might actually provide ground for co-operation between the two governments: whatever his ministers thought, the conservative, military-minded King Umberto regarded it as a cloak for republican propaganda, and detested it as heartily as Andrássy did. Even at this level, however, so long as Umberto had not been recognised by the Vatican as King of Italy, he hardly seemed to the conservative clericals who came to power in Vienna in 1879 to be an appropriate ally for His Apostolic Majesty. In fact, Haymerle's rather short-sighted decision to arrange a state visit from King Umberto to Vienna in 1881 was to cause endless trouble to his

7. Ibid., p. 127.
8. Ibid., p. 134.
9. Salvatorelli, *Triplice alleanza*, p. 30.
10. Ramm, 'European Alliances', p. 165.

successors; and fear of offending the Pope remained an insuperable obstacle to Franz Joseph's returning the visit at the Italian capital throughout the thirty-four years of the existence of the Triple Alliance.

Yet even if the Triple Alliance was never to be a thing of the heart, for either the Austrians or the Italians, in 1880 the idea had its attractions in terms of hard political advantage. The Italians were desperate to escape from isolation; and Haymerle – he had not been ambassador at Rome for nothing – was certainly prepared to consider an alliance, both in February 1880, when he was striving to turn the Dual Alliance into the anti-Russian bloc envisaged by Andrássy, and in February 1881, when he was trying to strengthen his hand to drive a hard bargain in the impending negotiations with Russia. The general diplomatic situation was unfavourable, however. Bismarck, totally unsympathetic to Haymerle's aspirations on both occasions, poured cold water on the idea, and the negotiations faded away. In the summer of 1881 even the Austrians lost their enthusiasm: they had managed to reach agreement with Russia; and if the French occupation of Tunis in May made Rome even more frantic to escape from isolation, it was for Vienna a serious obstacle to agreement. The Austrians had no more desire to be dragged into Italy's quarrels with France than into Germany's. The Italians only began to make progress at the end of the year when, in the atmosphere of tension created by the Bosnian imbroglio, they advanced an additional argument that carried some weight with the conservative Kálnoky: an alliance would give a much-needed boost to the prestige of the monarchy in Italy; and the Central Powers themselves must have an interest in preventing the spread of the contagion of republicanism from France to the whole Latin world.

This latter argument, important though it was to Kálnoky, was not in itself enough to clinch the issue. Kálnoky still refused to back the Italian monarchy to the extent of concluding a treaty of territorial guarantee: that would have implied the adoption by Franz Joseph, the leading Catholic monarch, of the Italian view in the quarrel between Quirinal and Vatican; and his own suggestion of a simple neutrality treaty in turn offered the Italians too little – in fact, no more than they already had in practice. It was Skobelev's visit to Paris, raising, not only in Vienna, but in Berlin, the spectre of a France in league with Russia, that broke the deadlock and determined Kálnoky to offer Italy some support against France. As he explained to the Austro-Hungarian ambassador at Rome on 1 April, the chief justification for the alliance from his point of view lay in 'the dreadful confusion [*Zerrüttung*] prevailing in Russia'.[11]

In this respect, the terms of the Triple Alliance (see Appendix IV), drafted by Kálnoky and concluded in Vienna on 20 May 1882,[12] suited Austro-Hungarian interests well enough. Austria-Hungary was committed to help Italy only in the extremely unlikely event of an unprovoked French attack; and she maintained her freedom from any obligation to help Germany in the event of a Franco-German war. It is true that Italy had gained security against both her potential enemies, and had offered Austria-Hungary nothing beyond neutrality in return. The Austrians, however, were not in the least interested in securing positive help from Italy: this would be of little value, and might entail greater commitments against France, or an Italian demand for a voice in Near Eastern affairs. Kálnoky's main preoccupation in the spring of 1882 had been simply to make sure of Italy's neutrality, so as to free all the resources of the Monarchy to cope with events in the east if the Three Emperors' Alliance should fail.

At the same time, the Alliance was undoubtedly a useful reinforcement of the conservative bastion in central Europe. Indeed, in contrast to the Dual Alliance and the Three Emperors' Alliance, the Triple Alliance emphasised explicitly in its preamble the determination of the contracting sovereigns 'to fortify the monarchical principle and thereby to assure the unimpaired maintenance of the social and political order in their respective states'. Kálnoky stressed this aspect in his efforts to dispel the indignation the alliance had aroused in the Vatican. Against the two great revolutionary threats of the day – the Orthodox Church in league with Panslavism, and revolutionary socialism emanating from France – all conservative elements, including, he reminded the Pope, the Italian monarchy, must stand together in defence of the principle of authority, 'qui en dernière analyse est la base de tous les états'.[13] By the same token the alliance was, in the eyes of the leading socialist newspaper in Austria, 'an offensive alliance [*Trutzbündnis*] against the working class . . . a defensive alliance of exploiters [*ein Schutzündnis der Ausbeutung*].[14]

Yet in terms of the external security of the Monarchy it must be said that the Triple Alliance was of only limited significance. It was never much more than a reinsurance treaty, to be kept in reserve in case Russia should break loose from the Three Emperors' Alliance.

11. P.A. I/457, Kálnoky to Wimpffen, private, 1 April 1882.
12. Text in Pribram, *Secret Treaties*, I, pp. 37–47.
13. P.A. XI/226, Kálnoky to Paar, private, 7 December 1883.
14. Kletecka, 'Parteien und Gruppen', in *Habsburgermonarchie VI*, p. 453.

Deterrence would only be resorted to if *détente* should fail. Moreover, whereas Germany, who had been promised Italy's active assistance in war with France, wished to see Italy militarily and financially strong, Austria-Hungary, if she was to feel really sure of Italy's neutrality in the event of war with Russia, wished to see her as weak as possible. This divergence between the German and Austro-Hungarian attitudes towards Italy was never to be resolved, and was to cause serious disharmony within not only the Triple, but also the Dual Alliance. Even in its agreed, 'conservative' function the Triple Alliance had serious weaknesses. Like the Serbian alliance and the Three Emperors' Alliance, it had no roots in popular feeling on either side. For example, in December 1882, after the execution of Guglielmo Oberdank (a deserter from the Austrian army who had planned to assassinate Franz Joseph during his visit to Trieste), vast demonstrations were held in Italy, where every town of any significance soon had its 'Piazza Oberdan'. True, the Italian government, like those of Alexander III and Prince Milan, was scrupulously correct in its behaviour, but Kálnoky was certainly being sanguine when he expressed the hope, in April 1884, that it would only be a matter of time before the Triple Alliance came to earn that popular approval in the member states that he regarded as 'the final cement [*den letzten festen Kitt*]'.[15]

In fact, only one of Austria-Hungary's alliances ever received this 'final cement': the Dual Alliance. After the Skobelev crisis this alliance was further strengthened by a military understanding. Since 1871, the German military had regarded it as axiomatic that France and Russia would fight together, should Germany become involved in war with either; and in 1879 they had decided to concentrate on eliminating Russia first in such an eventuality. They had not discussed their plans with the Austrians, however. The Dual Alliance had brought no co-ordination of military planning between the Central Powers. It was only the Skobelev crisis that convinced the Germans of the need at least to find out something about Austria-Hungary's plans. The Austrians, meanwhile, came to a similar conclusion. A war with Russia, Beck declared in April 1882, given her widespread Panslav ramifications, would be like a return to the *Völkerwanderungen*, and the Monarchy would need all the help it could get.[16] The impending Italian alliance would be a great help; but the Balkan states would need watching; and there was an urgent need for more fortifications in Galicia, and for more

15. P.A. I/457, Kálnoky to Ludolf, 15 April 1884.
16. Rutkowski, 'Skobelev', pp. 140–2.

strategic railways to reduce the Austro-Hungarian mobilisation time. Equally urgent, however, was the need to discover Germany's intentions. In preparing for talks with his German counterparts in the summer, Beck boldly declared for an Austro-German pincer movement deep in Russian Poland, to encircle and destroy the main Russian army there at the first sign that Russia was making serious preparations for war.[17] By the autumn, the two general staffs had in fact agreed on a strategy based on a strong joint offensive into Poland, the Germans even promising to put more than half their forces in the East.

True, these military agreements imposed no binding commitments on the two allied governments. As Beck himself observed,[18] there were limits to the trust one could put in even the best of allies; and if Austria-Hungary wanted a worthwhile share of the spoils, it was urgent to regroup the Cracow army further east, and to do everything possible to speed up the mobilisation timetable. It would never do to allow the Germans to win the early victories unaided, the Monarchy itself appearing late in the day with a sort of reserve army. Moreover, speedy Austro-Hungarian victories would be of vital importance in holding the Balkan states to an awed neutrality. Kálnoky gave Beck his full support in persuading the council of ministers of the necessity for more strategic railways, and by 1885 the Austrians had in fact succeeded in reducing the time needed for mobilisation from 40 to 21 days. In the military field, the understanding reached in 1882, together with the measures subsequently taken by the Austrians themselves, constituted an important addition to the effectiveness of the Dual Alliance against Russia.

For the rest, however, once the Skobelev affair proved to be a mere passing phenomenon, Austro-German relations did not develop at all. For example, Kálnoky was firm in resisting Bismarck's attempts to extend the Dual Alliance to cover the case of a Franco-German war: the Magyars were insistent that Hungary could not conceivably have any quarrel with France; and besides, Kálnoky said, in the event of a Franco-German war the Monarchy would have to put all its forces in the east to keep Russia quiet. In respect of economic relations, the two allies even drifted apart in the 1880s.[19] With Germany's adoption of protection in 1878 restrictive measures reduced German cattle imports from the Monarchy from

---

17. Ibid., pp. 142–3.
18. P.A. I/466, Beck memorandum, secret, 11 November 1881.
19. L. Höbelt, 'Die Handelspolitik der österreichisch-ungarischen Monarchie gegenüber dem deutschen Reich', in *Habsburgermonarchie VI*, pp. 567ff.

1,254,000 to 458,000 by 1880; and in 1881, on the pretext of an outbreak of cattle plague, the Germans imposed a total ban. This drove the Hungarian government in turn – and at some risk to the Monarchy's influence in Serbia and Romania – to close the frontier to livestock from the Balkan states. In 1881 the Monarchy was subjected to the full German tariff on cereals, and Kálnoky was seriously alarmed at the prospect of a tariff war, which he feared would have a most baleful effect on the popularity of the Alliance in both empires.[20] Bismarck's perspective was narrowly diplomatic, however. Economic questions (like colonial questions) he insisted could be kept on an entirely different plane from diplomatic relations; and in any case, he said that German agriculture could not possibly face the competition of Hungarian and Romanian cereals since the railway network had been extended in south-east Europe. In the end, since to continue a free-trade policy would certainly have entailed the utter ruin of Austrian and Hungarian industry in the face of German competition, Austria-Hungary had no alternative but to follow her best and most powerful trading partner, and adopt protection likewise.

The results were not an unmitigated disaster either for Austria-Hungary or for the Alliance. Despite the raising of Austro-Hungarian tariffs to correspond with German rates, total trade with Germany increased during the 1880s. And the Great Powers, unlike the Balkan states, did not usually allow commercial considerations to determine their diplomatic and military alignments. Indeed, the Monarchy's internal market enjoyed a measure of prosperity under the shelter of the new tariff policy – there was a steady increase in domestic consumption, and, as a result of railway development in Hungary and the Balkans, quite a boom in the iron industry. On the other hand, the Monarchy's exports on the whole stagnated; and there was certainly no perceptible strengthening of its hold over foreign markets against a competition from the stronger industrial economies of western Europe that would soon grow increasingly fierce. Even in the Balkan states, where a position of relative economic strength reinforced by commercial treaties mitigated the Monarchy's losses, it was to a great extent living on the capital of a past pre-eminence. The Monarchy enjoyed, in fact, only a mediocre prosperity in the 1880s; and this at least partly accounts for its relatively feeble performance in the field of military expenditure. There were limits to what diplomacy could do to redress the balance.

20. P.A. XL/294, Ministerratsprotokoll, 7 April 1885.

In Romania, at least, Kálnoky managed to salvage something from the fiasco of Haymerle's policy. True, at first relations got still worse before they got better – not surprisingly, given that Kálnoky worked on the principle that small states like Romania 'lick the hand that beats them, or that they fear will beat them'.[21] In the Danubian question the Romanians bitterly resented the decision of the Great Powers to circumvent their obstruction by summoning a special conference of signatories of the Treaty of Berlin in London (at which Romania, of course, was not represented); and their wrath was concentrated on Austria-Hungary as the Power chiefly concerned in the affair. Irredentism added fuel to the flames, and matters came to a head in June 1883, when, at a state banquet held in the presence of the king and queen of Romania speeches were made expressing regrets for 'the pearls still missing from the crown of St Stephen the Great', and the royal guests accepted a toast to 'the king and queen of the Romanians'.[22] This, Kálnoky decided, was too much for a Great Power to tolerate; and on 1 July he sent what was virtually an ultimatum to Bucharest: 'we must now insist on an explicit and clear declaration that the government condemns this unlawful agitation against the peace of our border territories, and, as is its duty, will not tolerate it . . . We are completely in the right and will pursue this matter, if necessary to the point of war [*bis in den letzten Konsequenzen*].'[23] The Romanian government at last saw into the abyss that yawned before it, and presented an apology virtually dictated by Kálnoky. The success of the firm, not to say overbearing, approach had been amply demonstrated. Kálnoky's 'ultimatum' had set a precedent that was to be imitated several times, sometimes with less happy results for the Monarchy, in the next thirty years.

Kálnoky, at any rate, was prepared to rest content with this achievement; and it was only at the urging of Bismarck – again temporarily worried about Russia's armaments – that he agreed to consider the possibility of extending the 'league of peace' eastwards by bringing in Romania. (He also took this opportunity to inform the Germans of Haymerle's Serbian alliance.) Even now, as in the case of the Dual and Triple Alliances, a catalyst was needed, in the form of a temporary scare about Russia. On this occasion it was provided by a serious row between the tsar and Prince Alexander of Battenberg; and the prospect of a Russian invasion of Bulgaria

21. Rutkowski, 'Kálnoky', p. 54.
22. Idem, 'Oesterreich-Ungarn und Rumänien 1880–83', in *Südost-Forschungen*, 25 (1966), p. 228.
23. Ibid., pp. 242–3.

alarmed the Romanians even more than the Austrians. The upshot, the Austro-Romanian alliance of 30 October 1883, negotiated by Kálnoky and Bratianu, gave a measure of reassurance to both parties. It gave the Monarchy cover in the south-east in the event of a Russian attack; and, perhaps more important, Germany's immediate accession to the alliance constituted in effect that very extension of the Dual Alliance to cover Romania that Haymerle had sought in vain from Bismarck in 1881. For the rest, however, Kálnoky was under no illusions. The alliance depended entirely on the king and Bratianu – not even the whole Romanian cabinet knew about it, and it had no roots in public opinion. It was significant that Kálnoky could not get Bratianu to accept a clause similar to that in the Serbian treaty which explicitly forbade the toleration of irredentist activities. Nor did he manage to bring Romania to modify by one jot her stubborn attitude on the Danube question. Indeed, Bucharest remained absolutely unyielding on this even after the alliance was signed; and Kálnoky in turn was only irritated by Bismarck's glib advice to humour Romania: 'no one outside Austria can have any idea what patience is needed when one is surrounded by a collection of half-barbarian states whose arrogant interpretation of their newly-acquired independence gives rise to perpetual friction'.[24]

The one bright spot on the horizon was Bulgaria, a state with which Austria-Hungary had no alliance at all, but where that same nationalism that undermined her position in Romania and Serbia worked in her favour, or, at least, worked against the attempts of her Russian rivals to preserve their political predominance. Indeed, by January 1883, Kálnoky was toying with the idea that a strong, united Bulgaria might not be a Russian satellite (as many people had feared after San Stefano), but perhaps the best means of driving Russia out of the Balkans altogether – an extremely dangerous ambition, even if only a long-term one. For the present, however, Austro-Hungarian interests in Bulgaria seemed to be secure enough; in the spring of 1883 agreement was at last reached with Turkey and Bulgaria for the construction of railway links with the Serbian network (which were to be given priority over the strategic lines desired by Russia). Kálnoky felt confident enough to hold to his policy of abstaining from open opposition to Russia. In the crisis of August 1883 he stayed calm, and advised Prince Alexander to avoid provoking a showdown with the tsar. If Russia was so foolish as actually to invade Bulgaria, he calculated, this would

24. Idem, 'Kálnoky', pp. 488–9.

only compromise her further, and keep the other Balkan states in the Austrian camp. Besides, if the worst came to the worst, other Powers, notably Great Britain, might pull the chestnuts out of the fire. At any rate, he was not prepared to risk his own relations with St Petersburg by coming forward himself; and he took care at this time not to respond to some British suggestions for joint opposition to Russian designs in Bulgaria.

More active intervention was called for, by contrast, to bolster the Austrian position in Serbia. When the collapse of the Union Générale Bank, in January 1882, dealt a severe blow to Prince Milan's prestige, and almost brought the Russophile Liberals and Radicals to power, the Austrians stepped in with timely financial aid; and in March they readily gave their approval when, in a move to strengthen the dynasty, Milan took the title of King. But nothing they did could alter the fact that Milan's pro-Austrian orientation continued extremely unpopular, associated as it was with higher taxation resulting from the governments' railway projects and disastrous financial ventures, and even more with the negation of cherished national ambitions in Bosnia and the Herzegovina. The Austrians, for their part, preferred to adopt a conspiracy theory, and blame Russian agents for fomenting all the opposition to King Milan. Kálnoky, certainly, seems to have been convinced that this was the root of the trouble. In January 1883, he lectured Giers on the need for co-operation between the great monarchies in support of the minor dynasties in the Balkans. None of these dynasties had any roots in its adopted country, and all of them were confronted with the same international revolutionary movement – which only assumed different guises (socialist, nationalist or liberal) according to varying circumstances.[25] Given the narrowly monarchical nature of most of Austria-Hungary's alliances, it was natural enough for Kálnoky to insist that it was a 'vital necessity [*Lebensnotwendigkeit*]' for Austria-Hungary to oppose challenges to the monarchical principle wherever they arose.[26] The argument was also a good one to use with the eminently conservative Giers, who promised to support the dynasty in Belgrade despite Milan's shortcomings. As far as the rather depressing outlook in Serbia was concerned, therefore, it made good sense for the Austrians to cultivate the Three Emperors' Alliance.

This was certainly Kálnoky's view. Far from attempting to incite anti-Russian feeling in Belgrade – that could only weaken the Three

25. P.A. I/469, Liasse XXIII/a, Kálnoky, memorandum, 20 May 1883.
26. Rutkowski, 'Kalnoky', p. 274.

Emperors' Alliance, his chief means of keeping Russia in order – he was in the summer of 1883 urging a very recalcitrant Milan to improve his relations with St Petersburg. It was perhaps just as well that Kálnoky had this order of priorities, for the Russians certainly retained an interest in Serbia. This was clear from their protests when Kálnoky tried to argue that Austria-Hungary could not, for reasons of her own security, tolerate openly hostile governments on her southern frontier in Montenegro or, especially, in Serbia, 'which lies so completely within our sphere of influence': 'we must insist on a friendly government in Belgrade', and in the last resort the Monarchy would intervene by force of arms to secure it.[27] In reply, Giers boldly advanced the claim that the spirit of the Three Emperors' Alliance (which, of course, technically applied only to Turkey and Bulgaria) forbade Austria-Hungary to intervene in Serbia without the consent of her treaty partners. At this, Kálnoky made an astonishing retreat, accepting this new interpretation of the treaty;[28] and it was a retreat that again demonstrated that for Kálnoky salvation lay, not in the Serbian alliance or in direct action in Belgrade, but in close co-operation with 'official' Russia within the framework of the Three Emperors' Alliance.

The military, it is true, still had their doubts about Russia, and Beck continued to emphasise the need to improve the Monarchy's defences and reduce the time needed for mobilisation. But even he was prepared to acknowledge the value of improved relations with Italy and Romania, and to admit that, all in all, 'the year 1883 has brought a real change for the better'.[29] Kálnoky, for his part, as the negotiations for the renewal of the Three Emperors' Alliance demonstrated, was very well content with the existing state of affairs. He turned down a Russian proposal, which Bismarck put to him, to alter the alliance in the sense of the Reichstadt Agreement of 1876, to take account of the eventual collapse of the Ottoman Empire; and he was equally firm in rejecting Bismarck's favourite idea of spheres of influence in the Balkans – Russia would not observe the principle in Serbia and Montenegro, so it would be just pure loss for the Monarchy to abandon Bulgaria. He also rejected Bismarck's suggestion that Italy might be brought in: this would overthrow the whole basis of existing treaties, in which Italy's role was only as part of the wall he had built up against the danger of Russian attack if the Three Emperors' Alliance should fail. (Besides, he said, the Near East was no business of Italy's; she would

27. Ibid. p. 303–4.
28. Ibid., p. 308.
29. P.A. I/466, Beck, memorandum, dated '1884'.

only complicate matters.) When the treaty was renewed for three years, on 27 March 1884, Kálnoky made only one alteration. That was a concession to Russia, and an important one: the text was amended to extend the prohibition of military action without prior consultation from Turkey proper and Bulgaria to the whole of the Balkan peninsula. Admittedly, he had sold that particular pass to Giers in the summer of 1883; but this formal amendment constituted a serious restriction on the Monarchy's freedom of action against Serbia, and one which Haymerle had resolutely resisted in 1881. To this extent, there was some justification for Andrássy's complaint that 'whereas the Congress of Berlin led Russia out of the Balkans, my successors brought her back in again'.[30] But this was a price that Kálnoky, of all Andrássy's successors the keenest devotee of a conservative alliance with St Petersburg until Aehrenthal, was prepared to pay.

Yet, valuable though the Three Emperors' Alliance might be as a means of reconciling Austro-Russian differences, it was, after all, an alliance of three Powers; and the attitude of the third party was of crucial importance to the other two. For Austria–Hungary, for example, diplomacy on the basis of the tripartite alliance could prove disastrous if she found herself placed in a minority of one to two. Hence Kálnoky's concern either to deal with Russia *à deux*, or, if the Germans insisted on pushing their way in, to bring Berlin into line with Vienna beforehand. There were disturbing signs, in the summer of 1884, that this might not be easy. Bismarck was supporting the Russians in their attempts to persuade the sultan to appoint a Russophile governor of Eastern Rumelia in succession to Aleko Pasha (whose term of office was due to expire); and Kálnoky was worried lest Russia might then be tempted to expel Alexander of Battenberg from Sofia, and unite the 'two Bulgarias'. He kept in step with his alliance partners to the extent of not actually opposing the Russian nominee for Eastern Rumelia; but he rejected out of hand Bismarck's bland suggestion that he should simply recognise that Bulgaria lay in Russia's sphere. Again he declaimed against the doctrine of spheres of influence, which, as he rightly observed, Russia herself did not accept. Austria–Hungary could never give Russia a free hand in Bulgaria: to do so would be to create that same big Slav state under Russian control that Andrássy had so tenaciously opposed. Such a state would dominate the whole Balkans; and besides, Austria–Hungary had a great material stake in Bulgaria.

30. Kab. 19, Andrássy to Franz Joseph, 24 November 1885.

In these circumstances, it was not surprising that the Austrians were disconcerted when the Germans sought to participate in a meeting between Franz Joseph and Alexander III, planned for September at the tsar's hunting lodge of Skiernewice in Poland. On the other hand, it would do no good to snub the Germans, especially at a time when the Russians were so disturbingly assiduous at Berlin. In the end, the Austrians had to give way; but they tried to square the Germans in advance, and managed to persuade them to agree to separate Austro-German talks at Ischl and Varzin to precede the Skiernewice meeting. This would put the Dual Alliance in the foreground, and give the public the impression that Skiernewice was merely a subsidiary reinforcement of Austro-German solidarity. In the intervening weeks, Kálnoky did his best to humour the Germans. He supported their opposition to an Anglo-Portuguese treaty about the Congo basin, and impressed strongly on Károlyi in London that it was vitally important, in the London conference then meeting on Egypt, to lend Bismarck wholehearted support against Gladstone. The latter's policy was in any case 'a disaster [*höchst unheilvoll*]' for Austria-Hungary, who had no interest whatever in seeing him continue in office.[31] As for Skiernewice, he was still apprehensive about the spectacular form it had assumed: 'You can imagine what a noise it will make', he complained to Károlyi.[32] Franz Joseph, always more sceptical than Kálnoky about the Three Emperors' Alliance, did not expect much of any value at all to emerge from the meeting: 'my distrust of conditions in Russia is so deep-rooted'.[33]

As it turned out, the Germans did not repeat, at Ischl or Varzin, their obnoxious advice of the summer, but, most encouraging of all, the Skiernewice meeting (15–17 September) surpassed all expectations in terms of cordiality, and was a good example of summit diplomacy at its most successful. This first personal contact brought a real improvement in the relations between Franz Joseph and the tsar; and Kálnoky's faith in the possibility of lasting co-existence with Russia was given a tremendous boost. The view that Skiernewice was merely 'the electrifying of a corpse, which . . . could deceive only the shortsighted'[34] certainly underrates the importance of the meeting. The Italians, for example, were not short-sighted in discerning a significant downgrading of the Triple Alliance, the raison d'être of which was, for the Aus-

---

31. P.A. I/460, Liasse XXII/a, Kálnoky to Károlyi, private, 28 July 1884.
32. Ibid.
33. Ibid., Franz Joseph to Kálnoky, 26 July 1884.
34. Sosnosky, *Balkanpolitik*, II, p. 68.

trians at least, the possible collapse of the Three Emperors' Alliance.[35] The latter was, in fact, very much in the ascendant.

Kálnoky had no doubts about this. Indeed, when, in October, Tisza allowed the Hungarian parliament to express its suspicion of Russia in a formal vote, his rage knew no bounds. He even went so far as to tender his resignation. Not only was it intolerable, he complained to the emperor, that Tisza should allow any debate at all in the Hungarian parliament, rather than in the Delegations, where the minister for foreign affairs would at least have a chance to defend his policy; the content of the Hungarian declaration was even more serious: 'for Austria-Hungary today it is a question of life and death to avoid war with Russia'.[36] At Skiernewice he had managed to secure peace and friendship with Russia without even a written agreement, 'with a handshake, so to speak'; and here were the Hungarians giving the impression that the Monarchy was now drawing back.[37] In the end, Franz Joseph refused to accept Kálnoky's resignation; and Tisza promised to behave more correctly in future. But the incident is as eloquent of Kálnoky's renewed faith in Russia as of the continuing distrust of that Power in Hungary.

The Hungarians were at the same time undermining Kálnoky's efforts to improve the Monarchy's relations with the Balkan states. Agrarian Hungary gained little from the Monarchy's commercial treaties with these states, and occasionally resentment at the admission of cheap Balkan livestock to the Hungarian market got the upper hand in Budapest. When in October 1884, for example, the Serbs persisted in sending animals infected with foot-and-mouth disease into Hungary, the Hungarians reacted drastically, and closed the frontier to all livestock from Serbia, Romania and Bulgaria. Although by December Franz Joseph and Kálnoky prevailed on them to relent and re-open the frontier, the affair had done nothing to raise the popularity of Hungary among the ordinary peasants who made up the bulk of the population in those states. Worse still, in February 1885, when infected cattle from Romania passed through Hungary to Germany, a major disruption of the international cattle trade resulted, and Hungary again closed the frontier to Romania. (Budapest wanted to extend the ban to Serbia too; but Kálnoky and the emperor insisted that the Monarchy could not ignore its treaty obligations towards Serbia just because a third party had made difficulties.) Relations with Romania, of course,

35. Salvatorelli, *Triplice alleanza*, p. 89.
36. P.A. I/467, Kálnoky to Franz Joseph, 13 October 1884.
37. Ibid., Kálnoky to Franz Joseph, 22 October 1884.

became seriously strained. Bucharest threatened not to renew the commercial treaty, due to expire in 1886, and Kálnoky's dismayed appeals to Budapest went unheeded. He was again feeling the shackles of the 1867 constitution, which allowed the foreign minister only an advisory function in internal and economic questions. He had no means of enforcing his views about a commercial policy which was made by others, but which none the less had important consequences in foreign policy.

On top of all these difficulties came a political crisis in Serbia. In the summer of 1885 Prince Milan proposed to amend the Austro-Serbian treaty to provide for his eventual abdication: if the Austrians would provide him with a pension, he would allow them to annex Serbia if they saw fit. Kálnoky, however, was interested only in stability, not expansion, and sternly reminded Milan of his duty to remain in Belgrade and govern his people. No one in the Monarchy had the faintest desire to intervene in Serbia unless an openly hostile regime should establish itself there and threaten the tranquillity of Austria-Hungary's South Slav provinces. 'A flourishing and independent Serbia on friendly terms with us suits our . . . intentions best – in any case better than the possession of an unruly province.'[38] Not that Kálnoky had any illusions about the vital importance of Serbia, 'the key to the Monarchy's position in the Near East'.[39] For if Austria-Hungary did not control Serbia, Russia would; and 'that moral encirclement by the leading Slav Power, which will always remain the chief danger for Austria-Hungary, would then extend from Montenegro to the banks of the Vistula; Austria-Hungary would be cut off from the Near East'.[40] Worse still, the South Slav idea would then have found a material basis for its political activity, and would soon penetrate deep into the Monarchy – which would then find foreign problems turning into domestic problems. This prophecy of doom was remarkably perceptive; but for the time being, if Kálnoky could only console himself with the thought that the personality of the abject creature on the Serbian throne was the 'surest and almost the only guarantee against these dangers',[41] it was all the more important to preserve the good relationship with Russia achieved at Skiernewice.

Certainly, there seemed to be little hope of salvation elsewhere – from the Western Powers, for example. On the contrary, Italy's tiresome adventures in East Africa were threatening to embroil her

38. P.A. I/456, memorandum by Kálnoky, 9 June 1885.
39. Ibid., memorandum drawn up by Kálnoky for Taaffe, September 1885.
40. Ibid.
41. Ibid.

with France. Kálnoky would have liked Bismarck to tell Italy straight out that she could expect no help from the Triple Alliance in such a conflict; and both he and Bismarck were agreed that while the Alliance was probably worth renewing, there must be no question whatever of any extension of their support for Italy. The British seemed equally reckless, toying with the idea of fighting out in the Black Sea their dispute with Russia over remote Afghanistan. This prospect filled Kálnoky with alarm: for if Turkey allowed a British fleet through the Straits, Russia would take this as an act of war; and the conflagration would spread to the whole Balkans. Even the prospect of a war confined to Great Britain and Russia worried Vienna (in contrast to Berlin): it might lead to an uncomfortable increase in Russian prestige, or to defeat, revolution, and an adventurist Panslav regime in St Petersburg.[42] It was in an effort to ward off such dangers, therefore, and in accordance with their obligations under the Three Emperors' Alliance, that the Austrians joined the other continental Powers in reminding the Turks that they must in no circumstances open the Straits to British warships. This effectively paralysed the activists in London, and the crisis faded away.

France meanwhile, although never the military threat to the Monarchy that she was to Germany, seemed to Kálnoky, as he set increasing store by the Three Emperors' Alliance and monarchical solidarity, less a potential source of support than a menace to the Monarchy's alliance system, and hence to its security. 'The long continued existence of a French republic', he declared to Bismarck in August 1885,[43] 'is a dangerous matter for the monarchical principle' – especially if republicanism spread to infect France's Latin neighbours: 'the realisation of the well-known idea of the *confédération de races latines*'. It would be a very serious matter, he explained, if some eighty million people from Cadiz to Lake Constance, from Syracuse to the North Sea, came to live under a republican system of government. One dream of the Revolution would be realised; and this would pose a threat to the three eastern empires, for the Confederation of Slav States and the United States of Germany were inscribed on the same programme. Clearly, it was more than ever important that the three empires stand together. A few days later, a very cordial return visit by Alexander

---

42. P.A. I/469, Liasse XXIII, Teschenberg memorandum on the possibility of an Anglo-Russian war, April 1885.
43. P.A. I/460, Kálnoky, notes on a conversation with Bismarck at Varzin, August 1885.

III to Franz Joseph at Kremsier (25–6 August) proclaimed again the Austrians' renewed faith in the Three Emperors' Alliance.

It is true that the Three Emperors' Alliance, by virtue of its very nature as a negative, self-denying agreement, could never exercise much positive direction over events in the little Balkan states; but the desire of both Vienna and St Petersburg to preserve the alliance was to prove, as in the 1870s, invaluable in ensuring that these events did not lead to a conflict between Russia and Austria-Hungary. This was clearly demonstrated in the crisis that followed the nationalist coup of 18 September 1885 in Eastern Rumelia, and Prince Alexander's acquiescence in the union of the 'two Bulgarias'. For a short time, Franz Joseph and Kálnoky seemed to lose their nerve, suspecting that Russia might have engineered the coup in an attempt to revive the Big Bulgaria of San Stefano: on no account, they declared, must the movement be allowed to spread to Macedonia; and the emperor stressed the need to bear in mind the claims to compensation of Serbia and Romania, two states which 'we must at all costs keep within our sphere of influence and on good terms with us'.[44] When, however, on 4 October, Russia demonstrated her innocence by condemning Prince Alexander and demanding the undoing of the union, and when the Germans supported her, Kálnoky brought the Monarchy into line with its allies. After all, a policy of upholding the Treaty of Berlin would have the advantage of relieving the Powers of the task of constructing a new Balkan balance of power. Unfortunately, this policy was to prove impracticable in the long run, as was shown by the failure of the ensuing Constantinople conference to restore the status quo ante in the face of British obstruction and Turkish reluctance to undertake the conquest of Eastern Rumelia. But Kálnoky, despite Andrássy's pleas for support for Bulgaria in her defiance of Russia, still put his faith in co-operation with St Petersburg within the framework of the Three Emperors' Alliance.

He clung to this policy even in November, when the Serbs, whom he had been trying desperately to restrain, were provoked by the deadlock at Constantinople to invade Bulgaria in a foolhardy attempt to redress the Balkan balance themselves. That Austria-Hungary's protégé, Serbia, had attacked Russia's – albeit erring – protégé, Bulgaria, was certainly embarrassing for Vienna. But it was on Great Britain, who had frustrated the efforts of the Constantinople conference, that Kálnoky's wrath was concentrated: she seemed to be trying to break up the Three Emperors' Alliance and

44. P.A. XL/55, Franz Joseph to Kálnoky, 20 September 1885.

set Russia and Austria-Hungary by the ears; but she would not succeed.[45] These sentiments were echoed in the Austro-Hungarian embassy at St Petersburg, a notable shrine of the Three Emperors' Alliance. Great Britain, the ambassador Wolkenstein declared, was a greater enemy of the Monarchy in the Near East than Russia was: 'she is striving for our commercial annihilation'.[46] And the military attaché had little sympathy for the Serbs: 'it is a pity these nationalist pigs think they have a right to boast of our protection'.[47] The embassy was relieved, therefore, when on 19 November Kálnoky agreed to a Russian proposal for diplomatic intervention by the Powers to stop the Serbian invasion of Bulgaria.

Kálnoky was all the more ready to co-operate when, on that same day, Prince Alexander defeated the invaders at Slivnitsa and in turn invaded Serbia, whereupon the panic-stricken Milan appealed to Vienna for help. When a joint appeal from the Powers for a cease-fire was rejected by Alexander, Kálnoky resorted to the famous Khevenhüller mission, instructing the Austro-Hungarian minister at Belgrade to go to Alexander's headquarters, and, using such arguments as he felt necessary, persuade the prince to call a halt. In the spirit of the Three Emperors' Alliance, Kálnoky took care to secure Russian approval of these instructions beforehand; but in the event the arguments by which the ebullient Khevenhüller brought Alexander to heel gave some offence in St Petersburg: if the Bulgarian invasion caused a revolution in Serbia, Austria-Hungary would occupy the country, whereupon Russia would occupy Bulgaria and depose Alexander. As Austro-Hungarian diplomats in St Petersburg complained, 'Khevenhüller's *coup* was a great surprise for us here at the embassy. No wonder Russia didn't like the threat of a Russian occupation of Bulgaria (which nobody here is thinking of).'[48] But Kálnoky did not take the contretemps too seriously, assuring the Russians that Khevenhüller had exceeded his intructions, and that nobody in Vienna had talked of occupying Serbia;[49] and he irritably reminded the complaining Bismarck that he had acted in order to forestall, not to precipitate, a situation that might lead to strife within the Three Emperors' Alliance.[50]

It must be said that Kálnoky's policy did not meet with universal

45. P.A. XV/98, Kálnoky to Károlyi, Tel. 117, 24 November 1885.
46. Aehrenthal MSS, Karton 4, Wolkenstein to Aehrenthal, 27 October 1885.
47. Ibid., Karton 2, Klepsch to Aehrental, 15 October 1885.
48. Ibid., Karton 4, Wacken to Aehrenthal, 13 December 1885.
49. P.A. XV/85, Kálnoky to Wolkenstein, private, 2 December 1885.
50. Ibid., Kálnoky to Széchényi, 14 December 1885.

approval at home. Andrássy, for example, like the Empress Elizabeth and Crown Prince Rudolf,[51] thought the whole policy of co-operation with Russia misguided, and in a long memorandum to the emperor (24 November) urged that the Monarchy should seize the initiative and work for the complete independence of a united Bulgaria.[52] Even Kálnoky wavered momentarily, and at the turn of the year thought of summoning Russia to explain her intentions in Bulgaria. But in the end he thought better of it; and it was not just the frowns of Bismarck that constrained him to operate within the Three Emperors' Alliance. Fundamentally, he was of one mind with his former colleagues in the St Petersburg embassy, who were as assiduous as ever in extolling the virtues of peace, the Monarchy's only really vital interest. According to Wolkenstein, there was in Europe 'a great revolutionary subversive party just waiting for the crash and for the great conservative Powers to weaken and exhaust each other in the conflict, and then the radical reform can begin'.[53] This being the case, it seemed wiser to avoid precipitating a confrontation with Russia.

Kálnoky's patience was rewarded. The Bulgarian military victory had in any case helped matters, by bringing even Russia to recognise that the status quo ante was an unrealistic aim, and by disposing of any Serbian hopes of compensation. In the event, Kálnoky was able to leave it to Great Britain and Russia to arrange the details of Turkish recognition of the new state of affairs in Bulgaria; and to play an equally self-effacing role in the naval demonstration by which the Powers brought Greece to abandon her claims to compensation. The Austrians only came forward in the negotiations affecting their Serbian protégés, when they managed to secure their main point: Serbia was not to be burdened with a war indemnity. Altogether, the crisis had not ended too badly for the Austrians, or for the Three Emperors' Alliance, which continued in good health until the autumn of 1886. In August, Archduke Karl Ludwig paid a highly successful visit to St Petersburg; and Kálnoky took care to dispel any doubts among the public by announcing that 'Austria-Hungary has no intention of weakening the relationship that was sealed at Skiernewice and Kremsier, and which came into practical operation in the last Bulgarian crisis.'[54]

Kálnoky's continuing faith in the Three Emperors' Alliance both accounts for and reflects his lack of interest in alternative align-

---

51. Brigitte Hamann, *Elisabeth, Kaiserin wider Willen* (Vienna 1982) pp. 533ff.
52. Kab. 19, Andrássy to Franz Joseph, 24 November 1885.
53. Aehrenthal MSS, Karton 4, Wolkenstein to Aehrenthal, 16 December 1885.
54. P.A. I/469, Aehrenthal memorandum 1895.

ments in the summer of 1886. On the one hand, reinsurance in the west against the collapse of the Alliance seemed less necessary. Kálnoky and Bismarck again agreed that if the Triple Alliance were renewed, they would resist any attempt by Italy to bring Balkan affairs within its purview; and Kálnoky, to oblige St Petersburg, rejected a British invitation to join in denouncing Russia's unilateral abrogation of the clause of the Treaty of Berlin that de-fortified Batum. On the other hand, the Monarchy's Balkan alliances hardly offered an alternative source of salvation. In Serbia, King Milan had now shown himself to be completely devoid of political, and – a failing that counted for much with Franz Joseph and Kálnoky – of military virtues. Indeed, in the aftermath of Milan's defeat Kálnoky told the emperor that he had 'always thought it would be wrong to base our position in Serbia' too exclusively on Milan or on 'ephemeral' public opinion.[55] Of course, if Milan abdicated, it would be important to ensure the continued rule of the dynasty in the form of his son, even under a regency, and to keep the Russophile Nikita of Montenegro off the throne. Apart from that, however, Kálnoky placed his hopes in what he rather optimistically termed a hard political fact, namely, Serbia's 'inevitable' dependence on her powerful northern neighbour. Whether lulled by the apparent success of the Three Emperors' Alliance, or simply at a loss for an alternative policy, he henceforth adopted a decidedly passive line towards Belgrade, steering clear of all involvement in the maelstrom of Serbian domestic politics. The problems besetting the Romanian alliance moved him to greater activity; but his desperate efforts to move the Hungarians to some concession, such as the reopening of the frontier to Romanian livestock, all came to nothing. In June 1886 the Austro-Romanian commercial treaty duly expired, and the Monarchy's imports from and exports to Romania fell by 90 per cent and 40 per cent respectively between 1885 and 1887. The tariff war was to last for seven years; and although it brought some benefits to Hungarian agriculture, now sheltered from Romanian competition, its consequences were wholly prejudicial both for Austrian industry – which lost most of the Romanian market to Germany, Belgium and Great Britain – and, as Kálnoky had tirelessly warned Budapest,[56] for the alliance.

In Bulgaria, admittedly, the prospects were somewhat brighter, and although Kálnoky was somewhat sceptical of Alexander's more effusive protestations of loyalty, he nevertheless recognised in

55. P.A. I/456, Kálnoky to Franz Joseph, 22 November 1885.
56. P.A. XL/294, Ministerratsprotokoll, 7 January 1886.

the prince 'a convinced and sincere enemy of Russian influence', whom it was in Austria-Hungary's interest to support.[57] For Kálnoky was never prepared to tolerate Russian control of Bulgaria and the encirclement of the Monarchy that he feared would follow. On the other hand, the chief guarantee against such a danger still remained for him not the prince's independent attitude, but the restraining effect of the Three Emperors' Alliance on the tsar; and for the sake of the Alliance, even Prince Alexander was expendable. At any rate, when the prince was kidnapped by Russian officers on 19 August 1886 and released from Russia into Austria a week later, Kálnoky advised him not to return to Bulgaria without the blessing of the tsar; and when this was crushingly refused, and Alexander abdicated, Kálnoky obligingly agreed with Giers that the simplest solution would be the speedy election of a new prince.

In the summer of 1886, therefore, Austria-Hungary seemed to enjoy a reasonable measure of security. This was in great part due to the alliances she had built up since 1879. True, Andrássy's and Haymerle's original simple idea of a grand alliance, including Germany, Great Britain and Italy, to resist Russia had proved unrealisable, owing to the vagaries of British policy and Bismarck's obsessive concern for good relations with Russia. Kálnoky had, in fact, inherited a basically dualistic system of alliances. In this, his own handling of affairs over the next five years had placed the emphasis decidedly on the Three Emperors' Alliance, the embodiment of the desire to co-operate with 'official' Russia, and, by the exercise of mutual restraint, to avoid a conflict over the Balkans that could only prove disastrous to all three great monarchies. So long as this Alliance seemed to be working, there was, naturally, less emphasis on the Dual Alliance and its ramifications, designed to assist the Monarchy in war if the Three Emperors' Alliance should fail to keep the peace. Of these alliances, the Dual Alliance was clearly the most important, with its promise of German military assistance. Little support could be expected from the Romanian alliance; and the Triple Alliance promised none at all. The military value of the Serbian, Italian and Romanian alliances lay chiefly in their giving the Monarchy cover to concentrate all its resources on the Russian front in the event of war. In normal peacetime circumstances they were certainly useful in bolstering up the monarchical principle and conservative interests generally; but that was about all. All three alliances were plagued with irredentist counter-currents. Even the Dual Alliance, in normal peacetime

57. P.A. XV/99, Kálnoky to Károlyi, 11 February 1886.

circumstances, was proving to be of little practical value: on the contrary, Bismarck's determination to stand well with Russia, and his tiresome advocacy of the doctrine of spheres of influence in the Balkans, were a distinct embarrassment to Vienna at a time when the struggle for influence was focused on Bulgaria.

In sum, therefore, of the alliances concluded between 1879 and 1883 the Three Emperors' Alliance offered Austria-Hungary a fair chance of peaceful co-existence with Russia, provided the pacific Alexander III continued to direct Russian policy; the other alliances offered her as strong a military position as she was ever likely to attain in the event of a final armed confrontation with Russia. There remained, however, the problems of day-to-day diplomacy; perhaps of less obvious urgency than the risk of actual war and annihilation, but, none the less, of vital importance when taken together over a number of years. The perpetual struggle for influence in the Balkan states had immense implications for the whole Great Power position of the parties concerned. At least, this was the conviction of those directing policy in Vienna and St Petersburg. It might happen that a diplomatic crisis would prove severe enough to estrange even 'official' Russia from the Monarchy and to destroy the Three Emperors' Alliance, but would yet stop short of that war which would bring the other alliances into operation. Such a crisis would not only intensify the contradictions in the Balkan alliance system, given the conflicting ambitions of the Monarchy's friends and allies in the peninsula; it would also reveal the inadequacy in diplomacy of alliances designed for use in war.

Just such a crisis occurred in the autumn of 1886, when, without prior consultation with his partners in the Three Emperors' Alliance, Alexander III suddenly sent General Kaulbars on a mission to Sofia to pressurise the Bulgarians into electing as Prince Alexander's successor a candidate agreeable to St Petersburg. To Vienna, this looked suspiciously like a bid for the political control of Bulgaria, and Kálnoky at once took alarm. Bismarck's bland suggestion that Bulgaria was after all in Russia's sphere of influence, he rejected out of hand: the prospect of Russian control of Bulgaria was 'unthinkable for Austria-Hungary. The question of what would happen to Romania is automatic and unanswerable.'[58] But these views, in turn, met with no sympathy whatever in Berlin. Nor did Kálnoky have enough confidence in the firmness of purpose of the distant British to throw in his lot with them and

---

58. P.A. I/469, Aehrenthal memorandum 1895.

abandon the Three Emperors' Alliance.[59] Hence his rejection of a British proposal of 30 September for Anglo-Austro-Italian co-operation at Sofia and Constantinople to support the Bulgarians against Kaulbars. After all, if it came to a war the Monarchy might well find itself bearing the main burden. Like Andrássy after San Stefano, therefore, he first tried to bring the Russians to reason within the framework of the three emperors' combination.

As in 1878, however, it soon became clear that the gulf that had suddenly opened up between Vienna and St Petersburg was un-bridgeable. Kálnoky's views, stated openly by Tisza in the Hunga-rian parliament in October – that no European treaty gave any Great Power a special position in the Balkan states, and that the latter should be left to settle their own affairs without interference – caused immense irritation in St Petersburg, where memories of the sacrifices Russia had made less than ten years before were still fresh. Tension rose further when on 13 November Kálnoky declared in the Delegations at Budapest that the Bulgarian question could be settled only by Europe, not by General Kaulbars; and threatened Russia pretty clearly with war if she proceeded to use force against Bulgaria. The Russians, for their part, claimed to be seeking to liberate Bulgaria from 'a regime of terror and violence', and ac-cused the Austrians of collaborating with 'cosmopolitan radicalism to transform Bulgaria into a hotbed of anarchy and hostility to Russia'[60] – a neat variation on Kálnoky's favourite theme. They were not in the least mollified by such conciliatory gestures as Kálnoky felt at liberty to make – for example, his promise to refrain from actually opposing Russia's candidates for the Bulgarian throne. After all, the Bulgarian regents refused to consider these candidates in any case; and they were stiffened in their defiance by Kálnoky's public utterances and by similar ones from Salisbury in London. By late November the tsar's policy had collapsed in ruins, and the Kaulbars mission – his own brainchild, infuriatingly enough – was recalled to St Petersburg.

In the atmosphere of frustration that now prevailed in the Russian capital the Three Emperors' Alliance came to grief. By December the Austro-Hungarian embassy, which had had no business to transact for some weeks, gloomily concluded that diplomatic relations between Russia and Austria-Hungary had for

59. W.N. Medlicott, 'British Foreign Policy in the Near East, from the Congress of Berlin to the Accession of Ferdinand of Coburg', MA thesis, London, 1926, pp. 320ff.
60. P.A. I/469, Aehrenthal memorandum 1895.

all practical purposes been broken off.[61] The new year brought no improvement. On the contrary, the news of the existence of the Three Emperors' Alliance, leaked to the press by Saburov, called forth a Panslav outcry that almost drove Giers from office. Kálnoky viewed these developments with sorrow but with resignation: 'I cannot boast that my years of effort to establish stable and friendly relations with Russia have been successful', he wrote to Wolkenstein on 7 May 1887, 'but I do not regret them and can say with a good conscience that I have done what I could' – there had never been any spirit of reciprocity in St Petersburg.[62] He instructed Wolkenstein to raise the question of the renewal of the Alliance none the less; but he was never prepared to pay the price of surrendering Bulgaria to Russian control. Indeed, he gave further proof of this in June, when his refusal to co-operate frustrated yet another Russian proposal, whereby the three empires would secure the replacement of the recalcitrant council of regents in Sofia by a single provisional regent, namely, the Russian General Ehrenroth; and the Russians found his repeated advice to allow the regents to proceed with an early election exasperating in the extreme. Kálnoky was regretful but not surprised, therefore, when the tsar, mortally offended by the Monarchy's opposition to his Bulgarian schemes, and impressed by the public outcry in Russia against the Alliance, refused to renew it. With the expiry of the Three Emperors' Alliance, on 18 June, Kálnoky's hopes of security through an *entente* with Russia that he had cultivated so assiduously ever since 1880/1 had failed. The question was, whether the Monarchy would be able to find an adequate substitute elsewhere.

Deterrence: The Mediterranean Entente, 1887–1895

The Dual Alliance had proved of no use at all in the recent crisis, and Kálnoky never succeeded in winning Germany's moral support over Bulgaria, even when he warned Berlin that the attitude of the German press in defending Russia's machinations was destroying the faith of the populations of the Monarchy in the Alliance.[63] Bismarck's famous 'Hecuba' speech of 11 January 1887, proclaiming to the *Reichstag* and the world that 'it is a matter of complete indifference to us who rules in Bulgaria and what becomes of

61. Aehrenthal MSS, Karton 4, Wacken to Aehrenthal, 23 December 1886.
62. P.A. I/460, Kálnoky to Wolkenstein, private and confidential, 7 May 1887.
63. P.A. I/464, Liasse XVI, Kálnoky memorandum on a conversation with the German ambassador, 6 October 1886.

her',[64] finally convinced Kálnoky of Germany's diplomatic useless-
ness. And this was matched by doubts as to her military reliability.
On 7 March Archduke Albrecht proposed[65] that, unless Germany
would give a binding promise to put eighteen divisions on the
eastern front in the event of war, Austria-Hungary should consider
freeing herself from all obligations to her ally. Kálnoky had more
understanding for the predicament of the Germans, who, he reminded the archduke, had to provide against the recent expansion
of French military power.[66] Moreover, in his view, France was in
her own way quite as dangerous as Russia, and quite as much in
need of watching. For if she ever defeated Germany, 'the republican and socialist menace would sweep through Europe like a flood
when a dam has been broken'. As things turned out, Kálnoky was
right not to panic, and by the summer could rejoice that Bismarck
had been able to give France 'a real fight' in 'the ridiculous Schnae-
bele affair'; and he calculated that once Boulanger was out of office,
Russia too would begin to behave with more circumspection.[67]
Nevertheless, as he confided to Széchényi, the ambassador at
Berlin, grave doubts had taken root among the public about the
value of the Dual Alliance. And this, he said, was no wonder,
considering the ostentatious indifference towards Near Eastern
questions paraded in official speeches and the semi-official press in
Germany, and Germany's continuing 'harshly negative' attitude
towards the Monarchy in commercial questions.[68]

The Monarchy's Balkan alliances presented if anything an even
gloomier picture. In Serbia, the political scene was one of complete
confusion, and the legation at Belgrade lamented the advancing
decay of Austria-Hungary's connections there: the ministry for
foreign affairs, formerly very co-operative, was now always difficult to handle. Perhaps Kálnoky feared that active interference
might only make things worse; at any rate, he continued to take
refuge in the bland assumption that Serbia, 'despite all her dislike of
us, does not want to become Russian and in the long run will not be
able . . . to escape from our influence'.[69] Relations with Romania
were still bedevilled by the tariff war, described by the Austro-

64. O. von Bismarck-Schönhausen, *Gesammelte Werke*, Vol. 13, p. 213.
65. P.A. I/466, Memorandum by Archduke Albrecht on military co-operation
between Germany and Austria-Hungary, 7 March 1887, with comments by
Kálnoky.
66. Ibid.
67. P.A. I/460, Kálnoky to Wolkenstein, private and confidential, 7 May 1887.
68. P.A. I/464, Kálnoky to Széchényi, private and secret, 12 May 1887.
69. P.A. I/460, Kálnoky to Wolkenstein, private and confidential, 7 May 1887.

Hungarian legation at Bucharest as 'a disaster' for the Monarchy.[70] Even Count Agenor Goluchowski, appointed to Bucharest in February 1887, and, thanks to his geniality and his august connections (his wife was a Princess Murat, and a distant relative of King Carol) a great personal success there, 'could not move mountains' in the commercial question, which for Romania was 'more important than all others'.[71] It was small consolation that Russia's bullying of Bulgaria brought the Romanians to renew their assurances of loyalty to Vienna. The very crisis that highlighted the importance of the alliance also showed its limitations: in February 1887 Archduke Albrecht had to confess to Bucharest that if it came to a war the Monarchy would need all its forces for the crucial offensive in Galicia, and would have none to spare to assist Romania directly.

The Triple Alliance, meanwhile, had had to undergo the ordeal of a formal renewal, which considerably increased the distrust between Vienna and Rome. By October 1886 Bismarck, alarmed by the progress of Boulangism in France, was willing to look with favour on certain amendments proposed by Rome – that the allies should support Italy if she got into war with France over North African questions, and that in the event of changes in the status quo in the Balkans Italy should be granted compensation. Kálnoky, however, was as determined as ever not to increase Austria-Hungary's commitments against France, and almost as unwilling to bind the Monarchy's hands *vis-à-vis* Italy in the Near East or to recognise an Italian sphere of influence there – especially when the cloven hoof of irredentism was all too evident in the compensations proposal. Indeed, after Bismarck's 'Hecuba' speech, which Kálnoky said had disheartened Austria-Hungary's friends and supporters everywhere, and showed that she would have to rely on her own resources to defend her Near Eastern interests, he refused point-blank to assume any new commitments in the west.[72] Bismarck, however, pointed out that although Italy might not be able to give Austria-Hungary much help, she could do her a good deal of harm by going over to France and Russia. This argument was unanswerable. There was no denying that the eastern crisis had completely transformed Italy's bargaining position since the summer of 1886. Kálnoky, with bitter reflections on Italy's *Trinkgeldpolitik*, gave way.[73]

The Triple Alliance was renewed, therefore, and supplemented by

70. Aehrenthal MSS, Karton 1, Heidler to Aehrenthal, 3 October 1886.
71. Ibid., Heidler to Aehrenthal, 16 February 1886.
72. P.A. I/462, Kálnoky to Széchényi, secret, 20 January 1887.
73. P.A. I/461, Széchényi to Kálnoky, private and secret, 1 April 1887.

an additional Austro-Italian treaty, similar in form to an additional Italo-German treaty on Tripoli, but covering the Balkans. (When the alliance was renewed in 1891 this treaty was to be incorporated into the main text [see Appendix V] to form the famous Article VII.) Franz Joseph was most emphatic that the annexation of Bosnia must not be held to constitute a change in the status quo warranting compensation under the new treaty; and that whatever compensation Italy might receive must not come from Austro-Hungarian territory. The Italian ambassador at Berlin stated that this was 'obvious'.[74] It was, nevertheless, somewhat naïve – or slipshod – of Kálnoky to content himself with an ambassador's verbal gloss as a sufficient guarantee. It was certainly not binding on any Italian government – as the Austrians were to find to their cost in 1915. The Alliance had survived. Indeed, its existence was at last announced to the world in March 1887. But it had gained nothing in internal strength nor, from an Austro-Hungarian point of view, in usefulness. Kálnoky still doubted whether Italy could be relied on to observe even neutrality if the Monarchy ever got into war with Russia.[75] Széchényi agreed: 'but what can one expect from a country where the mob rules the sceptre?'[76]

In one respect, however, Italy was undoubtedly useful: through her connections with Great Britain. The British, after the failure of their soundings at Vienna in September 1886, had managed to establish a link with Italy, in an agreement of 12 February 1887 providing for diplomatic co-operation to maintain the status quo in the Mediterranean and neighbouring seas. This the British saw as a chance to resume contact with Austria-Hungary. Already on 8 February the British ambassador at Vienna, Paget, had suggested to Kálnoky that Great Britain might be able to help Austria-Hungary in a war with Russia; and Kálnoky, by now despairing of the Three Emperors' Alliance, had enthusiastically agreed: if it really came to a war, Great Britain and Austria-Hungary might not be able to destroy Russia, but they could at least secure a lengthy breathing space by co-operating to bleed her white.[77] On 19 February, the British took a further step, informing Vienna of the Anglo-Italian agreement, whereupon Kálnoky enquired in London as to the possibility of a similar Anglo-Austrian agreement. According to Károlyi in London, Salisbury's assurance that he would

74. Salvatorelli, *Triplice alleanza*, p. 117.
75. P.A. I/462, Kálnoky to Bruck, private and secret, 15 February 1887.
76. Ibid., Széchényi to Kálnoky, secret, 12 February 1887.
77. P.A. I/461, Kálnoky, memorandum on a conversation with Paget, 8 February 1887.

stake his political existence on coming to the aid of the Monarchy in a war with Russia was as good as an alliance in principle, and Kálnoky was well content to accede on 24 March to the Anglo-Italian agreement. Its limited character as 'an agreement to agree' suited the Austrians well, in that it entailed no onerous commitments for them in the western Mediterranean, and yet ensured that British policy would not 'wander away again', as it had in the Bulgarian union crisis in 1885. In May the group was further reinforced by the addition of Spain: the Italo-Spanish exchange of notes on general lines of policy was welcomed in Vienna as strengthening conservative and monarchical ideas in Spain against 'the dangerous idea of a republican brotherhood of Latin races'.[78] Austria-Hungary formally acceded on 21 May.

If the disappearance of the Three Emperors' Alliance freed the Austrians from even a moral obligation to humour St Petersburg, the co-operation they had established with Great Britain and Italy put them in a good position to deal with the Bulgarian question in terms of confrontation, rather than compromise, with Russia. On 7 July Russia suffered another defeat when a special *Sobranje* unanimously elected Prince Ferdinand of Saxe-Coburg-Koháry to the Bulgarian throne. As an Austrian army officer, as a member of the Hungarian branch of the Saxe-Coburg family, as a relative of the British ruling house, and especially as a Roman Catholic, Ferdinand was from the point of view of St Petersburg the most obnoxious candidate conceivable. A Russian circular of 13 July declared the election to be illegal, 'an unworthy comedy staged by the most wretched rabble'.[79] At first, even the Austrians were not entirely happy about such a spectacularly anti-Russian choice: Franz Joseph thought it politic to refrain from receiving Ferdinand at Ischl; and Kálnoky warned him that before he could be legally installed in Bulgaria he would need the approval of the signatory Powers, which was not likely to be forthcoming. But they still found the election itself perfectly legal and correct; and once Ferdinand had established himself in Sofia and was clearly popular there, they decided to support him.

In the diplomatic battle that now ensued at Constantinople, as Russia began to press the sultan to invade Bulgaria and expel Ferdinand, the Austrians found the Mediterranean Entente of more use than all their alliances put together. Indeed, the Germans, competing with the French for the favours of St Petersburg,

78. Ibid., Kálnoky to Bruck, private and very secret, 19 March 1887.
79. P.A. I/469, Aehrenthal memorandum, 1895.

actually lent Russia their full diplomatic support. The Austrians were, of course, unaware of Germany's formal pledges to Russia on this score in the Reinsurance Treaty, and Kálnoky could only complain in bewilderment that Germany's behaviour was completely confusing the sultan's view of Great Power alignments, and was 'the most harmful element in the present situation'.[80] But the Mediterranean Agreement Powers held a trump card in the sultan's general inclination towards inertia, and their sustained campaign of passive resistance gradually gave Ferdinand time to establish his position. By November, Russia was ready to abandon her efforts at Constantinople. The long campaign that had started with her bid to control Bulgaria in the autumn of 1886 had ended in her total defeat, and in something of an Austrian victory. In Bulgaria, at least, the Mediterranean Entente had proved a more than adequate substitute for the Three Emperors' Alliance.

In other areas the prospects for the success of 'our group' – as the Austrians liked to refer to the Anglo-Austro-Italian combination – were more problematical. At Constantinople and in the Straits, for example, the sultan's natural tendency towards inaction sometimes played into the hands of their opponents: in the summer of 1887, for example, the frowns of France and Russia had easily persuaded him to abandon the 'Drummond–Wolff Convention', which provided for the evacuation of Egypt on terms favourable to the British. Moreover, by the late 1880s Russia was beginning to build a significant battle fleet in the Black Sea, and was pressing the sultan to permit the passage of the occasional Russian warship through the Straits. Constantinople was impressed. Indeed, according to the Austro-Hungarian ambassador, France and Russia ruled the sultan 'by intimidation'.[81] In the autumn, therefore, the Austrians took the initiative in suggesting an extension of the Mediterranean agreements to counter French and Russian influence in these specifically eastern questions. They were encouraged, for once, by Bismarck, who, despite or perhaps because of the Reinsurance Treaty, could only welcome it if another group of Powers were to assume the task of deterring Russia from actually precipitating a crisis. In October, Kálnoky sent to London an eight-point draft, together with a warning. This last – to which he often referred in subsequent crises – reflected the usual Austrian fear that the British might be tempted to push Austria-Hungary forward and shelter behind her (*zu sehr hinter uns verkrieche*):[82] at the Straits and at Constantinople,

80. P.A. I/458, Liasse VIII/b, Kálnoky to Calice, 18 August 1887.
81. Ibid., Calice to Kálnoky, 24 September 1887.
82. Ibid., Kálnoky to Calice, 25 September 1887.

he insisted, it was Great Britain who was in the front line, Austria-Hungary in only a supporting role. If Great Britain withdrew Austria-Hungary too would have to retreat, and concentrate on guarding her more immediate interests in the Balkan peninsula. That said, however, the proposed agreement would still give Vienna the confidence to hold to a policy of keeping Russia out of Constantinople. These arguments, and a letter of commendation from Bismarck, impressed Salisbury; and the resultant 'Second Mediterranean Agreement' of 9–12 December 1887 was an encouraging sign of the continuing co-operation of 'our group', not only in Bulgaria, but at Constantinople and in the Straits.

Striking as such successes might be in terms of the security of the Monarchy's position in the Near East, whether the Mediterranean agreements could offer an adequate replacement for the Three Emperors' Alliance in terms of the Monarchy's security in the European states system as a whole was a much more open question. Certainly, the condition of the Monarchy's formal alliances at the end of 1887 left much to be desired; and when Russia responded to her defeat in Bulgaria by massing troops in Poland, the reaction of Berlin was confusing, to say the least. True, Bismarck advised the Austrians to look to the defences of Galicia; but, for him, this was merely the military counterpart to blessing the Mediterranean Entente – a militarily prepared Austria-Hungary could more effectively deter the Russians from blundering into war. The military in Berlin went much further: on 12 December Moltke actually proposed to Vienna a joint preventive attack on Russia, drawing the response from Beck that the Monarchy would be ready to fight by 15 January 1888. Franz Joseph and Kálnoky, however, confined themselves to a few precautionary troop movements, whereupon the Russians assured Vienna on 23 December that they were not contemplating war or the shedding of a single drop of blood for Bulgaria. At this, Bismarck professed himself completely satisfied, and proclaimed in the Reichstag on 11 January that all danger of war had now disappeared.

The Austrians, by contrast, took a decidedly pessimistic view of the future. In a memorandum of 1 January 1888, Kálnoky analysed the nature of Russia's grievances,[83] concluding that they stemmed from the rise of Germany to Great Power status and the formation of the Dual Alliance. These events had ousted Russia from the artificially inflated status she had enjoyed in Europe since the Napoleonic wars. Hence, as both the German Empire and the Dual

---

83. P.A. I/469, Kálnoky, memorandum, 1 January 1888.

Alliance were there to stay, there could be no real prospect of an end to Russia's hostility. On the next day he told the Russian ambassador that the time was not right to discuss the restoration of lasting good relations; and at the end of the month he was still telling the Germans that 'Russia desires war'.[84] In fact, at the turn of the year ministerial conferences in Vienna had been much exercised with the question of a preventive war.[85] Kálnoky was always firmly against such 'madness': the Monarchy was neither militarily nor, above all, diplomatically prepared. The Dual Alliance was strictly defensive (and Germany, preoccupied in the west, would in any case be unable to render much assistance); relations with Great Britain and Italy were on a purely defensive basis; and as the Monarchy relied on an army of conscripts, public opinion would also have to be considered. Although Tisza argued that the Monarchy could only lose by delay – the Slavs were as yet still loyal, but might not be so after a few more years of Russian propaganda – Kálnoky remained of the view[86] that the Central Powers stood to gain by delay, as both Germany's armaments and Russia's financial embarrassments would grow. In sum, although he admitted that the situation was 'bad, because the basic causes of the evil have not disappeared', he was forced to the conclusion that 'at present there is nothing we can do but put up with it'.

One thing the Austrians nevertheless tried to do was to clear up a contentious aspect of the Dual Alliance, namely, the political status of the plans made by the military in Vienna and Berlin since 1882 for an offensive thrust into Poland if war with Russia became inevitable. In mid-January Kálnoky instructed a hesitant Széchényi to raise the matter with Bismarck in Berlin.[87] It was not a question, he was at pains to stress, of changing the defensive character of the Alliance, or of waging a preventive war. The military simply needed to know in advance – for there would be no time to start planning in a crisis – whether it would be at all permissible to take the offensive. The extremely unfavourable geographical conformation of Galicia rendered the Austro-Hungarian line of march hazardous in any case; but the allies would give up enormous advantages of territory and morale and severely compromise the whole issue of the war if they simply waited for the Russians to attack. The only guarantee of success lay in an immediate offensive

---

84. Glaise-Horstenau, *Beck*, p. 316.
85. P.A. XL/294, Ministerratsprotokoll, 18 December 1887.
86. Ibid., Ministerratsprotokoll, 5 January 1888.
87. P.A. I/464, Liasse XIX/d, Kálnoky to Széchényi, No. 2 secret, 12 January 1888.

and a simultaneous thrust from Germany. If on the other hand, Austria-Hungary knew definitely that she would have first to wait and let the Russians into the country, she would have to think hard about whether she could possibly go to war with Russia at all. To all these arguments Bismarck turned a completely deaf ear. The alliance, he insisted, was strictly defensive, and there could be no question of taking the offensive in any circumstances. It is true that, even after this, the soldiers went on making their plans regardless: in February 1888 Moltke was still talking of a common offensive into Poland; and although the Germans could not put up so many men as in 1882, the improvements in the Austro-Hungarian army since then ensured to the allied armies a superiority of some 178,000 men over Russia. At the political level, however, the Dual Alliance had certainly suffered a setback; and Kálnoky and Franz Joseph, if resigned, were bitter. It was time Berlin realised, the emperor observed, 'that "politically defensive" and "military offensive" are not contradictory terms'.[88] For the present, however, it seemed that there was indeed nothing more to be done.

In other respects too, the Germans made it abundantly clear that any support they might give the Austrians through the Dual Alliance would be strictly limited. Their publication of the terms of the Alliance in February 1888 was less a gesture of solidarity than an attempt to reassure Russia and to emphasise the purely defensive character of the Alliance for the better information of the chauvinist Hungarian press. And all this was at a time when Austro-Russian relations showed no sign of improvement: 'How we are supposed to get out of this without a war is not clear to me', Franz Joseph remarked to Waldersee, the German chief of staff, in June 1888.[89] Kálnoky, for his part, proved himself Bismarck's equal in the strict interpretation of treaties: in the military discussions between the Triple Alliance Powers in Berlin in January, he scrupulously upheld the Monarchy's treaty rights to observe neutrality in certain wars against France. It is true that Italy's accession to the Austro-Romanian alliance in the summer of 1888 was a success for Kálnoky, who felt that closer co-operation between the two Latin races against the Slav flood could only weld the alliances together. But this was of very limited practical importance. Kálnoky himself thought Italy so ramshackle that she would probably not be able to spare a man from the French front in the event; and Archduke Albrecht thought it positively dangerous to foster any links

88. Wagner, 'Kaiser Franz Joseph', p. 162.
89. Glaise-Horstenau, *Beck*, p. 324.

whatever between two irredentist states with claims on the Monarchy. Nor had the Austrians themselves any use for Italy's military assistance; and when this was mooted in military talks at Berlin Kálnoky, seeing in it, as usual, only a Trojan horse for irredentist claims, turned the idea down flat.

Moreover, although the alliances would clearly have their uses in the event of actual war, that was a contingency which Austro-Hungarian policy was very much concerned to avoid. Indeed, the outbreak of war would in itself indicate a failure of the very important deterrent function of the alliances. The Austrians had always hoped, however, that the alliances would serve another function – and this was to assume greater importance in Austrian minds in the decade after 1888, when there were no major confrontations between the continental Powers – namely, to serve the interests of the Monarchy in the humdrum, but hardly less essential, diplomacy of peace, and to ensure good relations with its neighbours. In this respect, the alliances were proving a sad disappointment. It was not merely that Germany's equivocal attitude at Constantinople was still confusing the Turks and disheartening Great Britain and Italy; or that nothing much could be done with the unstable governments in Belgrade and Bucharest. In the summer of 1888 the Dual and Triple Alliances too were plagued with mistrust. Indeed, Germany and Italy seemed almost to be engaged in something resembling a conspiracy against the Monarchy.

The new German Emperor, Wilhelm II, for example, not only chose demonstratively to honour St Petersburg with his first state visit, but followed this up with a visit to the king of Italy at Rome. There, he spent much of his time discussing the internal affairs of Austria with Crispi, who joined him in deploring the pro-Slav and clerical policies of the Taaffe government. Worse, the Germans tried to interfere in a minor frontier dispute between Italy and Austria, provoking Kálnoky to ask bitterly whether Germany for her part would consider ceding Lorraine to France 'in the interests of general European peace'.[90] Irredentism was at this time threatening to become quite a serious problem in Austro-Italian relations. In January 1889, Kálnoky took the gravest umbrage at an Italian law enfranchising Italian-speakers outside the kingdom. In November, it was only under pressure from Rome and Berlin – and with perhaps understandable bad grace – that Franz Joseph intervened to stop the trial for sedition of the editor of the Trieste

---

90. A. Sandona, *L'irredentismo nelle lotte politiche e nelle contese diplomatiche italo-austriache*, 3 vols (Bologna 1932), III, p. 146.

Independente; and in July 1890 the closing down of *Pro Patria*, the leading national association for Italian Austrians, was interpreted in Italy as another wicked plot by Taaffe and the clericals to undermine the Triple Alliance. Italy still needed the Alliance, of course, and it was under this banner that in the autumn of 1890 Crispi at last launched a great onslaught on the irredentists, after closing down all the societies dedicated to Oberdank. Kálnoky was relieved; but the ensuing Italian elections showed that the irredentists were still as powerful as ever. Meanwhile, the first state visit of Wilhelm II to Vienna in October 1888 was a disaster in every respect. He infuriated Franz Joseph with his blatant intrusions into the domestic affairs of the Monarchy. For example, his decision to present Tisza with the Black Eagle – the highest German order – while refraining from giving Taaffe any decoration at all, seemed to the emperor and Kálnoky monstrous. Nor were they impressed when Herbert Bismarck took the opportunity to preach the doctrine of spheres of influence in the Balkans. 'I know this is your father's idea', Franz Joseph told him, 'but I could never accept it in the past; and I must also reject it today.'[91]

In these circumstances, it was perhaps just as well that the Monarchy should look to its own defences. In the summer of 1888 the troop concentrations in Galicia were strengthened; and in April 1889 an Army Bill, envisaging the eventual doubling in size of the Common Army, was voted by both parliaments. True, this was not achieved without a struggle. There were people in Budapest who thought even the *Ausgleich* of 1867 a needless sacrifice of Hungary's liberty; and who regarded the creeping growth of the Common institutions as an even graver menace than the power of Russia. Thanks partly to the support of the German ambassador, Tisza eventually prevailed in parliament over what Kálnoky termed the 'radical rabble';[92] but he had to buy them off. To Beck's dismay the title of the Imperial General Staff was altered to 'Imperial and Royal' – a minor change, but another ominous sign of things to come. For the struggle over the Army Bill in Hungary marked the beginning of an instability in Hungarian politics that was seriously to weaken the Monarchy as a Great Power in the next decade. And it was to be the last Army Bill the government could extract from Budapest until 1912. For the present, however, the new law afforded proof enough that the Monarchy was firmly determined, as the German military attaché rather patronisingly put it, 'to become

91. Wagner, 'Kaiser Franz Joseph', p. 166.
92. Aehrenthal MSS, Karton 6, Kálnoky to Aehrenthal, 4 June 1888.

a real Great Power [*ebenbürtig zu werden*]'.[93]

Important though such efforts were, the fact remained that for a Great Power of the second rank such as Austria–Hungary, security depended even more on the international situation than on its own military capacity. It was only when the attitude of the Monarchy's chief ally, so disheartening in 1887–8, underwent a radical change in 1889 that the situation really improved – albeit only for a brief spell of about four years – and the Monarchy was able, perhaps for the last time in its existence, to maintain a deterrent posture against Russia with some confidence and with a fair amount of support from its friends and allies.

In the first place, Wilhelm II, whose effusive gestures had been rebuffed by the dour tsar, fell into an anti-Russian mood. He also became increasingly unwilling to listen to the Russophile Bismarck. In the second, with France paralysed by the aftermath of the Boulanger affair, it was Russia's military efforts in Poland that began to absorb the German military mind. In these circumstances, Franz Joseph's return visit to Berlin in July 1889 proved a tremendous success, surpassing even the Austrians' wildest hopes. True, Bismarck was not particularly forthcoming, refusing to lift the ban on pig imports from the Monarchy, and making tactless remarks about the growth of Slav influence in Austrian politics. But the Austrians could afford to ignore Bismarck, for the military conversations could not have gone better. Waldersee declared that Russia was definitely the chief enemy of Germany, which would evacuate Lorraine if necessary to finish the war in the east with all speed. More important still, the Germans now suddenly and enthusiastically adopted the Austrian view on the Alliance. The words of the war minister, Verdy du Vernois, to Beck – 'Your mobilisation will be for us the signal to come in with all we have got [*mit Allem einzusetzen*]'[94] – were perhaps nothing unusual from a military quarter. But now the Emperor Wilhelm himself declared: 'whatever reason you may have for mobilising, whether Bulgaria or anything else, the day of your mobilisation will be the day of mobilisation for my army, whatever the Chancellors [*die Kanzler*] may say'.[95]

The Austrians could hardly have wished for a more explicit assurance. Their only doubt was to its real value, coming from one so volatile as Wilhelm II, and at a time of growing political instability in Berlin. (Within a matter of months, for example, Verdy

93. Glaise-Horstenau, *Beck*, p. 330.
94. Ibid., p. 337.
95. Ibid., p. 338.

had been removed from the war ministry.) These misgivings account for the mixed feelings with which the news of the fall of the Bismarcks, in March 1890, was received at Vienna. The military, of course, were jubilant: 'Thank God we are rid of the whole family', Archduke Albrecht wrote to Beck.[96] Kálnoky, too, who had always been discouraged by the thought that the Bismarcks were really more Russian than Austrian in sympathy, noted with relief that there was now nobody with 'Russian feelings' in office at Berlin;[97] and he and Franz Joseph both hoped that Austria-Hungary might now be able to speak with more weight in the Alliance. Indeed, Franz Joseph lost no time in reminding Wilhelm II that the two German Powers must stand up to Russia, 'because then she always retreats'[98] – a dangerous lesson to have drawn from the recent Balkan crisis. Yet the question remained – and it was one that was to plague the Austrians for the next twenty-five years – how long Wilhelm II could be relied on to remain in one frame of mind. Certainly, at the Rohnstock manoeuvres, in September 1890, he again gave the Austrians his strong backing, but again only verbal backing, in the Near East. He agreed that a solution to the Straits question along the lines desired by Russia (viz. that Russia alone should gain a right of passage to and from the Mediterranean) was 'impossible';[99] and he endorsed the Austrian view that the question was one for Europe to handle. In the new year, however, the Austrians were much taken aback by the sudden and brutal dismissal of their old friend Waldersee and his replacement by the taciturn Schlieffen, who Archduke Albrecht feared was 'a slippery eel'.[100] For the time being, however, Schlieffen too continued to assure the Austrians that Russia remained Germany's chief enemy; and altogether, although the whims of Wilhelm II were hardly the best guarantee, it seemed that the Dual Alliance had gained considerably in effectiveness and importance.

The Triple Alliance experienced no such revival. Although Kálnoky recognised that for Germany the Alliance had acquired increased importance with the recovery of France in the middle eighties, he still felt that for the Monarchy Italy was only of interest as a link to Great Britain and for the diplomatic support she gave at Constantinople as a member of the Mediterranean Entente. As for

96. Ibid., p. 342.
97. Aehrenthal MSS, Karton 2, Kálnoky to Aehrenthal, 12 April 1890.
98. Wagner, 'Kaiser Franz Joseph', p. 175.
99. P.A. I/476, Liasse XXXIII/g, Szögyény to Goluchowski, very secret, 31 October 1896.
100. Glaise-Horstenau, *Beck*, p. 342.

the Triple Alliance, the Balkan clause was only a nuisance from the Austro-Hungarian point of view: all Vienna asked of the Italian ally was that she should refrain from harassing the Monarchy in a war with Russia. Hence whereas Germany, with her hopes of effective military aid from Italy, regarded the internal chaos in the kingdom with concern, the Austrians regarded it with aplomb, if not with satisfaction: 'the more uncomfortable Italy's domestic position is . . . the more secure we can feel'.[101] Above all, Kálnoky was determined not to be drawn by Italy into a war with France; and in the spring and summer of 1889 he firmly rejected Italian proposals (which enjoyed the support of Berlin) to reinforce the Triple Alliance with military and naval agreements.

Similarly, the alliances with Serbia and Romania showed no sign of developing into anything more than the narrowly monarchical agreements they had been from the start. Certainly, they still retained their importance in so far as they ensured that the rulers of those states would not actually join the Monarchy's enemies in the event of war; but Kálnoky had to be content with that. When King Milan of Serbia finally abdicated, despite the remonstrations of Vienna, in March 1889, the Austrians managed to establish tolerable relations with the regency that ruled for his thirteen-year-old son, despite its Russophile tendencies. At least it secured the preservation of the dynasty to the exclusion of more troublesome claimants; and it agreed to the prolongation of the Austro-Serbian treaty to 1895, for what it was worth. The Romanian alliance was for a time at a discount, owing to political instability in Bucharest, coupled with the timid king's refusal, despite Kálnoky's urgings, to renew the Alliance, to make it known to the leaders of both political parties, and to make the general drift of his policy clear to his people. Indeed, between 1889 and 1892 the Austro-Romanian alliance existed only by grace of the king, and had no foothold at all in the government. Things improved slightly with the renewal of the alliance in July 1892, which was followed by an Austro-Romanian commercial treaty which at last put an end to the long tariff war. The Monarchy gradually recovered its commercial position in Romania after this, although Germany, which had meanwhile established her position there, always remained a strong rival. On the irredentist front, however, there was no improvement. On the contrary, a *Liga Culturale* founded in 1891 was organising hatred of Hungary; and was helped in its task by a sensational trial of Romanian nationalists in Transylvania in 1894.

101. P.A. I/469, Kálnoky, memorandum, secret, July 1889.

Kálnoky did his best to keep the temperature low by paying no attention to complaints from either Bucharest or Budapest; but he only succeeded in displeasing both parties.

More important for the Monarchy's interests in the Near East than any paper alliances was its general political and economic influence in the area; and it was significant that Austria-Hungary's greatest success in these years was achieved in Bulgaria, a state with which she had no alliance at all. As Zwiedenek, head of the Eastern Department at the Ballhausplatz, insisted in March 1889, it was still 'of the utmost importance' to thwart Russian attempts to hinder Bulgaria's autonomous development; for a Bulgaria independent of Russia was 'the best guarantee against the success of Panslav and Great Serbian designs'.[102] He was, therefore, pleased to confirm that Kálnoky's policy of supporting the independent development of the Balkan states against Russia's attempts to establish her tutelage was meeting with success. The completion of the railway network to Constantinople in 1888 had strengthened Austria-Hungary's connections with the Balkan states, and her influence was growing. Altogether, 'the advancing development of the Balkan states forms an important obstacle to Russia's power-drive towards the west, and that is decidedly a success for our recent policy'.[103]

In Bulgaria itself Austria-Hungary still retained her commercial predominance, although her ruthless exploitation of what the Bulgarians regarded as an unequal treaty was often resented at Sofia. In the political field, there were still some obstacles to be overcome: Russia, assisted by France and Germany, had succeeded in convincing the sultan that Prince Ferdinand was an enemy who coveted Ottoman territory, and must not be accorded formal recognition as ruler. But even here, things changed markedly for the better when after the fall of Bismarck the Germans broke with his policy and started to support the Mediterranean Entente on Bulgarian questions: in July 1890 the four Powers together persuaded the sultan to give Ferdinand some satisfaction by appointing more Bulgarian bishops in Macedonia, to fortify the 'Bulgarian' Exarchist inhabitants against the propaganda of the Greek Patriarchate. At the same time Russia's persistent, and futile, efforts to embarrass the Bulgarian government by intriguing with its enemies at home were only grist to the Austro-Hungarian mill. In 1891 Franz Joseph graciously received the Bulgarian ruler in

---

102. Aehrenthal MSS, Karton 4, Zwiedenek to Aehrenthal, 15 August 1889.
103. Ibid., Zwiedenek to Aehrenthal, 28 March 1889.

Vienna; and Kálnoky blandly explained to the complaining Russians that 'little Ferdinand'[104] had been since his childhood a personal friend of the emperor. By the end of 1892 the Austrophile Stamboulov regime felt strong enough to abolish the stipulation in the constitution imposing the Orthodox religion on all rulers of Bulgaria after the first; and in January 1893 Ferdinand married the Catholic Marie Louise of Parma, who had Habsburg blood in her veins. By this time, the Russians were ready to wash their hands of Bulgaria. On the other hand, Kálnoky's assumption that, saving some catastrophe such as the assassination of Stamboulov, Russia would never be able to recover her influence in Bulgaria, was perhaps unduly sanguine. Although Austria-Hungary, assisted by her partners in the Mediterranean Entente, had succeeded in saving Bulgaria from Russian domination, she had been unable to secure what her protégé Ferdinand most craved – international recognition. That, only a change of heart in St Petersburg could secure. This fact was the Achilles' heel of the Austro-Hungarian position in Bulgaria.

That was a problem for the future. In 1891 the Monarchy still enjoyed the security of its *ententes*, and even – for what they were worth in terms of day-to-day diplomacy – of its alliances. In the spring, the Triple Alliance was renewed with less trouble than Kálnoky had expected. Although Crispi had had the alarming idea of amalgamating the three treaties of 1887 into one general treaty (which might have involved the Monarchy in commitments against France in North Africa) his successor Rudiní, in a weaker position at home, did not press the point. Although, when the Alliance was renewed on 6 May, the three treaties were inserted into one document – the Austro-Italian agreement on the Balkans duly becoming Article VII – they still remained distinct, and the Monarchy had thereby assumed only the most tenuous moral connection (being technically a signatory) with the Italo-German article on North Africa. It was to avoid assuming any further real commitments against France that Kálnoky in the summer again turned down an Italian suggestion for military and naval talks. It was to Great Britain that Italy should look for support in the Mediterranean, he said. He was, therefore, delighted when in June the British parliamentary under-secretary, Fergusson, acknowledged in the Commons that Great Britain had a common interest with Italy in maintaining the status quo in the Mediterranean; and he was even more encouraged by the resultant chorus of approval

---

104. Ibid., Karton 2, Kálnoky to Aehrenthal, 15 July 1891.

in the British press, declaring such open support from British public opinion to be worth far more than the secret declarations of a prime minister.[105]

In fact, the summer of 1891 saw something of a festival of the Triple Alliance and the Mediterranean Entente. Following on Fergusson's declaration came a flamboyant speech by Rudiní (29 June) proclaiming the renewal of the Triple Alliance and boasting of Italy's ties with Great Britain. Kálnoky thought this unduly sensational; but Franz Joseph himself had already caused a stir by going to Fiume to welcome a British squadron visiting the Adriatic; and King Umberto followed his example at Venice on 3 July. On the next day, Wilhelm II left for a ten-day visit to England. Nor was the western Mediterranean forgotten. The same month saw the settlement of an Anglo-Portuguese east African dispute, which Kálnoky, exercising his good offices at Salisbury's request, had been trying to smooth over. In fact, his good offices had consisted largely of urging the British to let Portugal down lightly. For if she were humiliated, and the monarchy fell, the monarchies of Spain and Italy would soon follow, and the international revolutionary parties (*Umstürzparteien*) would be correspondingly heartened to proceed against the great Germanic and Slav monarchies.[106] In April, Italy and Spain had extended the agreement of 1887 to include diplomatic co-operation to maintain the status quo against France in Morocco, and to this Kálnoky, ever keen to reinforce the influence of the Triple Alliance at Madrid, made haste to accede.

Nor was Kálnoky's confidence shaken when France and Russia, greatly disconcerted by the spectacular renewal of the Triple Alliance and the prospect of Great Britain's joining it, staged a counter-demonstration of solidarity in the form of the visit of a French squadron to Kronstadt at the end of July. Things would remain much the same, he calculated, when the smoke from this 'firework' had cleared.[107] After all, Russia had no reason to tie her hands *vis-à-vis* a France that could always be had for the asking; and the impending famine in Russia should at least give food for thought to any warmongers in St Petersburg. Indeed, Kálnoky advised a council of ministers at this time that it would be safe to reduce expenditure on armaments in order to balance the budget.[108] Similarly, he was content to bask in a policy of *quieta non movere* abroad. He showed no interest in German suggestions that the

105. P.A. I/461, Liasse XXIV/2, Kálnoky to Bruck, No. 1, secret, 22 June 1891.
106. P.A. VIII/172, Kálnoky to Deym, private, 21 March 1891.
107. Aehrenthal MSS, Karton 2, Kálnoky to Aehrenthal, 28 July 1891.
108. Ibid., Kálnoky to Aehrenthal, 19 October 1891.

sultan be initiated into the Mediterranean agreements: the Turks would only leak the agreements to France and Russia, who would then be spurred to even greater efforts at Constantinople. He was satisfied enough with the Mediterranean agreements as they stood – 'certain fundamental and general theoretical promises' – and he did not wish to enquire too closely into the exact extent to which they were binding, lest the British be moved to reduce it.[109] Salisbury's successor, Rosebery, for example, refused to read the agreements or put them before the Cabinet; but Vienna was still sanguine enough about the general diplomatic situation to be satisfied for the present with his rather less definite assurance that 'Anglo–Austrian relations must rest exclusively on reciprocal confidence'.[110]

Kálnoky's confidence was further increased when it at last proved possible in these years to bring the commercial policies of the allied Powers into line with their diplomatic commitments. This was, of course, only attainable once Bismarck, with his narrow diplomatic view of the alliances, was out of the way; and when Germany, Austria-Hungary's most important and most powerful trading partner, and still virtually the arbiter of her commercial policy, had had a change of heart. Caprivi's policy was designed partly to win the masses from socialism at home, by importing cheap food to lower the cost of living; and partly to reinforce the alliances by economic ties, with the ultimate objective of a central European customs union under German leadership. Hence, Caprivi lost no time in ending the commercial estrangement of Austria-Hungary, and between August 1890 and May 1891 negotiated a commercial treaty which from 1892 gave Austro-Hungarian agrarian exports increased access to the German market in return for a lowering of Austro-Hungarian tariffs on German industrial exports. The Monarchy in turn concluded treaties with Italy, Switzerland, Serbia and Belgium (1892); Romania (1894); and Japan (1896); and in 1897 forced Bulgaria to renew the 'unequal treaty' yet again. This plethora of treaties did not really mean a return to an era of free trade – many duties still remained high. But it was an improvement on the protectionist chaos of the autonomous tariff policy of the 1880s, and marked the start of a commercial armistice that lasted for the next ten years. For the Austrians, the political implications of the commercial treaties were undoubtedly of great importance. The Romanian and Italian treaties in particular – which, in the first case, subjected Hungarian agricul-

---

109. Jefferson, *Straits*, p. 87.
110. Ibid., p. 88.

ture, in the second, the Austrian wine industry, to severe competition – were notable examples of Kálnoky's willingness to sacrifice sectional economic interests to the strengthening of the alliances.

It is true that the commercial treaties did not lead to any spectacular boom in Austria-Hungary in the nineties. Although trade, particularly with Germany, increased, Austrian industry, already struggling to be competitive under the burden of what the founder of the Social Democratic Party described in 1891 as 'the best industrial worker legislation in the world'[111] (a burden from which the rival Hungarian industry was almost entirely free), now had to face severe German competition. Hungarian agriculture suffered even more severely from Serbian and Romanian competition – especially from the latter, when Hungary at last completed the navigation works on the Danube (1886–96). But, in general, the picture was healthy enough: the completion of the railway network to Constantinople furthered the Monarchy's Balkan trade – admittedly only about 6 per cent of the Monarchy's increased total trade – and the building of the Arlberg railway in 1896 gave a boost to Hungarian corn exports to the west. Moreover, particular industries enjoyed great prosperity – the Bohemian sugar-beet industry, for example, was by the 1890s producing one-fifth of the world supply; and years of crisis and tension, such as 1887 and 1888, were not without consolations for the iron and armaments industries. Besides, as general prosperity increased, government finance could be stabilised. The year 1888 saw the last of a long series of budget deficits; and after 1892 the government undertook a much-needed currency reform, and started buying up the remaining privately owned railways. In the 1890s Austrian government stock gradually became one of the most stable – though indeed hardly the most lucrative – commodities on the European exchange.

In the years 1889–92, therefore, the Monarchy was in a relatively strong position; and it is hardly surprising that these years saw no attempt to catch a rather questionable bird in the bush in the form of a *rapprochement* with Russia. True, there might have been a chance of success: the tsar and Giers certainly desired peace; and Russia's economic weakness (especially after the great famine of 1891–2) left her with little enough to spare to buy influence or undertake adventures in the Balkans. Even Russian public opinion, tiring of perpetual humiliations in Bulgaria, was beginning to concern itself with Russia's national interests elsewhere, particularly in the Far East. From Bucharest, Aehrenthal, who had made his career in

---

111. H. Benedikt, *Die wirtschaftliche Entwicklung in der Franz-Joseph-Zeit*, p. 131.

St Petersburg in the heyday of the Three Emperors' Alliance, pleaded with his chief to seek a *rapprochement* with Russia and to beware of German intrigues to foment ill will between Vienna and St Petersburg. But Kálnoky was sceptical. Russia's apparent retreat might not be permanent, he observed in June 1888; and Austria-Hungary must look to her armaments. Aehrenthal was sternly informed that there was simply no basis for a *rapprochement* with Russia, whose ultimate aims in Bulgaria were completely opposed to those of Austria-Hungary. This was also the emperor's view. When, in September 1890, a Russian diplomat was reported as saying that Russia would await an Austrian approach benevolently, but 'with proud reserve', he commented, 'then they can wait a long time';[112] and when, in the following year, the Russian press professed to discern signs that Austro-Hungarian policy was becoming more conciliatory towards Russia, Franz Joseph was most emphatic: 'I know absolutely nothing about a change in our policy.'[113] The general brandishing of diplomatic instruments in the summer of 1891 actually deepened the Austro-Russian estrangement; but Kálnoky trusted to the impending famine – 'may God continue to help' – to keep Russia in order.[114]

God did not help for much longer. The year 1893 was a bad one for Austria-Hungary, and was marked by a severe deterioration of the political situation in both halves of the Monarchy. In Hungary, where calm had never been really restored since the crisis over the Army Bill, the government was facing increasing opposition from magnates, clericals, and a motley collection of radical elements over such contentious issues as a civil marriage law. And this was personally embarrassing for Kálnoky himself, a notable clerical, and already in some ill favour at Budapest on account of his allegedly obsequious attitude towards Romania. In Austria, the stability of the Taaffe years was coming to an end as the prime minister's electoral reform proposals, designed to cut the ground from under the factious bourgeois nationalist parties by giving more weight to Christian Social and Social Democrat votes, alienated his conservative supporters. Kálnoky, too, was firmly opposed to anything that would strengthen Social Democracy; and his intervention – in the form of a complaint to Franz Joseph – was very probably a major factor in bringing Taaffe down (October 1893). As it was, however, Taaffe was followed by a succession of weak governments which for the rest of the nineties strove in vain

112. Wagner, 'Kaiser Franz Joseph', p. 186.
113. Ibid.
114. Aehrenthal MSS, Karton 2, Kálnoky to Aehrenthal, 15 July 1891.

to compose the increasingly violent quarrels of German, Czech and South Slav. This internal weakening of the Monarchy was accompanied by a serious deterioration in its military and international position after the end of 1892. The previous four years had been nothing more than an Indian summer.

It was in the military field that the Austrians felt the first tremors of the instability prevailing in Berlin. They had never found either Caprivi or Schlieffen particularly communicative – the Waldersee era was well and truly over. In August 1892 Schlieffen, who had little faith in the military capacity of Austria-Hungary, and did not wish German planning to depend too closely on that Power, began to shift the centre of gravity of German planning towards the western front. He had decided, as Russia steadily built up her armaments, that it would be impossible to defeat her in a quick war. Therefore, the only hope of salvation lay in a lightning strike against France. Consequently, the war in the east would become for Germany – at least in the opening stages – very much a side-show; and the Austrians would have to cope as best they could. This bomb-shell burst in Vienna at the end of 1892. For the time being, Beck kept his nerve and decided not to change his plans; but the future certainly gave cause for concern. As Kálnoky reminded a conference of ministers on 2 February 1893,[115] the military situation was becoming distinctly threatening; the Central Powers, who needed time to mobilise their civilian conscript armies, lived daily under the menace of Russia's huge professional army standing ready to strike at any moment; and with Germany concentrating so heavily on the west, Austria-Hungary would now have to do more in the east. Beck's figures showed that, despite the Army Bill, the Monarchy was not keeping pace with the other Powers. More should be done, and not only for the Common Army; the Austrian Landwehr was in a dreadful state and the Hungarian Honvéds existed only on paper. It was depressing, however, that his pleas made no impression on the cheese-paring Austrian and – particularly – Hungarian governments.

In the summer of 1893 came another surprise from Berlin, when Schlieffen decided that in the event of war the Germans would not attempt a thrust eastwards into north Poland, but would march south to join the Austro-Hungarian army. The Austrians, who had still been hoping to carry out their part of the original Austro-German pincer movement, did not like the new plan at all – especially as it threatened the draw the whole weight of Russia's

---

115. P.A. XL/296, Ministerratsprotokoll, 2 February 1893.

forces southwards on to Austria-Hungary. But Beck accepted even this. Two years later, however, Schlieffen changed his plans for a third time. In May 1895 he informed the bewildered Beck that the Germans would not now move south, but would make a small eastwards thrust into north Poland; and he suggested that the Austrians take on virtually the whole Russian army by means of a three-pronged offensive which would extend their left flank as far as Prussian Silesia. Beck was aghast, and insisted that such a hazardous dividing of the Monarchy's forces just did not bear contemplation. He pleaded with Schlieffen to stand at least by the plan of 1893; but he made no impression.[116] In terms of military planning the Dual Alliance had reverted to the position that had prevailed before 1882.

These highly unsatisfactory developments were accompanied by a sudden deterioration in the diplomatic situation, which caused a crisis of confidence in both the Triple Alliance and the Mediterranean Entente. In October 1893 Franco-Russian solidarity was startlingly demonstrated to the world in a spectacular visit by the Russian fleet to Toulon; and this was accompanied by rumours that Russia intended to establish a permanent squadron in the Mediterranean. The sultan was tremendously impressed; and by November Calice was reporting that France and Russia had once more gained the upper hand at Constantinople. To make matters worse Germany, dismayed by the growing solidarity of France and Russia and anxious not to provoke them, was becoming lukewarm in her support of the Mediterranean Entente at Constantinople. In Kálnoky's view,[117] the whole Mediterranean balance was now at stake, for Great Britain, confronted with such an imposing display of French and Russian power, might abandon the Mediterranean. It would not then be long before Italy, plagued with social and economic problems and in a state of 'collapse' since the Toulon visit, submitted to the threats and blandishments of France. With Great Britain and Italy gone, and Germany lukewarm, Austria-Hungary would be virtually isolated in the Near East.

In January 1894, therefore, Kálnoky instructed Deym in London to find out whether Great Britain would stand firm against Russia in the Mediterranean.[118] Of recent years, he explained, Russia had

---

116. Glaise-Horstenau, *Beck*, pp. 347–350, 377–9; G. Ritter, 'Die Zusammenarbeit der Generalstäbe Deutschlands und Oesterreich-Ungarns vor dem ersten Weltkrieg', in *Zur Geschichte und Problematik der Demokratie* (Berlin 1958), pp. 531–4.
117. P.A. VIII/174, Kálnoky to Szögyény, private and secret, 10 December 1893.
118. Ibid., Kálnoky to Deym, No. 1, secret, 25 January 1894.

shifted her pressure from Bulgaria to Constantinople and the Straits; and hence it was now Great Britain which was in the front line. Austria-Hungary still preferred to stand alongside Great Britain and Italy to resist Russia; but if Great Britain were to withdraw and allow Russia to have control of the Straits, Austria-Hungary too would retreat and secure her own immediate interests in the Balkan peninsula. Rosebery was not unforthcoming, and said that, if Constantinople were at stake, Great Britain would certainly not shrink from war with Russia. However, she could not cope alone with Russia and France combined, and he therefore asked for an assurance that the Triple Alliance would keep France neutral.

For this, Kálnoky had to appeal to Berlin – which he did with some apprehension. His misgivings were justified. The Germans were not only anxious to humour Russia, but almost obsessed with the fear that Great Britain, once the war started against France and Russia, would retreat to her island, leaving the Triple Alliance in the lurch. They therefore refused to give the required assurance; Great Britain must first show her seriousness of purpose by striking the first blow. They talked of allowing Russia to have Constantinople, and advised Kálnoky to secure compensation in the Balkans by means of a deal with St Petersburg. Worse was to come. In June the Germans tried to humour France too, and joined her in forcing the British to abandon a Congo treaty they had just concluded with King Leopold. This moved Rosebery to utter a chilling warning to Deym: 'If Germany continues to show herself so hostile to the Cabinet of St James I shall feel obliged to take back the assurances which I have given on the subject of Constantinople.'[119] In the event, he did not take them back; and all in all Kálnoky's soundings had evoked at least a promise of armed resistance to Russia, and of diplomatic support if France and Russia tried to raise the Straits question with the sultan. Kálnoky's policy, therefore, continued on course: diplomatic co-operation with Great Britain. In the Austrian view, the crisis of 1893–4 had shown that the *entente* with Great Britain, despite its limitations, could still serve Austro-Hungarian interests well enough. It had also shown that, so far as Austro-Hungarian interests in the Near East were concerned, the alliance with Germany was, at the most favourable estimate, useless. Much the same could be said of that with Italy, where Crispi since his return to power in December 1893 was becoming increasingly absorbed in a search for prestige in East Africa, and had even joined

---

119. H.W.V. Temperley and Lillian M. Penson, *Foundations of British Foreign Policy* (Cambridge 1938), p. 492.

the Germans against Great Britain in their disastrous campaign against the Congo treaty.

It was Germany who was causing the Austrians the most concern, however. With the *Neue Kurs*, Vienna had managed to interest her in the Eastern Question; but now, Kálnoky feared, she had reverted to Bismarck's policy of leaving the defence of Constantinople and the Straits to others. In December 1893 he lamented[120] the general aimlessness (*Zerfahrenheit*) that prevailed in the Wilhelmstraße: Caprivi had no understanding of foreign affairs, and Marschall no experience; and as a result 'the *Neue Kurs* has no policy at all', especially not in the Eastern Question. When his approach to Berlin failed in the spring of 1894 he characterised Germany's attitude as 'the worst feature' of the whole situation.[121] Of course, he understood Germany's great fear of a war with France and Russia; but if Russia were allowed to establish herself in the Mediterranean, that could only make matters even worse. Reports that Schlieffen, and even Wilhelm II himself, had said that Germany would not object if Russia seized Constantinople filled him with dismay; and he bitterly observed that this was in flagrant contradiction to the promises the Germans had made at the Rohnstock manoeuvres in 1890.[122] Indeed, German policy was now even more disastrous than it had been under Bismarck.[123] Although Bismarck had given Austria-Hungary no support in Bulgaria, he had at least helped her to win British support; and he had had too much sense actually to promote the preponderance of Russia in the Mediterranean. Now, the Germans seemed to be trying to frustrate Austria-Hungary's efforts in London. This was dangerous: whereas Austria-Hungary had been compelled by her own vital interests to stand guard in the Balkans whatever Germany did, Great Britain was by no means compelled to stay in the Mediterranean (and there were enough radicals in Great Britain urging a *rapprochement* with Russia and peace at any price). Moreover, if Great Britain abandoned the Mediterranean, it would not be long before Italy would be forced to come into line with France. The European balance was at stake, Kálnoky insisted; and the Germans should realise that it was only in this context, after all, that such issues as the Straits – and Alsace-Lorraine and Bosnia and the Herzegovina as well – were of any importance.[124] But his pleadings fell on deaf ears in Berlin; as

120. P.A. VIII/174, Kálnoky to Szögyény, private and secret, 29 December 1893.
121. Ibid., Kálnoky to Deym, No. 3, secret, 19 February 1894.
122. P.A. I/468, Kálnoky to Szögyény, No. 3, secret, 27 February 1894.
123. Ibid.
124. P.A. VIII/174, Kálnoky to Szögyény, very confidential, 21 March 1894.

did Franz Joseph's attempts at Abbazia in March 1894 to convince Wilhelm II of the threat to the balance of power. Wilhelm's vague and effusive protestations of loyalty 'as a true ally' only exasperated Kálnoky in turn: 'such general phrases do not really have any place in a serious discussion of great political questions'.[125]

Kálnoky's concern about Germany's efforts to blunt the edge of the Franco-Russian *rapprochement* by cultivating St Petersburg was intensified, in that unhappy winter of 1893/4, by the news that Germany and Russia had at last reached agreement on a commercial treaty. Commercial negotiations between the Monarchy and Russia, by contrast, had made no progress in the face of the opposition of the Austrian and Hungarian governments – especially the latter – to Russia's demands for a reduction in the rye duty. On 4 March 1894 Kálnoky seized the initiative, and summoned a special conference of the Austrian and Hungarian ministers to impress on them the need for agreement with Russia. Not only would it be generally desirable in the interests of peace, he argued,[126] to establish tolerable commercial relations with Russia for a decade or so; the developing Russo-German *rapprochement* meant that there was actual danger in delay. For Germany now had no quarrel with Russia; whereas the conflicting interests of Austria-Hungary and Russia could lend serious dimensions to any incident that might crop up – say in Bulgaria. 'Without expressing any lack of confidence in Germany's loyalty as an ally', he wryly observed, 'a state of cordiality between Germany and Russia on the one hand, and a state of bitterness resulting from a tariff war between Russia and ourselves on the other, would put us in a very unfavourable, if not dangerous position.' A failure to conclude a treaty would therefore be very bad for 'the most vital interests of Austria-Hungary'. He insisted on a more flexible attitude. On 7 March the treaty was finally concluded.

Kálnoky could congratulate himself on having staved off the danger of isolation in the face of a threatening Russo-German alignment; and he calculated that, good commercial relations having been established for ten years with Russia, tension would be reduced and a generally more friendly atmosphere created. But, as he observed on 21 March, he did not expect this to lead to any real change in Russia's policy. In the event, relations with Russia improved steadily for the rest of the year. In the first place, the Mediterranean scare faded away during the summer, and Russia

---

125. Ibid., Kálnoky to Szögyény, No. 1, 20 April 1894.
126. P.A. XL/296, Ministerratsprotokoll, 4 March 1894.

continued to display an almost ostentatious restraint in the Balkans. In the second, one of the great obstacles to any *rapprochement* with Russia, Hungarian public opinion, was undergoing a change in the early nineties.[127] Not only were the Magyars becoming increasingly and passionately preoccupied with domestic politics, but the generation that had experienced the trauma of 1849 was passing away (Andrássy had died in 1890). True, Hungarian opinion was still very much on the defensive; but Russia seemed to have stopped inciting the Balkan states against the Monarchy, and even Andrássy had held that the Slavs could only be a serious threat if Russia supported them. By the summer of 1894, therefore, there was generally more willingness in Vienna and Budapest to consider at least an accommodation with Russia.

It was at this juncture that the Russians took a positive step towards a *rapprochement*.[128] When, at the beginning of 1894, the chaos in Serbia developed to the point where the regents declared the constitution suspended, Giers seems to have feared that Vienna might be tempted to intervene. On 5 May, therefore, he appealed to Kálnoky: Austria-Hungary and Russia, he proposed, should agree on a policy of non-intervention, and should not let the Serbian crisis trouble their 'relations de confiance et d'amitié'. In return, Russia would abstain from interfering in Bulgaria. This suited Kálnoky well enough – after all, he was being asked to say nothing that he had not said before. He assured Giers, therefore, that he would certainly not depart from the principle of non-intervention (with the usual rider, 'sans y être forcés dans l'intérêt de notre sécurité'); and he too expressed the hope that Austro-Russian relations would continue to improve. The Austrians were, in fact, genuinely gratified: Russia had at last accepted their principles of non-intervention and the maintenance of the status quo. Admittedly, no formal agreement had been concluded; and the bare principle of non-intervention was strictly negative. There had been no return to Reichstadt, or even to the Three Emperors' Alliance, which had envisaged certain changes in the status quo. Nevertheless, summing up a year later, Aehrenthal remarked that it was at this point that Russia and Austria-Hungary had 'found their way back to an agreement in principle to treat the maintenance of peace, a vital interest, as more important than their own rivalries or the teething-troubles [*Kinderkrankheiten*] of the Balkan peoples'. To this extent, the Austro-Russian Entente, usually associated with the

127. I. Diószegi, 'Einige Bemerkungen zur Frage der österreichisch-ungarischen Außenpolitik', in Klein, *Weltpolitik*, pp. 240ff.
128. P.A. I/469, Aehrenthal Memorandum 1895.

name of Goluchowski, could already be discerned on the horizon – at least as a possibility – in Kálnoky's last year of office.

Not that the Austrians yet felt confident enough to lower their guard against Russia. Even the death, in November 1894, of their old opponent Alexander III was no unmixed blessing: the new tsar was an unknown quantity, and for Kálnoky, 'what is incalculable is always unwelcome to a foreign minister'.[129] The military, with a duty, of course, to prepare for the worst, were always inclined to look on the dark side, as Beck's memorandum of 18 December [130] bore witness: although the forces of the Central Powers were superior in quality to those of Russia, the latter had a superiority of numbers. In war, therefore, it would be a question of somehow dividing Russia's forces without dividing those of the Monarchy. Other Powers, such as Great Britain, Turkey, Bulgaria and Sweden might be of some assistance here. It is striking that none of the Monarchy's allies figured in Beck's calculations. Romania could not be relied on – according to Beck's information, the Russians even expected Romanian support. As for German and Italian cover, Beck was resigned to the prospect that this 'will become less and less effective'. Indeed, the whole memorandum was a remarkable comment on the insignificant role of the Monarchy's allies, Germany, Italy, Romania and Serbia, in Austro-Hungarian military planning. Of course, Beck was trying to convince the Austrian and Hungarian governments that the only sure guarantee was the Monarchy's own strength, and that there was a need for a new Army Bill. But in the view of the increasingly difficult parliamentary situation in both halves of the Monarchy, there was virtually no hope of this.

The civilian authorities took an equally sceptical view of the value of the alliances at the end of 1894, and on 30 November Kálnoky took the German ambassador, Eulenburg, roundly to task:[131] although a new era might have dawned, in which peaceful rivalry would be the keynote of international relations, it was no less important for success to keep alliances and friendships in good repair. Germany's policy, therefore, was disturbing: there seemed to be no guiding hand in Berlin; and junior officials could not make high policy, no matter how clever they might be. Germany's display of hostility to Great Britain in colonial questions was jeopardising the Monarchy's relations with the latter Power; and

---

129. Aehrenthal MSS, Karton 2, Kálnoky to Aehrenthal, 31 August 1894.
130. P.A. I/466, Beck, Memorandum on the general military situation, 18 December 1894.
131. P.A. VIII/174, Kálnoky to Szögyény, Nos. 1 and 2, 30 November 1894.

this, given Italy's dependence on Great Britain, was weakening the whole Triple Alliance. He castigated the spiteful tone of the German press towards Great Britain – its making fun of her abortive efforts to mediate in the Sino-Japanese War, for example – and observed with some acuity that the worst aspect of all this was the disastrous long-term effect it must have on British public opinion. Germany should not underestimate the danger of estranging Great Britain: some people in the Liberal party there wanted peace at any price, and would even come to terms with France and Russia to get it. It was highly dangerous for Germany to imagine that she could isolate Great Britain 'and force her to recognise Germany as a colonial equal'.[132] In all this, Kálnoky was certainly more far-sighted than those who, like Szögyény in Berlin or Aehrenthal in Bucharest,[133] shared the German view that Great Britain's differences with France and Russia were too vast ever to admit of a settlement. But the awkward fact remained that the Dual Alliance had never given the Monarchy any control over Germany's day-to-day policy, and Kálnoky was in the last resort helpless to do anything about it.

The fact that by the following spring Kálnoky was able to take an altogether calmer view of the international scene was due less to any renewal of confidence in the Monarchy's allies, than to an improvement in the general situation and the continuance of the *détente* with Russia. In April 1895 the appointment of Lobanov, the long-standing Russian ambassador to Vienna, to succeed Giers at the Foreign Office was a blessing the Austrians had hardly dared to hope for. On 17 April Kálnoky drew the attention of the council of ministers to the general reduction in tension,[134] which he attributed to the determination of all monarchs to avoid war and the shocks it would administer to the social order, and to the preoccupation of the other European Powers with Asian and African questions. True, Russia was increasing her armaments; but the Monarchy should try to counter this by improving the quality, rather than the quantity of its forces. In fact, he now found the general situation so satisfactory that he was even prepared to recommend a reduction in the armaments budget.

On this occasion, Kálnoky even seemed unperturbed by the deficiencies of the Monarchy's alliances. Serbia might be completely rotten, but she was isolated and hardly able to harm the Monarchy (the *détente* with Russia helped here). Romania too was a

132. Ibid., Kálnoky to Szögyény, No. 4, 30 November 1894.
133. Aehrenthal MSS, Karton 3, Szögyény to Aehrenthal, 8 December 1894.
134. P.A. XL/297, Ministerratsprotokoll, 17 April 1895.

harmless neighbour, even if, thanks to irredentism, an uncomfortable one. But he urged his Hungarian listeners to try to smooth over any incidents that might crop up, and to be thankful that the Bucharest government was at least outwardly correct. The Italian ally was in exceedingly poor shape – commercially and financially ruined and politically shattered – but this need not disturb Austro-Italian relations. After all, the Monarchy's relations with all the other Great Powers were 'excellent'. This being the case, the internal troubles of Turkey need not cause any great concern: the Great Powers were determined not to be misled by Christian propaganda campaigns into interfering in Macedonia; and as for the growing complaints of the Armenians, in respect of which the British had been keeping him closely informed of their dealings with France and Russia, the Monarchy could be well content to leave this problem to the three Powers most concerned.

The state of the alliances was, in fact, a good deal less happy than Kálnoky was prepared to admit openly. In the first place, the informal agreement of 1887 between the Triple Alliance Powers and Spain, renewed in 1891, was on the verge of collapse; and this threatened to have repercussions on the Mediterranean Entente generally. Since the end of 1894 Italy, with German support, had been trying to bully the Spaniards, on pain of non-renewal, into openly declaring their position by publishing the agreement. Kálnoky disapproved entirely, and urged Rome and Berlin to leave well alone:[135] the Triple Alliance should be trying to make friends in Spain, and to strengthen the hands of the monarchists and the Habsburg queen regent; all this bullying could only play into the hands of the French ambassador at Madrid. It was no wonder that Great Britain was becoming reserved either, when she saw Germany and Italy treating Spain in this way. But his warnings made scant impression in either Rome or Berlin. In fact, the atmosphere within the Triple Alliance was, by the spring of 1895, altogether deplorable. Italy was trying to amend the alliance to bind her Allies to more positive support of her designs in Tripoli. This the Central Powers turned down flat. The Alliance was an insurance company, Berlin declared, not a joint stock venture.[136] Indeed, for Kálnoky, above all anxious lest Italy's ambitions drag the Monarchy into war with France, it was hardly even that. He was intensely irritated[137] by a whining list of complaints from the Italian foreign office,

135. P.A. I/463, Liasse XXVI, Kálnoky to Bruck, secret, 11 January 1895; to Szögyény, secret, 23 March 1895.
136. Pribram, *Secret Treaties*, II, p. 104, n. 228.
137. P.A. I/470, Kálnoky to Szögyény, No. 55, secret, 23 March 1895.

according to which all the Powers of Europe were abetting France against Italy; and when the Germans tried to put in a word for Italy he finally lost patience. He now dismissed[138] even the German argument that the Alliance was valuable to the Monarchy as a guarantee against the irredentist threat. True, the cover Italy offered was of some use; and the Alliance had a certain moral value. But Italy was in no state to present a threat to the Monarchy: one had only to look at her – her internal collapse and her total lack of statesmen. Indeed, he concluded, Italy's defection would not be that much of a disaster for the Monarchy.

Nor had the Romanian alliance much to offer. The Austrians accepted the German view that it would never be of much practical value in war unless it was supplemented in advance by a military convention; but they felt that there was not the slightest hope of persuading Romania to strengthen the alliance in this way so long as feeling there was running so high against Hungary. Indeed, the Austro-Hungarian legation at Bucharest was, by the spring of 1895, becoming seriously alarmed at the ill feeling aroused by the magyarisation of Transylvania: unless Vienna intervened to restrain the Hungarian nationalists 'there will be a serious row here sooner or later'.[139] The Hungarians, for their part, insisted that irredentism spreading from Romania was the cause, not the symptom of the disease, and that the remedy lay in Kálnoky's taking a stern line with the government at Bucharest. Already in 1893 this attitude had helped to drive Goluchowski to give up his post in despair; and it was to be a contributory factor to Kálnoky's sudden resignation on 15 May.

Pusillanimity in dealing with Romanian irredentism had been the theme of a guerrilla campaign against Kálnoky in the Hungarian press since 1894. But already for some years he had been increasingly disheartened by the deepening domestic confusion inside the Monarchy. It was the old problem, and the one which had at first made him shrink from taking office in 1881, namely, that it was intolerable for a foreign minister to see his policies obstructed by domestic problems over which the constitution of 1867 denied him any control. Since the early nineties he had been dismayed by the growth of more intransigent varieties of Hungarian and Czech nationalism. The meetings of the Delegations tended to drag on endlessly while these parties ranted and raged about matters which, in Kálnoky's view, were not the fault of the Common Ministers at

---

138. Ibid., Kálnoky to Szögyény, private and very confidential, 4 April 1895.
139. Aehrenthal MSS, Karton 5, Welsersheimb to Aehrenthal, 28 February 1895.

all.[140] (It should be said, however, that he was himself a staunch defender of the Dualism that was in a sense the root cause of the nationalist fury, in so far as it ratified the supremacy of the Magyars in Hungary, and of the cosmopolitan aristocracy and – socially at least – the Germans in Austria.) In 1895, however, Kálnoky came under attack from even the relatively moderate government faction in Hungary, when a quarrel blew up between Budapest and the contumacious papal nuncio, Agliardi, who had launched a campaign against the Hungarian government's civil marriage bill. A few tactless remarks soon served to bring Kálnoky, a notorious clerical, into deep disgrace at Budapest; and when the prime minister attacked him openly he suddenly resigned.

As he wrote later, he could have defended himself in the Delegations; but, a strict conservative to the last, he felt that the sight of the minister for foreign affairs standing up and contradicting the Hungarian prime minister in public debate would have been nothing less than a scandal. He thought it especially unfortunate that there was no strong government in Austria to keep the Hungarian politicians in order: 'the gang need watching'.[141] Certainly, he had fallen victim to the growing intensity of national feeling in Hungary – even the government had to play to the gallery. And after all, as was to be demonstrated again eleven years later, Hungary's position under the dual constitution was so strong that no foreign minister could long survive once Budapest was really determined to get rid of him. Kálnoky, for his part, was glad to be out of the fray; and he retired to live as a country squire on his estate at Prodlitz in Bohemia. 'There is such a *fin de siècle* air about politics, I can hardly bear to watch', he wrote to his friend Aehrenthal in May 1896.[142] And although Franz Joseph appointed him to the house of peers in 1897, he thought this a bore, and said he would attend as little as possible.[143] Still, after years of hard work at the Ballhausplatz (unlike Andrássy, he wrote most of his own dispatches, in a painstaking, cramped hand) he found it difficult to adjust to life at Prodlitz, and his last years until his death in 1898 were spent in melancholy loneliness. The great ones he had served for so long soon forgot about him – his sister was extremely bitter about this, and asked Aehrenthal to put on record 'the shameful way in which he was treated after his retirement . . . The thanks of

140. Ibid., Karton 2, Kálnoky to his brother, 21 May 1895.
141. Ibid., Kálnoky to Aehrenthal, 11 June 1895.
142. Ibid., Kálnoky to Aehrenthal, 3 May 1896.
143. Ibid., Kálnoky to Aehrenthal, 27 May 1897.

the House of Austria should go down as a fearful warning for future generations.'[144]

The House of Austria certainly owed something of a debt to Kálnoky, even if, as usual in the case of servants it had once discarded, it did not pay it. He had steered the Monarchy through fourteen anxious years, and seemed in the end to have dispelled the most dangerous of the threats to it – encirclement by a ring of Russian satellites in the south. And this result was due, at least in part, to his own determination, hard work, and patient diplomacy. On assuming office, he had been prepared to work through the alliance system he had inherited, centred – in matters of day-to-day diplomacy at least, and failing the catastrophe of a general war – on the Three Emperors' Alliance. When, at the time of the Skobelev affair, the latter seemed to be failing, he had strengthened the Monarchy's position by securing cover from Italy, through the Triple Alliance, and from Romania; and had reinforced the Dual Alliance with a military understanding. But he still preferred to seek a diplomatic solution to the problem of encirclement by working within the Three Emperors' Alliance – as he showed at Skiernewice and in the Bulgarian crises of 1885 and 1886. By 1887 this policy had failed. The Three Emperors' Alliance lay in ruins; and the glaring inadequacy in diplomacy of the other alliances, designed for use in war, seemed to leave the Monarchy dangerously exposed. This was hardly Kálnoky's fault. The Dual Alliance could never be of much use in defending the Monarchy's Near Eastern interests by diplomacy so long as Bismarck held to his narrow interpretation of it and preached the facile and unrealistic doctrine of spheres of influence in the Balkans. And the decline of the Monarchy's Balkan alliances was perhaps inevitable, given the underlying economic and political conflicts between Magyar chauvinism and Serbian and Romanian irredentism. In the event, Kálnoky was resourceful enough to devise other means of safe-guarding the Monarchy's position. The Mediterranean Entente of 1887 served Austria-Hungary well, and with the menace of a Russian-controlled Bulgaria apparently dispelled, she could face the future with more confidence – all the more so as it at last proved possible after 1889 to reinvigorate the Dual Alliance and to re-inforce it with economic and military agreements. But the year 1893 showed that the Monarchy was not Atlas, but Sisyphus. Germany slipped away again, and a worsening international situation was compounded by the start of a long period of political

144. Ibid., Karton 4, Christina Thun to Aehrenthal, 28 December 1898.

instability inside the Monarchy. Again, Kálnoky was resilient enough to meet the situation. He struck the right note of informal co-operation in cultivating Great Britain (although he found his partners in the Triple Alliance a hindrance rather than a help in this); and at the same time he made an important contribution, by his handling of commercial and Balkan questions, to establishing a *modus vivendi* with Russia. For more than ten years after his fall the continental Powers were not confronted with any great crisis threatening an actual outbreak of war, such as might have activated the Monarchy's alliances; and the latter continued their decline. However, Kálnoky had bequeathed to his successor two other diplomatic instruments, rudimentary as yet, it is true, and ultimately incompatible, but either of which might be developed into an effective means of safeguarding the Monarchy's interests – the *entente* with Great Britain and the *détente* with Russia. It remained to be seen to which of the two his successor would turn.

Between Deterrence and *Detente*: the End of the Mediterranean Entente, 1895–1897

As Kálnoky's successor, Franz Joseph chose Agenor Count Goluchowski the younger, a rich Polish aristocrat and son of the author of the shortlived conservative-federalist constitution of October 1860. After serving for some seven years as a popular Austro-Hungarian minister at Bucharest, but finding his admonitions about the handling of Romania ignored at Budapest, Goluchowski had withdrawn from the diplomatic service in 1893 to live the life of a great provincial nobleman on his Galician estates. He was certainly sensitive where his vanity was concerned. No pushing career diplomat he: indeed, he was if anything easy-going to a fault, as his methods of work, or rather, lack of them, at the Ballhausplatz were to show. Nevertheless, some of his colleagues[145] found his bonhomie, tact, sincerity and charm a pleasing contrast to the 'frosty aristocratic manner' of his predecessor, and to the 'dry bureaucratic tone' of his successor. His geniality in handling the prickly Delegations was especially felicitous; and despite his 'Romanian heart' he managed to remain in favour at Budapest for ten years. The Magyar onslaught on Kálnoky proved, in fact, to have been a spontaneous outburst rather than a move in a sustained campaign to seize control of foreign policy. It was never followed

145. Hohenbalken, *Lützow*, p. 76.

up – all the more so as Franz Joseph issued a stern reminder to Budapest that the appointment of the minister for foreign affairs rested entirely within the prerogative of the Crown. And with Goluchowski, whom he came to call his 'Minister vom angenehmen Äußeren'[146] the emperor remained long content.

The new appointment was not universally popular abroad. True, Goluchowski was *persona gratissima* in France, whither he was wont to retire for most of the summer to the family estates of his wife – to the great annoyance of the Ballhausplatz officials, who had then to refer all important business by telegraph to Vittel. But as a notable ultramontane he was suspect at Rome; and as a Pole, at Berlin and St Petersburg. Admittedly, his views on foreign policy were conservative enough. As his father's son, he was always acutely conscious of the complexities of the domestic situation in the Monarchy, and always regarded a quietist foreign policy as the best palliative (in contrast to the vigorous exercise later prescribed by Aehrenthal and Conrad). Like Kálnoky, he abjured all thought of territorial expansion, or even any attempt to develop the *détente* with Russia in a positive, ambitious direction – for example, by finally carving up the Balkans into spheres of influence. In Goluchowski's view, a Russia established in Constantinople would exercise an irresistible attraction over the Orthodox subjects of the Monarchy, and this must be prevented at all costs. Indeed, the transition from Kálnoky to Goluchowski was initially marked by a distinct shift towards a more negative attitude to Russia. To Kálnoky, watching anxiously from the wings, it seemed by the autumn of 1895 that 'we could easily get back into the track of hostility towards Russia'.[147] He was dismayed to learn, during a visit to Vienna, that Beck and the military were pressing for further troop concentrations in Galicia as a counterweight to Russia's growing armaments – a futile gesture that could only anger St Petersburg to no purpose. He tried to stiffen Goluchowski to resist: to allow the military a voice in politics would indeed be 'to make the goat the gardener'.[148] But he found the minister himself strongly of the view that Russia was planning for war within two years. It certainly seemed that, of the two embryonic policies Goluchowski had inherited from Kálnoky, it would not be the *détente* with Russia that would be developed.

---

146. This is a play on the words 'Minister der Äußeren Angelegenheiten' (Minister for external affairs) and 'Minister vom angenehmen Äußeren' (Minister of pleasant external appearance).
147. Aehrenthal MSS, Karton 2, Kálnoky to Aehrenthal, 27 October 1895.
148. Ibid.

On the contrary, the striking feature of Goluchowski's first two years of office was the tenacity with which the minister, in the face of growing pressure both at home and abroad for an accommodation with Russia, clung stubbornly to a policy of deterrence based on the Mediterranean Entente. In the summer of 1895, for example, Salisbury's public criticisms of the sultan's government, and somewhat exaggerated reports from Berlin of his casual remarks about a possible partition of Turkey, had caused a stir in Austrian diplomatic circles. From Bucharest, Aehrenthal warned[149] of the hazards of relying on a Great Britain which would throw Austria-Hungary over at the first opportunity to come to terms with the increasingly awesome Franco-Russian bloc. He urged that Austria-Hungary should herself make haste to square Russia – perhaps only on a basis of the status quo for the present; but ultimately, should Turkey fall to pieces, by partitioning the Balkans into Austro-Hungarian and Russian spheres. The Monarchy might absorb Serbia, and establish a strong Albania at the expense of the Slavs. Beck, whose influence had increased since he had taken over some of the functions of Inspector General of the Army on the death of Archduke Albrecht in February, was of similar mind, and used his position to send memoranda in this vein to the emperor behind Goluchowski's back.[150] Even Calice at Constantinople questioned[151] the value of a simple renewal of the Mediterranean Agreements now that Russian pressure had shifted from Bulgaria to Constantinople and the Straits, areas of greater importance to Great Britain than to Austria-Hungary. All this made no impression in the Ballhausplatz. There, Zwiedenek sternly insisted[152] that a lasting agreement with Russia was out of the question. That Power was ultimately bent on world domination (*Weltherrschaft*). She already exerted enormous pressure on the Monarchy; and if she advanced any further she would not only establish a disastrous influence over the Slavs of the Monarchy, but also strangle Austria-Hungary's commercial development. With Russia established at Constantinople, Bulgaria, and then Romania and Serbia, would soon be lost. A binding agreement with Great Britain would be ideal; but failing that, the vaguer agreements of 1887 would do well enough. At any rate, Goluchowski declared himself satisfied with them when Salisbury assured him in November

149. P.A. I/461, Liasse XXV, Aehrenthal memorandum, September 1895.
150. Glaise-Horstenau, *Beck*, p. 380.
151. P.A. I/462, Liasse XXV/b, Calice to Goluchowski, private and secret, 12 September 1895.
152. Ibid., Zwiedenek to Calice, private, 25 September 1895.

1895 that London regarded them as still in force.

After all, the Mediterranean Entente had so far served Austria-Hungary's interests better than any of the alliances of the 1880s, because it represented a community of interests that found expression in a common line of action in day-to-day diplomacy. By the same token, however, the future of the Mediterranean Entente would depend on whether this continued to be the case in the crises of the middle nineties, crises that arose, not from any external Russian threat, but from the internal disintegration of the Ottoman Empire. In one instance, the Macedonian rising of July 1895, the Mediterranean Entente did not have to be put to the test, because unanimity prevailed among the Great Powers. Since 1893 a Bulgarian-controlled terrorist and propaganda organisation had been preparing a rebellion in Macedonia. The aim was to provoke the Turks into committing atrocities there. The Great Powers might then intervene and constitute Macedonia into an autonomous province, which might later be added to Bulgaria, after the fashion of Eastern Rumelia. In contrast to the 1870s, however, the governments of all the Great Powers now took a distinctly sceptical view of the aspirations of the Balkan Christians. The rising proved a complete fiasco: not even the Bulgarian government dared move in its support, so strong was the united disapproval of the Great Powers. After all, the raising of the whole Eastern Question – and this would certainly have been the consequence of Bulgarian intervention, bringing Greek and Serbian counter-claims in its wake – was the last thing the Great Powers desired.

The Armenian massacres of August 1895 presented a more dangerous problem, in that they threatened to divide the Great Powers. Whereas the Monarchy's partners in the Mediterranean Entente, under strong pressure from public opinion, demanded drastic measures of coercion to bring the sultan to heel, Russia (who had potentially troublesome Armenian subjects of her own), supported by France, would have none of this. Goluchowski, for his part, shrank from a confrontation between the Mediterranean Entente and the Franco-Russian bloc. This, he feared, could only increase the risk of a general war, a war which would, after all, bring far more death and destruction than any number of Armenian massacres. He decided, therefore, that a united Concert would provide the best safeguard for the essentially conservative interests on the Monarchy. He directed his efforts, therefore, to restraining his own Entente partners, while using the bogyman of a separate Anglo-Italian initiative to keep St Petersburg in line. In October, for example, he successfully took the lead in persuading the powers

1. Clemens Prince Metternich

2. Felix Prince Schwarzenberg

KARL GRAF ZU BUOL-SCHAUENSTEIN.

3. Karl Ferdinand Count Buol

4. Johann Bernhard Count Rechberg

5. Alexander Count Mensdorff

6. Friedrich Ferdinand Baron (1868 Count) Beust

7. Julius Count Andrássy

8. Heinrich Baron Haymerle

9. Franz Joseph I

10. Gustav Count Kálnoky

11. Agenor Count Goluchowski

12. Alois Baron (1909 Count) Aehrenthal

13. Leopold Count Berchtold

14. Stefan (1900 Baron, 1918 Count) Burián

15. Karl I

16. Ottokar Count Czernin

to agree that the Armenian question was a matter for the Concert; and in December he brought the Russians to join with the other Powers in a mild naval demonstration at Constantinople – although the Germans, ever anxious to humour the sultan, abstained in the end. The outcome – some vague promises of reform from the sultan – was exceedingly meagre from an Armenian point of view. Nevertheless, Goluchowski in a conference of ministers in April 1896 made much of the fact that he had achieved his main aim, namely, to preserve the unity of the Powers.[153] Not that his efforts earned him much credit abroad. The Russians resented his collaboration with Great Britain; and in Berlin, where hopes of an Anglo-Russian war had prevailed, the Kaiser angrily observed that Goluchowski 'ought to go to school again'.[154]

The Austrians, for their part, were in no mood to take advice from a Germany whose own behaviour seemed to them misguided, not to say perverse. The era of the *Neue Kurs*, when the Monarchy had been able to count on German backing for the Mediterranean Entente, was now clearly over. On the military front, the uncoupling of the Dual Alliance moved a stage nearer at the end of 1895, when Schlieffen decided to concentrate almost everything in the west, and advised the Austrians to look to their own salvation. In April 1896 Beck resignedly asked the Germans to bind as many Russian forces as they could in north Poland. For the next thirteen years there was no further co-ordination of strategy between the Austro-Hungarian and German general staffs, and each went ahead with its own plans without consulting the other. By 1908 they were completely out of touch, an Austro-Hungarian plan of that summer blithely assuming that Germany intended to concentrate her initial attack in the east.[155] On the diplomatic front, the Germans were showing an almost obsessive concern to stand well with their increasingly powerful French and Russian neighbours. True, in November 1895 the Kaiser declared somewhat patronisingly that Germany would come to the rescue of Austria-Hungary if she were ever in mortal peril; and even that it would be for Franz Joseph alone to decide when such a peril existed. Goluchowski and Franz Joseph, who felt that 'war with Russia must come sooner or later',[156] decided that this was the 'most important declaration as to the scope of the alliance since its foundation'.[157]

153. P.A. XL/297, Ministerratsprotokoll, 13 April 1896.
154. J. Andrássy, *Bismarck, Andrássy and their successors*, p. 244.
155. Ritter, 'Die Zusammenarbeit', in *Zur Geschichte und Problematik* pp. 537–8.
156. Wagner, 'Kaiser Franz Joseph', p. 203.
157. Ibid., pp. 201–2.

But they were soon to learn yet again that the Kaiser's grandiose words meant little in terms of practical politics, and Goluchowski found the Germans as exasperatingly useless as Kálnoky had done in his efforts to persuade Italy to cultivate Spain. Worse, in the Near East, they still insisted that Constantinople was not worth a war, and were conspicuously absent – to Goluchowski's great annoyance – from the international naval demonstration in December. Equally tiresomely, they seemed to be trying actively to hinder his efforts to bind Great Britain more securely to the Mediterranean Entente.

In November 1895 the Germans reverted to warning Vienna against co-operation with Great Britain, who they alleged had now abandoned the defence of the status quo and was plotting with Russia to partition Turkey. In December, the German Chancellor Hohenlohe came to Vienna, and urged Goluchowski to square St Petersburg: Constantinople must fall to Russia in the long run, and the Monarchy would be wise to make sure of some compensation for itself in the western Balkans. This idea was still anathema to Goluchowski. Any policy of compensation could only be fatal for the Monarchy: for once Russia was established in Constantinople, she would inevitably dominate the whole of the Balkans sooner or later. Even so, Goluchowski was himself not entirely free from doubts about Great Britain's devotion to the status quo – her drastic Armenian proposals had seemed to him cavalier, to say the least. Besides, 'in political action, one must base one's position on certainties'; vague agreements such as those of 1887 might draw Austria-Hungary into a posture of hostility to Russia, while yet providing her with no effective assistance if it came to war.[158] In January 1896, therefore, Goluchowski decided to ask London for assurances that Great Britain was still devoted to the status quo, and to resisting the aggression of Russia. These assurances must be given not in the form of a mere renewal of the 1887 'agreement to agree', but in the form of what would in fact be a new and far-reaching treaty, containing definite pledges to fight.[159]

His doubts as to British intentions were, in fact, largely groundless. Salisbury was not thinking of abandoning Turkey, let alone of making a deal with Russia. As he reminded the cabinet in February, he was still 'strongly against any policy that would cut Austria

158. P.A. I/461, Liasse XXV, Goluchowski to Deym, private and very secret, 9 December 1895.
159. J.A.S. Grenville, 'Goluchowski, Salisbury and the Mediterranean Agreements, 1895–1897', in *Slavonic and East European Review*, 36 (1958), pp. 340–69.

adrift. It would reconstitute the *Dreikaiserbund* – a state of things which must be injurious to Great Britain.'[160] Nevertheless, the awkward fact was that, given the sultan's unpopularity in Great Britain as a result of the Armenian massacres, Salisbury simply could not promise to fight in his defence on absolutely any occasion. It would all depend on the mood of parliament at the time – a mood which, as he consolingly told Deym on 4 February, might still change in Turkey's favour if Russia actually moved against her. For the present, however, he could consider nothing more than a simple renewal of the 1887 agreements, although – indeed, precisely because – they did not commit him to much. This did not satisfy Goluchowski, who felt that it would be dangerous to commit himself to an anti-Russian stance conjointly with Great Britain on such an uncertain basis – after all, it was Austria-Hungary, not the island kingdom, who would have to bear the brunt of any war over the Near East. But although he decided against proceeding to a renewal of the 1887 agreements, he consoled himself with the thought that, in terms of practical politics, the British were still inclined 'to go hand in hand with the Triple Alliance'.[161] This being the case, he was still not disposed to abandon the British and seek agreement with St Petersburg.

This was clear from his reaction to recent developments in the Balkans, notably the ending of the Russo-Bulgarian estrangement after the fall of the Russophobe Stamboulov government in 1894, and the return of Russian diplomatic agents to Bulgaria in the spring of 1895. At first, the Austrians had reacted philosophically: although Goluchowski felt it necessary to warn the Russian ambassador that, whereas the Monarchy sought no special position for itself in Bulgaria, it would concede none to any other Power, he on the whole shared Zwiedenek's sanguine view that so long as Russia respected Bulgaria's independence the ending of the tiresome Russo-Bulgarian quarrel was only welcome. Austrian reactions became distinctly less favourable, however, when Russia began to strengthen her position in Bulgaria in the spring of 1896. Indeed, when Crown Prince Boris was baptised into the Orthodox church in February, Franz Joseph and Goluchowski were besides themselves with rage, resolving that the ungrateful 'ape' Ferdinand should never again be received at court.[162] Goluchowski now directed his efforts to constructing a counterweight to the developing Russo-Bulgarian bloc

---

160. Jefferson, 'Straits', p. 197.
161. P.A. XL/297, Ministerratsprotokoll, 13 April 1896.
162. Aehrenthal MSS, Karton 1, Goluchowski to Aehrenthal, 24 March 1896.

by furthering a *rapprochement* between Serbia, Romania and Greece. The prospects were hardly inviting. Greece was not worth much; and Serbia, in a state of complete chaos, even less. (It had mattered little to Vienna that she had allowed the alliance to expire in 1895; and Goluchowski was content to note that she had become completely harmless as a neighbour.) Romania's renewed enthusiasm for the alliance was more positively encouraging; Franz Joseph and Goluchowski were determined to establish really cordial relations with Romania, and Magyar opinion would have to come into line. In April, they arranged a spectacular state visit to Bucharest, to follow on King Carol's visit to Hungary for the celebration of the completion of the Danube navigation works in the autumn. In short, the Ballhausplatz remained set on an anti-Russian course. When, in February, the German ambassador made so bold as to recommend a *rapprochement* with Russia, *Sektionschef* Welsersheimb sharply reminded him that the Russian threat constituted the only *raison d'être* of the Triple Alliance: after all, Austria-Hungary did not care who held Alsace-Lorraine.

The acerbity of this last remark was a measure of the frustration of the Austrians at the failure of their efforts to build up a really effective anti-Russian front. The failure was due, in part, to internal factors beyond the control of the Ballhausplatz: notably, the spectacle of domestic weakness which the Monarchy now presented to the world. Strife between Czech and German still paralysed parliamentary life in Austria; and this was particularly embarrassing as the negotiations for the renewal of the commercial *Ausgleich* loomed up, at a time when Hungarian chauvinism had been fired to fever heat by a Millenial Exhibition and other celebrations of the entry of the Magyars into Europe in 896. Such a state of affairs was bound to undermine the authority with which Austria-Hungary, at the best of times only a Great Power of the second rank, could speak on the international scene in these years; and it made her all the more dependent on external support. That the Dual Alliance was so patently failing to provide it was a source of immense exasperation in Vienna.

On 3 March, Goluchowski took Eulenburg severely to task:[163] Germany's whole policy of coquetting with Russia and fobbing the Monarchy off with fair words was intolerable. Altogether, Germany's behaviour was destroying the authority of the Triple Alliance. Friendly Powers were becoming estranged from it. Germany

---

163. P.A. I/476, Goluchowski, memorandum on a conversation with Eulenburg, 3 March 1896.

had been 'very stupid' in refusing to press Italy to humour Spain; and with the ending of the Italo-Spanish link the Triple Alliance was 'facing a grave diplomatic defeat'. In similar vein, Welsersheimb told the ambassador that it was Wilhelm II's 'Kruger telegram' of 3 January that had caused the failure of Goluchowski's approach to London: 'now England will not make agreements with Germany's allies'.[164] Franz Joseph, too, had considered the Kruger telegram 'frivolous and irresponsible'.[165] He approved heartily of all that Goluchowski had said to Eulenburg, and it was with his express approval that Goluchowski explained his aims frankly and at length during a visit to Berlin in March:[166] like the Germans, he wanted good relations with Russia; but the Monarchy would never tolerate a Russian preponderance in the Balkans – hence Russia must never be allowed to acquire Constantinople or special privileges in the Straits. Although it might be just as well to know that the Monarchy could not definitely count on the British, he would still seek to work with them, and he hoped that Berlin would help by humouring them and by restraining the German press. Italy, after her recent defeat at Adowa, was in need of comfort and consolation from her allies; for should the House of Savoy be sacrificed as a scapegoat, the way would then be clear for a confederation of Latin republics as planned by Leo XIII and the Francophile Cardinal Rampolla. Spain might yet be brought back into the fold of the Mediterranean Entente; and as for the Balkans, Austria-Hungary was for the present chiefly concerned to bring about a Greco-Romanian *rapprochement* to balance Russia's growing influence in Bulgaria. Germany should help in this. The Germans listened, and were effusive in their expressions of sympathy; but they promised nothing very specific.

The ensuing months only partially fulfilled Goluchowski's hopes of reviving the old system of a Mediterranean Entente supported by Germany. True, this system seemed to make a brief reappearance – for the last time, in fact – in April, when, in the face of frantic opposition from France and Russia, the Mediterranean Entente Powers and Germany granted money from Egyptian revenues to cover the cost of a British military expedition to Dongola in the Sudan; and in May the Triple Alliance was renewed virtually without a hitch. Yet Goluchowski's assumption[167] that the more Great Britain was 'nailed down' in Egypt, the more she would feel

---

164. P.A. I/461, Szögyény to Goluchowski, Tel. 40, secret, 4 March 1896.
165. Wagner, 'Kaiser Franz Joseph', p. 215.
166. P.A. I/476, Goluchowski, Memorandum, March 1896.
167. Aehrenthal MSS, Karton 1, Goluchowski to Aehrenthal, 7 April 1896.

constrained to defend her own (and Austria-Hungary's) interests in the Eastern Mediterranean was to prove mistaken. Indeed, it was precisely Great Britain's strong position in Egypt that was to render Constantinople less vital to the defence of the Mediterranean route to India. Spain proved an even greater disappointment, raising her price to include a guarantee of her possession of Cuba. This was too much even for Goluchowski, and the Spanish link with the Mediterranean Entente was now finally dropped. Romania was more amenable, and during the very successful state visit of Franz Joseph, Goluchowski and Beck to Bucharest in September the alliance was duly extended to run to 1903. But even here the Germans, ever-fearful of Russia, dragged their feet, and only acceded to the Protocol after several reminders in 1899. The unlimited German support of the early years of the *Neue Kurs* was clearly not forthcoming.

Nor, unfortunately, could Goluchowski have complete confidence in the British. It was not a question of the character of their obligations under the 1887 agreements. Salisbury had recently yet again reaffirmed his desire to lean on the Triple Alliance without belonging to it. The problem was that certain British activities were causing Vienna to wonder whether Great Britain was in fact pursuing the same aims as Austria-Hungary in the Near East, namely, the defence of the status quo. The Cretan question was a case in point. Since the Turks had restricted the constitutional rights of the Christians in Crete in 1889, tension in the island had increased until Christian and Muslim came to blows in the spring of 1896. The crisis was potentially dangerous, in that it might drag in Greece, spread to Macedonia, and open up the whole Eastern Question. Indeed, by July Goluchowski was so alarmed that, in a desperate effort to contain the conflagration, he suddenly seized the initiative with a proposal that the Powers should send a collective warning to Athens and blockade the island. His proposal came to nothing, however, when the British government, under strong pressure from a Grecophile public opinion, refused to co-operate. In the end, Goluchowski set to work with the French to examine the demands of the rebels, and temporary relief arrived in September when the sultan promised some concessions. But the British rejection of his blockade proposal had dealt a rude blow both to his vanity – it still rankled a year later – and to his confidence in the reliability of the Mediterranean Entente.

Not that, even now, he had the slightest intention of abandoning it – if only because he had even less confidence in Russia. His view of that Power had not changed since the spring, when, while admitting to a council of ministers[168] that relations were tolerably good he had laid great stress on the dangers that still threatened the Monarchy from that quarter. There was still plenty of inflammable material in the Near East; Russia's unceasing build-up of armaments must give food for thought. Her involvement in the Far East had produced no reduction at all in the troops she maintained on the Austro-Hungarian frontier; and she was now more interested than ever in the Mediterranean route to the Far East through the Straits and the Suez Canal – witness her renewed activity in Egyptian affairs. There was every need to keep a sharp eye open. Not all Goluchowski's countrymen agreed with his analysis by any means: Wolkenstein, now ambassador at Paris, but still an ardent champion of an Austro-Russian *entente*, was in despair: 'why are they always talking about a Russian attack on Constantinople?' he complained to Aehrenthal.[169] Kálnoky, too, thought that a chance was being missed. The emperor's speech to the Delegations on 1 June, extolling the Triple Alliance, he thought deplorable:[170] for what had the Triple Alliance ever done in the Near East? Did it even have a policy there? Goluchowski talked far too much. This situation was not changed by the state visit to Vienna in August of Nicholas II, accompanied by Lobanov. Goluchowski was sceptical of Russia's professed devotion to the status quo, especially when Lobanov turned down his suggestion that an international control of the Ottoman finances might put Turkey on her feet again. In Goluchowski's view, this just showed that Lobanov was not interested in a real cure for Turkey's ills, but only in letting her stagger on for another two or three years until the Trans-Siberian railway was completed.[171] Then – and this was a constant refrain in the Ballhausplatz in these months – Russia would suddenly raise a whole complex of 'questions' – Constantinople, the Straits, and Suez. With such a Russia there could be no accommodation.

That the Monarchy, with only limited expectations of external support, was still faced with a serious Russian threat was not Goluchowski's only cause for concern in the summer of 1896. As he reminded a council of ministers on 29 August,[172] the Monarchy's own defences left much to be desired: the strategic railways of Galicia and Hungary were still mostly single-track. Moreover,

168. P.A. XL/297, Ministerratsprotokoll, 13 April 1896.
169. Aehrenthal MSS, Karton 4, Wolkenstein to Aehrenthal, 31 May 1896.
170. Ibid., Karton 2, Kálnoky to Aehrenthal, 1 June 1896.
171. P.A. I/476, Goluchowski, Memorandum on a conversation with Lobanov, August 1896.
172. P.A. XL/297, Ministerratsprotokoll, 29 August 1896.

even in the event of a crisis involving the *casus foederis*, the Monarchy could not hope for too much from its allies. Certainly Germany, squeezed between France and Russia, would have little to spare. Beck was, if anything, even more gloomy:[173] if war with Russia arose, not from a direct clash, but from events in the south-east, Germany might refuse to recognise the *casus foederis*; and if the Monarchy, already engaged in the south, had to turn and cope alone with Russia, it would be in mortal peril indeed. In his view, this was another argument for an agreement with Russia, which would at least have the advantage of securing the Monarchy's rear for local military operations in defence of its Balkan interests. But that was not a course that Goluchowski was as yet prepared to pursue.

He preferred, rather, to adopt a cautious, waiting attitude when, as a result of a further round of Armenian massacres at the end of August – this time in the Turkish capital itself – the Ottoman Empire was again plunged into a potentially fatal crisis. Like the other ambassadors on the spot, Calice was appalled by the carnage, and even warned the sultan that the powers would depose him if he could not provide better government. But most statesmen in the distant European capitals were above all concerned to maintain the status quo and play down the crisis. All the Concert could agree on was virtual inaction. Austria-Hungary, certainly, was in far too weak a position both at home and abroad to take any bold initiatives: as Kálnoky remarked,[174] she had recently moved away from Great Britain without moving any closer to Russia; her German allies were strictly abstentionist, the Italians, weak; and a major domestic crisis was looming up over the renewal of the commercial *Ausgleich*. Goluchowski gave a mildly favourable reception to a new batch of reform proposals from London in October. But he was only too relieved when early in 1897 the Powers, distracted by a revival of the Cretan crisis, decided that matters were becoming too hot to handle, and that at least the Armenian question could be shelved.

The Armenian affair had, nevertheless, raised grave problems, notably the possibility of the early collapse of the Ottoman Empire; and in the ensuing months statesmen in Vienna were much preoccupied with the dreaded issue of the partition of Turkey-in-Europe. On 26 August, Goluchowski informed a council of ministers[175] that the decay of Turkey, clearly no longer capable of

173. Ibid., Memorandum of 14 August 1896.
174. Aehrenthal MSS, Karton 2, Kálnoky to Aehrenthal, 20 September 1896.
175. P.A. XL/297, Ministerratsprotokoll, 26 August 1896.

saving herself by reform, was proceeding apace. The Monarchy must be prepared to act in the event of her final disintegration. For although Austria-Hungary had no further claims to make on Turkish territory, Bosnia and the Herzegovina would have to be finally incorporated. This posed an awkward constitutional problem: it would be impractical to divide the provinces between the two halves of the Monarchy; and impossible to bring either half to renounce them in favour of the other. In the end, Goluchowski persuaded the Magyars to agree to their being incorporated into the Monarchy as a Reichsland, and governed as a colony common to both halves; and a draft protocol along these lines was duly drawn up.

More problematical was the fate of the rest of Turkey-in-Europe, which was the subject of a series of conferences of experts held in the Ballhausplatz at the end of 1896.[176] In Goluchowski's view, the general picture was fairly clear: the Monarchy had little interest in predominantly Serbian or Bulgarian areas; but in Albania it had vital interests to guard. That area must under no circumstances come under the influence of another Power – such as Italy (who would then control both coasts of the narrow Straits of Otranto, and be in a position to close the Adriatic). Nor must Serbia or Bulgaria be permitted be expand to the Adriatic: this would mean the completion of Russia's 'iron ring' encircling the Monarchy. If Serbia expanded into northern Macedonia or the eastern Sanjak, the Monarchy would have to retain the western Sanjak, if only to prevent a future union of Serbia and Montenegro into one big Slav state, anathema to the Monarchy since the days of Andrássy. The Monarchy's concrete aim would be, therefore (granted that a direct occupation of Albania was not desirable), the creation of an independent Albania under the moral protection of Austria-Hungary.

Albania, like Bosnia, seemed to call for immediate policy decisions. The Albanians, mere tribes who had as yet never formed a state, would clearly need help if they were to survive amongst their greedy neighbours. The conferences of experts decided, therefore, to bolster the Monarchy's position in the area by developing the consular service, spending more on subsidies, and making more of the Monarchy's rights – dating back to an Austro-Turkish treaty of 1606 – as protector of the Catholic tribes of northern Albania. Goluchowski was not indisposed to enlisting Greece in the cause,

---

176. P.A. I/473, Liasse XXXI/a, Protocols of confidential discussions of 17 November; 18, 23 December 1896.

and rewarding her with a slice of southern Albania. But the main emphasis was to be on encouraging a sense of Albanian national consciousness and independence among all Albanians, rather than simply among the northern Catholics – especially as some 77 per cent of the inhabitants of central Albania were Muslim. Even so, the matter would need skilful handling. As Calice warned, any display of Austro-Hungarian interest in the Albanians was always liable to arouse the suspicions of Constantinople. Indeed, when in the spring of 1897 the Cretan question developed into a Greco-Turkish war, and several Albanian chieftains seized the opportunity to rise in open rebellion against the sultan, Vienna wisely decided to defer the implementation of the new policy, and advised the consuls in Albania to lie low.

Meanwhile, Goluchowski's plans for rallying external support for the Monarchy's Balkan interests were running into difficulties. His efforts to unite Greece and Romania against the Slav menace as exemplified by the Russo-Bulgarian *rapprochement*[177] made painfully slow progress in the face of the harassment of Romanian 'Koutzo-Vlachs' by Greek nationalists in Macedonia; and in any case, the Balkan kaleidoscope was such that a displacement of power in one area usually produced a countervailing realignment in another: by the spring of 1897 Bulgaria had concluded a secret treaty with Serbia providing for co-operation against Greek and Austro-Hungarian influence in Macedonia. In the new year Goluchowski met with another disappointment when he tried to clarify relations with London. Citing Kálnoky's comments of October 1887 on the Mediterranean Agreements, he instructed Deym to remind the British that it was they, not Austria-Hungary, who stood in the first line of defence of the Straits: if they would give a clear promise to fight, Austria-Hungary would be ready to agree as to how best to support them; but the Monarchy could not even consider fighting Russia unless it was absolutely clear beforehand that Great Britain would fight. The risk would be far too great, especially as Germany could no longer be counted on. In reply to Deym, Salisbury, who still regarded Austria-Hungary as Great Britain's 'only friend in Europe',[178] repeated his assurances of 1896. But he could still give no clear pledge to fight. Public opinion was for the moment, he had to confess, most unlikely to fight in defence of the slayers of the Armenians. There were, moreover,

---

177. P.A. I/476, Goluchowski, Memorandum on a conversation with the King of the Hellenes, November 1896.
178. Jefferson, 'Straits', p. 229.

practical reasons to doubt – since the Turks had fortified the Dardanelles against Great Britain, but not the Bosphorus against Russia – whether Great Britain could do much to save Constantinople from Russia anyway. In these arguments, Deym rightly perceived a change in Salisbury's position since the previous winter. His personal policy might be the same, but he was several degrees less confident of being able to carry it out. He had moved, under pressure from public opinion, the cabinet, and strategic realities, from confidence in 1887, to mere hope by 1896, and by 1897 to almost hopeless gloom. As for Goluchowski, he declared that he would henceforth have to keep a completely free hand, and that he would 'be forced to forget' the Mediterranean Agreements.[179]

Goluchowski's wisdom has been questioned.[180] By insisting on a clear, all-or-nothing commitment, he had abandoned a basis of co-operation which, for all its vagueness, might yet have been developed into something more definite: even a mere renewal of the 1887 agreements would have been a more positive achievement than anything France was to extract from Great Britain in 1904 or Russia in 1907. Yet, although Goluchowski was perhaps unrealistic in aiming for a formal treaty commitment, the significance of the incident should not be exaggerated. Even as regards the Straits, Goluchowski still hoped that Russia would not come to hear of the change in Great Britain's position; and that if Russia actually moved, 'the British guns might yet go off by themselves'.[181] For the rest, he still hoped to work with Great Britain in practical questions: for instance, he continued to co-operate with the British in bringing the other Powers to agree on measures of coercion to be adopted if the sultan rejected their proposals for Armenian reform. What was to prove fatal to the Mediterranean Entente was not the failure to reach agreement about the agreements of 1887 – the Straits question continued to remain dormant in the event – but the appearance, as the Cretan question replaced the Armenian question at the centre of the stage in the spring, of a wide rift between London and Vienna in respect of their aims in the Near East generally.

When, in February 1897, fighting resumed in Crete, the Greek government this time lent its support officially to the rebels; and an incident on the Greco-Macedonian frontier, ominously symptomatic of the connection between Cretan and Balkan affairs and the

---

179. Ibid., p. 232.
180. Grenville, 'Goluchowski, Salisbury', pp. 367–8.
181. Jefferson, 'Straits', p. 238.

whole Eastern Question, sparked off a Greco-Turkish war. Within weeks, to the surprise of the Powers, the Greek aggressors were soundly defeated; but the crisis proved of lasting importance for the future of the Mediterranean Entente. Goluchowski's policy with regard to the war was threefold. First, to prevent the escalation of the conflict into a general Balkan war. Here, he found Russia, who co-operated in restraining the Balkan states from intervention, surprisingly helpful – the first notable example of Austro-Russian co-operation since the Serbian crisis of 1894. Second, to preserve peace between the Great Powers by maintaining the unity of the Concert. Third, to ensure that Greece did not profit in any way from her reckless adventure: that would set a deplorable precedent for the other Balkan states, and would be tantamount to the moral bankruptcy of the Concert. Still smarting under the rebuff of the previous summer, Goluchowski was reluctant to take the initiative; but he did his best to promote harmony within the Concert, on the one hand joining the other Powers in sending 'fire-brigade' detachments of troops to Crete in February, and on the other rebuking the Germans for their unnecessarily harsh opposition to some of Salisbury's suggestions.

But maintaining the unity of the Concert was a soul-destroying business; and it was particularly galling for Goluchowski that, of the Powers whose support he had recently been striving to enlist, Greece had started the conflagration in the first place, and Great Britain showed little sign of wishing to co-operate with Austria-Hungary in extinguishing the flames. On the contrary, the British government, under pressure from a Grecophile court and public opinion, and anxious to avoid obstruction from a Turcophile Germany, suggested in May that Great Britain, France and Russia, as the protecting Powers of Greece, should alone attempt to mediate peace between Greece and Turkey. In the end, the belligerents came to terms before the disunity of the Concert could be fully revealed (July), leaving the fate of Crete to be decided by the Powers. But Salisbury's proposal was for Goluchowski the last straw: Russia's loyalty to the status quo was by no means above suspicion, and could only be weakened by association with such Grecophile Powers as France and Great Britain. Franz Joseph, visiting St Petersburg at the time, expressed his disappointment to the British ambassador, and insisted that the matter was one for the Concert to deal with. Both the content and the timing of Salisbury's proposal had given Goluchowski food for thought. By the early summer of 1897, it was beginning to seem that, on the practical issues of the day, Austria-Hungary was more in line with the two northern empires than with her erstwhile friends in London.

The failure of Goluchowski's hopes of ad hoc co-operation with Great Britain on issues of the day was the last of a series of disappointments; and it forced him reluctantly to recognise the non-viability of a policy based on the Mediterranean Entente, unsupported, even disapproved of, by Berlin, and relying in the Balkans on a rickety Greco-Romanian *entente*. Just as in 1880 Gladstone's anti-Turkish activities had forced a reluctant Haymerle to yield to German pressure for a *rapprochement* with St Petersburg, so now it was force of circumstances (notably the disturbing behaviour of London and Athens), not doctrinaire considerations, that led Goluchowski to consider a reorientation of policy. In another sense, too, circumstances had conspired to favour such a reorientation. In 1896, when Turkey had seemed to be on the point of collapse and the maintenance of the status quo an impossibility, it had seemed urgently necessary to construct a bloc of anti-Russian forces for use when the general scramble occurred. In 1897, however, Turkey's success in the war with Greece had shown that she was by no means on the point of collapse, and that the maintenance of the status quo might indeed be a viable basis for a policy. The recent behaviour of Great Britain and Russia suggested equally clearly that if the Austrians committed themselves to such a policy, they would find more support in St Petersburg than in London.

6
The Austro-Russian Entente, 1897–1908[1]

Austro-Russian Co-existence, 1897–1902

The opening months of 1897 had not seemed to offer much hope of any significant improvement in Austro-Russian relations. Then, the constant threat of the dissolution of the Ottoman Empire had kept the ultimate incompatibility of Russian and Austro-Hungarian interests to the forefront of Austrian minds. Beck could make no headway with his suggestions that a partition of Turkey might provide a fruitful basis for co-operation: that the Monarchy should resign itself to Russia's acquisition of Constantinople and domination of the eastern Balkans in exchange for the annexation of the occupied provinces and Austro-Hungarian control of Serbia, Montenegro and Albania, leaving Macedonia as an autonomous province.[2] Franz Joseph and Goluchowski would have none of this: they had no intention of abandoning Bulgaria and Romania to Russia; and they feared that an autonomous Macedonia might in the end only swell Bulgaria's territory and ambitions to a dangerous degree. Temperamentally, too, as Kálnoky observed, Goluchowski was totally lacking in self-confidence in dealing with Russia.[3] At any rate, even in the train to St Petersburg at the end of April, he told Beck that he doubted whether Russia would be interested in negotiations, drawing from Beck the exasperated

---

1. The following works are of particular relevance to this chapter: F.R. Bridge, 'Izvolsky, Aehrenthal, and the end of the Austro-Russian entente', in *Mitteilungen des österreichischen Staatsarchivs*, 29 (1976), pp. 315–62; W.M. Carlgren, *Iswolsky und Aehrenthal vor der bosnischen Annexionskrise*, (Uppsala 1955); D. Dakin, *The Greek Struggle in Macedonia* (Salonika 1969); H. Hantsch, *Leopold Graf Berchtold*, 2 vols (Graz 1963); N. Stone, 'Constitutional Crises in Hungary, 1903–1906', in *Slavonic and East European Review*, 45 (1967); and the works by A. Wandruszka and P. Urbanitsch (eds), C.A. Macartney, A.J.P. Taylor, A. Sked and I. Diószegi cited in Chapter 1, note 1; by Barbara Jelavich, and F.R. Bridge and Roger Bullen cited in Chapter 2, note 1; by T. von Sosnosky, E. von Glaise-Horstenau, and A.F. Pribram cited in Chapter 4, note 1.
2. Glaise-Horstenau, *Beck*, pp. 380ff.
3. Aehrenthal MSS, Karton 2, Kálnoky to Aehrenthal, 23 February 1897.

retort that in that case it would have been better not to have undertaken the journey at all.[4]

In the event, Franz Joseph's visit to St Petersburg (27–29 April) proved to be a real turning point in Austro-Russian relations. Certainly, this was very much a consequence of changes in the international situation: Salisbury's unfortunate attempt to settle the Greco-Turkish crisis to the exclusion of the Central Powers dealt a shattering blow to the Austrians' faith in the Mediterranean Entente at the same time that Turkey's display of military resilience pointed to the feasibility of co-operation with Russia to prolong the existence of the Ottoman Empire rather than to grapple with the thorny problem of its dissolution. But the visit itself was an important catalyst. Nicholas II extended a remarkably cordial welcome to his Austrian guests, and declared that he regarded as 'self-evident [*selbsverständlich*]'[5] Goluchowski's entire catalogue of Austro-Hungarian interests that Russia must respect.

Although there was no written protocol agreed by both sides, broad agreement was reached, as Goluchowski was to explain to a council of ministers in October,[6] on four principles: first, the maintenance of the status quo in the Near East for as long as possible; second, the strict observance of the principle of non-interference with the independent development of the Balkan states (a reaffirmation of Kálnoky's doctrine); third, co-operation between the representatives of the two Powers in the Balkans, to show the Balkan states that they could gain nothing by trying to play off the two Great Powers against each other; fourth, that if the maintenance of the status quo should prove impossible, the two Powers, while expressly renouncing all designs of conquest for themselves, would come to a direct agreement as to the future territorial configuration of the Balkans – and would, moreover, impose this agreement on the other Powers. For Goluchowski, always inclined to treat the Balkan states (except perhaps Romania) with a high hand, the third principle, designed to destroy their capacity to set the Great Powers by the ears as Bulgaria had done in the 1880s, always remained one of the most valuable aspects of the agreement with Russia. The fourth point certainly gave the measure of the distance Austria-Hungary had travelled from her former partners in the Mediterranean Entente. The Italians were

4. Glaise-Horstenau, *Beck*, p. 385.
5. P.A. I/475, Liasse XXXII/i, Memorandum by Count v. Rhemen, dated '1903', on 'The agreements concluded between Austria and Russia . . . 1872–1902'.
6. P.A. XL/298, Ministerratsprotokoll, 5 October 1897.

informed only in the vaguest terms of the self-denying aspects of the agreement – to which Rudiní not unnaturally acceded; the British were not informed at all.

The Austro-Hungarian view of the practical implications of the four principles for the Balkans was summarised by Goluchowski on his return.[7] The Straits question had been excluded from the discussions, as the Austrians insisted that it was a matter for Europe to settle, and as the Russians professed themselves content with the status quo for the present. If the Balkan status quo could no longer be preserved, Austria-Hungary must insist on the possession of Bosnia, the Herzegovina, and the Sanjak of Novibazar (for Serbia and Montenegro must at all costs be kept apart); a large Albanian state must be created; and Russia and Austria-Hungary must later come to some agreement to ensure that no Balkan state grew so big as to upset the Balkan balance. These points he set out in a dispatch of 8 May to St Petersburg, emphasising particularly that the occupied provinces could not form the subject of any debate, and that the Monarchy reserved the right to annex them whenever it saw fit. The Russian reply of 17 May in fact expressed important reservations: Russia recognised only the position of 1878 in Bosnia and the Herzegovina – the annexation of the provinces would raise wider European issues and would require special examination; the territorial extent of the *Sanjak* was as yet undefined; and as for the future territorial configuration of the Balkans, Russia would take her decisions when the situation arose. The Austrians, for their part, held to their original position, especially as the Russian ambassador, Kapnist, admitted that his government's view of the annexation question was wrong; and as to pursue the argument might seem to suggest that a further Russian declaration would be needed to legitimise the annexation.[8] No reply was sent, therefore, to the Russian counter-note. From the start, the Austro-Russian Entente rested on an equivocation.

Even so, the agreements of 1897 marked a notable development in both the internal and the external affairs of the Monarchy. The renewed emphasis on Habsburg–Romanov solidarity was especially valuable to Vienna at a time when strife between Czech and German had been augmented by a quarrel with the Hungarians over the renewal of the commercial *Ausgleich*, to produce a crisis which in Goluchowski's opinion was the worst for forty years, and

---

7. P.A. I/474, Goluchowski to Pasetti, tel. 74, secret, 4 May 1897; to Szögyény, No. 731, secret, 5 May 1897.
8. P.A. I/475, Liasse XXXII/i, Rhemen, Memorandum.

apparently insoluble.[9] Externally, the Entente of 1897 – like the renewal of the Three Emperors' Alliance in 1884 – marked a devaluation of the Triple Alliance in Austro-Hungarian eyes. True, in surveying the international scene in a conference of ministers in October,[10] Goluchowski still described the Triple Alliance as the basis of his policy; but he had been as cavalier about initiating the Italians into the 1897 agreements as Kálnoky had been about Skiernewice; and Beck had been working on contingency plans for war against Italy since the end of 1896, the Tauern railway being extended to the Isonzo. The fact that the 1897 agreements were made over the head of Germany too, and that this was rather resented in Berlin, was another symptom of the decline in importance of the Monarchy's alliance system. Most striking of all was the complete abandonment of the link with Great Britain, a Power not even mentioned by Goluchowski in his survey of the situation. Indeed, according to Aehrenthal and his friends, the shedding of all 'illusory proclivities'[11] as regards Great Britain – a Power which, as they saw it, would never be able to give Austria-Hungary any effective help – was one of the most cheering features of the 1897 Entente, even if it as yet stopped disappointingly short at the mere maintenance of the status quo.

This last note of criticism was indicative of a debate over the scope and purpose of the Entente that was to continue throughout Goluchowski's tenure of office. Goluchowski was satisfied with the agreements as they stood. The St Petersburg visit had shown that there was really no fundamental reason why Russia and Austria-Hungary could not agree; Russian suspicions about Austria-Hungary's legendary plans of expansion as far as Salonika had been dispelled; and Austria-Hungary in turn now seemed to have nothing to fear from Russia – especially as she was so deeply engaged in the Far East. As he assured the conference of ministers on 5 October,[12] there was now reason to hope 'that we can avoid conflict with Russia without giving up any of our vital interests'. For Aehrenthal and the partisans of a more positive *entente*, however, this was not enough. Whereas for Goluchowski and the officials of the Ballhausplatz the Entente was primarily an instrument for safeguarding Austria-Hungary's particular Balkan interests from Russian encroachment, for Aehrenthal and his friends the Entente was the starting point for a positive, far-reaching understanding with

9. Aehrenthal MSS, Karton 1, Goluchowski to Aehrenthal, 30 June 1897.
10. P.A. XL/298, Ministerratsprotokoll, 5 October 1897.
11. Aehrenthal MSS, Karton 1, Hengelmüller to Aehrenthal, 26 May 1897.
12. P.A. XL/298, Ministerratsprotokoll, 5 October 1897.

Russia, extending eventually to close co-operation in Great Power politics generally. For the sake of this ambitious long-term aim, the exponents of a positive *entente* were prepared to sacrifice some of the Monarchy's narrower particular interests. Thus, whereas Goluchowski tended to put the emphasis on 'without giving up any . . . vital interests', they stressed the need to 'avoid conflict with Russia'. Which view of the Entente would eventually prevail would depend to some extent on developments in the area with which the Entente was specifically concerned.

The conclusion of the tedious Cretan affair, for example, showed that Goluchowski was certainly not prepared to take risks with Austro-Hungarian interests for the sake of the Entente. At the end of 1897 Russia, jealous of Germany's growing influence at Constantinople, suddenly sought to demonstrate her own power by putting forward the candidature of Prince George of the Hellenes for the governorship of Crete, now to be granted autonomy under the supervision of the Great Powers. This concession to aggressive Panhellenism was as much resented in Berlin as in Vienna, and in January 1898 Germany withdrew her contingent of troops from Crete and washed her hands of the question. Goluchowski was faced with a dilemma.[13] On the one hand, the maintenance of the status quo was undoubtedly jeopardised by Prince George's candidature, in so far as it seemed to be a step towards the union of Crete with Greece, an event that would certainly whet the appetites of the other Balkan states. Indeed, Goluchowski regarded Russia's action as a violation of the spirit of the 1897 agreements. On the other hand, as any weakening of the credibility of the new Entente, or any clear division within the Concert, could equally tempt troublemakers in the Balkans to further attacks on the status quo, Goluchowski wished to avoid an open breach with Russia. In the end, he decided to take that risk, and withdrew the Austro-Hungarian contingent from Crete. He was careful to explain in a circular to the Powers that Austria-Hungary still retained an interest in Crete, and intended to participate, along with the other members of the Concert, in any final solution of the question. But the exponents of a more positive *entente* with Russia were by no means mollified: Prince Liechtenstein, for example, when Goluchowski rejected a scheme of his whereby Russia would guarantee the integrity of Turkey in return for Austria-Hungary's co-operation in the Cretan

---

13. Aehrenthal MSS, Karton 4, Zwiedenek to Aehrenthal, 29 January 1898; P.A. XL/298, Ministerratsprotokoll, 3 April 1898.

question, went so far as to resign his post as ambassador at St Petersburg.[14]

Franz Joseph and Goluchowski, for their part, felt they had genuine reason for complaint about Russia's behaviour. In August 1898 the visiting Russian foreign minister, Mouraviev, was taken to task by the emperor himself, while Goluchowski berated Kapnist about Russia's disloyalty.[15] The tsar had recently given a large present of arms to Nikita of Montenegro, notoriously the most anti-Austrian of all the Balkan princes; the Russian press was forever engaged in a 'mad campaign' against the Austro-Hungarian administration in Bosnia and the Herzegovina, and was accusing Austria-Hungary of meddling in Serbia, whither ex-King Milan had just returned from his Austrian exile. Finally, far from being co-operative in accordance with the 1897 agreement, Russian diplomats recently transferred from the rough and tumble of Asian posts to the Balkan capitals – particularly Bachmatiev at Sofia – were guilty, Goluchowski claimed, of 'quite incredible' intrigues against Austria-Hungary. Indeed, he was finding it increasingly difficult to justify the Entente to public opinion; and was beginning to think it might be simpler if the two Powers reverted to their old methods, safeguarding their own interests and checkmating each other at every turn.

Although this outburst cleared the air, and drew promises of better behaviour from St Petersburg, the early years of the Entente saw Austro-Hungarian influence in retreat in all three Slav Balkan states. Montenegro, for instance, remained a thorn in the side of the Monarchy despite the Entente. Indeed, Prince Nikita had become increasingly bold in his efforts to influence Russian policy through two of his daughters who were married to Russian grand dukes. Minor frontier incidents and commercial disputes continually supplemented the bitterness felt at Cetinje towards the Dual Monarchy, by tradition the tiresome watchdog, the eternal creditor, and the destroyer of the treaty of San Stefano.[16] Vienna in turn maintained a stiff, cold attitude towards Nikita: Franz Joseph absolutely refused to receive him at court. In the Austrian view, the Monarchy would always have enough influence at Cetinje, simply by virtue of its geographical position, however bad relations might be.[17] The Ballhausplatz put its trust in this and in the new *entente* to restrain

---

14. Aehrenthal MSS, Karton 3, Liechtenstein to Aehrenthal, 28 December 1898.
15. P.A. I/476, Goluchowski, Memorandum on a conversation with Kapnist, August 1898.
16. Aehrenthal MSS, Karton 3, Macchio to Aehrenthal, 2 May 1901.
17. Ibid.

Montenegro. Indeed, it seemed for a time in 1901 that this policy was succeeding: the Russian minister at Cetinje, Vlassov, was an ardent supporter of the Entente, and determined that Nikita should not lead Russia by the nose.[18] But by the autumn of 1902, Nikita and Panslav elements at St Petersburg had secured Vlassov's recall. Within six months his successor, a man of the Ignatiev school, who, according to his Austrian colleague, treated the Entente as 'a social game', and shunned all discussions, had re-established a virtual Russian protectorate over Montenegro.[19]

Serbia, Montenegro's sister-state and rival in the struggle for leadership of the South Slav world, continued for a time under Austro-Hungarian influence. Between 1897 and 1900 an Austrophile government under Georgević managed to restore a measure of political and financial stability. True, the young King Alexander was as unstable as his father, and his wild boasts of Austro-Hungarian support were something of an embarrassment to Vienna, as when he publicly declared in 1899 that 'the enemies of Serbia are the enemies of Austria-Hungary'.[20] Equally, the return to Belgrade early in 1898 of ex-King Milan was by no means an unmixed blessing for the Austrians. His ill-judged intervention in favour of severe sentences for the accused in a spectacular treason trial of Russophile radicals at the end of 1899 – despite Vienna's urgent pleas for clemency – only caused problems for the Ballhausplatz. The infuriated Russians withdrew their diplomatic representatives from Belgrade, complaining that Austria-Hungary could have done more to check Milan's influence, or even to get rid of it altogether. But this Goluchowski refused to do: such pressure would contravene the 1897 agreement on non-intervention. Besides, it would be politically suicidal for the Monarchy to do anything to help Russia to establish her predominance in Serbia; and to cast the Monarchy in the role of a mere tool of Russia in this way would gravely compromise Austro-Hungarian prestige throughout the Balkans.[21]

Events beyond the control of Vienna soon conspired to undermine that prestige, however. In August 1900 King Alexander married his former mistress, Draga Masin, provoking both the fall of the Georgević ministry and the voluntary – and final – exile of

18. Ibid., Macchio to Aehrenthal, 2 September 1901.
19. Ibid., Macchio to Aehrenthal, 9 October 1902, 27 April 1903.
20. Ibid., Karton 2, Jettel to Aehrenthal, 18 August 1899.
21. P.A. I/475, Liasse XXXII, Goluchowski to Aehrenthal, No. 2, 10 January 1900; Liasse XXXII/h, Goluchowski to Aehrenthal, private and very confidential, 29 December 1901.

the enraged Milan. The Russians now made haste to restore diplomatic relations with Serbia, and by July 1901, according to a Ballhausplatz assessment,[22] the energetic Russian minister, Charykov, ruled in fact both King Alexander and his kingdom, thanks to his contacts with the powerful Radical party. The volatile king had meanwhile swung completely into the Russian camp, going so far as to describe the Monarchy, in speaking to a journalist in 1902, as 'the arch-enemy of Serbia'.[23] The Austrians were, not unnaturally, disconcerted by these events. But Goluchowski proved his loyalty to the non-interventionist principles of 1897 in bad times as in good. This loyalty was perhaps ultimately to cost the Monarchy dear. However, it could hardly be said that anything that had happened in Serbia so far necessitated heavy-handed intervention at the cost of damaging the Entente with St Petersburg. Certainly, if ever the dynasty fell and Panslav elements attempted to bring about a union between Serbia and Montenegro – a step towards a big Slav state that would cut off Austria-Hungary from the south-western Balkans – Goluchowski was prepared to prevent such a union by force, 'because when the vital nerve of the Monarchy is in question, we cannot yield'.[24] For the time being, however, he put his faith in the bland assumptions of the Kálnoky era: if Serbia became too troublesome she could always be brought to heel 'as by virtue of geography she is so dependent on us financially and economically'.[25]

Meanwhile, developments in Bulgaria did nothing to redress the Balkan balance in the Monarchy's favour. In the commercial field, the Monarchy maintained, even slightly increased, its trade with Bulgaria; but the greater part of the growth in Bulgaria's total trade was absorbed by the Monarchy's increasingly powerful competitors, Great Britain and Germany. Politically, the Austrians proceeded to commit the very error the Russians had committed in the 1880s: when, in July 1897, the Bulgarian prime minister publicly criticised Austro-Hungarian policy, Goluchowski summarily withdrew all Austro-Hungarian consuls and diplomatic agents from Bulgaria. Franz Joseph and Goluchowski continued to ostracise Prince Ferdinand, and after 1900 warmly supported Romania's complaints about the sufferings of the Koutzo-Vlachs of Macedonia at the hands of Bulgarian terrorists. All this left the field clear for

22. Aehrenthal MSS, Karton 5, Musulin to Aehrenthal, 12 July 1901.
23. Glaise-Horstenau, *Beck*, p. 391.
24. P.A. I/475, Liasse XXXII, Goluchowski to Aehrenthal, No. 242, 19 August 1900.
25. Ibid.

Russia, and the assiduous Bachmatiev was soon boasting that he occupied at Sofia a position comparable to that of Cromer at Cairo. It was cold comfort for Goluchowski when, in response to his testy enquiry at St Petersburg about rumours of an impending Bulgarian coup – either an incursion into Macedonia or a declaration of independence – the Russian government somewhat loftily assured him that Bulgaria was not planning any kind of coup, and that Russia could vouch for her future good conduct. He could only console himself with the thought that, as Russia boasted so openly of her control of Bulgaria, the Monarchy need be less restrained elsewhere.[26]

With Serbia and Bulgaria drifting away, Goluchowski attempted to make Romania the pivot of his Balkan policy. Initially, the news of the Austro-Russian Entente had been ill received at Bucharest, and not without reason. Aehrenthal, for example, had heaved a sigh of relief when Franz Joseph's speech to the Delegations in 1897 dwelt on the new *entente* and contained hardly a word about Romania. He hoped that Goluchowski's 'Romanian heart' would not be in evidence again for a long time.[27] But Goluchowski, after his experiences of the following three years, was by no means disposed to stake everything on the *entente* with Russia, and made a determined effort to cultivate Romania. In the autumn of 1900 he spoke encouragingly to King Carol:[28] the 1897 agreements were by no means contrary to Romania's interests; indeed, they constituted a guarantee of the future free development of Romania. Nor would they in the least prevent Austria-Hungary's standing up for Romanian interests in the event of changes in the status quo. He urged Bucharest to come to terms with Athens (but no longer, as in 1897, with Belgrade).[29] True, he refused to extend the alliance to give Romania a free hand to attack Bulgaria in the event of the latter's attempting to expand in Macedonia: Romania should continue to rely on Austria-Hungary to safeguard her interests in the event of a general redrawing of the Balkan map.[30] But more immediately, Vienna agreed to supply Romania with military instructors and equipment; and even if Goluchowski's doctrine that the irredentist question, being merely a matter for negotiation between Bucharest

26. Aehrenthal MSS, Karton 1, Goluchowski to Aehrenthal, 26 March 1900.
27. Mérey MSS, Aehrenthal to Mérey, 19 November 1897.
28. P.A. I/472, Liasse XX/e, Goluchowski to Pallavicini, No. 290, secret, 9 October 1900.
29. Ibid., Goluchowski to Pallavicini, No. 374, secret, 12 December 1900.
30. Ibid., Goluchowski to Pallavicini, No. 51, secret, 29 January 1901.

and Budapest, had 'nothing to do with the alliance'[31] had something of an unrealistically legalistic air about it, the alliance itself was in a fair state of health. In April 1902, it was renewed to run for five years, and then automatically for a further three.

Meanwhile, Goluchowski's dogged insistence that the *entente* with Russia was no more than a means of safeguarding Austria-Hungary's interests against a supposed threat from the *entente* partner herself exasperated the partisans of a more positive approach. The stronghold of the latter remained, as usual, the embassy at St Petersburg, where Liechtenstein had been followed by the even more assiduous Aehrenthal; but Aehrenthal also enjoyed the support of Szögyény, ambassador at Berlin (who may in fact have had an eye on Goluchowski's position for himself)[32] and of a small but influential group of people at home, including such notable Slav politicians as Kramář.[33] In the Ballhausplatz itself, Jettel von Ettenach, head of the Literary Office, strove untiringly to influence public opinion in favour of the Entente by a judicious placing of articles in the press.[34] In the foreign office as a whole, however, Russia remained an object of deep suspicion; not only for Goluchowski, but for his very powerful confidant, Baron Doczy, who, according to a lament of Jettel's of May 1900, was closer to the minister than anyone else, and whose word was law.[35] (As a Jew, Doczy naturally had little love for Tsarism.) The emperor, too, found Russia's behaviour intensely irritating, and often complained of her 'unreliability'.[36] He tended to dismiss Aehrenthal's criticisms of Goluchowski's policy as the expression of some personal animus against the minister, or as evidence that the ambassador had become 'ganz russisch'.[37]

Matters came to a head in the summer of 1901. First, Szögyény went in person to see the emperor to complain about Goluchowski's 'impossible' ways.[38] Even in his technical organising of the service and in his choice of personnel, Goluchowski was gravely at fault: in Szögyény's view, almost all the Austro-Hungarian representatives in the Balkan capitals were worthless. The minister's notorious indolence was equally exasperating: diplomats were constantly left

31. P.A. I/479, Liasse XXXIV/a, Goluchowski to Szögyény, No. 515, secret, 4 December 1901.
32. Aehrenthal MSS, Karton 2, Jettel to Aehrenthal, 2 November 1900.
33. Ibid., Kramář to Aehrenthal, 6 February 1899, 2 February 1900.
34. Ibid., Jettel to Aehrenthal, 28 June 1899.
35. Ibid., Jettel to Aehrenthal, 23 May 1900.
36. Ibid., Karton 6, Szögyény to Aehrenthal, 12 May 1899.
37. Ibid., Karton 2, Jettel to Aehrenthal, 5 January 1900.
38. Ibid., Karton 4, Szögyény to Aehrenthal, 10 July, 6 October 1901.

without instructions, and had to glean what they could of their government's policy from the newspapers. This tirade did little good, however; and in August the Russophile party were further enraged by the publication in *Pester Lloyd* of an alarmist article – the concluding paragraph of which had apparently been written by Goluchowski himself after consultation with the emperor – harshly summoning Russia to explain her recent behaviour and to state whether she wished to continue the Entente or not.[39] At this, Aehrenthal himself went to see the emperor.[40] He complained at length about Goluchowski's 'aimless' and suspicious attitude towards Russia, and pleaded strongly for a more positive approach to the Entente. The Monarchy should cultivate St Petersburg, both as a means of gaining more independence from Berlin within the Dual Alliance, and – as the days of the Triple Alliance might well be numbered – in order to avoid finding itself some day in the grip of a Russo-Italian vice. But he got the impression that his arguments were only wearying the old emperor, and so, in November, he repeated them in a long letter to Goluchowski.[41] Again he emphasised that minor questions and particular interests of the Monarchy must be subordinated to the need to preserve cordial relations with Russia at all costs. Goluchowski was not completely convinced, and defended his attitude[42] towards specific issues such as Crete and Serbia on grounds of political necessity. The purpose of the Entente, he reiterated, was to protect Austro-Hungarian interests: it would be quite wrong for the Monarchy to sacrifice those interests for the Entente, simply accepting every Russian advance just for the sake of avoiding a clash. That would place the Monarchy in a worse position than before the Entente existed, when at least it had had the freedom to take appropriate countermeasures to defend its interests.

In the event, Goluchowski was to be forced – as in 1897 – by internal and external factors outside his control at least to consider the possibility of more positive co-operation with Russia. In the first place, the situation in Macedonia, where Bulgarian terrorist atrocities alternated with Turkish reprisals, was becoming daily worse, and threatened to precipitate a war between Turkey and Bulgaria that would open up the whole Eastern Question. To this

39. Ibid., Karton 2, Jettel to Aehrenthal, 23 August, 6 September 1901.
40. Ibid., Karton 4, Aehrenthal to Szögyény, 27 September 1901 (copy).
41. P.A. I/475, Liasse XXXII/k, Aehrenthal to Goluchowski, private and secret, 15 November 1901.
42. Ibid., Liasse XXXII/h, Goluchowski to Aehrenthal, private and very confidential, 29 December 1901.

situation the Austrians felt they would have to devise some response, if only for the sake of their prestige (*Vormachtstellung*) in the Balkans. Goluchowski, therefore, while he sternly warned Aehrenthal that, if Russia refused to co-operate, he would return to his pre-1897 policy of opposing her at every turn, now authorised the ambassador to approach the Russian foreign minister, Lamsdorff, with a view to coming to some agreement to contain the developing crisis in Macedonia.[43] This need not entail any departure from the conservative principles of 1897: it would be quite in order to interfere in Turkey to make the sultan modify the obviously unsatisfactory political and administrative status quo in Macedonia for the greater good of preserving the territorial status quo. In fact, St Petersburg responded favourably, at least to the extent of joining Vienna in warning the Bulgarian government to refrain from intervention. It seemed that the Austro-Russian Entente might well be about to develop in a more positive direction after all.

One factor that was practically forcing Goluchowski to rely more on the Entente with Russia was the apparent lack of any feasible alternative source of support. In the first place, the later nineties were dominated by extra-European or world issues that hardly provided much common ground between the Monarchy's narrow interests in south-east Europe and the preoccupations of the other Great Powers. True, when the Boxer rising broke out in China in 1900 Franz Joseph, more prestige-minded and more in tune with public opinion than the Ballhausplatz,[44] insisted on sending a couple of ships and a detachment of marines, who, according to Austrian reports, fought better than the Italians.[45] In the Spanish–American dispute of 1898 Vienna had taken an even keener interest. Goluchowski had from the start been disposed to assist the Habsburg queen regent of Spain by offering to mediate – a last echo of Kálnoky's policy of supporting the Iberian monarchies;[46] and, under pressure from Franz Joseph,[47] he had tried to mobilise the Concert of Europe to put pressure on the United States. In the end, however, he had had to content himself with organising, through the diplomatic corps at Washington, a fruitless appeal to President McKinley's humanitarian sentiments. For Germany frowned on his efforts; and Great Britain, according to the

43. Ibid., Goluchowski to Aehrenthal, No. 556, 29 December 1901.
44. Mérey MSS, Szécsen to Mérey, 12,22,27 July 1900.
45. Glaise-Horstenau, *Beck*, p. 389.
46. P.A. XX/68, Goluchowski to Wolkenstein, tel. 8, 13 March 1898.
47. Bavarian State Archives, M.A. III, 1898 Wien, Podewils to Äußenministerium, No. 209 XXVII, 6 May 1898.

Austro-Hungarian minister at Washington (a staunch supporter of Aehrenthal) was worse than useless, being solely concerned to appease the United States – a Power which ultimately represented a greater threat to Europe than even the so-called Yellow Peril: 'we shall all be ruined commercially and brutalised politically'.[48]

Even in the European theatre, it seemed that the old system based on co-operation with Great Britain in the Mediterranean Entente was now lost beyond recall. It is true that Vienna wished the British a speedy victory in the South African War, in the hope that they might return all the sooner to look after their interests in the Mediterranean. The emperor, for example, made no bones about telling the British ambassador, at a ball and in the presence of several witnesses, that 'dans cette guerre je suis complètement Anglais';[49] and the Hungarian government – partly no doubt as a sound economic proposition at a time of depression – pressed ahead with the sale of large numbers of horses for use by the British against the Boers. These gestures were not insignificant at a time when public opinion in the Monarchy, as throughout Europe (except perhaps for certain Magyar and Italian patriots who remembered 1849 and 1860), was so violently anti–British. Despite a considerable uproar in the press, and especially in the Austrian parliament, the governments of Vienna and Budapest steadily ignored this opinion.[50] But nothing much grew out of all this. Although Goluchowski welcomed the Anglo-German alliance negotiations of 1901, as a chance to bind Great Britain closer to the Triple Alliance, he could do nothing to influence their outcome. He was, of course, blissfully unaware that reluctance to underwrite the tottering Dual Monarchy was one of the reasons for the British refusal to join the Triple Alliance as Germany was demanding; whereas Germany for her part rejected anything less – for example, what was virtually a British offer to revive the Mediterranean Agreements with the pivot in Berlin rather than in Vienna. At any rate, these very tentative contacts, even failures, could give Goluchowski no reason to contemplate reverting from the Russian to a British connection.

The other major components of Kálnoky's defensive system, the Dual and Triple Alliances, hardly offered any more hope of salvation. The Dual Alliance was seriously troubled in these years by the

48. Aehrenthal MSS, Karton 1, Hengelmüller to Aehrenthal, 12 May 1898.
49. F.O. 7/1297, Rumbold to Salisbury, No. 11, confidential, 10 January 1900.
50. F.R. Bridge, 'British Official Opinion and the Domestic Situation in the Habsburg Monarchy, 1900–1914', in B.J.C. McKercher and D.J. Moss (eds), *Shadow and Substance in British Foreign Policy* (Edmonton, 1984) pp. 77, 82–3.

intensification of national feeling in both Germany and Austria. Even temporary successes of the Slavs on the whirligig of Austrian politics after 1897 were liable to cause friction between the increasingly anti-Slav Germany and its polyglot ally. When, in 1899, the Prussian government arbitrarily expelled some Czech and Polish seasonal workers, the Austrian prime minister, Count Franz Thun, a Bohemian nobleman of Czech sympathies, hinted sharply in parliament at the possibility of retaliatory measures. At this, indignant complaints flowed in from the German embassy, and even from Wilhelm II himself; but Franz Joseph gave them short shrift and supported Thun. Meanwhile, the German unofficial, and even semi-official, press described the Slav tendencies allegedly prevailing in Austria as a threat to the Alliance. All this only exasperated Goluchowski, who pointed out that no Austro-Hungarian government could afford to ignore such important sections of opinion as the Czechs and the Poles, whatever Berlin might say. And the Austrians were not without their own grievances against Germany,[51] whence nationalism of a virulent Pan-German variety was spreading its tentacles across the frontier, linking up with the protestant-nationalist *Los von Rom* movement, denouncing Catholicism and the House of Habsburg, and demanding a speedy completion of Bismarck's great work. In November 1898 a German nationalist deputy proclaimed in the Reichsrat itself and amidst cheers from like-minded colleagues, that his loyalty lay with the emperor at Berlin. Such demonstrations, which became commonplace in the following years, could do the reputation of Germany and the Alliance no good in clerical and monarchist circles; and commercial circles were appalled when Germany reverted to a highly protectionist tariff in 1902. In Jettel's opinion, 'Germany has injured us far more commercially than Russia has done politically.'[52] Personal factors deepened the estrangement. Goluchowski, as a Pole, was never really *persona grata* in Berlin; whereas Franz Joseph was finding the flamboyant Wilhelm II increasingly tiresome: 'if only the German emperor could keep silent! He talks far too much. It is better that we should keep quiet and let our ministers do the talking.'[53] After 1900 he paid no more visits to Berlin.

The lamentable state of Austro-German relations at the turn of the century was no doubt also a reflection of differences over issues

---

51. P.A. I/480, Goluchowski to Szögyény, private, 17 January 1902.
52. Aehrenthal MSS, Karton 2, Jettel to Aehrenthal, 5 January 1900.
53. J. Andrássy, *Bismarck, Andrássy and their successors*, p. 291.

of foreign policy. The Austro-Russian Entente, itself very much a product of Austrian irritation at Germany's unreliability and pro-Russian proclivities, aroused in turn a good deal of jealousy in Berlin. For although the Germans now had no more stomach than they had had in Bismarck's day for an Austro-Russian war and all the burdens and dilemmas that it would entail, they had equally no desire to see their imperial neighbours on such close terms that Germany's services as broker could be dispensed with. Not that Goluchowski was intimidated by Bülow's blustering speech in the *Reichstag* in January 1902, hinting that Germany needed the Triple Alliance less than her allies did, and could make her own deal with St Petersburg. He rightly calculated that so long as the Franco-Russian alliance continued, the continental alliance system was too rigid to permit of a Russo-German alliance, or even of a restored Three Emperors' Alliance. But he was immensely irritated by Bülow's gratuitous downgrading of the Triple Alliance; and he was equally dismayed by Germany's treatment of Great Britain, remarking that 'friend Bülow richly deserved' the verbal drubbing he received from Chamberlain at this time in an exchange of polemics over the South African War.[54] Worst of all, the Germans were proving highly uncooperative in the Near East. In their obsessive concern for their economic interests in Turkey, they ostentatiously took the sultan's side against all the other Powers in a dispute over the foreign post offices in Turkey. Goluchowski, who felt that the very status of the Great Powers in Turkey was at stake, was much exercised about this. Even more serious, the Germans – in marked contrast to the Russians – showed no sympathy at all for Goluchowski's plans to stabilise the situation in Macedonia by forcing the sultan to make life tolerable for his subjects.

The Triple Alliance was hardly in any better shape. The year 1902 saw the usual crisis over its renewal, with the Italians demanding the incorporation into the Alliance of the Austro-Italian self-denying agreement of 1897. (In 1900, this had been formalised in an exchange of notes pledging the two Powers, in the event of Turkey's disappearance, to eschew all selfish desires of conquest and to work for the creation of a large independent Albania.) Goluchowski, however, at first refused to countenance any changes at all, insisting that the Alliance was concerned solely with the status quo, not with possible future developments. Nor would he pre-empt the decision of the Austrian and Hungarian governments

---

54. P.A. I/480, Liasse XXXIV/b, Goluchowski to Szögyény, private, 17 January 1902.

by committing himself to continue the favourable tariff accorded to Italian wine imports, due to expire in 1903. In the end, the only concession Goluchowski made was to give the Italians a declaration (similar to those just made by France and Great Britain) stating that as far as Austria-Hungary was concerned, Italy could have a free hand in Tripoli if ever the Ottoman Empire collapsed.

It was not a concession that did much to enhance the value of the Alliance in Italian eyes. Already in 1900 the assassination of the conservative soldier-king Umberto had weakened the ties between Rome and Vienna; and official contact between the Austro-Hungarian and Italian general staffs now virtually came to an end. The fact that the new king, Victor Emmanuel III, was married to a daughter of Nikita of Montenegro augured ill for Goluchowski's hopes of restricting Italy's interests and influence in the Balkans. And the elections of 1902 brought to power an anti-clerical and pro-French government under Zanardelli. Not that the Austrians – unlike the Germans – resented the Francophile inclinations of the new government, or even the Franco-Italian agreements of 30 June 1902: anything that diminished the risk of a Franco-Italian war which might entail unpleasant duties for Austria-Hungary was welcome to Vienna. But certain delicate questions which had troubled the Alliance in the past had undoubtedly become more difficult to handle. For example, a *modus vivendi* between Quirinal and Vatican, still the essential precondition of an Austro-Hungarian state visit to Italy, was under the new anti-clerical government further off than ever; and although the new king soon paid a state visit to Berlin, and even to St Petersburg, he and Franz Joseph were still complete strangers to each other – a state of affairs which was, as Goluchowski pointed out, hardly normal between allied monarchs.[55] Such issues undoubtedly weakened the hold of the Alliance over public opinion at a time when irredentism was still rife in Italy, and when the sharpening of national conflicts inside the Monarchy was awakening the hostility of the South Slavs of the Austrian and Hungarian coastlands towards both their Italian fellow-subjects and the Italians of the kingdom. In terms of practical diplomacy the Triple Alliance meant very little, for all Goluchowski might resent Bülow's public depreciation of it. In Albania, rivalry between Austrian and Italian propagandists, consular and religious, raged unabated; and Goluchowski was adamant in his refusal to initiate Rome into such plans as he was considering with

55. P.A. I/476, Goluchowski, Memorandum ·on a conversation with Count Nigra, 15 September 1902.

St Petersburg to deal with the unrest in Macedonia.

Underlining the crumbling of Kálnoky's system of diplomatic defences against Russia was the deepening confusion that prevailed in the domestic affairs of the Monarchy in the decade around the turn of the century. By the end of 1897 increasingly violent rioting over linguistic and national issues by Czechs and Germans, in the Austrian parliament, the Bohemian Diet and the streets of Vienna and Prague, had brought parliamentary government in Austria to a complete standstill. No government could be found which could command a sufficiently stable majority to carry through the negotiations for the renewal of the commercial *Ausgleich* with Hungary; and after 1897 the old *Ausgleich* was provisionally extended from year to year by a variety of constitutional expedients, Hungary attaining, in theory at least, actual independence as a commercial unit (although in practice the same external tariffs were maintained in both halves of the Monarchy). It was in these years that Austria-Hungary earned the sobriquet of 'Dual Monarchy on short notice [*auf Kündigung*]'. A deep pessimism gripped those who were called on to find a way out: to some it seemed that 'an archangel could not solve our domestic problems', and that the Monarchy had now sunk to the position of a second-class Power such as Japan.[56] Naturally, this state of affairs did not go unnoticed abroad. The Monarchy's potential enemies, France and Russia, took its possible disintegration into account when they amended their alliance in 1899 to include co-operation 'to maintain the balance of power' – that is, to prevent Germany's acquiring too large a slice of the Habsburg dominions. In 1900 André Chéradame's sensational book, *L'Autriche au seuil du vingtième siècle* propounded the view that the Monarchy had succeeded Turkey as the sick man of Europe, and now bade fair to be an easy prey for Pan-German expansionism. As the British refusal to join the Triple Alliance in 1901 showed, even Austria-Hungary's friends were impressed by her apparently inexorably advancing decrepitude.

This decrepitude was reflected in a weakening of the economic position of the Monarchy in the years of depression at the end of the nineties. There was a slight improvement after 1900, thanks largely to an extensive programme of public works initiated by the government in an effort to divert public opinion from nationalist strife. But it was becoming increasingly clear – and this had serious implications for the political prestige of the Monarchy in the Near East – that Austria-Hungary was finding it increasingly difficult to

56. Aehrenthal MSS, Karton 1, Biegeleben to Aehrenthal, 26 February 1899.

maintain, let alone strengthen, her position against her Great Power competitors. Perhaps the problem was exacerbated by the proverbial inefficiency of the commercial departments of the government, after Andrássy's departure very much poor relations in a system essentially military and aristocratic in spirit. In 1903 the go-ahead Austrian journalist, Baernreither, drew a very unfavourable comparison between the Prussian Ministry of Trade (the head of which had just visited the United States) and its counterparts in Austria-Hungary, where most of the Sektionschefs never in their lives ventured further than a lunchtime stroll in the Ringstraße.[57] The commercial department of the Ballhausplatz exhibited some of the worst features of Austrian bureaucracy – although it should be said that the chaos affecting the whole government was partly to blame for grumblings among the diplomatic corps that 'unexampled delay now occurs in extracting answers from this government in which ministries other than the ministry for foreign affairs are involved' – particularly when reference to Budapest was necessary: 'The dilatoriness of this country, if continued in progressive ratio, will soon rival that of Turkey.'[58] But the real problem lay deeper, and was hardly one that could be remedied by administrative tinkerings. The fact was that the governments of Vienna and Budapest were often helpless in the face of the inexorable intensification of competition from richer, more advanced industrial states, with which the largely agrarian Monarchy could not hope to hold its own.

For example, the thriving Austrian sugar-beet industry was virtually ruined when, at the turn of the century, Great Britain and the United States imposed draconian punitive duties on sugar that was produced with the help of government subsidies, and secured international endorsement for this in the Brussels Sugar Convention of 1902. Even more disastrous was the behaviour of Germany, still far and away the Monarchy's most important trading partner, which in 1902 reverted to a fairly stiff protectionist tariff which hit Austrian and Hungarian cattle and grain exports directly and very hard. At the same time, she was steadily securing markets in the Balkans for her own light industrial goods at Austria-Hungary's expense. The Austrians for their part were holding their own, as yet, in Serbia; but in Bulgaria and Romania German competition was becoming increasingly severe.[59] For the time being, if the

57. Ibid., Baernreither to Aehrenthal, 27 June 1903.
58. F.O. 7/1355, Johnstone to Lansdowne, No. 3, commercial, 11 January 1904.
59. V. Paskaleva, 'Ueber den wirtschaftlichen Einfluß Oesterreich-Ungarns in

Monarchy was losing some of its traditional Balkan markets, it could still find others further afield in even more primitive areas in Asia Minor (where more cotton goods were sold than in Hungary in 1906) and Macedonia. The position was by no means desperate. A number of profitable factories were soon operating in Turkey, where by 1908 the Monarchy was running second only to Great Britain as a trading power. But the prospects were by no means brilliant.

Not that the Monarchy could expect any assistance in this field from its alliances or *ententes*. In 1900, for example, it was decided to extend the Monarchy's railway network into Bosnia. For Goluchowski, this was a matter of highest policy: in military-strategic terms it was vital that the Monarchy should be in a position to send troops to the frontier of the Sanjak; and it would ultimately be desirable – for commercial purposes too – to extend the Bosnian network into the Sanjak of Novibazar itself, thereby establishing a direct railway connection with Turkey independent of the Balkan states. (The existing line to Constantinople ran through Serbia and Bulgaria.) Admittedly, two months of conferences were necessary before the Austrian and Hungarian governments could be brought to agree which railways were to be built, and by which companies; but by 1905 the Bosnian network had been completed. No progress was made, however, towards a further extension into the Sanjak. Indeed, a mere rumour of such a project drew from the Russian embassy in November 1900 an anxious enquiry, which elicited a careless assurance from Sektionschef Szécsen to the effect that the Monarchy could not build railways in foreign territory.[60] Goluchowski lost no time in correcting this statement, and sharply reminded the Russian ambassador that the Monarchy had every good right to build railways in the Sanjak by virtue of the Treaty of Berlin. Such economic projects, he said, had nothing to do with the Entente of 1897, which was concerned only with the political status quo.[61] But when the question was again raised tentatively at the end of 1902 it again came to nothing in the face of the frowns of St Petersburg and the lethargy of Constantinople – and of Germany's ostentatious refusal to put in a word for her ally in either capital.

Political confusion and economic weakness combined during these years to reduce the military potential of the Dual Monarchy.

Bulgarien 1878–1918', in Klein (ed.), *Weltpolitik*, pp. 187–9; Palotas, 'Außenwirtschaftliche Beziehungen', in *Habsburgermonarchie VI*, pp. 620ff.
60. Aehrenthal MSS, Karton 5, Notiz, 5 November 1900.
61. P.A. I/476, Liasse XXXIII/39, Goluchowski, memorandum on a conversation with Count Kapnist, November 1900.

The Common Army could only be increased if a new Army Law were passed by both parliaments to increase the size of the contingents recruited annually in Austria and Hungary beyond the level fixed by the Army Law of 1889. Now with Austria in political chaos and much of Magyar opinion traditionally suspicious of the Common Army as a threat to the liberties of Hungary, this simply could not be done. Indeed, the two parliaments provided precious little money even for technical improvements to the existing army. This was, perhaps, a blessing in disguise; for when the money was eventually forthcoming, in the last years of peace, the Austro-Hungarian Army at least got some of the best and most modern equipment. But for the time being, army reform plans were a pure waste of time. 'In building up the Army, unfortunately no progress'; this was the monotonous refrain of Beck's annual reports.[62] Nor was much done for the navy, despite Goluchowski's warnings that it might be needed in a Near Eastern crisis, and despite Franz Joseph's pointing to its general importance in terms of trade and prestige in peacetime. The 1890s, when all the other Great Powers were arming fast, had seen the balance of military power shift steadily against the Dual Monarchy. Indeed, in a conference of ministers in June 1899, the emperor stated quite bluntly that if the Monarchy had to fight in existing circumstances it would not have a hope of success.[63]

In these circumstances, the Hague Peace Conference, summoned in 1899 at the wish of the tsar, was a source of acute embarrassment to Vienna.[64] The idea of an armaments freeze was not attractive to a Power which already had so much leeway to make up; and compulsory arbitration might well deprive the Monarchy of its only military advantage over Russia, that of speed of mobilisation. On the other hand, the tsar would naturally be offended if the conference produced nothing at all. In the event, Goluchowski managed to appear conciliatory on unimportant issues – he helped to persuade the Germans to accept the idea of voluntary arbitration and a permanent court; and in the armaments question he skilfully kept in the background, allowing the Germans to incur the odium of leading the opposition. The outcome relieved his worst anxieties as to the future: public opinion would see in the anodyne declaration on armaments and in the court of arbitration great guarantees of

62. Glaise-Horstenau, *Beck*, p. 408.
63. P.A. XL/299, Ministerratsprotokoll, 29 June 1899.
64. P.A. X/144, Edler von Kriegshammer to Goluchowski, No. 2002, 21 April 1899; protocol of meeting of 28 April 1899 to determine Austria-Hungary's attitude at the Hague conference.

peace, yet none of this would in practice impose the slightest restriction on the Great Powers.[65] But it did nothing to relieve the pressing anxieties of the present.

Nor did the next two years see any improvement in the military capacity of the Monarchy. On 29 November 1901 Beck warned a conference of ministers[66] that Austria-Hungary might well be compelled to take action in a way not envisaged by her alliances; and Franz Joseph remarked that as far as its Balkan interests were concerned, the Monarchy could not count on its allies anyway. It was essential, therefore, to strengthen the army. As Beck pointed out, a continuation of the standstill (*Stillstand*) amounted in fact to a relative decline. Goluchowski expatiated on the serious diplomatic consequences of the situation: indeed, it was the military weakness of Austria-Hungary that lay at the root of her diplomatic weakness – Germany and Italy might soon seek stronger friends elsewhere – and which made Russia so difficult to handle. But none of these arguments made much impression on the parsimonious governments of Austria and Hungary. They agreed to vote some money for the artillery, but beyond that they refused to go. It was quite impossible, the Austrian finance minister declared, to find large sums of money for the army, let alone the navy, in such a time of depression. There was thus still no immediate prospect of the Monarchy's acquiring a military potential that would permit of a strong policy involving the risk of a confrontation with Russia. In this situation of domestic weakness, and in the absence of any effective external support, it was perhaps prudent of Goluchowski to yield to the pleadings of Aehrenthal and the Russophiles, at least to the extent of agreeing to examine the possibility of establishing a more comprehensive *modus vivendi* with St Petersburg.

Austro-Russian Co-operation, 1902–1906

The practical basis for more positive co-operation between Russia and Austria-Hungary lay in their common interest in containing the crisis in Macedonia and in preventing the interference of other Powers in what they had come to regard since 1897 as their own particular sphere of interest. The idea of a joint Austro-Russian supervision of Macedonian affairs appealed to both Lamsdorff and Goluchowski.[67] The Austrians in particular saw in it a means of

65. P.A. X/145, Goluchowski to Szögyény, tel. 37, 14 June 1899.
66. P.A. XL/301, Ministerratsprotokoll, 29 November 1901.
67. Aehrenthal MSS, Karton 2, Kinsky to Aehrenthal, 17 May 1902.

preventing the creation of a large autonomous Macedonia extending to Albania and the Adriatic, which might some day join Bulgaria to create that big Slav state that had been a nightmare of the Ballhausplatz since the 1870s. A major step forward was taken when Lamsdorff visited Vienna in December 1902, after calling at Sofia and Belgrade and warning those governments that Russia was determined to maintain the status quo. Goluchowski was much impressed by Lamsdorff's evident sincerity[68] – and the upshot of the visit was the so-called Vienna Memorandum of February 1903. This document was modest enough. Whatever the sultan might think, the two Powers were not seeking to undermine or encroach on his authority, but rather to preserve Turkish rule in Macedonia by creating tolerable living conditions for the inhabitants. The Memorandum urged the sultan to strengthen the authority of his newly-created Inspector-General of Macedonia by making him irremovable without the consent of Russia and Austria-Hungary; and to accept some foreign advisers to help improve the Macedonian gendarmerie – who should also be assisted by regular Turkish troops in combating both Bulgarian terrorist bands and Albanian robbers. On an international level, the Vienna Memorandum virtually served notice on the other Powers (who were nevertheless asked to support it at Constantinople) that the affairs of Macedonia were to remain the prime concern of Russia and Austria-Hungary.

This development of the Entente met with a somewhat mixed reception in Austro-Hungarian diplomatic circles. The Russophiles, of course, were ecstatic. Szögyény in Berlin looked forward to a general *rapprochement* between the three empires, now all set to embark on 'a really conservative policy'.[69] In St Petersburg, the ultra-conservative minister of the interior, Plehve, discussed with Aehrenthal a possible restoration of the Three Emperors' Alliance, an idea that Aehrenthal had been toying with for some time as a weapon against the rising forces of democracy.[70] But the Entente in its new aspect still had something of an exclusively Austro-Russian air about it, and resembled more the Three Emperors' League of the 1870s than the Russo-German dominated Three Emperors' Alliance of the 1880s. For Aehrenthal, for example, one of the chief advantages of a good understanding with Russia was that the Monarchy could thereby avoid falling too much under the domination of Berlin; and Plehve used the argument that if Vienna

68. P.A. I/476, Liasse XXXIII/39, Goluchowski, Memorandum on a conversation with Lamsdorff, 2 December 1902.
69. Aehrenthal MSS, Karton 4, Szögyény to Aehrenthal, 7 March 1903.
70. Ibid., Karton 5, Aehrenthal to Goluchowski, private, 16 January 1903 (copy).

would keep the Magyars in order, Russia would readily co-operate in checking the growth of German influence in the Balkans.[71] Indeed, in the Ballhausplatz, traditionalists such as Zwiedenek were from the start somewhat wary of Lamsdorff's amiability, suspecting that it might conceal a desire to drive a wedge between Germany and Austria-Hungary, and ultimately to destroy German influence and paralyse Great Britain at Constantinople.[72]

Such fears were perhaps not without foundation. At any rate, the new emphasis on exclusive co-operation with Russia necessarily implied yet a further devaluation of the Dual Alliance and of the Monarchy's former partners in the Mediterranean Entente. Not that the behaviour of the latter did anything to retard the process. In Berlin, where fears were rife for Germany's position at Constantinople if her ally were to embark on a policy of harassing the sultan, the Vienna Memorandum came in for some very carping criticism in the press; and there were ominous hints from Great Britain and Italy that they too would have to be consulted about Macedonian affairs. To Italy, particularly, Goluchowski delivered a very sharp rebuff, refusing point-blank to enter into talks with her about the future of Albania. Now that the Monarchy had sacrificed its freedom of manoeuvre in Macedonia by embarking on a joint policy with Russia, it was all the more essential to keep a completely free hand elsewhere. At the same time, the last tenuous links that bound Vienna to London were dissolved when Goluchowski refused to join the British in protesting at the passage through the Straits of four Russian torpedo-boat destroyers (admittedly, as yet, unarmed). The incident coincided with Lamsdorff's visit to Vienna, and Goluchowski fobbed London off with the argument that the infringement was only a trivial one, and that the Straits question was chiefly Great Britain's concern in any case. The British were furious, and washed their hands of Goluchowski and the Mediterranean Agreements; and in February 1903 a state paper of the Committee of Imperial Defence declared that so long as Great Britain held Egypt, the Mediterranean balance could not be all that disastrously affected even if Russia got control of the Straits. Between Russia and Great Britain Goluchowski had made a clear, and in the long term perhaps a fateful, choice. But in the circumstances, given that the explosive situation in Macedonia, which could only be defused in co-operation with Russia, was a far greater danger to Austria-Hungary than a relatively trivial violation of the

---

71. Ibid., Aehrenthal to Goluchowski, private, 16 July 1903 (copy).
72. Ibid., Karton 4, Zwiedenek to Aehrenthal, 23 January 1903.

rule of the Straits, it was perhaps the only intelligible choice.

If closer co-operation with Russia entailed a weakening of Austria-Hungary's links with her old partners, it was by no means certain that it would provide an adequate safeguard for her interests in the Near East. True, the reform programme, in so far as it protected and preserved the Christian element in Macedonia as the eventual heirs of the Ottoman Empire, was a step in the direction of a Balkan peninsula consisting of free and independent states – perhaps the most effective obstacle to Russian preponderance in the area.[73] Nevertheless, as some Austro-Hungarian observers were quick to point out,[74] if Russia had renounced a chance to strengthen her influence at Sofia as patron of Bulgaria's ambitions, the Monarchy had by the same token done the same. If Russia should ever revert to an active policy – and this was always the great risk implicit in the Entente – the Monarchy might well discover that it had wasted valuable opportunities. At the same time, the Austrians were perhaps jeopardising their chances of building up an Albanian barrier against Slavdom. Since 1896 they had been struggling, by an astute use of the *Kultusprotektorat*, to encourage the development of an Albanian national consciousness – albeit in the face of opposition from the Turks, who countered by fostering mistrust between Muslim and Christian Albanians and by draconian laws against the teaching of the Albanian language. Now, it seemed, Vienna was wavering in its support of the Albanians. Indeed, the February Memorandum specifically required the sultan to check their depredations – which to many Albanians meant that Austria-Hungary was throwing in her lot with the Slavs against them. The murder by Albanian soldiers in April 1903 of the Russian consul at Mitrovitsa produced the spectacle of Austria-Hungary joining with Russia – notoriously the arch-enemy of the Albanians – to demand the severe punishment of the guilty. This cost the Austrians a good deal of credit in the Albanian camp. Indeed, some in Vienna began to fear that the new *entente* policy would eventually drive the Albanians entirely into the arms of Italy.[75]

The collapse in 1903 of the Austro-Hungarian position in Serbia represented, it might be argued, an even more spectacular sacrifice on the altar of the Austro-Russian Entente. But this is a view of hindsight. In fact, the murder of King Alexander and his wife by military conspirators on 11 June 1903 hardly bore at the time the significance for Austro-Serbian relations that it was to acquire in

73. Ibid., Zwiedenek to Aehrenthal, 20 February 1903.
74. Ibid., Karton 3, Macchio to Aehrenthal, 27 April 1903.
75. Ibid., Karton 2, Jettel to Aehrenthal, 3,11 April 1903.

the light of Serbia's later behaviour under the Karageorgević dynasty. In the last months of Obrenović rule Austro-Serbian relations had been far from cordial. Although King Alexander, disappointed by St Petersburg's ostentatious devotion to the status quo, had sought early in 1903 to return to the Austro-Hungarian fold, Franz Joseph had had enough of his shiftiness, and refused to receive him, either at court or at manoeuvres; and Goluchowski, who had long regarded Alexander's regime as irretrievably lost, sharply rebuffed a Serbian request for help in promoting a league of Serbia, Romania and Turkey against Bulgaria. Russia and Austria-Hungary, he declared, wanted peace and quiet. Although the murder of the king, exceptional in its brutality even by Balkan standards, was personally shocking to the emperor, it caused no political misgivings in the Ballhausplatz. Nor did it seem in the least to threaten the Austro-Russian Entente. Indeed, the Russians even hinted that Austria-Hungary might march into Serbia and restore order there.

In the event, the Austrians took no action. In the first place, they were satisfied, on the basis of their own police reports, that 'we have every reason to believe in [*mit Vertrauen entgegenzukommen*] the Austrophile sentiments' of Petar Karageorgević, to whom the conspirators now offered the Serbian throne.[76] Despite his Parisian education and Montenegrin marriage, Petar had been born in Hungary, a son of the outspokenly Austrophile Alexander Karageorgević, and had always expressed great sympathy for the land of his birth. Moreover, intervention would have been difficult to justify on the pretext of restoring order, for the country was calm. Indeed, preparations for intervention might have been the very thing to cause disorder; and might have deterred Petar from accepting the throne. That would have raised the thorny question of an alternative head of state – probably Nikita of Montenegro or a republican president. In these circumstances,[77] therefore, the Austro-Hungarian government tolerated, even welcomed, the enthronement of King Petar, and was the first government to give its recognition and blessing to the new Serbian regime.

It was only after the new regime was firmly established that things began to go badly wrong for Vienna. King Petar, old, and above all anxious to avoid the fate of his predecessor, was determined to leave politics to the military conspirators and their allies in the Radical party. By November 1903 Austrians could see that 'the king is a nullity, . . . the whole show is run by the people of the

76. P.A. XL/316, Memorandum by Zwiedenek on the Karageorgević family, 14 June 1903 (based on a memorandum dated '1901').
77. Aehrenthal MSS, Karton 1, Dumba to Aehrenthal, 20 July 1903.

eleventh of June'.[78] As early as 27 September, Dumba, Austro-Hungarian minister at Belgrade, had described Austro-Serbian relations as 'as bad as possible . . . All our work and goodwill (as regards the coup) are now wasted.'[79] He ascribed much of the blame to the press, both in Serbia and in the Monarchy, which had been hurling abuse back and forth across the frontier since shortly after the coup; and he blamed the Austrian press particularly for starting the campaign. The newspapers ought to have been kept more in hand. (In fact, the Austrian press had at first adopted Goluchowski's cool approach to the murders; and it was Jettel in the Literary Office of the Ballhausplatz who had taken it upon himself to inject what he termed a more 'humanitarian' view of the situation into the newspapers.)[80] The Russians, meanwhile, exploited the situation, reminding the Serbs, according to Dumba, that their future lay in the west and on the Adriatic; and even advising them not to make a commercial treaty with Austria-Hungary, but to export their livestock to Germany instead. The Austro-Hungarian reaction to all this was unimaginative and entirely counter-productive. The boycott of the Serbian court was resumed: this was one thing on which the emperor, Goluchowski, and even Aehrenthal were all agreed. It was in vain that Sektionschef Mérey pointed out[81] that moral indignation expressed some six months after the event was hardly convincing; and that the Monarchy could not after all wish to see King Petar fall, if only because any alternative would be worse. By the end of 1903 Austro-Serbian relations were decidedly bad.

Not that this dismal turn of events could with justice be laid at the door of the Austro-Russian Entente. On the contrary, the Entente while it lasted offered some assurance that a Russian-controlled government at Belgrade would not assume an attitude so hostile to the Monarchy as to compel the latter to use force against it. Whether, even so, the Austrians would not have been wiser to intervene and bring Serbia to heel once and for all, is a question that can hardly be answered in the light of the situation in the summer of 1903. Certainly, once the new regime was established they would have had extreme difficulty in reconciling the adoption of a forceful, even violent, policy towards it with their desire to preserve the Austro-Russian Entente.

The Entente had in fact again proved its usefulness in these very

78. Ibid., Karton 3, Mérey to Aehrenthal, 27 November 1903.
79. Ibid., Karton 1, Dumba to Aehrenthal, 27 September 1903.
80. Ibid., Karton 2, Jettel to Aehrenthal, 24 June 1903.
81. Ibid., Karton 3, Mérey to Aehrenthal, 27 November 1903.

months. True, there were limits to the sacrifices the Austrians were prepared to make for it: when Wilhelm II visited Vienna in September 1903, he found both Franz Joseph and Goluchowski as resolutely opposed as ever to the Bismarckian doctrine of spheres of influence in the Balkans, and to the suggestion that the Central Powers might make sure of Russia by presenting her with Constantinople.[82] But there was much to be said for continuing and developing the Entente to cope with the pressing questions of the day, notably in Macedonia. There, the all too tentative February Memorandum had clearly proved inadequate. The summer had seen a good deal of marching and counter-marching in Bulgaria and Turkey; and in August the Bulgarian propaganda organisation in Macedonia at last managed to stage its long-planned rising. This was a miserable failure, owing to poor organisation and the lack of effective support from anybody but adherents of the Bulgarian Exarchate. (The other Christians of Macedonia – largely Greek or Serbian Orthodox – had been antagonised by years of Exarchist terrorism.) And although it was serious enough to provoke bloody reprisals by the Turks, and, indeed, the hoped-for European intervention, this last was by no means in the sense desired by the insurgents. Indeed, when the tsar's visit to Vienna at the end of September provided a convenient opportunity for Austro-Russian co-operation to devise new remedies for the ills of Macedonia, their purpose was very definitely the reinforcement of the territorial status quo.

The two monarchs, accompanied by Goluchowski and Lamsdorff (and also by Aehrenthal, who by threatening resignation forced his presence on the reluctant Goluchowski at the last minute) spent a few very enjoyable days at Franz Joseph's hunting lodge of Mürzsteg in Styria. The upshot was the Mürzsteg Punctation of 2 October 1903, essentially an elaboration of the February Memorandum, but envisaging a far more stringent control of the Ottoman authorities in Macedonia. The Ottoman Inspector General was to be assisted in his efforts to establish law and order by an Austro-Hungarian and a Russian 'Civil Agent'. The principle of Austro-Russian dual control was thus reaffirmed; but personnel from the other Great Powers were to assist in the reorganisation of the gendarmerie under the supervision of a European commander; and financial and judicial reforms were to be introduced by stages. For the time being, Macedonia was to be divided into zones, in each of

82. P.A. I/478, Liasse XXXIII, Goluchowski, memorandum on a conversation with Wilhelm II, late September 1903.

which a Great Power was to be entrusted with the task of seeing that the reforms were carried out; but ultimately, according to Article III of the Mürzsteg Punctation, Macedonia was to be reorganised into administrative districts more in accordance with ethnic realities.

Although Article III was later universally recognised to have made matters worse (in that it encouraged the Christians of Macedonia to adjust 'ethnic realities' by means of mutual massacres, against the day of its implementation) it seemed at the time quite a triumph for Goluchowski. Admittedly, it implied the abandonment of Albanian minorities in Serbian areas of Macedonia; but it guaranteed the consolidation of those areas that were predominantly Albanian; and as Goluchowski reminded a council of ministers in November 1903, 'the Albanian nation after all forms a dam against the flooding of the Porte's possessions in the Balkans by the Slav deluge.'[83] He had thus brought the Russians a step further than they had been prepared to go in 1897, when they would make no promises about the future territorial configuration of the Balkans. In immediate practical terms too, Goluchowski had reason for satisfaction, as in implementing the reforms the Great Powers managed at first to remain fairly united under Austro-Russian leadership. True, Berlin constantly complained that the Powers were encroaching too far on the sultan's sovereign rights; and this encouraged the Turks to obstruct the gendarmerie reform for some months. But they gave way in the end; and the summer of 1904 even saw a *détente* on the Turco-Bulgarian frontier. The immediate crisis, it seemed, had been safely overcome.

This success for the Entente was accompanied, as usual, by a further decline of the Monarchy's alliances. Admittedly, in personal terms, relations with Italy had improved somewhat in 1903, when Zanardelli had been replaced by the conciliatory Giolitti, with Tittoni at the Consulta. The new government was not only ever mindful of Italy's financial dependence on Germany, but anxious to reconcile the Liberals and the Church in a struggle against Socialism. This augured well for relations with Catholic Austria. Franz Joseph, for his part, managed, by exercising the ancient *jus exclusivae* (for the last time, incidentally: in 1904 Pius X forbade the practice on pain of excommunication) to veto the election to the papal throne of the arch-enemy of the Triple Alliance, Cardinal Rampolla. Tittoni, whom Goluchowski met at Abbazia in April 1904, seemed to Vienna a vast improvement on

83. P.A. XL/302, Ministerratsprotokoll, 19 November 1903.

his predecessor, professing his love of the Triple Alliance, his hatred of irredentism, and his ready acceptance of Goluchowski's very firmly stated view that an eventual annexation of Bosnia would not constitute a change in the status quo such as would entitle Italy or any other Power to compensation.[84]

Nevertheless, such meetings could not cover up the tension that arose from the Austrians' determination to resist Italy's growing Balkan aspirations. If the Italians were greatly irritated by the second-rank role assigned to them in Macedonia by the Mürzsteg Powers, the Austrians were concerned at Italy's determined efforts to set foot across the Adriatic and her increasingly close links with Montenegro, demonstrated in 1904 by the opening of Montenegro's first telegraphic station (built by Marconi in Antivari). Moreover, even at Abbazia Goluchowski had had to lecture Tittoni about Italy's misdeeds in Albania: whereas Austria-Hungary's activities there were of a purely religious and educational character, altruistically designed to build up the national consciousness of the Albanians, Italy's propaganda activities were of an essentially 'Italianising' nature.[85] In fact, in 1902 the Italians had been trying to persuade the Porte to abolish the Monarchy's *Kultusprotektorat*; and they made great play with an Albanian National Congress which was held at Naples in 1903. On the economic front, the future of the Austro-Italian commercial treaty was in some doubt. Goluchowski felt that its lapse would be 'a veritable catastrophe', as the Monarchy had a positive trade balance with Italy; and he would have been prepared to sacrifice the Austrian wine industry out of hand.[86] But the matter was one for the cumbersome governments of Vienna and Budapest to settle, and he could only await their commands.

The military was another complicating factor in relations with Italy. From 1903 onwards Beck began to think seriously of transferring troops from Galicia to Tyrol; and in the summer of 1904 Goluchowski had to ask him to desist, for the sake of the Alliance, from tours of inspection on the Italian frontier.[87] The autumn saw a fairly serious war scare in Austrian military circles, and some troops were called up in the south-west. As the war minister explained to a council of ministers in November,[88] it was in a sense

84. P.A. I/476, Liasse XXXIII/39, Goluchowski, memorandum on a conversation with Tittoni at Abbazia, April 1904.
85. Ibid.
86. P.A. XL/302, Ministerratsprotokoll, 19 November 1903.
87. Glaise-Horstenau, *Beck*, pp. 394ff.
88. P.A. XL/303, Ministerratsprotokoll, 28 November 1904.

only a question of redressing the balance of forces that had been distorted by a single-minded concentration on the Russian frontier since the 1880s; but recent outbreaks of irredentism in Italy were disturbing, and her latest frontier fortifications – of a temporary nature – indicated 'a definitely hostile intention'. On this occasion, even Goluchowski supported the war minister: although relations with Italy had recently 'much improved', there was no telling when Rome might revert to the attitudes of the Zanardelli ministry, 'when one had to be prepared for a coup at any moment'. This danger, coupled with the growing obstreperousness of Serbia and Montenegro, who were steadily intensifying their propaganda campaign against the Monarchy's position in Bosnia and the Herzegovina both at Constantinople and in the provinces themselves, meant that the Monarchy would have to keep a sharp eye open in the south.

The Monarchy's relations with its ally in the north, meanwhile, were anything but cordial. In Macedonia, Goluchowski's efforts to maintain a united front to overawe the sultan were even more seriously undermined by Germany's dragging her feet than by Anglo-Italian attempts to force a faster pace. In the economic field, the Austrians were having the greatest difficulty in extracting a satisfactory commercial treaty from Germany since she had raised her tariffs on agricultural imports in 1902. There was some truth in Jettel's despairing cry of December 1904: 'Germany is strangling us!'[89] Already in October Dumba at Belgrade had warned his German colleague that a failure to conclude a commercial treaty, together with Berlin's continuing persecution of the Poles, would seriously endanger the Dual Alliance – remarks which Goluchowski endorsed when asked by the German ambassador for a disavowal.[90] A commercial treaty was eventually concluded in 1906; but the higher tariffs involved did nothing for Germany's popularity in the Monarchy. And the Austrians continued to take deep umbrage at Germany's commercial activities in the Balkans. Perhaps Dumba went too far when he warned the Serbs that if they made a commercial treaty with Berlin before concluding one with Vienna and Budapest, Austria-Hungary would block the transit traffic between Serbia and Germany. As Goluchowski blandly explained to the complaining German ambassador, the Monarchy

89. Aehrenthal MSS, Karton 2, Jettel to Aehrenthal, 3 December 1904; Höbelt, 'Handelspolitik', in *Habsburgermonarchie VI*, pp. 575ff.
90. P.A. I/476, Goluchowski, Memorandum on a conversation with Count Wedel, 5 October 1904.

had no legal right to take such action.[91] But Dumba had been quite right, he insisted, to remind Belgrade that it was customary for Serbia to make her commercial treaties with Austria-Hungary first of all; nor would Vienna be browbeaten in negotiating with Belgrade by any Serbo-German fait accompli.

Of course, Austria-Hungary's economic embarrassments were bound to increase as Germany and Great Britain made ever greater inroads into her Balkan trade, and as tariff barriers were raised all over the continent. (It was a significant indication of the Monarchy's relatively weak position that emigration, which had been rising steadily since the 1880s, reached the level of 200,000 in 1903; and that by 1907 the Monarchy had attained the leading position among the European states supplying emigrants to the New World.) Yet the government's own economic policies also intensified its problems. The trade treaties which were eventually concluded in 1906, with Germany, Italy, Russia and Belgium, all embodied higher tariffs; and the most important consequence of this was to keep grain prices high inside the Monarchy. Now although high food prices boosted peasant consumption of Austrian industrial products in the internal market, they also made those industrial products increasingly uncompetitive abroad. At the same time, the protectionist demands of Hungarian agricultural producers, great and small, remained a formidable obstacle to the re-negotiation of the Monarchy's trade treaties with the Balkan states. The year 1906 was the last in which the Monarchy enjoyed a favourable balance of trade.

To add to – indeed, partly to cause – these difficulties, the domestic crisis had taken a very grave turn for the worse in 1903. The next three years saw a conflict between the Crown and the Hungarian Nation before which the mere paralysis of parliamentary government in Austria paled into insignificance.[92] When the Crown asked Budapest to increase the size of the contingent of troops supplied annually to the Common Army, a motley coalition of malcontent magnates and separatist politicians who looked back beyond 1867 to 1848 launched a campaign for concessions, aiming ultimately at creating a separate Hungarian army out of the Common Army. Franz Joseph would have none of this: 'common and united, as it is, My army shall remain', ran the famous Chlopy order of 16 September 1903. Deadlock resulted, and gradually degenerated into chaos by 1905, when Tisza's government was

91. Ibid.
92. Stone, *Crises*.

defeated at the polls by the coalition, following which the Hungarian parliament refused to supply even the normal contingent of
recruits to the Army. The king and his advisers stood firm,
subjecting Hungary to virtual martial law; and Beck began to work
on *Kriegsfall U*, a plan for the actual invasion of Hungary. Goluchowski showed himself not one whit backward where the unity of
the Monarchy was concerned: when an imposing delegation of
Hungarian politicians arrived from Budapest with compromise
proposals, he was instrumental in arranging their unceremonious
dismissal by Franz Joseph in the famous 'five-minute audience' of
September 1905. This incident destroyed his reputation in Hungary
at a blow.

The crisis threatened to destroy the Monarchy itself. In 1906
Franz Joseph remarked to the visiting ex-Empress Eugénie that the
empire would not survive him. Already in April 1905 the German
government had considered it timely to sound out the Russians as
to their reactions in the event of the sudden dissolution of the
Habsburg Monarchy. Certainly, the prestige of the Monarchy as a
Great Power reached a low ebb in these years. This was painfully
obvious in the military field too: the very existence of the army was
in jeopardy; and as the crisis affected all organs of the body politic,
even routine measures of strategic defence were held up – as late as
November 1905 Admiral Montecuccoli was still pleading for a
railway link between Pola and Dalmatia (as yet, troops would have
to rely on very hazardous and exposed sea-transport). It was all
very well, therefore, for patriotic Austrians to lament: 'what a fine
figure we could now cut in the Near East, were it not for our
domestic miseries [*Miseren*]'.[93] The political, military, economic,
and hence also diplomatic weakness of Austria-Hungary was glaring. She enjoyed neither the strength at home nor the respect
abroad to take advantage of Russia's growing involvement in the
Far East to re-establish her own influence in the Balkans.

It was hardly surprising, therefore, that the years 1903–6 saw the
high-water mark of the Austro-Russian Entente. If the Monarchy
was confronted with appalling difficulties at home and mistrustful
of its allies abroad, the Russians were involved in actual war with
Japan by February 1904. On 28 February the tsar remarked to the
Austro-Hungarian military attaché – perhaps somewhat hopefully
– that his faith in Franz Joseph was so complete that he would not
hesitate to move troops from Russia's western frontier to the Far
East should the need arise. Not surprisingly, the Austro-Hungarian

93. Aehrenthal MSS, Karton 3, Mérey to Aehrenthal, 15 July 1905.

embassy at St Petersburg made the most of this, and Aehrenthal began to press Goluchowski to broaden the Entente. Austria-Hungary, he said, was in a similar predicament, and might well have to move troops from Galicia to Tyrol if the Italian menace continued to grow. He went on to recommend a simple Austro-Russian neutrality agreement; and knowing Goluchowski's sensitivities, explained that this need not touch on Balkan matters – though he incautiously justified this restriction on the grounds that Russia might claim compensation in the Straits in return for her consent to the eventual annexation of Bosnia.[94] Goluchowski, for his part, was satisfied enough with the 1897 agreement as it stood, and certainly had no desire to restrict the Monarchy any further by elaborating it; and he was most emphatic – though he failed to convince Aehrenthal – that on no account could the eventual annexation of Bosnia give Russia any claim to compensation. But towards the idea of a simple neutrality agreement, he was fairly well disposed.[95]

Thus encouraged, Aehrenthal took the initiative in St Petersburg in May, urging on Lamsdorff that a neutrality agreement would be in the interests of both parties: the only war the Monarchy could expect to fight would be against an irredentist Italy striving to dominate the Adriatic; whereas Russia might have to fight Great Britain. The upshot was the Austro-Russian neutrality treaty of 15 October 1904 (see Appendix VI).[96] Although, as far as the Near East was concerned, this agreement only confirmed the negative principles of 1897, it very definitely marked the extension of the Entente into the field of general Great Power politics.[97] The treaty obliged the signatories to preserve benevolent neutrality in the event of war with 'a third Power'. Although such agreements behind the backs of allies might indeed be the normal way of proceeding in the Triple Alliance, in so far as the treaty referred to the possibility of an Austro-Italian war, and in so far as it pledged Austria-Hungary to neutrality not only in the event of a Russo-British war, but in the event of a Russo-German war, it went at least as far as anything the Germans had done in 1887 or the Italians in 1902. Indeed, it was altogether a devastating comment on the state of the Monarchy's alliances.[98]

94. P.A. I/475, Liasse XXXIII/k, Aehrenthal to Goluchowski, tel. 42, 29 February; and private letter, 24 March 1904.
95. Ibid., Goluchowski to Aehrenthal, private and secret, 13 April 1904.
96. Text in Pribram, *Secret Treaties*, I, pp. 237–9.
97. P.A. I/475, Liasse XXXII/k, Aehrenthal to Goluchowski, private and secret, 24 September 1904.
98. Stephan Verosta, *Theorie und Realität von Bündnissen*, pp. 195ff.

Certainly, Goluchowski had no time for Aehrenthal's idea of communicating the treaty to Germany, and announcing at the same time that the Three Emperors' Alliance had been restored.[99] A Three Emperors' Alliance, he insisted, would restrict the Monarchy's freedom of manoeuvre; and it would give Germany, as the strongest of the three parties (and no longer, as she had been in the 1880s, a disinterested party), a golden opportunity to push ahead against Austro-Hungarian interests in the Balkans. Indeed, he was coming to regard Germany, with her commercial ruthlessness, and her self-seeking encouragement of the sultan's resistance to the Mürzsteg reforms, as altogether a nuisance; and he was determined to do nothing to increase her influence in the Near East. But he was satisfied enough with the neutrality agreement as it stood – and above all, with Russia's increasingly obvious military weakness. At any rate, he was content to assure a council of ministers of 28 November that 'without wanting to prophesy . . . there is no threatening danger from the northern frontier of the Monarchy, and . . . we should have peace and quiet from Russia for a long time'.[100]

Whether, under Goluchowski, the Entente could have developed beyond negative principles into that co-operation to deal with future eventualities that had been hinted at in 1897 must be doubted, given the drift of the minister's views about the future development of the Balkan states.[101] By the end of 1904, Goluchowski was coming to the conclusion that, in the event of the collapse of Turkey-in-Europe, the expansion of Serbia and Montenegro, whose intrigues and propaganda activities in Bosnia were becoming increasingly tiresome, must be restricted as much as possible, despite – or, indeed, especially because of – Russia's inclination to count on those states as her obedient servants. The expansion of Bulgaria, by contrast, which, chastened by the wrath of the Turks and the Great Powers, was now behaving with studied correctness, would be quite in accordance with Austro-Hungarian interests (although Goluchowski was prepared to refrain from pressing for this if Russia would co-operate in restricting the growth of Serbia and Montenegro). Above all, however, it would be important to build up the non-Slav states, securing a big autonomous Albania as 'a strong wall' against the advance of Serbia, and compensations for Romania (from north-east Bulgaria) and for

99. Aehrenthal MSS, Karton 4, Zwiedenek to Aehrenthal, 14 November 1904.
100. P.A. XL/303, Ministerratsprotokoll, 28 November 1904.
101. P.A. I/477, Liasse XXXIII/35, Goluchowski to Calice, private and confidential, 31 December 1904.

Greece. Goluchowski's apparently sincere hopes of attaining complete agreement with Russia on such a programme were, it must be said, exceedingly sanguine.

Indeed, if 1904 had witnessed the apogee of the Entente, 1905 saw the beginning of its decline. Whereas in 1904 Austro-Russian co-operation in Macedonia, together with Russia's Far Eastern embarrassments, had served to consolidate the Entente, in 1905 these same factors assumed a character that made them a source of frustration and tension. In the first place, the new year saw Russia staggering towards catastrophic defeat and revolution; and this, together with the chaos in Hungary, emboldened the Turks to obstruct the efforts of the Mürzsteg Powers in Macedonia. At the same time, the Russians, only too painfully conscious of their internal and external collapse, began to doubt the wisdom of working exclusively with Austria-Hungary in Macedonia. For might not dual control now amount in practice to Austro-Hungarian control? They decided that they needed some counterweight to Austria-Hungary; and that it would be wise to vest control of the reforms – at least as regards the executive aspects – in all six Powers. To this the Austrians were not opposed in principle; they felt, in view of their own domestic troubles, that the other Powers might indeed bear a greater share of the burden of implementing the reforms – provided always that the Mürzsteg Powers retained overall control of their formulation; and in practice they allowed the others a fair amount of influence even over this. Even so, the future was to show that it would be infinitely more difficult to work out an effective programme between six Powers than between two.

More fundamentally, it was by no means clear that the Mürzsteg programme, whether operated by six Powers or by two, could cure the ills of Macedonia. For by 1905 the Macedonian problem was no longer what it had been when the Mürzsteg programme had been drawn up. It was no longer so much a problem of Turkish maladministration, which had indeed been mitigated by the reforms, as of ending the state of civil war that was developing between the Christians of Macedonia. Since 1904, increasing numbers of Greek terrorists, both native and imported, had been taking the field against the Exarchists and the Romanian Koutzo-Vlachs. This evil could be cured only by massive formations of Turkish troops, who could pursue the terrorists to their lairs in the hills – not by the local gendarmerie, nor by the administrative improvements envisaged at Mürzsteg. Indeed, Article III of the Mürzsteg programme acted as an actual incentive to the warring Christians to secure to themselves as much of the promised land as possible against the day when administrative boundaries would be re-drawn along ethnic lines. There was, in fact, some truth in the German complaint that the very principle of European control envisaged in the Mürzsteg programme, in so far as it undermined the sultan's authority and encouraged the Christians to look forward to its final extinction, was in itself a major cause of the worsening violence.

The Austrians and Russians nevertheless pressed ahead along the path laid down at Mürzsteg. But progress was slow. Indeed, it was something of a wonder that any scheme at all emerged from the interminable conferences of the six ambassadors at Constantinople. Discussion of the control of the Macedonian finances occupied the whole of 1905. Whereas the Germans dragged their feet and encouraged the sultan to resist, the British pressed enthusiastically for such stringent controls as might well have provoked Abdul Hamid to revolt against the whole Mürzsteg scheme. In the end, a compromise *règlement* was hammered out which accorded the representatives of the other Powers a position of equality with the Civil Agents – the first serious breach in the Mürzsteg principle of dual control – but which took more account of Turkish susceptibilities than the British would have liked. Even so, the Powers still had to stage a naval demonstration before the sultan would accept their proposals (December); and Germany's ostentatious absence from this demonstrated yet again to Constantinople that the Powers were far from united in their support of the reform programme.

The next item on the agenda, control of the administration of justice in Macedonia, was to occupy the Powers for two whole years. For it became mixed up in a wrangle over the Turks' request for a 3 per cent increase in the customs duties of the Empire (for which the consent of the Powers was necessary under the terms of the Capitulations). The Turks declared that without this extra revenue they would be unable to finance even the existing reforms for much longer, let alone any new ones. The Mürzsteg Powers were sympathetic, and filled with alarm at the prospect of the collapse of the reform programme; but the British, who stood to lose most by the proposed customs increase, pressed for drastic controls over Ottoman finances in return, if only to ensure that the new revenue really was spent on Macedonia, and not on the Ottoman army or the Baghdad railway project. Deadlock resulted, and until the 3 per cent customs increase was agreed, in April 1907, the exasperated Mürzsteg Powers refused, for their part, to proceed with any further reform proposals at all.

Goluchowski's frustration was intensified by the wayward behaviour of the allies in Rome and Berlin. The deterioration in Austro-Italian relations was reflected in a very strained meeting at Venice[102] in May 1905, when Goluchowski complained bitterly to Tittoni about Italian efforts to whittle away the leading role of the Civil Agents in Macedonia, and to undermine that special position of Russia and Austria-Hungary that was the essential basis of Mürzsteg. Albania, too, still rankled. According to a Ballhausplatz estimate of 1905, Italy was making very serious inroads into Austro-Hungarian influence in the coastal areas of Albania, and had even overtaken the Monarchy in terms of trade and shipping.[103] At the end of the year, Beck bleakly concluded that war with Italy had moved perceptibly nearer in 1905.

Germany, too, persisted in her tiresome behaviour. Despite all warnings from Vienna that the failure of the Mürzsteg programme might damage Austro-Hungarian and Russian prestige irreparably, and throw the Balkans into chaos, she continued to obstruct the reforms. Equally, her treatment of her Austro-Hungarian allies in the opening stages of the Moroccan crisis was insensitive to a degree. Here, Goluchowski had supported the German demand for an international conference, both as a loyal ally and as a party interested in maintaining the open door to trade in Morocco (where he ranked Austria-Hungary, by some strange calculation, third among the Great Powers).[104] At the same time, he was fully alive to the broader implications of the Franco-German confrontation. Indeed, so great was his anxiety that he interrupted his summer vacation at Vittel to visit the French prime minister, Rouvier, on 6 July, and, according to his own account, managed to persuade Rouvier to accept the idea of a conference.[105] He was much mortified, therefore, when the Germans left both Vittel and Vienna to learn from the newspapers of the final Franco-German agreement to hold a conference; and in retaliation he refused to help Germany any further, or to press the French to accept Tangier rather than Algeciras as the venue for the conference.[106] At the same time, Germany had embarked on another round of expulsions of Aus-

---

102. P.A. I/476, Goluchowski, memorandum on a conversation with Tittoni at Venice, May 1905.
103. P.A. I/473, Liasse XXXI/b, Consul Kral, Memorandum on Albania, 1901–5, April 1905.
104. P.A. XXXII/14, Goluchowski, Memorandum on a conversation with Rouvier, 6 July 1905.
105. Ibid., and Goluchowski to Franz Joseph (enclosing, Goluchowski to Welsersheimb), 5 December 1905.
106. Ibid., Goluchowski to Mérey, tel. 2, 17 July; to Szögyény, tel. 3, 17 July 1905.

trian and Hungarian seasonal workers, despite the remonstrations of Vienna; and she concluded a commercial treaty with Bulgaria, leaving her Austro-Hungarian ally with such scraps as most-favoured-nation treatment could provide.

This was especially embarrassing at a time when the Monarchy's own commercial relations with the Balkan states were in crisis. At the end of 1905, the Austrians were taken aback to learn that Serbia and Bulgaria had concluded a secret customs union. To Vienna, this seemed to show that the two states were preparing to drive a hard bargain in their forthcoming commercial negotiations with the Monarchy; and it was politically obnoxious as a pointer to a future Balkan league which would checkmate the Monarchy's timeworn policy of maintaining a state of balance between its South Slav neighbours.[107] For the first two months of 1906 the problem continued to worry the conference of ministers.[108] Although opinions were divided, one thing was agreed: the Monarchy must not take an equally tough line with both states, for that would only drive them together and promote a Balkan league; and as Goluchowski blandly observed when someone pointed to the inconsistency of differential treatment, 'in politics, the laws of logic do not always prevail'. Certainly, the Monarchy had a good case in international law against Bulgaria: her granting special terms to Serbia was a flagrant contravention of Article VIII of the Treaty of Berlin (even if it was soon to become clear that no other Great Power would help the Monarchy to enforce it); and the Austrian and Hungarian governments were both for taking a stiff line with Sofia and offering negotiations to Belgrade.

Goluchowski, however, was set on exactly the opposite policy. In the first place, the Monarchy could bring far more effective pressure to bear on Serbia than on Bulgaria. The Serbs sold far more to Austria-Hungary than they bought from her, whereas in Bulgaria's case, the Monarchy would be the chief loser if things came to a tariff war. In general political terms, too, Goluchowski had decided that Bulgaria was the most viable of the Balkan states. It would be wise, therefore, to draw this rising star into Austria-Hungary's orbit – especially as Bulgaria, unlike Serbia or Romania, had no racial brothers inside the Monarchy to give rise to an irredentist problem. Hence, he concluded, 'a good relationship with Bulgaria would always be preferable to one with Serbia, which has been intriguing incessantly against the Monarchy for a

107. P.A. XL/305, Ministerratsprotokoll, 10 January 1906.
108. Ibid., Ministerratsprotokolle, 16 January, 2 February 1906.

few years now, stirring up the Serbo-Croat population and agitating [*wühlen*] against Austria-Hungary in Bosnia and the Herzegovina'.[109] Goluchowski forced his policy through, and negotiations were started with Bulgaria. By March, the Serbs, threatened with the full rigour of the Austro-Hungarian veterinary regulations, had begun to climb down, abandoning the customs union and opening negotiations with a commercial treaty with Vienna. At this juncture, however, a new dispute arose, when Serbia insisted on placing a large order for weapons with the French firm of Schneider-Creusot, instead of with Skoda of Bohemia, as had been usual in the past. Negotiations were again broken off, and the Austrians resorted to economic sanctions, closing the frontier to imports of Serbian livestock.

The so-called 'Pig War' lasted for four years, and was nothing short of a disaster for Austria-Hungary. Not only did the Serbs successfully defy the Monarchy: they soon found markets overseas, in Turkey, Egypt, Russia and Western Europe – and above all in Germany, who was only too quick to move in and take over the lion's share of the trade which her ally had lost. All this only gave the Serbs more confidence and toughness in their negotiations with Austria-Hungary; and even Goluchowski's more conciliatory successor could not bring Belgrade to agree terms until July 1910. By then, Serbia had largely freed herself from her old commercial dependence on the Monarchy, to which she now exported only some 30 per cent of her produce, as opposed to some 80–90 per cent before 1906. The whole affair cost the Monarchy dear in terms of its general international standing as well. It was not just that the Monarchy's spectacular failure to overawe a state the size of Serbia dealt a heavy blow to its prestige throughout the Balkans. Austria-Hungary's bullying of Serbia won her no sympathy from either her allies or the Western Powers – most of whom were only too glad of the chance to develop their own trade with Serbia. Worst of all, perhaps, as not only public opinion in Russia, but the imperial government too, adopted a censorious attitude that Vienna found 'very worrying',[110] nothing but harm had been done to the Austro-Russian Entente.

The whole sorry episode not unnaturally obscured from the public eye what was in fact a very creditable performance by Goluchowski in the Moroccan crisis.[111] Unlike the Germans, who

109. Ibid.
110. Aehrenthal MSS, Karton 4, Zwiedenek to Aehrenthal, 20 February 1906.
111. F. Fellner, 'Die Haltung Oesterreich-Ungarns während der Konferenz von

at Algeciras were intent on winning a prestige victory over France by thwarting her plans to gain control of the Moroccan police, Franz Joseph and Goluchowski were above all concerned that the conference should not lead to a confrontation between the Powers. That, they feared, would poison the international atmosphere for years, and might even lead to a regrouping of the Powers and the isolation of Germany and Austria-Hungary. They made great efforts, therefore, as Franz Joseph put it to the French ambassador, 'to bring the Emperor Wilhelm to reason'[112] – pointing out to Berlin that if the Central Powers gave way on the police question, they would be able to take a firmer stand on the more important financial and commercial questions; and warning that the failure of the conference would be an absolute disaster.

By March, they had brought the Germans to accept a compromise Austro-Hungarian proposal which would leave the Moroccan police to Franco-Spanish control, but subject to an international authority established at Casablanca and supervised by the diplomatic corps. Although Goluchowski still had to work hard to get the French to accept any effective international control at all, and had to agree to the control body's sitting in the less important town of Tangier, it was in the end the Austro-Hungarian proposal that became the basis for the settlement of the police question – the most explosive issue at Algeciras. To that extent, Goluchowski could congratulate himself on having saved the conference from collapse – the gravest of the dangers he had feared. The French delegate's comment to his Austro-Hungarian colleague – 'c'est vous qui avez jeté le pont sur le précipice'[113] – was not undeserved. But more than fair words Goluchowski did not receive for his pains, either from France or from Germany, neither of whom paid the slightest attention to Austro-Hungarian requests – for a share in the control of the Moroccan Bank, for example – in settling such minor issues as remained. True, the open door was maintained by common consent. But any laurels Goluchowski had won were finally blighted by the publication – by the German embassy in Vienna, and despite Goluchowski's strenuous efforts to prevent it – of Wilhelm II's condescending 'brilliant second' telegram.

This was the least of Goluchowski's worries, given the alarming deterioration of the international situation as a result of the Moroccan crisis. Germany's bad-tempered reaction to her humiliation

Algeciras, 1906', in *Mitteilungen des Instituts für österreichische Geschichtsforschung*, 71 (1963) pp. 462–77.
112. *Documents diplomatiques français*, 2nd series, Vol. 9/1, No. 315.
113. P.A. XXXII/16, Welsersheimb to Goluchowski, tel. 64, 31 March 1906.

seemed almost calculated to conjure up that isolation of the Central Powers that Goluchowski most feared. The German emperor raged unrestrainedly not only against Great Britain and her 'satellite' Spain, but against Russia.[114] This last Power, he declared, would receive no more money from Germany to repair her shattered finances (whereupon the Franco-Russian alliance was promptly strengthened by a huge French loan). Equally worrying were Wilhelm II's tirades against Italy: 'this romance cat's-meat betrays us right and left'; and at a dinner party at the Austro-Hungarian embassy, he even talked in terms of war against the 'useless' ally.[115] All this alarmed the Austrians, for Austro-Italian relations were already bad enough; and Barrère, the French ambassador at Rome, was notoriously assiduous in his labours to weaken and divide the Triple Alliance. When Wilhelm II visited Vienna in May, therefore, Franz Joseph spared no effort to calm him down, insisting that he join him in sending telegraphic greetings to Victor Emmanuel as 'notre troisième et fidèle allié'; and emphasising that 'we two must hold on to [*festhalten*] the Italians; because otherwise these people could become a great nuisance, at least for us here'.[116] Goluchowski too, although he also had a rather sceptical view of the alliance with Italy – 'Austria-Hungary and Italy must either be full allies or latent enemies, sooner or later at war' – felt for that very reason that it was important to maintain it, in the interests of peace.[117]

If Goluchowski could think of no better means of warding off the threat of encirclement than clinging somewhat hopefully to the Triple Alliance, Aehrenthal in St Petersburg had far bolder remedies to propose. For him, the key to the situation lay, as usual, in Russia. He did not at all share the views of those in the Ballhausplatz who concluded from Russia's criticisms of the Monarchy's treatment of Serbia that the Entente had lost its usefulness.[118] True, the new Russian foreign minister, Izvolsky, was very much an unknown quantity; and there were signs that he wanted to wind up Russia's disastrous Far Eastern policy and come to terms with Great Britain and Japan.[119] Yet the risk that he might thereby be tempted to recoup Russia's shattered prestige by reverting to an

---

114. P.A. I/477, Liasse XXXIII/38, Szögyény to Goluchowski, tel. 79, 8 April 1906.
115. P.A. I/481, Liasse XXXIV/b, Lützow to Goluchowski, tel. 82, secret, 24 May 1906.
116. Wagner, 'Kaiser Franz Joseph', p. 227; *Die Große Politik der europäischen Kabinette, 1871–1914*, henceforth cited as G.P., Vol. XXI/2, No. 7155.
117. P.A. I/475, Liasse XXXII/c, Goluchowski to Aehrenthal, private and secret, 15 September 1906.
118. Aehrenthal MSS, Karton 4, Zwiedenek to Aehrenthal, 20 February 1906.
119. Ibid., Zwiedenek to Aehrenthal, 8 June 1906.

active policy in the Near East only made it all the more essential, in Aehrenthal's view, to continue to work closely with Russia in the Balkans to keep an eye on her, and to restrain her from participating in British manoeuvres to isolate and humiliate Germany.[120] Campbell-Bannerman's recent declared intention, for example, of raising the disarmament issue at the forthcoming Hague Peace Conference, seemed to Aehrenthal just such a manoeuvre.[121] Not that the merits of the disarmament issue were all that important to Aehrenthal. In fact, he felt that smaller, professional armies would actually be more useful than conscripted masses in suppressing proletarian rebellions. What was important was that Russia should align herself with the Central Powers on the issue; and in view of the Russo-German estrangement, it must fall to Austria-Hungary to bring about the *rapprochement*.

This was only part of the ambitious plan that Aehrenthal pressed on Goluchowski in long private letters in the summer of 1906.[122] First of all, Vienna should seek to strengthen the conservative forces in Russia generally. Perhaps Franz Joseph could send a message of encouragement to Nicholas II to stiffen him in the struggle that was just beginning between tsar and Duma. After all, if the tsardom succumbed, the revolutionary movement would not stop at the frontiers of Russia. The situation was like that of 1849; the two empires must stand together. But the only real solution would be the restoration of the Three Emperors' Alliance. This would, Aehrenthal admitted, involve a major diplomatic upheaval: Russia would first have to abandon her alliance with France. But he reckoned that the advantages to be gained would be well worth the effort: the Monarchy's whole international position would be strengthened; Germany would be compelled to support the Mürzsteg Powers, not Turkey, in the Near East; and the risk that a far-reaching agreement with Russia would tie the Monarchy's hands too firmly in the Balkans could be discounted – Russia would be too weak to undertake anything there for at least ten years.

Although Goluchowski took Aehrenthal's proposals seriously enough to write to the emperor at Ischl about them, the long reply he sent to Aehrenthal in September was essentially negative.[123] A friendly message to the tsar – perhaps timed to coincide with the

120. P.A. I/475, Liasse XXXII/c, Aehrenthal to Goluchowski, No. 1, private and secret, 20 July 1906.
121. Ibid., Aehrenthal to Goluchowski, private and secret, 23 August 1906.
122. Ibid., Aehrenthal to Goluchowski, No. 1, private and secret, 20 July; No. 2, private and secret, 25 July 1906.
123. Ibid., Goluchowski, report to Franz Joseph, 16 August 1906; to Aehrenthal, private and secret, 15 September 1906.

opening of the Hague Peace Conference in June 1907 – might possibly be of some use in restraining Russia from falling in with Great Britain's anti-German designs. The idea of reviving the Three Emperors' Alliance, however, seemed to Goluchowski quite unrealistic, possibly even harmful. For even in the unlikely contingency that Izvolsky, with his western proclivities and his extraordinary sensitivity to the criticism of Liberal politicians in the Duma, could be persuaded to abandon the alliance with France, the restoration of the Three Emperors' Alliance would certainly entail the dissolution of the Triple Alliance and the desertion of Italy to the Anglo-French camp, with disastrous consequences for Austro-Italian relations. Nor was he moved by Aehrenthal's general arguments, by the appeal to the timeworn doctrine of monarchical solidarity against the Revolution. In the first place, he felt that the Russian monarchy was in the long run doomed; and that it would not be wise to bind Austria-Hungary to such an unstable structure by an alliance. Indeed, he turned Aehrenthal's own arguments neatly against him: Russia's troubles might well be the result of the machinations of the international revolutionary party; but by the same token, a revived Three Emperors' Alliance, which would be widely regarded as a reactionary league for restoring tsarist autocracy, would be an extremely dangerous undertaking for the Central Powers, drawing on to them in turn the wrath of the international revolutionary movement. Besides, who in the Monarchy would support a restoration of the Three Emperors' Alliance? Clerical circles hostile to Italy perhaps, some Czechs, and a few conservatives who yearned for the days of the Holy Alliance; but not the Poles, the German Liberals, or the Radicals – even Czech Radicals; and certainly nobody at all in Hungary. With such a weight of public opinion opposed to the idea, it must be ruled out for a Dual Monarchy already embarking on a new age of democracy.

To the very end of his tenure of office, in fact, Goluchowski resisted all suggestions for a change of course. True, he admitted to a conference of ministers on 29 September 1906[124] that relations with Italy and Germany left much to be desired. Italy was arming fast and with determination; and her busy propaganda activities extended not only to Albania, Serbia and Montenegro, but even to Austro-Hungarian territory. As for Germany, it was significant that he thought it worthwhile to assure his colleagues that no danger threatened the Monarchy from that quarter. But he could

124. P.A. XL/305, Ministerratsprotokoll, 29 September 1906.

see no reason to jettison the Triple Alliance for a restored Three Emperors' Alliance – especially as the latter might only restrict the Monarchy's freedom of action in the Balkans. Admittedly, the threat from Russia had 'rather disappeared for the foreseeable future'; but for Goluchowski, the Austro-Russian Entente had always been only one means of safeguarding Austria-Hungary's interests, never in itself the end or everlasting basis of Austro-Hungarian policy. Perhaps in these months Goluchowski had let slip a chance to develop Austro-Hungarian foreign policy in a direction which might have averted the catastrophe of 1914. On the other hand, it might be said that his negative arguments made up in realism for what they lacked in imagination. Needless to say, Aehrenthal was not moved by them to abandon his ideas. Indeed, within a month he was in a position to make these ideas the basis of Austro-Hungarian policy.

On 23 October 1906 Goluchowski suddenly resigned his office. For some time he had been feeling ill at ease with trends in domestic policy in both halves of the Monarchy. In 1906 Franz Joseph had at last managed to resolve the Hungarian crisis – by threatening to introduce universal suffrage into Hungary (which would have shattered the carefully contrived electoral supremacy of the Magyars, 1867 Party and their radical opponents alike). The coalition had then agreed to take office on Franz Joseph's terms: the unity of the Common Army had been assured. In return for this the dynasty abandoned the Slavs and Romanians of Hungary, and no more was heard of universal suffrage in any meaningful sense. The fact that Franz Joseph now had a Hungarian government which offered, if well handled, a serious chance of calm and co-operation made Goluchowski's position difficult, however; for since his brush with the Hungarian politicians over the 'five-minute audience' in September 1905 it had been generally assumed that his head would be the first to be sacrificed to seal any reconciliation between the Magyars and their King.

Meanwhile, political developments in Austria were hardly more to Goluchowski's liking. Talk of introducing universal suffrage into Hungary had greatly increased the demand for it in Austria; and the emperor himself had begun to look back to Taaffe's project of 1893 – the bourgeois nationalist parties, which flourished under the five-class voting system, would under a system of universal suffrage be swamped by the great mass parties, Christian Socials and Social Democrats, as yet virtually uninfected with nationalism. Big public demonstrations at the end of 1905 – sparked by the Russian revolution – had given the final impetus for the Austrian government to prepare a new suffrage law with all speed. This had dismayed Goluchowski, by temperament an ultra-conservative, and one who had seen France at close quarters, and disapproved of what he saw.[125] But matters had not come to a head until the summer of 1906, when the Magyars gave him a very rough handling in the Delegations, and launched a sustained campaign against him in the press. By October, Goluchowski had decided that he had had enough of their 'ceaseless baiting'.[126] He had threatened to resign unless the Hungarian government would restrain his attackers; but he had got no satisfaction whatever – and this despite the fact that Franz Joseph had impressed on Budapest his express will that Goluchowski should continue in office.[127] At this, Goluchowski tendered his resignation to the emperor.

The End of the Austro-Russian Entente, 1906–1908

The autumn of 1906 saw a serious attempt to master the domestic situation by men of imagination. Max Vladimir von Beck, Austrian prime minister since February, and a close associate of Archduke Franz Ferdinand, was determined both to carry through the electoral reform in Austria and to take a firm stand against Magyar separatism in working out the details of the commercial *Ausgleich* already agreed in principle with the new Hungarian government. He was strongly supported by other nominees of the heir apparent, such as Conrad von Hoetzendorf, appointed Chief of the General Staff in November. For Aehrenthal, now summoned to succeed Goluchowski at the Ballhausplatz, a strong, constructive foreign policy and a stable, healthy domestic situation were just two sides of the same coin. For example, in a memorandum of February 1907, he proposed that Bosnia and the Herzegovina might one day be formally annexed, and joined to the South Slav lands of Austria and of Hungary, the whole new bloc being granted a genuine autonomy under the suzerainty of the Crown of St Stephen. The accretion of territory would flatter the Magyars (and perhaps develop their all too rudimentary consciousness of the Monarchy's interests as an Adriatic Power); the prospect of a common national development in a trialist direction would satisfy the South Slavs, and break the point of Panserbian propaganda. But these were as

125. P.A. XL/304, Ministerratsprotokoll, August 1905.
126. Mensdorff MSS, Karton 9, Goluchowski to Mensdorff, 4 November 1906.
127. T.M. Islamov, 'Oesterreichisch-ungarische Beziehungen am Anfang des XX Jahrhunderts', in F. Klein (ed.) *Weltpolitik*, pp. 113–14.

yet mere suggestions for the future. More immediately, the year 1907 saw the introduction of universal and direct suffrage into Austria, the electoral annihilation of the bourgeois nationalist parties by the clerical and socialist mass parties, and the conclusion of the commercial *Ausgleich* with Hungary in October. For the last time in its history the Monarchy was about to enjoy a respite of three years of relative domestic calm. This at least provided some basis for a more positive foreign policy; and the new foreign minister seemed to possess the necessary energy, drive and sense of direction.

Alois, Baron Lexa von Aehrenthal, although born in 1858 a member of the lesser German nobility of Bohemia, had excellent connections through his mother (a Thun) and his wife (a Széchényi) with the higher Bohemian and Hungarian aristocracy. Nevertheless, he owed his position largely to his own ability and industry, as evidenced by his career as Kálnoky's private secretary, as minister at Bucharest, and latterly as a most successful ambassador at St Petersburg. The brisk and businesslike tone he introduced into the Ballhausplatz was immediately remarked on by diplomats at home and abroad. The new minister was 'quite a different cup of tea [*ganz ein anderes Café*]' from the easy-going Goluchowski.[128] 'Just back from the Lion', wrote Prince Fürstenberg, 'he stamped his feet even while *seated*!!!'[129] According to a British ambassador, Aehrenthal would not permit his underlings at the Ballhausplatz even to express an opinion on foreign policy.[130] But this personal and centralised approach had disadvantages of its own. Aehrenthal was not without energy or ideas; but some observers thought him too much a statesman of the eighteenth century, prone to think too much in terms of governments and to ignore the great currents of public opinion;[131] and even his friend and colleague at St Petersburg, Berchtold, complained of his 'frightful tendency' to overlook awkward facts that did not fit into his bold designs.[132]

The general drift of his plans was fairly clear; and the instruments of Austro-Hungarian foreign policy – the alliance system and the *entente* with Russia – remained the same. But there were differences of emphasis from the Goluchowski era. Goluchowski had pursued an essentially negative, status quo policy, coping with problems on an ad hoc basis as they arose, viewing the Russian *entente* with a

---

128. Berchtold MSS, Hohenlohe to Berchtold, 19 May 1907.
129. Ibid., Fürstenberg to Berchtold, 14 July 1907.
130. Cartwright MSS, Cartwright to Chauncey, 6 July 1910 (copy).
131. Mensdorff MSS, Karton 1, Tagebuch, 31 October 1908.
132. Hantsch, *Berchtold*, I, p. 136.

caution bordering on suspicion, and alternating between fatalism and helpless irritation as the Dual and Triple Alliances continued their steady decline. In his eyes, the domestic ills of the Monarchy were so grave that, failing an actual threat to its vital interests, the best chance of survival lay in absolute calm and rest. Aehrenthal, by contrast, prescribed a vigorous foreign policy to sharpen the patient's self-confidence and interest in staying alive. Although he intended to use the same diplomatic instruments as his predecessor, he had a rather more purposeful and ambitious end in view – the positive strengthening of the prestige and independence of the Dual Monarchy.

For Aehrenthal, as for every Austro-Hungarian foreign minister since 1879, the Dual Alliance remained the ultimate safeguard of the Monarchy's security. His hypersensitive reaction in the summer of 1906 to what he regarded as British attempts to encircle and isolate Germany was a reflection of his concern for the pre-eminence of the Central European bloc. At the same time, however, he was determined to secure for Austria-Hungary a greater measure of independence within the Alliance – indeed, to take the lead in it. He was in a sense seeking for Austria-Hungary a position like that enjoyed by Germany in the 1800s and 1890s, when the dominant Power had been able to treat the Alliance as something to be held in reserve against an actual catastrophe, while retaining for itself considerable freedom of manoeuvre in day-to-day diplomacy. To this end, it would be essential – as he had been urging on Goluchowski for some six years – to reduce the Monarchy's dependence on Berlin by improving its relations with its potential enemies.

He lost no time in holding out an olive branch to Italy, in an ostentatiously friendly speech to the Delegations in November 1906. And he was quite undeterred by the clamour of Conrad, Franz Ferdinand and the clericals, who declared that war with Italy was inevitable, and that the sooner it came the better. By the spring of 1907 the Italians were beginning to respond. After a tour of Italy, Prince Liechtenstein reported that Austrophile feeling there was surprisingly strong, particularly – and this was a new if somewhat doubtful compliment – among left-wing circles, who were now afraid that if the Dual Monarchy fell to pieces Germany would expand as far as the Adriatic. A cordial meeting between Aehrenthal and Tittoni at Desio in July set the seal on the *rapprochement*.[133] Indeed, even world recognition was attained when Aehrenthal and

133. Mérey MSS, Aehrenthal to Mérey, 25 July 1907.

Tittoni were invited to accept the Nobel Peace Prize for 1907. But in Vienna it was felt that it would be quite improper for the emperor's foreign minister to accept a large sum of money from a foreign body merely for doing his duty. Besides, if war later broke out, *mauvais plaisants* might then ask whether the money should not be paid back.[134] So the offer of what was still considered a rather curious distinction was declined with much thanks.

In cultivating the Monarchy's other potential enemy, Russia, Aehrenthal was even more assiduous, and this not merely as a means to greater independence from Germany, but as an end in itself. He was still hoping ultimately for nothing less than the restoration of the Three Emperors' Alliance. He had never approved of Goluchowski's somewhat negative attitude towards the Entente, which had restricted the Monarchy's freedom of action while not providing the advantages that would accrue from a really cordial relationship with Russia. How far his hopes of far-reaching co-operation with St Petersburg could be reconciled with his determination to increase the prestige of Austria-Hungary in the Near East, only the future would show. Potential sources of friction were not far to seek. Even Aehrenthal continued Goluchowski's efforts to draw Bulgaria into Austria-Hungary's orbit; and although he was less averse than Goluchowski to granting commercial concessions to Serbia, this would only be done when that state came to heel and showed to Austria-Hungary 'the respect due to our Monarchy' as a Great Power.[135] Such language could hardly be music to Russian ears. Nevertheless, Aehrenthal seemed to get off to a good start when he returned to St Petersburg in November 1906 to take his leave as ambassador. He was able to sound the tocsin to some effect against Great Britain's alleged schemes to isolate and humiliate Germany at the forthcoming Hague Peace Conference, and against her attempts to steer the Macedonian reforms in a more radical direction. At any rate, the emperor and empress both responded warmly to his suggestion that the selfish designs of Great Britain might best be checked by a restoration of the Three Emperors' Alliance.

Izvolsky[136] was rather more difficult to handle, being a 'westerner' who accepted the new constitutional system in Russia, and who was, indeed, inordinately sensitive to criticism from press and Duma. Since his appointment in May 1906 the Entente had certainly lost something of its 'moral' content – that emphasis on

134. Aehrenthal MSS, Karton 3, Lützow to Aehrenthal, 24 December 1907.
135. P.A. XL/305, Ministerratsprotokoll, 6 January 1907.
136. Bridge, 'Izvolsky, Aehrenthal', p. 324.

monarchical solidarity by which Aehrenthal set such store. Yet even Izvolsky had not the slightest desire to abandon the Austrian *entente* in favour of an exclusively western alignment, as demanded by noisy sections of the public. Certainly, he had been appointed to wind up Russia's bankrupt Far Eastern policies; but the corollary of this was not an attempt to restore Russia's prestige by challenging the Central Powers in the Near East. Russia in 1906 was not in a position to challenge anybody, and Stolypin's demand for twenty years of peace to crush the Revolution at home had the force of law in the foreign office. In Izvolsky's view, both an exclusively western and an exclusively Austro-German orientation – and a revived Three Emperors' Alliance such as Aehrenthal hoped for was the most anti-British combination imaginable – were equally dangerous. He attempted, therefore, to tack, and to combine an *entente* with Great Britain, as demanded by the Duma, with the Austrian *entente* favoured by the court.

Aehrenthal, for his part, persisted with his efforts to establish really close relations with Russia and to draw her away from Great Britain. Indeed, British behaviour in the spring of 1907 seemed to make this urgently necessary. In the Macedonian negotiations at Constantinople[137] British demands for customs house reforms and control of Ottoman expenditure were delaying the granting of extra revenues to finance the existing reforms; yet at the same time the British were importunately pressing the Mürzsteg Powers to introduce still more reforms – in the judiciary – and were proffering radical suggestions as to their content. Now the Austrians, if they were prepared to concede to all six Powers an equal role in the implementation of the reforms, still insisted that their formulation was a matter for the Mürzsteg Powers alone; and they found the tendency of the Russian ambassador Zinoviev to ignore his Austro-Hungarian colleague, Pallavicini, and to lend an ear instead to British suggestions, distinctly disquieting. On the wider international stage, Edward VII's visits to the kings of Spain and Italy at Cartagena and Gaeta were rightly interpreted in Vienna as portending a new grouping in the Mediterranean; and agreements to safeguard the status quo there – obviously against Germany – followed in May. Meanwhile, Campbell-Bannerman's determined pursuit of his disarmament plans provoked Aehrenthal to renew his appeals to St Petersburg: it was essential that Russia should stand together with the Central Powers to prevent all discussion of the issue at the conference, or at least to siphon it off into a harmless

137. Bridge, *Great Britain and Austria-Hungary*, pp. 8–9, 42ff.

subcommittee on which the three empires need be represented. In May, he went a step further, hinting tentatively to France and Russia that they might join with the Central Powers to impose a moderate tempo in Macedonian affairs, confining the obstreperous British in a strait-jacket, as it were, inside the Concert.

This last plan misfired completely. Not only did Izvolsky shrink from supporting it, the French and Russians leaked it to the horrified British in a garbled form – as an attempt to exclude Great Britain from any voice in the Concert on Macedonian affairs; and it seriously damaged Aehrenthal's reputation in London. Meanwhile, the behaviour of the third member of Aehrenthal's projected Three Emperors' Alliance was equally disillusioning. In June, Aehrenthal felt obliged to send off another round of complaints to Berlin: Germany's encouragement of the violently anti-Catholic *Los von Rom* movement in Austria, and a projected Prussian law for the expropriation of Polish landowners in the Ostmark, posed serious threats to the popularity of the Dual Alliance inside the Monarchy. Worse, in the international field, where the Hague Peace Conference turned out to be less of a menace than Aehrenthal had feared – as it was soon clear that on the armaments issue the Conference would produce nothing more restrictive than the anodyne recommendations of 1899 – Germany was adopting an attitude of such inflexibility as seemed almost designed to contrive her isolation; indeed, she seemed, to Aehrenthal's intense irritation, to be trying to push Austria-Hungary forward as the intransigent Power. Altogether, it seemed by the summer of 1907 that Austria-Hungary, far from making progress towards restoring the Three Emperors' Alliance, was becoming uncomfortably isolated. It was for this reason that the Austrians, as so often in the past when they had been disappointed in St Petersburg and Berlin, tried to restore the wire to London. Aehrenthal now decided that, as the policy of Germany was 'rhapsodic', whereas that of Great Britain was cool and far-sighted, he would do well to associate the Monarchy with the cleverer Power;[138] and as for Russia, if Izvolsky would not go 'through thick and thin' with him, but insisted on flirting with the British, Aehrenthal would make his own approach to London ('so gehe ich lieber zuerst zu den Engländern').[139]

Consequently, at the Hague he accepted the British compromise proposals on armaments, and for the rest kept the Monarchy well in the background. He was also careful to receive the notification of

138. Berchtold MSS, Aehrenthal to Berchtold, 7 July 1907.
139. Ibid., Fürstenberg to Berchtold, 14 July 1907.

the new Mediterranean Agreements between Great Britain, France, Spain and Italy in good part, even though he regarded them as clearly directed against Germany, and was scarcely taken in by Grey's naïve explanation that they embodied the same principles as the Mediterranean Agreements of 1887. The British, for their part, showed themselves ready to forget the recent contretemps when Aehrenthal proceeded to sound out the terrain for a positive *rapprochement*. This could only be in Macedonia; but a highly successful visit by Edward VII to Franz Joseph at Ischl in August produced agreement even here, and Aehrenthal promised to speed up his proposals for judicial reform. It was a direct consequence of this meeting that the two Mürzsteg Powers bestirred themselves to check the internecine strife among the Christians of Macedonia and the depredations of terrorists entering the area from Bulgaria, Serbia and Greece, by issuing a solemn warning to the Balkan states concerned that Article III of the Mürzsteg Programme would not take any account of changes wrought by violence. By September, with the Mürzteg *entente* in good shape, even strengthened by the support of Great Britain, the Monarchy's interests seemed to be fairly secure.

In this situation, Aehrenthal could afford to take a benevolent view of the developing Anglo-Russian *rapprochement*. The Convention of 31 August 1907 he regarded as essentially an Asian affair, and certainly of no ominous portent for the Balkans. All the more so as Izvolsky, passing through Vienna in September, reiterated his determination to go hand in hand with Austria-Hungary in Macedonia.[140] More than this, Izvolsky went on to make a very bold proposal: 'If, despite its peace-loving and conservative policy in the Balkan peninsula, substantial changes occur, the Russian government will have to attend to the defence of its paramount interests', especially 'the question of free passage from the Black Sea to the Mediterranean'; and he asked Aehrenthal to specify 'the corresponding advantages which Austria-Hungary would seek in the event of the above-named circumstances occurring'. This was no less than a proposal to transform the Entente from a negative arrangement to maintain the status quo to a positive one to deal with those contingencies which in 1897 had been left in the air as too dangerous to handle; and Aehrenthal might have been expected to leap at the opportunity. In the event, however, although he immediately thought of the annexation of Bosnia as possible compensation, he decided for the present not to pursue the matter, as he

140. Bridge, 'Izvolsky, Aehrenthal', p. 325.

was as yet somewhat uncertain as to the genuineness of Izvolsky's loyalty to the Entente. There the matter rested until the Russians raised it again in 1908. In the meantime, the events of the autumn were to confirm Aehrenthal's misgivings.

In the negotiations that now got under way over the judicial reform,[141] Aehrenthal's hopes of the summer of co-operating with both Russia and Great Britain were to be dashed, and the Mürzsteg *entente* itself was to be seriously undermined. In a sense, the problem was one of a series of misunderstandings caused by the cumbersome diplomatic machinery of the Mürzsteg system, namely, conferences of ambassadors at Constantinople. Instructions from governments to ambassadors were often delayed; and when they arrived they had usually been overtaken by events. More serious, the ambassadors, susceptible to pressure from the Porte, and confident that they knew better than their distant masters, constantly flouted their instructions and sent back drastically modified proposals for the approval – or more often, the exasperated disapproval – of their governments. There were thus twelve, rather than six parties to the negotiations; and with the Germans incorrigible in their disparagement of the whole project as undermining the sultan's authority, and with the British, despite all their recent fine promises of co-operation, demanding extreme measures that nobody else thought the sultan could possibly accept, it was hardly surprising that it was not until January 1908 that ambassadors and governments finally reached agreement on a judicial reform project. Meanwhile, personal factors increased the friction: Pallavicini was constantly complaining of the attempts of the British ambassador to lure his Russian colleague from the straight and narrow path laid down at Mürzsteg. It is true that in December the Mürzsteg Powers united to reject a British proposal to send the gendarmerie and its European officers into action against the terrorist bands: this, they insisted, was a task for the Turkish regular army, not for the reform organisation. But this was their last display of solidarity. By the end of 1907 Aehrenthal, seriously disturbed by Great Britain's growing influence over Russia's attitude to the reforms, was coming to the conclusion that the days of the Mürzsteg *entente* were numbered.

Even so, some Russian goodwill still remained; and it was in an effort to capitalise on this while it lasted that Aehrenthal now decided to take action to secure Austria-Hungary's economic and political interests in the Balkans against the day when the *entente*

---

141. Bridge, *Great Britain and Austria-Hungary*, pp. 67ff.

should end. That his decision to launch a railway-building pro-gramme at this juncture might actually precipitate the final collapse of the Mürzsteg *entente* does not seem to have occurred to him.

Already for some thirty years the Monarchy had enjoyed, by virtue of the Treaty of Berlin, the right to build railways in the Sanjak of Novibazar. But there had so far been no urgency to exercise this right. The Turkish line to Mitrovitsa, at the southern end of the Sanjak, was not completed until the turn of the century, and the Austro-Hungarian line to Uvac, on the Bosnian frontier of the Sanjak, only in 1905. Now in the spring of 1907 Aehrenthal had drawn up a memorandum,[142] envisaging the construction of a whole series of Balkan railways to develop Austro-Hungarian commercial (and by implication political) influence in the penin-sula. These included: a link between the existing Greek and Turkish networks; a coastal railway for Montenegro; and, more important, a line to join the Serbian network on to the Bosnian line to the Adriatic. In Aehrenthal's view, Serbia's desire to reach the sea (*'Drang nach Westen'*) was a natural tendency which could not be halted in the long run. The Monarchy should simply accept this fact, and try to canalise the movement through Austro-Hungarian territory in Bosnia and Dalmatia. By this means, if the terms offered to Serbia were attractive enough, the counter-attraction of a Russian or Italian Danube–Adriatic railway skirting Austro-Hungarian territory and rendering Serbia even more independent might be overcome. Finally, the Monarchy should build a railway in the Sanjak of Novibazar: without it, the recently completed Bosnian lines would remain a mere cul-de-sac; whereas in terms of commerce and general political influence in Macedonia the Mon-archy stood to gain a great deal from a direct railway link of its own with Turkey.

As a portent of future events, Aehrenthal's handling of the Sanjak railway project[143] is instructive, and illustrative of his tend-ency, once he felt that either law or necessity gave the Monarchy a good case, to act boldly and with scant regard for the reactions of third parties. When his first approach to Constantinople, in De-cember 1907, produced the usual mutterings from the Russian government about the Entente of 1897 and the status quo, he brushed them aside, reiterating Goluchowski's arguments – that the Sanjak railway was a purely economic project, and hence outside the purview of the Entente, which was concerned only

142. S. Wank, 'Aehrenthal and the Sanjak of Novibazar Railway Project: a Reappraisal', in *Slavonic and East European Review*, 42, (1964), pp. 353–69.
143. Bridge, *Great Britain and Austria-Hungary*, Chapter IV.

with the political status quo; and – unlike Goluchowski – he pressed ahead, annnouncing his railway projects to the world in a speech to the Hungarian Delegations on 27 January 1908. This speech had an effect on Russian policy and on Great Power alignments in general that he had hardly bargained for, however. In St Petersburg the resultant gale of nationalist wrath swept Izvolsky completely off his feet; and this was duly noted in London: 'the struggle between Austria and Russia in the Balkans is evidently beginning and we shall not be bothered by Russia in Asia'.[144]

To make matters worse, a most unfortunate coincidence now occurred, which drove Great Britain and Russia still closer together in common indignation against Aehrenthal. On 5 February – the day following the issue of the Turkish *iradé* approving the Sanjak railway project – the ambassadors at Constantinople again defied their instructions and refused to present the judicial reform scheme to the Porte because they thought the Turks were not yet in a mood to accept it. In their reports, each ambassador took care to blame his colleagues for this decision; but the British and Russians now nursed the additional grievance (which was, in fact, without foundation)[145] that to secure the obnoxious railway project Vienna had 'played the mean game' of sabotaging Macedonian reform.[146] They consequently decided that Austria-Hungary was no longer to be trusted in Macedonian affairs. On 17 February Izvolsky told the British ambassador that he wished 'to get out of the dual action with Austria and to rally himself to . . . those Powers who are sincerely desirous of reforms'.[147] The British responded: 'this marks a very important development of the Anglo-French and Anglo-Russian agreement policy. Russia is now asking for our co-operation in the Near East.'[148] From this point, although Izvolsky talked of 'the abandonment of the dual co-operation and the merging of Russia in the general Concert',[149] Macedonian reform was in effect under a new dual control, that of Russia and Great Britain. Henceforth, Izvolsky discussed future reform projects with the British without any prior consultation in Vienna; and by early April it was noted with some satisfaction in London that 'the Mürzsteg Programme is as dead as a doornail'.[150]

Aehrenthal did not mourn it for long. He decided that it was

144. F.O. 371/581, Nicolson to Grey, No. 63, 4 February 1908, minute.
145. Bridge, *Great Britain and Austria-Hungary*, pp. 81–3.
146. *British Documents on the Origins of the War* (hereafter B.D.), V, No. 180.
147. F.O. 371/581, Nicolson to Grey, private tel., 17 February 1908.
148. Ibid., minute.
149. F.O. 371/582, Nicolson to Grey, private, 13 March 1908.
150. Hardinge MSS, XIII, Hardinge to Goschen, 7 April 1908 (copy).

after all a relief to be rid of the burden of civilising Macedonia. This task, he was prepared to leave to Great Britain and Russia, particularly as Izvolsky seemed to be exercising a salutary restraining influence over his British friends. The Russians forced the British to drop the idea of a Christian governor-general for Macedonia appointed by the Powers – which the Turks would in no circumstances have accepted. Consequently, Aehrenthal was not in the least put out by Edward VII's meeting with the tsar at Reval in June,[151] when the Anglo-Russian proposals were finally agreed. Unlike the Germans and the Turks, who took great alarm at this ominous Anglo-Russian combination, he professed himself ready to accept any Anglo-Russian proposals that were compatible with the sovereign rights of the sultan. Indeed, he angrily warned the Germans, who had been telling St Petersburg that Austria-Hungary's view of the matter was identical with Germany's, that he would not hesitate to issue a *démenti* if Germany ever again presumed to speak for Austria-Hungary. And he tartly reminded Berlin that Germany would have done better to lend more loyal support to the much milder Austro-Russian proposals in February. In fact, he was secretly quite pleased to see that Reval had given the Germans a fright: this could only increase their dependence on Vienna.

For similar reasons he was undismayed by the Young Turkish Revolution of 22–25 July, which overthrew the sultan's *camarilla*, and caused great despondency in Berlin. To the Austrians it seemed that Turkey, exasperated beyond endurance by the prospect of yet more drastic Great Power intervention after Reval, was at last making a serious effort to put her house in order. At least, the warring Christians of Macedonia seemed to think so, and laid down their arms to greet the new era of fraternity. This in itself rendered superfluous that reform programme which had been one of the chief bases of Anglo-Russian co-operation. Moreover, the fall of the *camarilla* and the collapse of Germany's position ought to give the Monarchy the chance to recover some of the ground lost of recent years to its ally and chief commercial rival in the Near East. Indeed, so heartened was Aehrenthal by this turn of events that he was even prepared to bury the hatchet with the British, and the meeting between Franz Joseph and Edward VII at Ischl in August 1908 was as cordial as that of the previous year. The emperor congratulated his old friend on Great Britain's restoration to 'that prominent position in the Turkish capital which, in his opinion, she

151. Bridge, *Great Britain and Austria-Hungary*, pp. 96–8.

should always have occupied'.[152] True, Aehrenthal refused to interfere at Berlin to restrain Germany's enthusiasm for the naval race, taking the somewhat ostrich-like view that this was no concern of Austria-Hungary's. But he told the British not to worry, as Germany's finances were not all that sound ('*nicht brilliant*').[153] The hoary legend that on this occasion the emperor had to rebuff an attempt by the king to seduce Austria-Hungary from the German alliance is not supported by any evidence in British or Austrian archives.[154] Nevertheless, Aehrenthal was well content to let the Germans believe the story, which would serve as a salutary reminder to them of their precarious situation and of the value of their alliance with Austria-Hungary.

In short, as the storms of the previous winter faded away the Monarchy found itself in a fairly comfortable position by the summer of 1908; and if Aehrenthal felt he could stand aloof – even benefit – from the anxieties of the Germans, he felt equally little need to run after the Russians. Although the Mürzsteg *entente* had indeed perished in the aftermath of the Sanjak railway affair, Aehrenthal was quite content to reaffirm, in an exchange of notes with St Petersburg in the early summer, his continued allegiance to the general conservative principles of the Entente of 1897.

It was the Russians who, in their craving for more positive successes, now took the initiative in an attempt to extend the Entente to cover changes in the status quo.[155] Izvolsky's famous note to Vienna of 2 July 1908 proposed in effect an Austro-Russian deal: if Austria-Hungary would promise her benevolent support to Russia in altering the rule of the Straits in Russia's favour (to allow the riverine states of the Black Sea, but no others, freedom of passage through the Straits) then Russia would assume a similarly benevolent attitude in the event of Austria-Hungary's annexing, not only Bosnia and the Herzegovina, but the Sanjak of Novibazar. It was indicative both of Aehrenthal's confidence in the international position of the Monarchy, and of his lingering distrust of Izvolsky, that he at first saw no advantage in binding himself to St Petersburg in this way. As he told the emperor on 8 July, Russia was simply trying to recover control over Austria-Hungary's Balkan policy. In his first draft reply, of 13 August, therefore, he firmly restated the traditional Austro-Hungarian position that the annexation of Bosnia was a matter that would be decided on by

152. Bridge, 'Izvolsky, Aehrenthal', p. 330.
153. Mensdorff MSS, Karton 4, Tagebuch, 15 August 1908.
154. Bridge, *Great Britain and Austria-Hungary*, pp. 102–3.
155. Bridge, 'Izvolsky, Aehrenthal', pp. 328ff.

Austria-Hungary alone – who had, moreover, no intention of annexing the Sanjak. That being the case, he had to say that there was no basis for an agreement in the terms proposed by St Petersburg.[156]

That within a week he changed his mind and decided to follow up the Russian proposal was due, not to the contents of the proposal, but to events in the Ottoman Empire. By mid-August it was becoming clear that the new rulers at Constantinople, encouraged by a vociferous nationalist press, were intent on reasserting Ottoman influence in the occupied provinces. There was talk of summoning representatives from Bosnia and the Herzegovina to the new Ottoman parliament; and even of giving the provinces a degree of autonomy under Ottoman rule. Besides, even if these dangers did not materialise, there was no denying the uncomfortable fact that Bosnia and the Herzegovina were now the only provinces in Europe that did not enjoy the benefits of constitutional government. For this deficiency, the only remedy acceptable to Austria-Hungary would be for Franz Joseph to grant a constitution. And this he could do only if he assumed full sovereign powers in the provinces by an act of annexation.

If these considerations alone were not cogent enough, military and prestige factors combined to clinch the arguments in favour of annexation. Within a month of the Young Turkish Revolution the Austrians had decided to renounce their rights to keep garrisons in the Sanjak of Novibazar. According to military opinion, the Sanjak, hemmed in between Serbia and Montenegro, was a useless, even potentially dangerous, cul-de-sac. After all, if it came to a showdown with Serbia, the Austro-Hungarian army would march directly on Belgrade. And to Aehrenthal it seemed that a military presence on Turkish soil burdened the Monarchy unnecessarily with the risk of immediate and unwelcome involvement in a morass of troubles should the Young Turkish Revolution merely prove the harbinger of perpetual chaos. (The Monarchy's economic interests in Turkey, however, were not to be abandoned. The Sanjak railway was still being discussed in the Ballhausplatz as late as 1912.) But to renounce treaty rights in the Sanjak would incur a loss of prestige, and this could perhaps best be offset by some move such as the annexation of Bosnia. What is more, the retreat from the Sanjak could be made to appear as a sort of compensation to Turkey for the loss of her sovereign rights in Bosnia. Finally, the annexation would put an end to an ambiguous situation which had

156. Ibid., p. 331.

appeared increasingly untenable since the Young Turkish Revolution; and by drawing a clear and final line between what was Austro-Hungarian and what was Turkish, the Monarchy would in fact be voluntarily setting a limit to its own frontiers and dispelling any lingering notions of its allegedly expansionist intentions.

Thus the annexation of Bosnia was essentially a conservative move, and – as even Izvolsky and his advisers were ready to recognise – anything but a forward thrust into the Balkans. Equally, the view that it was an attempt on the part of Aehrenthal to cut a fine figure on the international stage out of sheer desperation is a myth.[157] To him, the international position of the Monarchy seemed healthier in the summer of 1908 than it had been for some years. He had prestige enough: over-confidence, not desperation, would better account for the decidedly cavalier manner in which he determined to carry through the annexation – presenting Turkey with a *fait accompli*, and hardly taking the other Powers (except Russia) much more into his confidence. When he informed a conference of ministers of his plans on 19 August[158] he blandly oberved that Germany, being still in great terror of isolation, would not dare to make difficulties; and that Italy had no right whatever to claim compensation under Article VII of the alliance. France, preoccupied in Morocco, and Great Britain, who 'desires good relations with us', he did not propose to consult at all.[159] Only with Russia would there have to be negotiations, and these were progressing very well. On 27 August, he wrote to St Petersburg expressing his general agreement with Izvolsky's proposals.

However remiss Aehrenthal may have been in failing to give an inkling of the imminence of the annexation in his negotiations with his German and Italian counterparts in September, and whatever Izvolsky may have claimed later, the Russians were in no doubt as to his intentions.[160] This at least is clear from the correspondence – now published[161] – that passed, under the approving eye of the tsar, between Izvolsky and Charykov, the assistant left in charge of the St Petersburg foreign office when Izvolsky embarked on a lengthy European tour in August. From the moment they received Aehrenthal's reply of 27 August they were convinced that the decision to annex the occupied provinces in the very near future had been

157. Bridge, *Great Britain and Austria-Hungary*, p. 106.
158. *Oesterreich-Ungarns Außenpolitik* (hereafter OUA), Vol. I, No. 140.
159. F. Conrad von Hoetzendorf, *Aus meiner Dienstzeit* (Vienna 1921) I, p. 104.
160. Bridge, 'Izvolsky, Aehrenthal', p. 335.
161. I.V. Bestuzhev, (ed.), ' Borba v pravyaschikh krugakh Rossii po voprosam vneshnei politiki vo vremya Bosniiskogo krizisa', in *Istoricheskii Arkhiv*, 5 (1962), pp..113–47 (tr. Bridge, *Izvolsky, Aehrenthal*, pp. 343–62).

'finally and irrevocably taken'. There was nothing to be done about that; but, in any case, 'within the limits within which Baron Aehrenthal has planned it, it does not affect either our strategic or our economic interests' – on the contrary, it would free Russia once and for all from the nightmare of an Austro-Hungarian 'march on Salonika' through the Sanjak. Izvolsky and Charykov decided, therefore, with the tsar's approval, that they would do well to avoid the humiliation that would come from a futile protest, and concentrate on securing compensatory advantages for Russia.

Although there was no agreed written record of the discussions between Aehrenthal and Izvolsky at Buchlau on 16 September, both the Russian[162] and Austro-Hungarian sources show[163] that the agreement reached was a good deal more complete than Izvolsky was later to make out. In return for Russia's adopting a benevolent attitude towards the annexation of the occupied provinces (which Izvolsky was left in no doubt would occur early in October, when the Delegations were due to meet), Austria-Hungary would re-nounce all her rights in the Sanjak, support Russia's desiderata at the Straits, and consent to the granting of independence to Bulgaria (but decidedly not to the granting of territorial compensation to Serbia and Montenegro). These states, Aehrenthal insisted, – and, indeed, was hoping by the annexation to demonstrate once and for all to the whole world – had no *locus standi* in the affairs of Bosnia. Nothing much appears to have been said about the diplomatic method by which these various changes were to be incorporated into the Treaty of Berlin; and Izvolsky's correspondence with Charykov in the next few days about an international conference in which Austria-Hungary would appear as 'the accused' and Russia as the defender of the interests of aggrieved parties in Constantino-ple and Belgrade, throws a curious light on their concept of a 'benevolent attitude'. In this respect indeed, even if subsequent events had gone according to Izvolsky's plans, Europe would probably have witnessed a 'Bosnian crisis' of sufficient severity to destroy the Austro-Russian Entente anyway. But, as things stood in mid-September, the state of the Entente seemed healthy enough to the Austrians, to Izvolsky, and to the handful of cognoscenti in St Petersburg.

The sudden and irretrievable breakdown of the Entente two weeks later was partly the result of unpredictable developments in the Balkans. When Young Turkish attempts to emphasise the

---

162. Bridge, 'Izvolsky, Aehrenthal', pp. 348–51.
163. OUA, I, No. 79.

vassal status of Bulgaria as a province of the Ottoman Empire led Sofia to break off diplomatic relations with Constantinople, rumours began to spread of an impending declaration of Bulgarian independence. Now it had been Austro-Hungarian policy of recent years to cultivate Bulgaria as a potentially strong card to play against Serbia in the final scramble for Turkey; and it was in line with this policy that when Prince Ferdinand visited Budapest on 23–24 September, Franz Joseph made a point of receiving him with full royal honours; and Aehrenthal even gave him a broad hint that Austria-Hungary might soon annex Bosnia, in which case Bulgaria might take the opportunity to declare her independence. He was hoping thereby both to arrange a useful diversion to draw international attention away from the annexation after the event, and to tie Bulgaria closer to the Monarchy. Neither of these objectives was likely to prove congenial to St Petersburg, however. Indeed, Izvolsky and Charykov had been making their own plans for Bulgarian independence, which was to appear as a triumph for Russian diplomacy; and in no circumstances was Bulgaria to assume the role of the 'accomplice' of Austria-Hungary. In the event, Ferdinand was nobody's accomplice, and issued the anticipated declaration quite independently on 5 October – not after, but two days before, the annexation of Bosnia. Aehrenthal was somewhat put out: 'that Ferdinand has got ahead of me!'[164] The British were indignant, suspecting – especially when they learned of some loose speculative remarks made by the garrulous Khevenhüller to the French President – an Austro-Bulgarian conspiracy to discredit the Anglophile regime at Constantinople. The Russians were furious.

If Izvolsky and Charykov had failed to predict the actions of Prince Ferdinand, they had made a far more fearful miscalculation in respect of Russian public opinion, which proved in the event to care a great deal about the enslavement of Slav brothers in Bosnia, but nothing at all for the legalistic and strategic advantages which Izvolsky was hoping to gain for Russia at the Straits. In St Petersburg, Stolypin and his colleagues were acutely aware of these realities, however, and when they were informed, at the eleventh hour (3 October) of Izvolsky's policy of compensations, made no bones about disavowing it. At this, both Charykov and his imperial master abandoned Izvolsky. The latter, when he was informed of all this in Paris on the next day, was in a truly desperate position – all the more so as Khevenhüller, apparently inadequately briefed by Aehrenthal, but never at a loss for words, had already

---

164. Hantsch, *Berchtold*, I, p. 127 n. 14.

announced the impending annexation to President Fallières, adding that Russia concurred in it. Izvolsky was, moreover, in danger of losing his meagre pound of flesh, for although he had found the Italians and Germans accommodating enough, he soon discovered that the Western Powers were by no means anxious to harass Turkey, let alone in a cause that accorded ill with their own strategic interests. His first instinct was to resign; then he decided to blame the whole fiasco on Aehrenthal. He now protested that he had made no definite commitments at Buchlau: there must be a conference to call the perfidious Austrians to account before Europe, and to force them to pay compensation to Serbia and Montenegro. Here was the material for the most dramatic Austro-Russian confrontation since San Stefano. Owing to a combination of circumstances – haste, unfortunate coincidences and, above all, a fatal omission to take sufficient account of the broader currents of opinion outside the conference rooms of diplomacy, Izvolsky and Aehrenthal, in their efforts to develop the Austro-Russian Entente in a positive direction beyond the mere maintenance of the status quo, had ended by destroying it.

The Entente had always been a fragile instrument, only effective when it was not subjected to too great a strain or used for ambitious purposes for which it had not been designed. Like the Three Emperors' Alliance and the Three Emperors' League before it, it was essentially conservative, the product of the realisation by St Petersburg and Vienna that so long as Turkey-in-Europe existed, the Balkan situation was unlikely to become intolerable for either Russia or Austria-Hungary. Moreover, the Entente of 1897, like the earlier Austro-Russian agreements, not only arose from, but actually reinforced this appreciation of the situation. The very desire to preserve the Entente disposed Austria-Hungary and Russia to move with circumspection, and even to modify their policies on concrete issues that might precipitate major crises. It was in mitigating Austro-Russian rivalry in this way that the Entente of 1897 made its most important contribution to the maintenance of peace.

It could, however, provide no guarantee of permanent security. For the political situation on which it rested was impermanent. The expulsion of the Turks from Europe was generally recognised to be but a matter of time; sooner or later the map of the Balkans would have to be radically revised. The problem was that, whereas Vienna and St Petersburg could agree on the desirability of maintaining the Ottoman Empire in Europe, they would find it extraordinarily difficult to agree on what might replace it. The Russian government could never be reconciled to any settlement that exposed the land route to the Straits to control by an Austria-Hungary exercising a predominating influence in the Balkan peninsula; nor would Russian public opinion ever accept the subjection of the Slavs of the western Balkans to Austro-Hungarian control. Yet, by the same token, the prospect of Russia establishing control of the peninsula was anathema to Austria-Hungary. It would immensely increase the strategic threat from Russia, and would establish a link between a potentially hostile Great Power and irredentist states whose ambitions could only be realised through the destruction of the Dual Monarchy. Hence Vienna's anxiety to restrict the growth of Serbia and to dominate her; and to seek additional reinsurance by ousting Russian influence from Bulgaria. The fact was that, as regards the future territorial configuration of the Balkans and the diplomatic alignments of the heirs of the Ottoman Empire, it would be virtually impossible to devise a solution that would satisfy both Russia and Austria-Hungary. Obviously, neither Power could be expected to renounce its interests in favour of the other, or even to withdraw in the hope that the other would do so and establish a power vacuum in the area. That would have demanded of each a degree of trust in the future intentions of the other unprecedented in nineteenth-century diplomacy. The agreement of 1897 might gloss over the ultimate incompatibility of Russian and Austro-Hungarian interests, and even hint hopefully at an amicable solution of the underlying conflict; but it could never conjure it away altogether.

Of this, as the history of the Entente of 1897 shows, both governments were well aware. Goluchowski never had any illusions about the limitations of the *rapprochement*. He had only embarked on it after two years of fruitless striving to resuscitate the Mediterranean Agreements as the basis of a policy of opposing Russia and all her works. True, both for Russia with her Far Eastern preoccupations and for Austria-Hungary with her internal crises and her wayward allies, the Entente had its uses. But friction over its practical operation remained a constant reminder of the underlying conflict of interests. Rivalry for influence at Sofia and Belgrade continued to cause ill will between Vienna and St Petersburg; no significant progress was made towards an agreement regarding the future disposition of the sultan's territories in Europe; nor was Goluchowski ever tempted – even by the glittering prospect of a general diplomatic alignment with Russia – to do anything that might help Russia to establish her ascendancy in the Balkans (as Aehrenthal seemed to him to be recommending): that would be to sacrifice those very interests which the Entente was designed to safeguard. (Even Aehrenthal's proposals of 1906 for restoring the Three Emperors' Alliance were based on the assumption that Austria-Hungary would not need to sacrifice any of her interests in the Balkans, and that Russia would remain incapable of action there 'for the next ten years'.) The successes of the Entente were either negative – even Austro-Russian co-operation in Macedonia after 1903 was only designed to preserve the status quo by rendering it palatable to the sultan's Christian subjects – or peripheral to the main issue – the neutrality treaty of 1904 was made with an eye to possible wars in the Far East or in Tyrol, and expressly abstained from pronouncing on possible alterations to the status quo in the Near East.

Even so, despite their limitations, these various agreements all served to maintain an illusion of co-operation and to conceal the reality of the underlying conflict of interests. They helped to produce a situation tolerable for both parties, and rendered valuable service as a practical basis for policy for the best part of a decade. And given that the two governments, for all their future ambitions and apprehensions, felt for the time being an urgent need to keep the peace and maintain the status quo, they were perhaps wise to base their policies on a useful illusion rather than on a reality that lay, after all, in a distant and uncertain future.

Yet by 1905 even the negative *entente* was beginning to fail. The element of mutual trust on which it rested was undermined as Russia, weakened by war and revolution, and fearful of Austria-Hungary's predominance within an *entente à deux*, sought to bring other Powers – notably Great Britain – into the Balkan arena; and as, in the constitutional era, nationalist opinion began to make itself felt in Russian policy. All this in turn caused the Austrians to doubt Russia's devotion to the status quo, and to seek to secure their own interests. The Sanjak railway crisis marked the first serious rift in the Austro-Russian Entente, and the end of the Mürzsteg system. Yet even after this Izvolsky and Aehrenthal not only continued to profess their loyalty to the conservative principles of 1897, but sought to extend the Entente to take account of certain alterations in the status quo. Their objectives were limited – security at the Straits, and a formal change in the legal status of Bosnia and the Herzegovina. But their pains were ill rewarded. Both statesmen had badly miscalculated the effect the annexation of Bosnia would have on the mighty current of Slav feeling, which in Russia surged as far as the steps of the throne itself. By October 1908 the Entente lay in ruins.

Suddenly, the underlying incompatibility of Austro-Hungarian and Russian interests had been exposed to the glaring light of day. From this confrontation with reality Austro-Russian relations were never to recover. Russia and Austria-Hungary had gazed upon the Gorgon's head. After this, there was to be no question of their continuing to delude themselves with policies designed to conceal what was now known and felt to be a painful reality. Henceforth, both Powers based their policies on an assumption of frank hostility: whatever the one proposed was viewed by the other as part of some devious or openly hostile design. The years 1908–14 were the years of Austro-Russian confrontation – years which at first promised to be all the more difficult for Austria-Hungary, in that the annexation of Bosnia had not only brought the conflict with Russia into the open and destroyed the Entente, but also threatened to estrange her remaining friends and allies.

7

Austro–Russian Confrontation, 1908–1914[1]

Aehrenthal and the Independence of Austro-Hungarian Policy, 1908–1912

The immediate consequence of the annexation of Bosnia was the disgrace and isolation of Austria-Hungary. On the one hand, the German emperor, who learned of the annexation from the newspapers during a shooting trip in East Prussia, was aghast at Aehrenthal's 'fearful stupidity. . . . Thus my Turkish policy, so carefully built up over twenty years, is thrown away';[2] while in Italy the anti-Austrian street demonstrations that went on into the winter showed that two years of work on Aehrenthal's part to improve Austro-Italian relations had had little impact on public opinion. On the other hand, the Triple Entente Powers united to put forward a proposal for a conference to look into the whole question of the annexation – its validity, and the kind of compensation (possibly even territorial and at Austria-Hungary's expense) that could be paid to Serbia and Montenegro. The Monarchy's position among the Great Powers was, to say the least, uncomfortable.

That it improved in the autumn was due, not to any inherent strengths of its own, but to factors on the international scene that were beyond the Monarchy's control, above all, the German reaction to the conference proposal. In Berlin, the Entente's display of

1. The following works are of particular relevance to this chapter: N. Stone, 'Moltke–Conrad: Relations between the Austro-Hungarian and German General Staffs, 1909–14', in *Historical Journal*, 9 (1966), pp. 201–28; J. Redlich, *Schicksalsjahre Oesterreichs, 1908–1919. Das politische Tagebuch Josef Redlichs*, ed. F. Fellner. Veröffentlichungen der Kommission für neuere Geschichte Oesterreichs, 39/4. (Vienna 1953–4). E.C. Helmreich, *The Diplomacy of the Balkan Wars* (Harvard 1938); R.J. Crampton, *The Hollow Détente* (London 1979); and the works by A. Wandruszka and P. Urbanitsch (eds), C.A. Macartney, A.J.P. Taylor, A. Sked and I. Diószegi cited in Chapter 1, note 1; by Barbara Jelavich and F.R. Bridge and Roger Bullen cited in Chapter 2, note 1; and by H. Hantsch, cited in Chapter 6, note 1.
2. Minute on Bülow to Jenisch, 7 October 1908, G.P. XXVI, No. 8992.

solidarity immediately roused traumatic memories of the humiliating Algeciras conference: a repeat performance must be prevented at all costs. It was in fact simply a sudden panic about their general international position that moved the Germans, the senior and controlling partners in the Dual Alliance, to commit themselves to Vienna come what may – a somewhat similar situation was to arise, with infinitely more serious consequences, six years later. At any rate, the Germans now made haste to forget their initial anger with Aehrenthal and to promise him their full support. This in turn stiffened Aehrenthal in his determination that any conference must only be allowed to ratify, not discuss, let alone authorise, the annexation; and that there could be no question of territorial compensation for Serbia and Montenegro – whose disappointed hopes of some day acquiring Bosnia and the Herzegovina by no means gave them a *locus standi* in the dispute.

In the subsequent negotiations over the conference proposal Aehrenthal's task was made easier by the crumbling of the Triple Entente front. The French soon made it clear that they did not wish to make a big issue of the annexation. They were anxious at this time to secure the good offices of Austria-Hungary in a dispute with Berlin about Morocco; and it was in fact in appreciation of what he regarded as France's 'very correct' attitude towards the annexation that Franz Joseph in November persuaded Wilhelm II to submit the so-called Casablanca affair to arbitration.[3] Even with the British, Aehrenthal had reached a compromise agreement in principle by early December: the annexation might be put down for discussion at the conference, but preliminary agreements between the Powers would ensure that any discussion would be a mere formality. Only Izvolsky seemed hopelessly stubborn, insisting, in a circular of 19 December, that the Powers must go to the conference with their hands completely free, and citing the precedent of the London conference of 1871. Aehrenthal countered by circulating extracts from the confidential Austro-Russian exchanges of the summer, some of which contained highly embarrassing allusions to Russia's earlier commitments, dating back to the 1880s, to accept the annexation. Faced with this, Izvolsky collapsed, and nothing more was heard of the conference proposal for some months. But Aehrenthal's victory had been bought at a price: Austro-Russian relations were now worse than ever. Indeed, Izvolsky proceeded to declare normal relations with Austria-Hungary suspended: henceforth, he would receive only formal written communications from

3. Wagner, 'Kaiser Franz Joseph', p. 250.

the Austro-Hungarian embassy.

If the Austro-Russian Entente was now clearly lost beyond recall, it seemed that much the same could be said of the 'traditional friendship' with Great Britain. It was not simply that the British seemed to be encouraging the Turks in their stubborn refusal to recognise the annexation without financial compensation – a refusal which was backed up by a spontaneous but extremely effective boycott of Austro-Hungarian wares, which brought an embarrassing flood of complaints to the Ballhausplatz from Austrian and Hungarian traders. After all, British sympathy for the new regime at Constantinople was well understood; and in any case, Aehrenthal's failure to reach agreement with the Turks was chiefly attributable to the refusal of the impecunious governments in Vienna and Budapest to pay any compensation at all – despite Aehrenthal's cajolery (all the Monarchy's embarrassments would disappear once agreement was reached with Constantinople) and threats (the alternative would be a very expensive war to bring Turkey to heel). That Great Britain had also become Russia's chief supporter was perhaps similarly understandable. Quite incomprehensible to Anglophiles in Vienna, however, was British support for Serbia's and Montenegro's claims for compensation. Indeed, in Austro-Hungarian eyes this rendered the British at least morally responsible for the clamorous hostility displayed towards the Monarchy by those two states in demonstrations, the activities of propaganda societies (such as the Narodna Odbrana, founded in direct response to the annexation) and even military preparations. The Austro-Hungarian press was not slow to voice Aehrenthal's view that Great Britain was the chief troublemaker; and that she was perhaps even seeking to unleash a general war in order to settle accounts with Germany. Anglo-Austrian relations did not much improve even when Aehrenthal managed to persuade the Austrian and Hungarian governments to pay compensation to Turkey in January 1909, and when in the final Austro-Turkish Protocol of 26 February the Turks agreed to recognise the annexation in return for a payment of 2,500,000 Turkish pounds (disguised for prestige purposes as a payment for Ottoman property in the annexed provinces). On the contrary Great Britain and Russia now tiresomely insisted that the Austro-Turkish Protocol could not settle the international crisis, as the annexation had violated, not only Turkey's rights under the Austro-Turkish Convention of April 1879, but the rights of all the signatories of the Treaty of Berlin.

In the matter of the other principal violation of the Treaty of Berlin – Bulgaria's declaration of independence – the Triple Entente

Powers actually managed to inflict a defeat on the Monarchy. In St Petersburg Stolypin, never enamoured of Izvolsky's policy of compensations, had convinced the emperor that the best defence of Slav interests against the supposed ambitions of Austria-Hungary would be found in a league of Balkan states, including Turkey. When this aim proved unrealistic – the Balkan states being too jealous of each other, and more concerned to partition Turkey than to ally with her – the Russians and their British friends determined instead to try to reconcile at least Turkey and her wayward Bulgarian vassal under the auspices of the Triple Entente. At this, Berlin took great alarm; and Aehrenthal, although always sceptical of talk about Balkan leagues, tried to soothe the Germans with some gestures designed to keep Bulgaria out of the clutches of the Entente. After all, she might some day prove a useful pawn to play against Serbia. At the turn of the year, he actually offered Bulgaria a military convention. But the Triple Entente Powers could outbid the Central Powers in the economic field: and in so far as the settlement of 2 February 1909, by which Turkey recognised Bulgarian independence in return for financial compensation, was based on a Russo-Bulgarian loan transaction, it was a triumph for the Triple Entente and a defeat for the Central Powers. On the other hand, in so far as it cleared away yet one more complication from the diplomatic scene, it freed Aehrenthal's hands to deal with the one remaining contentious issue, the grievances of Serbia and Montenegro.

Here, Aehrenthal's victory was a foregone conclusion. That it was delayed for some two months was solely the consequence of his desire to bring Serbia and her Russian and British protectors to heel by diplomatic means alone. In fact, his reluctance to go to war was about the only playable card in his opponents' hand. Otherwise, Izvolsky's position was hopeless. In the first place, he had himself, at Buchlau, abandoned Serbia's claim to compensation, and lived in daily terror lest Aehrenthal should now reveal the fact. Diplomacy offered no salvation: he could no longer safely resort to a conference, being unsure of the French, who were all too anxious 'to give Austria a lift' in the hope of smoothing the course of their Moroccan negotiations with Germany.[4] Most important of all, Russia was in no condition to fight, even if Austria-Hungary invaded Serbia – and Izvolsky himself admitted this to Berchtold on 17 February. In this situation, Great Britain and Russia never had a chance of dictating to Austria-Hungary the line she should

---

4. F.O. 371/748, Nicolson to Grey, tel. 23, 20 January 1909, minute.

take towards Serbia – especially now that Aehrenthal was not only spurred on by his humiliation in the Bulgarian question, and fully aware of Russia's impotence, but also confident of the support and encouragement of Germany.

In the course of a correspondence between the German and Austro-Hungarian chiefs of staff authorised and supervised by the monarchs and governments of the two allied Powers, Moltke had assured Conrad on 21 January 1909 that if Austria-Hungary attacked Serbia, and Russia mobilised, then Germany would come to the Monarchy's assistance. This was, on the face of it at least, a most important extension of the defensive Dual Alliance.[5] How much such a sweeping promise was worth in practical military terms was another question. In fact, its very generosity was consciously designed to cloak a serious military deficiency.[6] For Moltke's letter was only one item in a three-month correspondence in which Conrad was trying – after a decade of virtually complete lack of communication between the two allied general staffs – to tie the Germans down to a specific commitment to undertake a substantial offensive in the east. Moltke, by contrast, was concerned to evade any such specific military commitment, while trying, by means of sweeping political promises, to keep the Monarchy from losing hope altogether and retiring into a defensive posture behind the Carpathians. This latter danger was by no means imaginary. As the likelihood increased that the Monarchy might find itself involved in war on either its northern or its southern frontier, or both, Conrad had devised two alternative plans to meet all contingencies. Minimal defensive forces were assigned to the south (*Minimal-Gruppe-Balkan* of 12 divisions) and to Galicia (*A-Staffel* of 30 divisions); and either of these could be brought up to offensive strength by the addition of a third bloc, *B-Staffel* of some 12 divisions. In the event of war with Russia, *A-Staffel* would be brought up to strength for an offensive in Galicia, and *Minimal-Gruppe-Balkan* would stand on the defensive. This was *Fall-R* (Russia). A war with Serbia would see the strengthening of *Minimal-Gruppe-Balkan*, while *A-Staffel* would stay on the defensive against Russia. This was *Fall-B* (Balkan); and this was naturally anathema to Moltke, who wanted a strong Austrian thrust into Poland to distract the Russians while Germany dealt with France.

In the end, a compromise was reached. Conrad promised to undertake an offensive even with the unstrengthened *A-Staffel* – but

5. Stephan Verosta, *Theorie und Realität der Bündnissen*, pp. 343–50.
6. Stone, 'Moltke–Conrad', pp. 201–28.

only on condition that the Germans would themselves launch a simultaneous offensive from East Prussia to take some of the weight off the Austrians. Moltke, for his part, in a letter of 19 March 1909 which remained decisive for Austro-Hungarian military planning until 1914, promised to launch an immediate offensive from East Prussia, albeit with fewer troops than the Austrians would have wished, and subject to an important escape clause: 'should the implementation of the plans of one of the allies be rendered impossible by the enemy' the other was to be informed immediately. In view of this clause – which in 1914 was to give rise to serious recriminations – Conrad had perhaps not obtained all that much. But he seemed satisfied enough, and throughout March remained an ardent advocate of a military solution to the Serbian crisis.

Aehrenthal, however, supported by the emperor,[7] was set on a peaceful solution. After all, the state of the Monarchy's military forces was far from brilliant, with the memory of the army crisis in Hungary still fresh, and with the Austrian and Hungarian parliaments still resolutely refusing to increase the recruiting contingents beyond the levels fixed in 1889. All the Monarchy had been able to do to meet the rumours of war emanating from Serbia was to transport a few extra battalions to Bosnia and to call up some reservists there. Aehrenthal decided, therefore, to summon Serbia to abandon her pretensions, accept the annexation, and live at peace with Austria-Hungary. If she complied, he was prepared to treat her generously in terms of commercial concessions: Serbia's drive towards the sea was a natural phenomenon, and it was for Austria-Hungary to come to terms with and canalise this energy. He proposed, therefore, to grant Serbia the use of a free port on the Dalmatian coast, a railway convention to cover the transport of all her products through Bosnia to the Adriatic, and a commercial treaty to last until 1917. After all, as he impressed on the Austrian and Hungarian prime ministers on 3 March,[8] it was a question of drawing Serbia into the Monarchy's orbit by a wise and far-sighted economic policy. Indeed, even if he had to resort to force – and this would only be in the nature of a punitive expedition, for there could be no question of incorporating Serbia into a Monarchy already overburdened with Slavs – it would be wise to treat the defeated kingdom with generosity. On the other hand, it was clear that the crisis must be settled soon: the tension and the prolonged

7. Wagner, 'Kaiser Franz Joseph', p. 252.
8. P.A. XII/354, Aehrenthal to Bienerth and Wekerle, 21464/9, 3 March 1909.

military preparations were exerting a strain on the economic life of the Monarchy that could not be allowed to go on indefinitely. And whatever happened, there could be no question of admitting Russia's 'mad claim' to act as protectress of Serbia; or of admitting that any 'Serbian question' concerning the Powers had arisen from the annexation.[9] Indeed, there would not be any negotiations, even with Serbia, until she abandoned her claim to territorial compensation.

Clearly, Aehrenthal was not prepared to allow much scope for British and Russian diplomatic intervention, and in the next few weeks Izvolsky and his British supporters found themselves pushed remorselessly to the wall. On 28 February Izvolsky told the Serbs to give up all hope of territorial compensation; and on 8 March, with a good deal of grumbling about the injustice of negotiations between 'giant and mouse', Great Britain and Russia at last admitted that even the commercial concessions that Austria-Hungary might make to Serbia were not a matter for the Concert to determine, but one for Vienna and Belgrade alone.[10] The situation became critical when the Serbs, in a note of 15 March that was considered insolent and unacceptable even in St Petersburg and London, flatly rejected Aehrenthal's offer of commercial negotiations. Grey now came forward to suggest that the Powers persuade Serbia to make submission in a note approved in advance by Aehrenthal; and the assiduous British ambassador at Vienna, Sir Fairfax Cartwright – acting, unfortunately, beyond his intructions – eventually persuaded Aehrenthal to agree to content himself with a Serbian promise to accept whatever the Powers might eventually decide about the annexation, the Powers for their part promising in advance to recognise the annexation at a conference.[11] The scheme suited Aehrenthal very well: Cartwright had in fact given him the chance to exploit the awkward predicament of Great Britain and Russia in the Serbian affair to extract from them their formal recognition of the annexation. At the last minute, however, Cartwright's superiors in London refused to concur in the arrangement, and it seemed as though the military chastisement of Serbia, with all its implications for Russian and British prestige, was about to begin.

The crisis was resolved by the diplomatic collapse of Russia. As the invasion of Serbia inexorably approached (and as Aehrenthal threatened to publish more material relating to Buchlau) Izvolsky

9. B.D., V, No. 657.
10. B.D., V, No. 627; OUA, II, No. 1083.
11. Bridge, *Great Britain and Austria-Hungary*, pp. 131ff.

lost his nerve and appealed desperately to Berlin to build a golden bridge out of the impasse. Now the energetic Kiderlen, temporarily in charge at the Wilhelmstraße, was only too pleased to seize the initiative, feeling that Vienna had called the tune in the Dual Alliance for long enough. Aehrenthal suspected as much; but he could hardly refuse the proffered German help, which came – in typical Kiderlen style – in the form of a rather peremptory request to St Petersburg to recognise the annexation without further ado; otherwise, Germany would do nothing to restrain Austria-Hungary from attacking Serbia. Izvolsky made haste to comply – all the more so as he could now assume in London and Paris the role of victim of a German 'ultimatum'. At this, the British, reluctant to appear more Russian than the Russians, also fell into line, Grey giving a verbal promise to recognise the annexation – albeit on condition that Aehrenthal gave the Powers time to arrange a peaceful settlement of the Serbian crisis. As this was what Aehrenthal wanted anyway, and as Serbia was to make submission on terms dictated by Aehrenthal, the condition imposed by Grey was, as Aehrenthal himself observed, hardly an onerous one.[12] On the advice of the Powers, Serbia at last delivered at Vienna, in a note of 31 March, the formal promise required by Aehrenthal 'to live in future on terms of friendly and neighbourly relations' with the Monarchy. Aehrenthal had got all he wanted; and that without the expense of a punitive expedition. The remaining issues were soon cleared up. Montenegro recognised the annexation in a note drafted in Rome and somewhat less humiliating than Serbia's; and the discomfiture of Izvolsky at finding himself excluded from this Italo-Austro-Montenegrin arrangement was complete. By mid-April, all the Great Powers, taking note of an amendment to Article XXV of the Treaty of Berlin, had formally recognised the annexation of Bosnia.

That it had proved possible both to carry through the annexation and to keep the peace was initially a source of immense satisfaction to Aehrenthal, who, in a council of ministers six months later, spoke of a 'text-book example [*Schulbeispiel*] of how success is only certain if the *strength* [*Kraft*] is there to get one's own way. . . . It has now become easier for us to uphold the peace in the future, . . . We are no *quantité négligeable*. We have reconquered again the place that belongs to us among the Powers.'[13] Before long it became clear, however, even to Aehrenthal, that the annexation

---

12. P.A. XII/357, Aehrenthal to Wekerle, 31 March 1909.
13. Erb MS.

had by no means resolved – if it had not, indeed exacerbated – the Monarchy's problems, both at home and 'among the Powers'.

On the domestic front, for example, Aehrenthal was soon forced to abandon his hopes of making the annexation the starting point for a remodelling of the Dual Monarchy on a more viable basis. The Magyars remained adamant in their opposition to anything smacking of Trialism; and neither Vienna nor Budapest would consider renouncing its share in the government of the newly annexed provinces. So they continued under the ultimate control of the Common Finance Ministry – 'floating like Mahomet's coffin in the air', as the younger Kossuth put it[14] – even after a constitution had been granted in 1910. Altogether, the annexation had probably sharpened the differences between the two halves of the Monarchy.

Nor had it done much to mitigate the strife within them. The relative calm that had followed the settlement of the great Hungarian crisis was ending. Even in February 1909, when the Serbian crisis had created something of a national emergency, the Reichsrat in Vienna had been totally preoccupied with the Czech–German language dispute, and one session, 'made hideous by a concert of foghorns and other instruments', ended in a mêlée reminiscent of the boisterous nineties, and had to be closed by imperial decree.[15] By 1911 nationalism had begun to infect even the great mass parties, and Czech and German Social Democrats determined to go their separate ways. Finally, the crisis left an embarrassing legacy of political trials, starting with the indictment at Agram – apparently as part of the government's attempts to orchestrate anti-Serbian opinion during the Bosnian crisis – of some Croatian deputies on a charge of high treason. The verdict of guilty had to be reversed when the charges were found to have been based on forgeries. Worse, the historian, Friedjung, who at the height of the Serbian crisis had written an article accusing some South Slav politicians of treasonable links with Belgrade, was sued for libel; and the documents on which the article had been based, which had been supplied by the Ballhausplatz itself, also proved to be forgeries. Aehrenthal's reputation recovered somewhat when a further trial in 1910 revealed that the forgeries had been supplied to an unwitting foreign ministry by one Vasić (acting indeed, it now appears,[16] as the agent of a well-planned Serbian disinformation campaign). But the whole affair – although contemporary expressions of indignation came ill from the France of Dreyfus, the Russia of Beyliss, the

14. F.O. 371/829, Howard to Grey, No. 83, 18 November 1910.
15. F.O. 371/599, Cartwright to Grey, No. 20, 6 February 1909.
16. Lavender Cassels, *Archduke and Assassin* (London 1984), pp. 117–19.

Germany of Harden and Eulenburg, and even, perhaps, the England of Parnell – did nothing for the Monarchy's reputation as a civilised great Power.

As for the long-term external results of Aehrenthal's victory, Serbia's formal submission, and her promise to live on good-neighbourly terms with Austria-Hungary, soon proved an empty gesture. Anti-Austrian propaganda continued to flood into the South Slav territories of the Monarchy from the neighbouring kingdom; the Narodna Odbrana pursued its activities unabated; and more extreme organisations continued their campaign of terrorism on Austro-Hungarian soil. From here, the road led straight to Sarajevo. Not that the Austro-Hungarian government could have done much to control the activities of terrorist organisations beyond the frontier. Indeed, such conciliatory gestures as Vienna made towards the South Slav population – and they were few enough – only served to increase the determination of nationalist hotheads in Serbia to wrest the South Slav provinces from the Monarchy, by violent means if necessary, before they could become reconciled to Habsburg rule. But apart from this, even the ordinary peasant population of Serbia was now hopelessly embittered against the Monarchy – all the more so as the 'Pig War' dragged on into its fourth year. Not that there was any desire – at least in Budapest – to end it. It was in vain that Aehrenthal pleaded for a far-sighted policy of economic conciliation: the old Magyar fears of Serbian agrarian competition were too strong. By the time an Austro-Serbian commercial treaty could be concluded in July 1910 the Austrians had finally lost their Serbian armaments contracts to Schneider-Creusot, and most of their remaining Serbian trade to their German allies. In short, Serbia had completely freed herself from her old commercial dependence on the Monarchy.

The Monarchy could ill afford such setbacks. One direct consequence of the annexation, the Turkish boycott, had already had disastrous effects, which were to prove permanent. Whereas to a contemporary British observer of Austria-Hungary's Turkish trade, 'it seemed in the spring of 1908 as if it only remained for Austria-Hungary to enter into her kindom',[17] the Monarchy now found itself ousted from many of its best markets – to the advantage, as usual, of the German ally. In the Balkan states, too, German competition was growing daily more severe, particularly in Bulgaria, where, although Austria-Hungary managed to retain her lead down to 1914, Germany now replaced Great Britain as her

17. G. Drage, *Austria-Hungary* (London 1909), p. 210.

chief competitor. True, the world depression of 1910 affected Austria-Hungary, a state producing largely for the internal market, less severely than the more advanced industrial states of the West; but the Monarchy's economic prospects in these years were by no means bright. The year 1907 saw the last budget surplus in the history of the Monarchy; and 1909, with the cost of military preparations incurred in the crisis added to such burdens as the re-nationalisation of the railways, saw a deficit of 42 million Kronen. By 1910 the government was actually planning for a deficit, and resorted to loans; but the two that were raised were emitted at 90, the lowest rate since 1892. In sum, the economic situation was not such as to encourage costly adventures.

Not that the diplomatic situation was such as to tempt Aehrenthal in that direction. Indeed, the Monarchy emerged from the Bosnian crisis with its diplomatic options more severely restricted than at any time since the 1870s: the Russian and British alignments that had occasionally proved so useful in the past thirty years were simply no longer available. The Bosnian crisis had caused a hardening of diplomatic fronts; and, like the Central Powers, the Entente Powers had drawn the conclusion that security lay only in absolute diplomatic solidarity backed up by massive armaments. The naval arms race began to dominate Anglo-German relations; and as regards Austria-Hungary, the immediate concern of the Entente Powers was now to counter her supposed further ambitions by means of a defensive bloc of Balkan states, and particularly to encourage Serbia to resist siren-songs from Vienna. Admittedly, the Triple Entente did not remain united on this programme for long; and even Anglo-German rivalry abated after 1912. But one factor henceforth remained a constant in European diplomacy until the outbreak of war in 1914: Austro-Russian hostility. The myth that the annexation of Bosnia was merely a harbinger of the legendary march on Salonika – or at least that, given a chance, the Monarchy would lose no opportunity to extend its influence, or even its frontiers – now acquired in St Petersburg the force of an immutable political law. And although Russia's plan to forestall the danger by means of a league of Balkan states was essentially defensive, it became in turn, in so far as its realisation would inevitably imply the absorption of the whole area into a Russian sphere of influence, the chief nightmare of Vienna.

Yet simply to rely on the Dual Alliance to meet this danger did not seem to Aehrenthal either practicable or desirable. True, the Alliance had recently proved its value, perhaps for the first time, as a diplomatic instrument. For Aehrenthal, however, with his almost obsessive concern for the independence of the Monarchy, this was perhaps a mixed blessing. The appointment of the forceful Kiderlen as German foreign minister in June 1910 raised the prospect that the Dual Alliance would be directed from Berlin, and not from Vienna. The awkward fact was that, given the deterioration of the Monarchy's relations with Russia and Great Britain, any policy of action would now be bound to increase its dependence on Berlin. Only a policy of self-sufficient inaction, studiously avoiding anything that might endanger the status quo or provoke hostile counter-combinations, could offer the Monarchy a fair measure of independence among the Great Powers.

The first major task confronting Aehrenthal after the Bosnian crisis was to dispel the general suspicion with which Austria-Hungary was regarded in almost every European capital except Berlin: to convince the Powers that the annexation of Bosnia had not been the first step in the march to Salonika, but the final rounding off of the Monarchy's southern frontiers; and that Vienna was now genuinely desirous of maintaining the status quo. With Turkey, the Power most directly affected, he had a fair measure of success. The Young Turks, whose relations with Great Britain and Russia were deteriorating as a result of Turkish interference in Persia and Egypt and Anglo-Russian criticism of the brutal Otto-manisation policies emanating from Constantinople, were in any case anxious to lean on Vienna. Indeed, on several occasions in 1909 and 1910 they even sought an alliance with Austria-Hungary. Aehrenthal would not consider an alliance with a Power so unstable as Turkey; but he nevertheless regarded the Young Turkish re-gime, despite all its faults and its revolutionary origins, as a useful 'lid on the pot that prevents the stuff inside from boiling over'.[18] For his own part, the studied caution he displayed towards the three Turkish 'questions' that arose in 1909–10 – in Crete, Albania and Macedonia – went a good way towards convincing both the Turks and most of the other Powers of his sincere devotion to the status quo.

As regards Crete, for example, where the remaining four pro-tecting Powers found themselves in a most unenviable position, between the insistence of Constantinople on the maintenance of Ottoman sovereign rights and the demands of the Greek Cretans for union with the Hellenic Kingdom, Aehrenthal withdrew into a posture of complete abstention.[19] After all, the Monarchy had

18. Grey MSS, II, Cartwright to Grey, 28 September 1910.
19. Bridge, *Great Britain and Austria-Hungary*, pp. 142ff.

nothing to lose if the Cretan question estranged Turkey from the protecting Powers. Indeed, he now abandoned even Goluchowski's formal claim to a voice in any discussions of fundamental issues, such as the ultimate destiny of the island; and refused to be drawn by Grey's argument that the recurrent Greco-Turkish quarrels were partly the consequence of the revival of Greek propaganda activity in Macedonia – and hence a matter for all six Powers to tackle. (A revival of international intervention in Macedonia he was determined to prevent at all costs.) Nor would he move in the very serious crisis of the summer of 1910, when an attempt by the Greek Cretans to impose an oath of loyalty to the King of the Hellenes on Muslim deputies in the Cretan assembly was used by Turkey as a pretext to launch a boycott aiming ultimately at the annihilation of Greek trading interests throughout the Ottoman Empire. He merely tendered the advice – unpalatable to the protecting Powers, but very much appreciated in Constantinople – to re-occupy the island. After this, the protecting Powers ceased to bother him about Crete. They were wistfully envious of his 'comfortable inertia';[20] but at least he did not seem to be actively fishing in troubled waters.

Comfortable inertia was not an attitude that Aehrenthal could assume towards developments in Albania at this time. There the centralising and Ottomanising policies of the Young Turk regime had by the spring of 1910 produced a major rebellion among the Catholic tribesmen in the North; and Constantinople's clumsy efforts to suppress it in a welter of blood confronted the Austrians with a major dilemma. On the one hand, observance of the principle of non-intervention had borne fruit – Austro-Turkish relations were better than they had been for years. On the other, the Catholic press of Vienna, notably the *Reichspost* (behind which stood Franz Ferdinand and a powerful circle of clericals and aristocrats) was loud in its denunciation of Turkish 'atrocities' and in its demands that Aehrenthal take action in the name of the Monarchy's three-hundred-year-old *Kultusprotektorat*. Other important considerations pointed in the same direction: if Austria-Hungary did nothing, the Albanians might turn in their despair to Italy; and in any case, indiscriminate massacres of Albanians could only leave the Serbian inhabitants of the area to inherit the land. In June, therefore, Aehrenthal gave some stern advice to Constantinople: Turkey would do well to preserve the Albanian race, which might prove an invaluable source of assistance in any future conflict with Slavs and

20. F.O. 371/654, Russell to Grey, No. 200, 16 December 1909.

Greeks. For Austria-Hungary had finally withdrawn from the Sanjak, and would be neither willing nor able to come to Turkey's assistance. Whether as a result of this advice or not, the Turks suddenly gave way and pacified the rebels with a commission of enquiry.

In one sense, the Austrians were simply very lucky, in that the summer of 1910 saw the Cretan and Albanian crises simply fade away, while in the rest of the Balkans an unusual calm prevailed.[21] The threat of a Russian-organised Balkan league was showing no signs of materialising. Serbia and Bulgaria seemed quite unable to agree on an equitable partition of Macedonia; the old dynastic quarrel between Serbia and Montenegro revived after plotters from Belgrade tried to assassinate Nikita in the spring of 1910; and although Sazonov, who in the autumn replaced the rancorous Izvolsky at St Petersburg, was as keen as his predecessor to organise a league to frustrate 'the ambitious designs of Austria-Hungary' – and even warned the Greeks that unless they looked to their defences they would see the Austrians at Salonika – he was equally unsuccessful. Negotiations between Greece and Bulgaria soon foundered on the Macedonian rock. Above all, the Austrians could take cheer from the fact that Russia was no longer finding the Western Powers so ready to support her efforts as they had been during and immediately after the Bosnian crisis. In another sense, however, it must be admitted that Aehrenthal had himself made a significant contribution to this favourable turn of events. In the summer of 1909, for example, he had sternly reminded the Serbs, when they sounded him about the future of the Sanjak, that this was Turkish property, and could not form the subject of any discussion. Similarly, he refused to respond to requests from Romania and Bulgaria for promises of support in the event of a Balkan conflagration, emphasising that the Monarchy's policy was one of strict non-intervention. Not surprisingly, such an ostentatious devotion to the status quo did not do much for the Monarchy's influence in the Balkan capitals – as was to become painfully clear in 1912; but it made its contribution to the stabilisation of the situation, and was much appreciated elsewhere – notably, in London. In this respect at least, Aehrenthal's new quietist policy was paying good dividends.

It is true that the Monarchy's relations with Great Britain remained clouded for some months after the Bosnian crisis. In the summer of 1909 injured pride on both sides prevented a visit by

21. Bridge, *Great Britain and Austria-Hungary*, Chapter VII.

Edward VII to Franz Joseph; and in August the king refused to congratulate Aehrenthal when Franz Joseph recognised his services with the title of Count. More serious, the British took umbrage at the Austrian decision – made in fact in response to the steady growth of the Italian navy – to build four dreadnoughts to restore the balance in the Adriatic. In London, this was seen as a concealed addition to the German fleet: Vienna's payment to Berlin for services rendered in the Bosnian crisis. But as it turned out, progress on the dreadnoughts was slow. The Monarchy was desperately short of money, and the Delegations did not meet to vote any until the autumn of 1910. Franz Ferdinand, an ardent supporter of naval expansion, managed to raise a certain amount; but in the meantime, all that could be done was to arrange for two dreadnoughts to be built as a speculative venture by the Stabilmento Tecnico of Trieste, on the chance that the government would eventually be able to buy them. This was by no means certain. Aehrenthal and Admiral Montecuccoli were confronted in the council of ministers by Austrian and Hungarian prime ministers who talked of the Monarchy's being actually bankrupt. At any rate, the question gradually ceased to trouble Anglo–Austrian relations, as the British became convinced, thanks partly to Cartwright's able dispatches, that Aehrenthal was in fact sincerely anxious both to lower the tension and to resist dictation from Berlin. They began to weary of Izvolsky's obsessive talk of Austrian plots, and to look askance at his projected Balkan leagues: these, by provoking Aehrenthal unnecessarily, seemed more likely to cause than to prevent a crisis in the Balkans. By the spring of 1910 London and Vienna were agreed that normal relations had been restored. Another royal visit, agreed in principle, was only prevented by the death of Edward VII in May; and it was significant that George V protested to his ministers at some length, if ultimately in vain, that the first state visit of his reign ought to be paid to Franz Joseph, as doyen of the European monarchs.[22]

The Italians, similarly, had for some months after the Bosnian crisis continued extremely anxious about the possibility of further surprises from Vienna. They encouraged Russia in her efforts to found a Balkan league, and in October 1909 gave a very cordial welcome at Racconigi to Izvolsky and the tsar, who had travelled from Odessa by an extraordinarily circuitous route through North Germany, demonstratively avoiding setting foot on Austro-Hungarian territory. Izvolsky and Tittoni agreed to co-operate to

22. Ibid., pp. 195–6.

maintain the status quo, and to make no Balkan agreements with a third party (sc. Austria-Hungary) without informing each other: there were to be no more Buchlaus. Indeed, Tittoni felt that Austria-Hungary could not be too carefully watched, and would have liked to secure similar pledges from all the other Powers. But the British felt that this would be too insulting to the Monarchy, and he had to desist. In fact, the Racconigi agreement gave no offence to Vienna. After all, it only endorsed principles which Aehrenthal himself professed; and he was in any case anxious to do something to improve Austro-Italian relations. In December 1909 a similar Austro-Italian agreement endorsed the status quo, and further confirmed the Monarchy's retreat from the Sanjak by bringing an eventual reoccupation of the territory within the purview of Article VII of the Triple Alliance. Much of the tension now went out of Austro-Italian relations; and within a year Aehrenthal was again speaking of them in the Delegations in strikingly glowing terms.

Yet welcome though *détentes* with Great Britain and Italy might be in terms of the Monarchy's freedom of manoeuvre, they could not really offset the disagreeable fact that its more important relationships with Russia and Germany were not improving at all. Of course, the intense personal animosity prevailing between Izvolsky and Aehrenthal (who now referred to each other in such terms as 'ce sale juif' and 'ce crapaud') was hardly conducive to a restoration of confidence between the two governments. And the two men added fuel to the flames in the autumn by reviving the whole Buchlau controversy in an acrimonious exchange of inspired articles in the *Fortnightly Review*. True, by the end of 1909 both parties were beginning to admit the desirability of restoring something like normal relations: Aehrenthal was temporarily worried about Turkey, where a new grand vizier, Hakki Pasha, was an unknown quantity; and the Russians were anxious about the activities of the United States and Japan in the Far East. But when negotiations started, on the basis of the conservative principles of 1897, the two governments were soon at cross purposes. Whereas Izvolsky tried to bind Aehrenthal over to keep the peace, by an elaborate document which could then be presented to the other Powers for safe keeping, Aehrenthal insisted that it was simply a matter of restoring normal relations, and that this was the concern of no other Power, not even of Germany. By March, normal relations were declared to have been restored; but Izvolsky's proceeding to circulate copies of the recent Austro-Russian exchanges to the other Powers without Aehrenthal's permission showed that what passed for normality in Austro-Russian relations still left much to be desired.

The Germans, meanwhile, had taken deep umbrage at Aehrenthal's determination to regulate Austro-Russian relations without Germany's brokerage – and, indeed, at his independent attitude generally. It was at this time that the German embassy at Vienna fired the first shots in what was to become a sustained campaign against Aehrenthal in the Viennese press, to which Franz Ferdinand's *Reichspost* lent its ready support. (The archduke's feelings towards Aehrenthal, who was accused of truckling to the Magyars at home and Italy abroad, while allowing the Monarchy's relations with its imperial neighbours to languish, now bordered on hatred.) As for the archduke's friend Wilhelm II, his patronising boast about 'shining armour' during his visit to Vienna in September 1910 was as embarrassing to Aehrenthal as his 'brilliant second' telegram had been to Goluchowski – and perhaps intentionally so. Certainly, the prospect, which had seemed to open up during the Bosnian crisis, that the Dual Alliance might become the basis of Austro-German co-operation in the diplomatic field, had once again proved a nine days' wonder. When Wilhelm II received the tsar and Sazonov at Potsdam in November, and the German Chancellor, Bethmann Hollweg, assured the Russians that Germany would not support any aggressive designs of Austria-Hungary in the Balkans, Franz Joseph was deeply hurt. Aehrenthal was less upset: he had no aggressive designs anyway; and besides, any confirmation of the fact that the Monarchy would have to stand on its own feet was quite welcome to him. After all, if Austria-Hungary received little help from her allies, she would be under equally little obligation to trim her sails to suit them, and could defend her own interests as she saw fit. In the first crises of 1911, over Albania and Morocco, Aehrenthal was indeed able to pursue a policy of a free hand. Its effectiveness was to be limited, however, by the absence of any co-operation between the Monarchy and either of its powerful imperial neighbours.

Certainly, the two German Powers were poles apart over the Albanian crisis that broke out in the spring of 1911, and for which Aehrenthal put the blame squarely on the Young Turks. They had persisted, despite his advice, in their brutal Ottomanisation policies in Albania; and they were doing nothing to facilitate the repatriation of a large body of Albanian refugees who had been imposing a heavy burden on the impecunious Montenegrin government ever since the revolt of 1910. By March, some 5,000 Albanian tribesmen were again in revolt; and the refugee issue was threatening to develop into a Turco-Montenegrin war. For two months, Vienna did nothing: Aehrenthal, his health sapped by advancing leukaemia, had retreated in March to seek recuperation at Abbazia, leaving the Ballhausplatz in the care of Pallavicini, a single-minded Turcophile. But for Aehrenthal, the religious and political considerations that had compelled him to speak up for the Albanians in 1910 had lost none of their force. Moreover, he was anxious to protect Montenegro, both as a potential counter to its arch-rival Serbia, and as a buffer-state between the Monarchy and the deepening chaos of Turkey-in-Europe.

His attempts to control the crisis single-handed were largely ineffective, however. On his return to Vienna in May he lost no time in speaking sternly to the Turkish ambassador; and on 8 June the semi-official *Fremdenblatt* carried a summons to the Young Turks to put their house in order. Constantinople, however, merely expressed its pained surprise and continued with its repressive policies – not surprisingly, when the Germans, to Aehrenthal's unconcealed 'great annoyance',[23] were proclaiming their wholehearted support for Turkey. The Concert proved equally unsatisfactory: Aehrenthal found Grey's proposal that Austria-Hungary, Italy and Russia pacify the rebels by 'guaranteeing' the implementation of Ottoman promises of reform all too reminiscent of the international intervention in Macedonia of unhappy memory; and the desultory discussions between the three Powers about the possibility of mediating between Turkey and Montenegro in no sense implied any real co-operation – the Russians being solely concerned to prevent any unilateral moves by Austria-Hungary. In the event, the crisis ended when the Turks suddenly accepted all the rebel demands (1 August). This was fortunate for Aehrenthal. His attempts to reconcile Turks and Albanians made sense in terms of any rational assessment of the Monarchy's interests. But his failure – given the irrational and intractable nature of national conflicts in the Balkans – to do more than arouse Turkish suspicions without satisfying the Albanians, and his failure – given the effective diplomatic isolation of Austria-Hungary – to control even a relatively minor crisis on the southern borders of the Monarchy, were ominous pointers to the future.

The Moroccan crisis of 1911 provided yet another illustration of the irrelevance of the Dual Alliance to the day-to-day diplomacy of these months. In the early stages it was perhaps fortunate for the French that the Ballhausplatz was in the care of Pallavicini, who,

---

23. F.O. 120/883, Cartwright to Grey, tel. 49, 28 May 1911.

being simply concerned to tide things over without complications until Aehrenthal returned, raised no objections to the French occupation of Fez in April, and allowed Paris considerable latitude in interpreting the Act of Algeciras. It was also of some significance that the Hungarian government was seeking to raise a loan in Paris at this time. At any rate, on 15 May the *Sonn- und Montagszeitung* carried an article – allegedly inspired by Aehrenthal from Abbazia – warning Germany not to make trouble in Morocco. The German ambassador made a fearful scene; but he could not persuade the Austrians to give Germany anything like positive support. Indeed, Aehrenthal on his return stoutly defended the Hungarian prime minister's announcement to parliament that the Moroccan question lay outside the scope of the Triple Alliance. For why should he support Germany? – after all, she had given him no advance warning of the *Panther's* expedition to Agadir; and he felt that her troubles were really of her own making – it was Germany's flirting with Russia at Potsdam that had provoked France to assert herself in Morocco. He was frankly at a loss to understand Germany's Moroccan policy, which seemed to him 'just Krupp and Mannesmann'.[24] As for the Monarchy: 'What more can I do? We can pursue no *Weltpolitik*.'[25] Austria-Hungary would loyally stand guard for Germany in the Near East; but she could not follow her to Agadir.

The charge made in Pan-German circles that in the Second Moroccan Crisis Aehrenthal simply 'remained as dumb as a fish'[26] is nevertheless perhaps unfair. As the crisis dragged on into August he tried to put in a word for the Germans in Paris; and in November he urged the British to help Spain in her negotiations with France for the sake of monarchical interests. (This was the last appearance of Kálnoky's doctrine – somewhat threadbare since the fiasco of the Spanish–American War and the fall of the Portuguese monarchy in 1910 – of supporting the Iberian monarchies.) In the hope of furthering the Hungarian loan he readily accepted the final Franco-German settlement in November. Yet if Austria-Hungary's membership of the Dual Alliance had hardly been the determining factor in Aehrenthal's policy in the affair, it nevertheless had an effect – in a negative sense – on its success. In the wake of the crisis a wave of chauvinism was welling up in France that was to last until 1914; and Poincaré, elected prime minister in January 1912, frowned on all special relationships that cut across existing alliance

24. Redlich, *Schicksalsjahre Oesterreichs*, 20 July 1911.
25. Ibid., 7 August 1911.
26. H. Kanner, *Kaiserliche Katastrophenpolitik* (Vienna 1922), p. 75.

systems as confusing and dangerous to peace.[27] It was becoming increasingly unlikely that any member of the Triple Alliance, whatever its behaviour, would succeed in securing loans from France now. In this atmosphere Aehrenthal's efforts indeed proved fruitless, and the Hungarian loan negotiations came to grief.

The resurgence of nationalism in France during the Second Moroccan Crisis was only one symptom of a general worsening of the international situation after 1911. Indeed, in a sense, the Moroccan crisis itself was only the first link in a chain of crises which was to sweep through Turkish North Africa into European Turkey and the Balkan states to engulf, after an uneasy nine months' truce, the Dual Monarchy and the other Great Powers. Diplomacy seemed to be helpless to check the spreading fashion for violent solutions to international problems – problems which in themselves were more than usually serious, complicated and interconnected. By January 1912 the British permanent under-secretary, Sir Arthur Nicolson had 'never seen the world in such a disturbed condition'.[28] In these circumstances Aehrenthal clung doggedly to the policy he had pursued since 1909, of containing as far as possible any threats to the Near Eastern status quo. His task was to prove no easy one, given that he had only his recently improved, but still rather distant, relations with London and Rome to set against a continuing lack of support from Berlin and St Petersburg.

Although Austria-Hungary, like all the other Powers, had recognised Italy's ultimate claims to Libya, Aehrenthal was certainly put out by her decision – a response to the French success in Morocco – to enter into her Turkish inheritance at this moment and by violent means: a war might bring about the total collapse of the Ottoman Empire. He was equally irritated by Italy's proclamation on 5 November of the formal annexation of Libya, which put an end to his hopes of mediating – perhaps in conjunction with Germany – a compromise settlement based on Ottoman suzerainty. He now fell back on the idea of a general mediation, in which all the Powers might share the odium or humiliation; and, finding Grey in agreement, was pleased to tell himself that he had 'restored the Concert of Europe' as a makeshift (*notdürftig*).[29] But his prime concern was not with the war in Africa (which might, in fact, serve as a useful distraction for Italy) or the health of the Concert, but with preventing the war from either spreading to the Near East, or damaging

27. J.F.V. Keiger, *France and the Origins of the First World War* (London 1983) pp. 85–6.
28. F.O. 800/185, Lowther MSS, Nicolson to Lowther, 15 January 1912.
29. Redlich, *Schicksalsjahre Oesterreichs*, 19 November 1911.

Austro-Italian relations. To the first end, he warned Italy formally against undertaking any operations in the Adriatic: even military or naval operations, he now told Rome, would entitle the Monarchy to claim compensation under the terms of Article VII of the Triple Alliance (a new interpretation which was to cause the Monarchy some embarrassment when it came to undertake military operations of its own in the Balkans in 1914).

Of equal importance to Aehrenthal, however, was the maintenance of those good relations with Italy by which he had always set such store. November saw his final triumph over Conrad von Hoetzendorf, who since the start of the Italo-Ottoman War had been declaiming against his policy and demanding a preventive strike against Italy to eliminate her as a potential opponent once and for all. Aehrenthal had the support of the emperor, who took Conrad to task in a stormy interview on 15 November: 'These incessant attacks on Aehrenthal, these pinpricks, I forbid them. . . . The ever-recurring reproaches regarding Italy and the Balkans are directed at me. Policy – it is I who make it! . . . My policy is a policy of peace. . . . It is possible, even probable, that such a war may come about; but it will not be waged until Italy attacks us.'[30] Conrad prepared himself to argue back in another interview on 30 November; but Franz Joseph forestalled him with the news of his dismissal from the post of chief of staff. It was in line with this that Aehrenthal emphasised to a conference of ministers on 6 December[31] that, particularly in view of the prevailing Anglo-German tension, which he felt would probably lead within two or three years to the 'now virtually inevitable [*kaum noch vermeidbaren*] European war',[32] the Monarchy must be careful to cultivate its relations with Italy. Hence there must be no big armaments programme that would give offence at Rome. The parsimonious governments of Austria and Hungary were, of course, delighted; but the government at Rome was not unappreciative either. All in all, Libyan war was tending to bring Italy back into the bosom of the Triple Alliance. For she was finding her allies on the whole more congenial, or at least less embarrassing, company than the Triple Entente Powers – France and Great Britain, who were both proving uncomfortable neighbours in the Mediterranean, and Russia, who in the autumn of 1911 was actually offering Turkey an alliance.

The idea behind the Charykov Kite, launched in October by the

30. F. Conrad von Hoetzendorf, *Aus meiner Dienstzeit*, II, p. 282.
31. P.A. XL/310, Ministerratsprotokoll, 6 December 1911.
32. Redlich, *Schicksalsjahre Oesterreichs*, 5 December 1911.

Russian ambassador at Constantinople, was that in return for a Russian guarantee of the Dardanelles against Italian attack, Turkey would not only join a Balkan league, but grant Russia sole rights of passage through the Straits. Of all the non-belligerent Powers, Austria-Hungary was the most determined in its opposition to the scheme. In Aehrenthal's view, Russia was aiming at nothing less than a protectorate over the Ottoman Empire: and if she were ever in a position to transfer her entire naval forces to the Black Sea, she would not only dominate the entire Balkan peninsula, but threaten the Monarchy's interests in the Mediterranean and the Adriatic. He decided, therefore, that as the Buchlau agreement could no longer be considered valid (in view of St Petersburg's unfriendly response to the annexation of Bosnia) he was by no means obliged to fall in with Russia's proposals. Indeed, he advised the Turks to beware of them. But he found little support elsewhere. The supineness of the Germans, who blandly asserted that the task of opposing Russia could well be left to the British, drove him into a fury. Ever since Potsdam, he told himself bitterly, the Germans had done nothing but truckle to Russia – and all because of their ridiculous obsession about Great Britain. In desperation, he himself appealed to London to restrain the Russians from pursuing the matter. But the British did not respond. Like Goluchowski in 1903, they rated an *entente* with Russia more highly than a few strategic advantages in the Eastern Mediterranean. Not that they liked Charykov's scheme, nor in the least resented Aehrenthal's appeal. On the contrary, they were very favourably impressed by Vienna's steady devotion to the status quo over the past few years. In January 1912 they even made a wistful suggestion that an Austro-Russian *entente* would be highly conducive to peace in the Balkans. But the French sharply reminded them of their Entente commitments, adding the warning – always effective in London – that an Austro-Russian *entente* would herald the return of the Three Emperors' Alliance. In the end the Austrians were lucky, in that the whole affair, like the Albanian crisis of the summer, suddenly faded away – in this case with Sazonov's disavowal of Charykov on 9 December. But it had afforded new proof of the inability of the Monarchy, in the existing constellation of Powers, to control the course of events in the Near East.

Perhaps the most ominous development of these months, in terms of Austrian hopes of maintaining the status quo, Aehrenthal did not even attempt to control: the sowing of the seeds of the Balkan League of 1912. Although since the late summer of 1911 Serbia, Bulgaria and Greece, encouraged by Turkey's embarrassments, had begun to draw together, Aehrenthal until the day of his death always regarded a Balkan League as an idle chimera – in view of the incompatibility of the interests of the Balkan states in Macedonia. But if events proved him right in the long run, he nevertheless disastrously misjudged the chances of a short-term combination. Moreover, his own strictly conservative and quietist policy, conducive though it might have been to the lowering of tension between the Great Powers, in the Balkan arena actually played into the hands of a Russia who seemed to have more to offer. For example, his advice to the visiting tsar Ferdinand in December 1911 to keep the peace only disappointed the Bulgarians, and made them more ready to listen to Russian and Serbian advice. Equally counter-productive were his efforts to intimidate the Balkan states into keeping the peace: for instance, when rumours circulated in the Balkan states from time to time that the Monarchy was only waiting to exploit any disturbance of the peace as a pretext to embark on the march to Salonika, he chose not to disavow them.[33] But the effect of this sphinx-like attitude was to induce in the Balkan states, not terrified paralysis, but feverish activity to create a defensive bloc against the evil day. When Aehrenthal died, on 17 February 1912, the Balkan League was well on the way to formation.

With hindsight, this might be seen as setting the seal on the deterioration of the international position of the Monarchy since 1906. But that deterioration was more a reflection of the harsh realities of the Monarchy's position among the Powers, than of a lack of statesmanship in Vienna. After all, the clearing up of the ambiguous status of Bosnia and the Herzegovina – a problem that had plagued successive foreign ministers since at least 1882 – was undoubtedly a notable achievement; and the deterioration of the Monarchy's relations with Russia was by no means solely Aehrenthal's fault. Certainly, Russian and Serbian hatred had been fired to white heat by the annexation; but, as the response of Russia and Serbia to Aehrenthal's conservative and pacific policy after 1909 amply demonstrated, this hatred was one which fed itself, and burned ever fiercer by a process of nationalist internal combustion. Equally, the sympathetic response of the British to that policy showed that if the Monarchy could no longer count on their active co-operation in the Near East, that was only because the British – like the French – had their own good reasons, quite unconnected with the activities of the Ballhausplatz, for preferring Russia to

33. OUA, III, Nos. 2774, 2883.

Austria-Hungary. And after all, the deterioration in relations with Russia had been to some extent offset by the marked improvement in relations with Italy. That was Aehrenthal's great achievement: the Russo-Italian pincer he had discerned on the horizon in 1901 had been broken up. Finally, if the Dual Alliance had only fleetingly proved of value in a diplomatic crisis, and if friction over Vienna's determination to pursue an independent policy, and over Berlin's pro-Russian proclivities, had all too soon recreated the familiar situation, in which an alliance designed for use in war proved to be of little use in day-to-day diplomacy, Aehrenthal's experience of it was perhaps no worse than that of any of his predecessors since 1879.

The difficult position in which the Monarchy found itself by 1912 was to some extent concealed by the great personal prestige of Aehrenthal, whom even former opponents in London now mourned as 'not only the doyen, but the most important of the continental foreign ministers'.[34] Even in St Petersburg he was respected, if hardly liked. Inside the Monarchy, the vigorous policy of his early years had been very favourably compared to the indolence of 'Goluschlafski', and had established his reputation as the Austrian Bismarck. In fact, the analogy would not be inappropriate to his whole term of office. Like Bismarck, Aehrenthal was essentially an extreme conservative; like the Treaty of Frankfurt, the annexation of Bosnia marked a final advance (if advance it may be called, marking as it did a retreat from the Sanjak and from all intervention in the internal affairs of Turkey); like Bismarck, Aehrenthal was the object of growing criticism at home in his later years – from Conrad and the military, from Archduke Franz Ferdinand and the clericals; and just as there were people in Austria who were seriously concerned, until well into the seventies, with fending off Bismarck's alleged designs on the German provinces of Austria, so it was hardly surprising that, a mere three years after the annexation, there were people in Russia and the Balkan states who credited Aehrenthal with plans of expansion as far as Salonika. Had he lived as long as Bismarck, he might have been able in time to dispel these fears. As it was, his death added yet another element of uncertainty to an unstable situation.

---

34. P.A. VIII/147, Mensdorff to Berchtold, private, 20 February 1912.

Berchtold and the Concert of Europe: 1912–1914

Leopold, Count Berchtold, although intelligent and hard-working, and possessed of a great personal charm, was entirely lacking in that self-confidence that had carried Aehrenthal through. Never an ambitious man, he had in 1905 given up his post as counsellor of embassy at St Petersburg (where the cold, damp climate was ruining his health); and it had taken a good deal of persuasion before Aehrenthal could get him to return to Russia as ambassador in 1906 – and then only on condition that the appointment was limited to two years. He served, in the event, for a very wearing four and a half, retiring again into private life in April 1911. Even as minister for foreign affairs he served chiefly from a sense of duty to his sovereign; and, as his diary reveals, was plagued constantly by the desire to resign and retire from the irksome tasks of office.[35] An aristocrat with great estates in Hungary and Bohemia, his views on domestic affairs were simple, unimaginative and faintly pessimistic – those of a conventional conservative supporter of the dualist system. He penned no long memoranda on the restructuring of the Monarchy as Aehrenthal had done. Nor was it simply that he had learned from the failure of Aehrenthal's grand designs in the face of Magyar opposition. He had himself, as a Hungarian magnate, on occasion supported this opposition – for example, in resisting Aehrenthal's plans to conciliate Serbia at the expense of Magyar agriculturalists.

The new appointment did not herald any radical changes in terms of the objectives of Austro-Hungarian foreign policy. Berchtold was no expansionist, but, like Aehrenthal, a firm believer in the Monarchy's role as a conservative, status quo Power. There were marked changes, however, in terms of the internal formulation of policy, and of the methods of making it effective among the Great Powers. In the Ballhausplatz Aehrenthal had always spoken with a firm voice that brooked no opposition; and the 'ginger group' of younger men whom he brought to prominence in the office in his later years[36] – men of the stamp of Forgách, Hoyos and Macchio, all advocates of a tough, confrontational approach towards the Monarchy's opponents – made no perceptible impact on the policy of *quieta non movere* that characterised his later years. Things were different under Berchtold. After two visits to the Ballhausplatz in September 1913 the ambassador

---

35. Hantsch, *Berchtold, passim.*
36. Rumpler, 'Rahmenbedingungen', in *Habsburgermonarchie*, p. 84.

to London, Count Mensdorff, lamented 'the indecisiveness and diffidence [*Unselbständigkeit*] of our excellent Leopold'; and prophesied that Sektionschef Forgách 'will shortly have the whole running of the foreign ministry in his hands and the minister entirely in his pocket'.[37] The story that when confronted with an enquiry Berchtold would simply press an electric button, whereupon the relevant official would appear and supply the answer, is probably apocryphal.[38] But one might see an ominous parallel between conditions in the Ballhausplatz as the conflict with Serbia sharpened after 1913 and those that had prevailed during the incumbency of Mensdorff's own father on the eve of the war of 1866. This should not be taken too far: all the evidence is, in Berchtold's case, of a unanimity of view between the minister and his officials over the South Slav question, particularly in the critical days of 1914; but if Berchtold was more inclined than Aehrenthal to seek the advice of his officials, they were certainly not inclined to restrain him from adopting a policy of confrontation. Similarly, outside the Ballhausplatz, Archduke Franz Ferdinand now looked forward to a voice in foreign affairs, and showered advice on the new minister, who he was sure would be very different from his 'frightful predecessors', Goluchowski and Aehrenthal.[39] This, since Berchtold, although hardly as Italophobe as the archduke, was not one to run after Italy, boded ill for the continuance of the Austro-Italian *rapprochement* so carefully tended by Aehrenthal.

Externally the most striking change, however, was a move away from the sturdy independence of Aehrenthal's regime to a preference for co-operative action within the Concert of Europe. Now this reflected, not Berchtold's alleged pliability, but firmly held convictions, acquired during the course of his diplomatic career. Both in his first post, in London in the 1890s, and in St Petersburg, he had developed a certain trust and respect for the British, even as opponents; and he was generally ready to work with Grey to resolve international problems by concert diplomacy. But his predisposition for the Concert stemmed essentially from his nerve-racking experiences at St Petersburg during the Sanjak railway and Bosnian crises, when Aehrenthal, to Berchtold's dismay and alarm, had stubbornly insisted on defending Austria-Hungary's interests by single-handed action, paying scant regard to the susceptibilities of the other Powers. Compared to these experiences, the frustrations inherent in concert diplomacy, even in wrestling with issues

37. Mensdorff MSS, Tagebuch, 29, 13 September 1913.
38. Kanner, *Katastrophenpolitik*, p. 89.
39. Berchtold MSS, Franz Ferdinand to Berchtold, 16 January 1913.

of such labyrinthine complexity as Macedonia, seemed to Berchtold infinitely more tolerable.

The problem confronting Berchtold, in his efforts to mobilise the Concert in defence of the Monarchy's interests, reduced itself in practice to one of persuading the other Great Powers to adjust their policies to take account of those interests – no easy task for a Power like Austria-Hungary, both relatively weak itself, and still largely isolated among the Great Powers. The Monarchy's interests were clearly threatened in the spring, for example, by Italy's operations near the Dardanelles, which brought the Tripoli War perilously close to the heart of the Ottoman Empire, and by her annexation of a whole series of islands in the Aegean, which was regarded in Vienna as a dangerous alteration of the whole Near Eastern balance of power. Yet not only were the Austrians quite unable to move Berlin to join in calling Italy to order – their exasperation being increased by a flamboyantly cordial visit by Wilhelm II to King Victor Emmanuel at this time. An appeal Berchtold made to London, with Franz Joseph's express and hearty approval,[40] also fell on deaf ears: the Germans, he explained, with their truckling to Russia since Potsdam, and their notorious designs on Turkey's Asian possessions, could no longer be regarded as a bulwark of the status quo in the Near East; nor, of course, could the Monarchy's Italian ally. Austria-Hungary would do well, therefore – without, of course, abandoning her allies – to keep in touch with Great Britain. But the only result was an exchange of compliments with Grey. The British would never be in two minds between the Anglo-Russian *entente* and a revival of the Mediterranean Agreements in such a vague and truncated form as Berchtold seemed to be hinting at. In fact, in the summer of 1912 the Monarchy seemed to be in some danger of falling between two stools: a marked deterioration in its relations with its allies had not been made good by closer relations with Great Britain. In July, a cordial meeting between Wilhelm II and the tsar at Port Baltic (where the Germans reiterated their assurances of Potsdam) was a renewed indication that Austria-Hungary, despite her alliances, was for practical purposes of day-to-day diplomacy, painfully isolated. None of this augured well for Berchtold's efforts to mobilise the Concert in defence of Austro-Hungarian interests as dangers arose in the Balkan peninsula.

It was only gradually that the Austrians became aware of the extent of the crisis developing on their southern borders. Not until

---

40. Wagner, 'Kaiser Franz Joseph' p. 260; OUA IV Nos. 3633, 3634.

late May did they learn, from Berlin and Bucharest, of the secret Serbo-Bulgarian treaty of 12 March; and, like their informants, they were unaware of its contents – of its defensive clauses aimed at Austria-Hungary, and offensive secret annexe providing for the partition of Macedonia. Indeed, Berchtold was content to accept Kiderlen's sanguine assurance that in so far as it was concluded under the patronage of Russia, a Power notoriously concerned to restrain the Balkan states, the treaty would actually serve to reinforce the status quo. (The Greco-Bulgarian treaty of 29 May, about which St Petersburg was known to be unenthusiastic, worried the Austrians even less; and they learned nothing of the negotiations between the rulers of Bulgaria and Montenegro, conducted under their very noses in the Vienna Hofburg in June.) By this time, however, there were alarming signs that the Balkan states were preparing to move, regardless of their treaty arrangements. As if the territorial problems of the Ottoman Empire – which by June had not only the Italian war, but another Albanian revolt and a frontier dispute with Montenegro to contend with – were not enough to tempt the Balkan states to action, a major political and military crisis soon gripped the government at Constantinople itself. There, the Young Turks were at last driven from power, and a new liberal, Anglophile government, in a desperate effort to settle at least the Albanian crisis, announced the grant of virtual autonomy to the rebels. This, however, only intensified the strife at Constantinople; and the government's efforts to draw the teeth of its Young Turk critics by instituting a major purge in the army, only added military disorganisation to its problems. The Balkan states, meanwhile, had taken great alarm at the concessions granted to the Albanians: clearly, now was the time to strike if Macedonia was to be saved for Greek and Slav. It was to contain this crisis that Berchtold made his first serious attempt to mobilise the Concert of Europe.

The experience was disheartening. His formal appeal to the Powers (13 August) to urge the Turks to extend their commendable decentralisation policy from Albania to the whole of Macedonia, while urging the Balkan states to give Turkey time to put her house in order, was certainly an attempt to take the lead in reviving the Concert in defence of peace and the territorial status quo. Yet even if the Germans had not taken umbrage at his attempt to demonstrate his independence of Berlin by omitting to consult them beforehand; and even if Russia and France had not been so obsessed about Entente solidarity, Berchtold's proposal could hardly have resolved the crisis. The hard-pressed Turkish government simply could not consider further concessions, if only for fear of provoking a chauvinist outburst that would bring the Young Turks back to power. (It was for this reason the Great Britain was reluctant to support any proposals involving pressure on Constantinople.) At the same time, the very fact that a Great Power had made a proposal, feasible or not, designed to preserve the Ottoman Empire, was to the Balkan states only a further incentive to strike before it was too late. The international situation had defeated Berchtold's efforts. In September, an attempt by Sazonov to mobilise the Concert came to grief for similar reasons: the difficult situation at Constantinople and the determination of the Balkan states. Not that Berchtold despaired of the Concert, even now: at the eleventh hour he readily fell in with a Franco-German proposal whereby Austria-Hungary and Russia should act as spokesmen of the Powers. On 8 October the two Powers informed Constantinople that the Powers would 'take reforms in hand'; and warned the Balkan states to keep the peace, for the Powers would permit no changes in the territorial status quo. But this belated appeal to the ghost of Mürzsteg made no impression at Constantinople; nor could it prevail against Balkan nationalism in full flood. On that very same day, Montenegro led the Balkan states into war against the Ottoman Empire.

Although the Austrians were undoubtedly disconcerted by the sudden collapse of the Balkan status quo, as the Turks retreated in confusion before the armies of the Balkan states, there was no question of any direct military intervention by the Monarchy to stop the process. At home, the treasury was empty and the army – as the Common War Minister, Auffenberg, had explained to a conference of ministers on 14 September – was by no means prepared for action. On this, not only Berchtold, but Franz Joseph and Franz Ferdinand were all agreed. Abroad, Berchtold felt there was little prospect of German or Italian support for intervention; and any move by Austria-Hungary in the direction of actual assistance for the Turks would only – as in the 1870s – have united the whole of the Christian Balkans against the Monarchy. Berchtold himself had in any case come to the conclusion that 'we have been Turcophile for decades and we have not got anything out of it'.[41] There certainly seemed no reason to deviate from the principles of non-intervention that Goluchowski had announced to the Russians in 1897 and Aehrenthal to the Italians in 1909. A series of

41. F.R. Bridge, 'Austria-Hungary and the Ottoman Empire in the Twentieth Century', in *Mitteilungen des österreichischen Staatsarchivs*, 1981, p. 258.

conferences in the Ballhausplatz in October decided, therefore, that the Monarchy had no interest in territorial acquisitions in the Balkans; nor in re-occupying the Sanjak of Novibazar. At the same time, however, the Austrians felt that they had certain interests to guard in the area – they had after all always insisted, at least since the agreement with Russia in 1897, that they must have a voice in any new arrangements in the Balkans.

That Berchtold was still hoping to safeguard these interests through concert diplomacy was seen when at the end of October he made haste to recognise – as first of the European foreign ministers – that the status quo was now lost beyond recall, and to inform the other Great Powers of the interests which Austria-Hungary had at stake in any final settlement.[42] The prospects at first looked good, when in most capitals Berchtold's list of desiderata was considered to be surprisingly moderate and reasonable: for example, the Monarchy would seek compensation for its non-combatant ally, Romania, according to the principle of Balkan balance of power; and security for its own commercial interests in formerly Turkish areas. More controversially, any territorial gains for Serbia must be accompanied by guarantees for her future good behaviour, perhaps in the form of close economic co-operation with the Monarchy (in which case the latter was prepared to be generous). Above all, in no circumstances must Serbia be allowed to expand to the Adriatic. Basically, this principle reflected the fear that a Serbian port might some day become a Russian port (or, as Franz Ferdinand feared, an Italian port); the well-founded apprehensions of Vienna as to the effect on the South Slavs of the Monarchy of too great an increase in Serbia's prestige; and the desire to restrict Serbia's economic independence by forcing her to channel her drive to the sea through Austro-Hungarian territory (as Aehrenthal had hoped to do in 1909). But the principle of 'the Balkans for the Balkan peoples', which Berchtold also fell back on in this connection, was not mere hypocrisy. Any port that Serbia acquired would of necessity lie in purely Albanian territory; and the creation of a viable Albania was another cardinal point in Berchtold's declaration of principles.

Well received though Berchtold's statement was in most capitals, it provoked a serious crisis in the Monarchy's relations with Serbia and Russia. The Serbs were absolutely determined to acquire an Adriatic port. Already their armies were fighting their way through to the coast and crushing the resistance of Austria-Hungary's Albanian protégés with a savagery that equalled anything the Turks had

---

42. OUA, IV, No. 4780.

done in the past. Russia, for her part, seemed determined to support Serbia's pretensions; and her military posture had been somewhat threatening from the very start of the Balkan crisis, at which time she had happened to carry out a trial mobilisation. At the end of October the Austrians had been moved to take some counter-measures, and decided to retain with the colours a portion of the third-year levy of troops due to be dismissed when the new recruits were called in. Already in the spring the government had at last managed – albeit at the price of police intervention in the riotous Hungarian parliament – to raise the size of the contingents recruited by the Common Army beyond the level fixed in 1888. In November, the forces facing the Russians in Galicia were stepped up; and on 12 December Conrad von Hoetzendorf was recalled as chief of staff. Meanwhile, as friction between Serbian military and Austro-Hungarian consular officials in Macedonia led to Serbian interference with communications between the Austro-Hungarian government and several of its consulates, culminating in the abduction by Serbian troops of the Austro-Hungarian consul in Prisren, something of a war psychosis – which the Ballhausplatz did nothing to restrain[43] – began to make itself felt in certain sections of the Austro-Hungarian press.

Fortunately for the peace of Europe the international situation was such that the Serbian port crisis could be resolved by the Concert of Europe in a sense favourable to Vienna. On the one hand, the Russians were disheartened by the distinct lack of enthusiasm displayed for the Serbian cause by their friends in Paris and London. On the other, the Monarchy, if its military measures were not enough, managed in this instance to put on an imposing diplomatic front. Germany, Italy and Austria-Hungary, notoriously united on the question of a Serbian port, emphasised their solidarity by formally renewing the Triple Alliance on 5 December. Already in November a demonstrative visit by Franz Ferdinand and the chief of staff to Berlin had given food for thought in the Entente capitals; and in the Reichstag on 2 December Bethmann Hollweg publicly pledged Germany to come to the aid of the Dual Monarchy should it be attacked by a third party while making good its interests in the Balkans. By then, Russia had largely given up hope of securing an Adriatic port for her protégé; the settlement of the Austro-Serbian consular dispute (with a formal apology from Serbia) lessened the tension further; and, in the most import-

---

43. Robert A. Kann, *Die Prochaska Affäre vom Herbst 1912: Zwischen kaltem und heißem Krieg* (Vienna 1977).

ant step of all towards preventing a major conflagration, the Great Powers accepted a proposal of Grey's for an informal conference of ambassadors to discuss those issues that impinged directly on the interests of the Great Powers in the Near East. Berchtold liked the idea of this kind of academic discussion, which offered the chance of positive results while yet avoiding the dangers involved in a formal conference (the failure of which might prove too great a strain on the international nerves). Moreover, he trusted in Grey as an impartial statesman, and readily agreed that the matter should be left to the ambassadors in London – rather than in Paris, where the rancorous Izvolsky might make trouble. By the end of December it seemed that Berchtold's faith in the Concert had been amply justified. At the very first meeting of the ambassadors, the vexed issue of a Serbian port finally disappeared when it was agreed that the frontiers of Albania should extend from Montenegro in the north to Greece in the south; and the decision to entrust Austria-Hungary and Italy with the task of devising a scheme of autonomous government for Albania seemed a further recognition of Austria-Hungary's interests in the area.

The new year, however, brought the first of a series of disappointments that led eventually to Berchtold's complete loss of faith in the Concert. Whereas at the end of 1912 concert diplomacy had served Austria-Hungary well, when she could count on the sympathy of a majority of the Powers and Russia had been virtually isolated, the position was reversed once the ambassadors proceeded, in the early months of 1913, to determine the inland frontiers of Albania. The Austrians wished to make the new state, a potential ally in any war against the Balkan Slavs, as big as possible; and they had a useful argument to hand in that the frontier they were demanding was in fact very much in accordance with the ethnic character of the area. They found themselves completely isolated, however. The other Great Powers were all unanimous in declaring that ethnic considerations could not be the sole criterion, and that some account must be taken of Serbia's and Montenegro's claims by right of conquest. The crucial issue in the debate was Scutari, which the Austrians, in view of its continuing and surprising resistance to Montenegrin besieging forces, now decided must go to Albania (although Berchtold had not dared hope for this in October). Russia, in a vengeful mood after her defeat on the Serbian port issue, was equally vociferous in defence of Montenegro. In London, Grey now argued that as St Petersburg had given way on the port question, it was up to Vienna to give way over Scutari; and Mensdorff received practically no support from his German and Italian colleagues in opposing this horse-trading and demanding a settlement according to the merits of the case. These were, after all, of less concern to the other Powers than the tension arising from Russia's and Austria-Hungary's continued military preparations; and from the failure of the mission to St Petersburg of Prince Gottfried Hohenlohe, sent by Franz Joseph, in a desperate attempt to invoke the spirit of monarchical solidarity, to assure the tsar personally of his goodwill. By February, the Germans began to put pressure on their allies: Bethmann Hollweg in a tactless – in Berchtold's view 'impertinent'[44] – message, urged Vienna to yield for the sake of Anglo-German co-operation; while Wilhelm II implored his friend Franz Ferdinand to consider whether for 'the grazing lands of the goats of Scutari' it really was worth keeping Russia and Austria-Hungary facing each other under arms and causing 'such hardship to so many poor families'.[45]

Isolated inside the Concert, the Austrians had to settle for a compromise. There could, after all, be no question of single-handed action. As the Common Finance Minister observed on 4 January, war might mean the total economic collapse of the Monarchy; and the emperor, Franz Ferdinand and Berchtold were equally determined to resist Conrad's incessant pleas for a military solution. Meanwhile, time was running out: if the Montenegrins were allowed to capture Scutari, the problem of evicting them from that inaccessible mountain fastness would complicate matters to a fearsome degree. In the event, Berchtold managed to persuade the Powers to award Scutari to Albania; but to secure this he had to make sweeping concessions in favour of Serbia and Montenegro on the north-eastern frontier of Albania, giving up not only all the areas which he had originally listed as possible bargaining counters, but the important market towns of Dibra and Djakova, which were notoriously purely Albanian in character. Yet although the settlement of the Scutari issue produced a temporary *détente* which at last enabled Russia and Austria-Hungary to start reducing their military establishments, the crisis had caused a further and lasting deterioration in their relations. In St Petersburg, it had finally dissipated any faith Nicholas II personally still had in the Habsburg Monarchy, and had intensified there – as in Vienna – that ingrained mistrust that since the Bosnian crisis had made it impossible for the ruling élites in the two empires to re-establish relations of mutual understanding, let alone co-operation. More immediately, there

44. Hantsch, *Berchtold*, I, p. 388.
45. Robert A. Kann, *Erzherzog Franz Ferdinand Studien* (Vienna 1967), p. 77.

was in Vienna both deep disillusionment over the high price paid in terms of Albanian (and thereby Austro-Hungarian) interests for the solution eventually devised by the Concert, and a fanatical determination that, having paid that price, the Monarchy must insist on the fulfilment of the bargain on the part of the Concert.

The futile efforts of the Powers in the next six weeks to bring Montenegro to desist from the siege of Scutari provided Berchtold with yet a second disillusioning lesson in concert diplomacy. Indeed, the naval demonstration that the Powers haltingly organised – under pressure of an Austro-Hungarian threat of separate coercive action – and in which Russia ostentatiously refused to participate, only demonstrated the disunity and ineffectiveness of the Concert. The actual surrender of Scutari to Montenegrin forces on 23 April was a devastating blow to Austro-Hungarian prestige: at Cetinje delirious demonstrators paraded a donkey, draped in black, in front of the Austro-Hungarian legation.[46] When, after another week, the Powers still proved incapable of uniting for action, the patience of Vienna was exhausted. Despite the risk of general war – an Austro-Hungarian action against Montenegro would almost certainly bring Serbian forces into the fray; and Russia had let it be known that she would not tolerate an Austro-Hungarian attack on Serbia – a conference of ministers decided on 2 May to put the forces in Bosnia, the Herzegovina and Dalmatia on a complete war footing: 'mobilisation was in full swing, even if it was not so labelled'.[47] These measures proved infinitely more effective than the notes and demonstrations of the Concert. News of them caused utter panic at Cetinje, and the Montenegrins immediately promised to withdraw from Scutari. That was enough for Berchtold and Franz Joseph. True, a council of ministers on 3 May would have liked to humiliate Montenegro further, by sending her an ultimatum with a formal summons to withdraw; and they even overruled Berchtold and compelled him to transmit their wishes to the emperor. But such was the power structure of the Monarchy in matters of foreign affairs that the wishes of the emperor and his foreign minister were decisive: only a warning telegram was sent to Cetinje. On 5 May the Montenegrins marched out of Scutari, tension relaxed, Austria-Hungary's latest military measures were countermanded, and Conrad lamented that yet another opportunity for war had been lost.

In dealing with the remaining issues that concerned the Monarchy,

46. Helmreich, *Balkan Wars*, p. 313.
47. Ibid., p. 322.

notably the final frontier and constitution of the new Albanian state, the Concert performed more to Berchtold's satisfaction. The Austro-Italian draft proposals for the constitutional ordering of Albania were by and large accepted by the London conference; and the choice of the German Prince, Wilhelm of Wied, a nephew of the queen of Romania, to be the first head of state, was another feather in the cap of the Triple Alliance. But the Austrians were by no means completely satisfied; and as the conference discussions on the southern frontier of Albania dragged on, with the French ardently championing the claims of Athens, and with the credibility of Austro-Italian support for Albania constantly undermined by Wilhelm II's notorious Grecophile sympathies, Mensdorff thought he could detect signs of growing bad temper in the 'peremptory' instructions he now began to receive from Vienna.[48] The London conference might have preserved the peace of Europe; but the cost in terms of Berchtold's disillusionment both with the Concert and with the Monarchy's allies had been high – witness his somewhat bitter observation on Mensdorff's difficult position 'between hostile Triple Entente colleagues and feeble Triple Alliance colleagues'.[49] Altogether, the truculent determination he now displayed, in making difficulties over minor issues in the Eastern Balkans that he admitted were primarily Russia's concern, 'to pay Russia back in her own coin'; and his almost casual observation[50] that Russia, 'although she has no real interests whatever [*gar keine reellen Interessen*] in the South Slav and Albanian questions', had nevertheless, pleading 'the – for us – unacceptable Panslav or Panorthodox idea, challenged the vital interests of the Monarchy in those areas', showed how fine was the line between a determined defence of Austro-Hungarian interests and a dangerously cavalier disregard for the interests of others. All this boded ill both for the future of Austro-Russian relations and for the peace. More immediately, however, the Monarchy's helpless frustration only intensified as a new conflict – between the victorious Balkan states over the division of the spoils in Macedonia – demonstrated yet again that the Balkan states were no longer inclined to take much account of the wishes of the Monarchy, and that, lacking the support of either the Concert or its allies, the Monarchy was in no position to compel them to do so.

Initially Berchtold, ever anxious to see a reduction of Serbia's prestige and a lessening of her attractive power over the increas-

48. Mensdorff MSS, Karton 4, Tagebuch, 6 July 1913.
49. Ibid., Karton 9, Berchtold to Mensdorff, 18 June 1913.
50. Ibid., Karton 1, Berchtold to Mensdorff, 16 July 1913.

ingly discontented South Slavs of the Monarchy, calculated that Bulgaria might pull Austria-Hungary's chestnuts out of the fire. Bulgaria was thought to be easily capable of defeating both Serbia and Greece if it came to a war. The trouble was, that she would not be able to cope with Romania as well. Berchtold, therefore, urged Sofia to make sure of Romania's neutrality by granting her some territorial concessions. Admittedly, his task was no easy one: the St Petersburg Protocol of 17 April, by which the Great Powers had assigned to Romania the Bulgarian town of Silistria as compensation for Bulgaria's anticipated gains, had left the two states on extremely bad terms. But he did not despair. After all, a Bulgarian–Romanian *rapprochement* under the auspices of the Triple Alliance would be a valuable prize indeed; and especially valuable to the Monarchy, now resigned to accepting Serbia's 'open hostility' as ineradicable. So convinced was Berchtold of this that on 24 June he went so far as to offer the Bulgarians 'sympathy and active support'[51] in resisting any further expansion of Serbia – but again, only on condition that they first squared Romania.

His grand design soon came to grief, primarily because the Bulgarians never paid the slightest attention to his advice to come to terms with Bucharest. They had a boundless – as it turned out, an ill-founded – faith in Russia to restrain Romania; and it was in consequence of this – and not, as was believed in Entente circles, as a result of Austro-Hungarian prompting – that they rashly attacked Greek and Serbian positions in Macedonia at the end of June. When both Turkey and Romania took advantage of the ensuing conflict to assert their own claims against Bulgaria, the latter was reduced in a matter of weeks to a state of utter prostration. Yet if the Austrians were dismayed by the outcome of these decisions taken in the Balkan capitals, they were if anything even more exasperated by the reactions of their allies in Berlin. The Germans had in fact never shown the slightest interest in Berchtold's projected Bulgarian–Romanian alignment. Indeed, since the death in December 1912 of Kiderlen (who had encouraged Berchtold's hopes of disrupting the Balkan League by winning over Bulgaria) German policy had become positively hostile to Bulgaria – largely a reflection of Wilhelm II's personal dislike of King Ferdinand. In April 1913 the Germans had sided with the Triple Entente Powers at the St Petersburg conference to thwart Berchtold's hopes of sugaring the Silistrian pill for Bulgaria by awarding Salonika to her as compensation. Salonika, the Germans declared, must go to Greece

51. OUA, VI, 7486.

(where, on 18 March, Wilhelm II's brother-in-law Constantine had ascended the throne). In fact, the Germans had a grand design of their own for the Balkans: a combination of Romania, Greece and Serbia. For this, of course, the Austrians had no time at all: Serbia was hopelessly hostile; and distant Greece, with her ingrained aversion to Bulgaria and Albania, could never be of much use to Austria-Hungary. But it was in vain that they warned Berlin against playing into the hands of the Triple Entente Powers, who were striving to build up just such a combination for their own purposes. To the Austrians, the spectacular triumph of this very group in the Second Balkan War was galling indeed.

Not that Vienna could do much about it. In the first place, the domestic situation, just calming down after six months of alarms, was anything but favourable to active intervention. Commercial circles were aghast at the prospect of further upheavals. The Balkan wars had severely disrupted Austria-Hungary's Near Eastern trade: goods had been held up at the frontiers, or even sent back; and the Balkan states had imposed moratoria on all payments. The mobilisation measures in May had caused a general crisis of credit; and the sum result was depression and a disturbing growth in unemployment. If all this did not give the government pause, the attitude of the public towards foreign affairs was marked by widespread apathy, even pacifism. On all sides, demands were raised for the demobilisation of the few troops still remaining on a war footing in the south. And anti-interventionalist feelings were by no means confined to the street. 'Sit back calmly and watch', Archduke Franz Ferdinand adjured Berchtold, 'while this rabble, these unreliable useless gentlemen break each other's heads';[52] and the emperor himself was equally strongly for peace. There was never the slightest chance that they would sanction a policy hostile to Romania, whose intervention in the war had in fact been decisive, sealing the fate both of Bulgaria and of Berchtold's schemes. In this situation, the exhortations of Wilhelm II to do nothing to jeopardise the alliance with Romania were unnecessary; and San Giuliano's famous remark about holding Austria-Hungary back 'by the coat-tails' was the result of a misunderstanding about her intentions.[53] There could be no question of military intervention by the Monarchy. Berchtold could only try to salvage what he could by diplomacy.

The upshot was merely a further demonstration of the Mon-

---

52. Berchtold MSS, Franz Ferdinand to Berchtold, 4 July 1913.
53. OUA, VI, No. 7748.

archy's isolation and helplessness, on this occasion the consequence of the failure of its allies to support it in a diplomatic contest between the two Power blocs rather than in concert diplomacy. Although both Russia and Austria-Hungary still claimed, as they had always done, a voice in the final re-ordering of the Balkan map, the other Powers, utterly weary after nine months of haggling in London, all insisted that the war between the Balkan states must be settled, not by the Concert, but by the Balkan states themselves.

Berchtold was not without hopes of the latter. After all, the Bulgarians, at last despairing of Russia, had appointed an Austrophile government. Even more encouraging, the Romanians seemed to be displaying a most commendable solicitude for the Balkan balance of power: deciding that Bulgaria had been weakened enough, they had forced their Serbian and Greek allies to agree to a peace conference, to meet, not at St Petersburg but at Bucharest. There, they assured Berchtold, they would look after the Monarchy's interests. This last promise, however, they singularly failed to fulfil: they allowed Serbia to take most of Macedonia, and, perhaps in response to Wilhelm II's appeals to King Carol, awarded the disputed areas of the Aegean coast, including Kavalla, to King Constantine. The Treaty of Bucharest of 10 August, confirming the triumph of expansionist Serbia and of Albania's other enemy Greece, and disastrously reducing in size and military potential the only Balkan state which had no conflict of interests with Austria-Hungary, was indeed a veritable disaster for the Monarchy. Berchtold could now only pin his hopes on the revision by the Great Powers of what, he rather tactlessly told the Romanians, was an 'arrangement préalable', to reduce Serbia's gains and to secure Kavalla for Bulgaria. On this latter point the Russians, hoping to recover lost ground in Sofia, supported him, or at least rivalled him in enthusiasm. The cut and thrust of Great Power diplomacy went against the Monarchy, however. Germany, struggling with France for influence at Athens, was resolutely opposed to any revision of the treaty; and when the French persuaded Sazonov to give way on the point of Kavalla, Russia too lost all interest in revision. Wilhelm II's lavish distribution of congratulatory telegrams and decorations to victorious Greek and Romanian notables proclaimed to the world that Germany regarded the Treaty of Bucharest as final and definitive. This, together with the fact that nobody else, not even the Italians, was interested in revision, ensured the final collapse of Berchtold's policy.

Clearly, the Monarchy could not count on its allies, either in the Concert or on the diplomatic fencing ground. Berchtold began to lose patience. Had Austria-Hungary no interests of her own to guard? he exasperatedly asked the Germans. Must she always submit to the common interest of Europe? It was particularly galling that Germany had persisted in her waywardness despite his repeated attempts to enlighten her. For example, on 1 August he had drawn up a long memorandum for the better information of Berlin:[54] Austro-Serbian hostility was irremediable (*unüberbrückbar*) and would soon end in war. It was essential, therefore, to win over Bulgaria by giving her some timely support – without, of course, losing Romania. It was high time that Germany gave up her independent Balkan policy. But his warnings of impending dangers, and his fears that the next Balkan league would be directed against Austria-Hungary, made no impression in Berlin. When, therefore, in September, Vienna faced yet another humiliation – as Serbia, on the pretext of suppressing disorders, continued in occupation of territory that the London conference had assigned to Albania, and as Russian obstruction continued to frustrate the efforts of the Concert to evict her – a conference of ministers decided on 3 October that the time had come for Austria-Hungary to take action unrestrained by the Concert or her allies. After all, even Tisza, with the Scutari crisis in mind, now admitted that the events of the past year had shown that whenever the Concert made a decision, nobody paid attention; whereas if a single Power showed that it would not shrink from the use of force, that made an impression. After somewhat perfunctory notice had been given to the allies of the Monarchy's determination to see the decisions of the London conference enforced; and after the Serbs had proceeded to reply evasively to several further warnings, an Austro-Hungarian ultimatum – of which the allies were only informed after the event – went off to Belgrade on 17 October, giving the Serbs eight days' notice to quit Albania.

The Serbs yielded immediately, and the Austrians had had their first significant diplomatic success since the Scutari crisis. As on the former occasion, they had only been acting to enforce an internationally agreed decision; and even the Russians had urged the Serbs to climb down. True, Rome was somewhat piqued; and the Triple Entente Powers were decidedly indignant at Berchtold's 'too precipitate' action,[55] the French going so far as to close the Paris bourse to Austria-Hungary's loans until her diplomatic manners improved. But all this was offset by the signs of a welcome change

54. OUA, VII, No. 8157.
55. B.D. X/1, No. 47.

of heart in Berlin. At the memorial celebrations to commemorate the hundredth anniversary of the Battle of Leipzig on 18 October, Wilhelm II was in an ebullient mood, and his language to Conrad betrayed a new and surprising hostility towards Serbia. His elation had not subsided when he harangued Berchtold for over an hour in Vienna a week later.[56] Although he still recommended economic concessions as the best way to bind Serbia to the Monarchy, he was certainly prepared to support stronger measures of compulsion:

> When His Majesty the Emperor Franz Joseph demands something the Serbian government must give way, and if it does not then Belgrade will be bombarded and occupied until the will of His Majesty is fulfilled. And of this you can be certain, that I stand beside you and am ready to draw the sabre whenever your action makes it necessary. (His Majesty accompanied these words with a movement of his hand to his sabre.)

The assurance that the Monarchy could 'fully and completely count on him' ran through the emperor's remarks, Berchtold was both impressed and gratified to note, 'like a red thread'. In short, the October crisis had convinced Berchtold that independent action was indeed an effective means of defending the Monarchy's interests; and had given him reason to hope that after eighteen disastrous months of dissension, the Dual Alliance had suddenly become a strong and serviceable diplomatic instrument.

In the event, Berchtold's confidence proved ill founded. When he resorted again to independent action in conjunction with Italy, summoning Greece on 31 October, and again on 8 March 1914, to evacuate territory which the Adriatic Powers were determined must go to Albania, even before the Concert had reached its final decision, the result was little short of a fiasco. None of the other Powers was anxious to jeopardise its position at Athens for the sake of insignificant Albania; and the peremptory language of the Adriatic Powers fell on completely deaf ears. As for their ways of proceeding, the Foreign Office in London noted with some irritation on the latter occasion that 'Austria and Italy do not seem to think that the Concert of Europe is any longer intact';[57] and even the Germans expressed their annoyance. In the euphoria of his success in the October crisis, Berchtold had failed to consider that independent action could only succeed if it had the subsequent endorsement or tacit acquiescence of the other Powers in the

---

56. OUA, VII, No. 8934.
57. Crampton, *Hollow Détente*, p. 147.

Concert. As for the support of the Alliance, Berchtold was soon to discover, like Kálnoky, Goluchowski and Aehrenthal before him, that Wilhelm II's effusive utterances did not always amount to much in terms of practical politics. Even in the October crisis the policy-makers in Berlin had been far less enthusiastic than their imperial master in their support of Vienna, acting largely out of fear lest yet another refusal of support might shatter the Alliance altogether. Once the crisis passed it became clear that the interests of Germany and Austria-Hungary had by no means been brought into line; and that for the Austrians the eternal problem of the Dual Alliance remained: how effectively could an Alliance designed to cope with the contingency of war serve the Monarchy's interests in the day-to-day diplomacy of peace?

In fact, the last nine months of peace saw the Dual Alliance descend to a new nadir as far as diplomatic achievements were concerned. The old conflicts of interest reappeared, now exacerbated by the fact that Germany, increasingly anxious for her own direct imperialist interests in Turkey – and who could tell whether Turkey-in-Asia and the Baghdad Railway would not soon follow Macedonia into the diplomatic market? – was less willing than ever to rely on the Austrians to stand guard over her Balkan interests. Germany was now set on building her own causeway to Constantinople, even if this meant shouldering her ally out of the way. Not that the Austrians, increasingly anxious for their own position after the recent disastrous events, felt either willing or able to serve as cat's-paws for the Germans. Nor were they anxious to involve themselves in quarrels where they considered only German interests to be involved. The fiasco of Germany's attempt to strengthen her influence in Turkey by the abortive military mission of General Liman von Sanders met with little sympathy in Vienna, where it was regarded as an unnecessary provocation of Russia. (The Constantinople embassy advised Austrian participation; but Franz Joseph would not hear of his soldiers' serving under German command.)[58] More dramatically, when the Austrians in the spring of 1914 talked of intervening by force to prevent the realisation of a new Serbian plan to set foot on the Adriatic (by means of a union with Montenegro) Wilhelm II declared that a war for such a purpose would leave Berlin 'completely cold': Vienna was 'crazy' to consider it.[59] Far from standing by their effusive assurances of October 1913, the Germans seemed to have abandoned even the

58. Bridge, 'Austria-Hungary and the Ottoman Empire', p. 259.
59. G.P. XXXVIII, No. 15539.

position of December 1912.

Meanwhile, the two allies floundered about in a morass of Balkan diplomacy, with policies hardly less conflicting than those of the summer of 1913. The Monarchy's plans still revolved round Bulgaria, Germany's round Greece. In a sense, it was simply the intractable facts of the diplomatic situation that frustrated Berchtold's untiring efforts to reconcile Bulgaria with Turkey and Romania – in the first case, Bulgarian distrust of a new military regime at Constantinople and reluctance to get involved in Turkey's continuing quarrel with Greece over the future of the Aegean Islands; in the second, the deep hostility between Bulgaria and Romania resulting from their divergent attitudes towards the Treaty of Bucharest. But it was still a source of endless exasperation in Vienna that the Germans evinced not the slightest interest in Berchtold's projected Turco-Bulgarian *entente*: this would have had anti-Greek implications, and Wilhelm II, never in two minds between his Greek brother-in-law and the detested Ferdinand, persisted into the summer of 1914 with his vain efforts to reconcile Turkey and Greece. Not until June could Berchtold prevail upon Berlin even to grant a loan to Bulgaria – despite the fact that the Triple Entente Powers were pressing the Bulgarians to accept a French loan, dismiss the Austrophile government, and return to the Russian camp.

The possible defection of Romania to that camp was in these months a distinct possibility. Not only had Berchtold's wooing of revisionist Bulgaria been taken much amiss; that same Treaty of Bucharest that had made Romania, to Berchtold's chagrin, a pillar of the new order in the Balkans, had given a tremendous boost to her self-confidence and to Romanian irredentism, concentrated on Transylvania. The allied Monarchy was coming to be regarded in Romania as a source, less of support, than of booty. By the autumn of 1913 the Austrians were very worried indeed. Count Ottokar Czernin, a protégé of that great hater of Magyars, Archduke Franz Ferdinand, was sent as minister to Bucharest in an effort to cultivate goodwill. Even the Magyars seemed to be making an effort. In January 1914 Tisza announced an 'era of unity and well-being', and opened talks with the committee of the Romanian nationalist party in Transylvania. But there could be no compromise between Romanian nationalism and the iron principles of Magyar supremacy on which the Hungarian state was based, and the talks failed. Czernin reported that the alliance was not worth the ink and paper it was written on. (Indeed, it was something of a liability, in that its existence, even if only formal, prevented the Monarchy from undertaking any extensive frontier fortifications against Romania to make Transylvania secure.) In June, Tsar Nicholas and his family paid a state visit to King Carol at Constantsa; talk of a marriage between Prince Carol and one of the tsar's daughters seemed to threaten even the dynastic foothold of the Central Powers in Romania; and Tisza was enraged to hear that during the visit Sazonov and Bratianu had made a motor-car excursion across the frontier into Transylvanian territory. Yet not even these ominous developments could bring German and Austro-Hungarian policy into line.[60] The Germans, to whom the Romanians had vouchsafed a report of the Constantsa talks that they withheld from their Austrian allies, were pleased to put their faith in the Hohenzollern connection and their own strong economic position in the country. They viewed the discomfiture of the Austrians with astonishing aplomb, Bethmann Hollweg noting that it could only be to Germany's advantage if Austria-Hungary's position at Bucharest were weakened, as the centre of gravity of the Romanian alliance would then move from Vienna to Berlin.

In other areas Austria-Hungary had to contend with not merely the indifference, but the active opposition of her allies. At every turn she seemed to come up against the economic imperialism of Germany, which, according to Conrad, was aiming at nothing less than the complete annihilation of Austro-Hungarian commercial influence in the Balkans.[61] At the end of 1913, for example, Berchtold opened negotiations with Paris with a view to creating two international companies to run those sections of the Orient Railway recently incorporated into Serbia and Greece. As the controlling influence in both would be French and Austro-Hungarian, the plan offered a measure of economic influence in Serbia, as well as some security for the bond-holders of the Orient Railway Company. Berchtold also cherished the somewhat sanguine hope that Austro-French co-operation in this field might lead to the re-opening of the Paris Bourse to Austro-Hungarian loans – urgently needed for the modernisation and expansion of the army. In the end, however, the negotiations failed in the face of opposition from Serbia and demands from the other Powers for the internationalisation of the holding company – demands to which Germany did not fail to add her strident voice. Berlin's complacent reaction to

---

60. Brigitte Zwerger, 'The diplomatic relations between Great Britain and Roumania, 1913–14', MA dissertation, London 1971, p. 23.
61. F. Klein, 'Probleme des Bündnisses zwischen Oesterreich-Ungarn und Deutschland am Vorabend des ersten Weltkriegs', in Idem (ed.), *Weltpolitik*, pp. 159–60.

this fiasco – that it was high time the Austrians admitted the futility of their attempts to bully Serbia; and that financial links between Austria-Hungary and France were politically undesirable – was a telling comment on the contradictions between the Balkan policies of the allies, and between Germany's diplomatic aims and the military requirements of the Dual Alliance.

Equally damaging both to Austro-Hungarian prestige and to alliance solidarity was the stubborn opposition of both Germany and Italy to the Monarchy's attempts to secure a foothold in Asia Minor, where the Great Powers were engaged in marking out spheres of influence against the day of partition.[62] Not that Berchtold's efforts marked any real departure from the tradition whereby the Monarchy, alone among the Great Powers, had largely abstained from imperialist activity outside the Balkans. The Ballhausplatz was under no more pressure to act now than at the turn of the century, when its tentative excursions into *Weltpolitik* in the Caribbean and China had been solely dictated by the court's concern for the Monarchy's prestige among the other European Powers. Now too, Berchtold was able to arouse singularly little enthusiasm for his project in commercial circles; and his hopes that it might serve as a distraction from the eternal wranglings of the nationalities at home (*Nationalitätenhader*) were certainly over-optimistic. But his anxiety to do something for the Monarchy's ailing prestige, or at least to prevent yet a further loss of prestige, was both desperate and sincere: it would simply never do if the Monarchy were the only Power to receive nothing at all in the general scramble. Germany and Italy were unmoved, however, and refused to make room for their ally within their own spheres of interest – the Germans talked of co-operating with France and Great Britain, even of ending the alliance, if Austria-Hungary continued to pester them. Berchtold persisted nevertheless. But by June 1914 he was facing yet another defeat.

In Albania, the prospects were equally depressing. Not only did the Germans join with the Triple Entente Powers to frustrate the attempts of Austria-Hungary and Italy to gain control of the finances of the new state. Their Greek proclivities were anything but helpful at a time when Greek troops remained in illegal occupation of large areas of southern Albania despite the admonitions of the Adriatic Powers. The Italian allies soon proved an even greater worry to Vienna, however. For that very Albanian state which, so

---

62. F.R. Bridge '*Tarde venientibus ossa*: Austro-Hungarian Colonial Aspirations in Asia Minor, 1913–14' in *Middle Eastern Studies* (1970) pp. 319–30.

long as it had been a mere project for the future, had been a source of unity and co-operation between Vienna and Rome, became, once it was actually established, a veritable apple of discord. By the summer of 1914 the country was virtually in a state of civil war, with the prince looking to Vienna for support and the rebels looking to Rome. An Austro-Italian gentlemen's agreement of April 1914 to refrain from intrigues proved when it came to be applied in practice yet another source of wrangling between the two allies – to the great exasperation of Berlin. When at the end of June the Austrian authorities permitted the opening of a recruiting office in Vienna to enlist volunteers for the prince's army, the German ambassador lost all patience. Storming into the Ballhausplatz, he managed to secure the closure of the recruiting office; and he went off to discuss 'in harmonious unanimity' with his Italian colleague 'the irresponsible attitude of the government here'. The conclusion of his report on the incident, written on the day of the Sarajevo assassinations, that 'yesterday was a critical day in the history of the Triple Alliance' was a telling comment on German priorities, Austrian isolation and the state of relations between the allies in the summer of 1914.

Certainly, the belated honeymoon in Austro-Italian relations, characterised by Aehrenthal's wooing of Italy, the cooling of Italy's relations with the Entente Powers during the Tripoli War, and her co-operation with Austria-Hungary against Slav expansionism in the Balkan Wars, was well and truly over by 1914. When in the spring the Italians heard rumours that the Monarchy was planning to purchase Mount Lovčen – a strategic point dominating the bay of Cattaro – from Montenegro, they talked of going to war rather than permit this. Nor was irredentism dead. In August 1913 the hysterical reaction in Italy to the decree of the *Statthalter* of Trieste removing Italian nationals from the city council had shown that large numbers of Italians still took a sweeping view of what was their concern. True, some military men in Italy, notably the chief of staff, General Pollio, were still loyal to the alliance; and in the summer of 1913 an Austro-Italian naval agreement had provided for wartime co-operation against the French in the Mediterranean under an Austro-Hungarian supreme command. But the Italian military attaché left Conrad in no doubt as to the realities of the situation; and Conrad rightly regarded Austro-Italian military conversations as no more than window-dressing. As he told Franz Joseph in March 1914, one thing was certain: Italy would not fulfil any of her alliance commitments – in this respect, at least, she was a dependable ally.

The Triple Alliance being in such disarray, it was little wonder that the purposeful diplomacy of the Triple Entente Powers was making steady progress in all the Balkan capitals; and that in so far as this served to whet the appetite of Serbia, a situation of some menace to the Monarchy was developing. Not that there was any imminent danger of war: the Serbian government was for the present fully occupied with bludgeoning into submission its newly acquired subjects in Macedonia, where conflicts between the civilian and military authorities precipitated a full-scale political crisis in Belgrade by the middle of June. Serbia's ultimate aims were clear, however: Pašić had been convinced since the end of the Second Balkan War that Serbia, having dealt with Turkey, must prepare for 'the second round against Austria', and during his visit to St Petersburg in February 1914 he received from Nicholas II himself the promise that Russia would some day come to the rescue of Serbia's kinsmen held in bondage across the Save. In any case, even Serbia's normal peacetime behaviour seemed unsatisfactory enough to Vienna. Not only had the Serbian government, in flagrant violation of its promise of 1909 to live on good neighbourly terms with Austria-Hungary, continued to tolerate on its territory propaganda organisations, and even terrorist groups, who operated in the South Slav areas of the Monarchy. Equally objectionable, in general political terms, was the Serbian government's alleged plan to advance to the Adriatic by means of a union with Montenegro; and, by making concessions in Macedonia to Bulgaria, to reconstitute the Balkan League. Whether this last was envisaged as defensive or not, the Ballhausplatz was in no doubt as to its ultimate purpose – 'expansion at the expense of the territorial integrity of the Monarchy, by means of a step-like [*staffelweise*] shifting of frontiers from east to west'.[63] The press was almost obsessively sensitive on the point: a new Balkan League, the *Neue Freie Press* declared in February 1914, would be 'a dagger in the hands of Russia pointed straight at the heart of Austria'.[64]

It was significant, and ominous, that the press in sounding the alarm pointed its accusatory finger not so much at the Balkan states as at Russia. Indeed, the spring of 1914 witnessed a veritable press campaign against that Power in the Monarchy – perhaps partly a reflection of an equally ominous press campaign in Germany that both confirmed and reflected the growing conviction in ruling circles there that war with Russia was indeed not far off. In

63. OUA, VIII, No. 9918.
64. B.D., X/1, No. 346.

Austria-Hungary, as in Germany, the furore was augmented by an armaments race, the Monarchy countering the steady growth of Russia's forces with another army bill (June 1914) to increase the size of the contingents annually recruited to the Common Army. Even an Austro-Russian irredentist dispute came to light, with mutual recriminations about Catholic intrigues among Russia's Ruthenian subjects and Russian Orthodox propaganda flooding into the Ruthenian areas of Galicia. Berchtold himself declared in June 1914 that the Ruthenian question would be 'decisive' for Austro-Russian relations.[65] But 'the plans which Serbia is weaving in the Balkans under Russia's auspices'[66] continued to cause Vienna most concern of all. Whatever the cause, the cold war in which Russia and Austria-Hungary had been locked since the collapse of the Entente in 1908 intensified sharply in 1914. The conciliatory Thurn was recalled from the St Petersburg embassy; even the pacific Tisza was beginning to despair of Russia; and Franz Joseph himself decided, in view of her remorseless arming, that she was a hopeless case, and that nothing more could be done about her.[67] Meanwhile the press, foreign observers were dismayed to note, continued to use language that would have been more appropriate had Russia and Austria-Hungary been on the verge of actual war.

Berchtold decided to seek his salvation not in war, but in a diplomatic offensive. He was now convinced – and Franz Joseph agreed with him – that something would have to be done to arrest the steady and disastrous decline of the Monarchy's diplomatic position. In June he embarked on yet another campaign to call the wayward Germans to order, directing Baron Matscheko (one of his assistants in the Ballhausplatz) to draw up a memorandum on the Balkan situation for the enlightenment of Berlin.[68] It was essential that Germany should bring her policy into line with Austria-Hungary's if there was to be any hope of frustrating the efforts of the Triple Entente Powers to build up a new Balkan League, completing the encirclement of the Monarchy from the south. As for practical remedies, the Romanian government should be summoned to show its colours and announce the alliance to the public. If it did not dare do this, then Vienna would at least know the worst, and could take measures to defend Transylvania without regard for an alliance that had proved itself a worthless scrap of

---

65. Z.A.B. Zeman, *The Break-up of the Habsburg Empire* (London 1961), p. 12.
66. Mensdorff MSS, Karton 9, Forgách to Mensdorff, 5 February 1914.
67. Wagner, 'Kaiser Franz Joseph', p. 275.
68. M.B.A. Peterson, 'Das österreichisch-ungarische Memorandum an Deutschland vom 5 Juli 1914' in *Scandia* 30 (1964), pp. 138–90.

paper. Nor should Romanian susceptibilities be allowed to stand in the way of a serious effort to secure an alliance with Bulgaria – and possibly Turkey might be brought in too. Even Serbia might yet be brought to reason by economic concessions and Romanian advice: but the Matscheko memorandum was not very hopeful about this, and argued on the whole that Serbia was probably irreconcilable.

It must be emphasised that the Matscheko memorandum contained not the slightest hint of war. Certainly, it marks the end of a long period of drift and indecision in the Ballhausplatz, and an attempt by the Austrians to give a firm lead and to devise a feasible Balkan policy for the Dual Alliance. Nevertheless, this was still a long-term policy, an attempt to solve the problem by patient and persevering diplomacy. The Ballhausplatz was in no great hurry: Matscheko had completed his memorandum by 24 June; and four days later it was still lying on Berchtold's writing table, awaiting approval, when Archduke Franz Ferdinand and his consort arrived at Sarajevo.

The Sarajevo assassinations radically transformed the situation from the point of view of the decision-makers in Vienna. Suddenly and dramatically that brand of South Slav irredentism that flourished in Serbia and spread its tentacles into the Monarchy stood revealed as an immediate and mortal threat to the position of the dynasty as lords of Bosnia, and, by implication, to the very existence of the Monarchy among the ranks of the Great Powers. To most people in the Ballhausplatz, it now seemed that only military action against Serbia could counteract the effect on the public mind of the spectacular deeds of nationalist terrorism. A secret and laborious diplomatic offensive of the kind envisaged by the Matscheko memorandum would no longer suffice to redress the situation. On the contrary, as far as the public would be able to see, the Monarchy would appear to be doing nothing – to lack even the will to survive. True, Tisza was still for patience, arguing that the diplomatic situation might yet improve – for instance, given time, the Monarchy might be able to win over Bulgaria and make sure of Romania. But Berchtold was adamant: failure to take vigorous action now would be universally regarded as such a clear 'renunciation of our Great Power position'[69] as would itself deprive any diplomatic offensive of all hope of success. No Balkan government would dream of casting in its lot with such a feeble Power. On the contrary, the disastrous trends of the past six months would only be accelerated: a new Balkan League would soon be on the

69. Hantsch, *Berchtold* II, p. 562.

scene. The only hope was a military offensive, either to reduce Serbia to the vassal status she had had in the 1880s, or to annihilate her and partition her between Bulgaria, Albania and Greece (thereby neatly bringing those states into Austria-Hungary's orbit) – at any rate, as Franz Joseph wrote to Wilhelm II on 2 July, 'to eliminate Serbia as a political power-factor [*Machtfaktor*] in the Balkans'.[70]

Now such a course of action would have grave international implications. The very considerations that commended it to Vienna made it totally unacceptable to St Petersburg. To Vienna, it was obvious that the downfall of Serbia – and, even more, Russia's inability to prevent it – would serve as an object lesson to the Balkan states, and put an end to all talk of Balkan leagues directed from St Petersburg against the Dual Monarchy. More than this: it implied, as Berchtold himself admitted, the complete renunciation by Russia of all influence in the Balkans ('einem Verzicht Rußlands auf jeden Einfluß auf dem Balkan'). Rather than accept this, however, Russia was likely to fight, whatever threats Germany might utter: and herein lay the danger of a continental war. Even this, the Austrians were prepared to contemplate. Although in June 1914 no one in Vienna, Belgrade or St Petersburg had been thinking in terms of war, the terrorists at Sarajevo had contrived a situation that, given the mentality of the decision-makers of the time, hardly admitted of any other solution. Before Sarajevo, the Austrians had been thinking in terms of re-establishing in the Balkans the kind of balance of power, tolerable at least to all parties, that had existed before the Balkan wars. Now, to the statesmen of Vienna, the choice seemed stark and simple, and the facts of the situation inescapable. Inaction would mean the total collapse of Austria-Hungary's diplomatic position, and of any hopes of saving it by diplomacy: action would equally inevitably entail the destruction of Russia's diplomatic position – which St Petersburg could hardly accept without a fight. However the chancelleries might manoeuvre, there was no escaping this.

In this situation, internal political factors could hardly have any really determining effect on the government's decision either way. True, the view that the Dual Monarchy was by 1914 in a critical state bordering on dissolution, which rendered some foreign action imperative as a diversion or as a solution, is not without a certain plausibility. The problem of South Slav discontent, exacerbated by a major quarrel between Budapest and the Croatian Diet, had

70. OUA, VIII, No. 9984.

become more serious since 1912, and was anything but alleviated by the government's continuing to treat Bosnia and the Herzegovina essentially as a colony or militarily occupied territory unintegrated into the general political structure of the Monarchy. At the same time, the triumphs of Serbia in the Balkan Wars had enhanced the attractiveness to some South Slav enthusiasts inside the Monarchy of the self-styled 'Piedmont of the Southern Slavs'. Elsewhere, quarrels between Czechs and Germans over language issues had resulted in the suspension by the summer of 1914 of both the Diet in Prague and the Parliament in Vienna. Nor did there seem to be any way out by means of constitutional reform. Even if the decision-makers in Vienna had been prepared to contemplate it, any attempt to tamper with the dualist structure would involve – as Aehrenthal had reluctantly recognised after 1909, and as Archduke Franz Ferdinand had anticipated with some relish – the tremendous upheaval of a showdown with the Magyars, perhaps even civil war.

Yet observers such as the German ambassador, who in May 1914 declared that the Monarchy seemed to be 'falling apart at the seams [*in allen Fugen*]'[71] were perhaps unduly alarmist.[72] After all, apart from a brief spell in 1906–8 parliamentary life in Austria had hardly functioned properly for the past twenty years. The nationalist wrangles that paralysed it were merely squabbles within a political élite. The mass of the emperor's subjects in 1914 would have been very surprised to hear that the Monarchy was 'falling apart'. Indeed, it was yet to survive another four years of incomparably more serious crises, during which the Common Army – the sinews of the Monarchy – remained for the great part impeccably loyal. The outbreak of war saw no refusals to enlist, such as had occurred among Czech reservists in Galicia in 1913. The South Slav regiments, as if to wash their hands of all guilt for the Sarajevo murders (which had precipitated serious anti-Serbian riots in Bosnia and Croatia) were particularly zealous in their loyalty. And on no occasion did the government have to order its troops to fire on its subjects, as the British were to do in Ireland. It was hardly the threat of imminent collapse that drove the Monarchy to war in 1914. The threat in 1914 was an external one, to the Monarchy's prestige among the Great Powers. And although the Russo-Serbian threat certainly had domestic implications, these were only, in 1914 at least, that the South Slavs would become more tiresomely

71. G.P., XXXIX, No. 15734.
72. For the best recent summary of this debate, see Sked, *Decline*, pp. 229ff.

difficult, not impossible, to govern. Altogether, the domestic situation in 1914 was infinitely less grave than that of 1903–6: then, one of the master races had been in open revolt, and the result had been the virtual paralysis of the Monarchy in foreign affairs. In 1914 the situation was very different: war was a feasible option precisely because the domestic situation was not particularly serious (while still perhaps being serious enough to engender enough pessimism, or exasperation, to provide an additional incentive to action).

The Monarchy's military position was similarly ambiguous. The army bills of 1912 and 1914 had raised the wartime strength of the army to 1,500,000, compared with the million or so with which the Monarchy had had to manage for the previous twenty-four years. This was no doubt a significant improvement; but it was partly offset by the fact that, with the increase coming so late in the day, the Common Army was still in the throes of reorganisation in 1914. And even the relative improvement in the Monarchy's position was unlikely to be lasting, given the frantic activity of Russia and France. In May 1914 Moltke admitted to Conrad that the German army was not superior in numbers to the French – which naturally rendered the Schlieffen plan (and any Austro-Hungarian plans based on it) hazardous in the extreme. And the Russian armaments programme of December 1913 planned to increase the size of the army to a wartime strength of 2,000,000 within the next five years. The military situation in 1914 was hardly inviting, from an Austro-Hungarian point of view. Conrad was aware of the deficiencies, of the near certainty that Russia would intervene, and of the equal certainty that neither Italy nor Romania would lend the Monarchy any assistance. Nevertheless, he threw his weight behind Berchtold and against Tisza in demanding action. For the relatively healthy position of the Austro-Hungarian army, with its recent additions of strength, would be bound to deteriorate year by year in the face of Russia's armaments, with which the Monarchy could never hope to compete. As the unrepentant Conrad later observed: in 1909 it would have been a game with stacked cards, in 1912 with equal chances; by 1914 it was *va banque*.

Even so, it was by no means certain for a couple of weeks after Sarajevo that the Monarchy would be able to proceed to war. The attitude of Germany had yet to be ascertained. Her support would be absolutely essential against any Russian intervention; and in view of her recent behaviour, Franz Joseph felt there was reason to doubt whether she would lend any help at all. Berchtold consequently proceeded to redraft the Matscheko memorandum, turning it from a programme of long-term diplomatic action into a plea for immediate military action against Serbia. This, he saw, would involve a serious risk of a major war. Hence he dropped the proposal to summon Romania to show her colours: that would be needlessly risky at a moment when the Monarchy might find itself in desperate need of Romania's goodwill. At the same time, he expanded the section that dealt with the threat to the Monarchy from Serbia and from a new Balkan League under Russia's auspices. On 5 July Count Hoyos took the memorandum to Berlin, together with a letter from Franz Joseph to Wilhelm II asking whether, if Austria-Hungary moved against Serbia and Russia intervened, Germany would stand by her ally.

The Austrians need not have worried. The Germans had good reasons enough of their own to support Vienna in taking a strong line. In the first place, they had recently been coming to view the fiasco of their own Balkan diplomacy with a frustration and despair that rivalled that of the Austrians. The prospect of a Balkan League directed from St Petersburg, a causeway of Russian influence stretching from Romania to the Adriatic, and sealing off not only Austria-Hungary, but Germany too, with her vast stake in the Ottoman Empire, was not unnaturally a cause of some alarm to Berlin. Berchtold's arguments found ready ears. In the second place, and perhaps even more important, the Germans were coming to regard their position in the European states system in general as increasingly precarious, in view of the steadily growing military power of France and Russia. As in the days of the *Neue Kurs* and at the time of the Bosnian crisis, the general diplomatic position of the stronger partner in the Dual Alliance was such as to render it dependent on the weaker. In July 1914 the Germans feared that if, after all the friction of the past six months, they were to thwart their Austro-Hungarian allies yet again, the result might be the total isolation of Germany and the final destruction of her own position among the Powers – Austria-Hungary might either lose all patience with Germany, and seek her salvation in a deal with Russia; or she might lapse into a complete apathy and despair, virtually ceasing to count as a Great Power. Ironically enough, one of Berchtold's arguments for taking a strong line was that otherwise Germany might despair of Austria-Hungary and abandon her for lost. In the final crisis, the solidarity of the Dual Alliance Powers was more the product of their mutual mistrust than of *deutsche Treue*.

It is true that, even when they promised their full support, on 5 July, the Germans still hoped to exercise a measure of control over their ally. They cherished the vague hope that any Austro-Serbian war might be localised: hence, their emphatic advice that if Vienna decided to act against Serbia, there was every reason to act with all possible speed – it would be vital to make use of the shock effect which the Sarajevo assassinations had produced at Tsarskoe Selo if there was to be any hope of restraining Russia from intervention. But in the last resort they were prepared to go through thick and thin with their allies; and their analysis of the issues at stake was much the same. If France and Russia would rather fight than tolerate an Austro-Hungarian victory, then so be it. The military situation could only deteriorate from Germany's point of view; and in a war over a Balkan issue Berlin could feel more sure of Austria-Hungary's loyalty than in one arising from a Franco-German dispute. The essential point, on which both members of the Dual Alliance were for once agreed, was that there must be no retreat; and that this particular Near Eastern crisis must be resolved in favour of the Central Powers, whether at the cost of a European war or not.

Berchtold found the German expressions of support very useful. In the first place, they helped him to convince Budapest of the need for action.[73] In a conference of ministers as late as 7 July Tisza was still holding out against everybody else and demanding a diplomatic solution to the crisis. He had good reasons for opposing war: defeat would mean the annihilation of Great Hungary; whereas victory might, as had been feared in the years after the Austro-Prussian War, strengthen the hand of the dynasty to implement centralist or trialist policies that would be equally disastrous for Magyar supremacy. True, even Tisza was beginning to wonder whether Serbia was not perhaps a hopeless case, especially as the Serbian press had maintained an unrepentant, indeed boastful, attitude ever since the assassinations. But it was probably strong pressure from Berchtold, from the Common Finance Minister, Burián, and, above all, from the German ambassador, that by 14 July brought him to accept the necessity for strong action. The lesson of Sadowa, that the independence of Hungary depended in the last resort on the goodwill of Germany, was still valid after Sarajevo.

Not that Germany's pledge of support, essential though it might have been to any plan of action, determined the timing and manner of its implementation. The subsequent development of the Serbian crisis showed that Austro-Hungarian policy was still not made in

---

73. N. Stone, 'Hungary and the crisis of July 1914', in *Journal of Contemporary History*, I (1966), pp. 153–70.

Berlin. With scant regard for German advice the Austrians put their trust, not in sentimental appeals to monarchical – or even allied – solidarity, but in the element of surprise, to spread confusion among their potential opponents. They decided against informing their Italian and Romanian allies of their intentions, assuming – rightly – that they would refuse to recognise the *casus foederis* in any case; and fearing a leak of the news of the planned action to the Entente Powers. Similar considerations determined them to defer their *démarche* at Belgrade until 23 July, by which time the French president would have completed his forthcoming state visit to St Petersburg, and would be more or less incommunicado on the high seas.[74] Three long weeks were spent in a painstaking collation of evidence to prove that Serbia had blatantly violated her promise of 1909 to live on good neighbourly terms with the Monarchy – the charge on which the note of 23 July was to be based (no evidence having been found of Serbian complicity in the actual assassination) – in the vague hope that the resultant dossier might convince the Powers of the justice of the Austro-Hungarian demands. Yet all these devices were for the decision-makers in Vienna very much of a secondary order. On 18 July the council of ministers did not even bother to discuss the chances of Russian intervention; and Franz Joseph himself took it for granted that 'Russia cannot possibly swallow [*sich . . .gefallen lassen*] this note'.[75] After all, whether the note, with its demand that Austro-Hungarian officials be allowed to operate on Serbian territory to assist in suppressing seditious movements, was designed to be unacceptable or not; whether Serbia peacefully accepted her reduction to the status of a satellite of the Monarchy, or refused to submit and was overwhelmed, was immaterial. The result in all cases would be the annihilation of Russian influence in the Balkans. The issue was whether Serbia was to be allowed to continue to exist as a Russian outpost, indeed, the kingpin of the Russian position in the Balkans; or whether Austria-Hungary was to liberate herself from this menace, regardless of the risks involved, in an attempt to destroy both Serbia's liberty and Russia's prestige at one blow.

The Austrians had chosen the latter course; and once Belgrade refused to submit to the note of 23 July – fobbing Vienna off with a virtual repetition of the promises of 1909 with no guarantees as to their fulfilment – they set about the destruction of Serbia with great determination and speed. On 27 July diplomatic relations with

74. Keiger, *France and the Origins of the War*, pp. 152–3.
75. Robert A. Kann, *Kaiser Franz Joseph und der Ausbruch des ersten Weltkrieges* (Vienna 1971), p. 12.

Belgrade were broken off; war was declared on the following day; and although the army could not be mobilised for major operations for a further three weeks, Belgrade was bombarded on 29 July. True, Conrad would have preferred to delay the declaration of war until the army was ready to start operations; but Berchtold insisted that 'the diplomatic situation will not hold as long as that'.[76] He was anxious for some demonstrative military action that would transfer the crisis immediately and irrevocably from the diplomatic to the military sphere, and forestall any attempt by the other Great Powers to intervene with another face-saving but worthless diplomatic solution. There must be no more compromises, either direct as in 1909 or under the cloak of the Concert as in 1912 and 1913. On that the Austrians were determined: they had taken charge of events, and would accept no advice from others, friend or foe. Grey's attempts to invoke the Concert, and Wilhelm II's hints that the Austrians might for the moment content themselves with the bombardment of Belgrade, were brushed aside in Vienna. At the eleventh hour, and in what proved to be Vienna's last independent move before it lost control of events for ever, discussions were started with St Petersburg. But these proved to be less an echo of the *entente* of the days of Goluchowski and Aehrenthal, now truly lost beyond recall, than of the dialogue of the deaf that followed San Stefano. Berchtold was interested only in discussing the means by which the Powers might bring Serbia to submit to the terms of 23 July; and he refused to accept Sazonov's preliminary stipulation that the Monarchy first cease all military operations against Serbia. Nevertheless, these strange negotiations were still going on, or rather, the deadlock was still being discussed, when Russia's mobilisation and Germany's reaction to it announced the outbreak of European war.

This development, although hardly unpredictable, was highly unwelcome to Vienna at this juncture. From this point, the Dual Monarchy lost control of events – indeed, to a large degree, of its own destiny. Austro-Hungarian policy was made with an eye to the Near Eastern balance of power, not to a world balance (which became the issue when Great Britain joined the war against Germany on 4 August). The Austrians had been above all concerned to re-establish their position in the Near East by crushing Serbia and destroying the influence of Russia. And although they had been undeterred by the thought that this might well entail a European war, they had few interests of their own in such a war. Austria-

---

76. F. Conrad von Hoetzendorf, *Aus meiner Dienstzeit*, IV, p. 132.

Hungary's sense of priorities, therefore, was quite different from Germany's; and the resultant conflict of interests was to render the life of the Dual Alliance in war as turbulent and strife-ridden as it had been in thirty-five wearisome years of peace. Needless to say, the Triple and Romanian alliances did not operate at all. Not that Austria-Hungary's offensive operations raised the *casus foederis* anyway. King Carol and a few traditionalists would have liked to support the Monarchy; but they could not prevail against the rest of the government in Bucharest. Romania declared her neutrality on 4 August. Italy had already done so on 3 August. It was henceforth a question of what compensation the Monarchy would have to pay to hold her to mere neutrality; and as Rome began to talk at once about compensation from the territory of the Monarchy, Kálnoky's sins of omission of 1887[77] were now visited on his successors.

The Dual Alliance was hardly in any happier condition. It was not until 6 August, after a week of hectoring from Berlin, that the Monarchy declared war on Russia. Nor was there any desire in Vienna to force a Mediterranean confrontation with the fleets of the Western Powers. France and Great Britain, ironically enough, were afraid of the Austro-Hungarian fleet, which with four dreadnoughts was potentially dangerous so long as the French fleet was engaged in ferrying troops to Europe from North Africa. It was only on 12 August that the Western Powers declared war on Austria-Hungary.[78] An even more striking illustration of the divergent interests of Vienna and Berlin was the fact that whereas the Germans wanted an immediate and powerful Austro-Hungarian offensive into Poland to take on the weight of Russia's forces, Conrad persisted until 5 August in implementing 'Plan B', sending the supplementary *B-Staffel* not to Galicia but to the Balkan front. Like Berchtold, he was above all intent on re-establishing the Monarchy's position in the Near East by finally crushing Serbia, and Germany's demands for action in the north were given short shrift. (After all, for Conrad, Germany was as much a threat to the Monarchy's position in the Near East as Russia was.) In the end, it was only an even more flagrant breach of faith by Germany – who refused to undertake any offensive at all from East Prussia – that forced Conrad to a belated and disastrous implementation of 'Plan R'. Berchtold's threats to denounce the alliance were at such a moment hardly convincing: there was nothing for it but to try to

---

77. See above, p. 178.
78. F.R. Bridge, 'The British Declaration of War on Austria-Hungary in 1914', in *Slavonic and East European Review*, (1969), pp. 400–22.

8
The World War and the End of Austria-Hungary, 1914–1918[1]

Compared with the Entente, the Central Powers were militarily well prepared for war, but they were not prepared for a long war. It was disastrous, therefore, when errors and confusion over the details of planning lost them the chance of a quick victory. If the Germans failed to put up enough men against the Russians, the Austrians' concentration of their efforts against Serbia fatally weakened their Northern Army in the critical early weeks. (This reflected Conrad's distrust of German ambitions in the Balkans, and his determination to establish Austro-Hungarian, not allied, control of Serbia.)[2] The Russians turned out to be far better prepared than the Austrians had expected. By 1 September, Lemberg was lost, and the whole of East Galicia by the end of the month. In December, the Austrians retreated from Serbia; and the offensive they started against the Russians in the Carpathians in January 1915 soon got bogged down in deep snow. These disasters were partly attributable to the inability of Germany, preoccupied with enormous Russian odds in the north, to lend the help that Conrad had expected; and to problems arising from the lack of a unified command – which were to bedevil Austro-German military co-operation for the next two years. Nevertheless, even at this early stage the Germans began to look patronisingly on the Austro-Hungarian ally as the 'schwachen Bruder'; whereas Conrad

1. The following works are of particular relevance to this chapter: M. Komjáthy (ed.) *Protokolle des gemeinsamen Ministerrates der österreichisch-ungarischen Monarchie 1914–1918* (Budapest 1966); F. Fischer, *Griff nach der Weltmacht* (Düsseldorf 1964); G. Silberstein, *The Troubled Alliance, German–Austrian Relations 1914–17* (Lexington 1970); L. Valiani, *The End of Austria-Hungary* (London 1973); J. Lilla, 'Innen- und außenpolitische Aspekte der austropolnischen Lösung, 1914–16', in *Mitteilungen des österreichischen Staatsarchivs* (hereafter cited as *MöSta*), 30 (1977), pp. 221–50; Robert A. Kann, *Die Sixtusaffäre und die geheimen Friedensverhandlungen Oesterreich-Ungarns im ersten Weltkrieg* (Vienna 1966); and the works by C.A. Macartney, A.J.P. Taylor, A. Sked and I. Diószegi cited in Chapter 1, note 1.
2. N. Stone, 'Die Mobilmachung der österreichisch-ungarischen Armee, 1914', in *Militärgeschichtlichen Mitteilungen*, 16, pp. 67–95.

was no less disillusioned about 'our underhanded enemy', Germany.[3]

Now tension with Germany could be dangerous for the Monarchy, if only because with the outbreak of war alternatives to the German alliance had largely ceased to exist. It was not merely the fact that the Monarchy had declared war on Russia on 6 August (Great Britain and France declared war on the Monarchy on 12 August), but that with the outbreak of war the aims of Austro-Hungarian policy developed in a direction totally incompatible with those of the Entente Powers. Fundamentally, of course, the aim was still the maintenance of Austria-Hungary as a Great Power – an aim which was, as later peace-soundings were to show, by no means uncongenial to at least Great Britain and France. But the means by which the Austrians decided to achieve this aim – the attainment of security in the south-east by the subjugation of Serbia, and, beyond that, as Berchtold told the Bulgarians in November 1914, 'the main aim . . . to weaken Russia lastingly'[4] – were hopelessly incompatible with Entente interests. They could only be secured through a victorious peace; and for this, German assistance and co-operation would be absolutely essential.

The question remained, however, of whether the means would not defeat the ends; whether the gaining of security against the Slav threat to integrity of the Monarchy might not undermine its existence as a Great Power in another direction, by reducing it to a state of total dependence on its powerful ally. The statesmen of the Monarchy had always been aware of this danger, and had managed in the previous forty years of peace to avert it. Under the stresses that developed in the struggle for existence that broke out in 1914, however, this danger assumed altogether different proportions, and proved within a mere four years irresistible. As the technological demands of war increased, so the more developed areas of central Europe increased in relative importance – Austria *vis-à-vis* Hungary, Germany *vis-à-vis* the Monarchy. The minutes of successive meetings of the councils of ministers document the growing awareness that Austrian industry could not manage without German capital.[5] In economic terms, the Monarchy was by no means well prepared for war: its gold reserves were relatively low, and it was not self-supporting in grain. The loss of Galicia, the granary of Cisleithania, led by June 1915 to the first imports of grain from Germany. As the Monarchy's economic dependence on Germany grew, and as it had to call repeatedly on German military assist-

3. Silberstein, *Troubled Alliance*, p. 265.
4. Fischer, *Griff*, p. 157.
5. Komjáthy, *Protokolle*, pp. 54–9.

ance, its statesmen had to take German views increasingly into account in their diplomacy. As the Monarchy's financial, economic, and military dependence on Germany increased, so the options open to its diplomacy diminished. By the summer of 1918 even the most Austrophile circles in the west, who had as late as January been promoting the idea of preserving the Monarchy as a useful element in the balance of power, despaired of it. It had been reduced from being an independent, if relatively weak, Great Power in 1914 to a helpless if resentful satellite of Germany.

Apart from the general problem of the Monarchy's role as an independent Power in the European states system, there was also the problem of whether risking falling into the position of a German satellite would secure even the Monarchy's more particular aims. For the war aims of the two allies were by no means identical. Fundamentally, the Austrians had no quarrel with the Western Powers, little interest in fighting for Germany's position in Alsace, and none in encouraging German schemes to strike at Great Britain in Persia or Egypt – where the Austrians still preferred to see the British, rather than the Germans, in control.[6] That suspicion of German commercial and political ambitions in the Balkans and the eastern Mediterranean that had been so marked a feature of Austrian thinking before 1914 remained so after the outbreak of the war; and it was to be exacerbated by an unending dispute with Germany over the future of Russian Poland. On the other hand, if Austria-Hungary's chief enemy was Russia, the Germans were very much preoccupied with the struggle against the British Empire, and were at times prepared, in 1915 and 1916, to consider a separate peace with Russia, even at the price of allowing her to retain her conquests in Galicia.

These differences were only symptomatic, however, of a broad difference of approach between the two allies. From 1914 to 1918 the fundamental principle of German policy was that the war must be won at all costs – even at the cost of the Monarchy's sacrificing territory in order to influence or appease potentially useful third parties such as Turkey, Italy or the Balkan states. The Austrians, for their part, while recognising the need to win the war, were equally concerned to do nothing that might prejudice their own position in the Near East after the war. They were above all determined to uphold the integrity of the Monarchy, which, as Berchtold testily reminded the Germans *à propos* Romanian claims,

6. F.G. Weber, *Eagles on the Crescent: Germany, Austria and the Diplomacy of the Turkish alliance, 1914–1918* (Ithaca 1970), p. 114.

was after all what the war was about: if the Monarchy was to be dismembered anyway, there was no point in fighting at all.[7]

The case of Italy was a good example of the divergence between German and Austrian attitudes. Italy was under no obligation to assist her allies: the war was not defensive, and in failing to inform Italy of the ultimatum in advance, Berchtold had violated the spirit of the Triple Alliance. Moreover, according to Aehrenthal's own redefinition of Article VII in 1911, even a temporary occupation by one party of territory in the Balkans entitled the other to claim compensation; and in 1887 Kálnoky had fatally omitted to secure written confirmation of Franz Joseph's view that Italy could not claim compensation in the territories of the Monarchy itself. True, the Germans were under an illusion when they advised concessions in the hope of securing actual military assistance from Italy, who, with her long coastline, could never contemplate fighting Great Britain and France. But the fact remained that, if the Austrians had been prepared to pay for Italy's connivance at the destruction of Serbia, this would have raised insurmountable barriers between Italy and the Entente; and, after all, Conrad admitted that he had not sufficient men available to fight Italy. Nevertheless, when the council of ministers discussed Italy's claim to Trentino on 8 August, Tisza, with Hungary's interests in mind, advised against setting any precedents for Romanian claims; and his Austrian colleague, Stürgkh, disingenuously suggested deceiving Italy with an insincere promise that territory would be ceded after the war: 'against brigands such as the Italians are now, no diplomatic swindle would be excessive'.[8] Perhaps with more honesty than wisdom, the conference decided to reject the Italian request.

By the spring of 1915 military developments were bringing the Austrians to reconsider. It was not simply that the defeat in Serbia had made the Monarchy less awesome to Italy – in January Sonnino increased his claim for compensation to include territory in Istria. The Monarchy was also faced with embarrassing problems in the south-east. Despite Pallavicini's advice that the defensive alliance of 2 August 1914 had given the Monarchy all it needed when Turkey had cut Russia off from her allies by closing the Straits in September, Berchtold had joined with the Germans in coaxing Turkey into the war on 11 November. His successor even swallowed the onerous obligations which Germany assumed in the second Turkish alliance of 11 January 1915. Austria-Hungary's – albeit reluc-

7. Silberstein, *Troubled Alliance*, p. 184.
8. Komjáthy, *Protokolle*, p. 163.

tant – accession to the treaty on 18 March certainly restricted her freedom of action in the future, committing her to support the Ottoman Empire against coalitions of Balkan states into the 1920s.[9] Yet all this brought very little in return. The Austrians deplored Turkey's decision to launch an Egyptian campaign – a purely German interest – instead of striking at Odessa. The Egyptian campaign was a fiasco anyway; and although the Entente's Dardanelles expedition in March was also to fail, the problem of maintaining the Central Powers' supply lines to Turkey was becoming serious by the spring of 1915. It was for this reason that the Germans now began to press for a Serbian campaign. This plan, however, not only cut across Conrad's plans for an offensive to relieve Russian pressure in the north: it increased the blackmailing power of Bulgaria and Romania, and it immeasurably increased Austria-Hungary's vulnerability to pressure from Italy.

Even so, the Austrians were fatally slow to face realities. True, on 9 January Berchtold, under strong pressure from Germany, steeled himself to advise Franz Joseph to cede the Trentino. But the emperor clung to it as stubbornly as he had clung to Venetia in 1866. The upshot was that when Berchtold persisted, pressing his views on Stürgkh and Tisza, the latter persuaded him that he would do better to resign (11 January). His successor was Stefan, Count Burián, who after a modest diplomatic career in the Balkans had risen to great heights in domestic politics, serving for nearly a decade (1903–12) as Common Finance Minister, and latterly as the Hungarian government's minister *a latere* at Vienna. He was not, however, the docile tool of Tisza that some supposed. On the contrary, according to one of Berchtold's assistants, it was he who had 'worked Tisza up' to oppose the proposed concessions to Italy;[10] and colleagues were struck, after three years of Berchtold's diffidence, by Burián's stubborn tenacity and excessive self-confidence. 'If he goes on like this', Forgách wrote on 24 February, 'in two months' time we shall be at war with Italy and Romania. He says he would prefer that to voluntarily surrendering one square metre.'[11] The conciliatory and experienced Italian ambassador found the new minister difficult to deal with: he had 'more the mentality of a disputatious, dogmatic lawyer than of a diplomat'.[12] Burián's judgment was certainly not above reproach. On 3 February, he

9. F.R. Bridge, 'Austria-Hungary and the Ottoman Empire in the Twentieth Century', *MöSta*, 1982, pp. 234–71, at pp. 265–6.
10. Macchio MSS, Forgách to Macchio, 25 April 1931.
11. Quoted in Valiani, *End of Austria-Hungary*, p. 59.
12. Ibid.

confidently advised a council of ministers that Italy was in no condition to fight, and that the Monarchy should trust to a favourable turn of events on the Russian front.[13]

This was a sheer gamble, and Burián was forced to admit to a council of ministers on 8 March that it had not paid off.[14] Italy was still using Article VII to maintain an effective veto on Austro-Hungarian operations in the Balkans; and her army would be ready for action by mid-April. On the other hand, if agreement could be reached over Article VII, Germany would guarantee that Italy would give Austria-Hungary a free hand in the Balkans in return. For these reasons, therefore, and 'because the military situation is so bad', Burián now advised giving way. Tisza, too, had changed his views since January: in Galicia, the great fortress of Premysl was about to fall to the Russians; the Dardanelles expedition might yet knock out Turkey; whereas an agreement with Italy might both isolate Romania and prepare the way for lasting co-operation with Italy against Slavdom after the war. The Austrian ministers took a tougher line – it was, after all, Austrian and not Hungarian territory that was at stake. On the whole they regarded Italy as a declared enemy, both now and in the future; and Conrad, even in this extremity, swore that he would fight to the death rather than yield the Isonzo line. Their views prevailed. The council decided to offer Italy only the Trentino, and that to be handed over only after the end of the war, when, as Stürgkh ominously observed, things would be different.[15]

The Italians were not deceived. They speedily concluded the Treaty of London with the Entente (26 April), denounced the Triple Alliance on 4 May, and declared war on Austria-Hungary on 23 May. It is true that, again under German pressure, the Austrians made an eleventh-hour bid to save the situation when the Austro-Hungarian and German ambassadors at Rome presented Giolitti, now out of office but still a neutralist statesman of some weight, with a list of concessions that included the Trentino, the Isonzo line and Albania. But apart from the fact that the Vienna government felt that the ambassadors had gone too far, even this offer was only to become operative after a successful conclusion of the war; and it was accompanied by a demand for a completely free hand in the rest of the Balkans. (It is significant that the Austrians refused to contemplate a papal guarantee of the implementation of the agree-

---

13. Komjáthy, *Protokolle*, p. 195.
14. Ibid., pp. 216ff.
15. Valiani, *End of Austria-Hungary*, pp. 62–3.

ment.)[16] If the offer had been made in March, it might conceivably have enabled Giolitti to carry the day. On the other hand, it may well be that the issue had already been decided by events beyond the control of Vienna, notably, Germany's failure on the Marne in the previous September[17] – witness the conviction of the French from the start that 'l'Italie volera au secours du vainqueur',[18] and the desperate and daily exhortations to the Ballhausplatz from the Austrophiles at the Italian embassy 'donnez-vous des victoires, des victoires!!'.[19] Even so, the failure of statesmanship at Vienna, where high principle rather than realism prevailed, and where the errors of the 1860s were repeated, made its own contribution to events.

Italy's entry into the war was less disastrous for Austria-Hungary than it might have been. True, Germany lent her ally no assistance, and it was, in fact, Italy who declared war on Germany in 1916. (The Germans had no reason to burden themselves gratuitously with an Italian war, and the strictly anti-Russian alliance of 1879 did not oblige them to do so.) But, in the first place, the Italians were slow to organise their offensive, allowing Conrad to transfer eight divisions to the Italian front, which remained stable until 1916. In the second place, Conrad managed to persuade his German counterpart, Falkenhayn, to defer his projected Serbian campaign, and to take the pressure off the north-eastern frontier of the Monarchy by a major joint offensive against Russia. The Gorlice–Tarnow offensive started on 2 May; Premysl was retaken on 2 June, Lemberg on 22 June; the whole Russian front was unhinged, and Russian Poland was cleared by the end of September. This was indeed victory in the grand manner. But it had been achieved by German, rather than by Austro-Hungarian efforts. For the 'schwachen Bruder' the consequences of victory were to prove hardly less embarrassing than the earlier problems of defeat.

The first danger that now arose was that the Germans might sacrifice the interests of the Monarchy for the sake of a separate peace with Russia. Ever since their failure on the Marne in September 1914 the Germans had been toying with the idea of such a peace – involving, possibly, the cession to Russia of East Galicia; and this despite Berchtold's insistence on the disastrous consequences for

---

16. Ibid., pp. 70–1.
17. W.A. Renzi, *In the Shadow of the Sword, Italy's Neutrality and Entrance into the Great War, 1914–15* (New York 1987); J. Gooch, *Army State and Society in Italy, 1870–1915* (Basingstoke 1989).
18. L. Villari, *The war on the Italian front* (London 1925).
19. Macchio MSS, Forgách to Macchio, 25 April 1931.

Austria–Hungary of leaving Russia unweakened after the war, and despite Austrian insistence that the crushing of Serbia was essential for the Monarchy's security in the south-east.[20] Faced with the entry of Italy, however, the Austrians were in no position to argue with Berlin; and in the end they had no reason to do so, when it turned out that the sort of peace the Germans, in the intoxication of victory, were now aiming for might suit them very well. Russia was both to cede her western territories and to accept a position of dependency on the Central Powers – indeed, Conrad enthusiastically declared that such a Russia might even be offered an alliance.[21] Of course, the very features that made the plan attractive to the Austrians made it totally unacceptable to the Russians, who had suffered a reverse but were no means beaten. The incident is worth noting, however, as an example of the lack of realism and the excessive self-confidence that came to mark the diplomacy, not only of Berlin, but also of Vienna, as the war progressed. It should also be said that in the whole affair it was the interests of Germany, and not of Austria-Hungary, that were paramount; and that in their soundings of the Japanese in 1916 the Germans were again speculating about a separate peace with Russia involving the cession by Austria of East Galicia.[22]

Meanwhile, more concrete problems had arisen, notably in Poland.[23] Already in the last days of July 1914 the Habsburg government had been preparing to assume the odd role of a revolutionary Power, and to foment rebellion in Russian Poland. But Berchtold disapproved of Conrad's proclamation simply promising liberation to the Russian Poles, and declared in August that any liberated Poland must be included within the frontiers of the Monarchy. An independent Poland, he insisted, would inevitably lead to the defection of Galicia from the Monarchy; for, unlike the cowed and dragooned Poles of Prussia, Austria's Poles were cultivated and politically conscious. Until the summer of 1915 the military situation made the question largely theoretical, and the Germans were content to consider Berchtold's 'obviously unacceptable' proposals 'dilatorisch'.[24] But with the success of the Austro-German offensive, the question became acute. On 13 August, ten days after the fall of Warsaw, Búrian asked the Germans straight out to agree to the incorporation of Russian Poland into the Monarchy.

20. Fischer, *Griff*, p. 233.
21. Ibid., p. 240.
22. Ibid. p. 290.
23. Lilla, 'Austro-polnische Lösung', pp. 221–50.
24. Fischer, *Griff*, p. 230.

The Germans, loath to consider incorporating so many Catholic Poles and Jews into the German Empire, decided to agree to this 'Austro-Polish solution'. But they imposed several very important conditions, the purpose of which was not only to give Germany military security, but to extend German power, in the guise of *Mitteleuropa*, into Poland and beyond: 'to force Austria to give us the military and economic guarantees we need to keep the whole Monarchy, including Poland, at our side'.[25] Austria–Hungary was to agree not only to cede to Germany a large 'frontier strip', and to guarantee German economic interests in Poland; she was also to give guarantees of the continued predominance of the influence of the Austrian Germans in the Monarchy, and to conclude with Germany a military convention providing for German participation in the reorganisation of the Austro-Hungarian army. Falkenhayn demanded an 'indissoluble bond' between Germany and the Monarchy; and 'in so far as this requires it, Austria will have to give up her sovereignty'.[26] Jagow, the German foreign minister, declared that 'only through the closest military and economic union shall we achieve a permanent chaining of the Monarchy to ourselves, and at the same time a strengthening of the German element in Austria'.[27] These demands, reminiscent of Bismarck's demands on the South German states in 1866, partly reflected the low opinion the Germans had come to hold of the military, political and economic strength of the Monarchy. They also show that, if in July 1914 the issue had been the maintenance of Austria–Hungary as a Great Power, by 1915 the control of Austria–Hungary as a satellite had become a German war aim.

The Austrians, for their part, were initially pleased to hear that Germany endorsed the Austro-Polish solution, and cheerfully discussed its implementation in a council of ministers on 6 October 1915.[28] There, the 'trialist' solution originally envisaged by Berchtold was rejected: for Tisza, the dualist structure was a *noli me tangere*; and he further argued that the German alliance, vital to the Monarchy's security, would be undermined if such a 'decidedly anti-German element' as the Poles were given equality with the Germans and Magyars. The council decided in favour of 'sub-dualism', according to the Poles in Cisleithania a status similar to that of the Croats in Transleithania. These plans began to appear somewhat academic, however, when the Austrians learned of

25. Ibid., p. 256.
26. Lilla, 'Austro-polnische Lösung', p. 233.
27. Fischer, *Griff*, p. 256.
28. Komjáthy, *Protokolle*, pp. 285ff.

Germany's conditions, spelt out to Burián in Berlin in November. Burián was quite unable to accept Jagow's premise that the 1879 alliance pre-supposed a 'built-in [*gesicherte*] predominance of Germans and Magyars', somehow fixed in law: such a thing was constitutionally impossible in the Monarchy; and he categorically rejected Jagow's assumption 'that Austria-Hungary is merely a Germanic *Ostmark*'.[29] The year 1915 closed with the future development of the Austro-Polish question in considerable doubt.

Equally contentious was a whole complex of Balkan questions that had arisen as a result of Bulgaria's entry into the war in October 1915.[30] For the first year of the war Bulgaria had been able to play a waiting game: the Central Powers could offer her more in Macedonia than the Entente, hamstrung by their alliance with Serbia; but they were still susceptible to blackmail. A Bulgarian threat to join the Entente proved sufficient to extract a loan from the Central Powers in 1915; and Germany's urgent desire for a Serbian campaign to relieve Turkey was another trump card in Bulgaria's hand. It should be emphasised, however, that Bulgaria's decision to join the Central Powers – in the hope of profiting from their victories in the summer of 1915 – was hardly a diplomatic success for Austria-Hungary. The Monarchy had interests of its own to pursue in Macedonia, and Burián had been holding out against Bulgaria's 'unacceptable' claims there. Great was his anger and dismay, therefore, when the Bulgarians went behind his back and concluded a treaty with the Germans (6 September) giving them almost all they wanted; and when Berlin, arguing as usual in terms of the overall war effort, rather peremptorily forced Austria-Hungary to accede. True, Bulgarian assistance was useful in the ensuing October campaign against Serbia: by November the railway through Belgrade to Constantinople was in allied hands, as was Serbia itself by the end of the year. But not only did the Austrians find themselves – as they had feared – in a dispute with Bulgaria over zones of occupation in Macedonia. The way in which Berlin had taken the lead in the September negotiations represented an ominous incursion by Germany into what had been before the war primarily an Austro-Hungarian sphere of interest.

The policies of the Central Powers in the Balkans were in fact not really aligned at all. The Germans, who, once the Serbian campaign had established a supply route to Turkey, wanted to close down the Balkan front, stood by in helpless rage as the Austrians proceeded

29. Lilla, 'Austro-polnische Lösung', p. 239.
30. Silberstein, *Troubled Alliance*, Chapters VI and VII.

in January 1916 to occupy Montenegro and part of Albania. Although ever since December 1914 the war had really been for the Monarchy simply a struggle for survival, the Austrians set their aims high: like the Germans, they grossly over-estimated their own strength and underestimated that of their opponents. At any rate, as Burián told Conrad on 25 December 1915, the Monarchy was aiming 'to get the greatest possible increase of power and security when things are re-arranged'.[31] In this sense, the council of ministers that met on 7 January 1916[32] to determine the Monarchy's war aims, opted for control of Serbia, Montenegro and Albania. Although Magyar objections – still as strong as in the 1870s – precluded the actual incorporation into the Monarchy of large numbers of Southern Slavs, Burián stated it as 'certain that Serbia and Montenegro must be made politically, militarily and economically subject to us'. Montenegro was to be cut off from the Adriatic, the Monarchy annexing Mount Lovčen and the coastal strip, as well as Scutari from Albania. The latter was to become an Austro-Hungarian protectorate. Finally, in the north, Congress Poland was to be incorporated into the Monarchy.

On this last point the Austrians were to be sharply disillusioned, for the Germans were in the process of deciding to revoke their consent to the Austro-Polish solution. This was not simply a result of Burián's stubborn refusal to consider Austria-Hungary as a Germanic *Ostmark*. There were strong military and commercial pressure groups in Berlin demanding direct German control of Poland; and they were gaining ground as Germany's hopes of large acquisitions in the west were beginning to fade. Even more important, as Austria-Hungary now seemed set on controlling the western Balkans, the Germans began to fear that if she controlled Poland too, she would become a Great Power of the first rank, no longer dependent on Germany. They decided,[33] therefore, to press for the direct annexation of a large frontier strip, and the establishment of the rest of Congress Poland as an autonomous kingdom. Anticipating opposition in Vienna – especially from Franz Joseph – they suggested an Austrian archduke for the Polish throne, and they put these proposals to Burián in April 1916. Burián was not impressed; he decided that 'this militarily and economically fettered buffer state Poland, gripped in Germany's powerful fist, would soon be very little different from direct German territory'.[34] The

31. Fischer, *Griff*, p. 402.
32. Komjáthy, *Protokolle*, pp. 352ff.
33. Fischer, *Griff*, pp. 299–300.
34. Ibid., p. 300.

Poles of the Monarchy would never forgive the Habsburgs if they handed over the majority of the nation to the hated Prussians; even the frontier strip project, amounting to a fourth partition, and anathema to the Poles, was impossible for any Austrian government to agree to. Finally, Burián found the Prussian argument that Austria-Hungary in control of Poland offered 'no adequate defensive rampart' for Germany in the east 'totally unacceptable'.[35] Jagow, for his part, insisted that Germany's military security was at stake, and that the Polish question was 'a matter of life and death' for Germany. The deadlock between the allies was complete.

The issue was resolved by military events. Despite the pleas of Falkenhayn, who wanted the Austrians to stand on the defensive in Italy and concentrate on the Russian front, so as to free German forces for the battle of Verdun, Conrad went ahead with an Italian offensive in May. After some initial successes he had to stop in June, however, when the Russians launched an offensive under General Brusilov. By 7 June the Austrian IV (northernmost) Army was shattered; and on 10 June the Russians broke through the Austrian VII (southernmost) Army and penetrated the Bukovina. Conrad had weakened the eastern front too much. The Monarchy was only saved when German troops came to the rescue, and managed to halt the Russian offensive in September – but not before Romania entered the war (2 August) and overran Transylvania. German faith in Conrad's judgement had been completely shattered, and Franz Joseph and Burián had at last to yield to German pressure and agree to the establishment of a unified command under Hindenburg (6 September).[36] Altogether these events amounted to a decisive shift of the balance of forces within the alliance to Austria-Hungary's disadvantage.

Certainly, the Austrians were no longer in any position to insist on their original Polish programme. 'The facts speak so plainly', Jagow noted with satisfaction, 'that even Baron Burián will be unable to ignore them.'[37] Domestic factors also played their part.[38] The German ambassador was pleased to discover that Burián was becoming increasingly isolated in his in intransigence. Whereas Stürgkh and other Austrians felt that the Balkans should be the Monarchy's first priority, Tisza, along with Andrássy and a powerful group in the Hungarian parliament, was distrustful of Polish influence in the Monarchy, and demanded a speedy solution

35. Lilla, 'Austro-polnische Lösung', pp. 244–5.
36. Silberstein, *Troubled Alliance*, Chapter XIII.
37. Fischer, *Griff*, p. 302.
38. Lilla, 'Austro-polnische Lösung', pp. 245–9.

of the Polish question in the interests of cordial relations with Germany. Under these external and internal pressures, therefore, Burián met Bethmann Hollweg in August and agreed to the creation of an independent kingdom of Poland. True, on a theoretical level, he managed to insist that the kingdom should be an Austro-German condominium, and it was as such that it was formally proclaimed by the two emperors' manifesto of 5 November. But the reality was very different: the Polish army was to be under German control; no agreement had been reached about the precise roles of the two allies in the administration of the condominium; and powerful military circles in Germany, particularly those round Ludendorff, remained resolutely determined to oust Austria-Hungary from Poland altogether.

German respect for Austria-Hungary had declined still further as a result of Romania's entry into the war.[39] In the first months of the war the Germans had been under the illusion – as in the case of Italy – that territorial concessions would secure actual assistance. Bethmann Hollweg even advised the cession of both Bukovina and Transylvania – which Wilhelm II described as 'a crumb' in comparison with the overriding necessity of winning the war.[40] The Austrians, however, for whom the integrity of the Monarchy was just as important as winning the war, held out. In fact, their analysis of Romanian intentions was probably right: most of Romania's irredentist ambitions, unlike Bulgaria's, could only be satisfied at the expense of Austria-Hungary; hence there was never any real chance of securing actual assistance from Romania. Concessions would only be interpreted in Bucharest as weakness; whereas at least Romania's fear of the Central Powers ensured her neutrality. Unfortunately this fear, which had grown with the Austro-German successes of 1915, was dissipated by the Brusilov offensive in 1916, whereupon Austro-German diplomacy at Bucharest collapsed. It was small comfort to the Austrians that their pessimistic estimate of Romania's intentions had been proved correct; and hardly much more that Germany's military rescue operation was so effective that Mackensen was in Bucharest by 6 December. The campaign was yet another victory for Germany, and marked a further shift towards Berlin of the balance of influence within the Dual Alliance.

Indeed, the psychological shock of the initial Romanian successes in Transylvania dealt a hefty blow to the confidence of ruling

39. Silberstein, *Troubled Alliance*, Chapter XIII.
40. Ibid., p. 187.

circles in the Monarchy in their ability to win the war. In Hungary, the reverberations were particularly severe.[41] Tisza was denounced for having consented to the plans of a – largely Austrian – Supreme Army Command, whereby all Hungarian regiments had been sent to the Russian, Serbian and Italian fronts, leaving Transylvania virtually undefended; and the old cry went up that Hungary's interests were being sacrificed to those of Austria. Tisza himself saw little hope of peace. His soundings of the Italians in April 1915 had convinced him that their claims were incompatible with the continued existence of Austria. And after all, for him, as for his father, 'Hungary can serve as a bulwark against the Slav tide that is threatening the western coast of the Adriatic only if it is united with Austria. . . . Hungary's fate is linked to the existence of Austria-Hungary as a Great Power.'[42] The crisis marked the end of the political truce that had prevailed in Hungary since the outbreak of the war, and swelled the growing undercurrent of opposition to the war in the Monarchy as a whole. In March 1917 Michael Károlyi told the emperor Karl straight out that the continuation of the war was a disaster, pushing Austria-Hungary into dependence on Germany and pushing the Entente into supporting the claims of Serbia and Romania; and although Karl did not have the courage to appoint Károlyi prime minister, he did at least, in May, force Tisza to resign.[43]

In fact, peace moves had been under consideration at an official level since the autumn of 1916. On 17 October Burián, increasingly aware of the growing economic difficulties of the Central Powers, and afraid lest the war might go on beyond the spring, told Bethmann Hollweg that it was essential 'to make an attempt, without abandoning real vital interests, to make an effort to bring about an end to the war' on a basis of 'reason'.[44] He was certainly sincere: a month later he was even considering abandoning Poland entirely to Germany if that would facilitate German concessions in the west and a general peace. But his hopes failed for two reasons. In the first place, Burián's basis of 'reason' – which included German control of Belgium, an independent kingdom of Poland, and Austro-Hungarian control of Serbia, Montenegro and Albania – still amounted to a victorious peace, if a comparatively modest

41. Valiani, *End of Austria-Hungary*, p. 165.
42. Tisza to Sonnino, April 1915, in Stefan Tisza, *Briefe, 1914–1918* (Berlin 1928), p. 193.
43. Valiani, *End of Austria-Hungary*, p. 187.
44. Bethmann Hollweg, Note, Berlin 18 October 1916, published as No. 317 in *L'Allemagne et les problèmes de la paix pendant la première guerre mondiale* (A. Scherer and J. Grünewald, (eds.)) (Paris 1962–78) I, p. 517.

one; and that the Central Powers were not yet in a position to impose on the Entente. In the second place, the Germans not only disliked the details of Burián's plan – they hoped, for example, to extend German influence into the Balkans by partitioning Albania between their Greek and Bulgarian clients; they were also not in the least interested in such modest terms as Burián's. Indeed, they only agreed to discuss them as an alternative to President Wilson's even more moderate proposals; and their reply to Wilson – of which they did not even deign to inform their Austrian allies in advance – was vague, and only intended as a cover for the resumption of unrestricted submarine warfare. By March 1917, therefore, the Austrian peace move had got nowhere; war with the United States seemed imminent; and the Central Powers were isolated and facing virtually the whole world.

This was not a situation that appealed to the new directors of Austro-Hungarian policy, Karl I, who had succeeded Franz Joseph on 21 November 1916, and Ottokar Count Czernin, foreign minister since December. The new emperor was well-meaning and conciliatory. He saw the Monarchy primarily in dynastic terms, and appreciated that its interests were not necessarily identical with those of German nationalists in Austria, let alone in Germany. He was also acutely aware – especially after the fall of the Russian monarchy in March – of the danger of revolution: hence his enthusiasm, in a council of ministers in January 1917, for the idea of a separate peace with Russia as a prelude to a restoration of the Three Emperors' Alliance;[45] hence his gestures in the direction of political conciliation, even federalism, at home – the re-summoning of the Austrian parliament, suspended since 1914, in May 1917, and the political amnesty he declared, despite Czernin's opposition, in July. These gestures did not fail to appeal to those circles in the Entente who wished to preserve the Monarchy provided it could reform itself and free itself from the grip of Germany.

They were, however, mere gestures; and it can hardly be said that Karl's vague yearnings ever amounted to a clear and consistent programme. Even if they had, it is doubtful whether the young emperor could have carried it through against the whole weight of a German and Magyar ruling élite that was – disastrously – coming to see the Monarchy in national rather than dynastic terms; or against the opposition of the mighty ally in the north. As regards the latter, if even the venerable figure of Franz Joseph had been unable to force Germany to pay much respect to the Monarchy's

45. Komjáthy, *Protokolle*, p. 451.

special interests, his young and inexperienced successor would carry even less weight in Berlin. Indeed, Karl's family connections were regarded by the German emperor with suspicion and alarm: 'The ultra-bigoted House of Parma', Wilhelm II wrote *à propos* the Austro-Polish solution, 'in league with its fanatical father-confessors, hates the Protestant House of Hohenzollern. . . . Under the leadership of Vienna, and *allied* with it, Italy, . . . France, Poland, Lithuania *to the sea* are to be united.'[46] In these circumstances, the change of ruler in Vienna amounted to a further weakening of Austria-Hungary's influence in the alliance.

Czernin was made of sterner stuff. He had made his career as a protégé of Archduke Franz Ferdinand, and had given ample proof of his drive and energy as minister at Bucharest from 1913 to 1916. Contemporaries compared him to Felix Schwarzenberg: 'He has an acute mind and pursues his aims ruthlessly. The same scorn for humanity and often fateful underestimation . . . and disregard of all the details relating to internal policy'[47] Redlich said he had 'the mentality of a man of the seventeenth century'.[48] Certainly, his vision was limited. Although hard-working and skilled in politics in the traditional sense, he failed to see the urgency of the situation, or to recognise that the age of popular self-government had arrived. At home, instead of manoeuvring among the nationalities for support, his unimaginative opposition to all demands for federal reform in the end drove Czechs and Slovaks, Croats, Serbs and Slovenes together in opposition to the Monarchy. In Czernin's view, the national structure of the Monarchy was such that no reform could satisfy everybody; therefore, none need be attempted – after all, 'the Czechs will scream anyway, so it does not matter how they are treated'.[49]

His negative attitudes cannot be explained simply in terms of his responsibility as foreign minister to cultivate the alliance with Germany, a state which he regarded with a mixture of admiration and fear; let alone in terms of the danger of a German invasion. After all, there were long periods – notably, during the Anglo-French offensive of the summer of 1917, and after the start of the German offensive of March 1918 – when Germany could not even contemplate military intervention in Austria. The roots of Czernin's immobility lay rather in his own German-Austrian *Weltanschauung*. He was not a slave of Germany: on the contrary, he hoped

46. Fischer, *Griff*, p. 568.
47. Kann, *Sixtusaffäre*, p. 19.
48. Redlich, *Schicksalsjahre Oesterreichs*, II, p. 212.
49. Kann, *Sixtusaffäre*, p. 19.

to use the German alliance in order to strengthen the Monarchy, and ultimately to make it independent of Germany. But in the last resort, it was his unwillingness to contemplate changes at home that might be detrimental to German-Austrian interests that led him to turn away from a possible peace with the Western Powers and to commit the Monarchy's fate to a gamble on the success of German arms.

Certainly, Czernin was more guarded than the emperor, who exclaimed to a visitor in April 1917: 'Every means of getting peace must be tried!'[50] But even Czernin was by then alarmed at the exhaustion of the Monarchy,[51] the chronic starvation and dull despair of the masses, together with the effects of the Russian Revolution on the Slavs. All this, he expected to lead shortly to revolution among the workers and revolts of the nationalities. It was with these dangers in mind that on 12 April he sent the emperor a long memorandum explaining that the Monarchy could not go on fighting beyond 1917:[52] 'if the Monarchs of the Central Powers are unable to conclude peace *in the next few months*, then the peoples will make it over their heads, and then the waves of revolution will sweep away everything for which our brothers and sons are still fighting and dying today'.

The emperor at once sent this memorandum to Wilhelm II, accompanied by a somewhat Metternichian warning: 'we are fighting against a new enemy, which is more dangerous than the Entente – against international revolution, which finds its strongest ally in general famine'.[53] The Germans, however, set on continuing the war for large annexations in the east, were in no mood to listen to such advice, even from the highest authority in an allied state. They simply dismissed the memorandum as a case of nervous pessimism.

The emperor, meanwhile, had embarked on his own attempt to secure peace, following some soundings his brother-in-law, Prince Sixtus of Bourbon-Parma, had made of Poincaré in March.[54] The

---

50. Ibid.
51. Cereal production in Austria fell from 91m quintals in 1914 to 28m in 1917; in Hungary from 146m quintals in 1914 to 98m in 1917. The cost of living rose from 100 in 1914 to 302 in July 1916, 616 in July 1917, and 1560 in July 1918. The armaments industry staggered on until mid-1918, but there was already a catastrophic shortage of manpower and materials. Cf. Robert J. Wegs, 'Transportation: the Achilles' Heel of the Habsburg War Effort' in Robert A. Kann, Béla K. Kiraly and Paula S. Fichtner, *The Habsburg Empire in World War I*, Studies on Society in Change, 2 (New York 1977), pp. 121–34, who attributes many of these difficulties to the deficiencies of the transport system.
52. Fischer, *Griff*, p. 460.
53. Ibid.
54. Kann, *Sixtusaffäre*, pp. 8ff.

purpose of the negotiations was never exactly clear: whereas the Bourbon-Parmas, living in the 'political and national no man's land of dynastic politics',[55] would have been prepared for a separate peace betraying all the Monarchy's allies, it is clear that Czernin would never have contemplated this, and it seems that Karl was hoping somehow to mediate a general peace. This was the context of the rather incautious letter he wrote to Sixtus on 23 March, offering his diplomatic support for what were somewhat ambiguously described as France's 'justes révendications' in Alsace-Lorraine. By May, however, the negotiations had petered out. On the one hand, Great Britain and France seem to have been hoping for a separate peace with Austria-Hungary, which was never really on offer; on the other, the Italians imposed their veto. Their claims under the Treaty of London could only be met by the destruction of the Monarchy, not by a separate peace with it; whereas the Austrians were determined not to cede an inch of territory to Italy. Meanwhile, the irrelevance of Karl's efforts was underlined by the redefinition of Austro-Hungarian war aims that Czernin was in the process of working out with the Germans.

Although in January 1917 the Austrians had failed to respond to German suggestions that they should abandon Poland entirely to Germany in exchange for a 'fat slice' of Romania,[56] a council of ministers on 22 March decided to accept this general idea. As Czernin pointed out, although the Monarchy's prime concern was now simply survival, it would not do to let Germany acquire Poland while the Monarchy, 'bleeding from a hundred wounds', came away empty-handed.[57] It was decided, therefore, to renounce Poland and concentrate on Romania – Burián's 'Milliardenobjekt'[58] – and control of Serbia. It must be emphasised that the council made this decision on the assumption that Germany, in return for acquiring Poland, would be prepared to renounce gains in the west in order to facilitate a general peace. As regards the east, Czernin, who had been hoping for a separate peace with Russia after the March revolution, was appalled at the extent of Germany's territorial claims. Characteristically, however, he decided to go along with Germany in the hope of persuading her to see reason – a dangerous game, which he was to play with even more disastrous results in 1918.

As it was, the Austro-German agreement on war aims, finalised

55. Ibid., p. 63.
56. Fischer, *Griff*, p. 422.
57. Ibid., p. 450.
58. Ibid., p. 404.

at Kreuznach on 17–18 May, marked a further subordination of Austro-Hungarian to German interests.[59] The Austrians found themselves endorsing German ambitions in areas as remote as Mesopotamia and Egypt; and, although Germany now agreed to Austro-Hungarian control of Serbia, Montenegro and Albania, the Austrians had to agree to the establishment of a German naval base in the Adriatic at Valona, to guarantee German control of oil, railways and shipping in Romania, and to give Germany a free hand to negotiate with Bulgaria for commercial concessions in Macedonia. This further intrusion into what had been primarily an Austro-Hungarian sphere of interest shows how far the relations between the two allies had altered since the days of Bismarck and the Pomeranian musketeer.

It was not concern about Germany's growing Balkan ambitions, however, so much as developments at home and on the western front that by the autumn convinced the Austrians that the Kreuznach agreement did not suit their purposes.[60] When the Reichsrat met on 30 May the Austrian government found that it could not get a majority without Polish support; and there was reason to fear an actual rebellion in Galicia if Vienna assigned Poland to Prussia. Moreover, since the fall of Tisza (18 May), Czernin was afraid the Poles might find ready allies in Budapest if Vienna let them down. To add to these difficulties, the Germans made it abundantly clear during the course of August that they were not in the least interested in a compromise peace in the west. This had been, in Austrian eyes, one of the main purposes of the Kreuznach agreement. Now the Germans were refusing to give up Belgium, let alone Alsace-Lorraine – although for this last the Austrians would have been prepared to compensate Germany by adding Galicia to German Poland. In September, therefore, Czernin asked the Germans to reverse the Kreuznach agreement, and to allow Poland – minus a modest frontier strip – to be incorporated into the Monarchy in return for German control of Romania.

The Germans were not opposed to this plan as such; but their conditions were now even more extreme than those they had put to Burián in 1915. Poland, albeit in a personal union with Austria, was to be tied to Germany by economic and military agreements, as was Austria-Hungary itself through a twenty-year offensive and defensive alliance and far-reaching economic and military arrangements. 'The kingdom of Poland', the Germans confidently told

---

59. Ibid., pp. 463ff.
60. Valiani, *End of Austria-Hungary*, pp. 180ff.

themselves, 'is to be attached to the German Empire in military, economic and financial respects, as is Austria-Hungary.'[61] Czernin's move towards acceptance of this deal, in the 'non-binding principles' of 22 October, marked a further capitulation of Austria-Hungary before Germany's claims to domination disguised as *Mitteleuropa*.

As for Czernin's motives,[62] it was not merely that a successful solution of the Polish question would be useful in domestic terms; or that until December he still clung to the hope that in return for large gains in the east Germany might yet be persuaded to renounce Belgium and settle for a compromise peace in the west. He was gambling on the chance that *Mitteleuropa* might be useful as a temporary device to regenerate the Monarchy, so weakened by the war, and to equip it, once it had revived, to take its place at Germany's side as an equal and independent partner. After all, after the war Germany would be 'the most hated state in the world', and would have need of Austria-Hungary.[63] The risk – that, as Tisza pointed out, the Monarchy might find itself reduced to a helpless pawn in Germany's ambitious eastern schemes – Czernin was prepared to take. True, for the time being, the application of the 'non-binding principles' remained in suspense: when Czernin discovered that Germany was claiming a 'frontier strip' that amounted to one-third of the Congress kingdom, and virtual economic control of the rest, he refused to proceed with any further discussion of *Mitteleuropa* until the matter was cleared up. Nevertheless, the peace negotiations that were about to open at Brest-Litovsk were amply to demonstrate the dangers inherent in Czernin's policy of co-operating with Germany in the hope of influencing and restraining her.

Although by late November the Austro-German victory over Italy at Caporetto and the Bolshevik decree on peace had convinced Czernin that in military terms 'the war can be regarded as won', the desperate supply situation at home convinced him equally of the need for a speedy peace in the east, even one without annexations. That he could not achieve this was not merely the result of Germany's inordinate desire for conquests. After Caporetto, and when the upheavals he had apprehended in the spring had not occurred by the autumn, Czernin too fell into the same error as the Germans – that of over-estimating the strength of the Central Powers. True, his demands now, with large-scale American intervention looming

61. Fischer, *Griff*, p. 574.
62. Ibid., pp. 574–5.
63. Ibid., p. 575.

on the horizon, were more moderate than in the spring, and were confined to control of Poland, annexation of the Montenegrin coast, and frontier rectifications in Serbia and Romania. But if even this programme presupposed a better military position than actually existed, perhaps the chief obstacle to a speedy peace was Czernin's own interpretation of the terms 'right to self-determination [*Selbstbestimmungsrecht*] and 'annexations'.[64] As he told the Russians at Brest on 25 December, the assimilation of territories that had been for some time under the control of the Central Powers was not to be regarded as 'annexation'; and the doctrine of self-determination could apply only to governments, not to peoples. By this device, the Central Powers could retain possession of Poland and of other areas of Russia where they had established puppet regimes; while established constitutional structures such as the Dual Monarchy would remain unscathed. At Brest, Czernin's enunciation of this doctrine caused the first of a long series of breakdowns in the negotiations; his use of it to deny the demands of the Czechs for self-determination finally drove the Czech parties at home to despair of the Vienna government, and to take up the struggle for complete independence.[65]

The domestic situation was deteriorating in other respects too. By mid-January 1918 there were only two months' supplies of grain in Austria, and a reduction in the flour ration led to a wave of potentially revolutionary strikes in Vienna and other major cities. Here, however, as in the naval mutiny at Bocche di Cattaro on 1 February, war-weariness was as much the issue as hunger. 'If peace is not made at Brest', the emperor wrote despairingly on 17 January, 'then the revolution will come here, no matter how much there is to eat.'[66] Czernin, therefore, on 22 January extracted the permission of a council of ministers to sign a separate peace with Russia if Germany's demands were such as to make an allied peace with Russia impossible. But as he still shrank from a direct clash with Germany, he also got permission to sign a peace with the self-styled government of the Ukraine, precariously established in Kiev. This, he hoped, would both secure much-needed grain supplies for the Monarchy and pressurise the Russians into an early peace. He was aware that the Ukranians were demanding not only the possession of the district of Cholm in Congress Poland, but the creation of a separate *Kronland* for the Ruthenes of East Galicia.

64. Wolfdieter Bihl, *Oesterreich-Ungarn und die Friedensschlüße von Brest-Litovsk* (Vienna 1970), p. 37.
65. Valiani, *End of Austria-Hungary*, pp. 209–10.
66. Bihl, *Brest-Litovsk*, p. 101.

Burián pointed out that to grant these concessions would so estrange the Poles of the Monarchy as to make any Austro-Polish solution illusory; but Czernin, arguing that Germany's demands in Poland were so burdensome as to make Austrian possession of the kingdom an illusion anyway, prevailed. Peace between the Central Powers and the Ukraine – conceding Cholm to the latter – was signed on 8 February, and the *Kronland* protocol issued on the same day. The results were disappointing. Civil war in the Ukraine and a strong local resistance to Austrian requisitioning forces meant that there was little grain to be had; and although this served as a pretext for Austria-Hungary's abrogation of the Cholm and *Kronland* concessions in June, the original treaty had alienated the Poles of the Monarchy beyond all measure. Like the Czechs, they too decided that their future lay in independence rather than with a House of Habsburg that so patently ignored their interests.

In the subsequent negotiations with the Russians at Brest-Litovsk and with the Romanians at Bucharest Austria-Hungary's influence on her powerful ally proved to be almost completely non-existent, and Czernin reaped the bitter rewards of his policy of co-operating with Germany in the hope of restraining her. He had spoken strongly to the Germans on 5 February:[67] Germany's exorbitant demands were ruining the chances of peace; the 1879 alliance did not commit the Monarchy to fight if Germany rejected all compromise; Germany's demands in Poland, which were making that country, like Romania, 'a squeezed-out lemon', were no proper basis for *Mitteleuropa*. He even threatened to terminate the alliance after the war. Actions spoke louder than words, however. When, two weeks later, the Germans proceeded to impose their draconian terms on the Russians by an ultimatum followed by a renewed military advance, all Czernin could manage was a resigned protest. The Austrians, informed of the peace terms but not consulted, duly signed the Treaty of Brest-Litovsk on 3 March.[68]

At Bucharest[69] Czernin did rather better, and Austria-Hungary's claims to frontier rectifications and protection of her commercial interests received a measure of consideration in the final treaty. But this was largely because the Austrians happened to have the support of the German civilian authorities against the ravings of Ludendorff. The German Chancellor, Hertling, reminded the generals that a resentful Austria-Hungary might prove an obstacle to Germany's post-war ambitions, whereas 'the strengthening and firm

67. Fischer, *Griff*, pp. 658–61.
68. Bihl, *Brest-Litovsk*, pp. 114–16.
69. Fischer, *Griff*, pp. 684ff.

establishment of the alliance on the basis of common interests would, on the other hand, create a Central European bloc of a strength never yet witnessed in the history of the world'.[70] But for these few scraps in Romania the Monarchy paid heavily. The whole Polish question was raised again when Ludendorff declared that as Germany had not got the complete control she needed in Romania, she revoked her consent to the Austro-Polish solution. Worse of all, perhaps, six weeks after Brest-Litovsk Austria-Hungary had for the second time put her signature to what was regarded in the rest of the world as a treaty of utterly unreasonable severity.

The negotiations at Brest and Bucharest were in fact only one aspect of a whole complex of missed opportunities for making something of the residual sympathies still felt for the Monarchy in Paris and London.[71] By December 1917, with Italy still reeling from Caporetto, and France still waiting for reinforcements from the United States, the British were in a far better position to pursue agreement with Austria-Hungary than at the time of the Sixtus mission. At the allied conference of 27 November to 3 December Lloyd George strongly advocated an Austro-Italian peace in which Italy would receive only the Trentino. But the Austrians, victors at Caporetto, confidently refused to cede anything whatever to Italy. The British nevertheless persisted. In secret talks in Switzerland in December General Smuts assured Czernin's emissary, Mensdorff, that Great Britain regarded Austria-Hungary, if reformed internally to give the nationalities their due weight against the Germans and Magyars, as a potential counterweight to Germany in the post-war balance of power. Lloyd George announced publicly on 5 January 1918 that 'the destruction of Austria-Hungary does not form any part of our war aims': Poland must be independent, but for the rest 'genuine self-government on truly democratic lines' would suffice; and President Wilson's Fourteen Points of 8 January said much the same thing. Czernin, however, uncompromisingly instructed Mensdorff to insist that there could be no question of the Monarchy's ceding any territory whatever, especially not to Italy; and that the Monarchy would not accept foreign advice about its domestic arrangements. Perhaps a man more far-sighted than Czernin, and less hopelessly negative about the possibility of domestic reform, might have seen that the external political constellation of January 1918 offered the Monarchy a better chance of survival as an

70. Ibid., p. 697.
71. Valiani, *End of Austria-Hungary*, pp. 225ff.

independent Great Power than a military gamble that subordinated Austria-Hungary's fate to the success of German arms. Czernin, however, was impressed by French stubborness over Alsace-Lorraine, irritated by allied demands for federalist reform, and, above all, blinded by his faith in Germany – apparently vindicated by Brest-Litovsk and the German March offensive in the west. It seemed to him now more than ever important to do nothing to weaken the Dual Alliance. In March 1918, therefore, he decided to abandon any further contacts with the British, and to stake everything on a German military victory.[72]

He announced this disastrous decision to the world in a defiant speech of 2 April, declaring that Austria-Hungary had no intention whatever of abandoning Germany, and was, indeed, prepared to continue the war for the sake of Alsace-Lorraine. This in turn provoked Clemenceau to publish the emperor Karl's letter of 23 March 1917 to Prince Sixtus, whereupon Czernin, both genuinely shocked and desperate to stem the ensuing outcry in Germany and among outraged German and Magyar partisans of the 1879 alliance at home, forced Karl publicly to deny ever having written the letter. The immediate consequence was the emperor's dismissal of Czernin – probably inevitable since the uproar over the Ukrainian treaty; but the emperor's authority had also suffered a severe blow. Worse still, his capitulation before the entrenched power of German and Magyar opinion had blighted the hopes that certain Entente circles had placed in his revisionist policies at home and abroad.[73] Whereas the decisions of the Rome Congress of nationalities (8–10 April) in favour of 'completely liberating' the peoples oppressed by the Habsburgs had at first received only the 'profound sympathy' of the Entente governments, the United States Secretary of State, Lansing, now began to make headway in his efforts to persuade Wilson that there was no point in looking to Vienna for peace, and that 'Austria-Hungary must be wiped off the map of Europe as an empire.'[74] On 27 June Wilson gave way; and Lansing's announcement on 28 June that 'all branches of the Slav race must be completely liberated from German and Austrian domination' was endorsed by the French government on 29 June and by the British on 9 August.[75] Together with Brest-Litovsk and Bucharest, the Sixtus affair had dealt the death-blow to the Monarchy's chances of salvation through a compromise agreement with

72. Ibid., pp. 229–1.
73. Kann, *Sixtusaffäre*, pp. 55–6.
74. Valiani, *End of Austria-Hungary*, p. 243.
75. Ibid., pp. 244.

the Western Powers.

There remained only the hope of a German military victory; but this itself promised to raise horrendous problems. For the Germans now determined to take advantage of the Sixtus affair to impose the *Mitteleuropa* plan on Austria-Hungary on their own terms. Karl and Czernin's successor, Burián, were to be summoned to accept a political alliance, a military treaty, and a customs union, without any compensating concessions whatever in Poland: they would have to agree if they were to dispel the doubts raised by the Sixtus letter. The German intention was now avowedly no less than 'to dominate [*beherrschen*] Austria-Hungary economically like Poland and Russia'.[76] However, when Karl and Burián made their *Canossagang* to Spa in May, they managed to insist that the *Mitteleuropa* treaties be made dependent on an agreement being reached over Poland (a concession the Germans had no intention of honouring); and when they discovered that the Germans were still intent on annexing part of Congress Poland, they refused to proceed any further with the *Mitteleuropa* treaties, despite a German 'ultimatum' of 6 July.[77] The alliance was threatening to break up. In other fields, too, victory brought its problems: the Austrians refused to support the German advance into Transcaucasia; the Germans feared that Austria-Hungary's grain-collecting activities in the Ukraine were alienating a valuable potential satellite; and, with their eyes fixed on the Black Sea, Persia and India, they looked askance at the presence of an Austro-Hungarian occupying force in Odessa. In September, Burián sent to Berlin a detailed exposé of his plans for the Austro-Polish solution – the most detailed ever worked out by the Ballhausplatz.[78] It met with a very clear and sharp rejection. Obviously, even in the event of a German victory, the Monarchy would be hard pressed to make good its aims as an independent Great Power.

As it turned out, the Monarchy was confronted with the problem of defeat. This was becoming increasingly clear to everybody by mid-August, when Karl, Burián and the Austro-Hungarian chief of staff, Arz, all made the journey to Spa to plead for peace: 'we are absolutely finished [*bei uns ist absolut Schluß*]', the emperor declared.[79] But even in this extremity they found their allies completely insensitive to the Monarchy's interests: although now prepared to consider a status quo peace in the west, the Germans still

76. Fischer, *Griff*, p. 704.
77. Ibid., p. 709.
78. Ibid., p. 713.
79. Ibid., p. 853.

refused to make any concessions whatever in the east. 'Poland', they declared, as late as 24 September, 'is the cornerstone of our policy in the south-east'.[80] Bulgaria collapsed four days later.

Meanwhile,[81] the moral effect of war-weariness and of Russian and allied propaganda on the troops of the Austro-Hungarian army was beginning to tell. There had been some ominous mutinies in May, especially among troops returning from Russia. A strategically unsound offensive launched on the Piave on 15 June cost the exhausted Imperial and Royal Army 150,000 men. By October, when the Italians took the offensive, whole regiments were deserting. In these circumstances, the emperor's manifesto of 16 October, promising federalist reform in Cisleithania (but not in Hungary, which, obstinate to the last, refused all concessions to the nationalities, and proclaimed the 1867 settlement replaced by a mere personal union), was irrelevant. It was now plain to all the nationalities that the Central Powers were lost, and that an Entente victory would bring them independence and unity. All the manifesto did was to make it easier for the subject peoples to proclaim their independence. At the end of October, when the revolutionary waves were overwhelming Vienna, Budapest and the state apparatus throughout the Monarchy, the Italians finally destroyed its army at Vittorio Veneto. The allies signed the armistice of 31 October with an empire that had effectively ceased to exist.

80. Ibid., p. 857.
81. Valiani, *End of Austria-Hungary*, pp. 245ff.

9
Conclusion

If the defeats of the autumn of 1918 finally destroyed the Habsburg Monarchy, the preceding four years of warfare had already destroyed its position as an independent Great Power, reducing it to the status of a helpless if reluctant satellite of the German Empire. The 'Flucht nach vorn' of July 1914, in a sense the apotheosis of Austro-German *Bündnistreue*, appeared by 1918 to have been indeed a case of *medicina peior malo*: by the end of 1918 both empires had ceased to exist.

Yet perhaps this outcome was not entirely unforeseeable. In 1918 it was the magnitude of the difficulties confronting the Monarchy, not their nature, that was unprecedented. Throughout the nineteenth century the statesmen of Vienna had been aware that the Monarchy, as of the weakest of the Great Powers, ran the risk, if it appealed for external support, of being exploited by a stronger partner for purposes alien to its own interests. Metternich and Schwarzenberg had always taken this into account in their dealings with Russia; Buol had borne it in mind in his attempts to align his diplomacy with that of the western Powers during the eastern crisis of the 1850s. When, after 1914, the Monarchy found itself involved in a life-and-death struggle at the side of an incomparably stronger German ally, the possibility that the existence of the Monarchy as an independent Great Power might be threatened not so much by the enemy as by the ally arose in an acute form.

In the wars of 1859 and 1866 the Monarchy had fought in isolation, and the result had been simply the loss of two provinces in Italy and of a (by 1866) largely formal primacy in Germany. The war of 1914–18 was a very different matter. Not only did the Austrians find their German allies alarmingly willing to countenance the cession of Austro-Hungarian territory to potential and even actual opponents; they were quite unable to vindicate their own interests in Poland and the Balkans in the face of a German imperialism that had worried them before 1914, and now seemed to be carrying everything before it. To the exhausted Monarchy's pleas for a compromise peace in 1917 and 1918 the Germans paid no

attention whatever; at Brest-Litovsk the Austrians found themselves dragged helplessly along behind their ally; and although to
the very end of the war they were refusing to accept the full
implications of the draconian Spa agreements, which assigned to
the Monarchy the role of a simple German satellite, it was clear that
the Germans were not inclined to yield an inch. Altogether, in the
war of 1914–18 the Monarchy faced the prospect perhaps for the
first time, and even more in the event of victory than of defeat, of
ceasing to be an independent Power within the European states
system.

Yet it was not just the Monarchy's commitment to the German
alliance that undermined its independence – after all, the Germans
were in the event defeated, and in no position to impose their terms
on Vienna. Even more disastrous, perhaps, was the fact that by
virtue of this commitment the Monarchy had finally isolated itself
from the other Great Powers of Europe who for the past hundred
years had generally had an interest in preserving it. True, by 1917,
both Russia and Italy were pursuing aims that were hardly compatible with the existence of the Dual Monarchy as a Great Power;
but equally, by 1917 Russia was staggering to defeat, and Italy
could have been controlled by its French and British allies. Even as
late as January 1918, influential voices in Paris and London were
advocating the preservation of the Monarchy as a potential check
on Germany in the balance of power of the future. But the assumption was always that Austria-Hungary must be genuinely independent of Germany; and this in turn would require some
strengthening of the non-German and non-Magyar elements in the
Monarchy by a measure of domestic reform. (For the opposite
reasons, of course, the Germans had been pressing for a strengthening of the German and Magyar elements, as a guarantee of the
continuance of the Dual Alliance and as a precondition of *Mitteleuropa*.) The decision of the ruling élite of the Monarchy, led by
Czernin rather than the emperor, and thinking in national rather
than in dynastic terms, to stake everything on a German victory
that would preserve the Monarchy as a German–Magyar state was
fatal. It drove the nationalities to seek outright independence rather
than federal reform, and drove the allies to endorse their aims. In
the event, the gamble failed. If the consequent prolongation of the
war to the point of defeat brought about the collapse of the
Monarchy from within, its wartime diplomacy had left it without
the support of any Power except defeated Germany. Whereas in the
peacemaking of 1814–15 the Monarchy had not lacked for external
support, when the peacemakers assembled at Versailles in 1919 no

one dreamed of suggesting that the now fragmented Monarchy might be re-created as the keystone of the new European order.

Ever since the 1815 settlement, which had left Austria with interests in Italy, Germany and the Near East that she was too weak to sustain unaided, the Monarchy had always been dependent on the support of at least one of the first-class Great Powers; and this meant that the Monarchy was dependent on shifts in an international situation that was more often than not entirely beyond its control. It was the weakest of the Great Powers, lacking the economic resources of the Western Powers and the human resources that sustained the Russian empire, and its relative position amongst the Great Powers, in economic and military terms, hardly improved as the century wore on. (By the 1890s even Italy had overtaken the Monarchy in terms of naval power.) The steady development of national feeling, not only among Germans and Magyars, but among the nationalities, and its repercussions in the domestic upheavals of the 1860s and at the turn of the century, made the Monarchy's future as a Great Power seem even more problematical. In the great crisis of 1897–1906 the Monarchy's impending disappearance was a topic of serious discussion in the chancelleries of Europe.

It should be emphasised, however, that for the élite that formulated the foreign policy of the Habsburg Monarchy the problem of nationalism was rather something 'given' than the determining factor in the Monarchy's relations with the Great Powers of Europe. It is idle to speculate as to whether a more enlightened handling of the nationalities by Vienna and Budapest could have quenched the fires of nationalism; certainly, the policies adopted by those governments helped to make the South Slav problem acute by 1914. But until then, these were essentially problems of internal policy. Although in the wars of 1859 and 1866 neither Cavour nor Bismarck had been above intriguing with disaffected elements in Hungary, so long as peace continued the other Powers of Europe did not attempt to interfere in what were regarded by universal consent as the internal concerns of the Habsburg government. (In 1848–9, indeed, the Habsburgs enjoyed the passive – and in Russia's case even the active – support of the Great Powers in re-establishing their authority.)

Admittedly, the problems arising from the multinational character of the Monarchy generally served to weaken its effectiveness as a Great Power. Magyar suspicion of the Common institutions established in 1867 was one factor in the government's failure to secure an increase in the size of the Imperial and Royal Army for twenty years after 1889 – years in which the rest of Europe was arming fast. The great Hungarian crisis of 1903–6 virtually paralysed the Monarchy for action beyond its borders at a critical time; and both the agrarian protectionism and the Magyarisation policies of Budapest fatally weakened the Monarchy's alliances with its Balkan neighbours. But these were all matters which the ministers for foreign affairs lacked the power – even if they had the will – to alter. Not that any of Franz Joseph's advisers ever seriously attempted to tamper with the constitutional arrangements of 1867 – even the energetic Aehrenthal abandoned all notions of trialist reforms when confronted with the adamant opposition of Budapest. All, even Czernin and Burián at the eleventh hour, accepted the internal arrangements of the Dual Monarchy as an unalterable fact of the situation.

It is true that successive foreign ministers sometimes alluded to the interests of this or that national group when they were called on to defend or justify particular policies – to Magyar devotion to the German alliance, to Polish or Magyar disapproval of too close relations with Russia. But when the international situation seemed to demand it, these currents of opinion were easily overridden or ignored. Foreign policy remained, throughout the period, part of the emperor's prerogative; and when it suited them both Franz Joseph and his foreign ministers could always enforce their will, often – especially in the 1860s and 1880s – against quite vociferous criticism in the parliaments of Vienna and Budapest.

Diplomatic history is the history of decision-making; and the élite that made the decisions about foreign policy – the emperor and his close advisers – thought primarily in terms of the international situation of the day. It was, after all, the external situation that determined the success or failure of the policies of a relatively weak Power such as Austria-Hungary. And as that situation was subject to changes quite beyond the power of Vienna to control, flexibility in the Ballhausplatz was a prerequisite for success. The wages of rigidity was invariably disaster.

Although the 1815 settlement was perhaps inherently unstable – in so far as it assigned to Austria responsibilities beyond her capacities – the Monarchy was fortunate in that for a generation after 1815 the leading Powers of Europe continued to see their own interest in co-operation to uphold the established order. In British eyes, the Monarchy was the keystone of an international structure designed to guard against both French revisionism and Russian ambition; whereas for the tsar it represented the first line of defence against the spread of liberal ideas from the west. Metternich, acutely aware of the Monarchy's inherent weakness, was careful to make the most of this – hence the emphasis he always placed on monarchical solidarity and the legitimacy of the international order as established by treaties.

Yet while he stood firm by these principles, Metternich was enough of a practical statesman to appreciate the need for flexibility in their practical application. In the first years of peace, he was generally inclined to lean on Great Britain against both France and Russia; but in 1820 he managed to establish his own working arrangement with the tsar at Troppau. True, even Metternich's plans were at the mercy of shifts in the international situation beyond his control: a bout of Anglo-Russian co-operation against Turkey in the 1820s left Metternich isolated and helpless. But in the 1830s and 1840s he made a good recovery, establishing tolerably good relations with both Great Britain and Russia. Both Powers were still fundamentally determined to uphold the 1815 settlement against France; and the Habsburgs were again able to profit, in meeting the challenge in Germany and Italy in 1848–9, from this fundamental disposition on the part of the two leading Great Powers.

The outbreak of war between Great Britain and Russia in 1854 destroyed the tacit alliance on which the 1815 system rested, and opened the door to the revisionist schemes of Napoleon III. Buol's policy during the Crimean War was intelligible enough: to lend diplomatic support to Great Britain and France in resisting the advance of Russian influence towards the south-eastern borders of the Monarchy, while not going so far as to involve the Monarchy itself in a war in which it might merely serve as a battering ram for the use of Powers which could themselves lend it no effective military assistance. The outcome was nevertheless disastrous for Austria: Russia seemed irretrievably lost and France and Great Britain had not been won, while Prussia and Piedmont continued to pose threats to the Austrian leadership of Germany and Italy.

Franz Joseph's reaction to this situation – a rigid insistence on Austria's legitimate rights and a refusal to seek allies by compromising anywhere – was consistent but unrealistic. The Austrians thereby condemned themselves to total isolation, and the wars of 1859 and 1866 finally demonstrated that the Monarchy was unable to sustain unaided the position in Germany and Italy that it had after all only achieved thanks to the help of a victorious coalition. True, in some respects the war of 1866 was beneficial: the Monarchy's responsibilities were brought more into line with its resources, and the Italian chimera was at last finally abandoned. But

Beust and Franz Joseph, while aware of a continuing threat in the Near East, continued to hanker after a role in German affairs, as protectors of the independence of the South German states. The international situation defeated them, however: reckless France proved an unsatisfactory partner, Great Britain had lapsed into isolation, and Russia was positively pro-Prussian. In 1871, Franz Joseph at last came to terms with reality and finally abandoned the five-hundred-year-old German mission of his House.

After 1871, Austro-Hungarian foreign policy was primarily concerned with safeguarding the Monarchy's position in the Near East – the one sphere of influence that now remained to it. There, the declining Ottoman Empire was all too likely to be replaced by a series of independent states, some of which might have irredentist claims against Austria-Hungary. True, the Imperial and Royal Army could cope with any of these states in isolation; but this might not be the case if a Great Power should back their ambitions. The chief danger now seemed to be that Russia might get control of the Balkans. This might portend, not merely the exclusion of the Monarchy from its important 'colonial' markets, but its military encirclement by Russia and her satellites; possibly, even – as was Russia's declared aim after 1914 – its actual dismemberment.

Of the foreign ministers who managed for almost half a century before Sarajevo to defend the Monarchy's interests without having recourse to war, all were confronted with the problem of an intractable diplomatic situation; yet all showed themselves versatile enough to overcome it. Although all took office with a blueprint for a policy which proved impractical owing to the harsh facts of the international situation, all managed without sacrificing any of the Monarchy's vital interests to adjust their policies to reality. Beust, who spent most of his years at the Ballhausplatz working for an alignment with France against Russia and Prussia over the Eastern Question, ended by accepting Prussia's domination of Germany, and laid the foundations for the Austro-German alliance, and even for a *modus vivendi* with Russia. Andrássy, who came to office with a plan for a grand alliance against Russia, had to abandon this when faced with British and German hesitations; and for most of the seventies worked in uneasy partnership with Russia herself. Even when, in 1879, he secured the alliance with Germany, he had by no means realised his ideal. Haymerle, who shared his objectives, was forced by the attitudes of Great Britain and Germany along the path of reconciliation with Russia. And Kálnoky, who took office with the firm intention of developing a really cordial relationship with Russia, spent most of his time in building up two imposing blocs against her – reinforcing the Dual Alliance with military agreements and Italian and Romanian alliances, and creating the Mediterranean Entente. Goluchowski, at first hopeful of developing the latter into something approaching an alliance, regretfully decided after two years to abandon it altogether, and seek some accommodation with Russia. Aehrenthal, the greatest partisan of the Austro-Russian Entente, presided over its collapse; and after spending three years on schemes and blueprints as bold as any of Andrássy's, then embarked on three years of the strictest conservatism. Only Berchtold, who on taking office had placed his hopes in concert diplomacy and co-operation with Great Britain, was moved by two years of disappointments to the conclusion that the best defence of the Monarchy's interests lay in recourse to war.

The case of Berchtold shows, of course, that however versatile and open-minded the statesmen of the Monarchy may have been as regards the means they adopted to defend its interests, versatility and open-mindedness were no sure guarantee of success. The international situation changed so often and so radically in the half-century after 1866 that it was hardly surprising that the makers of Austro-Hungarian foreign policy were often in difficulties. Even so, it is striking that the crisis of 1914 was in fifty years the only one that seemed to the decision-makers in Vienna to demand a military solution. For the rest, the diplomatic situation remained fluid enough, and the Monarchy's potential opponents cautious enough, to allow Austrian statesmen to cope with the Eastern Question by diplomatic means. The solutions they adopted fall into three broad categories.

First, there were direct agreements with Russia herself, usually on the basis of monarchical solidarity and mutual restraint in the tradition of Münchengrätz: the Three Emperors' League, the Three Emperors' Alliance, and the Entente of 1897–1908. This was the most satisfactory solution, and the one that prevailed for the greater part of the four decades of peace after 1871. But eventually, all these agreements broke down, as a result of the pressure of Panslav or nationalist opinion in Russia.

A second solution, sometimes pursued concurrently with the first, was the conclusion of agreements with Russia's potential clients, to restrain their irredentist tendencies, to prevent their combining together against the Monarchy, and, above all, to keep them out of Russian control. This category of agreement includes not only the Serbian and Romanian alliances, but also the Triple Alliance with Italy, in Austrian eyes primarily a means of neutralising a potential enemy. In the event, none of these alliances stood the test: in all three cases the principle of monarchical solidarity was swept away by the nationalist tide – although it is worth noting that as late as 1917 the Austrians were still talking in terms of a change of dynasty in Serbia as one means of achieving security in that quarter.

The third solution open to the Ballhausplatz was to construct blocs of Powers with a common interest in confronting Russia and resisting her advance. Here, Great Britain and Germany were the Powers to whom the Austrians generally turned when other means of restraining Russia failed. But as Franz Joseph, unlike Napoleon I, was in no position to command, but only to persuade, his efforts were only successful to the extent that the British and Germans chose to regard their interests as identical with Austria's.

In the British case, there was always the difficulty that London was usually unwilling to undertake an actual commitment to fight in unforeseen contingencies; and that even then Great Britain, as primarily a naval Power, could hardly protect Habsburg territory against the tsar's armies. Even when London lent diplomatic assistance – in 1878, or in the Mediterranean Entente of 1887–97, for example – the vagaries of British party politics made a British *entente* an unsteady star to steer by. By the turn of the century humanitarian and anti-Turkish currents in Great Britain were causing something of a cooling in Anglo-Austrian relations; and the conclusion of the Anglo-Russian agreements over Asia in 1907 put an end to any chance that Great Britain might support the Monarchy against Russia, and put her new-found imperial security at risk. It is true that the British were on the whole well-disposed towards the Monarchy, with which they had no quarrels, and which they wished to see preserved in the interests of stability and the balance of power. Indeed, in the closing stages of the war, when Russia had ceased to inspire awe in London, these ideas re-emerged in a series of British peace feelers to Vienna. But in the decade of Austro-Russian rivalry before the war, the Austrians, although inclined to see in Great Britain a friendly Power, discovered that she was not one on whom they could rely for much active support.

Their hopes of securing the active support of Germany were for the most part equally problematical. True, once the German quarrel had been wound up in 1871, Beust had seen in good relations' with the northern empire a potential source of security for the Monarchy – a view heartily endorsed by the mass of German and Magyar opinion. Andrássy went further, and aspired to make Germany serve Austro-Hungarian interests, and lend diplomatic, and even military, assistance against Russia. Bismarck, however, was determined never to jeopardise his relations with St Petersburg for the sake of Austria-Hungary's interests in the Balkans. His aim in conceding the alliance of 1879 was to make Austria-Hungary the servant of Germany, not vice versa; and this aim he largely achieved when Germany and Russia took Austria-Hungary prisoner in the Three Emperors' Alliance. Similarly, it was changes in German domestic politics, not Austrian appeals, which were the determining factor behind the brief shift of German policy towards support for Austria-Hungary after 1889, and which put an end to this, equally suddenly, after 1894.

The trouble with the Dual Alliance was that it was a defensive military agreement that could only prove its worth if the war it was designed to deter actually broke out. In normal times of peace it was, for diplomatic purposes, useless. Indeed, as Austro-Russian tension relaxed in the decade after 1897, Germany and Austria-Hungary were more often than not completely at odds in terms of day-to-day politics. In the era of *Weltpolitik* Germany was fast developing imperialist ambitions of her own in the Ottoman Empire and the Balkans – often at the expense of her Austro-Hungarian ally. By 1914 Conrad was convinced that Germany was striving to 'annihilate' Austro-Hungarian influence in the Near East; and, as Germany's plans for the Balkans, Poland and *Mitteleuropa* unfolded after 1914, Austrian alarm increased.

Already by 1909, however, there was little the Austrians could do to halt their decline into increasing dependence on Germany – much as Aehrenthal was determined to do so. The fact was that changes in the international situation – largely, but not entirely, independent of Austrian activities – had left the Monarchy with no other possible source of effective support but Germany. The Bosnian crisis and Russia's determined efforts to combine the Balkan states in a league under her own auspices had damaged Austro-Russian relations beyond repair. Great Britain and France, increasingly obsessed with the German threat, were determined to hold on to Russia at all costs. Italy, with her reckless ambitions at the expense of the Ottoman Empire and her intrigues in Albania, was actively undermining the status quo the Austrians wished to uphold. As for Germany, the Kaiser's theatrical assurances of support contrasted lamentably with the performance of his statesmen and diplomats in the field. In fact, Germany's behaviour only served to intensify the growing feeling of isolation and desperation in Vienna. The trouble for the Austrians was, however – and this was especially alarming after the disappearance of Turkey-in-Europe made the prospect of a Balkan peninsula under Russian control a real possibility – that the Monarchy had only Germany to turn to. The Matscheko Memorandum was an attempt to enlist German support for a diplomatic campaign to restore the Monarchy's position; Sarajevo drove the Austrians to attempt to do so by military means.

Once this decision had been taken, the Monarchy had no alternative diplomatic options open to it at all. It had sometimes been possible in the past for a weak Power such as the Monarchy to exert a measure of persuasive influence over a stronger Power if that Power had itself felt threatened and insecure in the context of the European states system as a whole. This had been the case with Germany in 1879, in 1908, and to some extent in July 1914. But this always implied that the Monarchy might, if disappointed, turn elsewhere for support. With the outbreak of war with the three Entente Powers in 1914, and with Italy in 1915, all such options had disappeared. Czernin's threats in 1918 to denounce the alliance made no impression whatever in Berlin. Moreover, until the summer of 1918 Germany was not the nervous and isolated Power of 1908 and 1914, but a powerful and victorious state intent on re-ordering the international system to its own permanent advantage. In that re-ordered system the Monarchy would be assigned its place as Germany saw fit. It had in fact ceased to exist as an independent Great Power.

This trend was confirmed by parallel developments within the Monarchy early in 1918, when the ruling élite decided not to pursue the possibility of a compromise peace, with its implications of federal reform, but to stake everything on a German victory. Perhaps it was not in 1914, but only in 1918, that the die was cast that determined the fate of the Monarchy. Its more far-sighted statesmen had for the past century striven more or less successfully to cope with the external problems of the Monarchy by diplomatic means; when no German victory arrived, the collapse of the Monarchy demonstrated what these men had always suspected: all they that take the sword shall perish with the sword.

Appendices

Appendix I The Schönbrunn Convention,
6 June 1873

His Majesty the Emperor of Austria and King of Hungary and His Majesty the Emperor of All the Russias:
Wishing to give a practical form to the sentiments that inspire Their close understanding [*entente*],
With a view to consolidating the state of peace that now exists in Europe, having at heart the elimination of the risks of war that might disturb it,
Convinced that this aim cannot be better achieved than by a direct personal understanding between the sovereigns independent of changes that may occur in their administrations, have agreed on the following points:

1. Their Majesties promise each other, in the event of the interests of Their countries appearing to diverge over particular [*spéciales*] questions, to concert together to ensure that these divergences do not prevail over the considerations of a higher order that are Their chief concern.
Their Majesties are determined to prevent anyone from dividing Them as in respect of the principles which They consider Themselves solely able to safeguard, and, if necessary, to enforce the maintenance of European peace against all disturbances from any quarter whatever.
2. In the event of a threat to the peace arising from the aggression of a third Power, Their Majesties promise each other to reach an understanding with each other first of all and, without seeking or contracting new alliances, to agree on a line of action to be pursued in common.
3. If in consequence of this understanding military action should become necessary it shall be regulated [*réglée*] by a special convention to be concluded between Their Majesties.
4. If one of the High Contracting Parties should wish to denounce this present agreement to recover his freedom of action, he must give two years' notice of his intention so as to allow the other Party time to make such arrangements as he finds convenient.

Schönbrunn, 25 May/6 June 1873.   Franz Joseph. Alexander.

His Majesty the Emperor of Germany, having taken note of the above agreement, drawn up and signed at Schönbrunn by Their Majesties the

Emperor of Austria and King of Hungary and the Emperor of All the Russias, and finding its content in conformity with the sentiments embodied in the agreement signed at St Petersburg between Their Majesties the Emperor William and the Emperor Alexander, accedes to its stipulations in every respect.

Their Majesties the Emperor and King William and the Emperor and King Franz Joseph in approving and signing this act of accession will bring it to the knowledge of the Emperor Alexander.

Schönbrunn, 22 October 1873.

William. Franz Joseph.

(*Source*: Translated from G.P. Vol. I, pp. 206–7)

Appendix II Treaty of Alliance between Austria-Hungary and Germany, 7 October, 1879

Inasmuch as Their Majesties the Emperor of Austria, King of Hungary, and the German Emperor, King of Prussia, must consider it Their imperative duty as Monarchs to provide for the security of Their Empires and the peace of Their subjects, under all circumstances;

inasmuch as the two Sovereigns, as was the case under the former existing relations of alliance, will be enabled by the close union of the two Empires to fulfil this duty more easily and more efficaciously;

inasmuch as, finally, an intimate co-operation of Germany and Austria-Hungary can menace no one, but is rather calculated to consolidate the peace of Europe as established by the stipulations of Berlin;

Their Majesties the Emperor of Austria, King of Hungary, and the Emperor of Germany, while solemnly promising each other never to allow Their purely defensive Agreement to develop an aggressive tendency in any direction, have determined to conclude an Alliance of peace and mutual defence.

For this purpose Their Most Exalted Majesties have designated as Their Plenipotentiaries:

His Most Exalted Majesty the Emperor of Austria, King of Hungary, His Actual Privy Councillor, Minister of the Imperial Household and of Foreign Affairs, Lieutenant-Field-Marshal Count Julius Andrássy of Czik-Szent-Király and Kraszna-Horka, etc., etc.,

His most Exalted Majesty the German Emperor, His Ambassador Extraordinary and Plenipotentiary, Lieutenant-General Prince Henry VII of Reuss, etc., etc.,

who have met this day at Vienna, and, after the exchange of their full powers, found in good and due form, have agreed upon the following Articles:

ARTICLE I

Should, contrary to their hope, and against the loyal desire of the two High Contracting Parties, one of the two Empires be attacked by Russia, the High Contracting Parties are bound to come to the assistance one of the other with the whole war strength of their Empires, and accordingly only to conclude peace together and upon mutual agreement.

ARTICLE II

Should one of the High Contracting Parties be attacked by another Power, the other High Contracting Party binds itself hereby, not only not to support the aggressor against its high Ally, but to observe at least a benevolent neutral attitude towards its fellow Contracting Party.

Should, however, the attacking party in such a case be supported by Russia, either by an active co-operation or by military measures which constitute a menace to the Party attacked, then the obligation stipulated in Article I of this Treaty, for reciprocal assistance with the whole fighting force, becomes equally operative, and the conduct of the war by the two High Contracting Parties shall in this case also be in common until the conclusion of a common peace.

ARTICLE III

The duration of this Treaty shall be provisionally fixed at five years from the day of ratification. One year before the expiration of this period the two High Contracting Parties shall consult together concerning the question whether the conditions serving as the basis of the Treaty still prevail, and reach an agreement in regard to the further continuance or possible modification of certain details. If in the course of the first months of the last year of the Treaty no invitation has been received from either side to open these negotiations, the Treaty shall be considered as renewed for a further period of three years.

ARTICLE IV

This Treaty shall, in conformity with its peaceful character, and to avoid any misinterpretation, be kept secret by the two High Contracting Parties, and only communicated to a third Power upon a joint understanding between the two Parties, and according to the terms of a special Agreement.

The two High Contracting Parties venture to hope, after the sentiments expressed by the Emperor Alexander at the meeting at Alexandrovo, that the armaments of Russia will not in reality prove to be menacing to them, and have on that account no reason for making a communication at present; should, however, this hope, contrary to their expectations, prove to be erroneous, the two High Contracting Parties would consider it their loyal obligation to let the Emperor Alexander know, at least confidentially, that they must consider an attack on either of them as directed against both.

ARTICLE V

This Treaty shall derive its validity from the approbation of the two Exalted Sovereigns and shall be ratified within fourteen days after this approbation has been granted by Their Most Exalted Majesties.

In witness whereof the Plenipotentiaries have signed this Treaty with their own hands and affixed their arms.

Done at Vienna, October 7, 1879.

Andrássy. H. VII v. Reuss.

L.S. L.S.

(*Source*: A.F.Pribram, *Secret Treaties*, Vol. I, pp. 25–31)

Appendix III   The Three Emperors' Alliance, 1881

(*a*) Convention between Austria-Hungary, the German
Empire, and Russia.
Berlin, June 18, 1881

The Courts of Austria-Hungary, of Germany, and of Russia, animated by an equal desire to consolidate the general peace by an understanding intended to assure the defensive position of their respective States, have come into agreement on certain questions which more especially concern their reciprocal interests.

With this purpose the three Courts have appointed: . . .

ARTICLE I

In case one of the High Contracting Parties should find itself at war with a fourth Great Power, the two others shall maintain towards it a benevolent neutrality and shall devote their efforts to the localization of the conflict.

This stipulation shall apply likewise to a war between one of the three Powers and Turkey, but only in the case where a previous agreement shall have been reached between the three Courts as to the results of this war.

In the special case where one of them should obtain a more positive support from one of its two Allies, the obligatory value of the present Article shall remain in all its force for the third.

ARTICLE II

Russia, in agreement with Germany, declares her firm resolution to respect the interests arising from the new position assured to Austria-Hungary by the Treaty of Berlin.

The three Courts, desirous of avoiding all discord between them, engage to take account of their respective interests in the Balkan Peninsula. They further promise one another that any new modifications in the territorial *status quo* of Turkey in Europe can be accomplished only in virtue of a common agreement between them.

In order to facilitate the agreement contemplated by the present Article, an agreement of which it is impossible to foresee all the conditions, the three Courts from the present moment record in the Protocol annexed to this Treaty the points on which an understanding has already been established in principle.

ARTICLE III

The three Courts recognize the European and mutually obligatory character of the principle of the closing of the Straits of the Bosphorus and of the Dardanelles, founded on international law, confirmed by treaties, and summed up in the declaration of the second Plenipotentiary of Russia at the session of July 12 of the Congress of Berlin (Protocol 19).

They will take care in common that Turkey shall make no exception to this rule in favour of the interests of any Government whatsoever, by lending to warlike operations of a belligerent Power the portion of its Empire constituted by the Straits.

In case of infringement, or to prevent it if such infringement should be in prospect, the three Courts will inform Turkey that they would regard her, in that event, as putting herself in a state of war towards the injured Party, and as having deprived herself thenceforth of the benefits of the security assured to her territorial *status quo* by the Treaty of Berlin.

[ARTICLES IV–VII relating to duration, secrecy, and ratification of the Treaty]

(*b*) Separate Protocol on the same date to the Convention
of Berlin, June 18, 1881

The undersigned Plenipotentiaries . . .

having recorded in accordance with Article II of the secret Treaty concluded today the points affecting the interests of the three Courts of Austria-Hungary, Germany, and Russia in the Balkan Peninsula upon which an understanding has already been reached among them, have agreed to the following Protocol:

I. BOSNIA AND HERZEGOVINA

Austria-Hungary reserves the right to annex these provinces at whatever moment she shall deem opportune.

2. SANJAK OF NOVIBAZAR

The Declaration exchanged between the Austro-Hungarian Plenipotentiaries and the Russian Plenipotentiaries at the Congress of Berlin under date of July 13/1, 1878, remains in force.

3. EASTERN RUMELIA

The three Powers agree in regarding the eventuality of an occupation either of Eastern Rumelia or of the Balkans as full of perils for the general peace. In case this should occur, they will employ their efforts to dissuade the Porte from such an enterprise, it being well understood that Bulgaria and Eastern Rumelia on their part are to abstain from provoking the Porte by attacks emanating from their territories against the other provinces of the Ottoman Empire.

4. BULGARIA

The three Powers will not oppose the eventual reunion of Bulgaria and Eastern Rumelia within the territorial limits assigned to them by the Treaty of Berlin, if this question should come up by the force of circumstances. They agree to dissuade the Bulgarians from all aggression against the neighbouring provinces, particularly Macedonia; and to inform them that in such a case they would be acting at their own risk and peril.

5. ATTITUDE OF AGENTS IN THE EAST

In order to avoid collisions of interests in the local questions which may arise, the three Courts will furnish their representatives and agents in the Orient with a general instruction, directing them to endeavour to smooth out their divergences by friendly explanations between themselves in each special case; and, in the cases where they do not succeed in doing so, to refer the matters to their Governments.

The present Protocol forms an integral part of the secret Treaty signed on this day at Berlin, and shall have the same force and validity.

In witness whereof the respective Plenipotentiaries have signed it and have affixed thereto the seal of their arms.

Done at Berlin, June 18, 1881

L.S.	Széchényi
L.S.	v. Bismarck
L.S.	Sabouroff.

(*Source*: A.F. Pribram, *Secret Treaties*, Vol. I, pp. 37–47)

Appendices

Appendix IV First Treaty of Alliance between Austria-Hungary, Germany, and Italy, Vienna, 20 May 1882

Their Majesties the Emperor of Austria, King of Bohemia, etc., and Apostolic King of Hungary, the Emperor of Germany, King of Prussia, and the King of Italy, animated by the desire to increase the guaranties of the general peace, to fortify the monarchical principle and thereby to assure the unimpaired maintenance of the social and political order in Their respective States, have agreed to conclude a Treaty which, by its essentially conservative and defensive nature, pursues only the aim of forestalling the dangers which might threaten the security of Their States and the peace of Europe.

To this end Their Majesties have appointed . . .

ARTICLE I

The High Contracting Parties mutually promise peace and friendship, and will enter into no alliance or engagement directed against any one of their States.

They engage to proceed to an exchange of ideas on political and economic questions of a general nature which may arise, and they further promise one another mutual support within the limits of their own interests.

ARTICLE II

In case Italy, without direct provocation on her part, should be attacked by France for any reason whatsoever, the two other Contracting Parties shall be bound to lend help and assistance with all their forces to the Party attacked.

This same obligation shall devolve upon Italy in case of any aggression without direct provocation by France against Germany.

ARTICLE III

If one, or two, of the High Contracting Parties, without direct provocation on their part, should chance to be attacked and to be engaged in a war with two or more Great Powers nonsignatory to the present Treaty, the *casus foederis* will arise simultaneously for all the High Contracting Parties.

ARTICLE IV

In case a Great Power nonsignatory to the present Treaty should threaten the security of the states of one of the High Contracting Parties, and the threatened Party should find itself forced on that account to make war against it, the two others bind themselves to observe towards their Ally a benevolent neutrality. Each of them reserves to itself, in this case, the right to take part in the war, if it should see fit, to make common cause with its Ally.

ARTICLE V

If the peace of any of the High Contracting Parties should chance to be threatened under the circumstances foreseen by the preceding Articles, the High Contracting Parties shall take counsel together in ample time as to the military measures to be taken with a view to eventual co-operation.

They engage henceforward, in all cases of common participation in a war, to conclude neither armistice, nor peace, nor treaty, except by common agreement among themselves.

[ARTICLES VI–VIII relating to secrecy, duration, and ratification of the Treaty]

Ministerial Declaration[1]

The Imperial and Royal Government declares that the provisions of the secret Treaty concluded May 20, 1882, between Austria-Hungary, Germany, and Italy, cannot, as has been previously agreed, in any case be regarded as being directed against England.

In witness whereof the present ministerial Declaration, which equally must remain secret, has been drawn up to be exchanged against identic Declarations of the Imperial Government of Germany and of the Royal Government of Italy.

The Imperial and Royal Minister of Foreign Affairs.
Vienna, May 28, 1882

(*Source*: A.F. Pribram, *Secret Treaties*, Vol. I, pp. 65–73)

Appendix V   Treaty of Alliance between Austria-Hungary, the German Empire, and Italy, Berlin, 6 May 1891

Their Majesties the Emperor of Austria, King of Bohemia, etc., and Apostolic King of Hungary, the Emperor of Germany, King of Prussia, and the King of Italy, firmly resolved to assure to Their States the continuation of the benefits which the maintenance of the Triple Alliance guarantees to them, from the political point of view as well as from the monarchical and social point of view, and wishing with this purpose to prolong the duration of this Alliance, concluded on May 20, 1882, and already renewed a first time by the Treaties of February 20, 1887, whose expiration was fixed for May 30, 1892, have, for this purpose, appointed as Their Plenipotentiaries, . . .

[ARTICLES I–V as ARTICLES I–V of the Treaty of 20 May 1882]

1. The Austro-Hungarian version of the so-called Mancini Declaration.

ARTICLE VI

Germany and Italy, having in mind only the maintenance, so far as possible, of the territorial *status quo* in the Orient, engage to use their influence to forestall, on the Ottoman coasts and islands in the Adriatic and the Aegean Seas, any territorial modification which might be injurious to one or the other of the Powers signatory to the present Treaty. To this end, they will communicate to one another all information of a nature to enlighten each other mutually concerning their own dispositions, as well as those of other Powers.

ARTICLE VII[2]

Austria-Hungary and Italy, having in mind only the maintenance, so far as possible, of the territorial *status quo* in the Orient, engage to use their influence to forestall any territorial modification which might be injurious to one or the other of the Powers signatory to the present Treaty. To this end, they shall communicate to one another all information of a nature to enlighten each other mutually concerning their own dispositions, as well as those of other Powers.

However, if, in the course of events, the maintenance of the *status quo* in the regions of the Balkans or of the Ottoman coasts and islands in the Adriatic and in the Aegean Sea should become impossible, and if, whether in consequence of the action of a third Power or otherwise, Austria-Hungary or Italy should find themselves under the necessity of modifying it by a temporary or permanent occupation on their part, this occupation shall take place only after a previous agreement between the two Powers, based upon the principle of a reciprocal compensation for every advantage, territorial or other, which each of them might obtain beyond the present *status quo*, and giving satisfaction to the interests and well-founded claims of the two Parties.

ARTICLE VIII

The stipulations of Articles VI and VII shall apply in no way to the Egyptian question, with regard to which the High Contracting Parties preserve respectively their freedom of action, regard being always paid to the principles upon which the present Treaty rests.

[ARTICLES IX–X, Italo-German clauses concerning North Africa]

[ARTICLES XI–XV, concerning secrecy, duration and ratification of the Treaty]

---

2. Identical with Article I of the Austro-Hungarian Italian Separate Treaty of 20 February 1887.

Appendices

PROTOCOL

At the moment of proceeding to the signing of the Treaty of this day between Austria-Hungary, Germany, and Italy, the undersigned Plenipotentiaries of these three Powers, thereto duly authorized, mutually declare themselves as follows:

1. Under reserve of parliamentary approval for the executory stipulations proceeding from the present declaration of principle, the High Contracting Parties promise each other, from this moment, in economic matters (finances, customs, railways), in addition to most-favoured-nation treatment, all of the facilities and special advantages which would be compatible with the requirements of each of the three States and with their respective engagements with third Powers.

2. The accession of England being already acquired, in principle, to the stipulations of the Treaty of this day which concern the Orient, properly so-called, to wit, the territories of the Ottoman Empire, the High Contracting Parties shall exert themselves at the opportune moment, and to the extent that circumstances may permit it, to bring about an analogous accession with regard to the North African territories of the central and western part of the Mediterranean, including Morocco. This accession might be realized by an acceptance, on the part of England, of the programme established by Articles IX and X of the Treaty of this day.

In witness whereof the three Plenipotentiaries have signed the present Protocol in triplicate.

Done at Berlin, the sixth day of the month of May, one thousand eight hundred and ninety-one.

Széchényi

v. Caprivi

Launay.

(*Source*: A.F. Pribram, *Secret Treaties*, Vol. I, pp. 151–63)

Appendix VI   Joint Declaration of Austria-Hungary and Russia in Regard to the Maintenance of Neutrality by Either if the Other is at War, St Petersburg, 2/15 October 1904

The undersigned, duly authorized by their August Sovereigns, have met together today at the Imperial Ministry of Foreign Affairs to sign the following Declaration:

Austria-Hungary and Russia, united by identical views as to the conservative policy to be followed in the Balkan countries, and much satisfied with the result obtained so far by their close collaboration, are firmly decided to persevere in this course. Happy to record once more this understanding, the Cabinets of Vienna and of St Petersburg attach great importance to offering each other in due form a mark of friendship and reciprocal confidence.

It is with this purpose that the two Powers have come to an agreement to observe a loyal and absolute neutrality in case one of the two Parties signatory to this Declaration should find itself, alone and without provocation on its part, in a state of war with a third Power which sought to endanger its security or the status quo; the maintenance of which constitutes the basis of their understanding, as pacific as it is conservative.

The engagement between Austria-Hungary and Russia stipulated in the above naturally does not apply to the Balkan countries, whose destinies are obviously closely attached to the agreement established between the two neighbouring Empires. The said engagement is understood to remain valid so long as these two great Powers shall pursue their policy of an understanding in the affairs of Turkey; it shall be kept secret, and cannot be communicated to any other Government, except after a previous understanding between the Cabinets of Vienna and of St Petersburg.

Done in duplicate at St. Petersburg, October 2/15, 1904.

L. Aehrenthal.   Count Lamsdorff.

(*Source*: A.F. Pribram, *Secret Treaties*, Vol. I, pp. 237–9)

Bibliography

A. Archive Sources

(i) Private papers

Aehrenthal MSS	Haus-, Hof-, und Staatsarchiv, Vienna.
Berchtold MSS	Haus-, Hof-, und Staatsarchiv, Vienna.
Cartwright MSS	Delapré Abbey, Northamptonshire.
Grey MSS	Public Record Office, London.
Hardinge MSS	University Library, Cambridge.
Kallay MSS	Haus-, Hof-, und Staatsarchiv, Vienna.
Mensdorff MSS	Haus-, Hof-, und Staatsarchiv, Vienna.
Merey MSS	Haus-, Hof-, und Staatsarchiv, Vienna.

(ii) Official papers

Foreign Office Correspondence in the Public Record Office, London.

Series F.O.	7, Austria
F.O.	120, Vienna embassy and consular archives
F.O.	368, Commercial
F.O.	371, Political
F.O.	800, Private papers.

Politisches Archiv, in the Haus-, Hof-, und Staatsarchiv, Vienna

Series P.A.	I Allgemeines
P.A.	III Preußen
P.A.	VIII England
P.A.	IX Frankreich
P.A.	X Rußland
P.A.	XII Türkei
P.A.	XV Bulgarien
P.A.	XXXII Marokko
P.A.	XL Interna.

Kabinettsarchiv.
Administrative Registratur.

Bibliography

Archives Nationales, Ministère des Affaires Étrangères, Paris Correspondance Politique, Autriche

Bayerisches Staatsarchiv, Munich
Series M.A. III Wien.

B. Published documents

I.V. Bestuzhev, (ed.), 'Borba v pravyaschikh krugakh Rossii po voprosam vneshnei politiki vo vremya Bosniiskogo krizisa', in *Istoricheskii Arkhiv*, 5 (1962), pp. 113–47. (English translation in the appendix to F.R. Bridge, 'Izvolsky, Aehrenthal, and the End of the Austro-Russian Entente', in *Mitteilungen des österreichischen Staatsarchivs*, 29 (1976), pp. 315–62.)

L. Bittner and H. Uebersberger (eds) *Oesterreich-Ungarns Außenpolitik von der bosnischen Krise 1908 bis zum Kriegsausbruch 1914*, 9 vols (Vienna 1930)

F.R. Bridge (ed.), *Austro-Hungarian Foreign Office Documents on the Macedonian Struggle, 1896–1912* (Salonika 1976)

G.P. Gooch and H.W.V. Temperley (eds), *British Documents on the Origins of the War, 1898–1914*, 11 vols (London 1926–8)

M. Komjathy (ed.), *Protokolle des gemeinsamen Ministerrates der österreichisch-ungarischen Monarchie, 1914–1918* (Budapest 1966)

J. Lepsius, A. Mendelssohn-Bartholdy and F. Thimme (eds), *Die Große Politik der europäischen Kabinette, 1871–1914*, 40 vols (Berlin 1922–7)

A.F. Pribram (ed.), *The Secret Treaties of Austria-Hungary, 1879–1914*, 2 vols (Cambridge, Mass. 1931)

C. General, 1815–1918

M.S. Anderson, *The Eastern Question, 1774–1923. A Study in International Relations* (London 1966)

J. Becker and A. Hillgruber (eds), '*Die deutsche Frage im 19. und 20. Jahrhundert*', Schriften der philosophischen Fakultät der Universität Augsburg, 24 (Munich 1963)

H. Benedikt, *Die wirtschaftliche Entwicklung in der Franz-Joseph-Zeit* (Vienna 1958)

F.R. Bridge, *From Sadowa to Sarajevo. The Foreign Policy of Austria-Hungary, 1866–1914* (London 1972)

—— and Roger Bullen, *The Great Powers and the European States System, 1815–1914* (London 1980)

I. Diószegi, *Hungarians in the Ballhausplatz. Studies in the Austro-Hungarian Common Foreign Policy* (Budapest 1983)

F. Engel-Janosi, *Geschichte auf dem Ballhausplatz. Essays zur österreichischen Außenpolitik, 1830–1945* (Vienna 1963)

F. Fellner, *Der Dreibund. Europäische Diplomatie vor dem ersten Weltkrieg*

(Vienna 1960)

E. von Glaise-Horstenau, *Franz Josephs Weggefährte. Das Leben des Generalstabschefs Grafen Beck* (Vienna 1930)

D. Goad, *The Economic Rise of the Habsburg Empire, 1750–1914* (Berkeley 1984)

B. Hamann, *Elisabeth, Kaiserin wider Willen* (Vienna 1981)

E.R. Huber, *Deutsche Verfassungsgeschichte seit 1789*, 7 vols (Stuttgart 1960–)

B. Jelavich, *The Habsburg Empire in European Affairs, 1814–1918* (Chicago 1969)

——, *History of the Balkans*, 2 vols (Cambridge 1983)

R.A. Kann, *A History of the Habsburg Empire, 1526–1918* (London 1974)

H. Lutz and H. Rumpler (eds), *Oesterreich und die deutsche Frage im XIX und im XX Jahrhundert*, Wiener Beiträge zur Geschichte der Neuzeit, 9 (Vienna 1982)

C.A. Macartney, *The Habsburg Empire, 1790–1918* (London 1968)

J. Redlich, *Kaiser Franz Joseph von Oesterreich, eine Biographie* (Berlin 1928)

G.E. Rothenberg, *The Army of Francis Joseph* (Lafayette, Indiana 1976)

L. Salvatorelli, *La triplice alleanza: storia diplomatica 1877–1912* (Milan 1939)

A. Sked, *The Decline and Fall of the Habsburg Empire* (London 1989)

T. von Sosnosky, *Die Balkanpolitik Oesterreich-Ungarns seit 1866*, 2 vols (Stuttgart 1913–14)

H. Ritter von Srbik, *Aus Oesterreichs Vergangenheit* (Salzburg 1949)

N. Stone, 'Army and Society in the Habsburg Monarchy', in *Past and Present*, 33 (1966), pp. 95–111

A.J.P. Taylor, *The Habsburg Monarchy 1809–1918. A History of the Austrian Empire and Austria-Hungary* (London 1949)

——, *The Struggle for Mastery in Europe, 1848–1918* (Oxford 1954)

W. Wagner, 'Kaiser Franz Joseph und das deutsche Reich, 1871–1914', unpublished Ph.D. thesis, Vienna 1951

A. Wandruszka and P. Urbanitsch (eds) *Die Habsburgermonarchie 1848–1918, V, Die bewaffnete Macht* (Vienna 1987)

—— (eds), *Die Habsburgermonarchie 1848–1918, VI, Die Habsburgermonarchie im System der internationalen Beziehungen* (Vienna 1989)

A. von Wittich, 'Die Rüstungen Oesterreich-Ungarns von 1866 bis 1914' in *Berliner Monatshefte*, 10 (1932), pp. 116–136

D. 1815–1856

R.A. Austensen, 'The Making of Austria's Prussian Policy, 1848–1852', in *Historical Journal*, 27 (1984), pp. 861–76

——, 'Felix Schwarzenberg: "Realpolitiker" or Metternichian? The Evidence of the Dresden Conference', in *Mitteilungen des österreichischen Staatsarchivs*, 30 (1977), pp. 97–118

——, 'Count Buol and the Metternichian Tradition', in *Austrian History*

Yearbook, 9–10 (1973–4), pp. 173–93

W. Baumgart, *The Peace of Paris, 1856* (Oxford 1981)

G. de Berthier de Sauvigny, *Metternich et al France après le congrès de Vienne*, 3 vols (Paris 1968–71)

R.D. Billinger, 'The War Scare of 1831 and Prussian–South German plans for the End of Austrian Dominance in Germany', in *Central European History*, 9 (1976), pp. 203–20

H. Contamine, *Diplomatie et diplomates sous la restauration* (Paris 1970)

E. Eyck, *The Frankfurt Parliament* (London 1968)

K. Hammer, *Die französische Diplomatie der Restauration und Deutschland* (Stuttgart 1963)

W. Heindl, *Graf Buol-Schauenstein in St Petersburg und London. Zur Genesis des Antagonismus zwischen Oesterreich und Russland*, Studien zur Geschichte der österreichisch-ungarischen Monarchie, 9 (Vienna 1970)

R.A. Kann, 'Metternich: a Reappraisal of his Impact on International Relations', in *Journal of Modern History*, 32 (1960), pp. 333–9

R. Kiszling, *Fürst Felix zu Schwarzenberg. Der politische Lehrmeister Kaiser Franz Josephs* (Graz–Cologne 1952)

E.E. Kraehe, *The Metternich Controversy* (New York 1971)

H. Müller, 'Der Weg nach Münchengrätz. Voraussetzungen, Bedingungen und Grenzen der Reaktivierung des reaktionären Bündnisses der Habsburger und Hohenzollern mit den Romanovs im Herbst 1833', in *Jahrbuch für Geschichte*, 21 (1980), pp. 7–62

I.C. Nichols, *The European Pentarchy and the Congress of Verona* (The Hague 1971)

A.J. Reinerman, 'Metternich, Alexander I and the Russian Challenge in Italy, 1815–20', in *Journal of Modern History*, 46 (1974), pp. 262–76

——, 'Metternich, the Papal States and the 1831 Italian Crisis', in *Central European History*, 10 (1977), pp. 206–18

——, *Austria and the Papacy in the Age of Metternich: I, Between Conflict and Co-operation, 1809–1830* (Washington 1979)

N. Rich, *Why the Crimean War? A Cautionary Tale* (London 1985)

K.W. Rock, 'Schwarzenberg versus Nicholas I, Round One: The Negotiation of the Habsburg–Romanov Alliance against Hungary in 1849', in *Austrian History Yearbook*, 6/7 (1970–1), pp. 109–42

——, 'Felix Schwarzenberg, Military Diplomat', in *Austrian History Yearbook*, 11 (1975), pp. 85–100

H. Rumpler, *Die deutsche Politik des Freiherrn von Beust, 1848 bis 1850*, Veröffentlichungen der Kommission für Neuere Geschichte Oesterreichs, 57 (Vienna 1972)

——, 'Felix Schwarzenberg und das "dritte Deutschland"', in H. Fichtenau and E. Zöllner (eds), *Beiträge zur neuere Geschichte Oesterreichs* (Vienna 1974), pp. 371–82

P.W. Schroeder, 'Metternich Studies since 1945', in *Journal of Modern History*, 33 (1961), pp. 237–60

——, *Metternich's Diplomacy at its Zenith, 1820–3*, (Austin, Texas 1962)

——, *Austria, Great Britain and the Crimean War. The Destruction of the European Concert* (Ithaca 1972)

——, 'A Turning Point in Austrian Policy in the Crimean War: The Conferences of March 1854', in *Austrian History Yearbook* 4/5 (1968–9), pp. 159–202

——, 'Austria and the Danubian Principalities, 1853–6', in *Central European History*, 2 (1969), pp.213–36

A. Sked, *The Survival of the Habsburg Empire: Radetzky, the Imperial Army, and the Class War, 1848* (London 1979)

—— (ed.), *Europe's Balance of Power, 1815–48* (London 1979)

A.J.P. Taylor, *The Italian Problem in European Diplomacy, 1846–49* (Manchester 1934)

C.K. Webster, *The Foreign Policy of Castlereagh, 1812–22*, 2 vols (London 1925)

D. Wetzel, *The Crimean War, a Diplomatic History* (New York 1985)

E. 1856–1871

R.A. Austensen, 'Austria and the "Struggle for Supremacy in Germany", 1848–1864', in *Journal of Modern History*, 52 (1980), pp. 195–225

N.N. Barker, 'Austria, France and the Venetian Question, 1861–66', in *Journal of Modern History*, 36 (1964), pp. 145–54

L.R. Beaber, 'Austria and the Emergence of Roumania, 1855–61', in *East European Quarterly*, XI (1971)

R. Blaas, 'Il problema veneto e la diplomazia austriaca', in *Conferenze e note accademiche nel 1 centenario dell'unione del Veneto all'Italia*, (Padua 1967), pp. 39–157

——, 'Die italienische Frage und das österreichische Parlament, 1859–66', in *Mitteilungen des österreichischen Staatsarchivs*, 22 (1969), pp. 151–245

H.H. Brandt, *Der österreichische Neoabsolutismus: Staatsfinanzen und Politik, 1848–1860*, 2 vols, Schriften der historischen Kommission bei der Bayerischen Akademie der Wissenschaften, 15 (Göttingen 1978)

M. Dendarsky, 'Das Klischee von "Ces Messieurs de Vienne". Der osterreichisch–französische Geheimvertrag vom 12 Juni 1866', in *Historische Zeitschrift*, 235 (1982), pp. 289–353

I. Diószegi, *Oesterreich-Ungarn und der französisch–preußische Krieg, 1870–71*, (Budapest 1974)

R.B. Elrod, 'Austria and the Venetian Question, 1860–66', in *Central European History*, 4 (1971), pp. 149–71

F. Engel-Janosi, *Graf Rechberg. Vier Kapitel zu seiner und Oesterreichs Geschichte* (Munich 1927)

C.W. Hallberg, *Franz Joseph and Napoleon III, 1852–1864. A Study in Austro-French Relations* (New York 1955)

K.F. Helleiner, *Free Trade and Frustration. Anglo-Austrian Negotiations,*

1860–1870 (Toronto 1963)

W.A. Jenks, *Franz Joseph and the Italians, 1849–59* (Charlottesville 1978)

K. Koch, *Franz Graf Crenneville, Generaladjutant Kaiser Franz Josephs*, Militärgeschichtliche Dissertationen österreichischer Universitäten, 3 (Vienna 1974)

E. Kolb (ed.), *Europa vor dem Krieg von 1870. Mächtekonstellationen – Konfliktfelder–Kriegsausbruch*, Schriften des historischen Kollegs, 10 (Munich 1987)

W.E. Mosse, *The Great Powers and the German Question, 1848–71, with special reference to England and Russia* (Cambridge 1958)

H. Potthoff, *Die deutsche Politik Beusts von seiner Berufung zum österreichischen Außenminister Oktober 1866 bis zum Ausbruch des deutsch-französischen Krieges 1870–71*, Bonner historischen Forschungen, 31 (1968)

K.P. Schoenhals, *The Russian Policy of Count Friedrich Ferdinand von Beust, 1866–71* (Ann Arbor 1964)

P.W. Schroeder, 'Austro-German Relations: Divergent Views of the Disjointed Partnership', in *Central European History* (1978), pp. 302–12

F. 1871–1897

N. de Bagdasarian, *The Austro-German Rapprochement, 1871–77* (Rutherford-Madison-Teaneck NJ 1976)

A.H. Benna, 'Studien zum Kultusprotektorat Oesterreich-Ungarns in Albanien im Zeitalter des Imperialismus, 1888–1908', in *Mitteilungen des österreichischen Staatsarchivs*, 7 (1954), pp. 13–46

J.A.S. Grenville, 'Goluchowski, Salisbury and the Mediterranean Agreements, 1895–97', in *Slavonic and East European Review*, 36 (1958), pp. 340–69

M.M. Jefferson, 'The place of Constantinople and the Straits in British Foreign Policy, 1890–1902', unpublished MA thesis, London, 1959

B. Jelavich, 'Foreign Policy and the Nationality Question in the Habsburg Empire. A Memorandum by Kálnoky', in *Austrian History Yearbook*, 6–7 (1970–1), pp. 142–59

B.K. Kiraly and G. Stokes (eds), *Insurrections, Wars and the Eastern Crisis in the 1870s*, War and Society in East Central Europe, 17 (New York 1985)

F.J. Kos, *Die Politik Oesterreich-Ungarns während der Orientkrise 1874/5–1879*, Dissertationen zur neuere Geschichte, 16 (Vienna 1984)

W.L. Langer, *European Alliances and Alignments 1871–90* (New York 1962)

C.J. Lowe, *Salisbury and the Mediterranean, 1886–96* (London 1965)

W.N. Medlicott, *The Congress of Berlin and After*, 2nd edn (London 1963)

——, *Bismarck, Gladstone and the Concert of Europe* (London 1956)

A. Novotny, *Quellen und Studien zur Geschichte des Berliner Kongresses, 1878*, Veröffentlichungen der Kommission für neuere Geschichte

Oesterreichs, 49 (Graz 1957)

A.F. Pribram, 'Milan IV von Serbien und die Geheimverträge Oester-reich-Ungarns mit Serbien 1881–9', in *Historische Blätter* (1921), pp. 464–94

A. Ramm, 'European Alliances and Ententes, 1879–1885, A Study of Contemporary British Information', unpublished MA thesis, London

E.R. von Rutkowski, 'Gustav, Graf Kálnoky von Köröspatak. Oester-reich-Ungarns Außenpolitik von 1881–1885', unpublished Ph.D. thesis, Vienna, 1952

——, 'General Skobelev, die Krise des Jahres 1882 und die Anfänge der militärischen Vereinbarungen zwischen Oesterreich-Ungarn und Deutsch-land', in *Ostdeutsche Wissenschaft*, 10 (1963), pp. 81–151

H-D. Schanderl, 'Die Albanienpolitik Oesterreich-Ungarns und Italiens 1877–1908', in *Albanische Forschungen*, 9 (Wiesbaden 1971)

I. Scott, 'The Making of the Triple Alliance, 1882', in *East European Quarterly*, 12 (1978), pp. 339–423

P. Stein, *Die Neuorientierung der österreichisch-ungarischen Außenpolitik, 1895–97*, Göttinger Bausteine zur Geschichtswissenschaft, 44 (Göttingen 1972)

B. Sutter, 'Die Großmächte und die Erhaltung des europäischen Friedens zu Beginn der Kreta-Krise 1897', in *Südostforschungen*, 21 (1962), pp. 214–369

B. Waller, *Bismarck at the Crossroads, 1878–1880: The Reorientation of German Foreign Policy after the Congress of Berlin* (London 1974)

E. Walters, 'Unpublished Documents: Lord Salisbury's Refusal to Revise and Renew the Mediterranean Agreements', in *Slavonic and East European Review*, 29, (1950), pp. 268–86

——, 'Unpublished Documents: Austro-Russian Relations under Golu-chowski, 1895–1906, (I–III)', in *Slavonic and East European Review*, 31 (1953), pp. 503–27, 32 (1954), pp. 486–98

E. von Wertheimer, *Graf Julius Andrássy, sein Leben und seine Zeit*, 3 vols, (Stuttgart 1910–13)

G. 1897–1914

F. Adanir, *Die makedonische Frage. Ihre Entstehung und Entwicklung bis 1908*, Frankfurter Historische Studien, ·20 (Wiesbaden 1979)

W.C. Askew, *Europe and Italy's Acquisition of Libya 1911–12*, (Durham, N.C. 1942)

V.R. Berghahn, *Germany and the Approach of War in 1914* (London 1973)

F.R. Bridge, 'The British Declaration of War on Austria-Hungary in 1914' in *Slavonic and East European Review*, 47 (1969), pp. 401–22

——, '*Tarde venientibus ossa*: Austro-Hungarian Colonial Aspirations in Asia Minor, 1913–14', in *Middle Eastern Studies*, 6 (1970) pp. 319–30

——, *Great Britain and Austria-Hungary, 1906–14. A Diplomatic History* (London 1972)

——, 'Izvolsky, Aehrenthal, and the End of the Austro-Russian Entente, 1906–8', in *Mitteilungen des österreichischen Staatsarchivs*, 29 (1976), pp.315–62

——, 'Austria-Hungary and the Ottoman Empire in the Twentieth Century', in *Mitteilungen des österreichischen Staatsarchivs* 34 (1981), pp. 234–71

W.M. Carlgren, *Iswolsky und Aehrenthal vor der bosnischen Annexionskrise. Russische und österreichisch-ungarische Balkanpolitik 1906–8* (Uppsala 1955)

L. Cassels, *Archduke and Assassin* (London 1984)

R.J. Crampton, *The Hollow Détente. Anglo-German Relations in the Balkans 1911–14*, (London 1979)

D. Dakin, *The Greek Struggle in Macedonia* (Salonika 1969)

F. Fellner, 'Die Haltung Oesterreich-Ungarns während der Konferenz von Algeciras', in *Mitteilungen des Instituts für österreichische Geschichtsforschung*, 71 (1963), pp. 462–77

L.A. Gebhard Jr, 'Austria-Hungary's Dreadnought Squadron: the Naval Outlay of 1911', in *Austrian History Yearbook*, IV–V (1968–9), pp. 245–58

P.G. Halpern, *The Mediterranean Naval Situation 1908–14* (Cambridge, Mass. 1971)

H. Hantsch, *Leopold Graf Berchtold, Grandseigneur und Staatsmann*, 2 vols, (Graz 1963)

E.C. Helmreich, *The Diplomacy of the Balkan Wars* (Harvard 1938)

L. Höbelt, 'Schlieffen, Beck, Potiorek und das Ende der gemeinsamen deutsch–österreichisch-ungarischen Aufmarschpläne im Osten', in *Militärgeschichtliche Mitteilungen*, 36 (1984/2), pp. 7–30

P. Hohenbalken (ed.), *Heinrich Graf Lützow. Im diplomatischen Dienste der k.u.k. Monarchie* (Vienna 1971)

Institut für Oesterreichkunde (ed.), *Oesterreich am Vorabend des ersten Weltkriegs* (Vienna 1964)

J. Joll, *The Origins of the First World War* (London 1984)

R.A. Kann, *Erzherzog Franz Ferdinand Studien*, Veröffentlichungen des österreichischen Ost-und Südosteuropa Instituts, 10 (Vienna 1967)

——, 'Erzherzog Franz Ferdinand und Graf Berchtold als Außenminister 1912–14', in *Mitteilungen des österreichischen Staatsarchivs*, 22 (1969), pp. 246–78

——, *Kaiser Franz Joseph und der Ausbruch des ersten Weltkriegs*, Oesterreichische Akademie der Wissenschaften, Philosophisch-historische Klasse, Sitzungsberichte 274 (Vienna 1971)

——, *Die Prochaska Affäre vom Herbst 1912. Zwischen kaltem und heißem Krieg*, Oesterreichische Akademie der Wissenschaften, Philosophisch-historische Klasse, Sitzungsberichte 319 (Vienna 1977)

J.F.V. Keiger, *France and the Origins of the First World War* (London 1983)

M. Kent (ed.), *The Great Powers and the End of the Ottoman Empire* (London 1984)

F. Klein, 'Die Rivalität zwischen Deutschland und Oesterreich-Ungarn in der Türkei am Vorabend des ersten Weltkriegs', in *Politik im Krieg 1914–1918*, (Berlin 1964), pp. 1–21

—— (ed.), *Oesterreich-Ungarn in der Weltpolitik, 1900–1918* (Berlin, 1965)

——, *Studien zum deutschen Imperialismus vor 1914* (Berlin 1976)

D. Löding, 'Deutschlands und Oesterreich-Ungarns Balkanpolitik von 1912–1914 unter besonderer Berücksichtigung ihrer Wirtschaftsinteressen', unpublished Ph.D. thesis, Hamburg, 1969

A.J. May, 'The Novibazar Railway Project', in *Journal of Modern History*, 10 (1938), pp. 496–527

——, 'Trans-Balkan Railway Schemes', in *Journal of Modern History*, 1952 pp. 352–67

R. Möhring, 'Die Beziehungen zwischen Oesterreich-Ungarn und dem osmanischen Reich, 1908–12', unpublished Ph.D. dissertation, Vienna, 1978

A. von Musulin, *Das Haus am Ballplatz*, (Munich 1924)

M.B.A. Peterson, 'Das oesterreichisch-ungarische Memorandum an Deutschland vom 5 Juli 1914', in *Scandia*, 30 (1964), pp. 138–90

A.F. Pribram, *Austria-Hungary and Great Britain 1908–1914* (Oxford 1951)

J. Redlich, *Schicksalsjahre Oesterreichs, 1908–1919. Das politische Tagebuch Josef Redlichs*, (ed. F. Fellner), Veröffentlichungen der Kommission für neuere Geschichte Oesterreichs, 39/4 (Vienna 1953–4)

J. Remak, 'The Healthy Invalid: How Doomed the Habsburg Empire?' in *Journal of Modern History*, 42 (1969), pp. 127–43

——, '1914- The Third Balkan War. Origins Reconsidered', in *Journal of Modern History*, 43 (1971), pp. 353–67

B.E. Schmitt, *The Annexation of Bosnia* (Cambridge 1937)

N. Stone, 'Moltke–Conrad: Relations between the Austro-Hungarian and German General Staffs, 1909–14, in *Historical Journal*, 9 (1966), pp. 201–28

——, 'Hungary and the Crisis of July 1914', in *Journal of Contemporary History*, I (1966), pp. 153–70

——, 'Constitutional Crises in Hungary 1903–6', in *Slavonic and East European Review*, 45 (1967), pp. 163–82

P.F. Sugar, 'An Underrated event. The Hungarian Constitutional Crisis of 1905–6', in *East European Quarterly*, 15 (1981), pp. 281–306

J.D. Treadway, *The Falcon and the Eagle. Montenegro and Austria-Hungary 1908* (West Lafayette, Ind. 1983)

S. Verosta, *Theorie und Realität von Bündnissen. Heinrich Lammasch, Karl Renner und der Zweibund, 1897–1914* (Vienna 1971)

E. Walters, 'Franco-Russian Discussions on the Partition of Austria-Hungary 1899', in *Slavonic and East European Review*, 28 (1949), pp. 184–97

——, 'Unpublished Documents: Aehrenthal's Attempt in 1907 to Regroup the European Powers', in *Slavonic and East European Review*, 30 (1951), pp. 213–51

S. Wank, 'Aehrenthal's Programme for the Constitutional Transformation of the Habsburg Monarchy, Three Secret Mémoires', in *Slavonic and East European Review*, 41 (1963), pp. 513–36

——, 'Aehrenthal and the Sanjak of Novibazar Railway Project: A Reappraisal', in *Slavonic and East European Review*, 42 (1964), pp. 353–69

S.R. Williamson Jr. 'Influence, Power and the Policy Process: The Case of Franz Ferdinand', in *Historical Journal*, 17 (1974), pp. 417–34

B. Zwerger, 'The Diplomatic Relations between Great Britain and Roumania, 1913–14', unpublished MA Dissertation, London, 1971

H. 1914–1918

W. Bihl, *Oesterreich-Ungarn und die Friedensschlüße von Brest-Litovsk*, Studien zur Geschichte der österreichisch-ungarischen Monarchie, 8 (Vienna 1970)

G.A. Craig, 'The World War I Alliance of the Central Powers in Retrospect: The Military Cohesion of the Alliance', in *Journal of Modern History* 37 (1966), pp. 336–44

K. Epstein, 'The Development of German–Austrian War Aims in the Spring of 1917', in *Journal of Central European Affairs*, 17 (1957), pp. 24–47

F. Fischer, *Griff nach der Weltmacht. Der Kriegszielpolitik des kaiserlichen Deutschland 1914–1918* (Düsseldorf 1964), (trs. as *Germany's Aims in the First World War*, London, 1967)

R.A. Kann, *Die Sixtusaffäre und die geheimen Friedensverhandlungen Oesterreich-Ungarns im ersten Weltkrieg*, Oesterreich Archiv (Vienna 1966)

——, B.K. Kiraly and P.S. Fichtner (eds), *The Habsburg Empire in World War I. Essays on the Intellectual, Military, Political and Economic Aspects of the Habsburg War Effort*, Studies on Society in Change, 2 (New York 1977)

R.W. Kapp, 'Divided Loyalties. The German Reich and Austria-Hungary in Austro-German Discussions of War Aims, 1914–16', in *Central European History*, 17 (1984), pp. 120–39

M. Kitchen, 'Hindenburg. Ludendorff and Russia', in *Slavonic and East European Review*, 54 (1976), pp. 214–30

B. Krizman, 'Austro-Hungarian Diplomacy before the Collapse of the Empire', in *Journal of Contemporary History*, 4 (1969), pp. 97–116

J. Lilla, 'Innen- und außenpolitische Aspekte der austro-polnischen Lösung, 1914–16', in *Mitteilungen des österreichischen Staatsarchivs*, 30 (1977), pp. 221–50

G.W. Shanafelt, 'Activism and Inertia: Ottokar Czernin's Mission to Romania, 1913–16', in *Austrian History Yearbook*, 19/20 (1983–4)

——, 'The Secret Enemy. Austria-Hungary and the German Alliance, 1914–18', East European Monographs, 187 (New York 1985)

G.E. Silberstein, *The Troubled Alliance. German–Austrian Relations 1914–17*

(Lexington 1970)

N. Stone, 'Die Mobilmachung der österreichisch-ungarischen Armee, 1914', in *Militärgeschichtliche Mitteilungen,,* 16 (1974/2), pp. 67–95

G.E. Torrey, 'The Rumanian Campaign of 1916: Its Impact on the Belligerents', in *Slavonic and East European Review*, 39 (1980), pp. 27–43

U. Trumpener, 'Turkey's Entry into World War I, an Assessment of Responsibilities', in *Journal of Modern History*, 34 (1962), pp. 369–80

L. Valiani, 'Italo–Austro-Hungarian negotiations, 1914–15', in *Journal of Contemporary History*, 1 (1966), pp. 113–36

——, *The End of Austria-Hungary* (London 1973)

F.G. Weber, *Eagles on the Crescent: Germany, Austria and the Diplomacy of the Turkish Alliance, 1914–1918* (Ithaca 1970)

S.R. Williamson Jr and P. Pastor (eds), *Essays on World War I: Origins and Prisoners of War*, War and Society in East Central Europe, 5 (New York 1983)

Z.A.B. Zeman, *A Diplomatic History of the First World War* (London 1971)

Name index

Abdul Hamid II (1842–1918), Sultan of Turkey 1876–1909: 129, 179–80, 189, 196, 209, 245, 253, 259, 278

Aehrenthal, Alois Baron (1909 Count) Lexa von (1854–1912), Ballhausplatz 1883–6, St Petersburg embassy 1888–94, Ballhausplatz 1894–5, I. and R. minister at Bucharest 1895–9, ambassador at St Petersburg 1899–1906, minister for foreign affairs 1906–12:

character and general, 7, 10–11, 13, 15–16, 21, 47, 205, 208, 269–70, 310ff., 377, 379; and domestic affairs, 21, 24, 265, 296, 304, 337, 374; and the press, 22–3, 305–6; and Germany, 193–4, 270, 273, 278, 304–6, 309; and Dual Alliance, 270, 293, 298–9, 304; and Russia, 193–4, 200, 217, 233, 271, 303–4; and Austro-Russian Entente, 227–8, 233–4, 244–5, 250, 256–7, 264–7, 271–2, 274, 279, 286; and Italy, 270–1, 288, 303, 307–8, 310–11; and Triple Alliance, 303, 308, 348; and Great Britain, 202, 209, 227, 265, 271–4, 278–9, 281, 290, 301–2, 310–11; and Ottoman Empire, 280–1, 290, 299–301, 309–11, 316; and Bosnia, 13, 256, 268, 274, 279–84, 288–97; and Sanjak of Novibazar, 276–7, 280, 301; and Macedonia, 272–5, 277–8; and Albania, 300–1, 305; and Crete, 299–300; and Serbia, 262, 271, 276, 289, 291–5, 297, 301, 310, 317; and Montenegro, 295, 305; and Romania, 232; and Bulgaria, 283, 291; and Morocco, 305–6; and Spain, 306

Albert, Prince Consort (1819–61): 45, 63

Albrecht, Archduke (1817–95), Inspector General of I. and R. Army, 1869–95: 6, 96, 107, 118,

123, 149, 176–7, 187, 209

Alexander I (1777–1825), Emperor of Russia 1801–25: 30–33

Alexander II (1818–81), Emperor of Russia 1855–81: 58–9, 72, 93, 98–9, 106, 107, 109, 114–5, 117, 120–2, 133, 143, 148, 150

Alexander III (1845–94), Emperor of Russia 1881–94: 148, 152–3, 156, 164, 167, 172–4, 186, 193, 201

Alexander of Battenberg (1857–93), Prince of Bulgaria 1878–86: 159–60, 163, 168–9, 171–3

Alexander Karageorgević (1806–85), Prince of Serbia 1843–58: 248

Alexander Obrenović (1876–1903), King of Serbia 1889–1903: 188, 230–1, 247–8

Andrássy von Csik-Szent-Király u. Kraszna-Horka, Julius Count (1823–90), Hungarian minister-president 1867–71, I. and R. foreign minister 1871–9:

character and general, 4, 8, 10, 13–16, 20, 23, 50, 104, 132–3, 150–1, 200, 205, 241, 376, 378; and Germany, 103, 107–9, 148; and Dual Alliance, 133–6; and Russia, 12, 97–100, 102–3, 109–10, 114, 123, 149; and Three Emperors' League, 1909, 115–7, 121–2, 125, 136; and Great Britain, 103, 106, 118, 121, 124, 126–7, 129–30, 134, 136; and France 108, 134, 136; and Italy, 153; and Ottoman Empire, 92, 105–6, 110–11, 127–8, 163, 170; and crisis of 1875–8, 113–30 *passim*; and Bosnia, 13, 112–3, 116–9, 126–7, 129–31; and commercial policies, 105, 111, 128

Andrássy von Csik-Szent-Király u. Kraszna-Horka, Julius Count (1860–1929), Hungarian minister of interior 1906–10, I. and R. foreign

Vatican 1906–9, assistant to the foreign minister 1909–10, foreign minister 1910–16: 301, 304, 309, 316, 330, 342

Schäffle, Albert (1831–1903), Austrian minister of commerce 1870: 102–3

Schemua, Blasius (1856–1920), I and R. chief of general staff 1911–12: 318

Schlieffen, Alfred Count von (1833–1913), chief of the Prussian general staff 1891–1905: 187, 195–6, 211

Schmerling, Anton Ritter von (1805–93), Austrian minister of interior 1860–5: 17, 74, 78

Schwarzenberg, Felix Prince zu (1800–52), Austrian minister at Turin and Parma 1838–43, at Naples 1844–8, minister-president and minister for foreign affairs 1848–52: 5–8, 13–15, 43–51, 62–3, 86, 360

Sixtus, of Bourbon Parma, Prince (1886–1934), 361–2, 367–9

Skobelev, General Michael Dmitrievich (1843–82) 152–4, 156–7

Smuts, Jan Christiaan (1870–1950), minister of defence of South African Union 1910–19: 367

Sonnino, Giorgio Sidney, Baron (1847–1922), Italian foreign minister 1914–19: 348

Stamboulov, Stefan Nikolov (1854–95), Bulgarian prime minister and minister of the interior 1887–94: 190, 213

Stanley, Edward Henry (1869 15th Earl of Derby), British foreign secretary 1866–8, 1874–8: 150

Stolypin, Peter Arkadievich (1862–1911), Russian minister-president 1906–11: 272, 283, 291

Stürgkh, Karl Count (1859–1916), Austrian minister-president 1911–16: 348–50, 356

Széchényi von Sárvar u. Felsö-Videk, Emmerich Count (1825–98), I. and R. ambassador at Berlin 1878–92: 176, 178, 182

Szécsen von Temerin, Nicholas Count (1857–1926), Sektionschef in the Ballhausplatz 1895–1901, I. and R. ambassador at the Vatican 1901–11, at Paris 1911–14: 242

Szögyény-Marich von Magyar-Szögyen u. Szolgaegyháza, Ladislas Count (1841–1916), I. and R. ambassador at Berlin 1892–1914: 202, 233–4, 245

Taaffe, Eduard Count (1833–95), Austrian minister-president 1879–93: 132–3, 151, 184–5, 194–5, 267

Talleyrand-Périgord, Charles Maurice Duc de (1754–1838): 30

Tegetthof, Wilhelm von (1866 Vice-Admiral) (1827–71), head of the naval division of the I. and R. war ministry 1868–71: 112

Thun und Hohenstein, Franz Count (1911 Prince) (1847–1916), governor of Bohemia 1889–96, Austrian minister-president and minister of the interior 1898–9, governor of Bohemia 1911–15: 237

Tisza von Borosjenö u. Szegod, Kálmán (1830–1902), Hungarian minister-president 1875–90: 8, 104, 121, 124, 129, 165, 174, 182, 185

Tisza von Borosjenö u. Szegod, Istvan (1897 Count) (1861–1918), Hungarian minister-president 1903–5, 1913–17: 254, 307, 329, 334–5, 338, 340, 348–50, 353, 356, 358, 363–4

Tittoni, Tommaso (1855–1931), Italian foreign minister 1903–5, ambassador at London 1906, foreign minister 1906–9, ambassador at Paris 1910–16: 251–2, 260, 270–1, 302–3

Tschirschky u. Bögendorff, Heinrich von (1858–1916), German foreign minister 1906–7, ambassador at Vienna 1907–16: 306, 332, 337, 340

Umberto I (1844–1900), King of Italy 1878–1900: 153, 191, 239

Vasić, Vladimir, confidant of the I. and R. legation at Belgrade: 296

Verdy du Vernois, Julius von (1832–1910), Prussian war minister 1889–90: 186–7

Victor Emmanuel II (1820–78), King of Piedmont-Sardinia 1849–61, of Italy 1861–78: 81, 108

Victor Emmanuel III (1869–1947), King of Italy 1900–46: 239, 314

Subject index

Note: *Alliances and Ententes, Battles, Concepts, Meetings and Visits, Treaties and Agreements,* and *Wars* are grouped under separate headings.